수능특강

영어영역 **영어**

이 책의 **구성과 특징** Structure

본 교재는 고등학교 영어과 교육과정 성취 기준의 달성 정도와 대학에서 수학하는 데 필요한 영어 사용 능력을 측정하는 대학수학능력시험을 준비하는 데 도움을 주고자 제작되었으며, 교육과정에 부합하는 내용으로 구성되었다. 특히 학생들의 읽기 능력 신장을 목적으로 다양한 주제 · 소재 분야의 글과 정보를 제시하고 있으며, 교육과정상의 어휘 범주를 고려하여 개발되었다. '영어 I'과 '영어 II' 교과서를 통해 익힌 기본 개념을 중심으로 본 교재를 활용하여 실제 응용력을 키워 나간다면, 교육과정 성취 목표 도달과 함께 대학수학능력시험 대비에 크게 도움이 될 것으로 기대된다.

Gateway

출제 유형을 중심으로 구성된 유형편과 다양한 주제나 소재의 글을 중심으로 구성된 주제 · 소재편의 Gateway를 통해, 해당 유형 및 주제 · 소재에 부합하는 2024학년도 수능 혹은 모의평가 기출 문항을 제시하여 수능의 각 유형 및 다양한 주제 · 소재별 문항에 대비하는 능력을 높이고자 하였다.

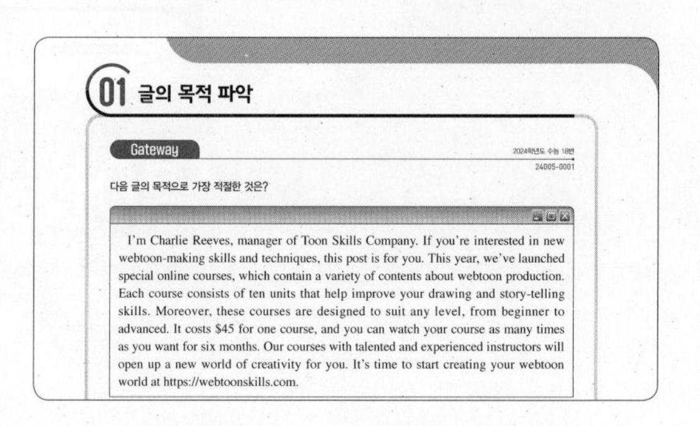
01 글의 목적 파악

Gateway

2024학년도 수능 18번

24005-0001

다음 글의 목적으로 가장 적절한 것은?

I'm Charlie Reeves, manager of Toon Skills Company. If you're interested in new webtoon-making skills and techniques, this post is for you. This year, we've launched special online courses, which contain a variety of contents about webtoon production. Each course consists of ten units that help improve your drawing and story-telling skills. Moreover, these courses are designed to suit any level, from beginner to advanced. It costs $45 for one course, and you can watch your course as many times as you want for six months. Our courses with talented and experienced instructors will open up a new world of creativity for you. It's time to start creating your webtoon world at https://webtoonskills.com.

Solving Strategies

유형편의 Gateway를 통해 소개된 기출 문항의 답을 도출해 가는 과정을 단계별로 제시함으로써 학습자의 유형별 문제 해결 능력을 신장하고자 하였다.

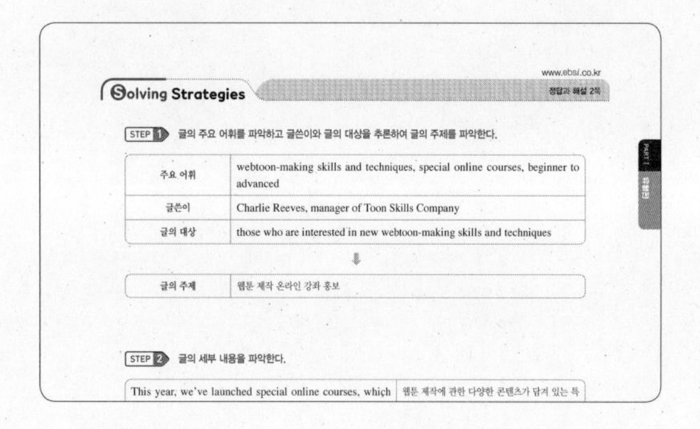
www.ebsi.co.kr

Solving Strategies

정답과 해설 2쪽

STEP 1 글의 주요 어휘를 파악하고 글쓴이와 글의 대상을 추론하여 글의 주제를 파악한다.

주요 어휘	webtoon-making skills and techniques, special online courses, beginner to advanced
글쓴이	Charlie Reeves, manager of Toon Skills Company
글의 대상	those who are interested in new webtoon-making skills and techniques

글의 주제	웹툰 제작 온라인 강좌 홍보

STEP 2 글의 세부 내용을 파악한다.

This year, we've launched special online courses, which	웹툰 제작에 관한 다양한 콘텐츠가 담겨 있는 특

Academic Vocabulary by Topic

주제 · 소재편에 소개된 주제 및 소재와 관련하여 읽기 지문에서 주로 다루어지는 필수 어휘를 영영 풀이와 예문을 통해 익히고, 간단히 복습해 볼 수 있도록 하였다.

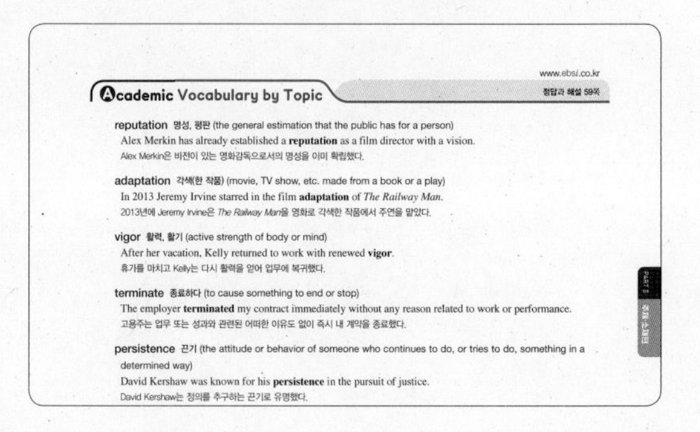
www.ebsi.co.kr

Academic Vocabulary by Topic

정답과 해설 59쪽

reputation 명성, 평판 (the general estimation that the public has for a person)
Alex Merkin has already established a **reputation** as a film director with a vision.
Alex Merkin은 비전이 있는 영화감독으로서의 명성을 이미 확립했다.

adaptation 각색(한 작품) (movie, TV show, etc. made from a book or a play)
In 2013 Jeremy Irvine starred in the film **adaptation** of *The Railway Man*.
2013년에 Jeremy Irvine은 *The Railway Man*을 영화로 각색한 작품에서 주연을 맡았다.

vigor 활력, 활기 (active strength of body or mind)
After her vacation, Kelly returned to work with renewed **vigor**.
휴가를 마치고 Kelly는 다시 활력을 얻어 업무에 복귀했다.

terminate 종료하다 (to cause something to end or stop)
The employer **terminated** my contract immediately without any reason related to work or performance.
고용주는 업무 또는 성과와 관련된 어떠한 이유도 없이 즉시 내 계약을 종료했다.

persistence 끈기 (the attitude or behavior of someone who continues to do, or tries to do, something in a determined way)
David Kershaw was known for his **persistence** in the pursuit of justice.
David Kershaw는 정의를 추구하는 끈기로 유명했다.

Exercises

각 강에서 다루어지는 문제 유형이나 주제 · 소재에 적합한 다양한 종류의 지문을 활용하여 읽기 문제를 제시하였다. 문제 풀이에 더욱 효과적으로 집중할 수 있도록 지문의 단어와 어구를 따로 떼어 '영단어 · 숙어'의 별책으로 제시하였다.

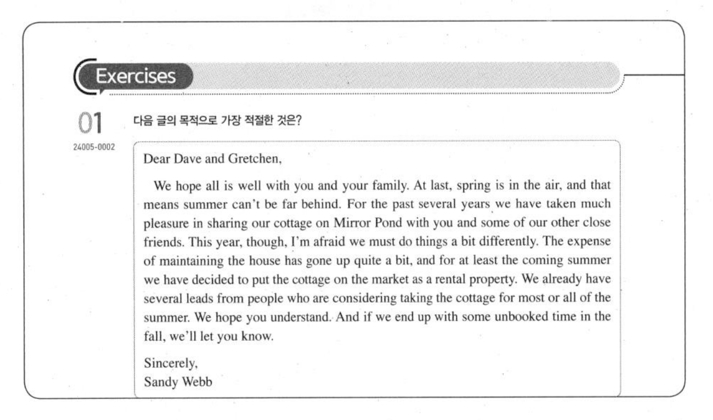

Exercises

01 다음 글의 목적으로 가장 적절한 것은?

24005-0002

Dear Dave and Gretchen,

We hope all is well with you and your family. At last, spring is in the air, and that means summer can't be far behind. For the past several years we have taken much pleasure in sharing our cottage on Mirror Pond with you and some of our other close friends. This year, though, I'm afraid we must do things a bit differently. The expense of maintaining the house has gone up quite a bit, and for at least the coming summer we have decided to put the cottage on the market as a rental property. We already have several leads from people who are considering taking the cottage for most or all of the summer. We hope you understand. And if we end up with some unbooked time in the fall, we'll let you know.

Sincerely,
Sandy Webb

Test

실전에 대비하여 자신의 읽기 능력을 스스로 진단해 볼 수 있도록 3회분의 테스트를 최신 수능 체제에 맞추어 구성하였다. 이 테스트를 통해 지금까지 학습한 내용을 총정리하고 실력을 점검하는 기회로 활용하도록 하였다.

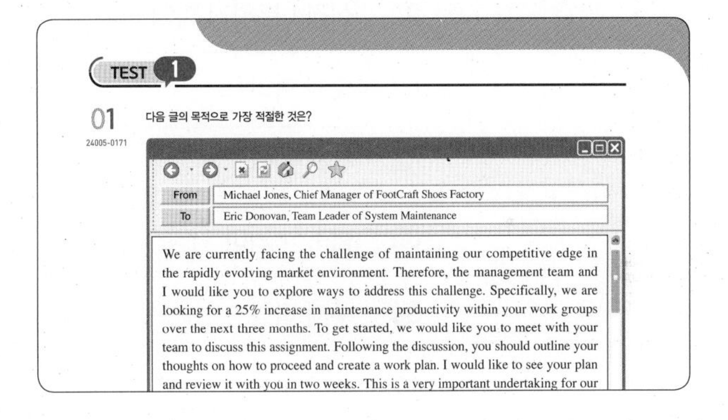

TEST 1

01 다음 글의 목적으로 가장 적절한 것은?

24005-0171

From: Michael Jones, Chief Manager of FootCraft Shoes Factory
To: Eric Donovan, Team Leader of System Maintenance

We are currently facing the challenge of maintaining our competitive edge in the rapidly evolving market environment. Therefore, the management team and I would like you to explore ways to address this challenge. Specifically, we are looking for a 25% increase in maintenance productivity within your work groups over the next three months. To get started, we would like you to meet with your team to discuss this assignment. Following the discussion, you should outline your thoughts on how to proceed and create a work plan. I would like to see your plan and review it with you in two weeks. This is a very important undertaking for our

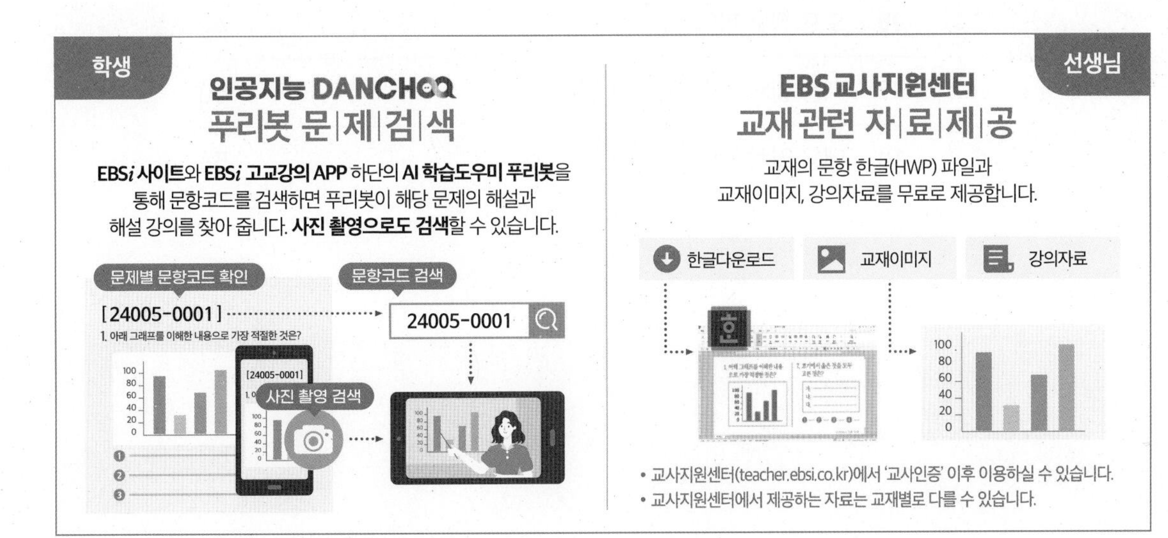

이 책의 **차례** Contents

Part I 유형편

이 책의 **차례** Contents

Part Ⅱ 주제 · 소재편

Part III 테스트편

www.ebs*i*.co.kr

Part I

유형편

01 글의 목적 파악

Gateway

2024학년도 수능 18번

24005-0001

다음 글의 목적으로 가장 적절한 것은?

I'm Charlie Reeves, manager of Toon Skills Company. If you're interested in new webtoon-making skills and techniques, this post is for you. This year, we've launched special online courses, which contain a variety of contents about webtoon production. Each course consists of ten units that help improve your drawing and story-telling skills. Moreover, these courses are designed to suit any level, from beginner to advanced. It costs $45 for one course, and you can watch your course as many times as you want for six months. Our courses with talented and experienced instructors will open up a new world of creativity for you. It's time to start creating your webtoon world at https://webtoonskills.com.

① 웹툰 제작 온라인 강좌를 홍보하려고
② 웹툰 작가 채용 정보를 제공하려고
③ 신작 웹툰 공개 일정을 공지하려고
④ 웹툰 창작 대회에 출품을 권유하려고
⑤ 기초적인 웹툰 제작 방법을 설명하려고

Words & Phrases in Use

- □ launch 시작하다, 개시하다
- □ consist of ~로 구성되다
- □ advanced 고급의
- □ instructor 강사

Solving Strategies

STEP 1 글의 주요 어휘를 파악하고 글쓴이와 글의 대상을 추론하여 글의 주제를 파악한다.

주요 어휘	webtoon-making skills and techniques, special online courses, beginner to advanced
글쓴이	Charlie Reeves, manager of Toon Skills Company
글의 대상	those who are interested in new webtoon-making skills and techniques

글의 주제	웹툰 제작 온라인 강좌 홍보

STEP 2 글의 세부 내용을 파악한다.

This year, we've launched special online courses, which contain a variety of contents about webtoon production.	웹툰 제작에 관한 다양한 콘텐츠가 담겨 있는 특별 온라인 강좌 시작
Each course consists of ten units that help improve your drawing and story-telling skills.	각 강좌는 10차시로 설계됨
Moreover, these courses are designed to suit any level, from beginner to advanced.	초급에서 고급까지 어떤 수준에도 맞도록 강좌가 구성됨
It costs $45 for one course, and you can watch your course as many times as you want for six months.	강좌당 45달러이며, 6개월 동안 원하는 만큼 볼 수 있음

STEP 3 글의 주제와 세부 내용을 종합하여 글의 목적을 파악한다.

Toon Skills Company의 경영자인 Charlie Reeves가 자신들이 새로 개설한 웹툰 제작 온라인 강좌의 구체적 내용과 비용에 관한 정보를 제시하며 수강할 것을 권유하는 내용이다.

→ 따라서 글의 목적으로 가장 적절한 것은 ① '웹툰 제작 온라인 강좌를 홍보하려고'이다.

Exercises

01

다음 글의 목적으로 가장 적절한 것은?

24005-0002

Dear Dave and Gretchen,

We hope all is well with you and your family. At last, spring is in the air, and that means summer can't be far behind. For the past several years we have taken much pleasure in sharing our cottage on Mirror Pond with you and some of our other close friends. This year, though, I'm afraid we must do things a bit differently. The expense of maintaining the house has gone up quite a bit, and for at least the coming summer we have decided to put the cottage on the market as a rental property. We already have several leads from people who are considering taking the cottage for most or all of the summer. We hope you understand. And if we end up with some unbooked time in the fall, we'll let you know.

Sincerely,
Sandy Webb

① 별장 이용 시 유의 사항을 전달하려고
② 별장 이용료 인상에 대해 양해를 구하려고
③ 별장 이용 후기를 써 준 것에 대해 감사하려고
④ 이번 여름에 별장을 이용할 수 없음을 알리려고
⑤ 휴가 기간에 별장에서 모임을 갖자고 제안하려고

02

24005-0003

다음 글의 목적으로 가장 적절한 것은?

Dear Mr. Butler,

I am James Franklin, principal of Grandview High School. Each year we provide engaging events to bring our school's community together. This year, we are trying to have a chess tournament. We think that it will create a healthy competitive atmosphere and help students make new friends. And some of the students in our school chess club are showing very promising results and are aiming to participate in the City Chess Tournament. They are practicing hard for the tournament. However, due to our school's budgetary constraints, we had to cut back on school supplies. To offer our students the best education possible, we need the supplies to keep our chess club running. We would like to ask that you help us continue the chess club by donating money. If you contribute to our school, you'll be a hero to the students who are pursuing their dream of becoming chess players.

Sincerely,
James Franklin

* budgetary: 예산상의

① 신학기에 열리는 학교 행사에 초대하려고
② 학교 동아리 예산 삭감 이유를 설명하려고
③ 체스 대회 개최를 위한 심의안 검토를 요청하려고
④ 체스 동아리 물품 마련을 위한 기부를 부탁하려고
⑤ 학교 체스 동아리의 지역 대회 참가를 홍보하려고

03 다음 글의 목적으로 가장 적절한 것은?

24005-0004

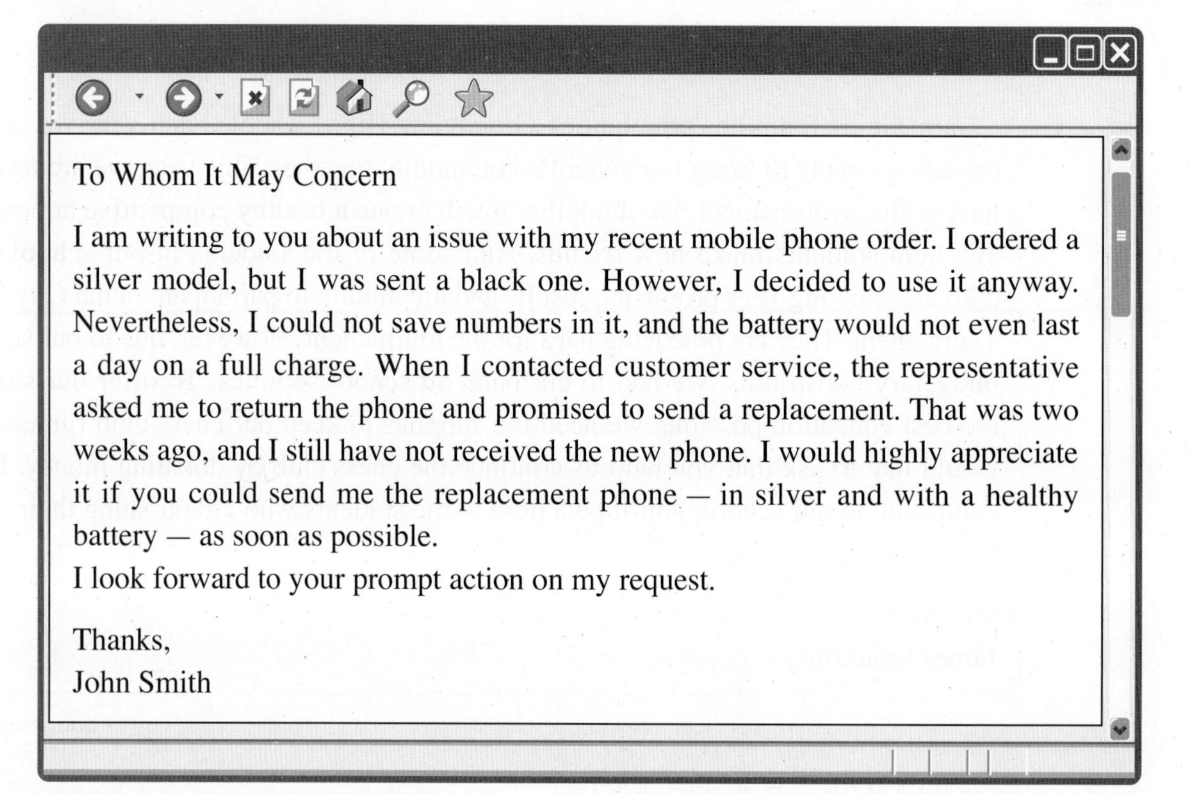

To Whom It May Concern

I am writing to you about an issue with my recent mobile phone order. I ordered a silver model, but I was sent a black one. However, I decided to use it anyway. Nevertheless, I could not save numbers in it, and the battery would not even last a day on a full charge. When I contacted customer service, the representative asked me to return the phone and promised to send a replacement. That was two weeks ago, and I still have not received the new phone. I would highly appreciate it if you could send me the replacement phone — in silver and with a healthy battery — as soon as possible.

I look forward to your prompt action on my request.

Thanks,

John Smith

① 휴대 전화 보조 배터리를 주문하려고
② 교체 상품의 신속한 배송을 요청하려고
③ 휴대 전화 수리 진행 상황을 문의하려고
④ 광고와 다른 제품 성능에 대해 항의하려고
⑤ 잘못 배송된 제품을 반송할 예정임을 알리려고

04 다음 글의 목적으로 가장 적절한 것은?

24005-0005

Dear Mr. Scott,

If you ask your administrative employees, they will probably agree that copier maintenance is critical to a successful office. Our research shows that the typical business will use copy equipment about six months before repairing or replacing it. Historically, when you have needed service, the only option has been to call a repairperson at a very high cost. Fortunately, there is now a service that can extend the life of your copier and save your company thousands of dollars during the next year. Lake Paperworx specializes in copier maintenance, successfully serving business and legal firms throughout the United States. We can significantly reduce your maintenance costs and your downtime. The enclosed brochure outlines our services. If you are interested in using our services, please call me directly at 920−4848−1212.

Sincerely,
James Palmer
Lake Paperworx Business Manager

① 신형 복사기의 추가 구매를 권유하려고
② 임대 복사기의 수리 지연을 사과하려고
③ 복사기 유지 관리 서비스를 광고하려고
④ 임대 복사기 정기 점검 계획을 안내하려고
⑤ 지역 복사기 판매 · 대여 업체를 추천하려고

02 심경 · 분위기 파악

Gateway

2024학년도 수능 19번

24005-0006

다음 글에 드러난 David의 심경 변화로 가장 적절한 것은?

David was starting a new job in Vancouver, and he was waiting for his bus. He kept looking back and forth between his watch and the direction the bus would come from. He thought, "My bus isn't here yet. I can't be late on my first day." David couldn't feel at ease. When he looked up again, he saw a different bus coming that was going right to his work. The bus stopped in front of him and opened its door. He got on the bus thinking, "Phew! Luckily, this bus came just in time so I won't be late." He leaned back on an unoccupied seat in the bus and took a deep breath, finally able to relax.

① nervous → relieved
② lonely → hopeful
③ pleased → confused
④ indifferent → delighted
⑤ bored → thrilled

Words & Phrases in Use

☐ direction 방향
☐ feel at ease 마음을 놓다, 안도하다
☐ lean back 등을 기대다
☐ unoccupied 비어 있는
☐ take a deep breath 숨을 깊이 들이쉬다

Solving Strategies

정답과 해설 4쪽

STEP 1 등장인물에게 일어난 일을 중심으로 상황을 파악한다.

- 밴쿠버에서 새로운 일을 시작하게 된 David는 버스를 기다리고 있었다.
  David was starting a new job in Vancouver, and he was waiting for his bus.
- David는 바로 자신의 직장으로 가는 다른 버스가 오고 있는 것을 보았다.
  When he looked up again, he saw a different bus coming that was going right to his work.

STEP 2 등장인물의 심경을 추측할 수 있는 표현을 찾는다.

- David는 "내가 탈 버스가 아직 오지 않아. 내가 첫날 지각할 수는 없어."라고 생각했다. 그는 마음을 놓을 수가 없었다.
  He thought, "My bus isn't here yet. I can't be late on my first day." David couldn't feel at ease.
- David는 버스에 오르며, "휴! 다행히도 내가 지각하지 않도록 이 버스가 딱 맞춰 왔네."라고 생각했다.
  He got on the bus thinking, "Phew! Luckily, this bus came just in time so I won't be late."
- David는 버스의 비어 있는 좌석에 등을 기대며 숨을 깊이 들이쉬었고, 마침내 긴장을 풀 수 있었다.
  He leaned back on an unoccupied seat in the bus and took a deep breath, finally able to relax.

STEP 3 등장인물이 처한 상황과 심경 관련 표현을 종합적으로 고려하여 등장인물의 심경 변화를 판단한다.

David는 첫 출근길에 버스가 오지 않아 지각할까 봐 마음을 놓지 못하다가, 마침내 직장으로 가는 다른 버스에 타고 좌석에 앉아 숨을 깊이 들이쉬며 지각하지 않을 것이라는 생각에 긴장을 풀 수 있었다는 내용이다.

→ **따라서 David의 심경 변화로 가장 적절한 것은 ① '초조한 → 안도한'이다.**

② 외로운 → 희망에 찬
③ 기쁜 → 혼란스러운
④ 무관심한 → 즐거운
⑤ 지루한 → 뛸 듯이 기쁜

01

다음 글에 드러난 Olivia의 심경 변화로 가장 적절한 것은?

24005-0007

Olivia pulled a piece of bright yellow silk from the display. In her free hand she held a sample of beaded lace and tried to imagine the sound it would make whispering around her ankles as she danced. Now that the war was over, there would be a lot of dancing. Anticipation bubbled in her chest. She'd meet a real gentleman this season, and who knew? Maybe she would get married. "May I help you?" A shopkeeper stood beside her. "I would like five yards of this silk and a roll of this lace," Olivia said. "I'm very sorry, miss. They are already reserved." What a letdown! No other fabric would make her as beautiful as the yellow silk, and no other pearls would make such a charming whisper. With a sigh, she returned the items to the display.

① grateful → frustrated
② curious → pleased
③ worried → jealous
④ expectant → disappointed
⑤ nervous → confident

02

다음 글에 드러난 'I'의 심경으로 가장 적절한 것은?

24005-0008

Mr. Garcia walked to his closet and pulled a trumpet out of its case. He blew into it, you know, like he was clearing it all out. He ran his fingers along the valves and played a scale. And then he said, "Okay, Zach, ready?" And then he started playing. I mean the guy could play. He played this really soft and beautiful song. I never knew a trumpet could whisper. I kept looking at his fingers. I wanted him to keep playing forever. It was better than any of the poems he'd read to us in class. It was like the whole loud world had gone really, really quiet and there was nothing but this one song, this one sweet and gentle and brilliant song that was as soft as a breeze blowing through the leaves of a tree. The world just disappeared. I wanted to live in that stillness forever. I wanted to clap. And then, I just didn't know what to do or what to say.

① proud and confident
② bored and indifferent
③ scared and frightened
④ disappointed and angry
⑤ moved and overwhelmed

03 다음 글에 드러난 Benny의 심경 변화로 가장 적절한 것은?

24005-0009

A very large warrior approached and stood in front of Benny. The warrior took him by the arm, and Benny was convinced that he was going to be punished. He shivered with fear while being dragged. The warrior brought Benny to an open area of the village. There sat an old man. He seemed to be incredibly respected by all of the warriors. He introduced himself as Ailani, meaning "Highest Chief," and surprisingly enough, he spoke in the English language. He told Benny, "I have decided that we are not going to punish you. We do not punish good men, so you can relax." The chief continued, "I heard what you did for us. Your kindness makes me say welcome. Welcome to Life Island." Tears of relief poured down Benny's face.

* shiver: (몸을) 떨다

① satisfied → frustrated
② pleased → angry
③ terrified → relieved
④ regretful → moved
⑤ calm → excited

04 다음 글에 드러난 Charlotte의 심경으로 가장 적절한 것은?

24005-0010

"I think everyone is here now! Shall we all sit down?" Everyone was more than happy to cooperate and soon the whole group was settled in their chairs around the long dining room table, passing dishes filled with Charlotte's cooking. Soon, everyone had a full plate and conversation buzzed around the table between bites. Charlotte took a careful bite of her stuffing and found that the seasonings had all blended together beautifully to create a flavorful experience. She relaxed a bit more as she sampled the dishes on her plate and found that everything tasted good. Or, at least, she thought so. She just hoped everyone else felt the same way. As if reading her mind, Addison leaned over to her. "Everything tastes so delicious," she said quietly, patting her belly and indicating her already half-eaten plate. "You're going to have to roll me out of here when all is said and done." "Eat as much as you like," Charlotte replied with a laugh. "There's no judgment, especially on Thanksgiving!"

* pat: (가볍게) 두드리다, 쓰다듬다

① relieved and pleased
② nervous and annoyed
③ calm and determined
④ ashamed and regretful
⑤ confused and panicked

03 요지 파악

Gateway

2024학년도 수능 22번

24005-0011

다음 글의 요지로 가장 적절한 것은?

Being able to prioritize your responses allows you to connect more deeply with individual customers, be it a one-off interaction around a particularly delightful or upsetting experience, or the development of a longer-term relationship with a significantly influential individual within your customer base. If you've ever posted a favorable comment — or any comment, for that matter — about a brand, product or service, think about what it would feel like if you were personally acknowledged by the brand manager, for example, as a result. In general, people post because they have something to say — and because they want to be recognized for having said it. In particular, when people post positive comments they are expressions of appreciation for the experience that led to the post. While a compliment to the person standing next to you is typically answered with a response like "Thank You," the sad fact is that most brand compliments go unanswered. These are lost opportunities to understand what drove the compliments and create a solid fan based on them.

* compliment: 칭찬

① 고객과의 관계 증진을 위해 고객의 브랜드 칭찬에 응답하는 것은 중요하다.
② 고객의 피드백을 면밀히 분석함으로써 브랜드의 성공 가능성을 높일 수 있다.
③ 신속한 고객 응대를 통해서 고객의 긍정적인 반응을 이끌어 낼 수 있다.
④ 브랜드 매니저에게는 고객의 부정적인 의견을 수용하는 태도가 요구된다.
⑤ 고객의 의견을 경청하는 것은 브랜드의 새로운 이미지 창출에 도움이 된다.

Words & Phrases in Use

- ☐ prioritize 우선순위를 매기다, 우선시하다
- ☐ one-off 일회성의
- ☐ interaction 상호 작용
- ☐ acknowledge 감사하다, 인정하다
- ☐ recognize 인정하다
- ☐ appreciation 감사
- ☐ solid 확고한, 탄탄한

Solving Strategies

정답과 해설 6쪽

STEP 1 유사한 표현으로 반복되거나 특정 개념과 관련되어 반복되는 어구를 통해 글의 내용을 추측해 본다.

a favorable comment, positive comments, a compliment	고객의 칭찬
to connect with individual customers, to create a solid fan	고객과의 관계 증진
acknowledged by the brand manager, recognized, answered with a response	응답받기

➡ 고객과의 관계 증진을 위해 고객의 칭찬에 응답하는 것에 관한 내용의 글인 것을 알 수 있다.

STEP 2 글의 세부 내용을 확인하면서 글의 요지를 추론한다.

■ Being able to prioritize your responses allows you to connect more deeply with individual customers, ~.
➡ 응답에 우선순위를 매길 수 있는 것은 고객들과 더 깊은 관계를 맺을 수 있게 해 줌

■ ~, people post because they have something to say — and because they want to be recognized for having said it.
➡ 사람들은 인정받기를 원하기 때문에 글을 올림

■ These are lost opportunities to understand what drove the compliments and create a solid fan based on them.
➡ 고객의 칭찬에 응답하지 않는 것은 그것을 바탕으로 하여 확고한 팬을 만들어 낼 기회를 잃은 것임

STEP 3 글의 결론을 통해 글의 요지를 확인한다.

■ **결론**: 고객은 인정받기를 원하기 때문에 제품이나 서비스에 대해 호의적인 의견을 올리는 것이며, 이러한 칭찬에 응답함으로써 고객들과 더 깊은 관계를 맺을 수 있다는 내용의 글이다.

→ 따라서 글의 요지로 가장 적절한 것은 ① '고객과의 관계 증진을 위해 고객의 브랜드 칭찬에 응답하는 것은 중요하다.'이다.

Exercises

01

다음 글의 요지로 가장 적절한 것은?

24005-0012

One of the biggest misconceptions about creativity is that it takes a brilliant idea to solve a complex problem. While this may be true in pure sciences, in most commercial contexts, or even in day-to-day living, it is never that one silver bullet that does the magic. It is, in fact, a series of seemingly simple ideas that counts. The key is to have enough ideas that solve specific parts of the overall problem, and then the thorny task looks very much tenable. Since creativity comes from combining concepts in an unusual fashion, and since it is exceedingly difficult to trace the origins of ideas, you are better off generating as many ideas as possible with the hope that some of them would click. That is what great scientists and artists do. As the author Walter Isaacson notes, 'The sparks come from ideas rubbing against each other rather than as bolts out of the blue.'

* thorny: 골치 아픈, 까다로운 ** tenable: 참아 낼 수 있는

① 평범한 사고 과정으로는 창의적인 아이디어를 창출하기 어렵다.
② 뛰어난 성과를 달성하려면 창의력뿐만 아니라 끈기도 필요하다.
③ 복잡한 과업을 효율적으로 해결하려면 탁월한 창의력이 필요하다.
④ 다른 이의 아이디어를 도용하는 것은 결코 창의적이라 할 수 없다.
⑤ 많은 단순한 아이디어가 있으면 창의적으로 문제를 해결할 수 있다.

02

다음 글의 요지로 가장 적절한 것은?

24005-0013

Sometimes it is hard to know the right thing to do for the planet. What sounds good may not necessarily be so. Rooftop solar panels, for example, are one of the most expensive and least effective ways to help the environment. Buying local food can actually increase water pollution and waste. According to research from the Danish and UK governments, plastic grocery bags may actually be better than cotton bags for the climate and for water. You may disagree with all or some of those claims, and you may be right. It depends on your individual circumstances. If you live in Phoenix, Arizona, for example, solar panels could be a smart choice. Using your own cotton bags continuously and without exception for shopping for several years is probably better for the environment than the alternatives. Each of these choices depends on personal circumstances and behavior. The best solutions for the environment are personal.

① 기술 발전에 따라 소비가 환경에 미치는 영향이 줄고 있다.
② 재활용보다 사용을 줄이는 것이 환경 보호에 더 효과적이다.
③ 개인의 상황과 행동에 따라 환경에 더 나은 선택이 달라진다.
④ 개인의 친환경 실천보다 정부 차원의 정책이 더 큰 효과가 있다.
⑤ 환경 보호의 지속적 실천에는 가치관의 근본적 변화가 필요하다.

03 다음 글의 요지로 가장 적절한 것은?

24005-0014

Consider people with disabilities. Often they are judged using criteria of competence that are *biased* in favor of nondisabled people. Compare, for example, an average blind person with an average sighted person. Who will be more competent in walking from one place to another? You might think that the sighted person will be more competent because the sighted person can see where he or she is going, but this is using an unfair criterion. If you think about competence based on the fairer criterion of who can best walk with the eyes closed, then the blind person will definitely be more competent. Such knowledge about people who are blind and, by extension, other socially marginalized people, can make us appreciate them and celebrate their unique abilities as they really are, rather than discriminate against, pity, or patronize them for some incompetence that does not exist except as a figment of our traditional, prejudiced imaginations.

* marginalize: 소외시키다 ** patronize: 깔보는 듯한 태도로 대하다 *** figment: 꾸며 낸 것

① 소외 계층이 겪는 어려움은 사회의 구조적 모순에 기인한다.
② 지금까지의 장애인 인식 개선 교육은 형식적인 경우가 많다.
③ 장애인의 입장을 고려하여 제도와 시설을 정비할 필요가 있다.
④ 사회 소외 계층의 정치 · 경제적 권리는 충분히 보장되지 못했다.
⑤ 편견 없이 장애인을 이해하면 그들의 능력을 제대로 인정할 수 있다.

04 다음 글의 요지로 가장 적절한 것은?

24005-0015

When you think, you are using your imagination to create an image or picture in your mind of an event rather than the real thing. If you are driving home from a football match, reviewing the game in your mind, you are merely imagining what the game was like. The game is no longer real; it's now only in your mind, in your memory. It was real once, but not any longer. Similarly, if you are thinking about how bad your marriage is, you are considering it in your mind. *It's all in your imagination*. You are literally 'making up' your relationship. The thoughts you are having about your relationship are just thoughts. This is why the old saying, 'Things aren't as bad as they seem' is almost always true. The reason things 'seem so bad' is because your mind is able to recreate past events, and preview upcoming events, almost as though they were happening right in front of you, at that moment — even though they're not. To make matters worse, your mind can add additional drama to any event, thereby making that event seem even worse than it really is, or was, or will be.

① 상상력을 발휘하면 창의적인 해결책을 생각해 낼 수 있다.
② 여러 사건 간의 복잡한 인과 관계를 파악하면 통찰력이 생긴다.
③ 상상은 사건의 본질을 정확히 파악하는 데 중요한 역할을 한다.
④ 생각을 많이 하는 것보다 무엇이든 일단 시작하는 것이 중요하다.
⑤ 상상은 상황을 더 안 좋아 보이게 할 수 있는 마음속 생각일 뿐이다.

04 주장 파악

Gateway

2024학년도 수능 20번

24005-0016

다음 글에서 필자가 주장하는 바로 가장 적절한 것은?

Values alone do not create and build culture. Living your values only some of the time does not contribute to the creation and maintenance of culture. Changing values into behaviors is only half the battle. Certainly, this is a step in the right direction, but those behaviors must then be shared and distributed widely throughout the organization, along with a clear and concise description of what is expected. It is not enough to simply talk about it. It is critical to have a visual representation of the specific behaviors that leaders and all people managers can use to coach their people. Just like a sports team has a playbook with specific plays designed to help them perform well and win, your company should have a playbook with the key shifts needed to transform your culture into action and turn your values into winning behaviors.

① 조직 문화 혁신을 위해서 모든 구성원이 공유할 핵심 가치를 정립해야 한다.
② 조직 구성원의 행동을 변화시키려면 지도자는 명확한 가치관을 가져야 한다.
③ 조직 내 문화가 공유되기 위해서 구성원의 자발적 행동이 뒷받침되어야 한다.
④ 조직의 핵심 가치 실현을 위해 구성원 간의 지속적인 의사소통이 필수적이다.
⑤ 조직의 문화 형성에는 가치를 반영한 행동의 공유를 위한 명시적 지침이 필요하다.

Words & Phrases in Use

- ☐ maintenance 유지
- ☐ distribute 퍼뜨리다, 배포하다
- ☐ concise 간결한
- ☐ description 설명, 기술
- ☐ critical 중요한, 결정적인
- ☐ visual 시각적인
- ☐ representation 표현, 묘사
- ☐ specific 특정한, 구체적인
- ☐ playbook 플레이북(팀의 공격과 수비 작전을 그림과 함께 기록한 책)
- ☐ transform 바꾸다

Solving Strategies

STEP 1 **반복되거나 특정 개념과 관련되어 반복되는 어구를 통해 글의 내용을 추측해 본다.**

Values alone, Living your values	가치, 문화
Changing values into behaviors, those behaviors	가치를 행동으로 바꾸기
a clear and concise description, a visual representation of the specific behaviors, a playbook with specific plays, a playbook with the key shifts	구체적 행동의 시각화

➡ 가치를 행동으로 바꾸되, 구체적 행동은 플레이북처럼 시각적으로 표현되어야 한다는 내용의 글임을 알 수 있다.

STEP 2 **글의 세부 내용을 확인하면서 글의 요지를 추론한다.**

- Values alone do not create and build culture.
  ➡ 가치만으로는 (조직) 문화를 창조하거나 구축할 수 없음
- Changing values into behaviors is only half the battle.
  ➡ 가치를 행동으로 옮기는 것으로는 (조직) 문화 창조와 유지가 이루어질 수 없음
- ~, but those behaviors must then be shared and distributed widely throughout the organization, along with a clear and concise description of what is expected.
  ➡ 행동은 명확하고 간결한 설명과 함께 조직 전체에 공유되고 퍼져 나가야 함
- It is critical to have a visual representation of the specific behaviors that leaders and all people managers can use to coach their people.
  ➡ 구체적 행동을 시각적으로 표현한 것을 갖는 것이 중요함
- ~, your company should have a playbook with the key shifts needed to transform your culture into action and turn your values into winning behaviors.
  ➡ 조직의 문화를 행동으로 바꾸고 가치를 승리하는 행동으로 바꿀 수 있는 핵심 변화를 담은 플레이북이 있어야 함

STEP 3 **글의 결론을 통해 필자의 주장을 확인한다.**

- **결론**: 조직의 문화를 창조하고 유지하기 위해서는 가치를 반영한 행동을 플레이북처럼 시각적으로 표현한 것을 갖는 것이 중요하다는 내용의 글이다.

→ **따라서 필자가 주장하는 바로 가장 적절한 것은 ⑤ '조직의 문화 형성에는 가치를 반영한 행동의 공유를 위한 명시적 지침이 필요하다.'이다.**

Exercises

01

다음 글에서 필자가 주장하는 바로 가장 적절한 것은?

24005-0017

Most people don't equate silence with appreciation. People whose work is always good still need to hear it from you occasionally. Let them know you've noticed they are meeting their goals. Acknowledgement and appreciation create a supportive work environment and keep motivation alive. Make your appreciation specific and positive by noting what was done well and why it matters. This makes people feel good and it also ensures that the behaviour you identify is repeated. So, don't just say, "That was great!" Say, "That was great because ..." Both teams and individuals need positive, specific information about their accomplishments. Use your imagination: post graphs showing what the team has achieved; mark the achievement of major milestones or goals by bringing in sandwiches for lunch for everyone to share or putting up balloons; send thank you notes. When you ignore success, people think it doesn't matter and stop trying.

① 모든 직원이 단합할 수 있는 다양한 계기를 마련해야 한다.
② 경쟁보다는 협력을 통해 성과를 높일 수 있도록 유도해야 한다.
③ 훌륭한 성과는 긍정적이고 구체적인 방식으로 인정해 주어야 한다.
④ 구성원 전체가 동의할 수 있는 공정한 보상 체계를 마련해야 한다.
⑤ 성과 향상을 위해 근무 환경 개선 노력을 꾸준히 기울여야 한다.

02

다음 글에서 필자가 주장하는 바로 가장 적절한 것은?

24005-0018

The quality of news is difficult to measure because there are no agreed-upon standards that satisfy everyone's definition of high quality. The term *quality* generally refers to any attribute, service, or performance that is highly valued within a group or a community. Defining quality is thus context-dependent, field-specific, and subject to individual preferences and tastes. It is important to note, however, that compared to other cultural products such as music and paintings, journalistic content is unique because it has a strong civic and democratic component. The idea of the press as the "fourth estate" stems from the expectation that high-quality journalism promotes democratic ideals by playing the role of a watchdog, providing a public forum, and serving as a reliable information provider. Therefore, when discussing news quality, normative aspects cannot be overemphasized.

* normative: 규범적인

① 뉴스의 질은 민주주의의 이상을 실현하도록 규범적 측면에서 판단해야 한다.
② 뉴스의 질을 판단하려면 취재 과정이 적절했는지를 먼저 평가해야 한다.
③ 뉴스 매체의 질 향상을 위해서 대중의 다양한 인식을 수용해야 한다.
④ 개인의 상황과 취향에 따른 다양한 뉴스 선택권이 보장되어야 한다.
⑤ 각 개인은 저널리즘의 질을 분별할 수 있는 능력을 길러야 한다.

03

24005-0019

다음 글에서 필자가 주장하는 바로 가장 적절한 것은?

One thing that managers have to keep in mind is that they should mend fences after any fight. Opponents are not necessarily enemies. An opponent disagrees with you on the issue, of course, but enemies are ones with whom you also have a negative relationship. That makes it personal. You can often work with opponents and strategize toward mutually successful outcomes, but enemies are far more difficult and consequently far more dangerous. Try to keep opponents from becoming enemies, and work to turn enemies into mere opponents. Find points of agreement, and find ways you can legitimately support those who were your opponents. The subject of the fight will eventually recede, but you still need the relationships.

* legitimately: 정당하게 ** recede: (기억이) 희미해지다

① 말다툼을 더욱 깊게 상대방을 이해할 수 있는 기회로 삼아야 한다.
② 방어적인 태도를 취할수록 싸움에서 지기 쉽다는 점을 명심해야 한다.
③ 의견이 다른 사람과 긍정적 관계를 도모하여 적이 되지 않게 해야 한다.
④ 단순 반대자와 진정한 적을 구분하는 방법은 경험을 통해 습득해야 한다.
⑤ 말다툼에서 자신의 주장을 펴기 전에 먼저 반대자의 의견을 경청해야 한다.

04

24005-0020

다음 글에서 필자가 주장하는 바로 가장 적절한 것은?

Political decisions and management decisions about how much of any given species can be harvested are often based on the amount of money there is to be made. Profit leads to economic growth, which is the goal of many politicians and business leaders. But the problem with seeking continuous economic growth is that our economy is not separate from our environment. Everything in our economy comes from our environment. We extract resources from the world around us, consume them as products we eat or use, and then dump the waste back into the Earth. Our Earth is a finite ecosystem, which means there is only so much that we can take from the natural world to feed our economy, and only so much waste that the Earth can absorb, before natural processes stop functioning properly. The constant effort to extract more and more resources is actually an ecological impossibility over the long term. Our survival depends on learning to live within the limits of ecosystems.

① 기술 혁신을 통해 천연자원의 한계를 극복해야 한다.
② 환경의 한계를 무시하고 경제 성장을 추구해서는 안 된다.
③ 인간 사회의 번영을 위해 지속적으로 성장을 추구해야 한다.
④ 친환경 제품의 생산과 소비에 실질적인 혜택이 주어져야 한다.
⑤ 환경 문제에 대처하기 위해서는 국제적인 연대를 강화해야 한다.

05 함축적 의미 파악

Gateway

2024학년도 수능 21번

24005-0021

밑줄 친 a nonstick frying pan이 다음 글에서 의미하는 바로 가장 적절한 것은?

How you focus your attention plays a critical role in how you deal with stress. Scattered attention harms your ability to let go of stress, because even though your attention is scattered, it is narrowly focused, for you are able to fixate only on the stressful parts of your experience. When your attentional spotlight is widened, you can more easily let go of stress. You can put in perspective many more aspects of any situation and not get locked into one part that ties you down to superficial and anxiety-provoking levels of attention. A narrow focus heightens the stress level of each experience, but a widened focus turns down the stress level because you're better able to put each situation into a broader perspective. One anxiety-provoking detail is less important than the bigger picture. It's like transforming yourself into a nonstick frying pan. You can still fry an egg, but the egg won't stick to the pan.

* provoke: 유발시키다

① never being confronted with any stressful experiences in daily life
② broadening one's perspective to identify the cause of stress
③ rarely confining one's attention to positive aspects of an experience
④ having a larger view of an experience beyond its stressful aspects
⑤ taking stress into account as the source of developing a wide view

Words & Phrases in Use

☐ scatter 분산시키다, 흩뜨리다 ☐ let go of ~을 해소하다[놓아주다] ☐ fixate on ~에 집착하다
☐ attentional spotlight 주의의 초점, 주의의 집중
☐ put ~ in perspective ~을 균형 있는 시각으로 보다 ☐ tie down to ~에 옭아매다
☐ superficial 피상적인 ☐ anxiety-provoking 불안감을 유발하는
☐ the bigger picture 더 큰 전체적인 상황, 큰 그림 ☐ transform 탈바꿈시키다
☐ nonstick 눌어붙지 않는

Solving Strategies

정답과 해설 11쪽

STEP 1 글의 핵심 문장을 통해 요지를 파악한다.

- **핵심 문장**: When your attentional spotlight is widened, you can more easily let go of stress.
- **요지**: 주의의 초점이 넓어지면, 여러분은 스트레스를 더 쉽게 해소할 수 있다.

STEP 2 글의 전체 흐름을 파악한다.

- **핵심 소재**: 주의를 집중하는 방식은 스트레스에 대처하는 방식에 중요한 역할을 함 ➡ 주의가 분산되더라도, 경험 중 스트레스가 많은 부분에만 집착할 수 있음
- **요지**: 주의의 초점이 넓어지면, 여러분은 스트레스를 더 쉽게 해소할 수 있음 ➡ 초점이 좁으면 각 경험의 스트레스 수준이 높아지지만, 초점이 넓으면 각 상황을 더 넓은 시각으로 더 잘 볼 수 있으므로 스트레스 수준이 낮아짐
- **부연**: 불안감을 유발하는 하나의 세부 사항은 더 큰 전체적인 상황보다 덜 중요함 ➡ 프라이팬의 비유 ➡ 달걀이 프라이팬에 눌어붙지 않음(스트레스로 인해 크게 영향을 받지 않음)

STEP 3 글의 요지와 관련하여 밑줄 친 부분의 함축적인 의미를 추론한다.

주의의 초점이 넓으면 불안감을 유발하는 측면에 얽매이는 것에서 벗어나 상황을 더 넓은 시각에서 볼 수 있으므로, 스트레스 수준이 낮아진다는 것이 글의 중심 내용이다.

→ **따라서 밑줄 친 부분이 글에서 의미하는 바로 가장 적절한 것은 ④ '스트레스를 주는 측면을 넘어 경험에 대한 더 넓은 시각을 갖는 것'이다.**

① 일상생활에서 스트레스를 주는 어떤 경험에도 절대 직면하지 않는 것
② 스트레스의 원인을 파악하기 위해 시각을 넓히는 것
③ 경험의 긍정적인 측면에 주의를 거의 제한하지 않는 것
⑤ 넓은 시각을 개발하는 원천으로 스트레스를 고려하는 것

Exercises

01 밑줄 친 It is like walking on thin ice가 다음 글에서 의미하는 바로 가장 적절한 것은?

24005-0022

There are no black-and-white issues in life. No categorical answers. Everything is a subject for endless debate and compromise. This is one of the core principles of our current society. Because that core principle is wrong, the society ends up causing a lot of problems when it comes to sustainability. There *are* some issues that are black and white. There are indeed planetary and societal boundaries that must not be crossed. For instance, we think our societies can be a little bit more or a little bit less sustainable. But in the long run you cannot be a little bit sustainable — either you are sustainable or you are unsustainable. It is like walking on thin ice — either it carries your weight, or it does not. Either you make it to the shore, or you fall into the deep, dark, cold waters. And if that should happen to us, there will not be any nearby planet coming to our rescue. We are completely on our own.

* categorical: 단정적인

① A balance between extremes is needed to maintain sustainability.
② We should not think of technology as either beneficial or harmful.
③ Our survival depends on keeping an open mind about global issues.
④ In the climate change debate, it is vital to keep a practical perspective.
⑤ Sustainability is a critical situation where failure means the end of life on Earth.

02

24005-0023

밑줄 친 the rebellion went too far가 다음 글에서 의미하는 바로 가장 적절한 것은?

The modern corporation as a child of laissez-faire economics and of the market society is based on a creed whose greatest weakness is the inability to see the need for status and function of the individual in society. In the philosophy of the market society there is no other social criterion than economic reward. Henry Maine's famous epigram that the course of modern history has been from status to contract neatly summarizes the belief of the nineteenth century, that social status and function should be exclusively the result of economic advancement. This emphasis was the result of a rebellion against a concept of society which defined human position exclusively in terms of politically determined status, and which thus denied equality of opportunity. But the rebellion went too far. In order to establish justice it denied meaning and fulfillment to those who cannot advance — that is, to the majority — instead of realizing that the good society must give both justice and status.

* laissez-faire: 자유방임의 ** creed: 신조, 신념 *** epigram: 경구(警句)

① No economic reward was actually made.
② The social status of the masses grew too much.
③ Society defined individuals only as social beings.
④ Status was overshadowed by economic advancement.
⑤ The new order overemphasized individuals over groups.

03

밑줄 친 "closing the loop"가 다음 글에서 의미하는 바로 가장 적절한 것은?

24005-0024

The notion of a "circular economy" — in which materials circulate continuously, being used and reused time and time again — is an appealing vision. However, it is crucial to highlight just how far we are from that goal at present. Although most textiles are entirely recyclable, 73 percent of waste clothing was incinerated or went to landfills globally in 2015. Just 12 percent was recycled into low-value textile applications such as mattress stuffing and less than 1 percent was recycled back into clothing. Some would question how realistic the idea of "closing the loop" can be; the complexity of the fashion system means that there are multiple opportunities for materials to "leak" from the reuse cycle. Furthermore, it must be noted that fiber recycling is not without its own environmental footprint. Even the reuse of secondhand clothing has implications in terms of resource use and waste, particularly if items are transported over long distances, dry cleaned, and repackaged.

* textile: 직물 ** incinerate: 소각하다

① producing new fashion products every season
② sustainable textile recycling that has zero waste
③ a continuous effort to invent recyclable materials
④ creating and supplying only enough to meet demand
⑤ the end of exclusively producing certain fashion goods

04

24005-0025

밑줄 친 compel Time to give money in advance가 다음 글에서 의미하는 바로 가장 적절한 것은?

When anticipating the effects of time, we should mentally forecast what they are likely to be; we should not practically stop them from happening, by demanding the immediate performance of promises which time alone can fulfill. The man who makes his demand will find out that there is no worse or stricter usurer than Time; and that, if you compel Time to give money in advance, you will have to pay a rate of interest much higher than any usurer would require. It is possible, for instance, to make a tree burst forth into leaf, blossom, or even bear fruit within a few days, by the application of unslaked lime and artificial heat; but after that the tree will wither away. So a young man may abuse his strength — it may be only for a few weeks — by trying to do at nineteen what he could easily manage at thirty, and Time may give him the loan for which he asks; but the interest he will have to pay comes out of the strength of his later years; indeed, it is part of his very life itself.

* usurer: 고리대금업자 ** unslaked lime: 생석회(生石灰) *** wither away: 시들어 죽다

① pass on your responsibilities to someone else
② seek premature results before the time is right
③ aim to predict the success or failure of your work
④ ask for enough time to get your work done successfully
⑤ want to get paid for tasks you've completed ahead of schedule

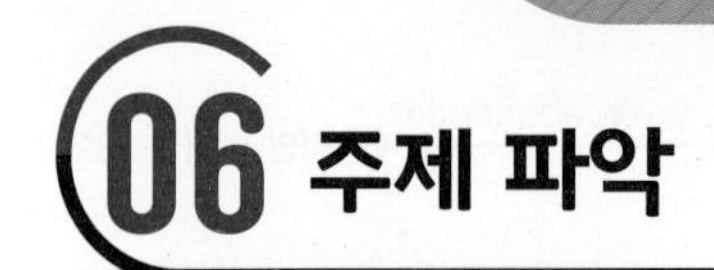

06 주제 파악

Gateway

2024학년도 수능 23번

24005-0026

다음 글의 주제로 가장 적절한 것은?

Managers of natural resources typically face market incentives that provide financial rewards for exploitation. For example, owners of forest lands have a market incentive to cut down trees rather than manage the forest for carbon capture, wildlife habitat, flood protection, and other ecosystem services. These services provide the owner with no financial benefits, and thus are unlikely to influence management decisions. But the economic benefits provided by these services, based on their non-market values, may exceed the economic value of the timber. For example, a United Nations initiative has estimated that the economic benefits of ecosystem services provided by tropical forests, including climate regulation, water purification, and erosion prevention, are over three times greater per hectare than the market benefits. Thus cutting down the trees is economically inefficient, and markets are not sending the correct "signal" to favor ecosystem services over extractive uses.

* exploitation: 이용 ** timber: 목재

① necessity of calculating the market values of ecosystem services
② significance of weighing forest resources' non-market values
③ impact of using forest resources to maximize financial benefits
④ merits of balancing forests' market and non-market values
⑤ ways of increasing the efficiency of managing natural resources

Words & Phrases in Use

- □ market incentive 시장 인센티브, 시장 유인
- □ carbon capture 탄소 포집
- □ habitat 서식지
- □ exceed 초과하다
- □ initiative 계획
- □ estimate 추정하다
- □ tropical 열대의
- □ regulation 조절
- □ purification 정화
- □ erosion 침식
- □ extractive 채취의, 채광의

STEP 1 도입 부분을 읽고, 반복적으로 제시된 핵심 개념을 파악한다.

- **market incentives** that provide financial rewards for **exploitation**
- market incentive to cut down trees

➡ **핵심 개념 1**: 산림 개발을 통해 얻는 시장 인센티브(**market incentives** that are gained through **forest exploitation**)

- **manage the forest** for carbon capture, wildlife habitat, flood protection, and other **ecosystem services**
- **These services** provide the owner with **no financial benefits**
- based on their **non-market values**

➡ **핵심 개념 2**: 산림 관리로 제공되는 생태계 서비스의 비시장적 가치(**non-market values of ecosystem services** provided by **forest management**)

STEP 2 핵심 개념 혹은 핵심 개념들의 관계에 대해 필자가 제시하는 견해를 찾는다.

- But the economic benefits provided by these services, based on their non-market values, may exceed the economic value of the timber.
  그러나 이러한 서비스가 그것들의 비시장적 가치에 근거하여 제공하는 경제적 이익은 목재의 경제적 가치를 초과할 수도 있다.
- Thus cutting down the trees is economically inefficient, and markets are not sending the correct "signal" to favor ecosystem services over extractive uses.
  따라서 벌목하는 것은 경제적으로 비효율적이며, 시장은 채취 이용보다 생태계 서비스를 선호하라는 올바른 '신호'를 보내지 않고 있다.

STEP 3 핵심 개념과 필자의 견해를 종합하여 글의 주제를 추론해 낸다.

천연자원의 관리자들이 삼림지가 주는 생태계 서비스의 비시장적 가치는 목재의 경제적 가치를 초과할 수도 있다는 점에 주목해야 함을 다루고 있는 글이다.

→ **따라서 글의 주제로 가장 적절한 것은 ② '산림 자원의 비시장적 가치를 따져 보는 것의 의의'이다.**

① 생태계 서비스의 시장 가치 산정의 필요성
③ 재정적 이익을 극대화하기 위한 산림 자원 이용의 영향
④ 숲의 시장 가치와 비시장 가치의 균형을 맞추는 것의 장점
⑤ 천연자원 관리의 효율성을 높이는 방법

01

다음 글의 주제로 가장 적절한 것은?

24005-0027

There are disturbing changes underway in today's school systems. Funding is frequently tied to scores achieved on standardized tests, which primarily evaluate rote memory. Teaching "to" tests like these inevitably focuses resources and curriculum on the lower-scoring students. The pressure to bring up test scores for these struggling students limits time for the kinds of individualized learning that challenges all students to reach their highest potential, and teachers have less opportunity to encourage creative thinking and incorporate hands-on activities. When education is not enriched by exploration, discovery, problem solving, and creative thinking, students are not truly engaged in their own learning. Because teachers are required to emphasize uninspiring workbooks and drills, more and more students are developing negative feelings about mathematics, science, history, grammar, and writing. Opportunities to authentically learn and retain knowledge are being replaced by instruction that teaches "to the tests."

* rote memory: 기계적 암기 ** authentically: 진정으로

① ways of helping students to stay focused during a test
② approaches of teaching to help develop students' creativity
③ dangers of associating students' test scores with their personality
④ problems of focusing on preparing students for standardized tests
⑤ impacts of hands-on activities on students' academic performance

02

다음 글의 주제로 가장 적절한 것은?

24005-0028

For many years, it was indeed widely believed that the adult brain was essentially 'set', with all the neurons and major connections we'd need. Sure, we learn new things and update our understanding of things all the time, meaning new connections are regularly being formed and turned over in networks governing learning and memory. But in terms of overall physical structure and major connections, the stuff that makes us 'what we are', the adult brain was long thought to be 'done'. However, in recent years there's been a steady stream of evidence revealing that the adult brain *can* change and adapt, even create new neurons, and experiences can still reshape the brain, even as we head into our twilight years. Consider the taxi driver study, where constant driving and navigation of chaotic London streets leads to increased hippocampus size, revealing the adult brain structure is somewhat malleable.

* hippocampus: (대뇌 측두엽의) 해마 ** malleable: 적응성 있는

① effects of negative life experiences on brain activity
② the solid connectivity of neural pathways in the brain
③ differences between the brain of an adult and that of a child
④ the parts of the brain used for analytic and creative thinking
⑤ the flexibility of the adult brain in adapting to new experiences

03 다음 글의 주제로 가장 적절한 것은?

24005-0029

Often ideological principles crystallize in laws, rules, and institutions that threaten to block deals. Nationalism requires that all resources belong to the state and that no one else may own them. Islamic fundamentalism prohibits interest payments on loans. Egyptian socialism demands that workers participate both in the management and the profits of an enterprise. Each of these principles can be an obstacle to deal making in particular cases. Yet, with some creativity, it is possible to structure a deal in such a way that the ideological principle is respected but business goes forward. For example, worker participation in management need not mean a seat on the company's board of directors, but simply an advisory committee that meets regularly with an officer of the company. And a petroleum development contract could be written in such a way that the ownership of oil is transferred not when the oil is in the ground but at the point that it leaves the flange of the well.

* crystallize: 구체화되다 ** flange: (철관 끝의) 테두리

① issues in sticking to original deal-making principles
② ideological barriers to universally accepted agreements
③ the impossibility of applying ideological principles universally
④ the critical role of business in breaking down ideological biases
⑤ the need to creatively design deals to navigate ideological hurdles

04 다음 글의 주제로 가장 적절한 것은?

24005-0030

The unquestioned assumption that any and all scientific knowledge — and associated technology — contributes to sustainability derives from faith in the importance of objective knowledge for solving global problems. Scientists obtain power and become the priests of our era to the extent that they provide a special form of knowledge that can be used to do such wonderful things. And we often consider that the final test of scientific knowledge: we can *do* things with its results, such as applying it to reverse the decline of an endangered species. Regardless, we know now that the linear view of the relation between science and social outcomes is flawed. Science may allow us to do things, but we can assess its contribution to sustainability only by incorporating broader contextual and socio-ecological questions. We typically think of sustainability as doing something out there in the world, when in fact we may need to first reassess the way we are setting the problem.

① concern about biodiversity loss and its impact on humanity
② constant scientific progress central to a sustainable future for all
③ requirements for science to solve problems of economic development
④ different scientific methods to justify the usefulness of technological innovation
⑤ necessity of integrating socio-environmental factors into science to achieve sustainability

07 제목 파악

Gateway

2024학년도 수능 24번

24005-0031

다음 글의 제목으로 가장 적절한 것은?

The concept of overtourism rests on a particular assumption about people and places common in tourism studies and the social sciences in general. Both are seen as clearly defined and demarcated. People are framed as bounded social actors either playing the role of hosts or guests. Places, in a similar way, are treated as stable containers with clear boundaries. Hence, places can be full of tourists and thus suffer from overtourism. But what does it mean for a place to be full of people? Indeed, there are examples of particular attractions that have limited capacity and where there is actually no room for more visitors. This is not least the case with some man-made constructions such as the Eiffel Tower. However, with places such as cities, regions or even whole countries being promoted as destinations and described as victims of overtourism, things become more complex. What is excessive or out of proportion is highly relative and might be more related to other aspects than physical capacity, such as natural degradation and economic leakages (not to mention politics and local power dynamics).

* demarcate: 경계를 정하다

① The Solutions to Overtourism: From Complex to Simple
② What Makes Popular Destinations Attractive to Visitors?
③ Are Tourist Attractions Winners or Losers of Overtourism?
④ The Severity of Overtourism: Much Worse than Imagined
⑤ Overtourism: Not Simply a Matter of People and Places

Words & Phrases in Use

- ☐ overtourism 과잉 관광(지역 규모에 비해 너무 많은 관광객이 오는 현상)
- ☐ rest on ~에 기초하다
- ☐ assumption 가정
- ☐ bounded 경계가 확실한
- ☐ stable 안정적인
- ☐ container 용기
- ☐ attraction (관광) 명소
- ☐ excessive 과도한
- ☐ out of proportion 균형이 안 맞는
- ☐ relative 상대적인
- ☐ degradation (질적) 저하
- ☐ leakage 유출

Solving Strategies

정답과 해설 17쪽

STEP 1 반복적인 어구 또는 특정 개념과 관련된 어구를 통해 글의 내용을 추측한다.

overtourism, people, places, physical capacity, more complex

➡ '과잉 관광, 사람, 장소, 물리적 수용력, 더 복잡한' 등의 어구가 반복해서 나오는 것으로 보아, '과잉 관광이 단순히 사람과 장소, 그리고 물리적 수용력의 측면에서 고려되는 것보다 더 복잡할 수도 있다'라는 내용의 글임을 알 수 있다.

STEP 2 글의 흐름을 따라가며 과잉 관광의 개념이 명확하게 정의되는 사람과 장소에 관한 특정한 가정에 기초하지만, 실제로는 그보다 더 복잡한 다른 측면과도 관련이 있을 수 있다는 필자의 견해를 파악한다.

■ 도입

- 과잉 관광의 개념은 관광학과 사회 과학 전반에서 흔히 볼 수 있는 사람과 장소에 관한 특정한 가정에 기초함(The concept of overtourism rests on a particular assumption about people and places common in tourism studies and the social sciences in general.)
- 그 둘(사람과 장소)은 모두 명확하게 정의되고 경계가 정해진 것으로 여겨짐(Both are seen as clearly defined and demarcated.)

■ 예시

사실, 수용력이 제한적이며 사실상 더 많은 방문객을 수용할 공간이 없는 특정 명소의 예가 있음(예: 에펠탑)(Indeed, there are examples of particular attractions that have limited capacity and where there is actually no room for more visitors. / ex) the Eiffel Tower)

■ 주제

그러나 도시, 지역 또는 심지어 국가 전체와 같은 장소가 목적지로 홍보되고 과잉 관광의 피해지로 묘사되는 상황에서는 사정이 더 복잡해짐(However, with places such as cities, regions or even whole countries being promoted as destinations and described as victims of overtourism, things become more complex.)

■ 결론

과도하거나 균형이 안 맞는 것은 매우 상대적이며, 물리적 수용력 이외에 (정치 및 지방 권력 역학은 말할 것도 없이) 자연의 질적 저하와 경제적 유출 같은 다른 측면과 더 관련이 있을 수도 있음(What is excessive or out of proportion is highly relative and might be more related to other aspects than physical capacity, such as natural degradation and economic leakages (not to mention politics and local power dynamics).)

STEP 3 선택지를 분석한 다음, 글의 주제를 정확하게 담고 있는 제목을 선택한다.

① 과잉 관광의 해결책: 복잡한 것에서 단순한 것으로
② 무엇이 인기 있는 목적지를 방문객에게 매력적으로 만드는가?
③ 관광 명소는 과잉 관광의 승자인가 아니면 패자인가?
④ 과잉 관광의 심각성: 상상했던 것보다 훨씬 더 나쁘다
⑤ 과잉 관광: 단순히 사람과 장소의 문제가 아니다

→ **STEP 2에서 확인한 글의 주제를 가장 정확하게 담고 있는 제목은 ⑤이다.**

01

다음 글의 제목으로 가장 적절한 것은?

24005-0032

According to research from the University of Arizona's Bureau of Applied Research in Anthropology, the average household ends up wasting an average of 14 percent of its grocery spending by throwing away unused or spoiled food. Even worse, 15 percent of that waste includes products that were never opened and were still within their expiration date! (This statistic really makes me cringe — why not just set dollar bills on fire while we're at it?) The study also found that a family of four ends up throwing away an average of $590 of perishable groceries per year, such as meat, produce, dairy, and grain products. You can save an average of $50 per month by avoiding overbuying perishable foods. Check your supplies before shopping and estimate the exact amount you'll need to buy for the next week. This is also a good time to throw away outdated leftovers, make sure perishable items are in view, and use up good leftovers for that day's meals.

* cringe: (겁이 나서) 움찔하다 ** perishable: 상하기 쉬운

① Patience Is a Strategic Shopping Virtue
② Don't Let the Low Food Prices Fool You
③ Creating a Health and Nutrition Shopping List
④ Stick to Your Grocery List and Shop as Quickly as Possible
⑤ Cut Food Waste Through Mindful Shopping and Meal Planning

02

24005-0033

다음 글의 제목으로 가장 적절한 것은?

Throughout history, human imagination has been a double-edged sword. On one hand, it pushes new discoveries, but for every newly established scientific fact, there are often multiple incorrect hypotheses, which must be corrected along the way or risk becoming myths. Thomas Edison is credited with saying: "I have not failed. I've just found 10,000 ways that won't work," implying that error is part of invention. Unfortunately, if errors or partial truths get circulated long enough, they can lead to a false echo chamber of repetition and suggest "truth" where none exists. For example, even though the *humors* have been discredited for centuries, some still believe in the myth that blood types (blood being one of the four *humors*) can determine personalities. A quick internet search finds more than five million websites related to this topic, meaning this myth is slow to die.

* echo chamber: 메아리 방 ** humor: 체액(인간의 기질을 정한다고 생각되었던 4가지 액)

① Scientific Efforts to Combat Harmful Myths
② Are Scientific Truths Proved or Just Believed?
③ Why Do We Believe That Personalities Are Inherent?
④ Diehard Myths Originating from Longstanding Errors
⑤ Blood Types as a Determinant of Personalities: A Plain Lie

03

다음 글의 제목으로 가장 적절한 것은?

24005-0034

Ideally, when we make art or engage in any creative activity by ourselves, we recognize its value and make time and space for it in our lives. The boom in coloring books and coloring pages in the past few years is one such example. It takes away the challenging part of visual art-making and skills and provides us with a level of challenge that is relatively easy and manageable. Our studies with cancer patients and caregivers showed that solitary activities like coloring helped in meditative and reflective ways by taking us to a space of distraction away from everyday concerns. Such activities do not necessarily help us resolve our problems; rather, they provide a time to rest and a way to focus our attention elsewhere until such time as we can address them directly. When we make art by ourselves, it can help us self-regulate; feel a sense of mastery, control, and agency over our lives; and engage in reflective, validating, contemplative, or meditative practices.

* meditative: 명상의 ** contemplative: 사색하는

① The Healing Effects of Cooperatively Making Art
② Lone Involvement in Creative Activities: A Mental Toolbox
③ Coloring Books: A Newly Emerging Pastime for Caregivers
④ Challenging Tasks Are More Enjoyable Than Manageable Ones
⑤ The Myth of Meditation: Does It Really Improve Concentration?

04 다음 글의 제목으로 가장 적절한 것은?

24005-0035

When Galileo rolled the balls down the inclined plane, he didn't merely look and see what happened. He very carefully measured the distance traveled and the time it took to travel that distance. From these measurements, he calculated the speed of travel. What he came up with was a mathematical equation relating numerical quantities. We can imagine that when he observed the moons of Jupiter, he didn't merely see some spots at various different places from night to night: he kept track of where the spots were, compared their positions from night to night, and perhaps did some calculations intended to compute what path they were traveling, to find out that their change in apparent position was consistent with their being bodies moving around Jupiter. Similarly, in my hypothetical bird experiment I imagined myself as a budding junior scientist weighing the stuff I put into the cage and calculating percentages by weight of what was eaten. It's obvious: numbers are important to science. Scientists measure and calculate; they don't just observe.

① Not Normal: The Uncertainties of Scientific Measurements
② The Fantasy of Accurate Calculation in Scientific Research
③ Who Is Responsible If a Scientist's Work Is Used for Harm?
④ What Is More Important in Science, an Experiment or a Theory?
⑤ True Scientific Activity: Pairing Measurements with Observations

08 도표 정보 파악

Gateway

2024학년도 수능 25번

24005-0036

다음 도표의 내용과 일치하지 않는 것은?

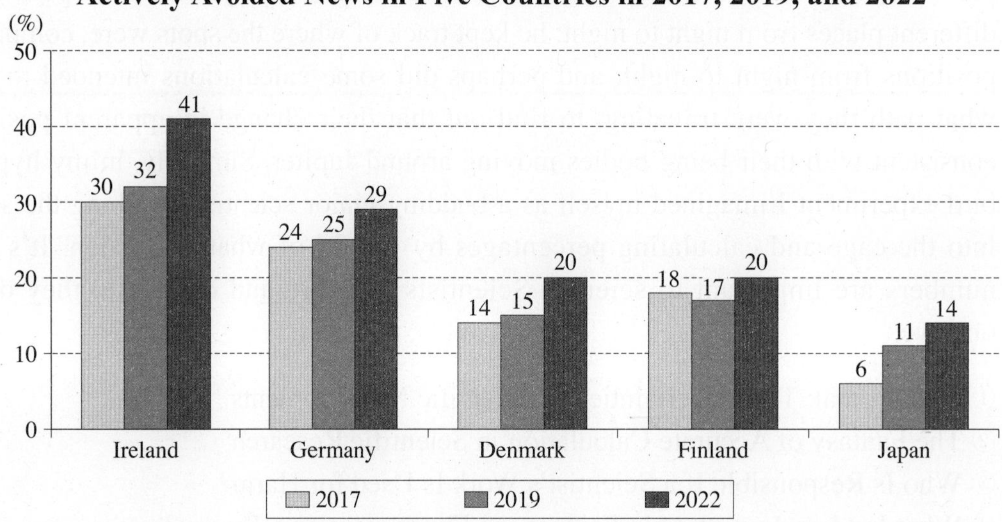

The above graph shows the percentages of the respondents in five countries who sometimes or often actively avoided news in 2017, 2019, and 2022. ① For each of the three years, Ireland showed the highest percentage of the respondents who sometimes or often actively avoided news, among the countries in the graph. ② In Germany, the percentage of the respondents who sometimes or often actively avoided news was less than 30% in each of the three years. ③ In Denmark, the percentage of the respondents who sometimes or often actively avoided news in 2019 was higher than that in 2017 but lower than that in 2022. ④ In Finland, the percentage of the respondents who sometimes or often actively avoided news in 2019 was lower than that in 2017, which was also true for Japan. ⑤ In Japan, the percentage of the respondents who sometimes or often actively avoided news did not exceed 15% in each of the three years.

Words & Phrases in Use

☐ respondent 응답자 ☐ actively 적극적으로 ☐ exceed 넘다

Solving Strategies

STEP 1 도표의 제목 및 내용을 파악한다.

- **도표의 제목**: Percentages of Respondents Who Sometimes or Often Actively Avoided News in Five Countries in 2017, 2019, and 2022(2017년, 2019년, 그리고 2022년에 때때로 또는 자주 적극적으로 뉴스를 회피한 다섯 개 국가의 응답자 비율)
- **도표의 내용**: 다섯 개 국가에서 2017년, 2019년, 그리고 2022년에 때때로 또는 자주 적극적으로 뉴스를 회피한 응답자들의 비율을 비교

STEP 2 글의 도입부를 통해 도표의 이해를 위한 개요를 파악한다.

The above graph shows the percentages of the respondents in five countries who sometimes or often actively avoided news in 2017, 2019, and 2022.

➡ 위 도표는 2017년, 2019년, 그리고 2022년에 때때로 또는 자주 적극적으로 뉴스를 회피한 다섯 개 국가의 응답자 비율을 보여 준다.

STEP 3 도표의 선택지 내용을 비교하여 일치 여부를 판단한다.

① 세 해 각각에 대해, 아일랜드가 도표의 국가 중, 때때로 또는 자주 적극적으로 뉴스를 회피한 응답자의 가장 높은 비율을 보여 주었음: 아일랜드가 세 해 각각 30퍼센트, 32퍼센트, 41퍼센트로 5개 국가 중 가장 높았음 ➡ 일치

② 독일의 경우, 때때로 또는 자주 적극적으로 뉴스를 회피한 응답자 비율이 세 해 각각 30퍼센트를 밑돌았음: 2017년 24퍼센트, 2019년 25퍼센트, 2022년 29퍼센트로 세 해 각각 30퍼센트를 밑돌았음 ➡ 일치

③ 덴마크의 경우, 2019년에 때때로 또는 자주 적극적으로 뉴스를 회피한 응답자 비율이 2017년의 비율보다는 더 높았으나 2022년의 비율보다는 더 낮았음: 2019년에 15퍼센트로 2017년 14퍼센트보다는 더 높았고 2022년의 20퍼센트보다는 더 낮았음 ➡ 일치

④ 핀란드의 경우, 2019년에 때때로 또는 자주 적극적으로 뉴스를 회피한 응답자 비율이 2017년의 비율보다 더 낮았으며, 이는 일본도 마찬가지였음: 일본은 2017년 6퍼센트, 2019년 11퍼센트로 핀란드의 경우와 같지 않았음 ➡ 불일치

⑤ 일본의 경우, 때때로 또는 자주 적극적으로 뉴스를 회피한 응답자 비율이 세 해 각각 15퍼센트를 넘지 않았음: 2017년 6퍼센트, 2019년 11퍼센트, 2022년 14퍼센트이었음 ➡ 일치

→ **따라서 도표의 내용과 일치하지 않는 것은 ④이다.**

01

다음 도표의 내용과 일치하지 않는 것은?

24005-0037

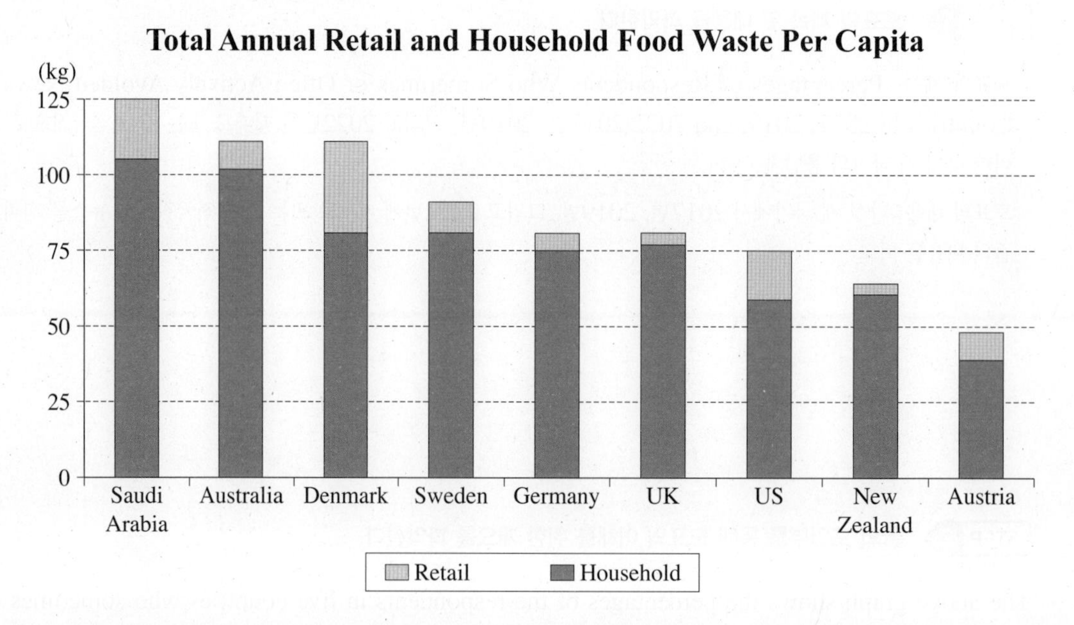

The above graph shows the total annual food waste at the retail and household stages, per capita, for nine selected countries. ① Among the countries, Saudi Arabia had the largest amount of total annual food waste per capita, immediately followed by Australia and Denmark. ② Austria was the only country whose total annual food waste per capita was less than 50 kg. ③ In terms of the annual food waste per capita at the retail stage, Denmark topped the list with more than 25 kg. ④ Germany had almost the same amount of total annual food waste per capita as the UK. ⑤ At the household stage, the US wasted almost as much as New Zealand; additionally, the former wasted even less than the latter at the retail stage.

* per capita: 1인당

02

24005-0038

다음 도표의 내용과 일치하지 않는 것은?

The World's Skiing Hotspots
Average Number of Skier Visits Per Season (Latest 5-Year Average)

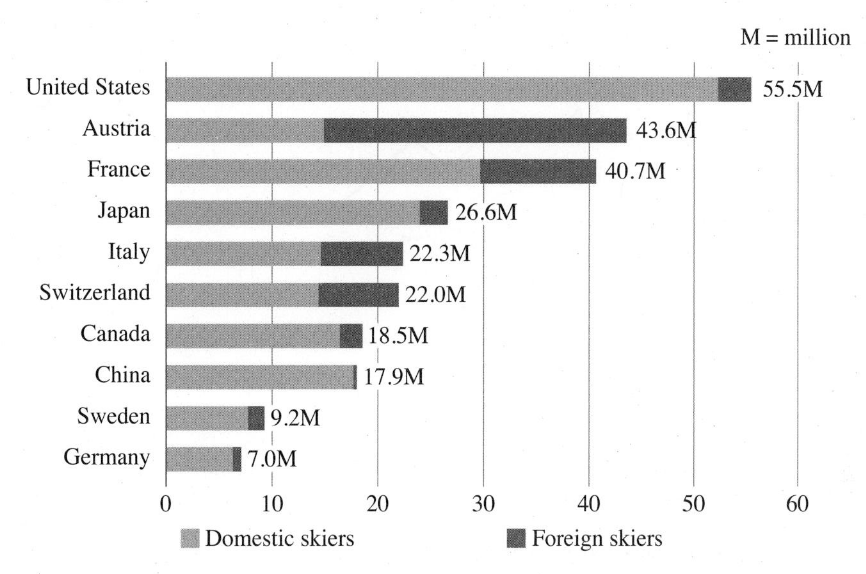

* Data from April 2022

The above graph shows the latest 5-year average number of skier visits per season in the world's skiing hotspots, as of April 2022. ① The United States had the largest average number of skier visits per season among the ten countries, with more than 50 million domestic skiers. ② Austria had the second largest average number of skier visits per season among the ten countries and recorded the most foreign skier visits. ③ The average number of domestic skier visits per season in Japan was more than that of domestic and foreign skier visits per season combined in Italy. ④ The average number of skier visits per season in Italy was more than that in Switzerland, with a difference of three hundred thousand visits. ⑤ The two countries with less than ten million average skier visits per season were Sweden and Germany, and the latter had more skiers than the former.

03 다음 도표의 내용과 일치하지 않는 것은?

24005-0039

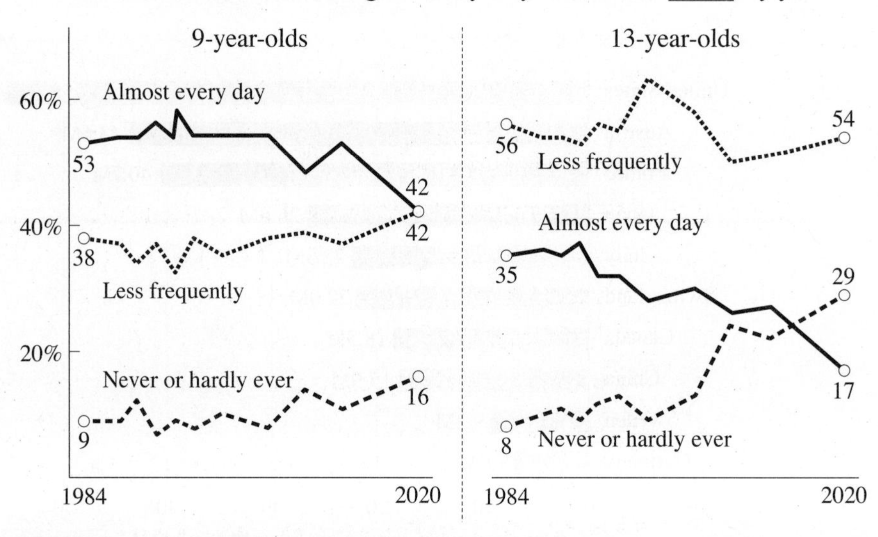

Note: Totals may not sum to 100% due to rounding.

The graphs above show the survey results on how often U.S. students aged 9 and 13 read for fun from 1984 to 2020. ① In 1984, more than half of 9-year-olds said they read for fun almost every day, but in 2020 the proportion dropped to the same level as that of 9-year-olds who said they read for fun less frequently. ② In 2020, the proportion of 9-year-olds who said they never or hardly ever read for fun was at its highest level in the survey period. ③ Among the 13-year-olds surveyed in 2020, 17% said they read for fun almost every day, which was less than half the percentage who said this in 1984. ④ In 2020, about three-in-ten students in this age group said they never or hardly ever read for fun, an increase of 21 percentage points compared to 1984. ⑤ In 2020, the share of 13-year-olds who reported reading for fun less frequently was 12 percentage points lower than that of their 9-year-old counterparts.

04 다음 도표의 내용과 일치하지 않는 것은?

24005-0040

Device Types Used by U.S. Adults for Their Online Shopping in 2022

% of U.S. adults who said, thinking about their general shopping habits, they ever bought things online using ...

	A smartphone	A desktop or laptop computer	A tablet
U.S. adults	76	69	28
Ages 18-29	87	69	20
30-49	92	71	29
50-64	69	67	32
65+	48	67	31
Upper income	81	86	36
Middle income	77	74	29
Lower income	74	51	23

Note: Those who did not give an answer are not shown.

The above graph shows the devices that U.S. adults used for their online shopping in 2022, including the distribution for each device by age and income. ① In 2022, smartphones were the most preferred method of online shopping for most Americans, with around three-quarters saying they used a smartphone for online purchases. ② In comparison, 69% reported using a desktop or laptop computer for online shopping, while only 28% said they used a tablet. ③ The use of smartphones for online shopping was more common among adults under 50 years old, especially with 92% of those aged 30 to 49 reporting that they shopped online using a smartphone. ④ Meanwhile, when it comes to age differences in online shopping using tablets, those aged 18 to 29 were more likely to use a tablet for online shopping than those aged 30 and older. ⑤ Device types for online shopping also varied by household income, with those with higher incomes more likely to use each device for online purchases.

09 내용 일치 · 불일치(설명문)

Gateway

2024학년도 수능 26번

24005-0041

Charles H. Townes에 관한 다음 글의 내용과 일치하지 않는 것은?

Charles H. Townes, one of the most influential American physicists, was born in South Carolina. In his childhood, he grew up on a farm, studying the stars in the sky. He earned his doctoral degree from the California Institute of Technology in 1939, and then he took a job at Bell Labs in New York City. After World War II, he became an associate professor of physics at Columbia University. In 1958, Townes and his co-researcher proposed the concept of the laser. Laser technology won quick acceptance in industry and research. He received the Nobel Prize in Physics in 1964. He was also involved in Project Apollo, the moon landing project. His contribution is priceless because the Internet and all digital media would be unimaginable without the laser.

① 어린 시절에 농장에서 성장하였다.
② 박사 학위를 받기 전에 Bell Labs에서 일했다.
③ 1958년에 레이저의 개념을 제안하였다.
④ 1964년에 노벨 물리학상을 수상하였다.
⑤ 달 착륙 프로젝트에 관여하였다.

Words & Phrases in Use

- ☐ influential 영향력 있는
- ☐ physicist 물리학자
- ☐ doctoral degree 박사 학위
- ☐ associate professor 부교수
- ☐ acceptance 인정
- ☐ be involved in ~에 관여하다
- ☐ contribution 공헌, 기여
- ☐ priceless 값을 매길 수 없는, 대단히 귀중한
- ☐ unimaginable 상상할 수 없는

Solving Strategies

정답과 해설 21쪽

STEP 1 **글의 전반부에서 누구에 관한 정보인지 확인한다.**

Charles H. Townes, one of the most influential American physicists, was born in South Carolina.

➡ 가장 영향력 있는 미국의 물리학자 중 한 명인 Charles H. Townes에 관한 글이다.

STEP 2 **선택지의 핵심 정보를 확인하고 글의 내용을 예측한다.**

① 농장에서 성장
➡ ~, he grew up on a farm, ~.

② 박사 학위를 받기 전 Bell Labs에서 일함
➡ He earned his doctoral degree from the California Institute of Technology in 1939, and then he took a job at Bell Labs ~.

③ 1958년에 레이저의 개념 제안
➡ In 1958, Townes and his co-researcher proposed the concept of the laser.

④ 1964년에 노벨 물리학상 수상
➡ He received the Nobel Prize in Physics in 1964.

⑤ 달 착륙 프로젝트에 관여
➡ He was also involved in Project Apollo, the moon landing project.

STEP 3 **글에 담겨 있는 정보 중에서 선택지의 서술 내용에 해당하는 부분을 찾아 비교하면서 일치하지 않는 진술을 찾는다.**

① In his childhood, he grew up on a farm, studying the stars in the sky.
➡ 어린 시절에 농장에서 성장하며 하늘에 있는 별을 연구했다고 했으므로, 글의 내용과 일치한다.

② He earned his doctoral degree from the California Institute of Technology in 1939, and then he took a job at Bell Labs in New York City.
➡ 1939년에 California Institute of Technology에서 박사 학위를 받았고 그 후 뉴욕시에 있는 Bell Labs에서 일자리를 얻었다고 했으므로, 글의 내용과 일치하지 않는다.

③ In 1958, Townes and his co-researcher proposed the concept of the laser.
➡ 1958년에 Townes와 그의 동료 연구자는 레이저의 개념을 제안했다고 했으므로, 글의 내용과 일치한다.

④ He received the Nobel Prize in Physics in 1964.
➡ 1964년에 노벨 물리학상을 받았다고 했으므로, 글의 내용과 일치한다.

⑤ He was also involved in Project Apollo, the moon landing project.
➡ 달 착륙 프로젝트인 아폴로 프로젝트에 관여했다고 했으므로, 글의 내용과 일치한다.

→ 따라서 ①, ③, ④, ⑤는 글의 내용과 일치하고, ②는 일치하지 않는다.

Exercises

01

24005-0042

Gladys West에 관한 다음 글의 내용과 일치하지 않는 것은?

Gladys West is an American mathematician. She was born in rural Virginia in 1930. She grew up on her family's small farm and dreamed of getting a good education. She worked hard and received a scholarship to Virginia State College (now Virginia State University), a historically black university. In 1956 she was hired as a mathematician at the naval base in Dahlgren, Virginia. She was the second black woman to be hired at the base and was one of only four black employees. There, West made significant contributions to the applied mathematics that deals with the measurement of the Earth's size, shape, and gravitational field. West and her team created a model that allows the GPS system to make accurate calculations of any location on Earth. West retired from the base in 1998 at the age of 68 but continued her education. She later completed a PhD in Public Administration at Virginia Tech by distance-learning.

* gravitational field: (지구의) 중력장

① 열심히 공부해서 Virginia State College에 갈 장학금을 받았다.
② Dahlgren에 있는 해군 기지에 수학자로 고용되었다.
③ 지구의 크기, 모양, 중력장 측정을 다루는 응용 수학에 기여했다.
④ 자신의 팀과 함께 GPS 시스템의 정확한 계산을 위한 모델을 만들었다.
⑤ 해군 기지에서 퇴직하며 자신의 교육을 그만두었다.

02

24005-0043

fado에 관한 다음 글의 내용과 일치하지 않는 것은?

Fado means "fate" in Portuguese, but is also the name of a form of music originating in Lisbon. It is usually performed by one singer, accompanied by dual *guitarras* (mandolin-shaped 12-string guitars) and a *viola* (Spanish guitar). Fado lyrics frequently focus on the hard realities of daily life, or the trials of love. Fado is also linked with the notion of *saudade*, which is a longing for something impossible to attain. *Fadistas*, as fado singers are known, often wear a black shawl of mourning, although songs can also be upbeat. Since the 19th century, fado has been performed in bars and clubs in working-class districts of Lisbon. It flourished during the Salazar years, before falling out of favour after the 1974 Revolution. In recent times, the genre has been revived and a new generation of musicians and singers can be heard in *casas de fado*, around Lisbon.

* lyrics: 가사 ** mourning: 애도

① 리스본에서 유래한 음악의 한 형태이다.
② 보통 한 명의 가수에 의해 공연된다.
③ 가사는 흔히 일상생활의 고단한 현실이나 사랑의 시련에 중점을 둔다.
④ 19세기 이후 리스본의 노동자 계층 구역에 있는 바와 클럽에서 공연되었다.
⑤ Salazar 시대에는 전혀 인기를 끌지 못했다.

03 Mayan ball game에 관한 다음 글의 내용과 일치하지 않는 것은?

24005-0044

The Mayan ball game was a very important part of Mayan culture. The ball games were played either by 2 players or by 2 teams of players. The object of the game was to put a ball through one of the stone rings while stopping the other team from putting the ball through the other stone ring. The ball was a little larger than a basketball and was made of solid rubber. For protection, players wore hard leather gloves, elbow and knee pads, masks, and belts that were made of wood or stone. Although not all historians agree, some think the rules did not allow players to touch the ball with their hands or feet. They used only their elbows, hips, and knees to hit the ball, and had to keep the ball from touching the ground. Spectators from all classes liked to watch and bet on the games.

① 두 명의 선수나 두 개의 팀으로 행해졌다.
② 공은 농구공보다 조금 더 컸다.
③ 선수들은 보호 장구를 착용했다.
④ 공이 땅에 닿는 것이 허용되었다.
⑤ 모든 계층의 관중들이 경기를 보며 내기하기를 좋아했다.

04 Lysippus에 관한 다음 글의 내용과 일치하지 않는 것은?

24005-0045

Lysippus was the most prominent, prolific and longest-lived of the great 4th-century BC sculptors. He was active, reportedly making 1,500 works, all of them in bronze. Considered the most accomplished artist of his age, Lysippus suitably became Alexander the Great's favourite — in fact, court-sculptor. The world-conqueror allowed almost no one else to sculpt him. Lysippus went on to make portrait busts of many of Alexander's warring successors, such as Cassander and Seleucus I. A native of Sicyon in the Peloponnese, Lysippus ran a workshop of almost industrial size that was continued after his death by his sons. Ancient writers such as Pliny relate that Lysippus invented an entirely new canon, or mathematically calculated ideal beauty, almost displacing that of Polyclitus.

* prolific: 다작의 ** bust: 흉상 *** canon: 규범

① 청동으로 된 1,500개의 작품을 만들었다고 전해진다.
② 당대의 가장 뛰어난 예술가로 여겨졌고 궁정 조각가가 되었다.
③ 알렉산더 대왕의 후계자들의 초상 흉상을 제작하였다.
④ 거의 산업적인 규모의 작업장을 운영했으나 그가 사망한 후에 문을 닫았다.
⑤ Pliny에 따르면 수학적으로 계산된 이상적인 미를 만들어 냈다.

10 내용 일치 · 불일치(실용문)

Gateway

2024학년도 수능 27번

24005-0046

Turtle Island Boat Tour에 관한 다음 안내문의 내용과 일치하지 않는 것은?

Turtle Island Boat Tour

The fantastic Turtle Island Boat Tour invites you to the beautiful sea world.

Dates: From June 1 to August 31, 2024

Tour Times

Weekdays	1 p.m.–5 p.m.
Weekends	9 a.m.–1 p.m.
	1 p.m.–5 p.m.

※ Each tour lasts four hours.

Tickets & Booking

- $50 per person for each tour
  (Only those aged 17 and over can participate.)
- Bookings must be completed no later than 2 days before the day of the tour.
- No refunds after the departure time
- Each tour group size is limited to 10 participants.

Activities

- Snorkeling with a professional diver
- Feeding tropical fish

※ Feel free to explore our website, www.snorkelingti.com.

① 주말에는 하루에 두 번 운영된다.
② 17세 이상만 참가할 수 있다.
③ 당일 예약이 가능하다.
④ 출발 시간 이후에는 환불이 불가능하다.
⑤ 전문 다이버와 함께 하는 스노클링 활동이 있다.

Words & Phrases in Use

☐ fantastic 환상적인 ☐ booking 예약 ☐ refund 환불
☐ feed 먹이를 주다

Solving Strategies

STEP 1 **안내문의 도입부 내용을 통해 소재를 파악한다.**

The fantastic Turtle Island Boat Tour invites you to the beautiful sea world.

➡ Turtle Island 보트 투어에 대한 안내문이다.

STEP 2 **선택지의 핵심 정보를 확인하고 안내문의 내용을 추측한다.**

① 주말에는 하루에 두 번 운영
 ➡ Tour Times, Weekends
② 17세 이상만 참가
 ➡ Only those aged 17 and over ~.
③ 당일 예약 가능
 ➡ Bookings must be completed ~.
④ 출발 시간 이후 환불 불가능
 ➡ No refunds after ~
⑤ 스노클링 활동
 ➡ Snorkeling with ~

STEP 3 **안내문에 포함된 정보 중에서 선택지의 서술 내용에 해당하는 부분을 찾아 비교하면서 일치하지 않는 진술을 찾는다.**

① Weekends 9 a.m.–1 p.m., 1 p.m.–5 p.m. 주말에는 하루에 두 번 운영
 ➡ 주말에는 투어 시간이 오전 9시~오후 1시, 오후 1시~오후 5시로 두 번 운영된다고 했으므로 안내문의 내용과 일치한다.
② Only those aged 17 and over can participate.
 ➡ 17세 이상만 참가할 수 있다고 했으므로 안내문의 내용과 일치한다.
③ Bookings must be completed no later than 2 days before the day of the tour.
 ➡ 예약은 늦어도 투어 당일 이틀 전에 완료되어야 한다고 했으므로 안내문의 내용과 일치하지 않는다.
④ No refunds after the departure time
 ➡ 출발 시간 이후에는 환불이 불가능하다고 했으므로 안내문의 내용과 일치한다.
⑤ Snorkeling with a professional diver
 ➡ 전문 다이버와 함께 하는 스노클링 활동이 있다고 했으므로 안내문의 내용과 일치한다.

→ **따라서 ①, ②, ④, ⑤는 안내문의 내용과 일치하고, ③이 일치하지 않는다.**

01

24005-0047

다음 Sunflower Gallery Renovation Notice의 내용과 일치하지 않는 것은?

Sunflower Gallery Renovation Notice

Renovation: March 1–31, 2024
The gallery will be closed during the renovation period.

Grand reopening exhibition (April 1–30): *Spring Flowers*

Gallery Membership Changes	Voucher Changes
20% Birthday Admission Discounts March birthdays can receive birthday discount in April. **Gallery Points Expiration Date** The expiration date of all gallery points expiring in March will be extended by 2 months.	All vouchers with March included in the term will be valid for an additional month. (e.g.: December 2023–June 2024 will be valid through July 2024.)

- The gallery information desk will be open during the renovation.
- As always, our digital gallery is open 24/7!

* voucher: 상품권 ** expiration: 만료

① Sunflower Gallery는 한 달 동안 보수 공사를 한다.
② Sunflower Gallery의 재개관 전시회는 4월 1일에 시작한다.
③ 3월이 생일인 회원은 4월에 입장료를 할인받을 수 있다.
④ 사용 기간에 3월이 포함된 모든 상품권은 두 달 연장된다.
⑤ Sunflower Gallery의 보수 공사 기간에 안내 데스크는 열려 있다.

02

24005-0048

Kids' Night Out에 관한 다음 안내문의 내용과 일치하는 것은?

Kids' Night Out

Kids' Night Out is an opportunity for children ages 5–12 to come to the Chester University Recreation Center to play, do crafts, watch a movie, interact with other children, and enjoy a pizza party.

Event Dates

- Every second Friday of the month from May through August

Schedule

5:00 – 6:15 p.m.: crafts
6:15 – 6:50 p.m.: pizza party
6:50 – 7:55 p.m.: watching a movie
7:55 – 9:00 p.m.: other activities
* Pickup starts at 8:30 p.m., 30 minutes before the end of the program.

Registration

- Registration is online at www.curc.edu and costs $30 per child.
- Registration is required by 5 p.m. the day prior to each event day.
- If you are a university faculty or staff member, use your university ID and password to log in.
- If you are not a university faculty or staff member, create a guest account by selecting "SIGN UP."

① 매주 금요일에 열리는 행사이다.
② 픽업은 오후 9시부터 할 수 있다.
③ 행사 참가 비용은 무료이다.
④ 각 행사 당일 전날 오후 5시까지 등록해야 한다.
⑤ 대학교 교직원이 아니면 등록할 수 없다.

03

2024 Sunrise Zoo Spring Camp에 관한 다음 안내문의 내용과 일치하지 않는 것은?

24005-0049

2024 Sunrise Zoo Spring Camp

Spring into a new season and discover the wonders of nature at the Sunrise Zoo Spring Camp! Participants will explore the Sunrise Zoo and learn about the plants, pollinators, and animals that return in the spring.

- All camps are 3 days long (March 6 – 8) and run from 9:00 a.m. to 3:00 p.m.
- Participants should wear outdoor clothing, including comfortable shoes.
- Participants should bring a sack lunch and beverage. Snacks will be provided.
- Cost: $120
- Camps: Four camps are run according to grade.
  - Zoo Tots (Pre-K & Kindergarten)
  - Zoo Buddies (grades 1 & 2)
  - Zoo Explorers (grades 3 & 4)
  - Zoo Investigators (grades 5 & 6)

Registration Details

- Please visit www.sunrisezoo.org to register and see complete program details.
- No phone registrations will be accepted.
- If you have any questions, please contact us by e-mail at education@sunrisezoo.org.

* pollinator: 꽃가루받이 매개자 ** tot: 어린아이

① 참가자는 봄에 돌아오는 동물에 관해 배우게 된다.
② 하루에 6시간씩 3일간 참여하게 된다.
③ 간식은 제공되지 않는다.
④ 학년에 따라 4개의 캠프가 운영된다.
⑤ 전화 등록은 받지 않는다.

04 Homer Elementary School Spelling Bee에 관한 다음 안내문의 내용과 일치하는 것은?

24005-0050

Homer Elementary School Spelling Bee

Are you a good speller? Do you like competing?
Then join the school spelling bee!

Who: Open to all students grades 1 through 4
When: Wednesday, March 20 at 4:30 p.m.
Where: The Homer Elementary School auditorium

How to participate
- You can sign up with your English teacher or post your application on the school website.

※ If you want to help set up, come to the English teachers' office and sign up.

Format
- There will be 5 rounds of spelling challenges.
- All students who pass the final round will be winners!

Prizes
- T-shirts, USB drives, pizza coupons, and medals

For questions or to sign up, please visit www.homeressb.ac.au, or the English teachers' office.

① 1학년부터 6학년까지 참가할 수 있다.
② 3월 20일 오전에 개최된다.
③ 학교 웹사이트를 통해서만 신청할 수 있다.
④ 다섯 판의 철자 맞히기 도전이 진행된다.
⑤ 상품에는 피자 쿠폰이 포함되지 않는다.

11 어법 정확성 파악

Gateway

2024학년도 수능 29번

24005-0051

다음 글의 밑줄 친 부분 중, 어법상 틀린 것은?

A number of studies provide substantial evidence of an innate human disposition to respond differentially to social stimuli. From birth, infants will orient preferentially towards the human face and voice, ① seeming to know that such stimuli are particularly meaningful for them. Moreover, they register this connection actively, imitating a variety of facial gestures that are presented to them — tongue protrusions, lip tightenings, mouth openings. They will even try to match gestures ② which they have some difficulty, experimenting with their own faces until they succeed. When they ③ do succeed, they show pleasure by a brightening of their eyes; when they fail, they show distress. In other words, they not only have an innate capacity for matching their own kinaesthetically experienced bodily movements with ④ those of others that are visually perceived; they have an innate drive to do so. That is, they seem to have an innate drive to imitate others whom they judge ⑤ to be 'like me'.

* innate: 타고난 ** disposition: 성향 *** kinaesthetically: 운동감각적으로

Words & Phrases in Use

- ☐ substantial 상당한
- ☐ infant 아기, 유아
- ☐ register 표현하다, 나타내다
- ☐ capacity 능력
- ☐ drive 욕구, 추진력
- ☐ differentially 구별하여, 달리
- ☐ orient 향하다
- ☐ protrusion 내밀기
- ☐ visually 시각적으로
- ☐ imitate 모방하다
- ☐ stimulus 자극 (*pl.* stimuli)
- ☐ preferentially 우선(적으로)
- ☐ distress 불편함, 괴로움
- ☐ perceive 지각하다

Solving Strategies

정답과 해설 26쪽

STEP 1 글의 내용을 파악하면서 읽는다.

인간에게는 타인을 모방하려는 타고난 성향이 있다는 것을 설명하는 글이다.

STEP 2 밑줄 친 부분이 포함된 문장의 구조를 파악하여 어법의 정확성을 판단한다.

① 분사구문을 이끄는 분사

From birth, infants will orient preferentially towards the human face and voice, seeming to know that such stimuli are particularly meaningful for them.

문장의 주어인 infants를 부가적으로 설명하는 분사구문을 이끄는 분사인데, infants가 seem이라는 행위의 주체이므로 현재분사 seeming은 적절하다. ➡ OK

② 관계절을 이끄는 관계사

They will even try to match gestures which they have some difficulty, experimenting with their own faces until they succeed.

관계사 which 다음에 이어지는 관계절이 필수 요소를 모두 갖추고 있다. ➡ STEP 3

③ 조동사 do

When they do succeed, they show pleasure by a brightening of their eyes; when they fail, they show distress.

do는 동사 succeed를 강조하는 조동사이다. ➡ OK

④ 대명사

In other words, they not only have an innate capacity for matching their own kinaesthetically experienced bodily movements with those of others that are visually perceived; they have an innate drive to do so.

those는 bodily movements를 대신하는 대명사이다. ➡ OK

⑤ 목적격 보어를 이끄는 to부정사

That is, they seem to have an innate drive to imitate others whom they judge to be ‘like me’.

to be는 judge의 목적격 보어 역할을 하는 to부정사구를 이끈다. ➡ OK

STEP 3 어법상 틀린 것으로 생각되는 ②를 정밀하게 분석하여 답을 확정한다.

They will even try to match gestures [which they have some difficulty], experimenting with their own faces until they succeed.

[ ]는 의미상 gestures를 수식하는 관계절이어야 하는데, 관계절이 필수 요소인 주어와 목적어를 모두 갖추고 있으므로, 전치사를 수반한 관계사 with which가 되어야 한다.

→ **which는 with which로 고쳐야 한다.**

Exercises

01

다음 글의 밑줄 친 부분 중, 어법상 틀린 것은?

24005-0052

A good way to make human-machine interaction more natural would be to develop a better metaphor. A computer metaphor is a familiar object or activity that your computer imitates with ① its commands, display arrangements, and behavior. The two main metaphors we have today are the desktop and the browser. In the desktop metaphor, the display screen mimics a typical desk; information ② is kept inside folders, which can be opened, closed, and slipped into other folders. With Web browsing, the metaphor is downtown window shopping; you gaze at various "storefronts," see ③ one you like, and (click) you enter. Inside, there are more options to browse, you choose another, and again you enter. Like a linguistic metaphor, the power of a good computer metaphor is that it makes a new system you don't know behave like an old "system" ④ which you are familiar. This lets you use the new system and ⑤ get useful results out of it easily, since you don't have to struggle learning new concepts and commands.

02

다음 글의 밑줄 친 부분 중, 어법상 틀린 것은?

24005-0053

Human activity on the landscape can significantly contribute to soil erosion. In a natural state, vegetation serves as natural protection against erosion because the network of roots ① helps hold the soil in place against various erosive forces, such as wind and water. Scientists estimate ② that, in the United States, 30% of erosion is due to natural forces and 70% is due to human impact. Oftentimes, when people use the land for farming, the protective covering of natural vegetation is destroyed, and the erosion process speeds up. In fact, studies have shown that ③ artificially created erosion played a big part in the downfall of many early civilizations. Poor land management practices degraded the soil until it was no longer productive enough to support the population ④ living in the area. Early civilizations that recognized the disastrous effects of erosion used devices such as terracing the land to keep from plowing, planting, and irrigating on hillside slopes ⑤ which water could wash the fertile soil away.

* erosion: 침식 ** plow: 쟁기질하다 *** irrigate: 관개 작업을 하다

03

다음 글의 밑줄 친 부분 중, 어법상 틀린 것은?

24005-0054

It used to be thought that Neanderthals were dim-witted, slouching cavemen completely covered with hair. But this reputation is based on just one fossil, which modern scholarship has proved happens to be ① that of an old, diseased, and injured man. He was approximately forty or forty-five years old when he died — very old for people at that time. Healthy Neanderthals probably walked erect. Objects ② were found at Neanderthal sites show that Neanderthals could make complex tools. The characteristics of their skulls suggest that they probably could speak, although perhaps not with the full range of sounds that modern humans make. Sites also show that they did not necessarily live in caves, but, if they did, they likely altered the caves to make them more ③ livable. Sometimes they built shelters rather than ④ settled in caves. In 1996, scientists digging at a Neanderthal site in Slovenia announced they had found ⑤ what appeared to be a musical instrument, a flute made from a bear bone.

* dim-witted: 우둔한 ** slouching: 구부정한 자세로 앉은[선]

04

다음 글의 밑줄 친 부분 중, 어법상 틀린 것은?

24005-0055

Discrimination occurs on two levels: institutional and individual. On the institutional level, discriminatory practices are embedded in the social structures of a society, whereas on the individual level, discrimination takes place ① during direct interactions among individuals or groups. Unlike individual discrimination, which tends to be overt, intentional, and direct, institutional discrimination is often covert and unintentional, and this invisibility makes ② them much harder to detect. Standardized testing in schools, for example, may exclude certain ③ historically marginalized groups from succeeding in academic settings. Although the government may not have intentionally established testing standards that ④ are culturally or class biased, in practice these standards tend to have a disproportionate negative effect on ethnic minority students. Furthermore, institutional discrimination often has a generational or cyclical impact on certain ethnic minority groups and therefore its consequences are as severe, if not more so, than for those ⑤ suffering individual discrimination.

* embed: 묻다, 끼워 넣다 ** overt: 공공연한 *** marginalize: (사회적으로) 소외시키다

12 어휘 적절성 파악

Gateway

2024학년도 수능 30번

24005-0056

다음 글의 밑줄 친 부분 중, 문맥상 낱말의 쓰임이 적절하지 않은 것은?

Bazaar economies feature an apparently flexible price-setting mechanism that sits atop more enduring ties of shared culture. Both the buyer and seller are aware of each other's ① restrictions. In Delhi's bazaars, buyers and sellers can ② assess to a large extent the financial constraints that other actors have in their everyday life. Each actor belonging to a specific economic class understands what the other sees as a necessity and a luxury. In the case of electronic products like video games, they are not a ③ necessity at the same level as other household purchases such as food items. So, the seller in Delhi's bazaars is careful not to directly ask for very ④ low prices for video games because at no point will the buyer see possession of them as an absolute necessity. Access to this type of knowledge establishes a price consensus by relating to each other's preferences and limitations of belonging to a ⑤ similar cultural and economic universe.

* constraint: 압박 ** consensus: 일치

Words & Phrases in Use

- □ bazaar 바자, 시장, 상점가, 시장 거리
- □ feature 특징으로 하다
- □ apparently 겉으로 보기에
- □ flexible 유연한
- □ mechanism 메커니즘(사물의 작용 원리나 구조)
- □ atop 위에, 맨 꼭대기에
- □ restriction 제약, 제한
- □ assess 판단하다, 평가하다
- □ financial 재정적인
- □ necessity 필수품, 필수 사항
- □ luxury 사치품
- □ possession 소유
- □ establish 형성하다, 수립하다

Solving Strategies

정답과 해설 29쪽

STEP 1 **글의 앞부분을 읽으며 중심 소재를 파악한다.**

중심 소재: 유연한 가격 설정 메커니즘을 특징으로 하는 바자 경제

STEP 2 **글의 논리적인 흐름을 따라가며 문장 간 또는 문장 내에서 근거를 파악하여 밑줄 친 낱말의 적절성을 파악한다.**

① restrictions: 제약에 대해 앎 → 흥정이 가능해짐
판매자와 구매자 둘 다 서로의 제약에 관해 알고 있어서 가격의 흥정이 가능하다는 맥락이므로, 적절하다.

② assess: 재정적 압박의 판단 가능 → 가격에 대한 의견 일치에 도달
판매자와 구매자는 둘 다 일상생활에서 상대방이 가지는 재정적 압박을 판단할 수 있으며, 따라서 서로 가격 일치에 도달할 수 있다는 맥락이므로, 적절하다.

③ necessity: 비디오 게임에 대한 이해 → 필수품이 아니라는 공감
비디오 게임은 식료품과 같은 필수품이 아니라는 이해가 공유되었다는 맥락이므로, 적절하다.

④ low: 서로의 제약을 알고 있음 → 비디오 게임의 가격 제시
필수품이 아닌 비디오 게임의 경우 너무 높은 가격을 제시하면 구매자가 구매를 포기하게 된다. 따라서 판매자는 적절히 낮은 가격을 제시하려 주의할 것이다. 그러므로 low는 문맥상 적절하지 않다.

⑤ similar: 판매자와 구매자의 공유하는 이해 → 비슷한 문화와 경제적인 배경에서 비롯됨
판매자와 구매자가 비슷한 문화적 경제적 세계를 공유하므로 가격 흥정이 이루어진다는 맥락이므로, 적절하다.

STEP 3 **문맥상 적절해 보이지 않는 ④low의 대안을 생각해 보고 문맥을 점검하여 답을 확정한다.**

델리에 있는 바자의 사례에서 구매자와 판매자가 서로의 제약을 알고 있으므로, 필수품으로 여겨지지 않는 비디오 게임의 경우에는 너무 높은 가격을 제시하지 않아야 구매자가 구매를 포기하지 않아 거래가 이루어질 수 있다는 맥락이 되어야 한다.
→ 따라서 ④ low(낮은)를 high(높은)와 같은 낱말로 바꿔야 한다.

Exercises

01

다음 글의 밑줄 친 부분 중, 문맥상 낱말의 쓰임이 적절하지 않은 것은?

24005-0057

One should perhaps ask why even very simple animals would prefer familiar stimuli or familiar other animals. A tendency to grow fond of the familiar would help stamp in the ① preference for a stable environment (so animals might learn to like their homes). It would certainly promote stable social bonds. Imagine, for example, that nature programmed animals in the ② opposite way, so that familiarity led to contempt or some other form of disliking. How would families stay together? How would friendships, alliances, or other partnerships ③ survive? If you always preferred a stranger to someone you knew, social life would be in constant turmoil and turnover. In contrast, if you automatically grew to like the people you saw ④ regularly, you would soon prefer them over strangers, and groups would form and stabilize easily. Given the advantages of stable groups (e.g., people know each other, know how to work together, know how to make decisions together, know how to adjust to each other), it is not surprising that nature ⑤ removed animals that grew to like (rather than dislike) each other on the basis of familiarity.

* contempt: 경멸 ** alliance: 동맹 *** turmoil: 혼란

02

다음 글의 밑줄 친 부분 중, 문맥상 낱말의 쓰임이 적절하지 않은 것은?

24005-0058

Social psychologist Irving Janis recognized the problems of groupthink, but felt that it could be avoided. It is most likely to develop when team spirit becomes more ① important than the opinions of individual members. It's also likely to form if the group is made up of like-minded people to begin with, and if they are faced with a difficult decision. To prevent groupthink, Janis proposed a system of organization that ② encourages independent thinking. The leader of the group should appear to be impartial, so that members do not feel any pressure to obey. Furthermore, he or she should get the group to ③ examine all the options, and to consult people outside the group, too. ④ Agreement, Janis argued, is actually a good thing, and he suggested that members should be asked to play "devil's advocate" — introducing an alternative point of view in order to provoke discussion. In addition to ⑤ ensuring that the group comes to more rational and fair decisions, allowing members to retain their individuality creates a healthier team spirit than the state of groupthink, which results from conformity and obedience.

* groupthink: 집단 순응 사고 ** provoke: 일으키다, 유발하다

03

다음 글의 밑줄 친 부분 중, 문맥상 낱말의 쓰임이 적절하지 않은 것은?

24005-0059

The alternative world provided by cyberspace is essentially an ideal private world in which each person controls the information that is revealed. In this world, the full identity of the person is not revealed, and the two people are physically ① remote from each other. Hence, it is much easier to keep private whatever areas the participants so wish. These circumstances do not lead the participants to remain completely ② mysterious — on the contrary, in many cases it leads the participants to reveal much more about themselves than they would usually do. When we can keep private that which seems to ③ threaten us, we can be more open concerning other matters. The greater degree of openness ④ generates a greater degree of emotional closeness as well. Accordingly, in online relationships we can find both greater privacy and greater closeness and openness — this considerably ⑤ maximizes the common conflict between openness and privacy.

04

다음 밑줄 친 부분 중, 문맥상 낱말의 쓰임의 적절하지 않은 것은?

24005-0060

People often have different definitions of education, as the nature of education is somewhat fluid. Nearly 600 years ago the printing press ① changed the way much of education occurred. Students began reading information, coupled with the information a teacher would share. To ensure that the student had retained the information, a test or paper was often required to make an ② assessment of that retention. This downloading of information is known as the banking model, and what the banking model does is it ③ reduces the student from being a critical and independent thinker to being a receptacle for facts. The process of the banking model ④ raises the power and control of the teacher while failing to recognize that students are more than simply unthinking blank slates. The concept, then, is placed squarely into the minds of students, who are taught that they are subservient and beholden to the keeper of information. As a result, students have ⑤ considerable control over their own thinking and their own education.

* subservient: 부차적인 역할을 하는, 보조적인 ** beholden: 신세를 진

13 빈칸 내용 추론

Gateway

2024학년도 수능 32번

24005-0061

다음 빈칸에 들어갈 말로 가장 적절한 것은?

A musical score within any film can add an additional layer to the film text, which goes beyond simply imitating the action viewed. In films that tell of futuristic worlds, composers, much like sound designers, have added freedom to create a world that is unknown and new to the viewer. However, unlike sound designers, composers often shy away from creating unique pieces that reflect these new worlds and often present musical scores that possess familiar structures and cadences. While it is possible that this may interfere with creativity and a sense of space and time, it in fact ________________. Through recognizable scores, visions of the future or a galaxy far, far away can be placed within a recognizable context. Such familiarity allows the viewer to be placed in a comfortable space so that the film may then lead the viewer to what is an unfamiliar, but acceptable vision of a world different from their own.

* score: 악보 ** cadence: (율동적인) 박자

① frees the plot of its familiarity
② aids in viewer access to the film
③ adds to an exotic musical experience
④ orients audiences to the film's theme
⑤ inspires viewers to think more deeply

Words & Phrases in Use

- ☐ layer 층
- ☐ composer 작곡가
- ☐ shy away from ~을 피하다
- ☐ reflect 반영하다
- ☐ present 내놓다, 제시하다
- ☐ structure 구조
- ☐ interfere with ~을 방해하다
- ☐ recognizable 쉽게 인식할 수 있는
- ☐ galaxy 은하계
- ☐ context 맥락, 환경

STEP 1 **도입 부분을 읽고, 글의 중심 소재를 파악한다.**

- 영화에서 악보의 역할: 영화 텍스트에 추가적인 층을 더함 → 보이는 연기를 단순히 흉내 내는 것 이상임
(A musical score within any film can add an additional layer to the film text, which goes beyond simply imitating the action viewed.)
- 미래 세계에 관한 영화에서의 작곡가: 관객에게 알려지지 않은 새로운 세계를 창조할 수 있는 자유를 가짐
(In films that tell of futuristic worlds, composers, much like sound designers, have added freedom to create a world that is unknown and new to the viewer.)

➡ **영화 음악 작곡가에 관한 글**임을 알 수 있다.

STEP 2 **전개 부분을 읽고, 영화 음악 작곡가에 대한 구체적 내용을 파악하여 빈칸에 기술되어야 할 내용을 추론한다.**

영화 음악 작곡가: 흔히 친숙한 구조와 박자가 있는 악보를 내놓음

(However, unlike sound designers, **composers** often shy away from creating unique pieces that reflect these new worlds and **often present musical scores that possess familiar structures and cadences.**)

⬇

빈칸에 기술되어야 할 내용: **영화 음악 작곡가가 친숙한 악보를 내놓는 것의 효과**

(While it is possible that **this** may interfere with creativity and a sense of space and time, **it in fact** ____________________.)

STEP 3 **중심 소재에 관한 글의 주제를 파악하고, 빈칸 이후의 내용을 바탕으로 정답을 확인한다.**

- **주제**: 영화 음악 작곡가는 관객에게 알려지지 않은 새로운 세계를 창조하는 데 있어 독특한 악곡을 피하고 친숙한 구조와 박자를 가지고 있는 악보를 내놓는 경우가 많은데, 이러한 친숙함을 통해 관객은 편안한 공간에 놓일 수 있게 되어 미래 세계에 대한 낯설지만 받아들일 수 있는 상상에 이르게 된다는 내용의 글이다.

→ **따라서 빈칸에 들어갈 말로 가장 적절한 것은 ② '관객이 영화에 다가가는 데 도움이 된다'이다.**

① 줄거리에서 그것의 친숙함을 없앤다
③ 이국적인 음악적 경험을 더한다
④ 관객을 영화의 주제에 익숙하게 한다
⑤ 관객을 더 깊이 생각하도록 고무한다

Exercises

01 다음 빈칸에 들어갈 말로 가장 적절한 것은?

24005-0062

In his 1967 book, Coopersmith first noticed a positive relationship between self-esteem levels in mothers and their children. But Bednar, Wells, and Peterson made considerable use of this factor by pointing out that parents actually *show* their children the route to self-esteem by how they handle their own challenges, conflicts, and issues. The impact of parents' behavior upon the child's self-esteem is undeniable; given the immaturity of children, however, parents' expression of their own resolution of the self-esteem question is far more influential than what they teach verbally. Parents who face life's challenges honestly and openly and who attempt to cope with difficulties instead of avoiding them thereby expose their children early to a pro–self-esteem problem-solving strategy. Those who avoid dealing with difficulties reveal a negative route for handling the challenges and problems of life. Either way, it is important to remember that ____________ helps set the stage for healthy self-esteem or problems with it.

① planning ② modeling ③ delaying
④ debating ⑤ supporting

02 다음 빈칸에 들어갈 말로 가장 적절한 것은?

24005-0063

Several different strategies will be used to get us to buy. For new products, marketers want to motivate us to try their product, so the job is to advertise it as much as possible to get the word out. With an established product, marketers will either want us to try it again (reminder advertising), or they may try to get us to consume more of their product. A good way to do this is to provide new ____________. One brand of baking soda is a good example. After women entered the job market en masse in the 1960s and there was less time for baking, the company promoted using the product to keep the freezer and refrigerator smelling clean — and to change the box every three months. Or when women started earning significant salaries and getting married later, the diamond industry started selling diamond rings to women, claiming that the left hand is for "we" and the right is for "me."

* en masse: 대거, 집단으로

① uses ② packages ③ names
④ designs ⑤ tools

03

다음 빈칸에 들어갈 말로 가장 적절한 것은?

24005-0064

When kids feel forced to do things — or are too tightly regulated in the *way* they do things — they're likely to become less interested in what they're doing and less likely to stick with something challenging. In an intriguing experiment, parents were invited to sit on the floor next to their very young children — not even two years old — who were playing with toys. Some of the parents immediately took over the task or barked out instructions ("Put the block in. No, not there. *There!*"). Others were content to let their kids explore, providing encouragement and offering help only when it was needed. Later, the babies were given something else to play with, this time without their parents present. It turned out that, once they were on their own, those who had ____________ parents were apt to give up more easily rather than trying to figure out how the new toy worked.

* intriguing: 아주 흥미로운

① playful ② democratic ③ respectful
④ controlling ⑤ unconcerned

04

다음 빈칸에 들어갈 말로 가장 적절한 것은?

24005-0065

It is critical, as we recreate mutual provision in a sustainable form, that we keep track of the line between needs and wants. While a permanent place for people on Earth requires that our needs be met, people gathering about themselves quantities of unnecessary goods, while others lack food and shelter, cannot be part of a durable order. A society that oppresses other people to bloat itself will not stop at undermining foreign nations. The ethic will express itself with exploitation at home. While ingenuity and hard work will still lead to improved circumstances as communities increase their effective use of local resources, when one's achieved wealth is at the expense of others, much goodwill, effort and resources will be lost to resentment, rebellion and repression. A huge bonus is available for everyone when the focus of development is ____________________________.

* bloat oneself: 자신의 배를 불리다 ** exploitation: 착취 *** resentment: 분노

① securing and improving the quality of life for all
② teaching individuals skills that benefit local communities
③ pursuing economic prosperity at the expense of inequality
④ becoming a successful individual through continuous efforts
⑤ encouraging less consumption of products to preserve resources

05 다음 빈칸에 들어갈 말로 가장 적절한 것은?

24005-0066

As Marshall McLuhan suggested so presciently in 1964, "the medium is the message," which means that, beyond the content that is conveyed, the medium itself has an impact by its very nature and unique characteristics. For example, the use of social media means that we have less need to interact with others directly. This distancing of communication has real implications for children's development. If learning to communicate with others is a skill that develops with practice, children's constant use of social media reduces the experiences they have with which to learn social skills. McLuhan asserts that we are so focused on the content of the technology that we neglect to notice the influence of the technology itself on people. This observation is certainly true today: we focus on what the technology provides (e.g., video, text messages, social media), but we fail to consider ________________________.

* presciently: 예지력 있게

① how much these technologies benefit us
② that technology is just a container for thought
③ how the very act of using these advances shapes us
④ why it is challenging for us to adapt to technological advances
⑤ that new technology helps children's development in multiple ways

06

24005-0067

다음 빈칸에 들어갈 말로 가장 적절한 것은?

Cities ______________________________. In the last few decades, many have worked to reduce pollution and create appealing modern spaces by restricting polluting vehicles, encouraging energy-efficient buildings, and planting trees. In 2020, another impetus for change came in the form of COVID-19, which saw retail centres empty, businesses send workers home, and some question whether crowded cities were a safe environment. Yet cities have responded to changing circumstances in the past. Through the first kingdoms of Mesopotamia, global expansion, and the Industrial Revolution, they have evolved to remain at the heart of politics, economics, and culture. The history of the world is very much a history of great cities, and whatever future we build, these sites of trade, creativity, and transformation are likely to be at the heart of it.

* impetus: (일의 추진에 필요한) 원동력, 자극

① keep causing cultural conflicts
② continue to reinvent themselves
③ attract people from all walks of life
④ act as engines of economic development
⑤ shift in response to the needs of their citizens

07 다음 빈칸에 들어갈 말로 가장 적절한 것은?

24005-0068

Human cultures seem to be infinitely variable, but in fact that variability takes place within the boundaries produced by physical and mental capacities. Human languages, for example, are tremendously diverse, differing in sound, grammar, and semantics. But all are dependent upon what appears to be a uniquely human capacity and predisposition for learning languages. While the range of sounds used in human languages extends from clicks and pops to guttural stops, the distinctive speech sounds that are meaningful in all the languages of the world are but a fraction of the sounds it is possible for humans to make. Another way that we might observe the intricate relationship between ____________________ is in the way an American boy and his Mixtec friends might react emotionally, even instinctively, to bee larvae and onion soup: whether they feel delight or disgust is determined by the way they learn to perceive food, but delight and disgust seem to be basic and universal human reactions to food.

* guttural stop: 후두 폐쇄음 ** intricate: 복잡한 *** larva: 애벌레 (*pl.* larvae)

① group size and conformity
② personal choice and collective decision
③ the culturally specific and the universal
④ the cultural behavior and the environment
⑤ subjective interpretation and objective reality

08

24005-0069

다음 빈칸에 들어갈 말로 가장 적절한 것은?

Think about what happens in a standard scientific experiment to find out how a certain laundry detergent bleaches. In normal use, there are several factors that may cause the detergent to act in a certain way. These will include its active ingredients, the type and temperature of the water in which the ingredients are mixed, the materials being cleaned and the machinery — if any — used to do the laundry. Any experiment that could hope to discover what *caused* bleaching would have to be devised in such a way as to ensure that ______________________________. So if, for example, the hypothesis is that it is the chlorine that does the bleaching, the experiment needs to show that *if all the other factors remain the same*, the presence or absence of the chlorine will determine whether the laundry detergent bleaches.

* detergent: 세제 ** bleach: 표백하다 *** chlorine: 염소

① the hypothesis could be rejected by unexpected variables
② the experiment was one that researchers have not tried before
③ the crucial factors were properly isolated from the other variables
④ the detergent being used could help any machinery do the laundry well
⑤ the factors in the experiment were all closely connected with each other

09 다음 빈칸에 들어갈 말로 가장 적절한 것은?

24005-0070

AI's effects on human knowledge are paradoxical. On the one hand, AI intermediaries can navigate and analyze bodies of data vaster than the unaided human mind could have previously imagined. On the other, this power — the ability to engage with vast bodies of data — may also ______________________. AI is capable of exploiting human passions more effectively than traditional propaganda. Having tailored itself to individual preferences and instincts, AI draws out responses its creator or user desires. Similarly, the deployment of AI intermediaries may also amplify inherent biases, even if these AI intermediaries are technically under human control. The dynamics of market competition prompt social media platforms and search engines to present information that users find most compelling. As a result, information that users are believed to want to see is prioritized, distorting a representative picture of reality. Much as technology accelerated the speed of information production and dissemination in the nineteenth and twentieth centuries, in this era, information is being altered by the mapping of AI onto dissemination processes.

* propaganda: 선전 ** deployment: 배치 *** dissemination: 전파, 보급

① establish standards for people to follow
② prohibit people from thinking creatively
③ ignore people's demands more thoroughly
④ generate data irrelevant to contemporaries
⑤ accentuate forms of manipulation and error

10

24005-0071

다음 빈칸에 들어갈 말로 가장 적절한 것은?

It is not a coincidence that children turn out like their parents. From the moment you come into the world, your mother and your father are your role models. As little girls grow, they try on their mother's clothes, put on her make-up, and pretend to be her. When little boys come of age, they play with their father's tools and try to build or fix something for real. The truth of the matter is that children look up to their parents as mentors. They praise them and hold them in high regard. The greatest compliment they can give their parents as they grow is to turn out just like them. If you stop to take a personal inventory, you may find that you are much like those that you emulate. A parent, a coach, a teacher, or a leader all leave their mark on the final package with your name on it. When you look in the mirror, you may ______________________.

* take a personal inventory: 자신을 성찰하다 ** emulate: (흠모하는 대상을) 모방하다

① judge them on the basis of familiarity
② see one or all of them in the reflection
③ turn away from any weaknesses in them
④ feel uncomfortable with the person in the mirror
⑤ be disappointed with your images different from them

11 다음 빈칸에 들어갈 말로 가장 적절한 것은?

24005-0072

We are all familiar with battles between reason and desire. Socrates asks whether there are thirsty people who don't wish to drink. Indeed there are. (A sign on a faucet that reads "nonpotable water, do not drink" won't take away a person's thirst, but she won't want to drink there.) Yet there is something paradoxical about this: the word "thirsty" means "wishes to drink." So we are imagining people who wish to drink and do not wish to drink. How could that be? "It is obvious that the same thing will not be willing to do or undergo opposites in the same part of itself, in relation to the same thing, at the same time. So, if we ever find this happening in the soul, we'll know that ______________." In other words, since no one thing can both wish to drink and not wish to drink (in the same way at the same time), no one thing can have both of those two characteristics; we thus manage this by being more than one: one part of the soul wishes to drink, and another does not wish to drink.

* faucet: 수도꼭지 ** nonpotable: 마실 수 없는

① what we end up doing is the better action
② we aren't dealing with one thing but many
③ our actions are rarely caused by our reason
④ doing one thing leads to doing another thing
⑤ thought and action can work together in harmony

12

24005-0073

다음 빈칸에 들어갈 말로 가장 적절한 것은?

Media executives understand that they must think of their audiences as consumers who buy their products or whom they sell to advertisers. The complaining individual might be successful in getting the content changed or even removed if he or she convinces the media executives that they might otherwise lose a substantial portion of their target market. But an individual's concern will garner little attention if it is clear that ______________________. The editors from *Cosmopolitan* magazine, which aims at 20-something single women, for example, are not likely to follow the advice of an elderly-sounding woman from rural Kansas who phones to protest what she feels are demeaning portrayals of women on covers of the magazine that she sees in the supermarket. Yet the magazine staff might well act favorably if a *Cosmopolitan* subscriber writes with a suggestion for a new column that would attract more of the upscale single women they want as readers.

* garner: 받다, 얻다 ** demeaning: 비하하는 *** subscriber: 구독자

① the issue is beyond the media outlet's control
② other consumers do not agree with the person
③ the person does not belong in the target audience
④ the concern has already been addressed by others
⑤ advertisers do not see the value of customer complaints

14 흐름에 무관한 문장 찾기

Gateway

2024학년도 수능 35번

24005-0074

다음 글에서 전체 흐름과 관계 없는 문장은?

Speaking fast is a high-risk proposition. It's nearly impossible to maintain the ideal conditions to be persuasive, well-spoken, and effective when the mouth is traveling well over the speed limit. ① Although we'd like to think that our minds are sharp enough to always make good decisions with the greatest efficiency, they just aren't. ② In reality, the brain arrives at an intersection of four or five possible things to say and sits idling for a couple of seconds, considering the options. ③ Making a good decision helps you speak faster because it provides you with more time to come up with your responses. ④ When the brain stops sending navigational instructions back to the mouth and the mouth is moving too fast to pause, that's when you get a verbal fender bender, otherwise known as filler. ⑤ *Um*, *ah*, *you know*, and *like* are what your mouth does when it has nowhere to go.

Words & Phrases in Use

- ☐ proposition 일, 문제, 제안
- ☐ maintain 유지하다
- ☐ persuasive 설득력이 있는
- ☐ sharp 예리한
- ☐ efficiency 효율(성)
- ☐ intersection 교차하는 지점
- ☐ come up with ~을 생각해 내다
- ☐ navigational 조종의, 항해의
- ☐ instruction 지시
- ☐ fender bender 가벼운 충돌

STEP 1 반복적인 어구 또는 특정 개념과 관련된 어구를 통해 글의 내용을 추측한다.

- speaking fast, high-risk, mouth, decision(s), brain
- 입이 제한 속도를 훨씬 초과하여 움직일 때 설득력 있고, 말을 정확하게 하고, 효과적이기 위한 이상적인 상태를 유지하는 것이 거의 불가능한데, 빠르게 말하면 가벼운 언어적 충돌을 겪게 되는 것처럼 그것은 위험 부담이 큰 일이다.

➡ **글의 요지**: 빠르게 말하는 것은 언어적으로 위험 부담을 가져올 수 있다.

STEP 2 글의 요지와의 연관성을 고려하면서 흐름에서 벗어난 문장을 찾는다.

첫 두 문장 ➡ **도입(주제)**: 빠르게 말하는 것은 위험 부담이 큰 일인데, 입이 제한 속도를 훨씬 초과하여 움직일 때 설득력 있고, 말을 정확하게 하고, 효과적이기 위한 이상적인 상태를 유지하는 것이 거의 불가능함

문장 ① ➡ 우리의 정신이 항상 최대의 효율로 훌륭한 결정을 내릴 수 있을 정도로 예리하지는 않다는 내용이므로 요지와 연관됨

문장 ② ➡ 실제로 뇌는 말할 가능성이 있는 것들 네다섯 가지가 교차하는 지점에 도달하고, 몇 초간 선택 가능한 것들을 고려하면서 아무것도 하지 않은 채로 있다는 내용이므로 요지와 연관됨

문장 ③ ➡ 훌륭한 결정을 내리면 더 빠르게 말할 수 있는데, 이는 그것이 반응을 생각해 낼 시간을 더 많이 주기 때문이라는 내용이므로 글의 요지와 무관함

문장 ④ ➡ 뇌가 입으로 조종 지시를 다시 보내는 것을 멈추고 입이 너무 빠르게 움직여 멈추지 못할 때, 가벼운 언어적 충돌을 겪게 된다는 내용이므로 요지와 연관됨

문장 ⑤ ➡ '음', '아', '저기', '있잖아'는 입이 갈 곳이 없을 때 하는 행동이라는 내용이므로 요지와 연관됨

STEP 3 글의 전개 방식을 환기하면서 문장 ③의 부적절함을 확인한다.

도입부(주제)	빠르게 말하는 것은 위험 부담이 큰 일임

⬇

논지 전개	우리의 정신이 항상 최대의 효율로 훌륭한 결정을 내리지는 않음

⬇

근거 1	뇌는 말할 가능성이 있는 것들의 교차 지점에 도달하면, 몇 초간 선택 가능한 것들을 고려하면서 아무것도 하지 않음

⬇

근거 2	뇌가 입으로 보내는 지시를 멈추었는데 입이 너무 빠르게 움직이면 가벼운 언어적 충돌을 겪게 됨

⬇

예시	'음', '아', '저기', '있잖아'는 입이 갈 곳이 없을 때 하는 행동임

→ **따라서 글의 전체 흐름과 관계가 없는 문장은 ③이다.**

Exercises

01 다음 글에서 전체 흐름과 관계 없는 문장은?

24005-0075

Rejecting any academic training they had experienced, Monet and the other Impressionists believed that their art, with its objective methods of painting what they saw before them, was more sincere than any academic art. ① They all agreed that they aimed to capture their "sensations" or what they could see as they painted. ② These sensations included the flickering effects of light that our eyes capture as we regard things. ③ In complete contrast to the Academie, the Impressionists painted ordinary, modern people in everyday and up-to-date settings, making no attempt to hide their painting techniques. ④ The academy system was started originally to raise artists' standing above craftsmen, who were seen as manual laborers, so emphasis was placed on the intellectual aspects of art. ⑤ They avoided symbols or any narrative content, preventing viewers from "reading" a picture, but making them experience their paintings as an isolated moment in time.

* flickering: 깜빡거리는

02 다음 글에서 전체 흐름과 관계 없는 문장은?

24005-0076

Plants assess when they need to be competitive and when it is more prudent to be collaborative. To make this kind of decision, they weigh the energy cost relative to the benefit for improved growth and persistence. ① For example, although a plant would generally attempt to grow taller than a closely situated neighbor for preferential access to sunlight, if the neighbor is already significantly taller and the race is likely to be lost, the plant will temper its competitive instinct. ② That is, plants compete only when competition is needed to improve their ability to support their own growth and reproduction and has some likelihood of success. ③ As in all organisms, the evolution, development, and growth of plants depend on the constant and intense competition. ④ Once competition yields the needed results, they cease competing and shift their energy to living. ⑤ For plants, competition is about survival, not the thrill of victory.

* prudent: 현명한 ** temper: 누그러뜨리다

03 다음 글에서 전체 흐름과 관계 없는 문장은?

24005-0077

Mechanisation speeded up vertical movement. Stairs and ramps were traditionally how you went up and down, so few buildings in frequent use exceeded five storeys. ① The Otis Company, founded in 1853 in New York, changed all that with the invention of the safety elevator (safe because it locked the car in place should the cables fail) that made taller buildings possible. ② Escalators came later bringing greater capacity to move more people over shorter vertical distance; they made their debut, and were a sensation, at the 1900 Paris Exposition. ③ World Expositions were a chance for companies, countries and innovators to learn from each other and to be inspired by each other. ④ With elevators and escalators cities could now spread underground, with deep basements, subways and tunnels, and upwards, with high rise buildings, as well as outwards. ⑤ The modern cityscape — of which Manhattan is still the iconic exemplar — was created.

* ramp: 램프(높이가 다른 두 도로나 건물 등의 사이를 연결하는 경사로) ** cityscape: 도시 경관 *** exemplar: 전형, 모범

04 다음 글에서 전체 흐름과 관계 없는 문장은?

24005-0078

If you wanted to be entertained in a theater before the nineteenth century, you could not avoid the fact that you were at some level participating in a dialog, a conversation, either with your fellow members of the audience, or with the actors. ① The idea of the audience sitting in the dark and watching the stage in silence is a new thing. ② Prior to the nineteenth century the audience were lit and often extremely vocal and active, even leaping on stage to fight with the cast. ③ In the nineteenth century, many working people were poor and could not afford to attend the theatre or have the time to join social groups, as they had families and children to look after. ④ It was the actor David Garrick in the eighteenth century who pioneered the idea that an audience should shut up and listen. ⑤ The passive and reverential silence in which today's actors can indulge themselves is a new phenomenon, as, of course, is the cinema, where our surrogates on the screen can unfold their stories unaware of our responses.

* reverential: 경건한 ** indulge oneself: 만끽하다 *** surrogate: 대리인

15 문단 내 글의 순서 파악하기

Gateway

2024학년도 수능 37번

24005-0079

주어진 글 다음에 이어질 글의 순서로 가장 적절한 것은?

Norms emerge in groups as a result of people conforming to the behavior of others. Thus, the start of a norm occurs when one person acts in a particular manner in a particular situation because she thinks she ought to.

(A) Thus, she may prescribe the behavior to them by uttering the norm statement in a prescriptive manner. Alternately, she may communicate that conformity is desired in other ways, such as by gesturing. In addition, she may threaten to sanction them for not behaving as she wishes. This will cause some to conform to her wishes and act as she acts.

(B) But some others will not need to have the behavior prescribed to them. They will observe the regularity of behavior and decide on their own that they ought to conform. They may do so for either rational or moral reasons.

(C) Others may then conform to this behavior for a number of reasons. The person who performed the initial action may think that others ought to behave as she behaves in situations of this sort.

* sanction: 제재를 가하다

① (A) – (C) – (B) ② (B) – (A) – (C) ③ (B) – (C) – (A)
④ (C) – (A) – (B) ⑤ (C) – (B) – (A)

Words & Phrases in Use

☐ norm 규범 ☐ conform to ~에 따르다, ~에 순응하다
☐ prescribe 지시하다, 규정하다 ☐ utter 말하다, 발화하다 ☐ prescriptive 지시하는
☐ alternately 다른 방법[방식]으로 ☐ conformity 따름, 순응 ☐ observe 관찰하다
☐ regularity 규칙성 ☐ initial 처음의, 최초의

Solving Strategies

STEP 1 **주어진 글을 통해 글의 소재와 핵심 어구를 파악하고 내용 전개 방향을 예측한다.**

주어진 글 ➡ **소재**: 규범 발생 과정
(규범은 다른 사람들의 행동에 따르는 결과로 집단에서 생겨나며 규범의 시작은 한 사람이 특정한 상황에서 특정한 방식으로 행동할 때 생겨남)

STEP 2 **주어진 글로부터 전개되는 내용을 바탕으로 연결 어구와 지시어, 반복되는 어구 등을 활용하여 논리적 흐름을 파악한다.**

(C) ➡ Others may **then** conform to **this behavior** for a number of reasons.에서 then은 규범의 시작이 생겨난 후를 가리키며, this behavior는 주어진 문장에서 말하는, 한 사람이 특정한 상황에서 특정한 방식으로 행동하는 것을 가리킴. 이어서 이 행동을 따르는 이유들을 설명함
- 처음 그 행동을 한 사람은 다른 사람들이 이런 종류의 상황에서 자신처럼 행동해야 한다고 생각할 수도 있음

(A) ➡ **Thus**, she may prescribe the behavior to **them** by uttering the norm statement in a prescriptive manner.에서 Thus는 (C)의 마지막 문장의 결과를 나타내는 문장을 이끌며, them은 others를 가리킴. 이어서 행동을 지시하는 방법과 그 결과가 제시됨
- 몸짓에 의한 것과 같은 다른 방식으로 따름이 바람직하다는 것을 전달할 수도 있음
- 자신이 원하는 대로 행동하지 않으면 제재를 가하겠다고 위협할 수도 있음
- 일부 사람들은 따르고 그 사람이 행동하는 대로 행동할 것임

STEP 3 **마지막 부분을 연결하여, 글의 전체적인 흐름이 자연스럽고 완결성이 있는지 확인한다.**

(B) ➡ **But** some others will not need to have the behavior prescribed to them.에서 But은 앞에 나온 내용과 대조되는 내용이 나오는 글을 유도함. 다른 일부 사람들에게는 그 행동이 자신에게 지시되게 할 필요가 없음
- 행동의 규칙성을 관찰하고 자신이 따라야 한다고 스스로 결정할 것임

→ 다른 순서도 가능한지 검토한 후, 정답을 최종적으로 결정한다.

01

24005-0080

주어진 글 다음에 이어질 글의 순서로 가장 적절한 것은?

Globalization has often been studied as a macro phenomenon. However, as the globalization process obviously affects individuals' lives, a need for alternative concepts has emerged.

(A) This requires the ability to question one's own assumptions and prejudices. Identity is in this context not essentialist or stable; rather, it is fragmented and constructed and reconstructed across the different practices and positions in which one participates.

(B) For instance, cultural sociologist John Tomlinson claims that being a cosmopolitan means that one has an active experience of "belonging to the wider world". As such, cosmopolitanism is closely connected to identity; a cosmopolitan obtains a reflexive awareness of the features that unite us as human beings.

(C) Concepts such as *cosmopolitanism* and *global citizenship* have therefore frequently been used to capture how globalization is experienced "from below", with individuals as the object of analysis. Here, cosmopolitanism is interpreted as having many similarities to global citizenship.

* fragment: 분해하다 ** cosmopolitan: 세계주의자 *** reflexive: 성찰의

① (A) – (C) – (B) ② (B) – (A) – (C) ③ (B) – (C) – (A)
④ (C) – (A) – (B) ⑤ (C) – (B) – (A)

02

24005-0081

주어진 글 다음에 이어질 글의 순서로 가장 적절한 것은?

On June 17, 1953, Mrs. Roosevelt traveled to Hiroshima, where she visited the Atomic Bomb Casualty Commission, an American research group that studied the effects of the nuclear attacks on bomb survivors. Many people had been injured by the fires that the bomb had caused.

(A) It led her to urge Americans to do more to help. Though she maintained that they were not America's direct responsibility, "as a gesture of goodwill for the victims of this last war, such help would be invaluable."

(B) After her official meetings, some girls were waiting to see her. The girls explained that they did not blame her for the atomic bomb; they only wanted to impress on her the need to ensure that these weapons were never used again on human beings, given their effects.

(C) Although she did not say so directly, the girls may have been among those whose faces were permanently disfigured by the attack. This must have been a powerful encounter because Mrs. Roosevelt called it a "tragic moment."

* casualty: 피해자, 희생자 ** disfigure: (외양을) 흉하게 만들다

① (A) – (C) – (B)　② (B) – (A) – (C)　③ (B) – (C) – (A)
④ (C) – (A) – (B)　⑤ (C) – (B) – (A)

03 주어진 글 다음에 이어질 글의 순서로 가장 적절한 것은?

24005-0082

Most philosophers accepted Plato's definition of knowledge as justified true belief until the 1960s, when Edmund Gettier showed that it didn't always provide a satisfactory explanation.

(A) He came up with several instances where we instinctively realize that someone doesn't really know something, even though that person's belief is both true and justified. For example, I have arranged to meet my friend Sue at her house, and when I arrive I see her through the window sitting in the kitchen.

(B) Examples such as this became known as "Gettier problems," and have prompted philosophers to ask if, in addition to belief, truth, and justification, there is a fourth criterion for knowledge. Gettier had cast doubt not only on Plato's definition, but also on whether or not it is possible to define completely what knowledge is.

(C) In fact, it is not Sue that I see, but her identical twin sister — Sue is actually in another room. My belief that Sue is home is true, and I have good reason to believe it because I am sure I have seen her, but it is wrong to say that I knew she was at home — I didn't know.

* criterion: 기준

① (A) – (C) – (B)　② (B) – (A) – (C)　③ (B) – (C) – (A)
④ (C) – (A) – (B)　⑤ (C) – (B) – (A)

04

24005-0083

주어진 글 다음에 이어질 글의 순서로 가장 적절한 것은?

On one level, it is helpful for individuals to identify which kind of ethical system they have and which kind they admire.

(A) If the answer is no, then don't do it yourself. For example, while you can easily imagine a situation in which it might be to your advantage to lie, you would not want everyone to lie, so you should not lie yourself.

(B) Immanuel Kant takes it one step further, adding an unusual rule for a deontologist. He believed that you can and should test your decisions for moral and ethical soundness and outlined a thought experiment he called the Categorical Imperative to help you do just that.

(C) When considering any course of action, ask yourself, "Would I want everyone else, if placed in my position, to do the same thing?" If the answer is yes, you're on the right path.

* deontologist: 의무론자 ** Categorical Imperative: 정언 명령(양심의 절대 무조건적 도덕률)

① (A) – (C) – (B)
② (B) – (A) – (C)
③ (B) – (C) – (A)
④ (C) – (A) – (B)
⑤ (C) – (B) – (A)

05

24005-0084

주어진 글 다음에 이어질 글의 순서로 가장 적절한 것은?

Life-forms work to evolve survival strategies but without necessarily being aware of the process. Consciousness is not a necessary condition of life — though it says much about the organism that happens to possess it.

(A) At present we see a host of rudimentary survival mechanisms in computers: we may expect these to develop and new ones to emerge. It is inevitable, at the present stage of their development, that computer survival strategies owe virtually everything to human involvement in computer design.

(B) Most biological species have evolved techniques and mechanisms for survival without reflecting on the fact, and this is what has happened so far with computer life-forms. We can speculate on how computers might ponder on their own survival but this is essentially a matter for the future.

(C) However, as machine autonomy develops there will be a progressive reduction in the extent of human influence on computer evolution. Computers will come to think about their own position in the world, and take steps to enhance their own security.

* rudimentary: 원시적인 ** ponder: 숙고하다

① (A) – (C) – (B) ② (B) – (A) – (C) ③ (B) – (C) – (A)
④ (C) – (A) – (B) ⑤ (C) – (B) – (A)

06

24005-0085

주어진 글 다음에 이어질 글의 순서로 가장 적절한 것은?

Since at least the late nineteenth century and the rise of industrial cities, the history of urbanism and urban planning has been a history of expertise — political, administrative, and technocratic.

(A) Degrees in hand, they were primed to lead both governments and businesses away from the era of laissez-faire and toward better outcomes for themselves and for workers and citizens. That meant safer food; safer water; better working conditions; safer and less expensive automobiles; expanded opportunities for education, leisure, and personal fulfillment; and so on.

(B) Both fueled by and fueling that problem/solution framework, the Progressive political movement of the early twentieth century relied heavily on trained and trusted experts, especially economists and other social scientists. Those experts were often educated in newly formed occupational disciplines and professional schools.

(C) Cities came to be seen as solutions to demands for wealth, health, safety, opportunity, and personal development, as society grew more economically, socially, and politically complex. Cities also came to be seen as posing new problems, often caused by their successes in meeting earlier social demands.

* technocratic: 기술 관료적 ** prime: (사용할 수 있게) 준비시키다 *** laissez-faire: 자유방임주의

① (A) – (C) – (B)
② (B) – (A) – (C)
③ (B) – (C) – (A)
④ (C) – (A) – (B)
⑤ (C) – (B) – (A)

16 주어진 문장의 적합한 위치 찾기

Gateway

2024학년도 수능 38번

24005-0086

글의 흐름으로 보아, 주어진 문장이 들어가기에 가장 적절한 곳은?

> Yes, some contests are seen as world class, such as identification of the Higgs particle or the development of high temperature superconductors.

Science is sometimes described as a winner-take-all contest, meaning that there are no rewards for being second or third. This is an extreme view of the nature of scientific contests. (①) Even those who describe scientific contests in such a way note that it is a somewhat inaccurate description, given that replication and verification have social value and are common in science. (②) It is also inaccurate to the extent that it suggests that only a handful of contests exist. (③) But many other contests have multiple parts, and the number of such contests may be increasing. (④) By way of example, for many years it was thought that there would be "one" cure for cancer, but it is now realized that cancer takes multiple forms and that multiple approaches are needed to provide a cure. (⑤) There won't be one winner — there will be many.

* replication: 반복 ** verification: 입증

Words & Phrases in Use

- □ identification 규명, 확인
- □ particle 입자
- □ superconductor 초전도체
- □ winner-take-all 승자 독식의
- □ reward 보상
- □ extreme 극단적인
- □ inaccurate 부정확한
- □ given that ~이라는 점을 고려할 때
- □ a handful of 소수의
- □ multiple 다양한, 복합적인
- □ cure 치료법

Solving Strategies

STEP 1 **글의 소재와 요지를 포함한 글의 전반적인 내용을 개략적으로 파악한다.**

- **소재**: 승자 독식의 경쟁으로 잘못 이해되는 과학
- **요지**: 과학은 때때로 승자 독식의 경쟁으로 묘사되는데, 그것은 극단적인 견해이자 부정확한 설명이며, 과학 분야의 경쟁에는 다양한 측면이 있고 그런 경쟁의 수는 증가하고 있을 수도 있다.

STEP 2 **글의 소재와 요지를 염두에 두고 글을 읽으면서 문장 사이의 흐름이 부자연스럽거나 단절되는 곳을 찾는다.**

문장 1	과학은 때때로 승자 독식의 경쟁으로 묘사되는데, 이는 2등이나 3등인 것에 대한 보상이 없다는 것을 의미한다.
문장 2	이는 과학 분야의 경쟁의 본질에 대한 극단적인 견해이다.
문장 3	과학 분야의 경쟁을 그런 식으로 설명하는 사람들조차도 반복과 입증이 사회적 가치를 지니고 있으며 과학에서 일반적이라는 점을 고려할 때, 이는 다소 부정확한 설명이라고 말한다.
문장 4	그것은 또한 소수의 경쟁만 존재한다고 시사하는 정도로 부정확하다.
문장 5	하지만 다른 많은 경쟁에는 다양한 부분이 있고, 그런 경쟁의 수는 증가하고 있을 수도 있다.
문장 6	예를 들어, 여러 해 동안 암에 대해 '하나'의 치료법만 있다고 생각되었지만, 이제는 암은 여러 가지 형태를 가지며 치료를 제공하기 위해 다양한 접근 방식이 필요하다고 인식된다.
문장 7	승자는 한 명이 아니라 여러 명이 있을 것이다.

STEP 3 **주어진 문장과 주어진 문장 앞뒤에 있는 문장의 단서를 활용하여, 주어진 문장이 들어가기에 가장 적절한 곳을 고른다.**

주어진 문장은 힉스 입자 규명이나 고온 초전도체 개발과 같은 몇몇 경쟁이 세계적인 수준으로 여겨진다는 내용으로, 이는 문장 4에서 언급한 소수의 경쟁만 존재한다는 내용의 사례이기도 하고, 문장 5에 나오는 many other contests의 내용과 대조를 이루기도 한다.

→ 따라서 주어진 문장은 문장 4와 문장 5 사이의 ③에 들어가야 한다.

Exercises

01

24005-0087

글의 흐름으로 보아, 주어진 문장이 들어가기에 가장 적절한 곳은?

City directories and telephone books from all cities in a reporter's area of coverage are valuable tools, as are internal directories of the organizations he or she will encounter on the beat.

As soon as a reporter is assigned to a specialized beat, he or she should read several basic books on that subject to become familiar in a general way with how the beat works. (①) If a governmental area is involved — for example, a state legislature or a court system — a reporter should not go on a first assignment without knowing how that particular unit operates. (②) Libraries contain such books, although it is better for reporters to buy their own copies for future reference. (③) No medical reporter can work successfully without a good medical dictionary, for example. (④) Nor should a business reporter be without a basic economics text. (⑤) Having such numbers — which are often impossible to obtain officially — will enable a reporter to bypass obstacles and reach potential sources quickly.

* beat: (관할) 구역 ** bypass: 우회하다

02

24005-0088

글의 흐름으로 보아, 주어진 문장이 들어가기에 가장 적절한 곳은?

But none of this intergroup variation and intragroup commonality would have anything to do with the workings of culture.

Cultural and behavioral diversity can result from humans' innate ability to flexibly respond to their environments, to engage in social learning, and to make culture (an ability which is itself a part of the social suite). (①) The diversity might conceal an underlying universality that, paradoxically, might relate more to our genes than to cultural exigencies. (②) Evolutionary psychologists John Tooby and Leda Cosmides provide a fanciful illustration of this idea. (③) They suggest a thought experiment in which aliens replace humans with jukeboxes, each of which has a repertoire of thousands of songs and the ability to play a particular song according to where and when it is. (④) We would then observe that jukeboxes in different parts of the world played different songs at different times, songs that were similar to those on the jukeboxes near them. (⑤) This is a way of illustrating that humans might have an inborn ability to respond flexibly — but also predictably — to their environment.

* innate: 타고난 ** exigency: 필요성, 본질적 요구

03

24005-0089

글의 흐름으로 보아, 주어진 문장이 들어가기에 가장 적절한 곳은?

Today, leaders must discipline themselves to look at problems and opportunities with a fresh eye.

When companies select leaders, two of the first questions they ask are, "Has he done anything like this before?" "What is his track record?" (①) We assume that if that person has done it before (and done it well), he can do it again. (②) Experience is still important for leaders, and there are times when it is the most effective predictor of future success. (③) The problem, however, is that because of constantly improving technology, processes, and best practices in a world that is constantly changing and where success is being continually redefined, experience can be a handicap. (④) This is difficult because people naturally want to repeat an approach that worked in a similar situation. (⑤) It is a challenge to consider an alternative to what brought you success in the past or to your current position in the present.

04

글의 흐름으로 보아, 주어진 문장이 들어가기에 가장 적절한 곳은?

24005-0090

> Yet biomedical pills and tablets are prepared in ways that deemphasize smells considered to be more palatable.

Smell is not just a sense that determines taste; it is also a powerful force that stimulates desire and may even overwhelm the other senses. In the past decade, aromatherapy has emerged as an alternative healing practice, as well as a new product to be advertised to consumers. (①) Some stores spread scents of freshly baked bread or apple pie to encourage shoppers to stay longer and buy more. (②) Smells are also important for distinguishing between edible and inedible foods. (③) Herbal medicine stores frequently have a wide variety of pungent odors. (④) The preparation of herbal medicines may include cooking plants into liquid form or distilling essences with alcohol, which often creates an odor. (⑤) The absence of smells further distances medicine from food.

* palatable: 맛이 좋은 ** pungent: 자극적인 *** distill: 증류하다

05

글의 흐름으로 보아, 주어진 문장이 들어가기에 가장 적절한 곳은?

24005-0091

> When it comes to social activities, such as whom to date and what clubs to join, they are more likely to discuss them with peers.

The divergence between parental and peer values does not necessarily lead to a hostile confrontation between parents and teenagers. (①) In fact, most youngsters are just as friendly with parents as with peers. (②) They simply engage in different types of activities — work and task activities with parents, play and recreation with peers. (③) Concerning financial, educational, career, and other serious matters, such as what to spend money on and what occupation to choose, youths are inclined to seek advice from parents. (④) This reflects the great importance placed by the peer group on *other-directed behavior*, looking to others for approval and support as opposed to reliance on personal beliefs and traditional values. (⑤) Peer groups, in effect, demand conformity at the expense of independence and individuality.

* divergence: 차이 ** hostile: 적대적인 *** confrontation: 대립, 대면

06

24005-0092

글의 흐름으로 보아, 주어진 문장이 들어가기에 가장 적절한 곳은?

> Even if not immediately intuitive, there are a (admittedly small) number of situations in which the ability to deliver painful stimulation comes in handy within mediated environments.

One important point related to the possibility of reproducing believable tactile sensations in virtual or machine-mediated environments lies in the role of "pain." (①) Certainly, a number of real interactions can never be entirely believable without the presence of painful stimulation. (②) However, one might wonder whether reproducing such kinds of stimulation would ever be of any use within virtual or mediated interactions. (③) Shouldn't a "virtual" world be, in some sense, "better" without pain? (④) In fact, numerous attempts have been made over the course of the last few years to reproduce these aspects of our perception as well. (⑤) This may occur in video games to increase the realism of the simulation or even more importantly in training programs for soldiers where pain is an occupational hazard and will need to be dealt with.

* intuitive: 직관적인 ** tactile: 촉각의 *** hazard: 위험

17 문단 요약하기

Gateway

2024학년도 수능 40번

24005-0093

다음 글의 내용을 한 문장으로 요약하고자 한다. 빈칸 (A), (B)에 들어갈 말로 가장 적절한 것은?

Even those with average talent can produce notable work in the various sciences, so long as they do not try to embrace all of them at once. Instead, they should concentrate attention on one subject after another (that is, in different periods of time), although later work will weaken earlier attainments in the other spheres. This amounts to saying that the brain adapts to universal science in *time* but not in *space*. In fact, even those with great abilities proceed in this way. Thus, when we are astonished by someone with publications in different scientific fields, realize that each topic was explored during a specific period of time. Knowledge gained earlier certainly will not have disappeared from the mind of the author, but it will have become simplified by condensing into formulas or greatly abbreviated symbols. Thus, sufficient space remains for the perception and learning of new images on the cerebral blackboard.

* condense: 응축하다 ** cerebral: 대뇌의

⬇

Exploring one scientific subject after another ＿＿(A)＿＿ remarkable work across the sciences, as the previously gained knowledge is retained in simplified forms within the brain, which ＿＿(B)＿＿ room for new learning.

	(A)		(B)
①	enables	……	leaves
②	challenges	……	spares
③	delays	……	creates
④	requires	……	removes
⑤	invites	……	diminishes

Words & Phrases in Use

- □ notable 주목할 만한
- □ embrace 포괄하다, 아우르다
- □ subject 주제
- □ attainment 성취, 성과
- □ sphere 영역
- □ amount to ~과 같다[마찬가지이다]
- □ proceed 나아가다, 진행하다
- □ formula 공식
- □ abbreviate 축약하다
- □ sufficient 충분한
- □ perception 인식

STEP 1 **요약문과 선택지를 먼저 훑어보면서 글의 주제를 추론해 보고 중심 내용에 대한 단서를 확보한다.**

이 글은 과학 주제를 차례로 탐구하게 되면 이전에 습득한 지식은 저자의 마음에서 단순화되어 새로운 학습을 위한 공간을 충분히 남겨 과학 전반에 걸쳐 주목할 만한 연구를 가능하게 한다는 내용의 글이다.

STEP 2 **요약문을 통해 얻은 단서들을 바탕으로 글을 읽는다.**

글의 요지	과학 분야에서 하나의 주제를 탐구한 다음에 다른 주제를 탐구하면 다양한 과학 분야에서 성과를 낼 수 있으며, 이것은 이전에 습득한 지식이 뇌 안에서 단순화된 형태로 유지되어 새로운 학습을 위한 충분한 공간을 남겨 두기 때문이다.

글의 요지를 뒷받침하는 내용

- 평균적인 재능을 가진 사람이라도 다양한 과학 분야에서 주목할 만한 성과를 낼 수 있음(Even those with average talent can produce notable work in the various sciences)
- 한 주제 다음에 다른 주제로 집중해야 함(they should concentrate attention on one subject after another)
- 더 이전에 얻은 지식은 확실히 저자의 머리에서 사라지지 않았을 것임(Knowledge gained earlier certainly will not have disappeared from the mind of the author)
- 그것은 공식이나 크게 축약된 기호로 응축되어 단순화되어 있을 것임(it will have become simplified by condensing into formulas or greatly abbreviated symbols)

STEP 3 **글을 읽으면서 파악한 요지를 바탕으로 요약문의 빈칸에 들어갈 말로 가장 적절한 단어를 선택지에서 고른다.**

(A) 하나의 과학 주제를 탐구한 다음에 다른 주제를 탐구하는 것은 과학 전반에 걸친 주목할 만한 성과를 가능하게 한다는 것을 알 수 있다. ➡ enables (가능하게 하다)

(B) 이전에 습득된 지식은 단순화된 형태로 유지되어 새로운 학습을 위한 공간을 남겨 둔다는 것을 알 수 있다. ➡ leaves (남겨 두다)

→ **그러므로 빈칸 (A), (B)에 들어갈 말로 가장 적절한 것은 ①이다.**

Exercises

01

다음 글의 내용을 한 문장으로 요약하고자 한다. 빈칸 (A), (B)에 들어갈 말로 가장 적절한 것은?

24005-0094

Consider a bar of soap, the kind you keep by the bathroom sink to wash your hands and face. How much meaning could such an innocuous object contain? While it may be tempting to answer "not much," or even "none," in fact, even soap can embody a rich set of symbols. Think about a particular brand of soap. By itself, that soap cleans like any other soap. But through some clever marketing, packaging, and advertising, the brand immerses its soap in a complex set of messages about the environment, personal empowerment, and progressive politics. The brand's website even says, "We are committed to animal protection, environmental protection and respect for human rights." These meanings allow the brand's customers to do more with the soap than just clean their faces: By using these products, they can make a statement about what kind of person they are and what kind of politics they embrace.

* innocuous: 눈에 띄지 않는, 재미없는 ** immerse: 담그다

⬇

An ordinary, everyday product can take on a(n) ______(A)______ meaning through clever marketing, packaging, and advertising; by using it, consumers can ______(B)______ their personal and political identity.

	(A)		(B)
①	symbolic	······	express
②	spiritual	······	conceal
③	innovative	······	explore
④	cultural	······	change
⑤	social	······	deny

02

다음 글의 내용을 한 문장으로 요약하고자 한다. 빈칸 (A), (B)에 들어갈 말로 가장 적절한 것은?

24005-0095

Comparative psychology finds that pointing (in its full-blown form) is unique to our species. Few nonhuman species seem able to comprehend pointing (notably, domestic dogs can follow pointing, while our closest relatives among the great apes cannot), and there is little evidence of pointing occurring spontaneously between members of any species other than our own. Apparently only humans have the social-cognitive infrastructure needed to support the kind of cooperative and prosocial motivations that pointing gestures presuppose. This suggests a new place to look for the foundations of human language. While research on language in cognitive science has long focused on its logical structure, the news about pointing suggests an alternative: that the essence of language is found in our capacity for the communion of minds through shared intentionality. At the center of it is the deceptively simple act of pointing, an act that must be mastered before language can be learned at all.

* presuppose: 전제로 하다 ** communion: 교감, 공유

⬇

Pointing, which indicates cooperative and prosocial motivations, is ______(A)______ to humans, and since the nature of language requires shared intentionality, mastery of pointing must ______(B)______ language learning.

	(A)		(B)
①	exclusive	……	precede
②	exclusive	……	follow
③	suitable	……	follow
④	suitable	……	cause
⑤	beneficial	……	precede

03

다음 글의 내용을 한 문장으로 요약하고자 한다. 빈칸 (A), (B)에 들어갈 말로 가장 적절한 것은?

24005-0096

We come into the world ready to start relationships and, as we gain control of our body, we're keen to take part in games and tasks that involve working with others. In this way, we're so different from young chimps. Experiments have shown chimps can understand collaborative tasks perfectly well, but they only bother to take part if they can see how it will result in their getting a piece of fruit or some other reward. Humans, by contrast, often work together just for the joy of it. Experiments have shown that working with others affects children's behavior. Afterward, they're more generous in sharing any treats the experimenters give them — as if working with others has put them in a better mood. It seems unlikely that children's greater willingness to share is simply the result of learning that they should pay people for working with them, but the way we feel about everything is strongly influenced by the experiences that shaped the development of our brain. Our childhood observations of others don't just help us learn how to behave; they help us understand how we're supposed to *feel*.

⬇

While young chimps collaborate solely for their own ______(A)______, humans derive pleasure from working with others, and through such experiences, they feel better and become more ______(B)______.

(A)		(B)
① benefit	······	productive
② benefit	······	charitable
③ learning	······	secure
④ learning	······	hopeful
⑤ interaction	······	righteous

04

24005-0097

다음 글의 내용을 한 문장으로 요약하고자 한다. 빈칸 (A), (B)에 들어갈 말로 가장 적절한 것은?

The theory of reasoned action maintains that a person's decision to engage in a purposeful activity depends on several factors, of which some are situational and some are mediated by personal dispositions or characteristics. At the core of the theory is the idea that when people engage in a given behavior it is because they formed an intention to do so and have reasons for their decision to actualize their intentions. Because of this, much of our behavior can be characterized as "reasoned action." Fishbein and Ajzen suggested that behavioral intentions are controlled by two factors: attitude toward an act and the normative component. Attitude toward an act is influenced by the beliefs that people have about the consequences of performing an act. The normative component is controlled by our beliefs about what valued others (i.e., people important in our lives) expect us to do. For some behaviors we rely more on our attitude toward an act, whereas for other behaviors we may rely more on the normative component for guidance on how to behave.

⬇

The theory of reasoned action explains that our behaviors result from the rational decisions to ____(A)____ our pre-formed behavioral intentions, which are influenced by beliefs about the ____(B)____ of the behaviors and the expectations of valued others.

	(A)		(B)
①	evaluate	……	purposes
②	modify	……	purposes
③	modify	……	outcomes
④	realize	……	outcomes
⑤	realize	……	contexts

18 장문 독해 (1)

Gateway

2024학년도 수능 41~42번

01~02 다음 글을 읽고, 물음에 답하시오.

One way to avoid contributing to overhyping a story would be to say nothing. However, that is not a realistic option for scientists who feel a strong sense of responsibility to inform the public and policymakers and/or to offer suggestions. Speaking with members of the media has (a) <u>advantages</u> in getting a message out and perhaps receiving favorable recognition, but it runs the risk of misinterpretations, the need for repeated clarifications, and entanglement in never-ending controversy. Hence, the decision of whether to speak with the media tends to be highly individualized. Decades ago, it was (b) <u>unusual</u> for Earth scientists to have results that were of interest to the media, and consequently few media contacts were expected or encouraged. In the 1970s, the few scientists who spoke frequently with the media were often (c) <u>criticized</u> by their fellow scientists for having done so. The situation now is quite different, as many scientists feel a responsibility to speak out because of the importance of global warming and related issues, and many reporters share these feelings. In addition, many scientists are finding that they (d) <u>enjoy</u> the media attention and the public recognition that comes with it. At the same time, other scientists continue to resist speaking with reporters, thereby preserving more time for their science and (e) <u>running</u> the risk of being misquoted and the other unpleasantries associated with media coverage.

* overhype: 과대광고하다 ** entanglement: 얽힘

01 윗글의 제목으로 가장 적절한 것은?

24005-0098

① The Troubling Relationship Between Scientists and the Media
② A Scientist's Choice: To Be Exposed to the Media or Not?
③ Scientists! Be Cautious When Talking to the Media
④ The Dilemma over Scientific Truth and Media Attention
⑤ Who Are Responsible for Climate Issues, Scientists or the Media?

02 밑줄 친 (a)~(e) 중에서 문맥상 낱말의 쓰임이 적절하지 <u>않은</u> 것은?

24005-0099

① (a) ② (b) ③ (c) ④ (d) ⑤ (e)

Words & Phrases in Use

- ☐ contribute to ~에 기여하다
- ☐ favorable 우호적인
- ☐ misinterpretation 오해
- ☐ individualize 개별화하다
- ☐ thereby 그렇게 함으로써
- ☐ unpleasantry 불쾌한 상황[사건]
- ☐ option 선택
- ☐ recognition 인정
- ☐ clarification 해명
- ☐ criticize 비난하다
- ☐ preserve 남겨 두다, 보존하다
- ☐ associated with ~과 연관된
- ☐ inform 알리다
- ☐ run the risk of ~의 위험이 있다
- ☐ controversy 논란
- ☐ resist 거부하다, 저항하다
- ☐ misquote (말이나 글을) 잘못 인용하다
- ☐ coverage (언론의) 보도

Solving Strategies

STEP 1 글의 전반적인 흐름을 파악한다.

도입	과학자의 미디어 접촉은 이점도 있지만 위험도 있다.

⬇

요지	과학자가 미디어와 접촉해야 하는지에 관한 결정은 개별화되는 경향이 있다.

⬇

부연1	1970년대까지는 과학자의 미디어 접촉은 흔치 않았고 권장되지도 않았다.

⬇

부연2	오늘날에는 각자의 이유로 미디어와의 접촉을 즐기는 과학자도 있고, 그것을 거부하는 과학자도 있다.

STEP 2 글의 내용을 종합적으로 파악하여 제목으로 적절한 것을 고른다.

과학자의 미디어 접촉은 이점도 있고 위험도 따르기 때문에, 그것은 개별화되는 경향이 있다는 내용의 글이므로, 글의 제목으로 가장 적절한 것은 ② '과학자의 선택: 미디어에 노출될 것인가 아니면 그러지 않을 것인가?'이다.

① 과학자와 미디어 간의 골치 아픈 관계
③ 과학자여! 미디어에 말할 때 조심하라
④ 과학적 진실과 미디어의 관심에 대한 딜레마
⑤ 누가 기후 문제에 책임이 있는가, 과학자인가 아니면 미디어인가?

STEP 3 글의 맥락을 살펴서 어휘의 적절성을 파악하고 문맥에 맞지 않은 단어를 고른다.

(e) 과학자들이 기자들과의 대화를 계속 거부하는 것은 미디어 보도와 연관된 위험과 불쾌한 상황을 피하기 위한 것이므로, (e)의 running을 avoiding과 같은 낱말로 바꾸어야 한다.

(a) 미디어와의 접촉은 과학자가 전달하고자 하는 메시지를 널리 알리고 미디어와 대중으로부터 인정을 받는 이점이 있을 것이므로, advantages는 문맥상 적절하다.

(b) 미디어와의 접촉이 기대되거나 권장되는 경우가 거의 없었던 것은 그들의 연구 결과가 미디어의 흥미를 끄는 경우가 드물었기 때문일 것이므로, unusual은 문맥상 적절하다.

(c) 오늘날의 상황과는 달리 1970년대에는 과학자가 미디어와 자주 접촉하는 것이 권장되지 않았다는 맥락이므로, criticized는 문맥상 적절하다.

(d) 오늘날 공개적으로 의견을 표명하는 데 책임감을 느끼는 많은 과학자는 주목과 인정을 즐기며 미디어와 접촉한다는 맥락이므로, enjoy는 문맥상 적절하다.

Exercises

01~02 다음 글을 읽고, 물음에 답하시오.

We trust our common sense largely because we are prone to *naive realism*: the belief that we see the world precisely as it is. We assume that 'seeing is believing' and trust our intuitive perceptions of the world and ourselves. In daily life, naive realism often serves us well. If you are driving down a one-lane road and see a tractor-trailer moving uncontrollably towards you at 120 kilometres per hour, it is a wise idea to get out of the way. Much of the time, we *should* (a) trust our perceptions. Yet appearances can sometimes be deceptive. The Earth seems flat. The sun seems to revolve around the Earth. Yet in both cases, our intuitions are (b) wrong. Sometimes, what appears to be obvious can mislead us when it comes to evaluating ourselves and others. Our common sense tells us that our memories (c) accurately capture virtually everything we have seen, although scientific research demonstrates otherwise. Our common sense also assures us that people who do not share our political views are biased, but that we are (d) objective. Yet psychological research demonstrates that we are all susceptible to evaluating political issues in a biased fashion. So our tendencies to believe appearances can lead us to draw (e) reliable conclusions about human nature. In many cases, 'believing is seeing' rather than the reverse: our beliefs shape our perceptions of the world.

* prone: (~의) 경향이 있는 ** deceptive: 판단을 그르치게 하는 *** susceptible: ~하기 쉬운

01

24005-0100

윗글의 제목으로 가장 적절한 것은?

① How Did Science Prove That the Earth Is Round?
② Comparison of Common Sense and Scientific Interpretation
③ Seeing Is Believing: Using Intuition to Make Better Decisions
④ Beyond Naive Realism: Is Our Perception of Reality Trustworthy?
⑤ When It Comes to Taking Risks, It's Dangerous to Trust Your Instincts

02

24005-0101

밑줄 친 (a)~(e) 중에서 문맥상 낱말의 쓰임이 적절하지 않은 것은?

① (a) ② (b) ③ (c) ④ (d) ⑤ (e)

03~04 다음 글을 읽고, 물음에 답하시오.

Some people claim that gratitude is just about thinking nice thoughts and expecting good things — and ignores the negativity, pain, and suffering in life. Well, they're (a) wrong. Consider our definition of gratitude, as a specific way of thinking about receiving a benefit and giving credit to others besides yourself for that benefit. In fact, gratitude can be very difficult, because it (b) requires that you recognize your dependence on others, and that's not always positive. You have to humble yourself, in the sense that you have to become a good receiver of others' support and generosity. That can be very hard — most people are (c) better givers than receivers.

What's more, feelings of gratitude can sometimes stir up related feelings of indebtedness and obligation, which doesn't sound like positive thinking at all: *If I am grateful for something you provided to me, I have to take care of that thing — I might even have to reciprocate at some appropriate time in the future*. That type of indebtedness or obligation can be perceived very negatively — it can cause people real (d) comfort, as Jill Suttie explores in her essay "How to Say Thanks Without Feeling Indebted."

The data bear this out. When people are grateful, they aren't necessarily free of negative emotions — we don't find that they necessarily have less anxiety or less tension or less unhappiness. Practicing gratitude magnifies positive feelings more than it (e) reduces negative feelings. If gratitude were just positive thinking, or a form of denial, you'd experience no negative thoughts or feelings when you're keeping a gratitude journal, for instance. But, in fact, people do.

* indebtedness: 부채 ** reciprocate: (비슷한 것으로) 보답하다

03

윗글의 제목으로 가장 적절한 것은?

24005-0102

① True Gratitude: Something Different from Debt
② Does the Gratitude of Others Truly Satisfy You?
③ Gratitude: Not an Absolute Form of Positive Thinking
④ The More Gratitude You Have, the More Benefits You Gain
⑤ Practice Gratitude to Please People Who Are Meaningful to You

04

밑줄 친 (a)~(e) 중에서 문맥상 낱말의 쓰임이 적절하지 않은 것은?

24005-0103

① (a) ② (b) ③ (c) ④ (d) ⑤ (e)

05~06 다음 글을 읽고, 물음에 답하시오.

In all social systems, it is true that people's behavior is influenced by social rules and they are extraordinarily adaptable. One natural experiment involving baboons is instructive. A study in 2004 examined how a troop of baboons dominated by large and aggressive males changed after all those dominant males caught a disease and died. With only smaller, gentler males remaining, the culture of that troop underwent a (a) dramatic shift, moving from a social structure characterized by widespread bullying and fighting to one with much more peaceful grooming. Conflict was still there, of course, but it tended to be resolved with peaceful methods, and the fighting that did happen was more between (b) equally matched baboons, instead of a big one picking on a small one. Remarkably, the culture of that troop persisted even after all those original males had died off and were replaced by others coming in from outside. The new males were acculturated to the group norms, and learned to behave less (c) generously.

Obviously, humans are not baboons. But it seems highly possible that this is basically (d) similar to why different human societies can have much different behavioral norms — consider premodern tribes who worshiped their ancestors and shared food in common, medieval peasants who accepted the divine right of kings and performed free labor for feudal lords, and people today who believe in democracy and corporate employment contracts. Human societies have much more complexity and choice than baboon societies, but the point is that behavioral norms are to a great degree the (e) product of culture and learning, not the other way around.

* baboon: 개코원숭이 ** groom: (서로) 털 손질을 해 주다 *** feudal: 봉건 (시대의)

05

윗글의 제목으로 가장 적절한 것은?

24005-0104

① Power of Social Pressure in Decision Making
② The Fluidity of Human Behavior: Socially Constructed
③ Learn Different Cultures and Broaden Your Perspective!
④ Survival of the Friendliest: A Universal Feature of All Societies
⑤ A Blind Spot of the Baboon Experiment: Animal Rights Protection

06

밑줄 친 (a)~(e) 중에서 문맥상 낱말의 쓰임이 적절하지 않은 것은?

24005-0105

① (a) ② (b) ③ (c) ④ (d) ⑤ (e)

07~08 다음 글을 읽고, 물음에 답하시오.

Not surprisingly, usage of unsafely designed and insecurely implemented software presents some risks. After distributed software reaches user sites, installation and administration of system and application software, when improperly performed, may adversely affect performance and proper functioning of such software. Due to the complexity as well as due to inadequate documentation of these systems, users (a) hardly understand effects of their attempts to "properly" use such systems. Consequently, users (b) disregard "trial and error" methods in learning to work with new features, rather than trying methodologically to understand which functions may have which effects, and which precautions should be taken to avoid unwished side-effects. This somewhat "explorative" way to use systems rather often leads to a (c) risky attitude with potentially harmful effects, e.g. by clicking on unknown attachments without due care.

Software manufacturers often argue that failure of software is mainly caused by (d) improper actions of users. But in many — if not most — cases, the human-computer interface (e.g. the display of functions and operations on the screen, or the handling of input devices such as mouse and keyboard) is inadequately designed and users are not properly supported by help functions (which when existing in many cases are so complex that users are further misled). While users are primarily interested in doing their work, one must admit that they rather often tend to (e) forget about any precaution and even sometimes bypass security measures when thinking that their work performance is reduced.

07

24005-0106

윗글의 제목으로 가장 적절한 것은?

① What Are the Real Causes of Software Failures?
② How to Avoid Unsuccessful Software Implementation
③ Cyber Security: The Digital Dilemma for Manufacturers
④ What Can We Expect from New Software Developments?
⑤ Social Responsibility Impacts on Software Development Processes

08

24005-0107

밑줄 친 (a)~(e) 중에서 문맥상 낱말의 쓰임이 적절하지 않은 것은?

① (a) ② (b) ③ (c) ④ (d) ⑤ (e)

19 장문 독해 (2)

Gateway

2024학년도 수능 43~45번

01~03 다음 글을 읽고, 물음에 답하시오.

(A) Emma and Clara stood side by side on the beach road, with their eyes fixed on the boundless ocean. The breathtaking scene that surrounded them was beyond description. Just after sunrise, they finished their preparations for the bicycle ride along the beach road. Emma turned to Clara with a question, "Do you think this will be your favorite ride ever?" Clara's face lit up with a bright smile as she nodded. "Definitely! (a) I can't wait to ride while watching those beautiful waves!"

(B) When they reached their destination, Emma and Clara stopped their bikes. Emma approached Clara, saying "Bicycle riding is unlike swimming, isn't it?" Clara answered with a smile, "Quite similar, actually. Just like swimming, riding makes me feel truly alive." She added, "It shows (b) me what it means to live while facing life's tough challenges." Emma nodded in agreement and suggested, "Your first beach bike ride was a great success. How about coming back next summer?" Clara replied with delight, "With (c) you, absolutely!"

(C) Clara used to be a talented swimmer, but she had to give up her dream of becoming an Olympic medalist in swimming because of shoulder injuries. Yet she responded to the hardship in a constructive way. After years of hard training, she made an incredible recovery and found a new passion for bike riding. Emma saw how the painful past made her maturer and how it made (d) her stronger in the end. One hour later, Clara, riding ahead of Emma, turned back and shouted, "Look at the white cliff!"

(D) Emma and Clara jumped on their bikes and started to pedal toward the white cliff where the beach road ended. Speeding up and enjoying the wide blue sea, Emma couldn't hide her excitement and exclaimed, "Clara, the view is amazing!" Clara's silence, however, seemed to say that she was lost in her thoughts. Emma understood the meaning of her silence. Watching Clara riding beside her, Emma thought about Clara's past tragedy, which (e) she now seemed to have overcome.

01 주어진 글 (A)에 이어질 내용을 순서에 맞게 배열한 것으로 가장 적절한 것은?

24005-0108

① (B) – (D) – (C) ② (C) – (B) – (D) ③ (C) – (D) – (B)
④ (D) – (B) – (C) ⑤ (D) – (C) – (B)

02 밑줄 친 (a)~(e) 중에서 가리키는 대상이 나머지 넷과 다른 것은?

24005-0109

① (a) ② (b) ③ (c) ④ (d) ⑤ (e)

03 윗글에 관한 내용으로 적절하지 않은 것은?

24005-0110

① Emma와 Clara는 자전거 탈 준비를 일출 직후에 마쳤다.
② Clara는 자전거 타기와 수영이 꽤 비슷하다고 말했다.
③ Clara는 올림픽 수영 경기에서 메달을 땄다.
④ Emma와 Clara는 자전거를 타고 하얀 절벽 쪽으로 갔다.
⑤ Emma는 Clara의 침묵의 의미를 이해했다.

Words & Phrases in Use

- □ beyond description 말로 표현할 수 없을 정도의
- □ destination 목적지
- □ hardship 고난
- □ constructive 적극적인, 건설적인
- □ tragedy 비극(적 사건)

Solving Strategies

STEP 1 주어진 글 (A)를 읽은 다음, 글 (B), (C), (D)의 앞부분을 살펴보며 전체적인 글의 순서를 추측해 본다.

글 (B): When they reached their destination, Emma and Clara stopped their bikes.
➡ 두 사람이 목적지에 도착하는 것으로 이어지는 것이 적절함

글 (C): Clara used to be a talented swimmer, but she had to give up her dream of becoming an Olympic medalist in swimming because of shoulder injuries.
➡ Clara의 비극적 사건에 대한 언급 다음에 이어지는 것이 적절함

글 (D): Emma and Clara jumped on their bikes and started to pedal toward the white cliff where the beach road ended.
➡ Emma와 Clara가 자전거 라이딩을 시작하려고 하는 내용 다음에 이어지는 것이 적절함

STEP 2 주어진 단서를 종합하여 글의 순서를 완성한다.

Emma와 Clara가 자전거 라이딩을 시작하려고 하는 내용인 (A) 다음에, 자전거를 타고 가면서 본 풍경과 Clara의 비극적 사건에 대한 언급이 있는 (D)가 오고, Clara의 비극적 사건의 내용을 구체적으로 설명하고 그것을 극복한 내용인 (C)가 온 다음에, 목적지에 도착하여 기쁨을 나누는 내용인 (B)가 마지막에 오는 것이 가장 적절하다.

STEP 3 글의 흐름에 맞추어 글의 내용을 이해하고 나머지 문제를 푼다.

- (a), (b), (d), (e)는 모두 Clara를 가리키지만, (c)는 Emma를 가리킨다.
- Clara는 어깨 부상으로 인해 올림픽 수영 메달리스트가 되겠다는 꿈을 포기해야만 했다고 했으므로, 글에 관한 내용으로 적절하지 않은 것은 ③이다.

Exercises

01~03 다음 글을 읽고, 물음에 답하시오.

(A)

Monica Padman left college in 2009 with two degrees in hand — one in theater and one in public relations. She moved to Hollywood to follow her dream of becoming an actor and comedian. Like most striving actors, she worked a variety of part-time jobs in between auditions and small roles. Padman scored a small part on Showtime's *House of Lies*, where she played the on-screen assistant to the actress Kristen Bell. They became friendly, and when Padman realized Bell had a young daughter, (a) she mentioned that she did some babysitting.

(B)

The job could be a detour. But Padman decided to take it. Over time, she became a friend and creative partner to Bell. She worked energetically wherever she saw a need. "Everything she does is at 110 percent," Bell said of Padman. Before long, Padman had become so essential that Bell wondered aloud, "How did I do any of this without (b) her?" While working for her family, Padman spent many hours sitting on the terrace debating with Bell's husband.

* detour: 돌아가는 길, 우회로

(C)

Bell and her husband, the actor Dax Shepard, took her up on the offer. As she saw the challenges Bell faced juggling multiple acting and producing projects, she offered to help (c) her with scheduling. Though it might have been tempting for the aspiring actress to ask the Hollywood A-lister to help her get on-screen roles, Padman worked where she was needed — ironically, as Bell's off-screen assistant. When Bell and Shepard asked her to work for them full-time, Padman was understandably reluctant — how would (d) she find time to audition?

* juggle: (일 · 활동 등을) 동시에 수행하다, 양립시키다

(D)

Their arguments were as fun as they were fierce, so when Bell suggested they develop their banter into a podcast, Padman was up for that too. Thus was born *Armchair Expert*. The podcast became 2018's most downloaded new podcast and has continued to grow in popularity. Padman could have pursued a direct path to her passion. Instead, (e) she worked wholeheartedly where she could be most useful. By working passionately in Bell's house, she found a bigger opportunity and, perhaps, her true purpose.

* banter: 재치 있는 농담

01

주어진 글 (A)에 이어질 내용을 순서에 맞게 배열한 것으로 가장 적절한 것은?

24005-0111

① (B) – (D) – (C)　② (C) – (B) – (D)　③ (C) – (D) – (B)
④ (D) – (B) – (C)　⑤ (D) – (C) – (B)

02

밑줄 친 (a)~(e) 중에서 가리키는 대상이 나머지 넷과 다른 것은?

24005-0112

① (a)　② (b)　③ (c)　④ (d)　⑤ (e)

03

윗글의 Padman에 관한 내용으로 적절하지 않은 것은?

24005-0113

① 배우이자 코미디언이 되기를 원했다.
② Bell의 친구이자 창의적인 파트너가 되었다.
③ Bell의 남편과 토론을 하면서 많은 시간을 보냈다.
④ Bell에게 자신이 영화 배역을 맡게 도와 달라고 부탁했다.
⑤ 팟캐스트를 해 보자는 제안을 받아들였다.

04~06 다음 글을 읽고, 물음에 답하시오.

(A)

An old and weak soldier was playing his violin one evening on the Prater, in Vienna. His faithful dog was holding his hat, in which passers-by dropped a few coppers as they came along. However, on the evening in question nobody stopped to put a small coin into the old soldier's hat. Everyone went straight on, and the joy of the crowd added to the sorrow in the old soldier's heart, which showed itself in (a) his withered face.

* withered: 활기 없는, 메마른

(B)

Then, having carefully tuned his violin, the gentleman said: "You take the money and I'll play." He *did* play! All the passers-by stopped to listen — struck with the distinguished air of the musician and fascinated by his marvelous genius. Every moment the circle became larger and larger. Not copper alone, but silver — and even gold — was dropped into the old soldier's hat. The dog began to growl, for it was becoming too heavy for him to hold. At an invitation from the audience, the old soldier emptied its contents into (b) his bag, and they filled it again.

* growl: 으르렁거리다

(C)

After a national melody, in which everyone present joined, with uncovered heads, the violinist placed the instrument upon the poor soldier's knees, and, without waiting to be thanked, disappeared. "Who is it?" was asked on all sides. "It is Armand Boucher, the famous violin player," replied someone in the crowd. "He has been turning his art to account in the service of charity. Let us follow (c) his example." And the speaker sent round his hat also, made a new collection, and gave the proceeds to the old soldier, crying, "Long live Boucher!" Deeply affected, the old soldier thanked everyone around him.

(D)

However, all at once, a well-dressed gentleman came up to where the old soldier stood, listened to his playing for a few minutes, and gazed compassionately upon (d) him. Before long, the old soldier's tired hand had no longer strength to grasp his bow. His limbs refused to carry him farther. He seated himself on a stone, rested his head on his hands, and began to weep silently. At that instant the gentleman approached, offered the old soldier a piece of gold, and said: "Lend me (e) your violin a little while."

* weep: 울다

04

24005-0114

주어진 글 (A)에 이어질 내용을 순서에 맞게 배열한 것으로 가장 적절한 것은?

① (B) – (D) – (C)
② (C) – (B) – (D)
③ (C) – (D) – (B)
④ (D) – (B) – (C)
⑤ (D) – (C) – (B)

05

24005-0115

밑줄 친 (a)~(e) 중에서 가리키는 대상이 나머지 넷과 다른 것은?

① (a)
② (b)
③ (c)
④ (d)
⑤ (e)

06

24005-0116

윗글에 관한 내용으로 적절하지 않은 것은?

① 노병의 충실한 개는 노병의 모자를 물고 있었다.
② 신사는 바이올린을 조심스럽게 조율했다.
③ 동전과 은화, 금화가 노병의 모자에 던져졌다.
④ 신사는 연주가 끝난 후 감사하다는 말을 듣고 사라졌다.
⑤ 노병의 손은 더 이상 활을 잡을 힘이 없었다.

07~09 다음 글을 읽고, 물음에 답하시오.

(A)

One day when I was little, my father told me the story of how Say Say had come to be with us. My father was talking to my mother about his work in the Kler Lwee Htu district, from where (a) <u>he</u> had just returned. It was far distant from us, and much closer to the front line where the Burmese military were attacking our villages. The Burmese regime had a notorious policy called the 'Four Cuts', which was designed to crush the Karen. It was brutally simple: it would cut off all supplies, information, recruits and food to the Karen resistance.

* regime: 정권 ** notorious: 악명 높은

(B)

My mother and father had only one child at this time — my older sister, Bwa Bwa — and my father felt a deep sympathy for (b) <u>his</u> friend. He agreed to take Say Say as one of his own children, and so Say Say became my parents' adopted son. Once a year Say Say's father would try to visit, if he could afford the time to make the long journey. Whenever (c) <u>he</u> did, he was so happy and proud to see how well his son was doing in his studies at school.

(C)

The Four Cuts policy was hurting people terribly, my father explained. As a small child I couldn't understand everything (d) <u>he</u> told us. I knew my people were starving to death, but I was scared, and I didn't want to think about it. I could see that my father was suffering, but I tried to close my mind to that. We were all closer to our mother at this time, for the simple reason that she was around. I'd grow close to my father when he was with us, but hurt, and distant, when he left.

(D)

The Four Cuts policy had driven families to ever more desperate measures. One day a man who worked for the resistance had approached my father. Over their time spent working together they had grown to like and respect each other. He told my father that he had seven children, and that he wanted one at least to get a proper education. But the Four Cuts policy had destroyed all the schools in the area. He asked my father if (e) <u>he</u> could take one of his older sons, Say Say, and give him an education in our home village.

07

24005-0117

주어진 글 (A)에 이어질 내용을 순서에 맞게 배열한 것으로 가장 적절한 것은?

① (B) – (D) – (C) ② (C) – (B) – (D) ③ (C) – (D) – (B)
④ (D) – (B) – (C) ⑤ (D) – (C) – (B)

08

24005-0118

밑줄 친 (a)~(e) 중에서 가리키는 대상이 나머지 넷과 다른 것은?

① (a) ② (b) ③ (c) ④ (d) ⑤ (e)

09

24005-0119

윗글에 관한 내용으로 적절하지 않은 것은?

① Kler Lwee Htu 지역은 'I'가 살고 있는 곳에서 멀리 떨어져 있었다.
② 버마 정권은 Karen 족을 탄압하기 위한 정책을 펼쳤다.
③ 'I'의 아버지는 Say Say를 양자로 받아들였다.
④ 'I'는 아버지의 고통을 외면하려고 했다.
⑤ Four Cuts 정책으로 'I'의 마을 아이들은 정규 교육을 받을 수 없었다.

10~12 다음 글을 읽고, 물음에 답하시오.

(A)

Long ago in New Orleans, there was an old gentleman named Raymond, who would sit on his porch every day. Raymond enjoyed his time outdoors, communing with nature and the neighbors and soaking up sunshine. Every day at the same time a kid would walk down his street on his way home from school. Raymond enjoyed talking to the local kid and the kid also loved talking with him. They kept an eye out for each other. However, this kid had developed a bad habit. On his way down the street every day, (a) he would beat on the metal trash cans with sticks.

* porch: (지붕이 얹혀 있고 벽이 둘러진) 현관 ** commune: 교감하다

(B)

The next week Raymond told the kid that he was short on money (even though that wasn't really true) and that he could only pay (b) him fifty cents a day for banging on cans. The kid was not happy about this new arrangement, but agreed anyway and got his fifty cents each day after banging cans. The week after that Raymond told the kid that money was even tighter and that he could only pay him twenty-five cents per day. Again, the kid was not happy about this new arrangement, but agreed anyway and banged cans and got his twenty-five cents each day.

(C)

After a week of paying the kid twenty-five cents a day, Raymond approached the kid and told him he couldn't pay him anymore but he still wanted (c) him to continue to bang cans. This time the kid did not agree. He was angry about not getting paid and refused to bang on cans anymore. Raymond continues to sit on his porch every day, enjoying nature, his neighbors, and soaking up the sun.

(D)

Raymond found this very annoying and tried to ask the kid to stop, but (d) he didn't want to listen to the old man on the porch. Raymond decided to put the concepts of intrinsic motivation and reinforcement theory to work. The next time the kid came down the street (e) he complimented him on the sound he made and said he would pay him a dollar a day if he promised to do it every day. The kid accepted and every day for the following week the kid banged on cans and Raymond paid him a dollar.

10

24005-0120

주어진 글 (A)에 이어질 내용을 순서에 맞게 배열한 것으로 가장 적절한 것은?

① (B) – (D) – (C)
② (C) – (B) – (D)
③ (C) – (D) – (B)
④ (D) – (B) – (C)
⑤ (D) – (C) – (B)

11

24005-0121

밑줄 친 (a)~(e) 중에서 가리키는 대상이 나머지 넷과 다른 것은?

① (a)
② (b)
③ (c)
④ (d)
⑤ (e)

12

24005-0122

윗글에 관한 내용으로 적절하지 않은 것은?

① Raymond는 야외에서 자연 및 이웃과 교감하는 것을 즐겼다.
② Raymond와 소년 모두 서로 대화하는 것을 좋아했다.
③ Raymond는 소년에게 줄 돈이 실제로 부족하지는 않았다.
④ 소년은 돈을 받지 못해도 자기 행동을 계속하기로 했다.
⑤ Raymond는 내재적 동기 부여와 강화 이론의 개념을 이용하기로 결심했다.

주제 · 소재편

20 인물, 일화, 기담

Gateway

2024학년도 6월 모의평가 26번

24005-0123

Jean Renoir에 관한 다음 글의 내용과 일치하지 않는 것은?

Jean Renoir (1894–1979), a French film director, was born in Paris, France. He was the son of the famous painter Pierre-Auguste Renoir. He and the rest of the Renoir family were the models of many of his father's paintings. At the outbreak of World War I, Jean Renoir was serving in the French army but was wounded in the leg. In 1937, he made *La Grande Illusion*, one of his better-known films. It was enormously successful but was not allowed to show in Germany. During World War II, when the Nazis invaded France in 1940, he went to Hollywood in the United States and continued his career there. He was awarded numerous honors and awards throughout his career, including the Academy Honorary Award in 1975 for his lifetime achievements in the film industry. Overall, Jean Renoir's influence as a film-maker and artist endures.

① 유명 화가의 아들이었다.
② 제1차 세계대전이 발발했을 때 프랑스 군에 복무 중이었다.
③ *La Grande Illusion*을 1937년에 만들었다.
④ 제2차 세계대전 내내 프랑스에 머물렀다.
⑤ Academy Honorary Award를 수상하였다.

Words & Phrases in Use

- ☐ outbreak (전쟁 등의) 발발
- ☐ serve in the army 군에 복무하다
- ☐ wounded 부상을 입은
- ☐ enormously 엄청나게
- ☐ invade 침공하다
- ☐ numerous 수많은
- ☐ achievement 업적
- ☐ overall 전체적으로 보아, 대체로
- ☐ endure 지속되다

reputation 명성, 평판 (the general estimation that the public has for a person)
Alex Merkin has already established a **reputation** as a film director with a vision.
Alex Merkin은 비전이 있는 영화감독으로서의 명성을 이미 확립했다.

adaptation 각색(한 작품) (movie, TV show, etc. made from a book or a play)
In 2013 Jeremy Irvine starred in the film **adaptation** of *The Railway Man*.
2013년에 Jeremy Irvine은 *The Railway Man*을 영화로 각색한 작품에서 주연을 맡았다.

vigor 활력, 활기 (active strength of body or mind)
After her vacation, Kelly returned to work with renewed **vigor**.
휴가를 마치고 Kelly는 다시 활력을 얻어 업무에 복귀했다.

terminate 종료하다 (to cause something to end or stop)
The employer **terminated** my contract immediately without any reason related to work or performance.
고용주는 업무 또는 성과와 관련된 어떠한 이유도 없이 즉시 내 계약을 종료했다.

persistence 끈기 (the attitude or behavior of someone who continues to do, or tries to do, something in a determined way)
David Kershaw was known for his **persistence** in the pursuit of justice.
David Kershaw는 정의를 추구하는 끈기로 유명했다.

transform 변화[변모]시키다 (to change completely the appearance or character of something or someone, especially so that that thing or person is improved)
Artificial intelligence has the potential to **transform** the entertainment industry.
인공지능은 엔터테인먼트 산업을 변화시킬 잠재력을 가지고 있다.

idol 우상 (someone who is admired and respected very much)
Baseball players are my son's **idols**.
야구 선수는 내 아들의 우상이다.

Quick Review 다음 각 문장의 빈칸에 들어갈 말로 가장 적절한 것을 〈보기〉에서 고르시오.

보기

transform   adaptation   idol   reputation   vigor

1. The young singer burst into tears when she finally met her ___________ backstage.
2. When it comes to dental health, chocolate has a bad ___________.
3. The musical ___________ of the beloved children's book delighted audiences of all ages.
4. Technological development will ___________ the weapons of war.
5. The speaker delivered her speech with ___________ and captivated the audience with her passion.

Exercises

01 Marcel Pagnol에 관한 다음 글의 내용과 일치하지 않는 것은?

24005-0124

Marcel Pagnol was born in Aubagne in 1895, and died in 1974. The son of a primary school teacher, whom he described so vividly in his *Souvenirs d'enfance* (childhood memories), this southern Frenchman began his professional life as an English teacher. However, he quickly earned a reputation for his plays in the 1920s: the extraordinary success of *Topaze* in 1927 and *Marius* in 1928 established him as a playwright. Marcel Pagnol had long been interested in the cinema, but had to wait for the development of talking picture techniques to use his full vigor as a dialogue writer. His first few films were adaptations of his theatrical works, for example the highly acclaimed trilogy *Marius*, *Fanny* and *César*. The public success was enormous at both national and international levels. This persuaded Marcel Pagnol to devote himself exclusively to the cinema. For his second film he set up his own production company, La societe des films Marcel Pagnol. He was certain that the dramatist of the past would be the film-maker of the future, a thesis which he controversially developed in a short-lived critical review entitled *Les cahiers du film.*

* acclaimed: 극찬[호평]을 받은 ** trilogy: 3부작 *** thesis: 논제(論題)

① 초등학교 교사의 아들로 태어났다.
② 1920년대에 희곡으로 빠르게 명성을 얻었다.
③ 국내와 달리 국제적으로는 대중적인 성공을 이루지 못했다.
④ 두 번째 영화를 위해 자기 자신의 제작사를 설립했다.
⑤ 과거의 극작가가 미래의 영화 제작자가 될 것이라고 확신했다.

02 다음 빈칸에 들어갈 말로 가장 적절한 것은?

24005-0125

When he was a Harvard student, world-famous cellist Yo-Yo Ma played often at concerts in and around Boston. He became very popular, and one day when one of his concerts was sold out, he gave a free concert for those who were unable to obtain tickets — he sat in the theater lobby and played Bach cello suites. Later in his career, when he was an international success, he still would often ______________________. For example, many guest cello soloists play in the first half of a concert, then they are finished for the night. However, Mr. Ma would sometimes play as part of the orchestra in the second half of the concert — doing this with the Philadelphia Orchestra was especially enjoyable for him. He says, "It is an honor to play the back stands of the Philadelphia Orchestra. It's incredible the way those players listen, the knowledge they have. I admire it so much. And I feel the thrill of being part of something that's greater than the sum of its parts — being accepted as part of the team."

① give more than required
② correct his unexpected mistakes
③ seek freedom in his performance
④ focus on the basics of playing music
⑤ teach people how to play instruments

03 주어진 글 다음에 이어질 글의 순서로 가장 적절한 것은?

24005-0126

In the summer of 1878, a thirty-year-old Dutch botanist named Hugo de Vries traveled to England to see Darwin. It was more of a spiritual journey than a scientific visit.

(A) With no more than a brief conversation, Darwin had inserted a sluice into de Vries's racing mind, completely redirecting it forever. Back in Amsterdam, de Vries suddenly terminated his prior work on the movement of tendrils in plants and threw himself into solving the mystery of heredity.

(B) He also had Darwin's persistence. The meeting must have been exhausting, for it lasted only two hours, and Darwin had to excuse himself to take a break. But de Vries left England transformed.

(C) Darwin was vacationing at his sister's estate in Dorking, but de Vries tracked him down and traveled out to meet him. Thin, intense, and excitable, with a beard that rivaled Darwin's, de Vries already looked like a younger version of his idol.

* sluice: 수문(水門) ** tendril: 덩굴손 *** heredity: 유전

① (A) – (C) – (B)
② (B) – (A) – (C)
③ (B) – (C) – (A)
④ (C) – (A) – (B)
⑤ (C) – (B) – (A)

21 철학, 종교, 역사, 풍습, 지리

Gateway

2024학년도 9월 모의평가 31번

24005-0127

다음 빈칸에 들어갈 말로 가장 적절한 것은?

In the post-World War II years after 1945, unparalleled economic growth fueled a building boom and a massive migration from the central cities to the new suburban areas. The suburbs were far more dependent on the automobile, signaling the shift from primary dependence on public transportation to private cars. Soon this led to the construction of better highways and freeways and the decline and even loss of public transportation. With all of these changes came a ____________ of leisure. As more people owned their own homes, with more space inside and lovely yards outside, their recreation and leisure time was increasingly centered around the home or, at most, the neighborhood. One major activity of this home-based leisure was watching television. No longer did one have to ride the trolly to the theater to watch a movie; similar entertainment was available for free and more conveniently from television.

* unparalleled: 유례없는

① downfall ② uniformity ③ restoration
④ privatization ⑤ customization

Words & Phrases in Use

- ☐ fuel 부추기다
- ☐ massive 대규모의
- ☐ migration 이주
- ☐ suburban 교외의
- ☐ public transportation 대중교통
- ☐ freeway 초고속 도로
- ☐ decline 감소
- ☐ loss 쇠퇴, 상실
- ☐ trolly 전차
- ☐ entertainment 오락(물)
- ☐ for free 무료로

consensus 합의 (general agreement or opinion reached by a group of people, typically after discussion or debate)
After hours of deliberation, the committee finally reached a **consensus** on the best course of action.
몇 시간의 심사숙고 끝에, 위원회는 마침내 최선의 행동 방침에 대한 합의에 도달했다.

morality 도덕(성) (principles or standards concerning the distinction between right and wrong, or good and evil)
Honesty, compassion, and fairness are basic values in the realm of **morality**.
정직, 동정심, 공정성은 도덕성 영역의 기본적 가치이다.

relative 상대적인 (considered or evaluated in relation to something else)
The concept of time is **relative** because it can be perceived differently depending on one's frame of reference.
시간의 개념은 기준의 틀에 따라 다르게 인식될 수 있어서 상대적이다.

fertile 비옥한 (capable of producing abundant vegetation, crops, or offspring)
The **fertile** land along the river was perfect for farming and produced abundant crops.
강변의 비옥한 땅은 농사를 짓기에 적합했고 풍성한 농작물을 생산했다.

constitute 구성하다, 이루다 (to form or make up a whole)
The various departments and teams **constitute** the organization.
다양한 부서와 팀이 그 조직을 구성하고 있다.

wilderness 황무지, 황야 (an uncultivated, uninhabited, and undisturbed area of land, typically characterized by its natural features and the absence of human development)
The adventurers set out to explore the vast **wilderness** of the national park.
모험가들은 국립 공원의 광활한 황무지를 탐험하기 위해 출발했다.

Quick Review 다음 각 문장의 빈칸에 들어갈 말로 가장 적절한 것을 〈보기〉에서 고르시오.

보기: wilderness relative fertile consensus morality

1. There is a growing __________ among scientists that climate change is real.
2. We have a responsibility to protect our __________ for future generations.
3. The Amazon's __________ soil is home to a wide variety of plants and animals.
4. __________ is important because it helps us live together in a harmonious society.
5. The concept of beauty is __________ and varies from person to person.

01

다음 글의 주제로 가장 적절한 것은?

24005-0128

It is uncontroversially true that people in different societies have different customs and different ideas about right and wrong. There is no world consensus on which actions are right and wrong, even though there is a considerable overlap between views on this. If we consider how much moral views have changed both from place to place and from age to age it can be tempting to think that there are no absolute moral facts, but rather that morality is always relative to the society in which you have been brought up. On such a view, since slavery was morally acceptable to most Ancient Greeks but is not to most Europeans today, slavery was right for the Ancient Greeks but would be wrong for today's Europeans. This view, known as moral relativism, makes morality simply a description of the values held by a particular society at a particular time. This is a meta-ethical view about the nature of moral judgements. Moral judgements can only be judged true or false relative to a particular society. There are no absolute moral judgements: they are all relative.

① the harmful effects of moral relativism
② the relative nature of moral judgements
③ considerations in making moral judgements
④ why moral judgments are not always desirable
⑤ moral behavior as a means of self-improvement

02 다음 빈칸에 들어갈 말로 가장 적절한 것은?

24005-0129

If the United States has one of the easiest geographies to develop, Mexico has one of the most difficult. The entirety of Mexico is in essence the southern extension of the Rocky Mountains, which is a kind way of saying that America's worst lands are strikingly similar to Mexico's best lands. As one would expect from a territory that is mountain-dominated, there are no navigable rivers and no large cohesive pieces of fertile land like the American Southeast or the Columbia valley, much less the Midwest. Each mountain valley is a sort of fastness where a small handful of oligarchs control local economic and political life. Mexico shouldn't be thought of as a unified state, but instead as a collage of dozens of little Mexicos where local power brokers constantly align with and against each other (and a national government seeking — often in vain — to stitch together something more cohesive). In its ______________________________, Mexico is a textbook case that countries with the greatest need for capital-intensive infrastructure are typically the countries with the lowest ability to generate the capital necessary to build that infrastructure.

* cohesive: 응집된, 결합력이 있는 ** oligarch: 과두 정치 독재자 *** infrastructure: 사회 기반 시설

① democratic atmosphere
② agricultural vastness
③ labor-intensive structure
④ regional disconnectedness
⑤ widespread industrialization

03 글의 흐름으로 보아, 주어진 문장이 들어가기에 가장 적절한 곳은?

24005-0130

Saltwater constitutes 97% of Earth's water, and of the 3% that is fresh, two-thirds is frozen in glaciers and polar ice.

When Samuel Taylor Coleridge wrote the words, "Water, water everywhere, but not a drop to drink" in *The Rime of the Ancient Mariner* in 1798, the dangers of drinking seawater had been known for thousands of years. (①) Seawater does indeed make men mad. (②) Historical evidence indicates the ancient Egyptians knew seawater was not potable, but the earliest realization that it was unsafe to drink has been lost to antiquity. (③) In pre-Columbian times, the greatest fear of venturing too far from land on the ocean was not falling off the surface of the Earth but lack of fresh drinking water. (④) From a human perspective, the oceans, which cover 70% of Earth's surface, are still the most extensive and unique desert wildernesses on the planet. (⑤) Thus, a mere 1% of all the water on the planet (in lakes and rivers, groundwater, and the atmosphere) is fresh and can be used by terrestrial plants and animals.

* potable: 마시기에 적합한 ** terrestrial: 육상의

22 환경, 자원, 재활용

Gateway

2023학년도 수능 22번

24005-0131

다음 글의 요지로 가장 적절한 것은?

Urban delivery vehicles can be adapted to better suit the density of urban distribution, which often involves smaller vehicles such as vans, including bicycles. The latter have the potential to become a preferred 'last-mile' vehicle, particularly in high-density and congested areas. In locations where bicycle use is high, such as the Netherlands, delivery bicycles are also used to carry personal cargo (e.g. groceries). Due to their low acquisition and maintenance costs, cargo bicycles convey much potential in developed and developing countries alike, such as the *becak* (a three-wheeled bicycle) in Indonesia. Services using electrically assisted delivery tricycles have been successfully implemented in France and are gradually being adopted across Europe for services as varied as parcel and catering deliveries. Using bicycles as cargo vehicles is particularly encouraged when combined with policies that restrict motor vehicle access to specific areas of a city, such as downtown or commercial districts, or with the extension of dedicated bike lanes.

① 도시에서 자전거는 효율적인 배송 수단으로 사용될 수 있다.
② 자전거는 출퇴근 시간을 줄이기 위한 대안으로 선호되고 있다.
③ 자전거는 배송 수단으로의 경제적 장단점을 모두 가질 수 있다.
④ 수요자의 요구에 부합하는 다양한 용도의 자전거가 개발되고 있다.
⑤ 세계 각국에서는 전기 자전거 사용을 장려하는 정책을 추진하고 있다.

Words & Phrases in Use

- ☐ urban 도시의
- ☐ vehicle 운송 수단
- ☐ density 밀도, 밀집 상태
- ☐ distribution 분포, 배치
- ☐ congested 혼잡한
- ☐ cargo 짐, 화물
- ☐ implement 시행하다
- ☐ gradually 점차
- ☐ adopt 채택하다, 도입하다
- ☐ restrict 제한하다
- ☐ access 접근(권)
- ☐ commercial district 상업 지구
- ☐ extension 확장
- ☐ dedicated 전용의

Academic Vocabulary by Topic

demographics 인구 통계 (statistical data relating to the population and particular groups within it)
The marketing team conducted thorough research on the **demographics** of their target audience.
마케팅팀은 목표 구매자층의 인구 통계에 대한 철저한 조사를 실시했다.

efficiency 효율성 (the quality of working well in an organized way, without wasting time or energy)
LED lighting has high energy **efficiency**, providing the same brightness as traditional bulbs but with significantly lower energy consumption.
LED 조명은 높은 에너지 효율성을 가지고 있어 기존 전구와 동일한 밝기를 제공하면서도 에너지 소비량은 현저히 더 낮다.

disproportionate 불균형적인 (too large or too small in comparison to something else)
The allocation of resources was considered **disproportionate**, with certain departments receiving significantly more funding than others.
특정 부서가 다른 부서보다 훨씬 더 많은 자금을 지원받아서, 자원 배분이 불균형한 것으로 간주되었다.

accommodate 수용하다 (to provide with a place to live or to be stored in)
The subway system is continually updated to **accommodate** the growing number of commuters.
지하철 시스템은 증가하는 통근자 수를 수용하기 위해 지속적으로 업데이트된다.

conscious 의식하는 (aware of and responding to one's surroundings)
The school implemented a recycling program to encourage students to be more **conscious** of the environment. 그 학교는 학생들이 환경을 더 많이 의식하도록 독려하기 위해 재활용 프로그램을 시행했다.

endangered 멸종 위기에 처한 ((of a species) seriously at risk of extinction)
The giant panda is an **endangered** species, and conservation efforts are being made to protect its declining population. 대왕판다는 멸종 위기에 처한 종인데, 감소하는 개체 수를 보호하기 위한 보존 노력이 이루어지고 있다.

conservation 보존 (the careful utilization of resources to prevent waste or depletion)
The establishment of national parks aims at the **conservation** of natural landscapes for public enjoyment while preserving biodiversity.
국립 공원의 설립은 생물 다양성을 보존하면서 대중이 즐길 수 있는 자연 경관을 보존하는 것을 목표로 한다.

Quick Review 다음 각 문장의 빈칸에 들어갈 말로 가장 적절한 것을 〈보기〉에서 고르시오.

보기
conservation disproportionate conscious demographics endangered

1. The city planners analyzed the ____________ of the city to make informed decisions about infrastructure development.
2. The use of eco-friendly fishing gear is encouraged for sustainable fishing practices and marine ____________.
3. The documentary aimed to make viewers more ____________ of the consequences of climate change.
4. Efforts to save the ____________ sea turtles include implementing measures to reduce accidental capture in fishing gear.
5. The media coverage of the event appeared ____________, focusing excessively on minor details rather than the overall significance of the occasion.

Exercises

01

다음 글의 주제로 가장 적절한 것은?

24005-0132

Shifting demographics, household structures, lifestyle preferences, and consumer values suggest a different built environment and urban fabric 30 years ahead compared with 30 years ago. More and more Americans, Australians, and Europeans are choosing to live in settings where they are less dependent on their cars because reducing air pollution and energy use matters to them. A 2011 survey of more than two thousand adult Americans found seven times more people said the neighborhood where a house is located is a bigger consideration in deciding where to live than the size of the house. Walking to restaurants, businesses, schools, and other amenities was the most appealing neighborhood feature for many respondents. To many 20- and 30-somethings, walkable communities are equated with a downsized environmental footprint and energy efficiency, with the added benefit of burning calories during everyday activities. If green buildings and solar panels dot the landscape and rooftops, all the better. Notes one economist with the Urban Land Institute, "Energy efficiency is becoming the new granite countertops; it's a necessary feature to sell the property."

* amenity: 생활 편의 시설 ** dot: (점으로) 덮다 *** granite: 화강암

① preferred housing types in urban areas by generation
② urban neighborhood facilities attracting young people
③ demographic differences between urban and suburban areas
④ growing preference for housing locations in walkable neighborhoods
⑤ factors to consider when buying a house in an inner city versus a suburb

02

24005-0133

다음 글의 밑줄 친 부분 중, 어법상 틀린 것은?

In recent years, there has been an increasing tendency of economists, scientists, and politicians to shift the focus from population growth to consumption as the more important underlying driver of biodiversity loss. For many, the emphasis on consumption avoids politically charged topics, such as population control, ① which most people oppose on ethical or moral grounds, and because it is associated with divisive topics such as xenophobia, racism, and eugenics. Others highlight that it is not the number of people per se, but how natural resources are consumed ② what is the main cause of environmental decline. Indeed, rich people and rich countries have a disproportionate impact on the natural environment because they consume a disproportionately large share of the world's natural resources. To use one example, the USA accommodates only 5% of the world's human population but uses 25% of the world's ③ harvested natural resources each year. In fact, decorative Christmas lights in the USA alone ④ use more energy than the annual energy usage of the entirety of Ethiopia or Tanzania. And yet, the average USA citizen uses less than half of the energy that an average citizen of Qatar uses, Qatar ⑤ being a small but wealthy Middle Eastern country.

* xenophobia: 외국인 혐오 ** eugenics: 우생학 *** per se: 그 자체로

03

24005-0134

다음 빈칸에 들어갈 말로 가장 적절한 것은?

Movies featuring wonderful natural landscapes and charismatic wildlife often increase the desire of moviegoers to visit natural areas where they can see these landscapes and animals first-hand. But they can also ____________________. While many documentaries are created with this purpose in mind, such benefits can also extend to blockbuster movies meant for broader audiences. For example, Disney's *Happy Feet* (2006) highlighted the threat of overfishing and plastic pollution to penguins; *The Jungle Book* (2016) exposed audiences to the endangered pangolins. Such exposure can even lead to environmentally conscious behavioural changes. For example, moviegoers were willing to donate 50% more money to climate mitigation after watching the apocalyptic movie *The Day After Tomorrow* (2004). Perhaps, in part, due to the influence of environmentally-orientated movies, an increasing number of movie stars (and other celebrities) have started using their stardom as a platform from where they promote biodiversity conservation efforts in Africa.

* pangolin: 천산갑(몸의 위쪽이 딱딱한 비늘로 덮여 있고 긴 혀로 곤충을 핥아먹는 작은 동물) ** mitigation: 완화
*** apocalyptic: 종말론적인

① emphasize the conservation of rare plant species
② have a positive influence on the lives of the natives
③ stimulate movie studios to make more blockbuster films
④ raise awareness of environmental issues in new audiences
⑤ motivate moviegoers to participate in fun activities in the wild

23 물리, 화학, 생명과학, 지구과학

Gateway

2024학년도 9월 모의평가 37번

24005-0135

주어진 글 다음에 이어질 글의 순서로 가장 적절한 것은?

Plants show finely tuned adaptive responses when nutrients are limiting. Gardeners may recognize yellow leaves as a sign of poor nutrition and the need for fertilizer.

(A) In contrast, plants with a history of nutrient abundance are risk averse and save energy. At all developmental stages, plants respond to environmental changes or unevenness so as to be able to use their energy for growth, survival, and reproduction, while limiting damage and nonproductive uses of their valuable energy.

(B) Research in this area has shown that plants are constantly aware of their position in the environment, in terms of both space and time. Plants that have experienced variable nutrient availability in the past tend to exhibit risk-taking behaviors, such as spending energy on root lengthening instead of leaf production.

(C) But if a plant does not have a caretaker to provide supplemental minerals, it can proliferate or lengthen its roots and develop root hairs to allow foraging in more distant soil patches. Plants can also use their memory to respond to histories of temporal or spatial variation in nutrient or resource availability.

* nutrient: 영양소 ** fertilizer: 비료 *** forage: 구하러 다니다

① (A) – (C) – (B)
② (B) – (A) – (C)
③ (B) – (C) – (A)
④ (C) – (A) – (B)
⑤ (C) – (B) – (A)

Words & Phrases in Use

- ☐ finely 섬세하게, 정교하게
- ☐ tune 조정하다
- ☐ adaptive response 적응 반응
- ☐ abundance 풍부
- ☐ risk averse 위험을 회피하는
- ☐ unevenness 불균등
- ☐ variable 가변적인, 변하기 쉬운
- ☐ availability 획득 가능성
- ☐ supplemental 보충의
- ☐ proliferate 급증시키다
- ☐ patch 구역, 작은 땅
- ☐ temporal 시간의
- ☐ spatial 공간의

Academic Vocabulary by Topic

정답과 해설 66쪽

predator 포식자 (an animal that lives by killing and eating other animals)

Hawks are skilled **predators**, soaring high in the sky before diving down to catch their prey.
매는 숙련된 포식자로, 하늘 높이 날아오른 후 급강하하여 먹이를 잡는다.

adaptation 적응 (형태) (the process of changing to suit different conditions)

The study of genetic **adaptations** in populations over time provides insights into how organisms have evolved to better suit their environments.
장기간에 걸쳐 개체군의 유전적 적응 형태를 연구하면 유기체가 자기 환경에 더 잘 적응하도록 어떻게 진화해 왔는지에 대한 통찰력을 얻을 수 있다.

inedible 먹을 수 없는 (not fit or suitable to be eaten; not edible)

After accidentally adding too much salt to the soup, the chef realized it had become **inedible**.
실수로 수프에 소금을 너무 많이 넣은 후 요리사는 수프가 먹을 수 없게 되었다는 것을 깨달았다.

angle 각도 (the inclination of a line or surface with the vertical or horizontal plane)

The triangle has three **angles**, and their sum equals 180 degrees.
삼각형에는 세 개의 각도가 있으며 그 합은 180도와 같다.

minute 미세한 (extremely small, tiny)

When studying sea level rise or fall, scientists may examine **minute** changes in sea level over time.
해수면 상승 또는 하강을 연구할 때, 과학자들은 장기간에 걸친 해수면의 미세한 변화를 조사할 수도 있다.

deposit 놓다, 두다 (to place or store in a specific location, typically for safekeeping)

Coastal storms have the potential to **deposit** large amounts of sand along the shoreline.
해안의 폭풍은 해안선을 따라 대량의 모래를 놓아둘 가능성을 갖고 있다.

variation 변화 (a change or difference in condition, amount, or level, typically with certain limits)

Chemists study the **variation** in reaction rates under different temperature and pressure conditions to understand the factors influencing chemical reactions.
화학자들은 화학 반응에 영향을 미치는 요인을 이해하기 위해 다양한 온도와 압력 조건에서 반응 속도의 변화를 연구한다.

Quick Review 다음 각 문장의 빈칸에 들어갈 말로 가장 적절한 것을 〈보기〉에서 고르시오.

보기

adaptation inedible variation predator minute

1. Due to the extreme temperatures, the food left in the car overnight became ____________.
2. There was a noticeable ____________ in the color of the leaves as the seasons changed from summer to autumn.
3. The domestic cat retains many traits of a(n) ____________, instinctively hunting small rodents and birds.
4. The ____________ of a species to its environment is crucial for its survival and reproductive success.
5. Tiny, ____________ particles of dust floated in the air when the old book was opened.

01

다음 글의 주제로 가장 적절한 것은?

24005-0136

Many aspects of an ant's appearance have likely evolved to meet a specific lifestyle requirement, although the extent to which this is true has not been fully explored for all aspects of its body structure. Adaptations could be due to environment, available food, or predators. Long legs and large eyes are commonly seen in ground-foraging ants that need to move quickly to avoid predators in open ground or be the first to acquire a food resource. In contrast, ants that forage and nest in leaf litter have shorter legs and antennae, alongside small eyes. This makes sense in the dark environment of leaf litter where moving through small spaces is easier with a compact body plan. Based on the unique combination of body size measurements, scientists can predict where an ant nests and forages or even what kind of food it eats. Predators have longer, flatter mandibles, while omnivores — those eating a diverse range of foods — have shorter, curved mandibles.

* forage: 먹이를 찾다 ** leaf litter: 낙엽 *** mandible: 아래턱뼈

① ants' behavior depending on what they eat
② ways scientists predict ants' reproduction cycles
③ adaptations in ants' appearance for specific lifestyles
④ ants' strategies to avoid predators in dark environments
⑤ relationship between ants' appearance and their movement

02

24005-0137

giant Pacific octopus에 관한 다음 글의 내용과 일치하지 않는 것은?

The largest species of octopus in the world, the giant Pacific octopus, usually grows to about 3 m in length and weighs up to 272 kg. It lives on the rim of the North Pacific Ocean, where it crawls about on the bottom, using its long, sucker-covered arms. It seeks out rocky dens on the seabed; youngsters will often dig holes under rocks in sand. Here, the octopus can take refuge from predators — seals, sharks, and other large fishes — too big to slip through the den mouth. Foraging mainly at night, this giant octopus looks especially for crabs and lobsters, but also takes shrimp and shellfish, smaller octopuses, and fishes. Often it will return to its den to feed, depositing empty shells and other inedible fragments of prey in piles at the entrance. Like its relatives, this octopus mostly lives alone, except for a brief period when adults come together for mating. The female lays her eggs in a den, and will tend them until her young emerge. She will not feed in all this time — and will die soon after her young emerge.

* rim: 가장자리 ** den: 굴, 동굴 *** fragment: 조각

① 빨판으로 덮인 긴 팔을 이용하여 바닥을 기어다닌다.
② 어린 것들은 모래 지대의 바위 밑에 굴을 파기도 한다.
③ 특히 게와 바닷가재를 찾지만 새우와 조개류도 잡는다.
④ 짝짓기를 위한 짧은 기간을 제외하고는 대부분 혼자 산다.
⑤ 암컷은 새끼들이 알에서 나오기 전에 죽는다.

03

24005-0138

다음 글에서 전체 흐름과 관계 없는 문장은?

However skilled you may be at bowling, there will always be minute changes in the angle at which you release the ball that will be magnified as the ball travels the length of the lane. ① As it strikes, the first skittle falls back either slightly to the right or the left, and the ball is deflected slightly in the other direction. ② From then on, within a fraction of a second, skittles start falling in different directions, sometimes hitting others as they fall. ③ The differences in the final arrangement of skittles each time are difficult to predict from the slight variation of angle as the ball leaves the bowler's hand. ④ Whereas most sports require participants to be in good physical shape and play with people around the same age, bowling allows a mixed group of all sizes, ages, and skill levels. ⑤ Even those who can achieve strike after strike actually achieve a different strike every time, for the skittles will never fall in exactly the same way twice.

* skittle: 볼링핀 ** deflect: 방향을 바꾸다

Gateway

2024학년도 6월 모의평가 25번

24005-0139

다음 도표의 내용과 일치하지 않는 것은?

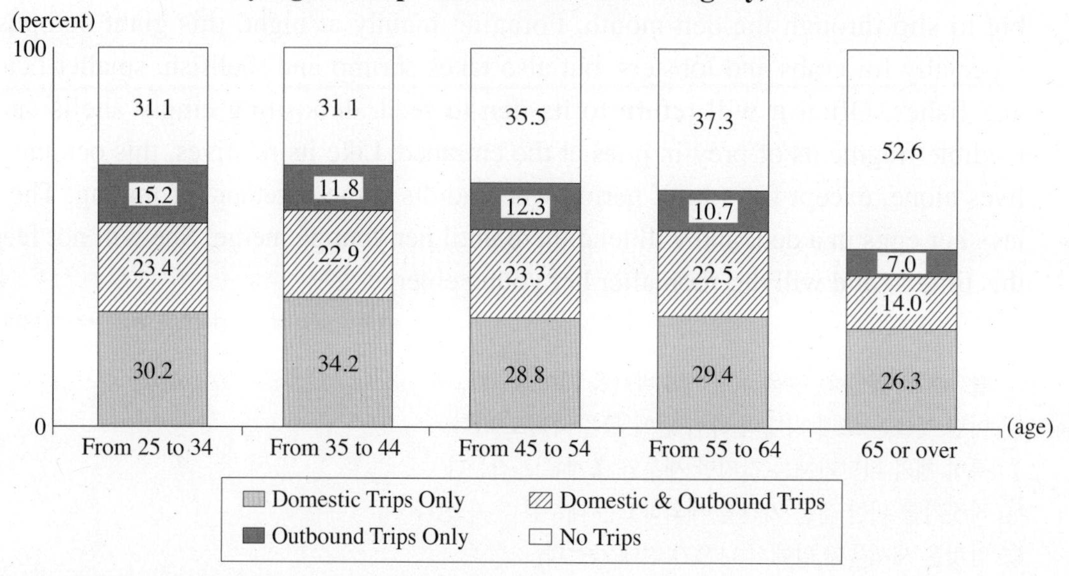

Note: Percentages may not sum to 100% due to rounding.

The above graph shows the share of the EU-28 population participating in tourism in 2017 by age group and destination category. ① The share of people in the No Trips category was over 30% in each of the five age groups. ② The percentage of people in the Outbound Trips Only category was higher in the 25–34 age group than in the 35–44 age group. ③ In the 35–44 age group, the percentage of people in the Domestic Trips Only category was 34.2%. ④ The percentage of people in the Domestic & Outbound Trips category was lower in the 45–54 age group than in the 55–64 age group. ⑤ In the 65 or over age group, the percentage of people in the No Trips category was more than 50%.

Words & Phrases in Use

☐ share 점유율 ☐ destination 목적지 ☐ domestic 국내의
☐ outbound 외국행의

spectator 관중, 관객 (a person who watches an event, show, game, activity, etc.)
The soccer stadium was packed with enthusiastic **spectators** cheering for their favorite teams.
축구 경기장은 자신이 좋아하는 팀을 응원하는 열광적인 관중들로 가득 찼다.

athlete 운동선수 (a person who is trained in or good at sports, games, or exercises that require physical skill and strength)
At the international competition, **athletes** from different countries gathered to demonstrate their skill in various disciplines.
국제 대회에서 각국의 선수들이 모여 다양한 종목에서 자신의 기량을 발휘했다.

nutrient 영양소, 영양분 (a substance that plants, animals, and people need to live and grow)
Plants absorb **nutrients** from the soil to support their growth and development.
식물은 토양에서 영양소를 흡수하여 자신의 성장과 발달을 지원한다.

physical 신체의, 육체의 (relating to the body of a person instead of the mind)
Regular exercise is important for maintaining good **physical** health and well-being.
규칙적인 운동은 좋은 신체 건강과 행복을 유지하는 데 중요하다.

comfort 편안함 (a state or situation in which you are relaxed and do not have any physically unpleasant feelings)
Wearing loose-fitting clothing contributes to a greater sense of **comfort**, especially during hot weather.
특히 더운 날씨에는 헐렁한 옷을 입는 것이 더 큰 편안함을 느끼게 해 준다.

satisfaction 만족(감) (a happy or pleased feeling because of something that you did or something that happened to you)
Completing the difficult project on time gave her a great sense of **satisfaction** and accomplishment.
어려운 프로젝트를 제시간에 완료한 것은 그녀에게 큰 만족감과 성취감을 주었다.

Quick Review 다음 각 문장의 빈칸에 들어갈 말로 가장 적절한 것을 〈보기〉에서 고르시오.

보기
nutrient spectator physical satisfaction athlete

1. Emma was recognized as an outstanding ___________ for her achievements in both track and field events.
2. ___________ imbalances in the body can lead to different health problems, highlighting the importance of a balanced diet.
3. Sufficient sleep is crucial for both mental and ___________ health, allowing the body to recover.
4. As a(n) ___________ at the film festival, she enjoyed herself watching a diverse range of masterpieces.
5. Maintaining a work-life balance is essential for overall well-being and job ___________.

Exercises

01 다음 글의 밑줄 친 부분 중, 문맥상 낱말의 쓰임이 적절하지 않은 것은?

24005-0140

Spectators are seen as a source of drive arousal. This ① heightened state of arousal is presumed to facilitate the performance of well-learned or simple skills. However, if a skill is not well-learned or complex, the increase in arousal will interfere with its performance. The underlying notion is that an increase in drive arousal ② favors the emission of the performer's dominant responses. In the case of a skilled performer, her dominant responses are presumed to be largely "correct" ones. Her performance stands to be ③ improved with an audience present. In a case where the performer is still struggling to master a skill, ④ correct responses are present in abundance and are thereby presumed to be dominant responses. As a consequence, onlookers can only worsen the performance of a beginner. Hence, the performer's level of skill and the complexity of the skill itself will ⑤ determine whether an audience helps or hinders a performance.

* hinder: 방해하다

02 다음 글의 요지로 가장 적절한 것은?

24005-0141

Athletes do require more protein (and all nutrients) than sedentary people, but there is no evidence that they require a higher percentage of protein compared to other macronutrients in their diet to perform more optimally. To put it another way, a diet with 10 percent protein is sufficient for most people, athlete and nonathlete alike. If an average adult female eats 2,000 calories, 10 percent is 200 calories from protein. If an average female athlete eats 3,000 calories, 10 percent is 300 calories from protein — that's a 50 percent increase in protein achieved by simply eating more of the same foods. So when you exercise, you don't need to change the composition of the food (i.e., consuming foods with higher concentrations of protein or consuming protein powders). You just need to eat more of the same foods. The increased athletic activity will work up your hunger drive. In response, you will consume more protein as well as nutrients of all types. This works well since physical activity likely requires more of all nutrients, not just protein.

* sedentary: 몸을 많이 움직이지 않는

① 운동선수는 일반인보다 더 많은 양의 단백질을 섭취해야 한다.
② 운동 후 과식을 피하려면 단백질이 풍부한 식단을 유지해야 한다.
③ 필요 이상의 단백질을 섭취하면 운동을 해도 체중이 증가할 수 있다.
④ 체력 향상을 위해 충분한 영양 섭취와 운동을 병행하는 것이 중요하다.
⑤ 운동에 필요한 단백질은 평소 식사의 양을 늘리는 것만으로도 충분하다.

03

24005-0142

다음 빈칸에 들어갈 말로 가장 적절한 것은?

Once production shifts to industrial methods, the leisure consumer is free to ______________________________. Typically, the technology itself enters one or more paths to pleasure as the market recognizes hobby demand: tools and materials are designed for comfort, beauty, and satisfaction. Both needlework tools and those of hobby woodworking have undergone this transition, to name only two of many possible examples. Fountain pens, considered obsolete as a production technology for writing, are selling at four-figure prices to people who simply enjoy the process of forming words with ink on paper and are willing to pay a premium for the pleasure. In the 1950s, the late Shelby Foote reportedly wrote his three-volume 1.5-million-word history of the Civil War with a dip pen, eschewing the then-dominant writing technologies — the manual typewriter and the fountain pen — thereby lending a new meaning to the term "belletristic history."

* obsolete: 구식의, 한물간 ** eschew: 멀리하다 *** belletristic: 순수 문학적인

① choose to replace or repair a product
② benefit from buying products at lower prices
③ seek pleasure in the older handcraft technology
④ try to regulate the speed of technological progress
⑤ choose less expensive forms of recreational activities

25 음악, 미술, 영화, 무용, 사진, 건축

Gateway

2024학년도 9월 모의평가 26번

24005-0143

Charles Rosen에 관한 다음 글의 내용과 일치하지 않는 것은?

Charles Rosen, a virtuoso pianist and distinguished writer, was born in New York in 1927. Rosen displayed a remarkable talent for the piano from his early childhood. In 1951, the year he earned his doctoral degree in French literature at Princeton University, Rosen made both his New York piano debut and his first recordings. To glowing praise, he appeared in numerous recitals and orchestral concerts around the world. Rosen's performances impressed some of the 20th century's most well-known composers, who invited him to play their music. Rosen was also the author of many widely admired books about music. His most famous book, *The Classical Style*, was first published in 1971 and won the U.S. National Book Award the next year. This work, which was reprinted in an expanded edition in 1997, remains a landmark in the field. While writing extensively, Rosen continued to perform as a pianist for the rest of his life until he died in 2012.

① 어려서부터 피아노에 재능을 보였다.
② 프랑스 문학으로 박사 학위를 받았다.
③ 유명 작곡가들로부터 그들의 작품 연주를 요청받았다.
④ *The Classical Style*이 처음으로 출판되고 다음 해에 상을 받았다.
⑤ 피아니스트 활동을 중단하고 글쓰기에 매진하였다.

Words & Phrases in Use

- □ virtuoso 거장, 명인
- □ distinguished 저명한, 성공한
- □ debut 데뷔, 첫 출연
- □ glowing 열렬한
- □ numerous 수많은
- □ recital 독주회
- □ expanded edition 증보판
- □ landmark 획기적인 것
- □ extensively 폭넓게, 광범위하게

Academic Vocabulary by Topic

정답과 해설 71쪽

catalog 분류하다 (to list or describe (something) in an organized way)

The librarian worked diligently to **catalog** the new books and add them to the library's database.
사서는 새 책을 분류하고 그것을 도서관 데이터베이스에 추가하기 위해 부지런히 일했다.

inquiry 탐구 (examination of facts or principles)

The scientific **inquiry** into the mysterious phenomenon led to a series of experiments and observations.
그 신비한 현상에 대한 과학적 탐구는 일련의 실험과 관찰로 이어졌다.

enormous 막대한, 거대한 (very great in size or amount)

The hurricane caused **enormous** damage to the coastal town, leaving many homes and buildings in ruins.
허리케인은 해안 마을에 막대한 피해를 끼쳤고, 많은 주택과 건물을 폐허로 만들었다.

architectural 건축의 (relating to the design and construction of buildings)

The city underwent a transformation with the implementation of new **architectural** designs and urban planning.
그 도시는 새로운 건축 디자인과 도시 계획의 시행으로 변화를 겪었다.

aesthetics 미학 (a branch of philosophy concerned with the study of the idea of beauty)

In the field of design, **aesthetics** plays a crucial role in creating products that are both functional and visually satisfying.
디자인 분야에서 미학은 기능적이면서도 시각적으로 만족스러운 제품을 만드는 데 중대한 역할을 한다.

component 요소 (a part or element of a larger whole)

The architect considered the aesthetic and functional aspects of each building **component** when designing the structure.
그 건축가는 구조물을 설계할 때 각 건물 요소의 미적, 기능적 측면을 고려했다.

Quick Review 다음 각 문장의 빈칸에 들어갈 말로 가장 적절한 것을 〈보기〉에서 고르시오.

보기

enormous　catalog　aesthetics　architectural　component

1. The fashion designer emphasized the importance of ____________ in creating clothing that not only fits well but also looks elegant.
2. The company achieved ____________ success with its innovative product, quickly dominating the market.
3. The engineer carefully examined each ____________ of the machine to identify the source of the problem.
4. The town's ____________ plan focuses on making neighborhoods friendly and accessible for residents of all ages.
5. The software developer designed a program to automatically ____________ files based on their content.

Exercises

01 다음 글의 밑줄 친 부분 중, 어법상 틀린 것은?

24005-0144

Responding to life with joy and sorrow is part of being human. At times when pain and suffering are inescapable, it is important ① to remember that this is part of the process by which we acquire knowledge. This does not mean that one must be in discomfort to make art, but stress can be channeled into a creative force if it produces a sense of inquisitiveness and an incentive for change. ② Think through making pictures can allow us to place our distress in context. The images we make can help us understand its source, catalog its scope, adapt ourselves to its presence, and devise ways to control ③ it. There are things in life, once called wisdom, ④ which we have to discover for ourselves by making our own private journeys. Stress can ⑤ be directed to open up possibilities for intelligent and imaginative inquiries and solutions that otherwise might have been ignored, overlooked, or refuted.

* inquisitiveness: 호기심 ** refute: 반박하다

02 글의 흐름으로 보아, 주어진 문장이 들어가기에 가장 적절한 곳은?

24005-0145

> The Oval Office in the White House is a good example of a place with enormous historic significance.

Architectural spaces become memorable through the architectural characteristics that define them. Qualities of scale, appropriateness for people, aesthetics, and visual impact are among the many components that give a place its character and feel. (①) The purpose of a space can make it a place. (②) The unique oval shape of this splendid room makes it memorable and gives it a special importance without being ostentatious. (③) Incidentally, George Washington had two rooms at Mount Vernon altered to include bowed ends so he could greet guests while standing in the middle as they circled around him. (④) Thomas Jefferson designed two oval meeting rooms in the main floor of the Rotunda at the University of Virginia. (⑤) Oval rooms were seen as being democratic because no person could be placed at a more important position in the room than anyone else.

* splendid: 훌륭한 ** ostentatious: 대단히 호사스러운

03 다음 글의 제목으로 가장 적절한 것은?

24005-0146

Museum and gallery exhibitions are 'hired' by or co-produced with other galleries; it is not uncommon for shows to be 'on the road' for two years or longer. Normally they are curated by one or more people, whose role includes researching the exhibition concept, the selection (or commissioning) of work, planning how the work will be hung within the exhibition space and writing a significant part of any accompanying book or catalogue. The power of the curator, operating regionally, nationally or internationally, has been questioned. Of course, curators take initiatives which contribute to the exposure of work. But they may also regularly favour certain artists, or types of work, at the expense of others. Furthermore, it has been suggested that curators often act more as 'creators', putting together themed exhibitions which, however relevant and interesting, serve as much to advance themselves as to showcase the work of artists. Indeed, all exhibitions and collections reflect the particular interests of their curators and archivists as well as the mission statement, priorities and terms of reference of particular organisations.

* archivist: 기록 보관인 ** terms of reference: 위임 사항

① New Ideas for Expanding Artistic Expression
② What Happens When Artists Take On the Role of Curators
③ The True Collaborative Power Between Artist and Curator
④ How to Become a Competent Curator in Today's Art World
⑤ Curatorial Influence: How Curators' Interests Shape Exhibitions

26 교육, 학교, 진로

Gateway

2024학년도 6월 모의평가 20번

24005-0147

다음 글에서 필자가 주장하는 바로 가장 적절한 것은?

Certain hindrances to multifaceted creative activity may lie in premature specialization, i.e., having to choose the direction of education or to focus on developing one ability too early in life. However, development of creative ability in one domain may enhance effectiveness in other domains that require similar skills, and flexible switching between generality and specificity is helpful to productivity in many domains. Excessive specificity may result in information from outside the domain being underestimated and unavailable, which leads to fixedness of thinking, whereas excessive generality causes chaos, vagueness, and shallowness. Both tendencies pose a threat to the transfer of knowledge and skills between domains. What should therefore be optimal for the development of cross-domain creativity is support for young people in taking up creative challenges in a specific domain and coupling it with encouragement to apply knowledge and skills in, as well as from, other domains, disciplines, and tasks.

① 창의성을 개발하기 위해서는 도전과 실패를 두려워하지 말아야 한다.
② 전문 지식과 기술을 전수하려면 집중적인 투자가 선행되어야 한다.
③ 창의적인 인재를 육성하기 위해 다양한 교육과정을 준비해야 한다.
④ 특정 영역에서 개발된 창의성이 영역 간 활용되도록 장려해야 한다.
⑤ 조기 교육을 통해 특정 분야의 전문가를 지속적으로 양성해야 한다.

Words & Phrases in Use

- □ hindrance 방해 요인
- □ multifaceted 다면적인
- □ premature 너무 이른
- □ specialization 전문화
- □ i.e. 즉(= id est)
- □ domain 영역
- □ enhance 높이다
- □ flexible 유연한
- □ generality 일반성
- □ specificity 특수성
- □ excessive 과도한
- □ underestimated 과소평가된
- □ fixedness 고정성
- □ chaos 혼돈
- □ vagueness 모호함
- □ shallowness 얕음
- □ tendency 경향
- □ pose a threat to ~에 위협이 되다
- □ transfer 이동
- □ optimal 최선인
- □ cross-domain 영역 간의
- □ discipline (학문의) 분야

Academic Vocabulary by Topic

flexible 유연한 (able or willing to change according to circumstances etc. or capable of bending or being bent)

A **flexible** approach to problem-solving promotes innovation.
문제 해결에 대한 유연한 접근은 혁신을 촉진한다.

discipline (학문의) 분야 (a branch of knowledge or teaching)

The scholars established psychology as an academic **discipline**.
그 학자들은 심리학을 하나의 학문 분야로 확립했다.

aptitude 적성, 소질 (a natural ability to do something or to learn something)

Aptitude for teamwork is crucial for project collaboration.
협동 작업에 대한 적성은 프로젝트 공동 작업을 위해 중요하다.

perspective 관점 (a way of thinking about and understanding something)

Literature allows readers to explore characters' diverse **perspectives** on life.
문학은 독자들이 등장인물들의 인생에 관한 다양한 관점을 탐구할 수 있게 해 준다.

consistent 일관성 있는 (always acting or behaving in the same way)

Consistent routines contribute to a balanced and healthy lifestyle.
일관성 있는 일상은 균형 잡히고 건강한 삶의 형태에 기여한다.

commitment 헌신, 전념 (a promise to be loyal to someone or something)

Mike has demonstrated exceptional **commitment** and dedication to education.
Mike는 교육에 대한 특출한 헌신과 전념을 보여 주었다.

integrate 통합하다 (to combine (two or more things) to form or create something)

We are trying to **integrate** the latest research findings into our project.
우리는 최신의 연구 결과를 우리의 프로젝트에 통합하려고 하고 있다.

Quick Review 다음 각 문장의 빈칸에 들어갈 말로 가장 적절한 것을 〈보기〉에서 고르시오.

보기

flexible　aptitude　consistent　commitment　integrate

1. Yoga promotes a(n) ____________ body and a calm mind.
2. Developing language ____________ enhances communication skills.
3. The student demonstrated a strong ____________ to academic success.
4. The artist's work aims to ____________ art and technology in innovative ways.
5. ____________ behavior builds trust in personal and professional relationships.

Exercises

01

다음 빈칸에 들어갈 말로 가장 적절한 것은?

24005-0148

A significant challenge arises when we ask whether ________________. Many people are terrific at calculus but couldn't write a good essay or paint a good picture if their lives depended on it. Some people can walk into a room full of strangers and immediately figure out the relationships and feelings among them; others may never learn this skill. As Will Rogers put it, "Everybody is ignorant, only on different topics." Clearly, individuals vary in their aptitude for learning any specific type of knowledge or skill taught in a specific way. A hundred students attending a lecture on a topic they knew nothing about beforehand will all walk away with different amounts and kinds of learning, and aptitude for that particular content and that particular teaching method is one important factor in explaining these differences. But would the students who learned the most in this class also learn the most if the lecture were on a different topic or if the same material were presented through hands-on experiences or in small groups?

* **calculus:** 미적분학

① intelligence is a product of genes
② styles of learning can change suddenly
③ aptitude is connected with intelligence
④ learning is a mutually purposeful activity
⑤ there is any such thing as general aptitude

02

다음 글의 요지로 가장 적절한 것은?

24005-0149

One implication of expectancy theory is that even though all students should have a chance to be rewarded if they do their best, no student should have an easy time achieving the maximum reward. This principle is violated by traditional grading practices, because some students find it easy to earn A's and B's, whereas others believe that they have little chance of academic success no matter what they do. In this circumstance, neither high achievers nor low achievers are likely to exert their best efforts. This is one reason why it is important to reward students for effort, for doing better than they have done in the past, or for making progress, rather than only for getting a high score. For example, students can build a portfolio of compositions, projects, reports, or other work and can then see how their work is improving over time. Not all students are equally capable of achieving high scores, but all are equally capable of exerting effort, exceeding their own past performance, or making progress, so these are often better, more equally available criteria on which to base reward.

* **exert:** 다하다, 발휘하다 ** **criterion:** 기준 (*pl.* criteria)

① 학생의 성취 수준에 따라 과제를 달리 부여해야 한다.
② 교사의 기대 정도에 따라 학생의 성취 수준이 달라진다.
③ 외적 보상만으로는 학생의 학습 동기를 촉진할 수 없다.
④ 협동 학습은 학생의 성취도 향상에 매우 큰 도움을 준다.
⑤ 학생은 점수만이 아니라 발전 노력에 대해 보상받아야 한다.

03

24005-0150

주어진 글 다음에 이어질 글의 순서로 가장 적절한 것은?

As students move into adolescence, they are developing capabilities for abstract thinking and understanding the perspectives of others. Even greater physical changes are taking place as the students approach puberty.

(A) But adolescence marks the first time that a conscious effort is made to answer the now-pressing question: “Who am I?” The conflict defining this stage is identity versus role confusion. Identity refers to the organization of an individual’s drives, abilities, beliefs, and history into a consistent image of self.

(B) So, with developing minds and bodies, young adolescents must confront the central issue of constructing an identity that will provide a firm basis for adulthood. They have been developing a sense of self since infancy.

(C) It involves deliberate choices and decisions, particularly about work, values, ideology, and commitments to people and ideas. If adolescents fail to integrate all these aspects and choices, or if they feel unable to choose at all, role confusion threatens.

* adolescence: 청소년기 ** puberty: 사춘기

① (A) – (C) – (B)
② (B) – (A) – (C)
③ (B) – (C) – (A)
④ (C) – (A) – (B)
⑤ (C) – (B) – (A)

27 언어, 문학, 문화

Gateway

2024학년도 9월 모의평가 22번

24005-0151

다음 글의 요지로 가장 적절한 것은?

The need to assimilate values and lifestyle of the host culture has become a growing conflict. Multiculturalists suggest that there should be a model of partial assimilation in which immigrants retain some of their customs, beliefs, and language. There is pressure to conform rather than to maintain their cultural identities, however, and these conflicts are greatly determined by the community to which one migrates. These experiences are not new; many Europeans experienced exclusion and poverty during the first two waves of immigration in the 19th and 20th centuries. Eventually, these immigrants transformed this country with significant changes that included enlightenment and acceptance of diversity. People of color, however, continue to struggle for acceptance. Once again, the challenge is to recognize that other cultures think and act differently and that they have the right to do so. Perhaps, in the not too distant future, immigrants will no longer be strangers among us.

① 이민자 고유의 정체성을 유지할 권리에 대한 공동체의 인식이 필요하다.
② 이민자의 적응을 돕기 위해 그들의 요구를 반영한 정책 수립이 중요하다.
③ 이민자는 미래 사회의 긍정적 변화에 핵심적 역할을 수행할 수 있다.
④ 다문화 사회의 안정을 위해서는 국제적 차원의 지속적인 협력이 요구된다.
⑤ 문화적 동화는 장기적이고 체계적인 과정을 통해 점진적으로 이루어진다.

Words & Phrases in Use

- □ assimilate 받아들이다
- □ host culture 주류 문화
- □ conflict 갈등
- □ multiculturalist 다문화주의자
- □ partial 부분의, 부분적인
- □ assimilation 동화
- □ immigrant 이민자
- □ retain 유지하다
- □ conform 순응하다
- □ migrate 이주하다
- □ exclusion 배척, 배제
- □ transform 변모시키다
- □ significant 중대한
- □ enlightenment 계몽
- □ recognize 인정하다

Academic Vocabulary by Topic

assimilate (자기 것으로) 받아들이다, 동화시키다 (to take into the mind and thoroughly understand)
We need to **assimilate** new information that will broaden our understanding of ourselves and of the world.
우리는 우리 자신과 세상에 대한 우리의 이해를 확장할 새로운 정보를 받아들일 필요가 있다.

conform 순응하다, 따르다 (to be obedient or compliant)
The artist refused to **conform** to traditional artistic norms.
그 예술가는 전통적인 예술 규범에 순응하기를 거부했다.

acceptance 수용 (the quality or state of being accepted or acceptable)
True happiness lies in the **acceptance** of oneself and others.
진정한 행복은 자기 자신과 다른 사람을 수용하는 데 있다.

relative 상대적인 (considered in comparison or relation to something else)
The beauty of art is often **relative** to personal taste.
예술의 아름다움은 흔히 개인 취향에 따라 상대적이다.

universal 보편적인 (done or experienced by everyone, existing or available for everyone)
Universal access to clean energy promotes sustainable development.
청정에너지에 대한 보편적인 접근성은 지속 가능한 성장을 촉진한다.

distinct 뚜렷이 다른 (noticeably different)
The painting had a **distinct** style that captivated viewers.
그 그림은 보는 사람의 마음을 사로잡는 뚜렷이 다른 스타일을 지니고 있었다.

reputation 명성, 평판 (the common opinion that people have about someone or something)
The city's **reputation** as a cultural hub drew artists and creatives.
문화 중심지로서의 그 도시의 명성은 예술가들과 창의적인 사람들을 끌어들였다.

interpretation 해석 (the act or result of explaining or interpreting something)
Cultural nuances affect the **interpretation** of gestures and expressions.
미묘한 문화적 차이는 몸짓과 표현의 해석에 영향을 미친다.

Quick Review 다음 각 문장의 빈칸에 들어갈 말로 가장 적절한 것을 〈보기〉에서 고르시오.

보기
assimilate conform relative reputation interpretation

1. Literary analysis involves a deep ___________ of the text.
2. ___________ happiness depends on one's perspective on life.
3. The committee will need time to ___________ this suggestion.
4. The artist's innovative work enhanced her artistic ___________.
5. The team had to ___________ to the guidelines set by their coach.

Exercises

01 다음 글의 주제로 가장 적절한 것은?

24005-0152

Some assumptions that notions of space (that is, a three-dimensional area in which events and objects occur and have relative direction and position) are universal — are being reexamined. Stephen Levinson showed that "systems of spatial reckoning and description can in fact be quite divergent across cultures, linguistic differences correlating with distinct cognitive tendencies." More specifically, languages vary in their use of spatial concepts and, in some instances, determine the cognitive categories relating to space concepts; also, the speakers of a number of languages do not use spatial terms corresponding to the bodily coordinates of left-right and front-back. One example comes from the Tenejapa Tzeltal of Mexico: Their language uses no relative frame of reference and therefore has no terms for spatial reference that would correspond to *left*, *right*, *front*, and *back*. Although terms exist for *left hand* and *right hand*, they do not extend to other parts of the body or to areas external to it.

* reckoning: 추정, 계산 ** divergent: 다른, 갈라지는 *** coordinate: 좌표

① impact of culture on business communication
② universal recognition of the concept of time and space
③ cultural differences in nonverbal signals related to space
④ variability in perception of spatial concepts across languages
⑤ nature of online communication beyond the limits of language

02 다음 글에서 전체 흐름과 관계 없는 문장은?

24005-0153

Languages are far more similar than had previously been thought, and that universality suggests that the human brain is designed to understand the world in certain ways, which may also correspond to the structure of reality. ① Thus, all languages have nouns and verbs, modifiers (adverbs and adjectives), and names and pronouns. ② Languages may differ as to the sequence of words in a sentence (e.g., verb in the middle or at the end), but sentences are always used. ③ Therefore, individuals belonging to a particular community may not follow the language habits of that community. ④ Even the sequence of words does not vary as widely as it could: Steven Pinker says that there are 128 possible orderings of the main parts of a sentence, but most languages use one of only two of those possibilities. ⑤ Crucially, most languages seem to have an almost identical list of concepts, and as a result nearly all words and sentences can be translated effectively from one language into another.

* modifier: 수식어

03 다음 빈칸에 들어갈 말로 가장 적절한 것은?

24005-0154

Some performers manipulate the style of their product to shift the incentives of critics to pay attention. Richard Posner cites Shakespeare, Nietzsche, Wittgenstein, and Kafka as figures who owe part of their reputation to the puzzling and perhaps even contradictory nature of their writings. Unclear authors, at least if they have substance and depth, receive more attention from critics and require more textual interpretation. Individual critics can establish their own reputations by studying such a writer and by promoting one interpretation of that writer's work over another. These same critics will support the inclusion of the writer in the canon, to promote the importance of their own criticism. In effect, deep and ambiguous writers are offering critics implicit invitations to ________________________________. Critics respond by examining these works more closely and spreading their fame more widely.

* canon: 주요 문헌 목록 ** ambiguous: 모호한

① ignore readers for a better textual analysis
② serve as coauthors of a broader piece of work
③ exclude paradoxical points from their arguments
④ compare their writing styles with those of classical writers
⑤ cooperate in a criticism of how writers copy each other's styles

28 컴퓨터, 인터넷, 정보, 미디어, 교통

Gateway

2024학년도 6월 모의평가 36번

24005-0155

주어진 글 다음에 이어질 글의 순서로 가장 적절한 것은?

The growing complexity of computer software has direct implications for our global safety and security, particularly as the physical objects upon which we depend — things like cars, airplanes, bridges, tunnels, and implantable medical devices — transform themselves into computer code.

(A) As all this code grows in size and complexity, so too do the number of errors and software bugs. According to a study by Carnegie Mellon University, commercial software typically has twenty to thirty bugs for every thousand lines of code — 50 million lines of code means 1 million to 1.5 million potential errors to be exploited.

(B) This is the basis for all malware attacks that take advantage of these computer bugs to get the code to do something it was not originally intended to do. As computer code grows more elaborate, software bugs flourish and security suffers, with increasing consequences for society at large.

(C) Physical things are increasingly becoming information technologies. Cars are "computers we ride in," and airplanes are nothing more than "flying Solaris boxes attached to bucketfuls of industrial control systems."

* exploit: 활용하다

① (A) – (C) – (B) ② (B) – (A) – (C) ③ (B) – (C) – (A)
④ (C) – (A) – (B) ⑤ (C) – (B) – (A)

Words & Phrases in Use

- ☐ complexity 복잡성
- ☐ implication 영향
- ☐ security 보안
- ☐ implantable medical device 이식형 의료 기기
- ☐ basis 근간
- ☐ malware 악성 소프트웨어
- ☐ take advantage of ~을 이용하다
- ☐ elaborate 정교한
- ☐ flourish 창궐하다, 번성하다
- ☐ suffer 악화되다
- ☐ nothing more than ~에 불과한
- ☐ attached to ~에 부착된
- ☐ bucketfuls of 수많은

Academic Vocabulary by Topic

automated 자동화된 (operated by largely automatic equipment)
The company is investing in **automated** customer service system to improve efficiency.
그 회사는 효율성을 개선하기 위해 자동화된 고객 서비스 체계에 투자하고 있다.

encode 부호화하다, 표현하다 (to convert from one system of communication into another)
The brain **encodes** sensory information into neural signals.
뇌는 감각 정보를 신경 신호로 부호화한다.

optimize 최적화하다 (to make the best or most effective use of something)
You should use the latest data to **optimize** your marketing campaigns.
마케팅 캠페인을 최적화하려면 최신 데이터를 사용해야 한다.

assistant 보조자, 보조 장치 (a person or a thing that helps in particular activity)
The research **assistant** categorized the data for the study.
연구 보조자는 연구를 위한 데이터를 분류했다.

transition 전환하다 (to make a change or shift from one state, subject, place, etc. to another)
The organization is **transitioning** to a new software system.
그 조직은 새로운 소프트웨어 시스템으로 전환하고 있다.

statement 진술 (something that someone says or writes officially, or an action done to express an opinion)
The police released a **statement** detailing the progress of the investigation.
경찰은 수사 진행 상황을 자세히 설명하는 진술을 발표했다.

currently 현재 (at the present time)
The company is **currently** working on a new product.
그 회사는 현재 새로운 제품을 작업 중이다.

Quick Review 다음 각 문장의 빈칸에 들어갈 말로 가장 적절한 것을 〈보기〉에서 고르시오.

보기

automated　　currently　　optimize　　statement　　transition

1. The suspect is ____________ being questioned by the police.
2. The athlete followed a strict training program to ____________ his performance.
3. The scientist issued a(n) ____________ confirming the results of the study.
4. The government is trying to ____________ to renewable energy sources.
5. The factory is highly ____________, with robots performing most of the tasks.

Exercises

01 다음 글의 주제로 가장 적절한 것은?

24005-0156

The proliferation of data brings with it many challenges for both reporting and consuming information. Social networks themselves are biased by their constituents, which never exactly mirror the population at large. Certain ethnicities are overrepresented, a significant challenge to social news as an equalizer. In addition, a growing number of algorithms make automated decisions on which content to recommend for people to read. Algorithms are generating top-news lists or hot trends and personalizing recommendations for readers. Algorithms leave the impression of being neutral, yet they are not. Algorithms are human creations. They encode political choices of their designers and have cultural values baked in. As curatorial power is enhanced by automated systems, we should understand the biases at play. Perhaps more important, we should work to make sure product engineers and designers are seeking to optimize the wanted outcome — an informed public — not just heightened traffic.

* proliferation: 급증 ** constituent: 구성원 *** curatorial: (데이터의) 선정, 조직 및 제시의

① inequality reflected in the volume of data on social networks
② danger of fake news generated by culturally biased algorithms
③ the increasing role of algorithms in news selection for individual needs
④ the recent trend of traditional media being threatened by news algorithms
⑤ importance of recognizing biases by data, algorithms, and algorithm creators

02 다음 빈칸에 들어갈 말로 가장 적절한 것은?

24005-0157

How much time are we spending not *truly* connected to other things or people, in the analogue or real sense of the word? Not much. We have turned ourselves into human wearables, attached to our phones nonstop, with additional sensors from our smart watches and AI assistant devices, while we patiently await to upload our memories, fantasies, and consciousness to the cloud. In a relatively short time frame, we quickly transitioned from the internet to the internet of things and now the "You of Things," a concept that sees our bodies as part of an enormous sentient digital network, and our entire existence ______________________. Since our selves have been largely reduced to the digital fragments of our reputation captured in the many devices that connect us to others and the world, it is hard to disagree with Yuval Harari's argument that "we are becoming tiny chips inside a giant data-processing system that nobody really understands."

* analogue: 아날로그적인 ** sentient: 지각이 있는 *** fragment: 파편

① raised to the level of a digital network operator
② ceasing to be relevant as a source of digital information
③ forgotten faster than the superior data-processing devices
④ downgraded to the status of our smart TVs and refrigerator
⑤ becoming separated from our reputations presented on social media

03

24005-0158

주어진 글 다음에 이어질 글의 순서로 가장 적절한 것은?

Much alarm and handwringing have occurred over the idea that the Internet allows you to lock yourself in an information bubble and see only facts that support your views.

(A) That was about it. We were all beholden to the views of a very few people. The Internet allows every statement to be fact-checked, every falsehood challenged. Anything you want to know is just a few keystrokes and a few clicks away.

(B) Well over 100,000 web searches are performed each second, and at their heart, they each represent a person who wants to know something they don't currently know. It is the great democratization of knowledge, which is an unquestionably good thing.

(C) I am sure this happens, but it would do us good to remember the alternative. In 1980, for instance, you got your daily dose of information from your local paper and your choice of any of three network news shows, which ran for an hour, all covering the same basic stories.

* handwringing: (걱정으로 인한) 손떨림 ** beholden: 갇힌, 신세를 진 *** dose: 분량

① (A) – (C) – (B) ② (B) – (A) – (C) ③ (B) – (C) – (A)
④ (C) – (A) – (B) ⑤ (C) – (B) – (A)

29 심리, 대인 관계

Gateway

2024학년도 9월 모의평가 29번

24005-0159

다음 글의 밑줄 친 부분 중, 어법상 틀린 것은?

Viewing the stress response as a resource can transform the physiology of fear into the biology of courage. It can turn a threat into a challenge and can help you ① do your best under pressure. Even when the stress doesn't feel helpful — as in the case of anxiety — welcoming it can transform ② it into something that is helpful: more energy, more confidence, and a greater willingness to take action. You can apply this strategy in your own life anytime you notice signs of stress. When you feel your heart beating or your breath quickening, ③ realizing that it is your body's way of trying to give you more energy. If you notice tension in your body, remind yourself ④ that the stress response gives you access to your strength. Sweaty palms? Remember what it felt like ⑤ to go on your first date — palms sweat when you're close to something you want.

* physiology: 생리 기능

Words & Phrases in Use

- □ resource 자산, 자원
- □ transform ~ into ... ~을 …으로 바꾸다
- □ biology 생명 작용
- □ courage 용기
- □ willingness 기꺼이 하려는 마음
- □ apply 적용하다
- □ strategy 전략
- □ quicken 빨라지다
- □ access 이용할 기회, 접근권
- □ sweaty 땀이 난
- □ palm 손바닥

Academic Vocabulary by Topic

absurd 터무니없는, 우스꽝스러운 (ridiculously unreasonable, unsound)
The notion that humans can fly like birds is **absurd**.
인간이 새처럼 날 수 있다는 생각은 터무니없다.

willingness 자발성 (the state of being prepared to do something; readiness)
The student demonstrated a **willingness** to learn and participate in class.
그 학생은 배우고 수업에 참여하려는 자발성을 보여 주었다.

deliberately 의도적으로 (with full awareness of what one is doing)
The child **deliberately** lied to his parents in order to get out of trouble.
그 아이는 곤경에서 벗어나기 위해 부모에게 의도적으로 거짓말을 했다.

identity 정체성 (the distinguishing character or personality of an individual)
It is important to accept and respect your own **identity**.
자기 자신의 정체성을 받아들이고 존중하는 것이 중요하다.

potential 잠재력, 잠재성 (something that can develop or become actual)
The new technology has the **potential** to revolutionize the industry.
이 새로운 기술은 그 업계를 혁명적으로 변화시킬 잠재력을 가지고 있다.

drain 소모, 소진 (depletion of strength or vitality)
The company's financial problems are a **drain** on its resources.
그 회사의 재정 문제는 자원의 소모이다.

indifferent 무관심한 (marked by a lack of interest, enthusiasm, or concern for something)
The universe is **indifferent** to the existence of humans.
우주는 인간의 존재에 무관심하다.

Quick Review 다음 각 문장의 빈칸에 들어갈 말로 가장 적절한 것을 〈보기〉에서 고르시오.

보기
absurd drain identity indifferent potential

1. Your ____________ is made up of your experiences, beliefs, and values.
2. The demands of her job are taking a(n) ____________ on her personal life.
3. The claim that the moon is made of cheese is ____________.
4. The research has the ____________ to cure a deadly disease.
5. The child was ____________ to the new toy, so his parents were disappointed.

Exercises

01 다음 글의 제목으로 가장 적절한 것은?

24005-0160

Unfortunately, as we age, we tend to avoid vulnerability by avoiding change, so our learning opportunities are reduced and new learning slows. We've all had the experience of a reunion with an old friend, when listening to them saying how they've been, noticing how he or she has held onto some old beliefs that we discarded long ago. Probably the friend has not put himself or herself into a state of vulnerable openness for a long time. Personal growth involves trying out new behaviors, attitudes, and beliefs. Trying out something makes us vulnerable to failure and ridicule. When learning, we make mistakes, we look foolish — even absurd. Who likes that? Willingness to take chances in life, to try new experiences, challenges or activities — even though the outcome is unsure — demands being vulnerable while doing so. Open-mindedness is one of those activities that we must do deliberately, because we are naturally inclined to avoid the vulnerability it entails.

* vulnerability: 취약성 ** discard: 버리다

① Why Failures Hurt More As You Grow Older
② Reflect on Yourself When You Feel Bad About Others
③ Jumping into Uncertainty: A Way of Proving Your Ideas
④ Good Old Friends: A Reliable Bridge to New Relationships
⑤ Avoiding Vulnerability: A Barrier to Lifelong Learning and Growth

02 다음 글의 밑줄 친 부분 중, 어법상 틀린 것은?

24005-0161

Expectations influence children's behavior. After observing the amount of litter in three classrooms, Richard Miller and colleagues had the teacher and others repeatedly ① tell one class that they should be neat and tidy. This persuasion increased the amount of litter placed in wastebaskets from 15 to 45 percent, but only ② temporarily. Another class, which also had been placing only 15 percent of its litter in wastebaskets, ③ being repeatedly congratulated for being so neat and tidy. After 8 days of hearing this, and still 2 weeks later, these children were fulfilling the expectation by putting more than 80 percent of their litter in wastebaskets. Tell children they are hardworking and kind (rather than lazy and mean), and they may live up to their labels. Tying the identity to the self is important: Children ④ who were asked to be "a helper" were more likely to help in later tasks than those asked to "help." When children think of ⑤ themselves as tidy and helpful, they become tidy and helpful.

* litter: (바닥에 버린) 쓰레기

03 글의 흐름으로 보아, 주어진 문장이 들어가기에 가장 적절한 곳은?

24005-0162

> But if one person only deposits and the other person only withdraws, checks are going to start bouncing.

If maintenance of a balance in a relationship requires much work, why bother aiming for the middle ground? The wonderful thing about relationships is that with the proper maintenance, the whole is greater than the sum of its parts. (①) Ideally, both members get support to realize their potential as individuals as well as realizing the potential of the team. (②) If things go sour, the tremendous energy drain of an irreparably damaged relationship can also mean that the whole is less than the sum of its parts. (③) Pooling resources — as in a joint savings account — makes them optimally large. (④) Similarly, if only one person in a relationship is performing maintenance and the other is indifferent, their joint account will also wind up with insufficient funds. (⑤) Overdraft protection might cover everyday necessities, but it won't help when something big comes around.

* bounce: (수표가) 부도 처리되다 ** irreparably: 회복할 수 없을 정도로 *** overdraft: (은행 계정 등의) 초과 인출

30 정치, 경제, 사회, 법

Gateway

2024학년도 9월 모의평가 30번

24005-0163

다음 글의 밑줄 친 부분 중, 문맥상 낱말의 쓰임이 적절하지 않은 것은?

Why is the value of *place* so important? From a historical perspective, until the 1700s textile production was a hand process using the fibers available within a ① particular geographic region, for example, cotton, wool, silk, and flax. Trade among regions ② increased the availability of these fibers and associated textiles made from the fibers. The First Industrial Revolution and subsequent technological advancements in manufactured fibers ③ added to the fact that fibers and textiles were no longer "place-bound." Fashion companies created and consumers could acquire textiles and products made from textiles with little or no connection to where, how, or by whom the products were made. This ④ countered a disconnect between consumers and the products they use on a daily basis, a loss of understanding and appreciation in the skills and resources necessary to create these products, and an associated disregard for the human and natural resources necessary for the products' creation. Therefore, renewing a value on *place* ⑤ reconnects the company and the consumer with the people, geography, and culture of a particular location.

* textile: 직물

Words & Phrases in Use

- □ fiber 섬유
- □ flax 아마 섬유
- □ associated 관련된, 연관된
- □ subsequent 뒤이은, 다음의
- □ advancement 발달, 진보
- □ bound 얽매인, 속박된
- □ on a daily basis 매일
- □ appreciation 올바른 인식[이해], 평가
- □ disregard 경시, 무시

civilization 문명(사회) (an advanced state of human society, in which a high level of culture, science, industry, and government has been reached)
A thriving **civilization** values diversity and inclusivity, creating a society where different cultures, beliefs, and perspectives coexist harmoniously.
번영하는 문명은 다양성과 포용성을 중시하여 다양한 문화, 신념, 관점이 조화롭게 공존하는 사회를 만들어 낸다.

promote 장려하다, 촉진하다 (to help or encourage the progress or development of something)
The government launched a program to **promote** education in disadvantaged communities.
정부는 사회적으로 혜택을 받지 못한 지역 사회의 교육을 장려하기 위한 프로그램을 시작했다.

inspector 검사[감독]관, 감시자 (a person designated to inspect and examine something, often for quality, safety, or obedience to regulations)
The food safety **inspector** visited the restaurant to check if all health practices were being met in handling and preparing food.
식품 안전 검사관이 음식을 취급하고 준비할 때 모든 위생 관행이 준수되고 있는지 확인하기 위해 그 식당을 방문했다.

regulate 규제[통제]하다 (to control or maintain the proper functioning of something)
Traffic signals are used to **regulate** the flow of vehicles at intersections, promoting orderly and safe movement on the roads.
교통 신호는 교차로에서 차량의 흐름을 규제하여 도로에서 질서 있고 안전한 운행을 촉진하기 위해 사용된다.

ownership 소유(권) (the state or fact of being an owner or the right to possess, use, and dispose of something)
The debate over the **ownership** and control of natural resources often shapes economic policies.
천연자원의 소유권과 통제권을 둘러싼 논쟁은 흔히 경제 정책을 형성한다.

financial 재정[금융]의 (related to the management of money, banking, investments, and credit)
Instabilities in **financial** markets, such as stock exchanges and currency markets, can significantly impact the global economy. 증권 거래소와 외환 시장과 같은 금융 시장에서의 불안정성은 세계 경제에 큰 영향을 미칠 수 있다.

Quick Review 다음 각 문장의 빈칸에 들어갈 말로 가장 적절한 것을 〈보기〉에서 고르시오.

보기

financial　ownership　inspector　promote　regulate

1. The artist retained ____________ of the original artwork while allowing limited reproductions for public enjoyment.
2. The government introduced policies to ____________ renewable energy sources, aiming to reduce reliance on fossil fuels.
3. The quality control ____________ identified and addressed manufacturing flaws to maintain product standards.
4. Individuals are encouraged to develop a(n) ____________ plan that includes budgeting, saving, and investing for future goals.
5. The city council passed a law to ____________ the use of plastic bags and tried to reduce environmental impact.

Exercises

01 다음 글의 제목으로 가장 적절한 것은?

24005-0164

The ancient Egyptian term for 'colour' was *iwn* — a word that also meant 'skin', 'nature', 'character' and 'being', and was represented in part by a hieroglyph of human hair. The members of that civilization had noticed a striking resemblance between colours and humans. To them colours were just like people — full of life, energy, power and personality. We now understand, as the Egyptians could only sense, how thoroughly the two are connected. Colour, after all, is ultimately made by its perceivers. Every hue we see around us is actually manufactured within us — in the same grey matter that forms language, stores memories, triggers emotions, shapes thoughts and gives rise to consciousness. Colour is a pigment of our imaginations that we paint all over the world. Larger than any city, more sophisticated than any machine, more beautiful than any painting, it might in fact be the greatest human creation of them all.

* hieroglyph: 상형 문자 ** hue: 색조 *** pigment: 빛깔, 색소, 안료

① The Seeds of Colour: Planted Within Humans
② Vividness: A Source of Inspiration for Painters
③ Colour Preference as an Indicator of Personality
④ What Roles Did Colours Serve in the Egyptian Civilization?
⑤ Similar but Different: Colour Symbolism in Different Cultures

02 다음 빈칸에 들어갈 말로 가장 적절한 것은?

24005-0165

Bentham, the eighteenth-century utilitarian philosopher who promoted the social benefits of mass surveillance, designed a panopticon, a circular building where those to be observed, whether prisoners, workers, patients, or students, were placed in cells or rooms lined along an outside wall. An "inspector" sat in a booth at the center of the circle, unseen by those being watched, but able to see them. According to Bentham, even though this inspector could not observe every resident at every moment, simply knowing that they could be seen would be enough to make prisoners behave and keep workers and students on task. The panopticon's physical design proved impractical, but the idea that behavior could be regulated by ________________ lived on. Closed-circuit television both on our streets and inside public and private spaces is the modern, subtle, and more practical version 2.0 of that first architectural panopticon.

* utilitarian: 공리주의의 ** surveillance: 감시

① stripping away privacy
② implementing legal forces
③ offering financial incentives
④ having people watch each other
⑤ improving architectural practicality

03 다음 글에서 전체 흐름과 관계 없는 문장은?

24005-0166

The mode of consumption has been changing from ownership to access during recent years because of the shift in consumers' perception of value and the advancement of technology. ① With the advent of online platforms that has made unlimited number of tangible and intangible resources accessible, ownership has lost its value in the consumers' mind. ② Consumers believe that access to resources is associated with fewer risks than ownership; for example, they believe that the potential financial and social loss is greater in the purchase of a product than in the free or fee-based access to the product. ③ However, a vast majority of consumers prefer shopping online on their mobiles or tablets from the comfort of their homes or offices rather than going to a physical store and facing a limited stock of items and pushy sales assistants. ④ All these new changes and beliefs have created a sharing practice named "sharing economy" in which individuals share their resources with others through online networks and promote the culture of collaborative consumption. ⑤ Sharing economy practices, which are seen in different sectors, have become very popular and started to disrupt traditional businesses.

* advent: 등장, 출현 ** tangible: 유형의

31 의학, 건강, 영양, 식품

Gateway

2022학년도 6월 모의평가 39번

24005-0167

글의 흐름으로 보아, 주어진 문장이 들어가기에 가장 적절한 곳은?

> This is particularly true since one aspect of sleep is decreased responsiveness to the environment.

The role that sleep plays in evolution is still under study. (①) One possibility is that it is an advantageous adaptive state of decreased metabolism for an animal when there are no more pressing activities. (②) This seems true for deeper states of inactivity such as hibernation during the winter when there are few food supplies, and a high metabolic cost to maintaining adequate temperature. (③) It may be true in daily situations as well, for instance for a prey species to avoid predators after dark. (④) On the other hand, the apparent universality of sleep, and the observation that mammals such as cetaceans have developed such highly complex mechanisms to preserve sleep on at least one side of the brain at a time, suggests that sleep additionally provides some vital service(s) for the organism. (⑤) If sleep is universal even when this potential price must be paid, the implication may be that it has important functions that cannot be obtained just by quiet, wakeful resting.

* metabolism: 신진대사 ** mammal: 포유동물

Words & Phrases in Use

□ responsiveness 반응성	□ adaptive 적응성의, 순응적인	□ pressing 긴급한
□ inactivity 비활동	□ hibernation 겨울잠	□ adequate 적정한, 적절한
□ predator 포식자	□ apparent 분명한	□ universality 보편성
□ cetacean 고래목의 동물	□ mechanism 기제	□ preserve 유지하다
□ vital 생명 유지에 필수적인	□ organism 생물체	□ implication 함의
□ obtain 얻다	□ wakeful 깨어 있는, 잠이 들지 않은	

Academic Vocabulary by Topic

정답과 해설 86쪽

clinician 임상의, 임상 의학자 (a doctor, psychologist, etc. who has direct contact with patients)
Some **clinicians** may be unaware of information about the safety of the new medical technology.
몇몇 임상의는 그 새로운 의학 기술의 안전성에 대한 정보를 모르고 있을 수도 있다.

adverse 부정적인, 해로운 (having a negative or harmful effect on something)
So far the drug is thought not to have any **adverse** effects.
현재까지 그 약물은 어떤 부작용도 없다고 여겨진다.

dysfunction (병리) 기능 장애[이상] (the fact of a part of the body not working as it should)
The inflammation can lead to organ **dysfunction** if not treated.
그 염증은 치료되지 않으면 장기 기능 장애를 초래할 수 있다.

disorder (신체 기능의) 장애, 혼란 (a condition or illness that causes problems with the way part of the body or brain works)
Mental **disorders** are typically diagnosed with a physical examination and a thorough interview.
정신적 장애는 보통 신체검사와 면밀한 인터뷰로 진단된다.

abuse 남용, 오용 (the use of something in a way that is wrong or harmful)
Chronic drug **abuse** can lead to gradual brain damage.
만성적인 약물 남용은 점진적인 뇌 손상을 초래할 수 있다.

genetic 유전(학)의, 유전자의 (belonging or relating to genes received by each animal or plant from its parents)
Most traits are determined by a combination of **genetic** and environmental factors.
대부분의 특성은 유전적 요인과 환경적 요인의 결합에 의해 결정된다.

nutrition 영양, 영양 섭취 (the substances that you take into your body as food and the way that they influence your health)
Milk, meat, fruits, and vegetables provide good **nutrition**.
우유, 고기, 과일, 채소는 좋은 영양을 공급해 준다.

Quick Review 다음 각 문장의 빈칸에 들어갈 말로 가장 적절한 것을 〈보기〉에서 고르시오.

보기: adverse　disorder　genetic　nutrition　abuse

1. She suffers from an eating ____________.
2. Black eyes and hair are ____________ characteristics of Koreans.
3. This food will provide all the ____________ you need.
4. He was seeking treatment for alcohol ____________.
5. Modern farming methods can have a(n) ____________ effect on the environment.

Exercises

01

다음 글에서 필자가 주장하는 바로 가장 적절한 것은?

24005-0168

Skilled clinicians pride themselves in their knowledge of diseases and treatments. Having an extensive command of anatomy and physiology, pharmacology, and the latest evidence-based breakthroughs is critical to providing competent care. But just as important is the knowledge of how illness can impact patient emotions. And although there is certainly room for individual variation, typical emotional reactions can often be anticipated. Having a sense of the normal emotions that accompany phases and stages of illness allows clinicians to think about how to incorporate the emotional domain into patient assessments and plans of care. Working with patients' emotions, from a place of understanding and acceptance, allows the clinician to skillfully address the emotions in a manner that best serves the patients' needs.

* anatomy: 해부학 ** physiology: 생리학 *** pharmacology: 약리학

① 임상의는 의학과 관련한 많은 학문 분야를 잘 알아야 한다.
② 임상의는 환자의 개인 정보가 유출되지 않도록 주의해야 한다.
③ 환자는 자신이 치료받는 방식에 대해 항상 잘 인지하고 있어야 한다.
④ 환자는 자신의 임상의를 절대 개인적인 감정으로 평가하지 않아야 한다.
⑤ 임상의는 환자 진단 및 치료 계획 시 환자의 감정적인 측면을 다뤄야 한다.

02

다음 빈칸에 들어갈 말로 가장 적절한 것은?

24005-0169

In medical sociology, a disease is considered an adverse physical state consisting of a physiological dysfunction within an individual, as compared to illness or sickness. In actual practice, the term disease is applied rather liberally to a wide variety of conditions that do not precisely fit the definition. One of the more controversial areas relates to mental illness. It could be argued that many, if not most, mental disorders would not be considered diseases under the definition above. The same could be said of other conditions that have been identified as "diseases" at various times. Examples include alcoholism and drug abuse. These conditions do not necessarily have the requisite clear-cut symptomatology and underlying biological pathology. They are nevertheless frequently treated as if they were diseases. One explanation for this is clear: In order for a condition to be treated by the healthcare system, it must be identified as a disease. Therefore, there is a tendency toward ____________________.

* symptomatology: 병 증상 ** pathology: 건강 이상

① the attribution of disease to social problems
② an overly broad conceptualization of disease
③ the differentiation of mental and physical illness
④ an emphasis on academic achievements in medicine
⑤ an oversimplification of very complex disease processes

03

24005-0170

주어진 글 다음에 이어질 글의 순서로 가장 적절한 것은?

Worldwide increases in IQ scores of about 3 points per decade over the last 100 years illustrate the potential for intellectual development. This increase in IQ scores, known as the Flynn effect, has occurred far too quickly to represent genetic changes.

(A) As nations become wealthier and more capable of battling disease, their citizens' IQ scores increase. Surprisingly, the test score gains are most pronounced in supposed culture-free tests such as the Raven's Progressive Matrices.

(B) Participants born after 1990 scored far better on these tests than did participants born in 1940. This change might reflect an improvement in the ability to manage dissimilar items that accompanies living in a modern society.

(C) Improvements in nutrition and other health factors probably account for some of the change. Using information from the World Health Organization, researchers have identified strong correlations between a nation's freedom from serious infectious diseases and its citizens' average IQ scores.

① (A) – (C) – (B)　② (B) – (A) – (C)　③ (B) – (C) – (A)
④ (C) – (A) – (B)　⑤ (C) – (B) – (A)

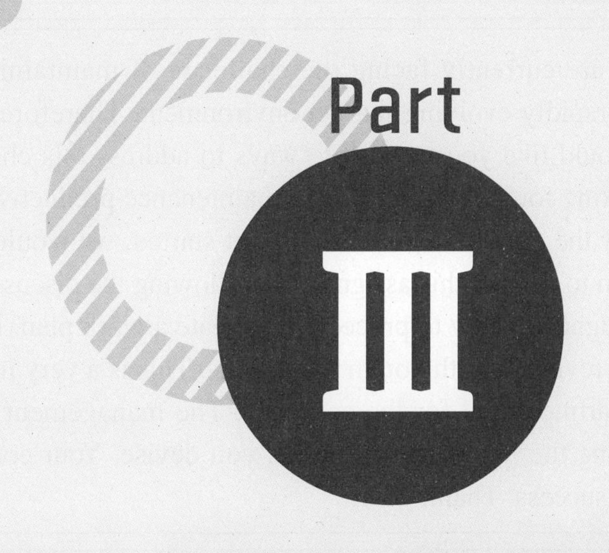

테스트편

01

24005-0171

다음 글의 목적으로 가장 적절한 것은?

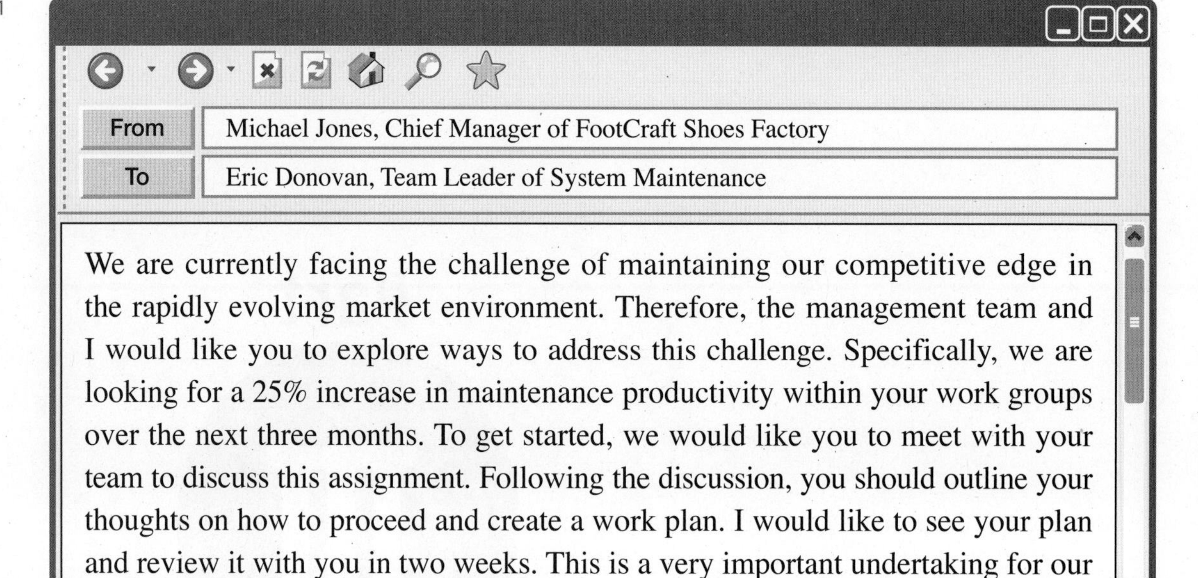

From: Michael Jones, Chief Manager of FootCraft Shoes Factory

To: Eric Donovan, Team Leader of System Maintenance

We are currently facing the challenge of maintaining our competitive edge in the rapidly evolving market environment. Therefore, the management team and I would like you to explore ways to address this challenge. Specifically, we are looking for a 25% increase in maintenance productivity within your work groups over the next three months. To get started, we would like you to meet with your team to discuss this assignment. Following the discussion, you should outline your thoughts on how to proceed and create a work plan. I would like to see your plan and review it with you in two weeks. This is a very important undertaking for our department and for the company. The management team and I look forward to seeing the innovative solutions you devise. Your contributions are invaluable to our success. Thank you.

① 생산비 절감을 위한 회의 개최를 안내하려고
② 경영팀과 관리팀의 협업 필요성을 강조하려고
③ 기술 혁신을 위한 프로젝트팀 합류를 제안하려고
④ 생산성 향상 아이디어 경연 대회 결과를 알리려고
⑤ 업무 생산성 향상을 위한 작업 계획 수립을 요청하려고

02 다음 글에 드러난 Kira의 심경 변화로 가장 적절한 것은?

24005-0172

Kira was playing with her doll when she heard a voice singing. "*Churi*, *churi*. Little girls, come and see." Kira ran to the window and saw a bangle seller with a basket on his head. He saw Kira and said, "Come little girl, come and buy some *churis*." She wanted to buy some, but she couldn't, because her mother had gone to the local market and there was no one there to give her money. Kira's heart sank at the thought of not being able to buy bangles. When she told the seller about her situation, he said, "Come and choose them at least. I'll take the money some other day." After thinking for a while, Kira went down. The bangle seller asked, "Child, which colour do you like best?" "Orange," said Kira and she selected some bangles. By then, Kira's mother returned from the market and had a few words with the seller before paying for the bangles. Kira was so glad. The sound of the bangles hitting each other sounded like music to her. She hummed her way back to her room.

* churi: 츄리(인도 팔찌) ** bangle: 팔찌

① bored → curious
② grateful → angry
③ jealous → regretful
④ frightened → relieved
⑤ disappointed → delighted

03 다음 글의 요지로 가장 적절한 것은?

24005-0173

There has been an effort by some economists to commodify ecosystem services, which refer to benefits and resources that humans obtain from natural ecosystems. Some ecosystem services are rival, such as the waste absorption capacity for greenhouse gases, so rationing is necessary. Making rationing possible requires excludable property rights, for example, through auctionable emission permits. If emissions are limited to absorption capacity and equitably distributed, commodification can be both sustainable and just. However, many ecosystem services are inherently non-excludable and non-rival and therefore cannot and should not be commodified. They should also not be ignored. Public services serve all members of the human community; economists recognize that these services are ill-suited to commodification and market allocation. Ecosystem services should not be defined as nature's benefits to people, but rather as fund-services that benefit all members of the biotic community, not simply humans. Ecosystem services in general are an even worse fit for commodification than public services.

* rationing: 배급 ** biotic: 생물의

① 공공 서비스와 생태계 서비스는 시장 원리에 의해 좌우된다.
② 생태계 서비스는 인간의 이익을 우선하여 활용하는 것이 중요하다.
③ 생태계 서비스는 생물 군집 구성원 모두의 것이므로 상품화할 수 없다.
④ 공공의 이익을 위해 생태계를 효율적으로 개발하려는 노력이 필요하다.
⑤ 생태계 서비스를 공평하게 활용하기 위해 배급 제도의 시행이 시급하다.

04

다음 글에서 필자가 주장하는 바로 가장 적절한 것은?

24005-0174

If we think about our feelings as being *part* of us but not *all* that we are, then our feelings can feel more manageable. This idea is captured in this metaphor: you are the blue sky; your feelings are the weather. If you are the blue sky and your feelings are the weather, then just as the worst hurricane or tornado can't damage the blue sky, and it eventually ends, your feelings can't damage you, and eventually they will pass. Sometimes we just have to wait out the storm. Does that mean it's fun to live through a tornado or a rainstorm? Of course not! Is it easier to live your life when it's sunny and 80 degrees Fahrenheit compared to when it's rainy and stormy? Of course! But if I let the weather determine what I can get done, I'll forever be at the mercy of something I can't control. Our job is to make space for our feelings, to be the blue sky, so we don't have to engage in unhealthy habits to cope with our feelings and we can continue to do the things that matter to us.

① 긍정적인 감정을 유지하기 위해 다양한 관점을 수용해야 한다.
② 감정을 우리 존재의 일부로만 받아들여 그것에 휘둘리지 마라.
③ 미래의 편안하고 안락한 삶을 위해 현재의 어려움을 이겨내야 한다.
④ 고난이 끝나기만을 기다리기보다 그것에 적극적으로 대처해야 한다.
⑤ 삶에 중요한 것과 그렇지 않은 것을 구분 짓지 않고 최선을 다해야 한다.

05

밑줄 친 They are stories가 다음 글에서 의미하는 바로 가장 적절한 것은?

24005-0175

In the lecture on memory, I ask my students to remember a list of words. It includes words like "dream" and "bed." Then I ask them to write down the words they remember. Invariably, they (mis)remember hearing the word "sleep" even though I never said the word "sleep." The idea of "sleep" is activated in the brain because other words in the same semantic network, words that have been associated with sleep through constant repetition, have also been activated. The word "sleep" is retrieved as if it were really *heard*. When people hear "bed," they cannot help but hear "sleep." When people hear "genes" or "intelligence" they cannot help but hear "race." A reader new to this topic might therefore be surprised to learn that there is zero evidence that genetics explains racial differences in outcomes like education. Currently, stories about genetically rooted racial differences in the complex human traits relevant for social inequality in modern industrialized economies — traits like persistence and conscientiousness and creativity and abstract reasoning — are just that. They are stories.

* semantic: 의미의 ** retrieve: 회상하다 *** conscientiousness: 성실성

① People are fond of stories related to racial equality.
② Words in the same semantic network are activated more easily.
③ People enjoy making up stories about dreams and social justice.
④ People's racial prejudices about human traits have no genetic basis.
⑤ Words associated with race trigger emotional responses among people.

06

다음 글의 주제로 가장 적절한 것은?

24005-0176

Simplifying a problem is what opens it up to mathematical analysis, so inevitably some biological details get lost in translation from the real world to the equations. As a result, those who use mathematics are frequently criticized as being too disinterested in those details. In his 1897 book *Advice for a Young Investigator*, Santiago Ramón y Cajal (the father of modern neuroscience) wrote about these reality-avoiding theorists in a chapter entitled 'Diseases of the Will'. He identified their symptoms as 'a facility for exposition, a creative and restless imagination, an aversion to the laboratory, and an indomitable dislike for concrete science and seemingly unimportant data'. Cajal also complained about the theorist's preference for beauty over facts. Biologists study living things that are abundant with specific traits and subtle exceptions to any rule. Mathematicians — driven by simplicity, elegance and the need to make things manageable — silence that abundance when they put it into equations.

* exposition: 설명 ** aversion: 혐오감 *** indomitable: 불굴의

① biological patterns explainable by mathematical models
② historical conflicts between biologists and mathematicians
③ misconceptions of mathematics as a discipline of abstraction
④ increasing importance of exceptional findings in biology research
⑤ criticisms of mathematicians for simplifying the richness of biology

07 다음 글의 제목으로 가장 적절한 것은?

24005-0177

It's important to distinguish what humans are doing, in following norms, from what other animals are doing in their related patterns of behavior. An animal that decides not to pick a fight is, in most cases, simply worried about the risk of getting injured — not about some abstract "norm against violence." Likewise, an animal that shares food with animals outside of its group is typically just trying to get future reciprocity — not following some "norm of food-sharing." The incentives surrounding true norms are more complex. When we do something "wrong," we have to worry about reprisal not just from the wronged party but also from third parties. Frequently, this means the entire rest of our local group, or at least a majority of it. Big strong Albert could easily steal from weak Bob without fearing trouble from Bob himself, but in human groups, Albert would then face punishment from the rest of the community. *Collective enforcement*, then, is the essence of norms. This is what enables the egalitarian political order so characteristic of the forager lifestyle.

* reciprocity: 호혜, 상호 이익 ** reprisal: 질책 *** egalitarian: 평등주의의

① What Makes Animals Share Food with Others
② Social Pressure: A Reason Humans Follow Norms
③ Group Size Impacts the Development of Social Norms
④ How Social Norms and Individual Thought Are Related
⑤ Difficulties of Establishing True Norms for a Healthy Community

08

24005-0178

Geoffrey Hinton에 관한 다음 글의 내용과 일치하지 않는 것은?

Geoffrey Hinton was born in England in 1947. He chose to study psychology as an undergraduate at Cambridge because he wanted to explore his growing interest in neural networks. He quickly realized, however, that his professors didn't actually understand how neurons learned or computed. While the science of the day could explain the mechanics of electrical signals traveling from one neuron to another, no one could offer Hinton a compelling explanation for the emergence of intelligence from these billions of interactions. He felt certain he could better understand the workings of the brain using tools from the growing field of artificial neural networks, so he went on to pursue a doctor's degree in artificial intelligence from the University of Edinburgh in 1972. In his subsequent research, he sought to create interconnected layers of information using hardware and software, just as the human brain spreads information around its dense web of connected neurons. Throughout his career, Hinton has held positions at various institutions, including Carnegie Mellon University and the University of Toronto.

① Cambridge 대학교에서 심리학을 공부하기로 했다.
② 지인에게서 지능의 출현에 대한 설득력 있는 설명을 들었다.
③ Edinburgh 대학교에서 인공 지능 박사 과정을 밟았다.
④ 하드웨어와 소프트웨어를 사용하여 상호 연결된 정보의 층을 만들려고 했다.
⑤ 경력 내내 다양한 기관에서 근무했다.

09 다음 도표의 내용과 일치하지 않는 것은?

24005-0179

Global Plug-in Vehicle Sales

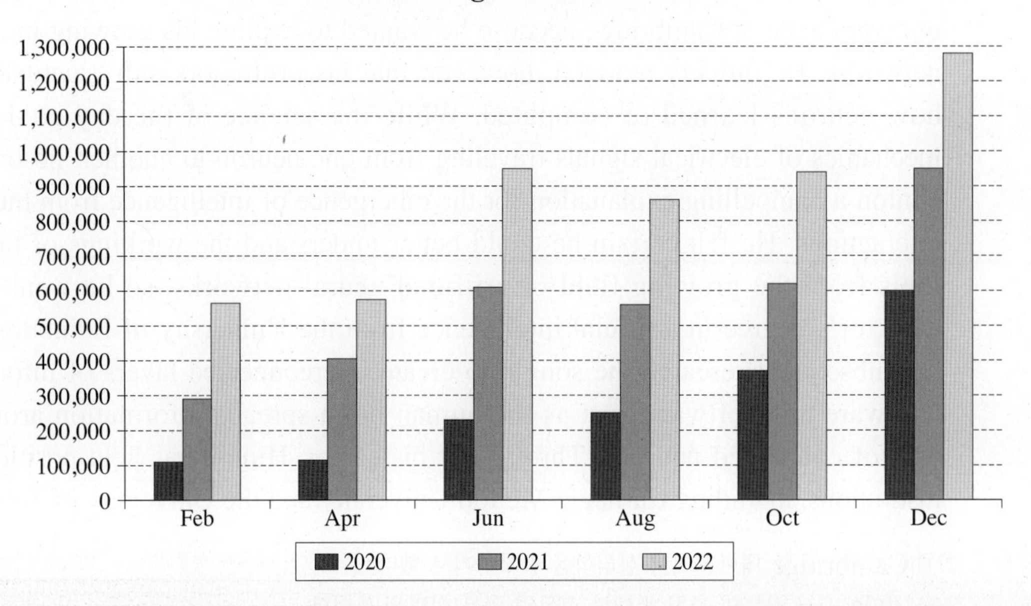

The above graph shows global plug-in vehicle sales from February 2020 to December 2022, represented by two-month intervals. ① In all three years, the sales were the least in February and the most in December. ② In 2021, each of the months showed an increase of more than 100,000 vehicles compared with the same month in 2020. ③ In 2020, global sales of plug-in vehicles increased to more than 200,000 in June, and in December, they reached around 600,000. ④ In 2021, global plug-in vehicle sales decreased from more than 600,000 in June to less than 600,000 in August, but then rose to more than 600,000 in October. ⑤ In 2022, August saw a sales decrease from June, but sales increased to more than 1,000,000 in October.

* plug-in: 플러그인의, 전기로 충전되는

10

24005-0180

2024 Python Basics Camp에 관한 다음 안내문의 내용과 일치하지 않는 것은?

2024 Python Basics Camp

Ages 11 to 19

Learn the basics of software development, animation, and games using Python!

In this 10-hour camp, kids will learn:

- Python syntax programming, one of the top 10 STEM skills for the 21st century
- How to create animations and games like Turtle Race, Hangman, and much more

Details

- Maximum of 8 students in a class
- Camp fee: $410 (with laptop rental) / $350 (without laptop rental)
- Time: 1:30 p.m. to 4 p.m. daily on Monday, Wednesday, Thursday, and Friday (no class on Tuesday)
- Start dates: Every Monday from March 18 to April 15
- Fees are non-refundable. If your child is sick during the camp, please provide a medical note and we will arrange for replacement classes.

* python: 파이썬(프로그래밍 언어) ** syntax: (컴퓨터 언어의) 문법
*** STEM: (science, technology, engineering, and mathematics) 과학 · 기술 · 공학 · 수학 융합 교육

① 10시간 동안 진행된다.
② 참가자는 애니메이션과 게임을 만드는 법을 배운다.
③ 학급당 최대 8명이 정원이다.
④ 월요일부터 금요일까지 매일 수업이 있다.
⑤ 진료 기록을 제출하면 대체 수업을 준비해 준다.

11

2024 Forest Park Annual Walking Tour에 관한 다음 안내문의 내용과 일치하는 것은?

24005-0181

2024 Forest Park Annual Walking Tour

This year's Forest Park Walking Tour is on Saturday, October 19 at 2:00 p.m. It is sponsored by the Albanios Historical Society. So put on your walking shoes, come out and learn about the history and legends of Forest Park!

Walking tour information:

- A reservation is required. You can make one by calling the Historical Society or leaving a message at 314–586–4023.
- Forest Park opens at 12 p.m., and parking is available outside the park.
- Parking is not permitted along Pinewoods Avenue or other nearby streets.
- This event is free, but a donation of any amount to the Albanios Historical Society Forest Park Restoration Project is appreciated.

In the event of bad weather, please check the Albanios Historical Society's website at 1:00 p.m. on the day of the event to know if the event will be held or not.

① 매달 열리는 행사이다.
② 행사 참가를 위한 예약은 필요하지 않다.
③ 공원 내에 주차할 수 있다.
④ 행사는 무료이나 기부금을 내는 것은 환영한다.
⑤ 악천후 시 행사 당일 오전 중에 행사 개최 여부를 확인해야 한다.

12

다음 글의 밑줄 친 부분 중, 어법상 틀린 것은?

24005-0182

From an evolutionary standpoint, ensuring the continuation of our species (specifically, our genetic descendants) ① is the meaning and purpose of life. But as intelligent animals, who can make decisions based on morality rather than biology, we could ask whether preserving our genome is worth any cost. Individual humans can and occasionally do make the choice ② to sacrifice their own lives in order to save the lives of other humans, or even non-human animals. But let's examine that choice, between biology and morality, on a global scale: What if preserving the human species means eliminating or ③ abandoning all other life on Earth? What if it means humankind exists only in a state of misery and deprivation, in an ④ eternally inhospitable and alien environment? This is not to argue that space settlement will definitely result in these worst-case scenarios, but rather to ask whether there is any imaginable case ⑤ what allowing or causing humans to become extinct is the more ethical choice.

* genome: 게놈(세포나 생명체의 유전자 총체) ** alien: 이질적인

13

다음 글의 밑줄 친 부분 중, 문맥상 낱말의 쓰임이 적절하지 않은 것은?

24005-0183

In most business settings it is desirable to put competitors out of business. Naturally, fewer competitors mean more ① available customers. However, this is not always the case in sport. In fact, sport organizations that compete in leagues actually rely on the health of their competitors for their own success. For example, fans are often more attracted to a game where there is a ② close contest, and the winner is unknown in advance. Dominating a league or competition can be self-defeating, because the interest of fans can ③ fade. When it is difficult to predict who will win a match, sport leagues attract higher attendances and viewers. Ironically, in order to remain successful, leagues and competitions need as many of their clubs to be ④ competitive as possible. When the outcome of a match is highly predictable, it will not attract large crowd numbers and eventually it will reduce ticket, media and sponsorship revenue. It is important for sport that there is a healthy, competitive balance between teams. This leads to ⑤ certainty about who will win a contest, and encourages fans to watch.

* revenue: 수익

14

다음 빈칸에 들어갈 말로 가장 적절한 것은?

24005-0184

The fact that the young brain is in a constant state of ____________ should give us pause. Regulations are in place to prevent certain types of companies from marketing directly to children. These are good measures, but they also provide a false sense of security. Why? Just like with language learning, young children don't need ads explicitly directed at them to learn about a product, or the consumer world in general. Think about ads on websites, TV, mobile, and social media, and in video games. Children are showered with repeated exposure to thousands of ads for hundreds of brands, and their spongy, malleable brains are constantly taking this information in. In a study, researchers discovered that kids are exposed to so many ads that they will have memorized three hundred to four hundred brands before their tenth birthday. Creepily, children grow up forming relationships with a select number of these brands that last well into the future, like friends you didn't know they had.

* malleable: 영향을 잘 받는 ** creepily: 오싹하게

① transition
② analysis
③ absorption
④ distraction
⑤ multitasking

15

다음 빈칸에 들어갈 말로 가장 적절한 것은?

24005-0185

People often think that personality traits such as kindness are fixed. But our research with groups suggests something quite different: the tendency to be altruistic or exploitative may depend heavily on how the social world is organized. So if we took the *same* population of people and assigned them to one social world, we could make them really generous to one another, and if we put them in another sort of world, we could make them really mean or indifferent to one another. Crucially, this indicates that the tendency to cooperate is ______________________________. Cooperation depends on the rules governing the formation of friendship ties. Good people can do bad things (and vice versa) simply as a result of the structure of the network which they belong to, regardless of the convictions they hold or that the group shares. It is not just a matter of being connected to "bad" people; the number and pattern of social connections is also crucial. Aspects of the social suite, such as cooperation and social networks, work together.

* altruistic: 이타적인 ** exploitative: 남을 이용해 먹는 *** vice versa: 그 반대도 마찬가지이다

① a basic desire unique to human beings
② a crucial requirement for community prosperity
③ a trait handed down from generation to generation
④ a property not only of individuals but also of groups
⑤ a kind of fixed structure, not an ever-changing aspect

16 다음 빈칸에 들어갈 말로 가장 적절한 것은?

24005-0186

Our natural survival instinct is to seek comfort in temperatures that keep us around 68 to 72 degrees Fahrenheit (20–22.2 °C). By getting outside of this comfort zone and stressing the cellular functioning of the body either by using heat and cold in the same session or focusing on one temperature extreme, we strengthen our physiological systems. We lower our daily breathing rate, improve our muscle tissue, and raise our threshold for handling stress. Evidence shows that we are at our best — physically harder, mentally tougher, and spiritually sounder — after experiencing the same discomforts our early ancestors were exposed to every day. The lack of temperature change caused by indoor lifestyles and misalignment with nature has taken us far from our ancestorial upbringing, and it continues to weaken the nervous system. By ____________________, we become our best physically, mentally, and even spiritually.

* physiological: 생리적인 ** threshold: 역(감각, 반응을 일으키는 경계에 있는 자극의 크기)
*** misalignment: 부정합(가지런히 들어맞지 않음)

① intentionally placing ourselves into the heat or cold
② understanding what effective breathing mechanics are
③ occasionally engaging in mindless and repetitive tasks
④ adjusting the indoor temperature to make us comfortable
⑤ carefully designing individualized physical exercise routines

17 다음 빈칸에 들어갈 말로 가장 적절한 것은?

24005-0187

Suppose a child plays at make-believe. She barks, crawls on all fours, and says, "I'm a puppy!" In order to make the claim, her brain must construct the key proposition "I'm a puppy" as well as contain the information that puppies bark and walk on all fours. And yet that information exists in a larger context. Her brain contains a vast net of information, including "I'm not really a puppy," "I'm making it up to play a game," "I'm a little girl," and so on. Some of that information is present at a cognitive and linguistic level. Much of it is at a deeper, sensory or perceptual level. Her body schema is constructed automatically, beneath higher cognition, and it describes the physical layout of a human body, not a puppy body. She sees her human hands in front of her, and the visual information confirms her human identity. She remembers eating breakfast cereal with a spoon, going to school, reading a book — all human activities. The claim "I'm a puppy" is a superficial proposition that ______________________.

* proposition: 명제 ** cognitive: 인지의

① reveals her personality and taste
② shows her strong affection for dogs
③ has nothing to do with her physical health
④ contradicts her tendency to play and learn
⑤ is inconsistent with her deepest internal models

18 다음 글에서 전체 흐름과 관계 없는 문장은?

24005-0188

Your children establish their social comfort and skills early in their lives by observing you in your own social life and through the social experiences they have. ① These first social experiences become the defaults that will guide and shape the quality and quantity of their relationships throughout their lives. ② Genetics clearly has an influence on these defaults; research has demonstrated that children are born with a certain temperament, including where they lie on the continuum of introversion to extraversion. ③ But, as the saying goes, "genetics are not destiny"; the messages that your children get from you early in their lives about how they should interact with others will influence how their genetic predispositions will be expressed. ④ What children do as they, for example, watch television or movies or play video games or surf the Internet, has no direct consequences on their lives or the lives of others. ⑤ In this interaction of genes and upbringing, your children will develop social defaults that trigger social ease, connectedness, and healthy relationships, or social anxiety, loneliness, and dysfunctional relationships.

* default: 기본 값 ** temperament: 기질 *** introversion: 내향성

19

24005-0189

주어진 글 다음에 이어질 글의 순서로 가장 적절한 것은?

When different cultures meet, whether at the societal level or in the company, ideas about how things should be done often clash. To resolve it, we typically make the assumption that others should change to be more like us.

(A) So when you ask people to do something not consistent with their cultural background, ask yourself whether you should be rethinking your assumptions about what works best. For example, free-flowing talk is usually considered the hallmark of a good meeting. Everybody just jumps in whenever they have a thought.

(B) And we can enforce this view because we are in power — either as the boss in an organization or as the dominant culture in a country. But assuming that the dominant person or country has the right rules and the right way is, in itself, anathema to innovating. Self-satisfied people are not good innovators.

(C) However, in some cultures, this is considered rude and pushy, so some people with excellent ideas may not speak up. One solution might be to strengthen their group skills but other methods are to occasionally ask everyone to express an opinion in turn, ask for ideas in writing, or table an idea on someone else's behalf.

* hallmark: 특징 ** anathema: 아주 싫어하는 것

① (A) – (C) – (B)
② (B) – (A) – (C)
③ (B) – (C) – (A)
④ (C) – (A) – (B)
⑤ (C) – (B) – (A)

20

24005-0190

주어진 글 다음에 이어질 글의 순서로 가장 적절한 것은?

Like some strange alien creature extending tentacles, each neuron is simultaneously connected to up to thousands of other neurons. It is the combined activity of information coming in that determines whether a neuron is active or not.

(A) And every time the neuron has such a conversation with its different neighbors or long-distance pals, it remembers the message either to spread the word or be silent, so that when the rumor comes round again, the neuron responds with more certainty. This is because the connections between the neurons have become strengthened by repeatedly firing together.

(B) When the sum of this activity reaches a tipping point, the neuron fires, discharging a small chemical electrical signal and setting off a chain reaction in its connections. In effect, each neuron is a bit like a microprocessor because it computes the combined activity of all the other neurons it is connected to.

(C) It's a bit like spreading a rumor in a neighborhood. Some of your neighboring neurons are excitatory and, like good friends, want to help spread the word. Other neurons are inhibitory and basically tell you to shut up.

* tentacle: 촉수 ** pal: 친구 *** tipping point: 급변점(극적인 변화의 시작점)

① (A) – (C) – (B)
② (B) – (A) – (C)
③ (B) – (C) – (A)
④ (C) – (A) – (B)
⑤ (C) – (B) – (A)

21

24005-0191

글의 흐름으로 보아, 주어진 문장이 들어가기에 가장 적절한 곳은?

> The cook and kitchen are approximately the same after making the pizza as before, though just a bit more worn out.

Conventional economics uses the phrase "factors of production." Factors of production are the inputs into a production process necessary to create any output. For example, when you make a pizza, you need a cook, a kitchen with an oven, and the raw ingredients. (①) If you think about it carefully, however, you will clearly see that the cook and kitchen are different in some fundamental ways from the raw ingredients. (②) The raw ingredients, however, are used up, transformed first into the pizza itself, then rapidly thereafter into waste. (③) The cook and kitchen are not physically embodied in the pizza, but the raw ingredients are. (④) Thousands of years ago, Aristotle discussed this important distinction and divided causation (factors) into *material cause*, that which is transformed, and *efficient cause*, that which causes the transformation without itself being transformed in the process. (⑤) Raw ingredients are the material cause, and the cook and kitchen are the efficient cause.

* embody: 담다, 구현하다

22

24005-0192

글의 흐름으로 보아, 주어진 문장이 들어가기에 가장 적절한 곳은?

> In the United States, the cost of educating children is borne collectively through the system of public education, but most other costs of raising children are treated as private costs of the parents.

A society needs to raise children to replace its members who die, or the society would disappear over a couple of generations. (①) One could, therefore, think of the production of children as a positive externality. (②) Those who do not have children benefit from the child-rearing labors of those who do; they enjoy a society of varied ages in which to live as they grow older, and a labor force of younger people is available to support them in their retirement. (③) Should all then share in the economic costs of raising the children? (④) In about half of the world's states, however, the full society assumes some of the responsibility for all costs of child rearing by giving direct grants to families with children. (⑤) These grants are often pegged to the median income of workers in the country: the government might give 10 percent of the country's median income to any family with two children, for example.

* positive externality: 긍정적인 외부 효과(경제적 거래의 결과로 제삼자가 누리는 이익) ** peg: (가격이나 임금 등의 수준을) 정하다

23 다음 글의 내용을 한 문장으로 요약하고자 한다. 빈칸 (A), (B)에 들어갈 말로 가장 적절한 것은?

24005-0193

Primates are capable of sophisticated forms of reasoning in naturalistic settings, especially when their food — or position in the social hierarchy — is in danger. However, it is unclear how versatile their relational reasoning might be. In the 1940s, the primatologist Harry Harlow made an interesting discovery. In a series of experiments, monkeys learnt to choose between two visual objects, one of which was rewarded and one was not. Harlow noted with surprise that each time the task was restarted with two entirely novel objects, the monkeys learnt slightly faster. In fact, their performance continued to accelerate over hundreds of new object sets, until eventually the monkeys could respond almost perfectly from the second trial onwards. Harlow argued that over the course of repeated pairings, the monkeys had *learnt how to learn*. It seems that the monkeys learnt something abstract about the relations between the two stimuli in each pairing — that if one was rewarded, the other was not. By generalizing this knowledge to new pairings, they could learn ever faster. Human children tested in a comparable fashion showed the same ability.

* primate: 영장류 ** hierarchy: 위계, 계층 *** versatile: 다방면적인

Harry Harlow's experiments show that primates, like humans, can ＿＿(A)＿＿ abstract relational reasoning in a different context, which happens faster with ＿＿(B)＿＿ exposure to stimuli.

	(A)		(B)
①	accept	……	occasional
②	acquire	……	brief
③	apply	……	increased
④	explain	……	regular
⑤	reject	……	repetitive

24~25 다음 글을 읽고, 물음에 답하시오.

In the 1930s, the English psychologist Sir Frederic Bartlett proposed that we gradually build up our knowledge of the world from events we experience, and that these experiences are then clustered in organized mental structures he called "schemata." In turn, these schemata (or "schemas") are used to help us understand new experiences and form frameworks in which to remember them. One potential (a) downside of this arrangement is that it is relatively difficult for us to understand and remember information and events that do not fit our current schemata. One of Bartlett's classic demonstrations was to present an unusual North American folktale to an English university student to learn and recall. The student's written recall differed from the (b) original by being shorter and omitting a number of details. This first student's written recall was then given to a second student to learn and recall with the result that more unusual details were dropped out of his reproduction, but other details were added, apparently to make the story (c) more coherent and comprehensible to English ears. This procedure was repeated until a series of ten students had learned the previous reproduction and produced their own versions. By the end of the series, the reproductions were much shorter, the supernatural details in the original had been (d) lost, and the whole tale was closer to the experience of English university students in the 1930s. This demonstration thus illustrates the constructive nature of remembering, and the effects of beliefs and attitudes on recollection and understanding. Gossip serves as a commonplace example that is (e) counter to Bartlett's findings, with a story progressively changing as it travels across tellings. To return to metaphors for a moment, human memory is *not* like a tape recorder!

* schema: 스키마(정보를 통합하고 조직화하는 인지적 개념 또는 틀) (*pl.* schemata) ** coherent: 일관된 *** metaphor: 은유

24 윗글의 제목으로 가장 적절한 것은?

24005-0194

① How Prior Knowledge Impacts Memory
② How Gossip Affects Personal Relationships
③ The Need for New Experiences for Storytelling
④ What You Should Do to Improve Your Memory
⑤ Why Your Experience Matters in Making Up a Story

25 밑줄 친 (a)~(e) 중에서 문맥상 낱말의 쓰임이 적절하지 않은 것은?

24005-0195

① (a) ② (b) ③ (c) ④ (d) ⑤ (e)

26~28 다음 글을 읽고, 물음에 답하시오.

(A)

Mary, a young violist, played a slow sarabande by Bach during a presentation Theresa Adams made at the Music Educators National Conference in San Antonio, Texas. The piece requires sustained control of the bow arm, a warm tone, and precise pitch. Being very shy, Mary was noticeably self-conscious playing before this large gathering of educators. While rehearsing for the performance, (a) she had a very hard time controlling her anxiety.

* sarabande: 사라반드(느린 춤곡)

(B)

Theresa then instructed Mary to imagine there was a video camera above the stage taping her performance. Theresa told Mary it didn't matter whether (b) she played out of tune or missed notes or had poor tone. All that mattered was that she should look the way Martha Katz looked while playing Bach. Theresa told Mary the camera was only recording the way she looked, and that her sound would be replaced by a CD of her role model playing the same piece.

(C)

Since Mary no longer had to worry about how she played, she felt free to throw (c) herself into the role of Martha Katz during the playing session. She not only looked confident, relaxed, and dignified — she also played with bow control, accuracy, and fine phrasing. She effectively "became" Martha Katz as she performed the Bach sarabande. The audience was shocked by her playing and curious to know what instructions Theresa had given her that had produced such a marked effect. And Mary realized that although she had been imagining she was Martha Katz, (d) she was still the one playing the viola.

(D)

Mary had difficulty keeping her bow from shaking, and her tone was thin and scratchy. Theresa could see that Mary had a warm feeling for the music she was playing but that she felt too inhibited to express it. Theresa spoke to Mary privately for a few moments so that the audience wouldn't know what instruction she had given to Mary. Theresa asked Mary who her favorite Bach violist was, and she replied that it was Martha Katz and she wanted to play the sarabande like (e) her.

* inhibited: 어색해하는, 억제된

26

24005-0196

주어진 글 (A)에 이어질 내용을 순서에 맞게 배열한 것으로 가장 적절한 것은?

① (B) – (D) – (C)　② (C) – (B) – (D)　③ (C) – (D) – (B)
④ (D) – (B) – (C)　⑤ (D) – (C) – (B)

27

24005-0197

밑줄 친 (a)~(e) 중에서 가리키는 대상이 나머지 넷과 다른 것은?

① (a)　② (b)　③ (c)　④ (d)　⑤ (e)

28

24005-0198

윗글에 관한 내용으로 적절하지 않은 것은?

① Mary는 교육자들 앞에서 연주하게 되었다.
② Theresa는 Mary에게 카메라가 연주 모습과 소리를 녹화한다고 말했다.
③ 청중은 Theresa가 Mary에게 어떤 지시를 했는지 알고 싶어 했다.
④ Mary는 활이 떨리지 않게 하는 데 어려움을 겪고 있었다.
⑤ Theresa는 Mary에게 바흐 곡 비올라 연주자로 누가 가장 좋은지 물었다.

01

다음 글의 목적으로 가장 적절한 것은?

24005-0199

Dear Mr. Cole,

Thank you for your offer of the pharmacist position. The position is attractive to me because I have a strong passion for healthcare and a desire to make a positive impact on patients' lives. As I indicated in our last interview, however, I was disappointed to learn that your company would not be in a position to reimburse tuition costs for my ongoing study toward a Doctor of Pharmacy degree, currently a primary professional goal of mine. On March 14, I was offered another position by a company whose benefits package includes tuition reimbursement. Because I expect these costs to be substantial in the next two years, I have decided to accept this position. I sincerely appreciate the time you have taken and the special interest you have shown in me during the interview. Thank you again for your consideration.

Best regards,
Julie Robinson

* pharmacist: 약사 ** reimburse: 변제하다, 상환하다 *** substantial: 상당한

① 약사 직위를 맡아달라는 제안을 거절하려고
② 대학원 학비 상환에 대한 도움을 요청하려고
③ 약학 박사 학위 취득을 위한 요건을 문의하려고
④ 새로운 직위에 대한 인터뷰 참석 의사를 밝히려고
⑤ 대학원 학위 과정 입학 허가에 대한 감사를 표하려고

02

다음 글에 드러난 Captain Hall의 심경 변화로 가장 적절한 것은?

24005-0200

One day, Captain Hall, the famous Arctic explorer, went in a small boat to visit a certain island which he wanted to explore. The boat was fastened to a piece of rock on the shore. When he returned from his expedition, he discovered the tide had risen and floated his boat, which was quite out of reach. Captain Hall feared the extreme danger in which he was placed. The boat was the only connecting link between him and the living world, and it was beyond his reach. What was to be done? To swim towards the boat was out of the question in such a climate. He did the only thing that seemed possible. He unwound the thongs that fastened his boots to create a line about twenty feet long. He attached a heavy stone to its end and threw it into the boat, pulling the boat to the shore. It was with unspeakable comfort that Captain Hall once more entered it and felt he was saved from inevitable starvation — saved by a shoe-string!

* arctic: 북극의 ** expedition: 탐험 *** thong: 가죽끈

① confused → ashamed
② terrified → relieved
③ excited → confident
④ indifferent → cheerful
⑤ nervous → disheartened

03

다음 글의 요지로 가장 적절한 것은?

24005-0201

Think about the changes that have taken place in our world over the past 100 years. The first to come to mind are probably the spectacular scientific and technological achievements of the past century — motor vehicles, aircraft, the telephone, radio and TV, computers and genetic engineering. Each new development creates its own demand for legal change. Consider, for example, the vast body of law which has grown up around the motor vehicle: there are regulations governing such matters as the construction and maintenance of motor vehicles, the conduct of drivers on the road and even where vehicles may be parked. Indeed, almost half of the criminal cases tried by magistrates' courts are directly related to the use of motor vehicles. The increasing volume of traffic on the roads and the resulting inexorable rise in traffic accidents have also led to developments in the civil law, especially in the areas of the law of tort and insurance.

* magistrates' court: 치안 판사 재판소 ** inexorable: 끊임없는 *** tort: 불법 행위

① 법률 제정만으로 사회의 모든 문제를 해결할 수는 없다.
② 과학과 기술이 새롭게 발전하면 법도 그에 따라 발전한다.
③ 시민 편익을 위한 법 개정으로 시민의 권리를 더욱 보장할 수 있다.
④ 새로운 이동 수단의 개발을 통해 당면한 교통 문제를 해결할 수 있다.
⑤ 새로운 기술이 반드시 사람들을 행복하게 만들어 주는 것만은 아니다.

04 다음 글에서 필자가 주장하는 바로 가장 적절한 것은?

24005-0202

Sometimes pursuing the truth about some question would be morally worse than not pursuing it. This may be because, as in the case of nuclear weapons research, the answer itself may prove dangerous or harmful. But it may also be because the manner of pursuing that truth is dangerous or harmful, or simply morally wrong independently of its consequences. Consider the Nazi or Tuskegee experiments: it is not the information pursued that is morally bad here, but *the manner in which that information is pursued.* And we need not resort to such dramatic cases. The National Institutes of Health and the National Science Foundation heavily monitor contemporary scientific research that involves any sort of experiment involving human subjects. In cases where the only way in which we can obtain certain scientific information is harmful to other people, we generally feel — rightly — that the information is not worth pursuing, all things considered. So in deciding whether to pursue a particular line of inquiry, we must first determine whether pursuing that line might conflict with our other values, moral or otherwise.

① 가치가 극한으로 대립할 때는 무엇보다도 도덕적 가치를 우선시해야 한다.
② 진리 추구를 방해하는 사회적 편견 이면의 복잡한 이해관계를 밝혀내야 한다.
③ 잘못된 정보로 인해 지속적으로 큰 혼란이 발생한 경우는 즉각 바로잡아야 한다.
④ 진리를 추구할 때는 외부의 개입 없이 독립적으로 탐구하는 태도를 견지해야 한다.
⑤ 특정한 방식의 진리 추구가 다른 가치관과 충돌하지 않는지 먼저 살펴보아야 한다.

05

24005-0203

밑줄 친 a circus elephant가 다음 글에서 의미하는 바로 가장 적절한 것은?

As parents, we spend countless hours debating on the freedoms we should allow our children. Too much freedom may lead to mischief while not enough may stifle their growth. How much should be allowed? I am always reminded of a circus elephant when in a discussion on freedom. When the elephant is a baby, it learns restriction by being tethered to a small stake with a four-foot piece of chain. The elephant is trained to know that its individual freedom is restricted to that small four feet. As the elephant grows stronger and larger, it still thinks that it has no more freedom outside of those four feet. Although the power to move that stake and run free is immense, it will not attempt to break the stake or the chains because of what it perceives as being able to. Are you a victim of your own restraints as well? Do you not move beyond your four feet circle because you think you are not allowed to? Be bold. Step outside your circle and see if you can grow. Without breakthroughs, there cannot be change.

* mischief: 나쁜 행동[짓] ** stifle: 억누르다 *** tether: (동물을 밧줄로 말뚝에) 매어 놓다

① a victor achieving freedom through personal effort
② a supporter of absolute freedom in all circumstances
③ a thinker who emphasizes responsibility for freedom
④ a critic who argues against too much freedom in childhood
⑤ a victim whose prior experience restricts his or her freedom

06 다음 글의 주제로 가장 적절한 것은?

24005-0204

The most effective way to defuse racial ideology is to bring people from different ethnic backgrounds together under conditions that enable them to deal with one another as individuals and discover that ideologies obscure important aspects of people and the realities of their lives. However, this is difficult when teachers, coaches and employers maintain a belief in the myth of black natural physical talent and a lack of cognitive skills. Social scientist Ellis Cashmore illustrates this with an experience of receiving a telephone call from a black journalist writing for a major newspaper. The journalist asked why no one actually expressed what he believed to be an absolute truth: that black athletes have a 'natural edge'. The very fact that a talented black journalist believed this defective theory is evidence to its power and the difficulties in escaping expectations based on racial ideology. When such myths maintain credibility in society, black people are regarded as unsuited to, or unwanted for, study, work and other activities that demand mental rather than physical skills.

* defuse: 완화하다 ** obscure: 보기 어렵게 하다

① the influence of media on racial stereotypes
② the need for racial diversity in the workplace
③ the role of education in challenging racial prejudice
④ the importance of sports in promoting racial harmony
⑤ the challenge of escaping racial ideology about black people

07

다음 글의 제목으로 가장 적절한 것은?

24005-0205

Negotiators can make options more palatable by enhancing the attractiveness of accepting them. This is a matter of placing emphasis on the positive rather than the negative. In the language of traditional carrot-and-stick tactics for motivating workers, the approach should make the carrot more attractive rather than enlarging the stick. Promises and offers can be made more attractive in several ways: maximizing the attractive qualities and minimizing the negative ones, showing how the offer meets the other party's needs, reducing the disadvantages of accepting the offer, making offers more credible by providing third-party references or factual support, or setting deadlines on offers so they expire if not accepted quickly. Many would argue that these are common sales tricks similar to discount coupons, two-for-the-price-of-one offers, "today only" sales, and extra-added-attraction elements. They are! Negotiators can and should use the same techniques that salespeople use to move their products.

* palatable: 마음에 드는

① Establishing a Neutral Position: A Starting Point for Negotiation
② In Negotiation, Sweeten the Offer Rather Than Intensify the Threat
③ Use Both Factual Support and Legal Authority to Win a Negotiation
④ Cases Where Negotiators Themselves Seek Third-Party Intervention
⑤ Negotiation as a Process of Distributing a Fixed Amount of Resources

08

Benny Goodman에 관한 다음 글의 내용과 일치하지 않는 것은?

24005-0206

Benny Goodman is one of the greatest clarinetists of all time. Born in 1909 in Chicago, he began taking lessons at the age of 10. With a natural inborn talent, he made rapid progress and was soon playing professionally. He was strongly influenced by New Orleans jazz, and it played an important role in his music throughout his life. At 16, he joined the Ben Pollack Orchestra in Chicago, which at the time was one of the top bands in the United States. He was soon making recordings, and it wasn't long before he formed his own band. Although Goodman was relatively well known before 1935, it was the change in his style that occurred in the Palomar Ballroom in Los Angeles that really caused his career to take off. And a few years later, he was playing in Carnegie Hall in New York City. At the time, this was something new for a jazz orchestra. The concert was a tremendous success. After years of appealing only to specialized audiences, jazz had finally broken through and was being accepted by mainstream audiences.

① 타고난 재능으로 빠르게 클라리넷을 배웠다.
② 뉴올리언스 재즈에 큰 영향을 받지 않았다.
③ 16세에 Ben Pollack 오케스트라의 단원이 되었다.
④ 음반을 녹음하고 나서 얼마 지나지 않아 자신의 밴드를 결성했다.
⑤ 뉴욕시의 카네기 홀에서 연주했다.

09 다음 도표의 내용과 일치하지 않는 것은?

24005-0207

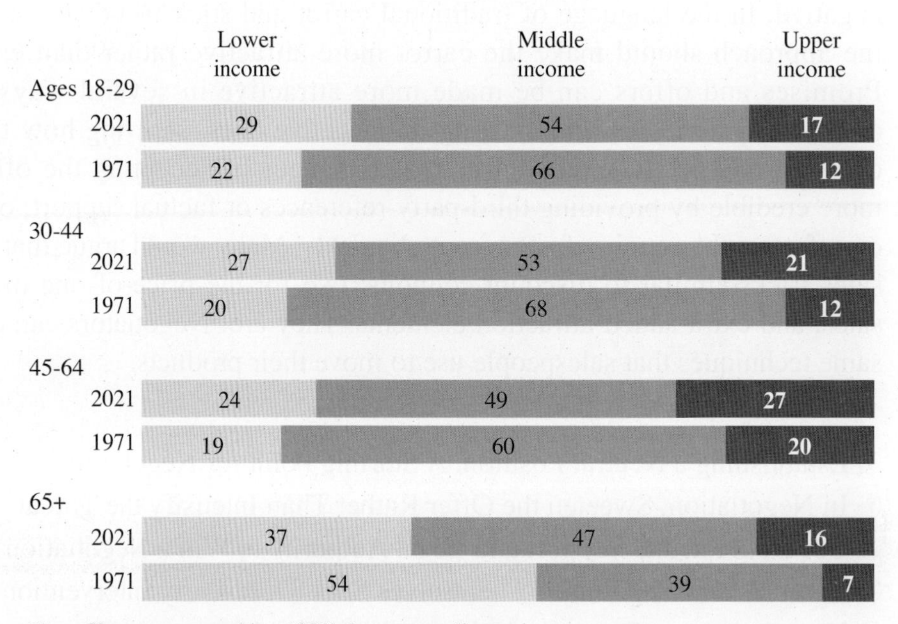

The graph above shows the share (%) of American adults in each income tier by age group in 1971 and 2021. ① Among American adults ages 18 to 29, the share in the upper-income tier increased by 5 percentage points from 1971 to 2021, whereas their share in the middle-income tier decreased by 12 percentage points during the same period. ② Among the 1971 middle-income tiers, the share of American adults ages 30 to 44 was higher than that of any other age group. ③ In 1971, more than two-thirds of American adults ages 45 to 64 were in the middle-income tier, and in 2021, more than half of the people in that age group were in the same income tier. ④ The share of American adults ages 65 and older in the lower-income tier fell from 54% in 1971 to 37% in 2021, while their share in the middle income tier rose from 39% to 47% during the same period. ⑤ However, American adults 65 and older were the only age group in which more than one-in-three adults were in the lower-income tier in 2021.

* tier: 층, 단계

10 2024 Kids' Quilt Challenge에 관한 다음 안내문의 내용과 일치하지 않는 것은?

24005-0208

2024 Kids' Quilt Challenge

Are you ready for a fun and exciting challenge?
Then join the Kids' Quilt Challenge and show off your creativity and design skills.

Contest Guidelines

1. The contest is open to all youth ages 15 and under.
2. The contest is limited to the first 50 people who submit a contest entry form.
3. Quilts must be no larger than 45" in diameter. Quilting may be done by hand or by machine.
4. Contest entrants must submit their quilts via postal delivery, and they must arrive by August 9.
5. Quilts will be displayed at The Great Wisconsin Quilt Show, September 5 – 7. Winners will be announced at the Show on Saturday, September 7.
6. Cash prizes will be awarded to the top three winners: $300 for first place, $200 for second place, and $100 for third place.

* diameter: 지름

① 신청서를 제출하는 맨 처음 50명으로 참가가 제한된다.
② 퀼트 작업은 손이나 기계로 해도 된다.
③ 참가작은 8월 9일까지 도착해야 한다.
④ 수상자는 퀼트 쇼 첫날 발표된다.
⑤ 상위 3명의 우승자에게 상금이 수여될 것이다.

11

24005-0209

Brownstone House Charity Volunteer Clinic에 관한 다음 안내문의 내용과 일치하는 것은?

Brownstone House Charity Volunteer Clinic

The Brownstone House Charity Volunteer Clinic is one of the many initiatives of Brownstone House, a nonprofit organization that focuses on promoting healthy lifestyles. The clinic is staffed by volunteers who provide basic medical care and support to those in need and has served more than 10,000 patients since opening in 2016.

Details

- Open on Saturdays and Sundays, 9 a.m. – 1 p.m.
- Where: Room 210 on the second floor of the Brownstone House (555 West Bellfort Avenue)
- Fee: $8 for first visit and $5 for each subsequent visit
- The clinic is run by appointment only. To schedule or cancel an appointment, please call Brownstone House during weekdays at 700 – 123 – 4567.

Note

- Please do not attempt to contact doctors directly at their private offices or on their cell phones.

For more information, please email us at cyn@brownstonehouseinc.org.

① 2016년에 개원한 이래 10,000명에 조금 모자라는 환자를 진료했다.
② 매주 토요일과 일요일 오후 1시에 시작된다.
③ 진료 비용은 무료이다.
④ 예약하지 않아도 진료를 받을 수 있다.
⑤ 의사의 개인 사무실로 직접 연락해서는 안 된다.

12

다음 글의 밑줄 친 부분 중, 어법상 틀린 것은?

24005-0210

In the worldview of the Cree hunter, humans do not control the hunt. The fish and game are not there simply ① to be taken. Rather it is the animals who control the success of the hunt by offering themselves ② willingly to people (or, conversely, choosing to withhold themselves from a hunter). The Cree credit animals with knowing the same things that people know and ③ being able to communicate and share that knowledge with people. Humans and animals are in a relationship of reciprocity, just as humans ④ do in relationship with other humans. Indeed, anthropologists argue even more generally that in all cultures, including those that are modern and postmodern, there are profound connections between the ways ⑤ that people engage with each other and with other species.

* Cree: 크리족(북아메리카 원주민) ** reciprocity: 호혜 *** anthropologist: 인류학자

13

다음 글의 밑줄 친 부분 중, 문맥상 낱말의 쓰임이 적절하지 않은 것은?

24005-0211

Stay-at-home parents have new employment options in our internet economy. Over the last few decades many women have been self-employed. Such an arrangement gives them greater flexibility over their hours and days of work. The rise of remote work could further ① increase opportunities for them. Internet platforms such as Withinwork are two-sided platforms as workers seeking employment post their resumes and employers seeking workers post their tasks. Artificial intelligence (AI) algorithms play a key ② matchmaking role here by gathering and presenting the set of job opportunities a person sees. I set up my profile on Withinwork and was impressed with the ③ alternative tasks that I was offered by the AI. As with any two-sided matching platform, the more job offerings an applicant sees, the more ④ likely that person will find value in the platform. In this sense, as remote work grows as a socially high-status activity, this process will ⑤ lose its own momentum.

* momentum: 힘, 탄력

14

다음 빈칸에 들어갈 말로 가장 적절한 것은?

24005-0212

Considerable debate exists as to the appropriate beneficiaries of affirmative action. In the United States, supporters of affirmative action hoped that, by expanding the coverage to apply to many minority groups, they would broaden the political base favoring such programs. In practice, however, the wider coverage has diluted, in the minds of some, the moral argument in favor of a program intended to help the most obvious victims of governmental discrimination: African Americans and Native Americans. Some argue that the ______________ matters. Thus, because Asian Americans and women are generally not under-represented among university student bodies, affirmative action admissions for them would now be inappropriate (though they should not be singled out for restrictions). On the other hand, among corporate executives or university faculties, blacks, Asians, Latinos, and women all faced exclusion in the past and remain under-represented today; therefore, in these areas all four groups ought to be beneficiaries of affirmative action.

* affirmative action: (인종 · 남녀 차별 등으로 인한) 사회적 약자 우대 정책 ** dilute: 약화하다 *** discrimination: 차별

① budget ② gender ③ context
④ education ⑤ personality

15

다음 빈칸에 들어갈 말로 가장 적절한 것은?

24005-0213

Predictions of technological unemployment have recurred since the onset of the Industrial Revolution. But the recurring reality was one of economic growth through ______________________________. Yes, machines destroyed lots of jobs, often with devastating effects on displaced workers for whom new jobs were often too late or out of reach. Over time, however, job destruction freed up labor and capital that went into new and usually better jobs and higher incomes. That is because technology both *substitutes* for labor — in particular, less-skilled labor — and *complements* labor, or makes it more productive, thus generating new demand for labor. Casual observers have often tended "to overstate the extent of machine substitution for human labor," which was readily observable; they "repeatedly underestimated the demand for the work of human beings that would remain."

* recur: 되풀이되다, 반복하다 ** onset: 시작, 개시 *** devastating: 치명적인

① idea generation ② enlarged marketing
③ creative destruction ④ controlled freedom
⑤ diversified demand

16

다음 빈칸에 들어갈 말로 가장 적절한 것은?

24005-0214

The most common situation in which musical equipment becomes an instrument is in live performance. Playing the piano is generally associated with performance in real-time, and computer-based musical instruments are increasingly being played in real-time. For example, laptop computers are increasingly used in performance by live electronic musicians even in preference to keyboard synthesizers, groove boxes, and turntables. One thing that changes in computer performances is that ______________________. In acoustic instrument performance the musician's gestures are translated into sound. Many instruments have a one-to-one gesture-to-sound relationship, including the press of the piano or synthesizer key, or the slide of the finger of the guitar fretboard; each translates gesture into a direct audible result. Many electronic and computer-based instruments have a one-to-many gesture-to-sound relationship when a mouse gesture or parameter movement changes the complexity of a rhythmic part, or the timbre and volume of an entire ensemble of musical voices.

* fretboard: (기타의) 지판 ** parameter: 파라미터, 매개 변수 *** timbre: 음색

① the gestural relationship with sound is sometimes less direct
② the results can be audio, visual or textual, all in one medium
③ musicians can express themselves more clearly using gestures
④ it is possible to use the computer as an instrument in classical music
⑤ computer music production reduces effort and offers many possibilities

17

다음 빈칸에 들어갈 말로 가장 적절한 것은?

24005-0215

Two Northwestern University marketing researchers, David Gal and Derek Rucker, conducted research using framing techniques to make people feel uncertain. For example, they told one group to remember a time when they were full of certainty, and the other group to remember a time when they were full of doubt. Then they asked the participants whether they were meat eaters, vegetarians, vegans, or otherwise, how important this was to them, and how confident they were in their opinions. People who were asked to remember a time of uncertainty were less confident of their eating choices. However, when asked to write their beliefs to persuade someone else to eat the way they did, they would ________________ than those who were certain of their choice. Gal and Rucker performed the research with different topics (for example, preferences for a Mac versus a Windows computer) and found similar results. When people were less certain, they would dig in and argue even harder.

* framing: 프레이밍(생각의 틀 짜기)

① write more and stronger arguments
② look for less proof for their opinions
③ change their opinions more willingly
④ suspect the researchers' motives more strongly
⑤ remember less supporting details about their choices

18

다음 글에서 전체 흐름과 관계 없는 문장은?

24005-0216

In the same way that it is sometimes advisable to take a momentary break, or "fast," from some of our food, beverages, and habits, a media fast may be good for your system. ① Spending a set period of time unplugged can clarify for you the advantages and disadvantages of your media practices. ② Life without electronic devices momentarily separates you from constant distraction, online advertisements, and artificial blue light. ③ You'll have more time for other things, like physical activity, face-to-face interaction, and even solitude. ④ What is most important is to think carefully about what is gained and what is lost when you choose to engage in face-to-face communication, computer-mediated communication, or some combination of the two. ⑤ You'll also have the opportunity to reflect critically on how life in the Communication Age differs from older modes of living and connecting and engaging with the world.

* solitude: 고독

19

24005-0217

주어진 글 다음에 이어질 글의 순서로 가장 적절한 것은?

To the extent that one can distinguish self-esteem from public esteem, the latter seems to be more important. The overriding motive of narcissists seems to be to obtain social approval from others.

(A) That is, they spend much of their time and energy seeking ways to get others to admire them. In terms of being liked by others rather than admired, they are somewhat indifferent. That is, narcissists are no more nor less interested than anyone else in being liked.

(B) For example, if given a chance to tackle a difficult task and find out how good they are, narcissists put forth minimal effort if no one is looking, which is a sign that they do not really care about demonstrating their brilliance to themselves, whereas if others are watching, they put forth maximum effort in order to shine.

(C) Being admired, however, is extremely important to them. In general, they do not seem overly concerned with proving something to themselves (possibly because they are already privately persuaded of their own good qualities), but they are quite interested in demonstrating their superiority to others.

* overriding: 최우선시되는

① (A) – (C) – (B)
② (B) – (A) – (C)
③ (B) – (C) – (A)
④ (C) – (A) – (B)
⑤ (C) – (B) – (A)

20

24005-0218

주어진 글 다음에 이어질 글의 순서로 가장 적절한 것은?

One obvious area where climbing and philosophy intersect is with regard to the normative dimension of climbing — the ethical or unethical behavior of climbers. Some of the ethical issues in climbing involve a straightforward extension of more general moral principles.

(A) For these sorts of questions, broader moral rules do not apply in any straightforward way, and climbers must work out for themselves what is right or wrong within the context of climbing.

(B) For example, it is wrong to lie about your climbing accomplishments because it is generally wrong to lie about accomplishments; it is wrong to needlessly endanger others at the cliff because, more generally, it is always wrong to needlessly endanger others.

(C) However, other ethical issues involve factors that are unique to climbing and thus cannot be resolved by invoking broader moral rules. Is it wrong to place bolts on rappel? Is it cheating to use pre-placed gear on a traditional pitch?

* invoke: (법 등을) 적용하다 ** rappel: (암벽에서) 줄을 타고 내려오기 *** pitch: (등반) 구간

① (A) – (C) – (B) ② (B) – (A) – (C) ③ (B) – (C) – (A)
④ (C) – (A) – (B) ⑤ (C) – (B) – (A)

21

24005-0219

글의 흐름으로 보아, 주어진 문장이 들어가기에 가장 적절한 곳은?

> Equally important to perception, however, is top-down processing, which involves previously acquired knowledge.

Sensation and perception almost always happen together. Researchers, however, have studied each process separately to determine how the two work together. (①) Perception can occur through bottom-up processing, which begins with the physical stimuli from the environment, and proceeds through transduction of those stimuli into neural impulses. (②) The signals are passed along to successively more complex brain regions, and ultimately result in the recognition of a visual stimulus. (③) For example, when you look at the face of your best friend, your eyes convert light energy into neural impulses, which travel into the brain to visual regions. (④) This information forms the basis for sensing the visual stimulus and ultimately its perception. (⑤) As a result, when you look at your best friend's face, brain regions that store information about what faces look like, particularly those that are familiar to you, can help you to perceive and recognize the specific visual stimulus.

* transduction: (에너지 등의) 변환 ** neural: 신경의 *** impulse: 자극

22

24005-0220

글의 흐름으로 보아, 주어진 문장이 들어가기에 가장 적절한 곳은?

> Gender mainstreaming is based on the understanding that all policies have the potential to impact social and demographic groups differently, thus creating and sustaining unequal power relations.

The European Union, since the late 1990s, has embraced gender mainstreaming as its main strategy for addressing gender inequality in policy making. (①) It is defined as the integration of the gender perspective into every stage of the policy process (design, implementation, monitoring, and evaluation). (②) For example, gender mainstreaming may explicitly consider the experiences of men, such as parental leave as a legal claim for men or labor policies for men in female-dominated occupations (e.g., nursing). (③) Gender mainstreaming can also apply to health care, equally promoting women's and men's health care needs. (④) In many countries, coronary heart disease is defined through a masculine lens, influencing all areas of medical care from prevention to recovery. (⑤) Not only does this lead to overlooking women's heart health needs, but it also may negatively impact men who do not seem to fit the model of hegemonic masculinity.

* demographic: 인구 통계학의 ** coronary: 관상 동맥의 *** hegemonic masculinity: 헤게모니 남성성

23

다음 글의 내용을 한 문장으로 요약하고자 한다. 빈칸 (A), (B)에 들어갈 말로 가장 적절한 것은?

24005-0221

Although a traditional textbook drawing suggests that neurons in the brain are happily packed next to one another like jelly beans in a jar, don't let the cartoon fool you: neurons are locked in competition for survival. Just like neighboring nations, neurons stake out their territories and persistently defend them. They fight for territory and survival at every level of the system: each neuron and each connection between neurons fights for resources. As the border wars rage through the lifetime of a brain, maps are redrawn in such a way that the experiences and goals of a person are always reflected in the brain's structure. If an accountant drops her career to become a pianist, the neural territory devoted to her fingers will expand; if she becomes a microscopist, her visual cortex will develop higher resolution for the small details she seeks; if she becomes a perfumer, her brain regions assigned to smell will enlarge.

* stake out: ~을 차지하다 ** cortex: (대뇌) 피질

Neurons constantly ___(A)___ with each other for existence, which leads to the ___(B)___ of the brain structure based on one's experiences and goals.

	(A)		(B)
①	struggle	……	unification
②	struggle	……	personalization
③	connect	……	simplification
④	connect	……	regeneration
⑤	collaborate	……	specialization

24~25 다음 글을 읽고, 물음에 답하시오.

In Singapore, due to road pricing, one can always expect to be able to achieve a speed of 40 miles per hour on the road. While the rich are more likely to afford this, buses can also achieve these speeds, and with the economies of scale of a bus this (a) lowers the per-person trip price for achieving this speed. The full cost of commuting includes not only the out-of-pocket expenditure on gasoline, parking, and road use fees but the value of the lost time. If a commute takes thirty minutes rather than fifteen minutes because of traffic congestion, then the commuter has lost fifteen minutes. Economists have adopted the rule of thumb of (b) valuing such lost time by half of the person's hourly wage. For example, if I earn $80 an hour and I lose fifteen minutes stuck in traffic, then this costs me $10 in lost time (.25 × 80 × .5).

To (c) conserve on such lost time due to congestion, cities such as Stockholm, London, and Singapore have adopted road pricing. Drivers in such cities move at higher speeds and save time but must pay more money out of pocket to travel at peak use times. One explanation for why so few cities have adopted road pricing focuses on behavioral economics: people are used to the roads being free. To an economist, this is a (d) puzzling explanation because congested roads cost us valuable time. This time cost means that free roads are not free to use. A second explanation for the (e) agreement to road pricing is that many poor people drive and they prefer to pay for their commute using their time rather than paying a road use fee.

* commute: 통근(하다) ** expenditure: 경비 *** congestion: 정체

24 윗글의 제목으로 가장 적절한 것은?

24005-0222

① Road Pricing: Is Time More Valuable than Money?
② Varying Compensations for Lost Time on the Road
③ Too Much Administration to Implement Road Pricing
④ Analysis of the Underlying Causes of Road Congestion
⑤ Efforts to Reduce Commute Times: Fighting a Losing Battle

25 밑줄 친 (a)~(e) 중에서 문맥상 낱말의 쓰임이 적절하지 않은 것은?

24005-0223

① (a) ② (b) ③ (c) ④ (d) ⑤ (e)

26~28 다음 글을 읽고, 물음에 답하시오.

(A)

One hot afternoon, little William and his dad were passing through a dusty village road. It was a dry season, so little William thought the whole village road looked lonely and deserted. After walking for a long while, (a) he asked his dad to stop somewhere for a short rest. Looking around, little William and his dad could not find a comfortable place to relax. Unable to find anywhere to rest, they were forced to keep walking under the hot bright sun.

(B)

Unknowingly to little William, his dad let him win. (b) He jumped for joy because he reached the huge coconut tree first. Little William and his dad breathed a deep sigh of relief because they were so exhausted from walking all day. They dropped all that they had with them on the ground and lay down under the huge coconut tree, which protected them from the sun. And they embraced the cool breeze in the air.

(C)

After a few minutes' walk, little William and his dad saw a huge coconut tree far off in the distance that could provide shade from the burning sun, so they started walking faster to reach the tree. "Dad, why don't (c) you race me to the tree?" little William asked his dad. After letting out a short smile, he agreed to the race and, at the count of three, he watched little William take off like a runner.

(D)

Then, they began to feel hungry. Little William looked up towards the huge coconut tree and said, "This huge coconut tree is useless. It doesn't have any coconuts we can eat." "My dear little William," his dad responded, "it is not good to be ungrateful to people and things around us. This tree, which (d) you are calling useless, saved us from the hot sun." Little William gently stood from where he lay and turned towards the tree. (e) He thanked it for protecting them from the sun. The coconut tree began to give little William and his dad a more pleasant wind.

26

24005-0224

주어진 글 (A)에 이어질 내용을 순서에 맞게 배열한 것으로 가장 적절한 것은?

① (B) – (D) – (C)　② (C) – (B) – (D)　③ (C) – (D) – (B)
④ (D) – (B) – (C)　⑤ (D) – (C) – (B)

27

24005-0225

밑줄 친 (a)~(e) 중에서 가리키는 대상이 나머지 넷과 다른 것은?

① (a)　② (b)　③ (c)　④ (d)　⑤ (e)

28

24005-0226

윗글에 관한 내용으로 적절하지 않은 것은?

① 어린 William은 마을 길 전체가 쓸쓸하고 황량해 보인다고 생각했다.
② 어린 William은 아빠가 달리기 경주에서 져 준 사실을 몰랐다.
③ 어린 William과 아빠는 모든 짐을 내려놓고 코코넛 나무 아래 누웠다.
④ 아빠는 어린 William이 달리기 선수처럼 잽싸게 출발하는 모습을 지켜보았다.
⑤ 코코넛 나무에는 코코넛이 매우 많이 열려 있었다.

TEST 3

01

다음 글의 목적으로 가장 적절한 것은?

24005-0227

Dear Members,

Thank you for always supporting our park's efforts to improve our community's health and social bonds. As we have announced, construction at Lions Park will begin as soon as the spring season allows. As an alternative place to play pickleball in town this summer, the lines for three pickleball courts will be painted on the blacktop surface at Rose Park, located at 201 Green Valley Road. The blue equipment bin with portable nets and extra balls from Lions Park will be relocated there as well. The combination to unlock the bin can be obtained by calling the front desk at the community center. If you have any questions regarding the alternative pickleball courts, please contact Mark Perkins at mperkins@ShakopeeMN.gov. We look forward to the completion of the new dedicated pickleball courts at Lions Park this summer.

Sincerely,
Mark Perkins

* pickleball: 피클볼(배드민턴, 테니스, 탁구의 요소가 결합한 새로운 패들 스포츠) ** blacktop: 아스팔트로 포장된

① 피클볼의 역사와 경기 방법을 소개하려고
② 회원 등록과 시설 이용 방법을 설명하려고
③ 임시 피클볼 경기장 마련 계획을 알리려고
④ 공사로 인한 피클볼 대회 취소를 공지하려고
⑤ 공원 내 신축 경기장의 개장식에 초대하려고

02

다음 글에 드러난 'I'의 심경 변화로 가장 적절한 것은?

24005-0228

I should have guessed things were not going to go well when I stepped off the train at Weston Station and there was no sign of my father. I was only fifteen, and there was no way I could go back home if he didn't show up. I wandered up and down the platform. The waiting felt like forever, and I began to anxiously wonder if something bad had happened to him. After a while, one of the station employees approached me and asked me if I was all right. I said I was fine, but inside, my concern was growing. Then I glanced to the left and noticed my dad. At that very moment, all my anxieties disappeared. 'Dad!' I shouted. I snatched my little bag from the floor and ran to him. 'Sorry to keep you waiting, Son,' he said, ruffling my hair and pulling me close to him. 'Let's go home.' He smiled, and I returned his smile with an even bigger one.

* snatch: 낚아채다 ** ruffle: 헝클어 놓다

① furious → satisfied
② confident → nervous
③ indifferent → thrilled
④ worried → relieved
⑤ ashamed → proud

03

다음 글의 요지로 가장 적절한 것은?

24005-0229

Urban agriculture is moving from just a practice for earning an income and small food-producing activities to a more sustainable practice that focuses on promoting local food production as an energy-saving resource that is central to creating vital urban communities. It needs to become even more central to city planning as food security and food safety become issues that cities need to address along with the increase in population that is creating a strain on a global level with regards to food availability and health. In current practice, the term *urban agriculture* does not necessarily mean that food production itself is based on a sustainable methodology or procedure but when combined with an ecological-based approach it does. With the recognition of natural resource decline and the advance of environmental degradation in cities today, urban agriculture is taking on new meaning in bringing ecological-based systems back into the city as a vital part of the solution to creating more sustainable cities. This does require a paradigm shift in thinking about food as an integral part of the city's framework.

* degradation: 저하

① 도시 농업이 기능을 제대로 발휘하려면 농지의 장기적인 확보가 중요하다.
② 도시 농업을 통한 소규모 식량 생산 활동은 지역 경제 발전에 도움이 된다.
③ 지속 가능한 도시 조성을 위해 생태 기반형 도시 농업을 활용할 필요가 있다.
④ 시민은 도시 농업에 적극 참여하여 녹색 공간 조성의 주체가 되는 것이 바람직하다.
⑤ 도시 농업을 통해 식량 안보와 식품 안전 문제를 해결하는 것은 현실적으로 불가능하다.

04 다음 글에서 필자가 주장하는 바로 가장 적절한 것은?

24005-0230

There is a tendency in some parents to treat small children as if they are much older. It seems as if they want to give the impression that their child is mature beyond his age. They ask a small child to make decisions about matters he is too young to decide. When a child is put in this situation, sometimes he will do what the parent wants him to do, and sometimes he will simply say, "No." This is his attempt to show his authority and to display his power. A small child should never be asked to make a decision he is too young to make. The parent should make the decision and then give instructions to the child. For example, if a parent thinks that a child should stop playing and eat, he should not ask the child, "Do you want to eat now?" He should tell the child to put his toys away and get ready to eat. If he thinks that the child should take a nap, he should not ask the child, "Do you want to take a nap?" He should tell the child that it is time for his nap.

① 부모는 자신의 아이가 어릴 때부터 스스로 결정할 수 있게 해 주어야 한다.
② 부모는 훈육할 때 자신의 아이에게 일관성 있는 모습을 보여야 한다.
③ 부모는 어린아이에게 권위적인 태도를 보이지 말아야 한다.
④ 부모는 아이가 무리한 요구를 할 때는 단호하게 거절할 수 있어야 한다.
⑤ 어린아이가 할 수 없는 결정은 부모가 내린 다음 아이에게 지시해야 한다.

05 밑줄 친 our diggings will meet in the middle of that huge Alp가 다음 글에서 의미하는 바로 가장 적절한 것은?

24005-0231

I think of neuroscience and the human sciences as like two very small miners energetically tunnelling in from opposite sides of an immense Alp. Although neuroscientists on their side of the Alp do not listen much to sounds of digging from the humanists on the other side, some humanists, those concerned with the brain's role in the arts, listen very closely to what the neuroscientists on the other side are saying. We draw hopefully on a great many researchers. We hope for answers from them to the questions that bother us. The neuroscientists and we of the human sciences, even if we are divided into two groups, share the same hope. Although dwarfed by the mountain, we hope our diggings will meet in the middle of that huge Alp, and there we will discover this mysterious, magical treasure, Mind. We hope.

* dwarf: 왜소해 보이게 만들다

① The human sciences and neuroscience will be more specialized.
② The humanists will make a discovery faster than the neuroscientists.
③ The direction of research in neuroscience and the human sciences will be altered.
④ The human sciences and neuroscience will encounter more problems than before.
⑤ The understandings of the mind in neuroscience and in the human sciences will come together.

06

24005-0232

다음 글의 주제로 가장 적절한 것은?

Modern broadcast media may have contributed to the perpetuation of the innate talent account of musical performance ability. The discovery of an exceptional child performer — "the next Mozart" is a common label — makes for a much better story than reporting how advanced musical learning has resulted from an unusually plentiful combination of environmental, educational, and economic factors. Beyond simple media sensationalism, however, the belief in talent offers other appealing effects. Giving the musically talented person the designation of specialness can turn the experience of a concert into a fantastic, even supernatural, happening. Plus, musicians themselves can benefit from the "gifted" label. Feeling special — or even divinely blessed — can contribute to musicians' self-esteem and motivation; consequently, many "talented" musicians feel an obligation to nurture their gift, which allows them to approach their musical activities with confidence and the expectation of success.

* perpetuation: 영구화 ** nurture: (재능 따위를) 기르다

① issues with broadcasting that focuses on gifted musicians
② potential of using broadcast media to promote music concerts
③ psychological benefits of believing that practice makes perfect
④ importance of music education in improving creative intelligence
⑤ positive effects of faith in innate musical talent reinforced by media

07 다음 글의 제목으로 가장 적절한 것은?

24005-0233

Many have observed that people often use mobile phones in waiting areas. It is a way to kill time but it is also a way to create a space within what is often a weak or poorly defined space. Spaces at the edge of a dead zone for making mobile calls are also prime spots for making calls or sending texts. So, when people touch down at an airport or leave a tunnel after having been out of contact with a cell tower, they are more likely to make calls or send texts. The mobile phone can be used to share a space with someone at a distance, for example, people at a concert who call others so they can hear part (or all) of the concert. At the extreme, people may be so immersed in the interaction with others on a mobile phone, that they lose contact with those in the physical space they occupy. Sherry Turkle calls this *alone together*; others have used the term *absent presence* to characterize this behavior.

* dead zone: 휴대 전화 불통 지역 ** cell tower: 무선 셀 기지국

① How Do Our Mobile Phones Redefine Our Physical Space?
② How Are Digital Devices Changing the Rules of Etiquette?
③ Digital Transformation: Towards a More Sustainable Future
④ Dead Connections: What Causes Them and How to Fix Them
⑤ Why We Expect More from Technology and Less from Each Other

08

24005-0234

W. E. B. DuBois에 관한 다음 글의 내용과 일치하지 않는 것은?

W. E. B. DuBois (1868–1963), an African American sociologist, graduated from Fisk University in Tennessee and became the first African American to receive a doctorate from Harvard University. Then, at Atlanta University, he founded the nation's second department of sociology. He soon began a highly productive academic career that included, among many other things, founding two scholarly journals and writing numerous books and articles. He focused his research and writing on the racial problems in the United States. At the same time, however, he worked hard to apply his enormous knowledge to improving society. He founded the Niagara Movement, an organization of African American intellectuals fighting for racial equality. He also helped create the National Association for the Advancement of Colored People (NAACP) and edited its influential magazine, *Crisis*. Later, he even advocated the use of force to achieve racial equality. Finally, seeing little improvement in race relations, he moved in 1961 to the African nation of Ghana, where he died 2 years later.

① Harvard 대학교에서 박사 학위를 받았다.
② Atlanta 대학교에서 미국 최초의 사회학과를 설립했다.
③ 아프리카계 미국인 지식인 단체인 Niagara Movement를 설립했다.
④ NAACP의 영향력 있는 잡지인 *Crisis*를 편집했다.
⑤ 인종 관계의 개선을 거의 보지 못하고 1961년에 아프리카 국가 가나로 이주했다.

09

다음 도표의 내용과 일치하지 않는 것은?

24005-0235

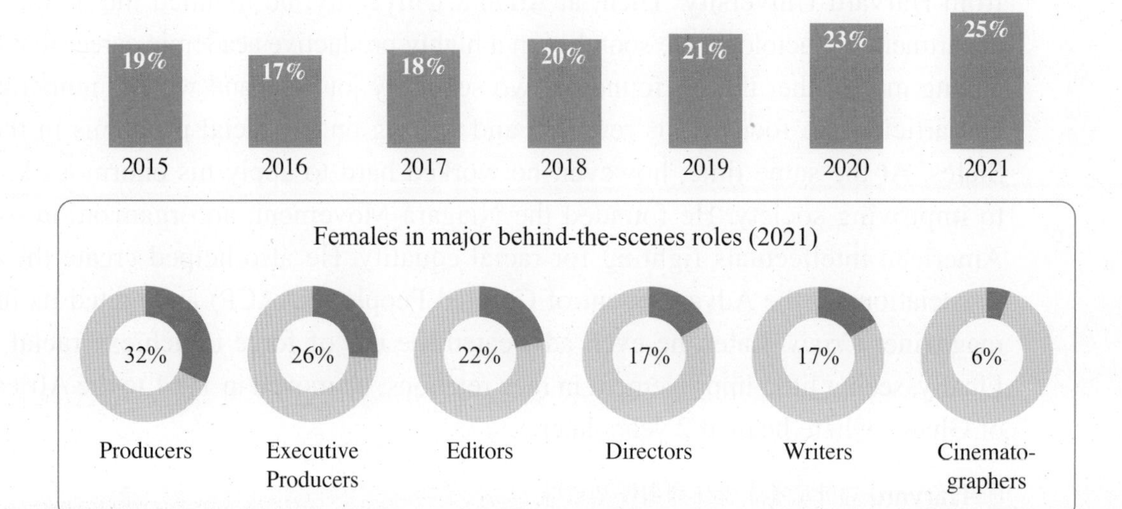

The charts above show the percentage of women who worked in major behind-the-scenes roles in the 250 highest-grossing U.S. films from 2015 to 2021 and the percentage of those women in 2021 by role. ① Compared to 2015, the percentage of women who worked in the 250 highest-grossing U.S. films was lower in 2016 and 2017, but it was higher in 2018. ② In 2021, the percentage of women who worked in the 250 highest-grossing U.S. films accounted for a quarter of the total. ③ In the same year, the percentage of female executive producers in these films was lower than that of female producers. ④ While the share of female directors and writers in the 250 highest-grossing U.S. films in 2021 stood at 17 percent each, 22 percent of all editors were female. ⑤ In the same year, among the major behind-the-scenes roles, cinematographers had the lowest percentage of women, at less than a third of the percentage of women who worked as writers.

* highest-grossing: 가장 높은 수익을 올린

10 Limber College Summer Softball Camp에 관한 다음 안내문의 내용과 일치하지 않는 것은?

24005-0236

Limber College Summer Softball Camp

Limber College is excited to host its annual summer softball camp from June 14 to 16.

There are two camp sessions:

Camp session	A	B
Ages	4–7 years old	8–18 years old
Time	9 a.m.–11:30 a.m.	10 a.m.–2 p.m.
Cost (per person)	$80	$160

Camp participants are required to bring a glove and bat, and wear baseball shoes. They are also encouraged to bring sun block, a water bottle, and extra clothing/socks.

Camp B participants should bring a sack lunch. (Lunch is at 11:30 a.m. daily.)

Snacks and drinks will be available for purchase.

To sign up for the camp, please contact coach Jessica Kershaw at jessica.kershaw@limbercollege.edu.

① 운영 기간은 6월 14일부터 6월 16일까지이다.
② Camp A는 4~7세 참가자를 대상으로 한다.
③ Camp B 참가비는 1인당 160달러이다.
④ 참가자는 글러브와 배트를 지참해야 한다.
⑤ 간식과 음료는 무료로 제공된다.

11

24005-0237

Sunflower Park Family Camp Outing에 관한 다음 안내문의 내용과 일치하는 것은?

Sunflower Park Family Camp Outing

To have a fun-filled family camping experience this summer, join the Sunflower Park Family Camp Outing! There will be activities such as a nature walk, fishing competition, campfire games and more!

Dates: Saturday, August 10 – Sunday, August 11
Cost: $35 for a family of four, $5 for each additional camper
Registration deadline: August 7
Location: Sunflower Park
General information:

- A park recreation pass is required for vehicles to enter the park.
- Each family can bring up to two small tents or one medium-sized tent.
- Check-in starts at noon on Saturday. Check-out is at 11 a.m. on Sunday.
- Our staff will transport your equipment to and from the campsite in a trailer. Pickup times are Saturday from noon to 1 p.m. and Sunday from 9 a.m. to 11 a.m.

Register before the deadline to reserve your place. Hope to see you there!

① 야영 활동에 낚시 대회는 포함되지 않는다.
② 4인 가족의 요금은 40달러이다.
③ 공원에 입장하는 차량은 별도 출입증이 필요하지 않다.
④ 가족당 중형 텐트 2개까지 가져올 수 있다.
⑤ 장비는 직원들이 트레일러로 운반해 준다.

12

24005-0238

다음 글의 밑줄 친 부분 중, 어법상 틀린 것은?

We are so easily impressed and make judgements based on superficial evidence, but sometimes luxury provides a psychological boost to confidence that improves our well-being. Wearing designer clothes can make us feel better about ① ourselves, which then becomes self-reinforcing. When we put on our luxury clothes we feel special and behave accordingly. Luxury goods light up the pleasure centres in our brain. If you think you are drinking expensive wine, not only does it taste better but the brain's valuation system ② associated with the experience of pleasure shows greater activation, compared to drinking exactly the same wine when you believe it to be cheap. What's important here ③ is the belief — not the actual luxury. Francesca Gino, a professor at Harvard Business School, found that people who wore ④ which they believed to be fake designer brand sunglasses (but were in fact genuine) felt like frauds and were more likely to cheat on tests. You may be able to fake until you make it, but deep down, if we ⑤ do, many of us feel like imposters.

* fake: 모조의; 속이다 ** fraud: 사기꾼 *** imposter: 사기꾼

13

24005-0239

다음 글의 밑줄 친 부분 중, 문맥상 낱말의 쓰임이 적절하지 않은 것은?

Overfishing is in large part a consequence of excessive effort and capacity in fisheries. Too often, fishery managers have been unable to control fishing effort, resulting in ① unsustainable levels of catch. This has been a particular problem for open-access fisheries where management does not ② limit the number of participants or high individual effort. In this situation, the economic incentives favor short-term exploitation over long-term sustainable use because the economic benefits of ③ sacrificing current catch to rebuild the stock are hard to perceive compared to short-term needs (bills to be paid), and long-term benefits may have to be shared with newcomers when the fishery recovers. As more people enter the fishery or improve their fishing capabilities, the future yield to the individual fisher ④ decreases. This often fosters competition to maintain or even increase individual catch levels even as stocks decline. In response, managers may ⑤ lengthen fishing seasons; participants then increase their fishing power, and effort becomes concentrated in time, sometimes resulting in "races for fish" or "fishing derbies."

* exploitation: 이기적 이용 ** derby: 시합, 경기

14 다음 빈칸에 들어갈 말로 가장 적절한 것은?

24005-0240

Typically, *homework* consists of any assigned task slated to be done outside the hours of class. What the word *homework* does not describe is the quality or quantity of the task, a reality that makes homework discussions challenging because it turns into a war of ____________. For example, if two people discuss their children's homework, one could be railing against mindless worksheets while the other is in favor of carefully crafted activities prompting students to reflect or create. But instead of naming the specific activity, they both refer to the tasks simply as "homework." And so one parent wonders why on earth anyone would be a proponent of (mindless) homework while the other can't understand why a parent *wouldn't* want their child to do (relevant and creative) work at home. Neither parent understands the other's point of view because they aren't speaking the same language about homework.

* slated: (일정이) 계획된 ** rail: 불평하다

① relationships ② vocabulary ③ responsibility
④ investment ⑤ manners

15 다음 빈칸에 들어갈 말로 가장 적절한 것은?

24005-0241

American sociologist William Julius Wilson has argued that an unintended consequence of African American suburbanization has been that inner cities ____________. As higher income minorities leave center cities, young people who remain are less likely to see and interact with adult men who work and have achieved upward income mobility. Research in development economics has documented, with data from the Dominican Republic, that when young people are informed about the wage gains that are possible by obtaining more education, this information increases their educational attainment. The explanation for this is that young people are more likely to underestimate the economic benefits of education when they never interact with people who look like them and have also attained a high level of education. The suburbanization of upwardly mobile people thus has social consequences for peer effects in the inner city.

* inner city: (흔히 대도시의, 사회적인 문제가 많은) 도심 지역

① have lost valuable role models
② have resolved a variety of conflicts
③ have spent too much money on education
④ have become indifferent to social injustice
⑤ have suffered from high levels of inequality

16 다음 빈칸에 들어갈 말로 가장 적절한 것은?

24005-0242

Because advertisers in the 1950s were interested in reaching baby boomers, many radio stations played music called rock 'n' roll with disc jockeys that specifically called out to them. Other stations targeted different age groups with different styles of music and DJs. This new sort of station that focused on particular music preferences caught on because radio ______________________________. The development in 1948 of the transistor, a much smaller replacement for the Audion vacuum tube, led to the miniaturization of radio receivers. Now radio became something that people could literally take with them throughout the day — to the park, to the beach, or wherever. All of a sudden, the medium had a new life, and companies rushed to get new licenses. The number of stations jumped dramatically, from about one thousand in 1946 to nearly 3,500 in the mid-1950s. The largest proportion of these played specific types of music.

* baby boomer: (특히 2차 세계대전 후의) 베이비 붐 세대인 사람

① featured stories from listeners
② was now more portable than ever
③ acted as a link between generations
④ became the stage for new musicians
⑤ gave listeners their favorite songs for free

17

다음 빈칸에 들어갈 말로 가장 적절한 것은?

24005-0243

In a study by Arthur Aron and myself, we created a fake computer dating service, but instead of romance, the goal was to help college students find friendship. All the subjects listed their interests, and we returned a week later to ask them to review a profile written by another person and judge whether they liked and wanted to meet them. Half of them were told that our ultra-reliable, matchmaker program determined that this new person was an ideal match for them. The other half weren't told anything. When people weren't given any information about whether a friendship was likely, they preferred people with interests just like theirs. But when they were told that a friendship was likely, they preferred people who complemented them with different interests. That is, when people ______________________, they wanted to spend time with people who were unique, interesting, and who offered a chance for them to expand their horizons.

* fake: 가짜의

① felt that their close friends would feel jealous
② already had friends from various backgrounds
③ were confident that a relationship was possible
④ were unable to judge the candidate based on the profile
⑤ received no information about the matchmaking algorithm

18

다음 글에서 전체 흐름과 관계 없는 문장은?

24005-0244

Many of our activities (arguing, solving problems, budgeting time, etc.) are metaphorical in nature. The metaphorical concepts that characterize those activities structure our present reality. New metaphors have the power to create a new reality. ① This can begin to happen when we start to comprehend our experience in terms of a metaphor, and it becomes a deeper reality when we begin to act in terms of it. ② If a new metaphor enters the conceptual system that we base our actions on, it will alter that conceptual system and the perceptions and actions that the system gives rise to. ③ Much of cultural change arises from the introduction of new metaphorical concepts and the loss of old ones. ④ A dead metaphor is a popular metaphor that has been used so frequently and for such an extended period that its original figurative meaning has faded. ⑤ For example, the Westernization of cultures throughout the world is partly a matter of introducing the time is money metaphor into those cultures.

* metaphorical: 은유적인, 비유적인

19

24005-0245

주어진 글 다음에 이어질 글의 순서로 가장 적절한 것은?

Animal damage control advocates often characterize *game animals* as *pest species.* Deer, for instance, do not kill farm animals but are blamed for destroying gardens, bringing disease, causing car accidents, and wreaking other forms of damage in suburbs.

(A) Yet the fact remains that as long as developers continue to build in suburban areas, humans and wildlife will come into contact. Sadly, animal damage control programs have just one way of solving these problems — hunting.

(B) So sport hunters are allowed to kill deer with public support — after all, no one wants to be involved in a collision with a deer. Unfortunately for deer, hunting does not necessarily control their populations. They can rebound soon after hunting season due to lessened competition for resources.

(C) And, of course, the animal damage control measures that wiped out many of their natural predators also play a role in their large numbers. There are numerous methods to prevent the damage that deer can cause, such as more responsible driving, speed limits, warning signs, roadside reflectors, as well as the use of fencing along roadways.

* pest: 유해 동물 ** wreak: (피해를) 가하다 *** collision: 충돌 (사고)

① (A) – (C) – (B)
② (B) – (A) – (C)
③ (B) – (C) – (A)
④ (C) – (A) – (B)
⑤ (C) – (B) – (A)

20

24005-0246

주어진 글 다음에 이어질 글의 순서로 가장 적절한 것은?

A gene can increase in frequency by making its bearers more likely than nonbearers to perform some fitness-enhancing behavior.

(A) So, as long as a gene makes some fitness-enhancing behavior more likely, that gene will increase in frequency in a population, and as a result the behavior may increase in frequency as well. For this reason, biologists frequently say that, from the standpoint of evolutionary biology, "behavioral traits are like any other class of characters."

(B) For example, females of many species choose a mate based on the quality of male courtship displays. If the courtship displays of males differ in quality and a genetic difference underlies the display difference, the gene for the superior display will increase in frequency. Of course, courtship behaviors are not the only behaviors that affect fitness.

(C) If parents differ in the quantity of care they give to their offspring, if the quantity of care affects the viability of offspring, and if a genetic difference underlies this difference in parental care, then the gene for higher quantity care will increase in frequency.

* courtship: 구애 ** viability: 생존 능력

① (A) – (C) – (B) ② (B) – (A) – (C) ③ (B) – (C) – (A)
④ (C) – (A) – (B) ⑤ (C) – (B) – (A)

21

24005-0247

글의 흐름으로 보아, 주어진 문장이 들어가기에 가장 적절한 곳은?

> Although the United States has always been a nation of immigrants, it managed, at least until World War II, to maintain a sense of itself as a whole, a European-derived, English-speaking nation.

A mark of postmodernity is the increasing mobility, both voluntary and forced, of human populations around the world. (①) The migration of whole societies, the problem of refugees, the incorporation of migrant workers, have created a global, multicultural society that challenges the ability of any nation to define a reasonably homogeneous cultural identity or a set of cultural norms. (②) The case of the failure of America's "melting pot" image is a telling example. (③) But new migrations — Asian, African, and Latino — have challenged this image and made it almost impossible to define a central cultural identity for the nation. (④) Moreover, the American experience has become the norm in other parts of the world as well. (⑤) People's identities have become fractured, pluralized, and hybridized, and populations that were silent and marginalized in the past have suddenly moved to the center of the historical and cultural stage.

* homogeneous: 동질의 ** fracture: 조각내다 *** pluralize: 복수로 만들다

22

24005-0248

글의 흐름으로 보아, 주어진 문장이 들어가기에 가장 적절한 곳은?

> This is not to say that there are not pristine-like nearshore waters left on Earth.

Human impacts are the most direct in the upper 500 meters of the ocean as commercial fishing is not conducted in deeper waters. (①) Indeed, geological extraction and construction of ports and windmill farms are typically conducted in waters of 50 meters depth or less. (②) In shallow and nearshore waters human impacts are palpable, even in remote parts of the world. (③) Animal life in Antarctic waters is abundant and has been protected from commercial use for decades, yet hunting in the early part of the twentieth century changed the ecosystem to a degree that it can no longer be considered a pristine ecosystem. (④) A case may be made for the northwest Hawaii islands, which have never been inhabited by humans and only very rarely have experienced fishing expeditions. (⑤) Such locations are few — in fact, probably less than 1% of the ocean surface is fully protected against fishing or other kinds of disturbing activities.

* pristine-like: 자연[원래] 그대로와 비슷한 ** palpable: 매우 뚜렷한 *** expedition: 원정, 탐험

23

다음 글의 내용을 한 문장으로 요약하고자 한다. 빈칸 (A), (B)에 들어갈 말로 가장 적절한 것은?

24005-0249

In a simple experiment conducted by Michael Ross, Cathy McFarland, and Garth Fletcher, college students received a persuasive message arguing the importance of frequent tooth brushing. After receiving the message, they changed their attitudes toward tooth brushing. Needless to say, this is not surprising. But here's what was surprising: Later that same day in a different situation, the students were asked, "How many times have you brushed your teeth in the past 2 weeks?" Those who received the message recalled that they brushed their teeth far more frequently than did students in the control condition. The students were not attempting to deceive the researcher; there was no reason for them to lie. They were simply using their new attitudes as a heuristic to help them remember. In a sense, they needed to believe that they had always behaved in a sensible and reasonable manner — even though they had just now discovered what that sensible behavior might be.

* heuristic: 휴리스틱(특정 상황에서 사람들이 신속하게 사용하는 어림짐작의 기술)

According to the experiment in the passage, the students' attitudes toward tooth brushing were ____(A)____ by a persuasive message for frequent tooth brushing, which caused them to revise their memories so that the memories could be ____(B)____ with their new beliefs.

	(A)		(B)
①	predicted	······	unassociated
②	expressed	······	consistent
③	predicted	······	blended
④	influenced	······	consistent
⑤	influenced	······	unassociated

24~25 다음 글을 읽고, 물음에 답하시오.

When it comes to the common belief fallacy in your own life, remember that scientists are always trying to reach better conclusions, and that is something you don't do as an individual, at least not by default, and by extension it is something your institutions are not so (a) great at either. You don't seek out what science calls the null hypothesis. That is, when you believe in something, you rarely seek out evidence to the contrary to see how it matches up with your assumptions. That's the (b) source of urban legends, folklore, superstitions, and all the rest. Having doubts is not your strong suit. Corporations and other institutions rarely set aside a division tasked with paying attention to the faults of the agency. Unlike in science, most human undertakings (c) include a special department devoted to looking for the worst in the operation — not just a complaint department, but a department that asks if the organization is on the right path. Every human effort should systematically pause and ask if it is currently mistaken. To (d) beat your brain, you need that department constantly operating in your cranium. You would do well to borrow from the lessons of the scientific method and apply them in your personal life. In the background, while you sew and golf and browse cat videos, science is fighting against your (e) stupidity. No other human enterprise is fighting as hard, or at least not fighting and winning.

* fallacy: 오류 ** null hypothesis: 귀무가설(기각될 것이 예상되는 가설) *** cranium: 두개골

24

24005-0250

윗글의 제목으로 가장 적절한 것은?

① Common Beliefs Complement Science
② Science Is Not a Value-Neutral Discipline
③ Common Sense Keeps Your Daily Life Smooth
④ Which Is More Powerful: Intuition or Scientific Evidence?
⑤ Apply Science to Your Life to Avoid Common Misconceptions

25

24005-0251

밑줄 친 (a)~(e) 중에서 문맥상 낱말의 쓰임이 적절하지 않은 것은?

① (a) ② (b) ③ (c) ④ (d) ⑤ (e)

26~28 다음 글을 읽고, 물음에 답하시오.

(A)

Jill was quite a sickly child, but she had always wanted to be like Madeleine Sharp, a famous dancer. One day Jill and her mom went to Miss Madeleine Sharp's class for young ladies in the ballroom of the Bell Hotel in Bromley. Madeleine Sharp was tall, slim, and powerful. There were eight other little girls, who all hung on Madeleine's every word and jumped to obey (a) her instructions. Madeleine came over to Jill and said, "Right, let's see what Jill can do." Jill began with the classic first rule for all dancers: How to hold the bar. Madeleine Sharp said, "Never grip it, dear."

(B)

Madeleine put her arm round Jill, returned to Jill's mom and said, "I'd like to teach Jill very much. Can you come again on Friday?" They exchanged a few more words but Jill didn't hear a thing. Jill's head was too alive with the events of the afternoon and the thrilling new world before her. (b) She was barely conscious of her mom saying, "Hurry up, darling. Let's get home and tell your dad!" But as her voice woke Jill up, Jill put her arms round her mom.

(C)

So Jill's mom was extremely nervous while her daughter was dancing, especially as some of the other mothers stayed there to see how this new child was going to do. Jill got carried away with the music and flew around the room. After a minute or so Madeleine clapped her hands and Jill stopped in front of her, panting and looking up at (c) her, full of hope.

* pant: 숨을 헐떡이다

(D)

Madeleine firmly continued to say to Jill, "Rest your hand lightly on it. It is there to steady you, not as a lifeline. Turn your feet out. This must not be feet only, but start in the hips so that your whole leg is turned out. Good." Madeleine Sharp wanted to explore her possibilities as a dancer. So (d) she asked the pianist to play a lyrical piece of music and said, "Jill, dear, let me see you run and enjoy yourself and see what the music tells you to do." Jill didn't know it at the time, but Madeleine Sharp was highly regarded and entry to (e) her classes was quite competitive as a result.

26

24005-0252

주어진 글 (A)에 이어질 내용을 순서에 맞게 배열한 것으로 가장 적절한 것은?

① (B) – (D) – (C)   ② (C) – (B) – (D)   ③ (C) – (D) – (B)
④ (D) – (B) – (C)   ⑤ (D) – (C) – (B)

27

24005-0253

밑줄 친 (a)~(e) 중에서 가리키는 대상이 나머지 넷과 다른 것은?

① (a)   ② (b)   ③ (c)   ④ (d)   ⑤ (e)

28

24005-0254

윗글의 관한 내용으로 적절하지 않은 것은?

① Jill은 엄마와 함께 Madeleine Sharp 씨의 수업에 갔다.
② Madeleine Sharp는 Jill에게 바를 절대로 꽉 잡지 말라고 말했다.
③ Madeleine Sharp는 Jill의 엄마에게 금요일에 다시 올 수 있는지 물었다.
④ Jill의 엄마는 자신의 딸이 춤을 추는 동안 마음이 매우 편안했다.
⑤ Madeleine Sharp는 Jill의 댄서로서의 가능성을 살펴보고 싶었다.

한눈에 보는 정답

Part Ⅰ 유형편

	G	01	02	03	04	05	06	07	08	09	10	11	12
01	①	④	④	②	③								
02	①	④	⑤	③	①								
03	①	⑤	③	⑤	⑤								
04	⑤	③	①	③	②								
05	④	⑤	④	②	②								
06	②	④	⑤	⑤	⑤								
07	⑤	⑤	④	②	⑤								
08	④	⑤	⑤	⑤	④								
09	②	⑤	⑤	④	④								
10	③	④	④	③	④								
11	②	④	⑤	②	②								
12	④	⑤	④	⑤	⑤								
13	②	②	①	④	①	③	②	③	③	⑤	②	②	③
14	③	④	③	③	③								
15	④	⑤	③	①	③	②	⑤						
16	③	⑤	⑤	④	⑤	④	④						
17	①	①	①	②	④								
18	01 ② 02 ⑤	④	⑤	③	④	②	③	①	②				
19	01 ⑤ 02 ③ 03 ③	②	③	④	④	③	④	③	③	⑤	④	⑤	④

Part Ⅱ 주제·소재편

	G	01	02	03
20	④	③	①	⑤
21	④	②	④	⑤
22	①	④	②	④
23	⑤	③	⑤	④
24	④	④	⑤	③
25	⑤	②	②	⑤
26	④	⑤	⑤	②
27	①	④	③	②
28	④	⑤	④	④
29	③	⑤	③	④
30	④	①	①	③
31	⑤	⑤	②	④

Part Ⅲ 테스트편

Test 1	01	02	03	04	05	06	07	08	09	10
	⑤	⑤	③	②	④	⑤	②	②	⑤	④
	11	12	13	14	15	16	17	18	19	20
	④	⑤	⑤	③	④	①	⑤	④	②	③
	21	22	23	24	25	26	27	28		
	②	④	③	①	⑤	④	⑤	②		
Test 2	01	02	03	04	05	06	07	08	09	10
	①	②	②	⑤	⑤	⑤	②	②	③	④
	11	12	13	14	15	16	17	18	19	20
	⑤	④	⑤	③	③	①	①	④	①	③
	21	22	23	24	25	26	27	28		
	⑤	②	②	①	⑤	②	③	⑤		
Test 3	01	02	03	04	05	06	07	08	09	10
	③	④	③	⑤	⑤	⑤	①	②	⑤	⑤
	11	12	13	14	15	16	17	18	19	20
	⑤	④	⑤	②	①	②	③	④	③	③
	21	22	23	24	25	26	27	28		
	③	④	④	⑤	③	⑤	②	④		

문제를 사진 찍고
해설 강의 보기
Google Play | App Store

EBS*i* 사이트
무료 강의 제공

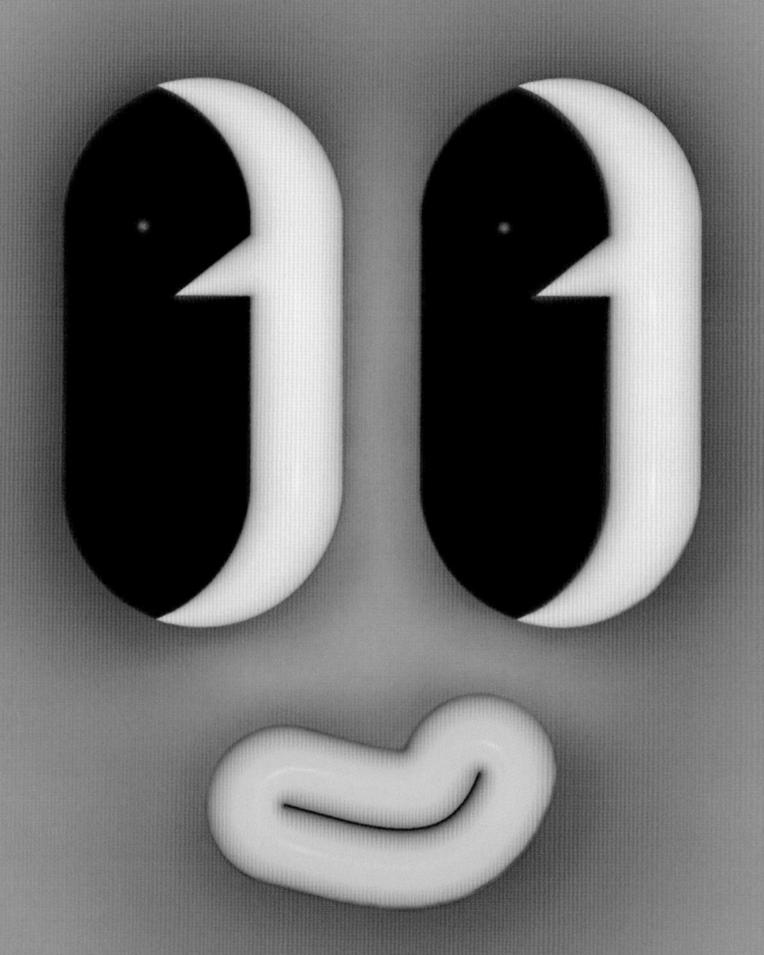

영단어·숙어

수능특강 | 영어영역 영어

2025학년도 수능 연계교재

본 교재는 대학수학능력시험을 준비하는 데 도움을 드리고자 영어과 교육과정을 토대로 제작된 교재입니다.
학교에서 선생님과 함께 교과서의 기본 개념을 충분히 익힌 후 활용하시면 더 큰 학습 효과를 얻을 수 있습니다.

수능특강

영어영역 **영어**

단어장

01 글의 목적 파악

본문 12~15쪽

01

□ in the air (어떤) 기운이 감도는
□ cottage 별장
□ expense 비용, 경비
□ maintain 유지하다
□ put ~ on the market ~을 시장에 내놓다
□ rental property 임대 부동산
□ lead 좋은 제의[정보]
□ unbooked 예약이 없는

02

□ engaging 재미있는, 매력적인
□ competitive 경쟁의
□ promising 전도유망한
□ constraint 제약, 제한

03

□ representative 담당자, 대표자
□ replacement 교체 상품, 교체물
□ prompt 신속한

04

□ administrative 행정의, 행정상의
□ maintenance 유지 관리
□ extend 연장하다
□ downtime (고장으로 인한) 작업 중단 시간
□ enclosed 동봉된
□ brochure 소책자
□ outline 개요를 기술하다

02 심경 · 분위기 파악

본문 18~19쪽

01

□ beaded 구슬이 달린
□ whisper 살랑거리다, 속삭이다; 살랑거리는 소리
□ anticipation 기대
□ bubble (감정이) 부풀다
□ roll 두루마리
□ letdown 낙담
□ fabric 직물, 천
□ pearl 진주
□ charming 매력적인

02

□ closet 벽장, 옷장
□ scale 음계
□ poem 시
□ gentle 부드러운, 온화한
□ brilliant 아주 멋진, 찬란한
□ breeze 산들바람
□ stillness 고요함
□ clap 박수를[손뼉을] 치다

03

□ warrior 전사
□ incredibly 엄청나게
□ relief 안도, 안심

04

□ cooperate 응하다, 협력하다
□ buzz 바쁘게 오가다, 윙윙거리다
□ stuffing (요리 속에 넣은) 소[속]
□ seasoning 양념
□ flavorful 풍미 가득한
□ sample 맛보다, 시식하다
□ indicate 가리키다, 보여 주다
□ roll 굴리다

□ when all is said and done 결국, 뭐니 뭐니 해도

□ discriminate 차별하다
□ incompetence 무능함
□ prejudiced 편견에 찬

04

□ rather than ~이 아닌
□ review 복기하다, 복습하다
□ merely 그저, 단지
□ literally 말 그대로
□ make up ~을 만들어 내다
□ old saying 옛말, 속담
□ recreate 재현하다, 되살리다
□ preview 미리 보다
□ to make matters worse 설상가상으로

03 요지 파악

본문 22~23쪽

01

□ misconception 오해
□ brilliant 기발한, 훌륭한
□ commercial 상업적인, 상업의
□ silver bullet 묘책, 특효약
□ exceedingly 매우, 극도로
□ generate 만들어 내다
□ click 성공하다, 잘 되다
□ bolt out of the blue 예상치 못하게 (난데없이) 발생하는 것

02

□ solar panel 태양 전지판
□ grocery 식료품
□ continuously 계속
□ exception 예외
□ alternative 대안

03

□ disability 장애
□ criterion 기준 (*pl.* criteria)
□ competence 능력
□ biased 편향된
□ in favor of ~에게 유리하게
□ sighted 앞을 볼 수 있는
□ competent 유능한
□ unfair 불공정한
□ definitely 분명히
□ by extension 더 나아가
□ appreciate 가치를 인정하다
□ unique 고유한, 독특한

04 주장 파악

본문 26~27쪽

01

□ equate 동일시하다
□ appreciation 인정, 감사
□ acknowledgement 감사, 인지
□ specific 구체적인
□ ensure 보장하다
□ mark 축하하다
□ milestone 획기적인 일

02

□ refer to ~을 일컫다[언급하다]
□ attribute 속성, 특성
□ civic 시민적인, 시민의
□ democratic 민주적인, 민주주의의
□ component (구성) 요소
□ press 언론

□ watchdog 감시자, 감시 단체
□ overemphasize 지나치게 강조하다

03

□ mend 고치다
□ fence 울타리
□ opponent 반대자, 반대편
□ strategize 전략을 세우다
□ mutually 서로, 상호 간에
□ consequently 따라서

04

□ management 관리
□ continuous 지속적인
□ separate 분리된
□ extract 채취하다, 추출하다
□ consume 소비하다
□ dump 버리다
□ finite 유한한
□ ecosystem 생태계
□ absorb 흡수하다
□ properly 제대로
□ constant 끊임없는
□ ecological 생태학적인
□ impossibility 불가능성

05 함축적 의미 파악

본문 30~33쪽

01

□ compromise 타협, 절충
□ sustainability (환경의) 지속 가능성
□ societal 사회의
□ boundary 경계
□ rescue 구조

02

□ corporation 기업
□ status 신분, 지위
□ criterion 기준
□ contract 계약
□ summarize 요약하다
□ exclusively 오로지
□ advancement (경제적) 성공, 향상, 발전
□ emphasis 강조
□ rebellion 반란
□ define 정의하다
□ in terms of ~의 관점에서, ~의 측면에서
□ deny 부정하다, 부여하지 않다
□ establish 확립하다
□ fulfillment 성취
□ majority 다수

03

□ material 재료, 자재, 직물
□ circulate 순환되다
□ crucial 매우 중요한
□ highlight 강조하다
□ landfill 매립지
□ stuffing 충전재
□ loop 루프, 고리
□ complexity 복잡성
□ leak 누출되다
□ environmental footprint 환경(에 악영향을 미치는) 발자국
□ secondhand 중고의
□ implication 영향, 함축
□ transport 운송하다

04

□ anticipate 예견하다, 예상하다
□ forecast 예측하다
□ practically 실제로
□ immediate 즉각적인

□ fulfill 이행하다
□ strict 가혹한
□ compel 강요하다
□ burst forth into 갑자기 ~하기 시작하다
□ blossom 꽃을 피우다
□ application 이용, 적용
□ artificial 인공적인
□ abuse 남용하다
□ loan 대출금, 융자금

06 주제 파악

본문 36~37쪽

01

□ disturbing 불안한, 어지럽히는
□ underway 진행 중인
□ funding 재정 지원, 자금 제공
□ standardized test 표준화 시험
□ primarily 주로
□ evaluate 평가하다
□ inevitably 필연적으로, 불가피하게
□ struggling 힘겨워하는, 분투하는
□ challenge 장려하다, 북돋우다
□ incorporate 포함하다, 통합하다
□ hands-on 체험하는
□ be engaged in ~에 참여하다
□ uninspiring 흥미를 주지 않는
□ workbook 워크북, 학습장
□ drill 반복 학습, 훈련
□ retain 기억하다, 간직하다

02

□ neuron 뉴런, 신경 세포
□ in terms of ~이라는 측면에서
□ steady 꾸준한
□ twilight 황혼기, 황혼
□ navigation 주행, 운항
□ chaotic 혼잡한, 혼란스러운

03

□ ideological 이념의
□ institution 제도
□ block 막다
□ nationalism 내셔널리즘, 민족주의
□ fundamentalism 근본주의
□ prohibit 금지하다
□ payment 지불(금)
□ loan 대출
□ profit 이익
□ enterprise 기업, 대규모 사업
□ obstacle 걸림돌, 장애(물)
□ board of directors 이사회
□ advisory committee 자문 위원회
□ petroleum 석유
□ contract 계약(서)
□ ownership 소유(권)
□ transfer 이전하다
□ well 유정(油井)

04

□ assumption 가정
□ associated 관련된
□ sustainability 지속 가능성
□ era 시대
□ to the extent that ~인 점에서
□ reverse 되돌리다
□ endangered 멸종 위기의
□ linear 선형의
□ flawed 결함이 있는
□ incorporate 통합하다
□ contextual 맥락적인
□ socio-ecological 사회 생태학적인
□ reassess 재평가하다

07 제목 파악

본문 40~43쪽

01

□ bureau	(관청의) 국(局), 부서
□ anthropology	인류학
□ end up	결국 ~하게 되다
□ spoiled	(음식물이) 상한
□ expiration date	유통 기한
□ statistic	통계
□ while we're at it	기왕 말 나온 김에
□ produce	농산물
□ overbuy	과도하게 사다
□ estimate	추정하다
□ outdated	오래된, 구식의
□ leftover	남은 음식
□ be in view	눈에 띄는 곳에 있다
□ use up	~을 다 써 버리다

02

□ double-edged sword	양날의 검
□ establish	확립하다
□ multiple	다수의
□ hypothesis	가설 (*pl.* hypotheses)
□ be credited with	~의 공이 있다고 여겨지다
□ imply	암시하다
□ partial	부분적인
□ circulate	유통하다
□ discredit	신빙성을 떨어뜨리다

03

□ ideally	이상적으로
□ engage in	~을 하다, ~에 참여[종사]하다
□ recognize	인정하다
□ challenging	어려운
□ solitary	혼자 하는
□ reflective	성찰적인
□ resolve	해결하다
□ address	해결하다
□ agency	주체성
□ validate	검증하다, 승인하다

04

□ inclined	경사진, 기운
□ plane	면, 평면
□ calculate	계산하다
□ come up with	~을 생각해 내다
□ equation	방정식
□ numerical	수의, 숫자로 나타낸
□ quantity	양, 수량
□ moon	(행성의 주위를 도는) 위성
□ compute	산출하다, 계산하다
□ apparent position	시위치(지구에서 볼 때, 천구(天球) 안에 놓이는 천체들의 겉보기 위치)
□ be consistent with	~과 일치하다
□ hypothetical	가상의, 가설의
□ budding	신예의, 신진의

08 도표 정보 파악

본문 46~49쪽

01

□ annual	연간의, 한 해의
□ retail	소매(의)
□ in terms of	~ 면에서는, ~에 관해서는
□ top the list	1위를 차지하다

02

□ domestic	국내의
□ as of	~ 현재
□ combine	합치다
□ the latter	후자
□ the former	전자

03

- □ frequently 자주, 빈번히
- □ survey 설문 조사
- □ proportion 비율

04

- □ device 기기, 장비
- □ income 수입
- □ distribution 분포
- □ prefer 선호하다
- □ common 흔한
- □ vary 다르다, 다양하다

09 내용 일치 · 불일치(설명문)

본문 52~53쪽

01

- □ naval 해군의
- □ significant 중요한
- □ contribution 기여
- □ PhD 박사 학위 (= Doctor of Philosophy)
- □ distance-learning 원격 교육

02

- □ originate in ~에서 유래하다
- □ accompany 반주[연주]하다, 동반하다
- □ longing 갈망
- □ upbeat 경쾌한, 낙관적인
- □ district 구역
- □ flourish 번성하다
- □ fall out of favour 인기가 떨어지다, 총애를 잃다
- □ revolution 혁명
- □ revive 부활시키다
- □ generation 세대

03

- □ object 목표, 목적
- □ solid 단단한, 고체의
- □ rubber 고무
- □ leather 가죽
- □ elbow 팔꿈치
- □ spectator 관중, 관객
- □ bet 내기를 하다

04

- □ prominent 저명한, 유명한
- □ sculptor 조각가
- □ reportedly 전하는 바에 따르면
- □ bronze 청동
- □ suitably 당연히, 적절하게
- □ portrait 초상, 초상화
- □ successor 후계자
- □ relate 말하다, 설명하다
- □ displace 대체하다

10 내용 일치 · 불일치(실용문)

본문 56~59쪽

01

- □ renovation 보수 공사
- □ notice 공지
- □ extension 연장
- □ extend 연장하다
- □ 24/7 연중무휴, 일주일 내내 24시간 동안

02

- □ craft 공예
- □ interact 교류하다

□ registration 등록
□ faculty or staff member 교직원

03

□ explore 탐험하다
□ comfortable 편안한
□ sack lunch 점심 도시락
□ beverage 마실 것
□ investigator 조사관
□ detail 세부 사항, 세부 정보
□ complete 전체의, 전부의
□ accept 받아 주다
□ contact 연락하다

04

□ auditorium 강당
□ application 신청서

11 어법 정확성 파악

본문 62~63쪽

01

□ metaphor 은유, 비유
□ imitate 모방하다
□ command 명령어, 명령
□ arrangement 배열
□ browser 브라우저(인터넷의 자료들을 읽을 수 있게 해 주는 프로그램)
□ folder (일부 컴퓨터 시스템에서 파일 보관용) 폴더
□ slip (재빨리 슬며시) 넣다, 놓다
□ gaze at ~을 응시하다[바라보다]
□ storefront 상점, 점포, 가게 앞
□ linguistic 언어적인, 언어의
□ struggle 애쓰다, 분투하다

02

□ landscape 자연 경관, 경치
□ vegetation 초목
□ hold ~ in place ~을 제자리에 고정하다
□ estimate 추정하다
□ artificially 인위적으로
□ downfall 몰락
□ degrade 악화시키다
□ productive 생산적인
□ disastrous 재앙의
□ device 방법, 장치, 기기
□ terrace 계단식으로 만들다
□ keep from ~을 못하게 막다
□ fertile 비옥한

03

□ caveman 원시인, 동굴 거주자
□ completely 완전히
□ reputation 평판, 명성
□ fossil 화석
□ injured 다친, 상처를 입은
□ approximately 대략
□ erect 직립한
□ skull 두개골
□ alter 개조하다, 바꾸다
□ shelter 주거지
□ settle 자리 잡다

04

□ discrimination 차별
□ occur 발생하다
□ institutional 제도적인
□ discriminatory 차별적인
□ covert 은밀한
□ invisibility 보이지 않는 특성
□ detect 감지하다, 발견하다

□ exclude 차단하다, 배제하다
□ establish 정하다, 마련하다
□ biased 편향된
□ disproportionate 균형이 맞지 않는
□ generational 세대의, 세대 간의
□ cyclical 순환적인, 주기적인
□ consequence 결과
□ if not more so 어쩌면 그보다 더

12 어휘 적절성 파악

본문 66~67쪽

01

□ stimulus 자극 (*pl.* stimuli)
□ tendency 경향
□ stamp in ~에 새겨 넣다
□ promote 촉진하다
□ bond 유대, 끈
□ program 길들이다, 조정하다
□ opposite 정반대의
□ constant 끊임없는
□ turnover 전복, 전환
□ automatically 자연히
□ adjust 적응하다

02

□ recognize 인식하다
□ opinion 의견
□ prevent 방지하다, 막다
□ independent 독립적인
□ impartial 공정한
□ obey 복종하다
□ consult 상의하다
□ devil's advocate 악마의 변호인((열띤 논의가 이뤄지도록) 일부러 반대 입장을 취하는 사람)
□ alternative 대안의
□ rational 합리적인
□ retain 유지하다
□ conformity 순응
□ obedience 복종

03

□ alternative 새로운, 대안적인
□ essentially 본질적으로
□ circumstance 상황
□ generate 만들어 내다
□ considerably 상당히
□ conflict 갈등

04

□ definition 정의
□ fluid 유동적인
□ retain (정보를) 기억하다, 잊지 않고 있다
□ retention (정보의) 기억
□ critical 비판적인
□ receptacle (내용물을 담는) 용기, 그릇
□ blank slate 백지상태
□ squarely 분명하게, 정면으로

13 빈칸 내용 추론

본문 70~79쪽

01

□ self-esteem 자존감, 자부심
□ considerable 상당한, 적지 않은
□ route 길, 방법
□ undeniable 부인할 수 없는, 명백한
□ immaturity 미성숙(함), 미발달
□ resolution 해답, 결의
□ verbally 말로, 구두로
□ thereby 그렇게 함으로써, 그것에 의하여

□ pro– ~에 친화적인, ~을 지지하는
□ set the stage for ~을 위한 장(場)을 마련하다

02
□ get the word out 입소문을 퍼뜨리다
□ established 자리를 잡은
□ promote 홍보하다
□ freezer 냉동고
□ refrigerator 냉장고
□ significant 상당한

03
□ tightly 엄격하게
□ regulate 통제[규제]하다
□ stick with ~을 계속하다
□ challenging 도전적인, 힘든
□ take over ~을 인계받다
□ bark out ~을 큰 소리로 외치다
□ instruction 지시 사항
□ content 만족한
□ explore 탐색하다
□ encouragement 격려
□ be apt to *do* ~하는 경향이 있다
□ figure out ~을 알아내다

04
□ critical 중요한
□ mutual 상호의, 서로의
□ provision 공급
□ keep track of ~을 파악하다
□ permanent 영구적인
□ shelter 거처, 주거
□ durable 영속성 있는
□ oppress 억압하다
□ undermine 해치다, 서서히 약화시키다
□ ingenuity 창의력
□ at the expense of ~을 희생하면서
□ rebellion 반란
□ repression 억압

05
□ medium 매체
□ content 콘텐츠
□ convey 전달하다
□ interact 상호 작용하다
□ distancing 거리 두기
□ implication 영향
□ constant 지속적인
□ assert 주장하다
□ neglect 게을리하다
□ observation 소견, 의견, 관찰

06
□ appealing 매력적인
□ restrict 제한하다
□ energy-efficient 에너지 효율이 높은
□ circumstance 상황
□ expansion 팽창, 확장
□ transformation 변혁

07
□ infinitely 무한히
□ variable 가변적인
□ variability 가변성
□ take place 발생하다
□ boundary 한계, 경계
□ capacity 능력
□ tremendously 엄청나게
□ semantics 의미, 의미론
□ uniquely 고유하게
□ predisposition 성향, 기질
□ range 범위
□ extend 펼쳐지다, 확장하다
□ click 흡착음, 딸깍 소리
□ pop 파열음, 터지는 소리
□ distinctive 특유의, 특이한

□ fraction 일부, 부분
□ disgust 혐오
□ determine 결정하다
□ perceive 인식하다
□ universal 보편적인

08

□ active ingredient 유효 성분(어떤 제품에 함유되어 있는 주가 되는 성분 물질)
□ discover 알아내다
□ devise 고안하다
□ hypothesis 가설
□ presence 존재
□ absence 부재

09

□ paradoxical 역설적인
□ intermediary 중개자
□ exploit 이용하다, 착취하다
□ tailor (특정한 목적 · 사람 등에) 맞추다[조정하다]
□ amplify 증폭시키다
□ inherent 내재한, 고유의
□ prompt 자극하다, 부추기다
□ compelling 흥미로운, 강력한
□ prioritize 우선순위를 차지하다
□ distort 왜곡하다
□ accelerate 가속하다
□ era 시대
□ alter 바꾸다
□ map 배치하다

10

□ coincidence 우연(의 일치)
□ make-up 화장
□ come of age 성년이 되다
□ for real 진짜의
□ hold ~ in high regard ~을 깊이 존경하다
□ compliment 찬사, 칭찬(의 말)
□ package 포장물, 꾸러미

11

□ paradoxical 역설적인
□ undergo 겪다
□ characteristic 특성

12

□ executive (기업 등의) 경영 간부, 이사
□ consumer 소비자
□ advertiser 광고주
□ content 콘텐츠
□ remove 삭제하다, 제거하다
□ convince 설득하다
□ substantial 상당한
□ portion 부분
□ rural 시골의
□ protest 항의하다
□ portrayal 묘사
□ favorably 호의적으로
□ upscale 고소득의

14 흐름에 무관한 문장 찾기

본문 82~83쪽

01

□ Impressionist 인상파 화가[예술가]
□ objective 객관적인
□ sincere 진실한
□ aim to *do* ~하는 것을 목표로 삼다
□ sensation 감각
□ regard 응시하다, 눈여겨보다
□ up-to-date 현대적인
□ originally 원래

□ standing	지위
□ craftsman	장인
□ emphasis	강조
□ narrative	서사적인
□ isolated	고립된

02

□ assess	가늠[판단]하다
□ collaborative	협력하는
□ weigh	따져 보다, 저울질하다
□ relative to	~과 비교하여
□ persistence	지속성
□ situated	위치한
□ preferential	우선적인
□ access	이용, 접근
□ instinct	본능
□ reproduction	번식, 생식
□ likelihood	가능성
□ yield	산출[생산]하다
□ cease	중단하다
□ thrill	짜릿함, 전율

03

□ mechanisation	기계화
□ vertical	수직의
□ exceed	넘다, 초과하다
□ storey	층
□ lock	고정시키다, 잠그다
□ in place	제자리에 (있는)
□ debut	첫선, 데뷔
□ sensation	돌풍(을 일으키는 것)
□ exposition	박람회
□ basement	지하층
□ iconic	상징적인

04

□ dialog	다이얼로그(연극이나 영화에서, 인물들 사이에 이루어지는 대화)
□ prior to	~ 이전에
□ vocal	말이 많은
□ cast	출연진
□ pioneer	주창하다, 개척하다
□ phenomenon	현상
□ unfold	펼치다
□ unaware of	~을 의식하지 않는

15 문단 내 글의 순서 파악하기

본문 86~91쪽

01

□ macro	거시적인
□ alternative	대안의
□ emerge	대두하다, 출현하다
□ question	의문을 제기하다
□ assumption	가정
□ prejudice	편견
□ essentialist	본질주의적인
□ stable	안정된
□ reconstruct	재구성하다
□ as such	따라서
□ awareness	인식
□ feature	특징
□ unite	결속[통합]시키다
□ capture	포착하다
□ analysis	분석

02

□ atomic bomb	원자 폭탄
□ commission	위원회
□ survivor	생존자
□ urge	촉구하다
□ maintain	주장하다
□ invaluable	매우 귀중한
□ impress	(중요성·심각성 등을 강조하여) 이해시키다

□ permanently 영구적으로
□ encounter 만남, 조우

03

□ accept 받아들이다
□ definition 정의
□ justified 정당화된, 정당한 이유가 있는
□ satisfactory 만족스러운
□ explanation 설명
□ come up with ~을 제시하다
□ instinctively 본능적으로
□ arrange 약속하다
□ prompt 유도하다, 촉발하다
□ cast doubt on ~에 의문을 제기하다, ~을 의심하다
□ identical twin 일란성 쌍둥이

04

□ ethical 윤리적인
□ soundness 건전성, 견실성
□ outline 개요를 설명하다, 윤곽을 그리다
□ thought experiment 사고 실험

05

□ evolve 진화시키다
□ strategy 전략
□ be aware of ~을 의식하다
□ consciousness 의식, 인식
□ organism 유기체
□ a host of 다수의
□ mechanism 기제, 방법
□ inevitable 불가피한, 필연적인
□ virtually 거의, 사실상
□ involvement 개입
□ reflect on ~을 숙고하다
□ speculate 짐작하다, 추측하다
□ essentially 본질적으로
□ autonomy 자율성
□ progressive 점차적인, 점진적인

06

□ urbanism 도시화, 도시 계획
□ expertise 전문 지식
□ administrative 행정의, 관리상의
□ degree 학위
□ expand 확대하다
□ fulfillment 성취, 달성
□ fuel 자극하다
□ occupational 직업의
□ discipline 분야, 학문
□ pose (문제를) 제기하다

16 주어진 문장의 적합한 위치 찾기

본문 94~97쪽

01

□ encounter 마주치다
□ assign 배정하다
□ specialized 전문의, 특화된
□ legislature 의회, 입법부
□ court 법원, 법정
□ reference 참조, 참고
□ obstacle 장애물
□ source 취재원, 정보원, 출처

02

□ variation 차이, 변화
□ intragroup 집단 내의
□ commonality 공통성
□ diversity 다양성
□ flexibly 유연하게
□ social suite 사회성 모둠
□ underlying 근본적인
□ universality 보편성
□ evolutionary 진화의
□ fanciful 기발한

□ alien 외계인
□ jukebox 주크박스(동전을 넣고 곡을 지정하면 저절로 음악이 나오는 장치)
□ illustrate 보여 주다, 실증하다

03

□ discipline 단련[훈련]시키다
□ track record 실적
□ predictor 예측 변수
□ constantly 끊임없이
□ redefine 재정의하다
□ handicap 불리한 조건
□ challenge 힘든 일
□ alternative 대안
□ current 현재의

04

□ biomedical 생물 의학의
□ pill 알약
□ tablet 정제
□ deemphasize 강조하지 않다, 경시하다
□ stimulate 자극하다
□ overwhelm 압도하다, 제압하다
□ aromatherapy 방향 요법
□ emerge 부상하다
□ alternative 대체의
□ advertise 광고하다, 선전하다
□ consumer 소비자
□ distinguish 구분하다
□ edible 먹을 수 있는
□ herbal medicine 한약, 한방약
□ odor 냄새, 향기
□ essence 진액, 에센스

05

□ when it comes to ~과 관련하여
□ peer 또래
□ engage in ~을 하다, ~에 참여하다
□ concerning ~과 관련하여
□ financial 재정적인
□ occupation 직업
□ be inclined to *do* ~하는 경향이 있다
□ reflect 반영하다
□ place importance on ~을 중요시하다
□ look to ~ for ... …을 ~에게 기대하다
□ approval 승인
□ as opposed to ~이 아니라
□ reliance 의존
□ conformity 순응
□ at the expense of ~을 희생하면서
□ individuality 개성

06

□ immediately 즉각적으로
□ admittedly 물론, 틀림없이
□ stimulation 자극
□ come in handy 유용하다, 쓸모가 있다
□ mediate 매개하다, 중재하다
□ reproduce 재현하다, 재생산하다
□ virtual 가상의
□ presence 존재
□ numerous 수많은
□ perception 지각
□ occupational 직업상의

17 문단 요약하기

본문 100~103쪽

01

□ tempting 하고 싶은 마음이 드는, 유혹하는
□ embody 담다, 구현하다
□ empowerment 자율권, 권한 부여
□ progressive 진보적인

□ be committed to ~에 매진하다
□ make a statement 자신의 생각을 표현하다
□ embrace 수용하다, 받아들이다

02

□ comparative 비교의
□ full-blown 완전한
□ comprehend 이해하다
□ notably 특히, 눈에 띄게
□ ape 유인원
□ spontaneously 자발적으로
□ apparently 분명히
□ infrastructure 토대, 기초 조직
□ prosocial 친사회적인
□ foundation 출발점, 토대, 재단
□ alternative 대안
□ capacity 능력
□ shared intentionality 지향점 공유
□ deceptively 놀랄 정도로, 믿을 수 없게

03

□ keen 열망하는
□ experiment 실험
□ collaborative 협력적인
□ bother to *do* ~하려고 애쓰다
□ generous 관대한
□ treat 간식
□ mood 기분
□ observation 관찰

04

□ purposeful 의도적인
□ situational 상황에 따른
□ mediate 조정[중재]하다
□ disposition 성향
□ actualize 실현하다
□ characterize 특징짓다
□ attitude 태도
□ normative 규범적인
□ component 요소
□ consequence 결과

18 장문 독해 (1)

본문 106~109쪽

01~02

□ common sense 상식
□ naive realism 소박실재론
□ precisely 바로, 정확히
□ intuitive 직관적인
□ perception 인식
□ uncontrollably 통제할 수 없게
□ appearance 겉모습
□ revolve 돌다, 회전하다
□ obvious 명백한
□ when it comes to ~에 관한 한
□ evaluate 평가하다
□ virtually 거의, 사실상
□ assure 확신시키다, 장담하다
□ biased 편향된
□ objective 객관적인
□ reverse 반대, 역

03~04

□ gratitude 감사
□ negativity 부정적인 것
□ definition 정의
□ give credit to ~에게 공로를 돌리다
□ humble 자신을 낮추다, 겸손하게 만들다
□ generosity 관대함, 너그러움
□ stir up ~을 불러일으키다
□ obligation 의무
□ grateful 감사하는

- □ perceive 인식하다, 지각하다
- □ bear out ~을 실증하다, ~을 뒷받침하다
- □ tension 긴장(감)
- □ magnify 크게 하다, 확대하다
- □ denial 부인, 부정, 거부
- □ journal 일기, 일지

05~06

- □ adaptable 적응력이 뛰어난
- □ instructive 시사하는 바가 큰, 유익한
- □ troop 무리
- □ dominate 지배하다
- □ aggressive 공격적인
- □ undergo 겪다
- □ widespread 만연한
- □ bullying 괴롭힘
- □ resolve 해결하다
- □ pick on ~을 괴롭히다
- □ acculturate (다른 문화에) 동화시키다
- □ norm 규범
- □ obviously 분명, 명백히
- □ premodern 전근대의
- □ worship 숭배하다
- □ medieval 중세의
- □ peasant 농민, 소작농
- □ divine 신성한
- □ lord 영주
- □ democracy 민주주의
- □ corporate 기업(의)
- □ contract 계약
- □ complexity 복잡성
- □ the other way around 그 반대

07~08

- □ insecurely 불안정하게
- □ implement 구현하다, 시행하다
- □ present 야기하다, 겪게 하다
- □ installation 설치
- □ administration 관리, 시행
- □ improperly 부적절하게
- □ adversely 불리하게, 반대로
- □ due ~으로 인한, 적절한, 마땅한
- □ inadequate 부적절한
- □ documentation 문서화
- □ feature 기능, 특징
- □ methodologically 방법론적으로
- □ precaution 예방 조치
- □ side-effect 부작용
- □ explorative 탐색적인
- □ attachment 첨부 파일, 부착물
- □ mislead 오도하다, 잘못 안내하다
- □ primarily 주로
- □ bypass 건너뛰다, 우회하다

19 장문 독해 (2)

본문 112~119쪽

01~03

- □ striving 노력하는, 애쓰는
- □ score (성공 등을) 얻다[거두다]
- □ energetically 열정적으로
- □ take ~ up on the offer 제안을 수락하다
- □ aspiring 장차 ~이 되려는
- □ A-lister 특급 배우, 대단히 인기 있는 사람
- □ reluctant 주저하는, 머뭇거리는
- □ fierce 치열한
- □ wholeheartedly 진심으로, 성실하게

04~06

- □ faithful 충실한
- □ passer-by 행인
- □ in question 문제의
- □ sorrow 슬픔

- □ distinguished 기품[위엄] 있는
- □ marvelous 놀라운
- □ contents 내용물
- □ uncovered 모자를 벗은
- □ instrument 악기
- □ disappear 사라지다
- □ turn ~ to account ~을 이용[활용]하다
- □ proceeds 수익금
- □ compassionately 연민 어린 눈으로
- □ limb 팔다리

07~09

- □ district 지역, 구역
- □ front line 최전선
- □ attack 공격하다
- □ crush 탄압하다, 진압하다
- □ recruit 신병
- □ resistance 저항 운동
- □ sympathy 연민
- □ adopt 입양하다
- □ desperate 절망적인
- □ measure 한계, 한도
- □ proper 제대로 된

10~12

- □ soak up ~을 빨아들이다
- □ beat 두드리다, 때리다
- □ bang (세게) 두드리다
- □ arrangement 합의, 조정
- □ approach 다가가다
- □ refuse 거부하다, 거절하다
- □ annoying 짜증스러운
- □ concept 개념
- □ intrinsic 내재의, 본래 갖추고 있는
- □ motivation 동기 부여, 동기
- □ reinforcement 강화
- □ theory 이론
- □ compliment 칭찬하다
- □ accept 수락하다

20 인물, 일화, 기담

본문 124~125쪽

01

- □ vividly 생생하게
- □ reputation 명성, 평판
- □ extraordinary 놀라운, 비범한
- □ playwright 극작가
- □ talking picture 발성 영화
- □ vigor 활력, 활기
- □ adaptation 각색(한 작품)
- □ theatrical 연극의
- □ devote oneself to ~에 전념하다
- □ exclusively 오로지 ~만
- □ dramatist 극작가
- □ controversially 논쟁적으로
- □ short-lived 단명한
- □ critical review 비평지, 평론지
- □ entitled ~(이)라는 제목의

02

- □ be sold out (표 등이) 매진되다
- □ Bach cello suites 바흐의 첼로 모음곡
- □ soloist 독주자, 단독 공연자
- □ admire 높이 평가하다, 존경하다
- □ sum 합

03

- □ botanist 식물학자
- □ spiritual 영적인
- □ brief 짧은
- □ insert 끼워 넣다, 삽입하다
- □ redirect 새로운 방향으로 돌려놓다
- □ terminate 종료하다
- □ prior 이전의
- □ persistence 끈기
- □ exhausting 진을 빼는, 기진맥진하게 만드는
- □ excuse oneself 자리를 뜨다
- □ transform 변화[변모]시키다
- □ vacation 휴가를 보내다
- □ estate 저택, 사유지
- □ track ~ down ~을 추적하다
- □ intense 열성적인, 진지한
- □ excitable 흥분을 잘하는, 감정적인
- □ beard 턱수염
- □ rival 필적하다
- □ idol 우상

21 철학, 종교, 역사, 풍습, 지리

본문 128~129쪽

01

- □ uncontroversially 논란의 여지없이
- □ consensus 합의
- □ considerable 상당한
- □ overlap 겹침
- □ tempting 솔깃한, 유혹적인
- □ absolute 절대적인
- □ morality 도덕(성)
- □ relative 상대적인, 관련되어 있는
- □ acceptable 용인되는
- □ relativism 상대주의
- □ description 설명, 기술
- □ meta-ethical 메타 윤리적인(윤리학의 본질에 대한)

02

- □ geography 지형
- □ entirety 전체
- □ extension 연장, 확대
- □ strikingly 눈에 띄게
- □ territory 지역, 지형
- □ mountain-dominated 산악 지대가 많은
- □ navigable 배가 다닐 수 있는
- □ fertile 비옥한
- □ much less ~은 말할 것도 없고

□ fastness 요새
□ unified 통일된
□ collage (여러 가지 것들의) 모음, 콜라주
□ power broker 실세, 유력 인사
□ align with ~과 손을 잡다, ~과 동조하다
□ in vain 헛되이
□ stitch together ~을 만들어 내다, ~을 봉합하다
□ capital-intensive 자본 집약적인

03

□ constitute 구성하다, 이루다
□ fresh 담수의, 신선한
□ glacier 빙하
□ polar 극지방의
□ antiquity 태고 (시대), 고대
□ venture 모험하다, 과감히 ~하다
□ surface 표면
□ extensive 광활한
□ wilderness 황량한 지역, 황무지
□ groundwater 지하수
□ atmosphere 대기

22 환경, 자원, 재활용

본문 132~133쪽

01

□ demographics 인구 통계
□ fabric 구조
□ consideration 고려 사항
□ appealing 매력적인
□ equate 동일시하다
□ efficiency 효율성
□ solar panel 태양 전지판
□ countertop 조리대 상판
□ property 부동산

02

□ underlying 근본적인
□ charged 격론을 불러일으키는
□ divisive 분열을 초래하는
□ racism 인종 차별
□ disproportionate 불균형적인
□ impact 영향
□ accommodate 수용하다

03

□ charismatic 카리스마 넘치는
□ overfish 물고기를 남획하다
□ endangered 멸종 위기에 처한
□ conscious 의식하는
□ celebrity 유명인
□ stardom 스타덤, 스타의 지위[신분]
□ conservation 보존

23 물리, 화학, 생명과학, 지구과학

본문 136~137쪽

01

□ specific 특정한
□ extent 정도
□ adaptation 적응 (형태)
□ predator 포식자
□ compact 작은, 소형의
□ body plan 몸의 구조
□ omnivore 잡식성 동물

02

□ crawl about 이리저리 기어다니다
□ sucker-covered 빨판으로 덮인
□ refuge 피신, 도피
□ deposit 놓다, 두다

- □ inedible 먹을 수 없는
- □ tend 돌보다
- □ emerge 나오다, 모습을 드러내다

03

- □ minute 미세한
- □ angle 각도
- □ magnify 크게 하다, 확대하다
- □ a fraction of a second 순식간
- □ arrangement 배열
- □ variation 변화

- □ composition 구성
- □ concentration 농도
- □ work up ~을 북돋우다, 불러일으키다

03

- □ recognize 인식하다
- □ comfort 편안함
- □ satisfaction 만족감
- □ transition 변화
- □ dip pen 잉크를 찍어 쓰는 펜
- □ lend (어떤 특징을) 부여하다

24 스포츠, 레저, 취미, 여행

본문 140~141쪽

01

- □ spectator 관중, 관객
- □ drive 추동, 동인
- □ arousal 각성, 환기
- □ heighten 고조시키다
- □ presume 추정하다, 간주하다
- □ facilitate 용이하게 하다
- □ interfere with ~을 방해하다
- □ emission 방출
- □ dominant 지배적인
- □ stand to *do* ~할 것이다
- □ abundance 다수, 과다
- □ onlooker 관중, 구경꾼

02

- □ athlete 운동선수
- □ nutrient 영양소, 영양분
- □ macronutrient 다량 영양소
- □ optimally 최적으로
- □ sufficient 충분한

25 음악, 미술, 영화, 무용, 사진, 건축

본문 144~145쪽

01

- □ inescapable 피할 수 없는
- □ acquire 습득하다, 얻다
- □ discomfort 고통, 불편
- □ incentive 동기, 자극
- □ distress 고통
- □ catalog 분류하다
- □ inquiry 탐구
- □ ignore 무시하다
- □ overlook 간과하다

02

- □ Oval Office (백악관의) 대통령 집무실
- □ enormous 엄청난, 막대한
- □ architectural 건축의
- □ appropriateness 적합성
- □ aesthetics 미학
- □ component 요소
- □ incidentally 덧붙여 말하자면
- □ bowed 굽은

03

- □ on the road 이리저리 옮겨 다니는
- □ curate 예술 작품을 선별하여 전시 구성을 하다
- □ commission (미술 · 음악 작품 등을) 의뢰하다
- □ initiative 주도권
- □ exposure 전시, 진열
- □ at the expense of ~을 희생하면서
- □ relevant 적절한
- □ mission statement (기업 · 조직의) 강령

26 교육, 학교, 진로

본문 148~149쪽

01

- □ significant 중요한
- □ arise 발생하다
- □ terrific 아주 잘하는
- □ immediately 즉시
- □ figure out ~을 파악하다
- □ ignorant 무지한
- □ aptitude 적성, 소질
- □ specific 특정한
- □ beforehand 사전에, 미리
- □ content 내용
- □ factor 요소, 요인
- □ present 제공하다
- □ hands-on 실습의, 직접 해 보는

02

- □ implication 함의
- □ reward 보상하다; 보상
- □ maximum 최대의
- □ principle 원칙
- □ violate 위배하다, 위반하다
- □ circumstance 상황, 환경
- □ progress 진전, 진보
- □ composition 작문
- □ exceed 뛰어넘다
- □ performance 성과

03

- □ capability 능력
- □ abstract 추상적인
- □ perspective 관점
- □ mark (어떤 것의 전형적인 특징이나 특성에) 해당하다
- □ conscious 의식적인
- □ now-pressing 당장 시급한
- □ conflict 갈등
- □ define 정의하다
- □ stage 시기, 단계
- □ confusion 혼란
- □ refer to ~을 말하다
- □ drive 욕구, 동기
- □ consistent 일관성 있는
- □ confront 직면하다
- □ construct 구축하다
- □ firm 확고한
- □ infancy 유아기
- □ deliberate 신중한
- □ commitment 헌신, 전념
- □ integrate 통합하다
- □ threaten 우려가 있다, 조짐이 있다

27 언어, 문학, 문화

본문 152~153쪽

01

- □ assumption 가정
- □ three-dimensional 3차원의
- □ relative 상대적인
- □ direction 방향
- □ universal 보편적인

□ reexamine 재검토하다
□ description 설명
□ correlate with ~과 연관되다
□ distinct 뚜렷이 다른
□ cognitive 인지적인, 인지의
□ tendency 성향
□ specifically 구체적으로
□ vary 각기 다르다
□ concept 개념
□ determine 결정하다
□ category 범주
□ term 용어
□ correspond to ~에 해당하다
□ reference 준거, 기준, 참조
□ extend 확장하다

02

□ previously 이전에
□ correspond to ~과 부합하다, ~과 일치하다
□ adverb 부사
□ adjective 형용사
□ pronoun 대명사
□ as to ~에서, ~에 관해
□ sequence 순서
□ particular 특정한
□ vary 다르다, 다양하다
□ ordering 순서
□ crucially 결정적으로
□ identical 동일한
□ concept 개념
□ translate 번역하다
□ effectively 효과적으로

03

□ manipulate 능숙하게 다루다, 조작하다
□ cite 언급하다
□ figure 인물
□ reputation 명성
□ contradictory 모순되는

□ substance 실체, 본질, 요지
□ interpretation 해석
□ inclusion 포함시킴
□ implicit 암묵적인

28 컴퓨터, 인터넷, 정보, 미디어, 교통

본문 156~157쪽

01

□ biased 편향된
□ ethnicity 민족
□ overrepresented 과도하게 대표된
□ equalizer 균형추, 평등하게 만드는 것
□ automated 자동화된
□ encode 부호화하다, 표현하다
□ bake in ~을 내재하게 하다[포함하다]
□ enhance 향상하다
□ make sure ~을 확실하게 하다
□ optimize 최적화하다

02

□ wearable 웨어러블 기기
□ assistant 보조자, 보조 장치
□ patiently 끈기 있게
□ await 기다리다
□ transition 전환하다
□ You of Things 인간 인터넷(사물 인터넷을 넘어, 이제 인간의 신체까지 인터넷 네트워크에 연결된 것을 가리킴)
□ chip 칩

03

□ information bubble 정보 버블
□ statement 진술
□ falsehood 거짓
□ keystroke (컴퓨터의) 자판 키 누르기

□ currently 현재
□ democratization 민주화
□ unquestionably 의심할 여지가 없이
□ alternative 다른 가능성, 대안
□ indifferent 무관심한
□ wind up with 결국 ~이 되다
□ insufficient 불충분한
□ necessities 필수품

29 심리, 대인 관계

본문 160~161쪽

01

□ reunion 재회, (오랫동안 못 본 사람들의) 친목 모임
□ openness 개방성
□ ridicule 조롱
□ absurd 터무니없는, 우스꽝스러운
□ willingness 자발성
□ deliberately 의도적으로
□ inclined to *do* ~하는 경향이 있는
□ entail 수반하다

02

□ amount 양
□ repeatedly 반복해서
□ neat and tidy 깔끔하고 정돈된
□ persuasion 설득
□ congratulate 칭찬하다
□ fulfill 부응하다
□ identity 정체성

03

□ deposit 예치하다
□ withdraw 인출하다
□ potential 잠재성, 잠재력
□ go sour (관계 등이) 잘못되다
□ tremendous 엄청난
□ drain 소모, 소진
□ optimally 최적으로, 가장 적절한 상태로

30 정치, 경제, 사회, 법

본문 164~165쪽

01

□ represent 표현하다
□ civilization 문명
□ striking 놀라운
□ resemblance 유사성
□ thoroughly 밀접하게, 완전히
□ manufacture 만들다, 제조하다
□ grey matter (두)뇌, 지성
□ trigger 불러일으키다
□ give rise to ~을 불러일으키다
□ consciousness 의식
□ sophisticated 정교한

02

□ philosopher 철학자
□ promote 장려하다, 홍보하다
□ observe 감시하다, 관찰하다
□ inspector 감시자
□ impractical 비현실적인
□ regulate 규제[통제]하다
□ closed-circuit television 폐쇄 회로 TV, CCTV
□ subtle 영리한, 교묘한
□ architectural 건축물의

03

□ consumption 소비
□ ownership 소유

□ perception 인식
□ be associated with ~과 관련되다
□ pushy 강요하려 드는
□ collaborative 협력적인
□ disrupt 와해시키다
□ pronounced 두드러진, 현저한
□ dissimilar 상이한, 닮지 않은
□ nutrition 영양
□ account for ~을 설명하다
□ World Health Organization 세계 보건 기구(WHO)
□ correlation 상관관계
□ infectious 감염성의

31 의학, 건강, 영양, 식품

본문 168~169쪽

01

□ clinician 임상의(직접 환자를 상대하는 의사)
□ extensive 폭넓은
□ command 지식, 능력
□ breakthrough 획기적 연구, 큰 발전
□ competent 만족할 만한, 유능한
□ accompany 수반하다, 동반하다
□ phase 양상, 국면
□ incorporate 포함하다, 통합하다
□ address 다루다
□ serve 만족시키다, 채우다

02

□ adverse 좋지 않은, 불운한
□ physiological 생리적인
□ dysfunction 기능 장애
□ condition 신체의 문제, 몸의 이상
□ precisely 정확히, 꼭
□ identify 인정하다, 확인하다
□ requisite 필수적인, 반드시 있어야 하는
□ clear-cut 명백한
□ underlying 기저의, 잠재적인

03

□ illustrate 여실히 보여 주다, 예증하다
□ intellectual 지적인
□ battle (~과) 싸우다

TEST 1

본문 172~191쪽

01

- □ maintenance 관리
- □ edge (약간의) 우위, 유리함
- □ address 다루다
- □ specifically 구체적으로
- □ assignment 과업
- □ outline 밑그림을 그리다
- □ proceed 진행하다

02

- □ hum 흥얼거리다

03

- □ commodify 상품화하다
- □ refer to ~을 가리키다[의미하다]
- □ obtain 얻다
- □ absorption 흡수
- □ excludable 배제성을 갖는
- □ auctionable 경매 가능한
- □ emission 배출, 배기가스
- □ equitably 공평하게
- □ sustainable 지속 가능한
- □ inherently 본질적으로
- □ ill-suited 적합하지 않은
- □ allocation 배분, 분할

04

- □ metaphor 은유, 비유
- □ wait out ~이 끝나기를 기다리다
- □ at the mercy of ~에 휘둘리는, ~ 앞에서 속수무책인
- □ cope with ~에 대처하다

05

- □ invariably 항상, 언제나
- □ activate 활성화하다
- □ cannot help but *do* ~하지 않을 수 없다
- □ genetics 유전학, 유전적 특성
- □ trait 특성
- □ relevant 관련 있는, 유의미한
- □ persistence 끈기
- □ abstract 추상적인
- □ reasoning 추론

06

- □ simplify 단순화하다
- □ translation 변환, 전환, 변형
- □ equation 방정식
- □ neuroscience 신경 과학
- □ theorist 이론가
- □ entitle 제목을 붙이다
- □ facility 재능
- □ restless 끊임없는, 쉬지 않는
- □ laboratory 실험실
- □ concrete science 형이하학(형체를 갖추고 있는 사물을 연구하는 학문. 주로 자연 과학)
- □ abundant 풍부한
- □ exception 예외

07

- □ norm 규범
- □ abstract 추상적인
- □ wrong 잘못된; 부당하게 취급하다
- □ party 당사자
- □ enforcement 강제, 집행
- □ essence 본질
- □ forager 수렵 채집인

08

- □ undergraduate 학부생
- □ neural 신경(계)의
- □ neuron 신경 세포
- □ compute 계산하다
- □ mechanics (일이 이루어지는) 방식, 방법

☐ electrical 전기의
☐ compelling 설득력 있는
☐ explanation 설명
☐ emergence 출현
☐ working 작동 방식
☐ artificial 인공의
☐ doctor's degree 박사 학위
☐ subsequent 이후의
☐ interconnected 상호 연결된
☐ layer 층
☐ dense 촘촘한
☐ various 다양한
☐ institution 기관

09

☐ vehicle 차량, 탈것
☐ represent 표시하다
☐ interval 간격
☐ decrease 감소하다; 감소

10

☐ maximum 최대
☐ non-refundable 환불이 안 되는
☐ medical note 진료 기록
☐ arrange for ~을 준비하다, 배열하다
☐ replacement 대체

11

☐ annual 연례의
☐ legend 전설
☐ reservation 예약
☐ donation 기부금, 기부
☐ restoration 복원
☐ appreciate 환영하다, 감사하다

12

☐ standpoint 관점
☐ ensure 보장하다
☐ continuation 지속
☐ descendant 후손
☐ occasionally 때때로
☐ scale 규모
☐ deprivation 궁핍, 박탈
☐ definitely 반드시
☐ imaginable 상상할 수 있는

13

☐ setting 환경
☐ attract 마음을 끌다, 끌어들이다
☐ close 박빙의
☐ dominate 지배하다
☐ self-defeating 자멸적인
☐ fade 서서히 사라지다
☐ attendance 관중, 관객
☐ sponsorship (재정적) 후원, 협찬

14

☐ constant 지속적인
☐ regulation 규정
☐ explicitly 명확하게
☐ exposure 노출

15

☐ tendency 성향, 동향
☐ organize 구성하다
☐ assign 배치하다, 배정하다
☐ generous 관대한
☐ regardless of ~과는 관계없이
☐ conviction 신념
☐ aspect 양상, 측면
☐ social suite 사회성 모둠

16

☐ instinct 본능

☐ stress 긴장을[스트레스를] 주다, 강조하다
☐ strengthen 강화하다
☐ spiritually 영적으로
☐ sound 건전한
☐ upbringing 양육 방식

17

☐ make-believe 가장(假裝)
☐ crawl 기어다니다
☐ construct 구성하다
☐ context 맥락, 환경
☐ make up ~을 꾸며 내다
☐ sensory 감각의
☐ perceptual 지각의
☐ body schema 신체 도식(신체의 위치와 움직임에 대한 인지적 지식과 신체의 움직임을 조절하는 능력)
☐ layout 구조
☐ superficial 피상적인

18

☐ establish 확립하다, 설정하다
☐ observe 관찰하다
☐ quality 질
☐ quantity 양
☐ genetics 유전적 특징, 유전학
☐ demonstrate 보여 주다
☐ continuum 연속체
☐ extraversion 외향성
☐ destiny 운명
☐ predisposition 성향
☐ express 발현시키다
☐ upbringing 양육
☐ trigger 촉진하다, 유발하다
☐ dysfunctional 역기능적인

19

☐ clash 충돌하다
☐ assumption 가정
☐ consistent with ~과 일치하는
☐ background 배경
☐ enforce 강요하다
☐ in itself 그 자체로
☐ pushy 강압적인
☐ strengthen 강화하다
☐ occasionally 가끔
☐ in turn 차례대로
☐ table 상정하다
☐ on one's behalf ~을 대신하여

20

☐ alien 외계의
☐ simultaneously 동시에
☐ combined 합친, 결합된
☐ certainty 확실성
☐ strengthen 강화하다
☐ discharge 방출하다
☐ electrical 전기의
☐ chain reaction 연쇄 반응
☐ compute 계산하다
☐ inhibitory 억제적인

21

☐ approximately 거의
☐ worn out 닳은
☐ conventional 전통적인
☐ ingredient 재료
☐ fundamental 근본적인
☐ distinction 차이, 구별

22

☐ bear 떠맡다, 감당하다
☐ collectively 공동으로
☐ rearing 양육
☐ varied 다양한
☐ retirement 퇴직, 은퇴

□ grant 보조금
□ median 중위의, 중간의
□ income 소득

23

□ sophisticated 정교한, 세련된
□ reasoning 추론
□ primatologist 영장류학자
□ experiment 실험
□ reward 보상을 주다
□ note 언급하다, 주목하다
□ accelerate 빨라지다, 속도를 높이다
□ onwards (특정 시간부터) 계속, 앞으로
□ pairing (둘이 짝을 이룬 한) 쌍
□ abstract 추상적인
□ stimulus 자극 (*pl.* stimuli)
□ generalize 일반화하다
□ comparable 비슷한, 비교할 만한
□ fashion 방식

24~25

□ cluster 결집시키다
□ downside 단점, 불리한 면
□ arrangement 방식, 배열
□ demonstration 실증, 설명
□ folktale 민간 설화
□ omit 생략하다
□ apparently 겉보기에 (~인 것 같다), 분명히
□ supernatural 초자연적인
□ constructive 구성적인
□ commonplace 일반적인, 흔한

26~28

□ sustained 지속된
□ bow arm 활을 쥔 팔
□ pitch 음의 높이
□ noticeably 눈에 띄게
□ self-conscious 남의 시선을 의식하는
□ out of tune 음이 맞지 않는
□ session 시간, 회
□ dignified 위엄 있는
□ phrase 악구를 구분하다, 표현하다
□ scratchy 긁는 듯한 소리가 나는

TEST 2

본문 192~211쪽

01

□ passion 열정
□ healthcare 보건 의료, 의료 서비스
□ indicate 간단히 말하다
□ Doctor of Pharmacy 약학 박사
□ degree 학위
□ primary 가장 중요한, 첫째의
□ benefits package 복리 후생 제도

02

□ float 떠오르게 하다
□ extreme 극도의
□ out of the question 불가능한
□ comfort 안도감, 안심, 위로
□ inevitable 피할 수 없는

03

□ spectacular 눈부신, 장관의
□ genetic engineering 유전 공학
□ vast 방대한
□ regulation 법규, 규정
□ govern 규제하다, 지배하다
□ maintenance 정비, 유지
□ conduct 행동, 행위

- □ criminal case 형사 사건
- □ try 재판[심리]하다
- □ civil law 민법
- □ insurance 보험

04

- □ pursue 추구하다
- □ morally 도덕적으로
- □ nuclear weapon 핵무기
- □ manner 방식
- □ independently of ~과는 별개로
- □ consequence 결과
- □ subject 피실험자
- □ all things considered 모든 것을 고려해 볼 때
- □ inquiry 탐구
- □ conflict with ~과 충돌하다

05

- □ restriction 제한
- □ stake 말뚝
- □ immense 엄청난
- □ chain 사슬
- □ victim 희생자
- □ breakthrough 돌파구

06

- □ effective 효과적인
- □ racial ideology 인종 이데올로기
- □ ethnic 인종의, 민족의
- □ deal with ~을 다루다
- □ aspect 측면, 양상
- □ employer 고용주
- □ maintain 유지하다
- □ myth 근거 없는 믿음
- □ natural 타고난
- □ cognitive 인지의, 인지적인
- □ illustrate 분명히 보여 주다
- □ express 표현하다
- □ absolute 절대적인
- □ edge 장점
- □ defective 결함이 있는
- □ escape 벗어나다
- □ credibility 신뢰성
- □ unsuited 적합하지 않은
- □ unwanted 불필요한

07

- □ negotiator 협상가
- □ enhance 높이다
- □ attractiveness 매력(도)
- □ place emphasis on ~을 강조하다
- □ carrot-and-stick 당근과 채찍의
- □ tactic 전술
- □ enlarge 크게 하다
- □ maximize 극대화하다
- □ minimize 최소화하다
- □ disadvantage 불이익
- □ credible 신뢰할 수 있는
- □ third-party 제삼자의
- □ reference 추천, 언급, 참고
- □ factual 사실에 근거한
- □ deadline 마감 기한
- □ expire 만료되다
- □ two-for-the-price-of-one 1+1의, 하나의 가격으로 두 개를 주는

08

- □ professionally 전문적으로
- □ relatively 비교적
- □ tremendous 엄청난
- □ specialized 전문적인
- □ mainstream 주류

09

- □ share 점유율
- □ income 소득, 수입

10

□ entrant 참가자
□ announce 발표하다

11

□ charity 자선 (단체)
□ initiative 계획
□ nonprofit 비영리의
□ promote 장려하다, 촉진하다
□ subsequent 이후의
□ appointment 예약, 약속
□ contact 연락하다

12

□ willingly 기꺼이
□ conversely 반대로
□ withhold ~ from ... …에게 ~을 허락하지 않다
□ credit ~ with ... ~이 …인 것으로 생각하다
□ profound 지대한
□ engage with ~과 관계를 맺다

13

□ stay-at-home 가사 전담의, 가사를 돌보는
□ employment 직장, 고용
□ decade 10년
□ self-employed 자영업을 하는
□ arrangement (처리) 방식
□ flexibility 유연성, 융통성
□ remote work 원격 근무
□ resume 이력서
□ matchmaking 매칭의, 중매의
□ applicant 지원자
□ high-status 높은 지위의

14

□ considerable 상당한
□ debate 논쟁
□ appropriate 적절한
□ beneficiary 수혜 대상
□ expand 확대하다
□ coverage 적용 범위
□ apply to ~에 적용되다
□ minority group 소수 집단
□ favor 지지하다
□ argument 논거
□ in favor of ~을 지지하는
□ obvious 명백한
□ victim 피해자, 희생자
□ matter 중요하다
□ under-represented 불충분하게 대표되는
□ admission 입학
□ single out ~ for ... ~을 …의 대상으로 삼다
□ restriction 제한
□ corporate 기업의
□ executive 임원
□ faculty 교수진
□ exclusion 배제

15

□ displaced 실직한
□ income 소득, 수입
□ substitute 대체하다
□ complement 보완하다
□ generate 만들어 내다, 창출하다
□ overstate 과장하다
□ extent 정도
□ underestimate 과소평가하다

16

□ equipment 장비
□ be associated with ~과 관련되다
□ electronic 전자의
□ in preference to ~에 우선해서
□ audible 들을 수 있는
□ volume 음량
□ ensemble 앙상블, 전체적인 효과

17

□ vegetarian	채식주의자
□ vegan	엄격한 채식주의자
□ uncertainty	불확신
□ persuade	설득하다
□ dig in	단호하게 행동하다, 변화하기를 거부하다

18

□ advisable	바람직한
□ momentary	잠시의, 일시적인
□ fast	단식, 금식
□ beverage	음료
□ unplugged	언플러그드 상태의, 전원을 차단한
□ clarify	명료하게 하다
□ separate	떼어 놓다, 분리하다
□ distraction	주의 산만
□ artificial	인공의
□ face-to-face	대면의
□ engage in	~을 하다
□ mediated	매개되는
□ reflect on	~을 고찰하다

19

□ to the extent that	~하는 한
□ distinguish	구분하다
□ self-esteem	자존감
□ motive	동기
□ obtain	받다, 얻다
□ approval	인정, 승인
□ admire	존경하다
□ in terms of	~이라는 측면에서, ~의 관점에서
□ indifferent	무관심한
□ tackle	(문제를) 다루다
□ put forth	~을 기울이다, 발휘하다
□ minimal	최소한의
□ demonstrate	입증하다, 보여 주다
□ brilliance	탁월함
□ maximum	최대한의
□ extremely	매우, 극도로
□ in general	일반적으로
□ be persuaded of	~을 확신하다
□ superiority	우월성

20

□ intersect	교차하다
□ normative	규범적인
□ dimension	차원
□ ethical	윤리적인
□ straightforward	직접적인, 간단한
□ extension	연장
□ accomplishment	업적
□ cliff	절벽
□ factor	요인, 요소
□ gear	장비

21

□ perception	지각
□ sensation	감각
□ separately	개별적으로
□ bottom-up processing	상향식 처리
□ successively	잇따라서, 연속적으로
□ convert	변환하다, 바꾸다

22

□ impact	영향을 미치다
□ sustain	유지하다
□ embrace	받아들이다
□ strategy	전략
□ address	해결하다
□ inequality	불평등
□ define	정의하다
□ integration	통합
□ gender perspective	성 인지 관점
□ implementation	실행
□ evaluation	평가

□ explicitly	명시적으로, 분명하게
□ parental leave	육아 휴직
□ occupation	직업
□ promote	증진하다
□ prevention	예방
□ overlook	간과하다
□ negatively	부정적으로

23

□ jelly bean	콩 모양 젤리
□ jar	병, 단지, 항아리
□ territory	영역
□ persistently	끈질기게, 끊임없이
□ rage	맹렬히 계속되다
□ redraw	다시 그리다
□ accountant	회계사
□ devoted to	~에 (전적으로) 할애된
□ microscopist	현미경 사용 전문가
□ resolution	해상도
□ region	영역

24~25

□ road pricing	도로 혼잡 통행료 징수제
□ economies of scale	규모의 경제
□ out-of-pocket	자기 부담의, 자비의
□ adopt	채택하다
□ rule of thumb	경험 법칙
□ hourly wage	시급
□ conserve	줄이다, 절약하다, 보존하다
□ peak	절정
□ explanation	설명
□ puzzling	당혹스러운, 의아한

26~28

□ deserted	황량한
□ relief	안도
□ embrace	맞다, 맞이하다, 수용하다
□ breeze	바람
□ ungrateful	감사하지 않는
□ pleasant	상쾌한, 기분 좋은

TEST 3

본문 212~231쪽

01

□ support	지지하다
□ bond	유대
□ announce	공지하다
□ construction	(건설) 공사
□ alternative	대체의, 대안의
□ equipment	장비
□ bin	보관함
□ portable	휴대용의
□ relocate	이전하다
□ combination	비밀번호
□ unlock	잠금을 해제하다
□ dedicated	전용의

02

□ sign	흔적, 자취
□ wander	(정처 없이) 돌아다니다, 거닐다
□ platform	(기차역의) 승강장, 플랫폼
□ anxiously	걱정스럽게
□ glance	훽[흘긋] 보다
□ anxiety	걱정, 불안

03

□ sustainable	지속 가능한
□ promote	촉진하다, 홍보하다
□ vital	활력이 넘치는, 중요한
□ security	안보
□ strain	부담
□ methodology	방법론

□ procedure	절차
□ recognition	인식
□ advance	진행
□ integral	필수적인
□ framework	체제, 구조

04

□ tendency	경향
□ mature	성숙한
□ authority	권위
□ instruction	(보통 복수로) 지시
□ take a nap	낮잠을 자다

05

□ neuroscience	신경 과학
□ human science	인문[인간] 과학(인류학 · 언어학 · 문학 등의 총칭)
□ miner	광부
□ tunnel	터널을 뚫다
□ opposite	(정)반대의
□ immense	거대한, 엄청난
□ dig	굴을 파다
□ closely	열심히, 면밀히

06

□ contribute to	~에 기여하다
□ innate	타고난
□ exceptional	비범한, 보통이 아닌
□ plentiful	풍성한
□ combination	결합
□ sensationalism	선정주의
□ appealing	흥미로운, 매력적인
□ designation	명칭, 지명
□ divinely	신의 힘으로
□ self-esteem	자존감
□ motivation	동기 부여
□ consequently	결과적으로
□ obligation	의무

07

□ edge	가장자리
□ prime	가장 적합한
□ touch down	착륙하다
□ immersed	몰두한, 깊이 빠진
□ physical	물리적인
□ occupy	점유하다, 차지하다
□ characterize	~의 특성을 나타내다

08

□ doctorate	박사 학위
□ found	설립하다
□ productive	왕성한, 생산적인
□ scholarly journal	학술지
□ numerous	다수의
□ article	소논문, 기사
□ enormous	방대한, 막대한
□ organization	단체, 조직
□ racial equality	인종 평등
□ influential	영향력 있는
□ advocate	옹호하다
□ improvement	개선

09

□ behind-the-scenes	무대 뒤의
□ cinematographer	영화 촬영 기사
□ account for	~의 비율을 차지하다

10

□ host	주최하다
□ annual	연례의
□ session	수업
□ participant	참가자
□ extra	여분의
□ sack lunch	점심 도시락
□ purchase	구매
□ sign up for	~에 등록하다

11

- □ outing 야유회
- □ competition 대회
- □ additional 추가의
- □ pass 출입증, 허가증
- □ vehicle 차량
- □ transport 운반하다
- □ equipment 장비
- □ reserve 예약하다

12

- □ superficial 피상적인
- □ luxury 고급(품); 고급(품)의
- □ boost 증진, 증가
- □ self-reinforcing 자기 강화의
- □ accordingly 그에 따라
- □ light up ~을 밝히다, ~을 빛나게 하다
- □ pleasure centre 쾌락 중추
- □ associated 관련된, 연관된
- □ activation 활성화
- □ business school 경영 대학원
- □ genuine 진품인, 진짜의
- □ cheat 부정행위를 하다

13

- □ overfishing 어류 남획
- □ excessive 과도한
- □ fishery 어장, 양식장
- □ catch 어획량
- □ incentive 유인, 동기
- □ rebuild 복원하다, 재건하다
- □ stock 자원
- □ foster 조장하다, 촉진하다

14

- □ consist of ~로 구성되다
- □ assign 지정하다
- □ discussion 토론
- □ prompt 유도하다, 자극하다
- □ refer to ~ as ... ~을 …이라고 부르다
- □ proponent 지지자
- □ relevant 유의미한, 관련된

15

- □ sociologist 사회학자
- □ unintended 의도치 않은
- □ suburbanization 교외화
- □ income 소득
- □ minority 소수 집단[민족]
- □ mobility 이동성
- □ document 상세히 기록하다
- □ gain 인상
- □ attainment 성취(도)
- □ underestimate 과소평가하다
- □ peer effect 동료 효과(동료의 사고관이나 가치관에 영향을 받아 개인의 사고방식이 변하는 것)

16

- □ disc jockey 디스크자키, 디제이
- □ specifically 특히
- □ preference 선호
- □ catch on 인기를 끌다
- □ transistor 트랜지스터
- □ replacement 대체물
- □ vacuum tube 진공관
- □ miniaturization 소형화
- □ receiver 수신기
- □ literally 그야말로, 글자 그대로
- □ all of a sudden 갑자기
- □ medium 매체
- □ dramatically 급격하게
- □ proportion 비율

17

- □ subject 실험 대상자

□ profile (인물의) 약력
□ ultra-reliable 매우 신뢰할 수 있는
□ ideal 이상적인
□ complement 보완하다
□ horizon 시야

18

□ budget 할당하다
□ concept 개념
□ characterize 특징짓다, (~의) 특징이 되다
□ perception 인식, 지각
□ give rise to ~을 만들어 내다, ~을 일으키다
□ arise 발생하다
□ extended 오랜, 장기간의
□ figurative 비유적인
□ fade 희미해지다

19

□ advocate 옹호론자
□ characterize ~ as ... ~의 특징을 …이라고 묘사하다
□ suburb 교외
□ come into contact 접촉하게 되다
□ be involved in ~에 연루되다
□ population 개체 수
□ rebound 원래대로 되돌아가다, 다시 튀어 오르다
□ measure 조치
□ wipe out ~을 말살하다
□ predator 포식자
□ numerous 수많은
□ reflector 반사경, 반사기

20

□ frequency 빈도, 횟수
□ bearer 보유자
□ fitness 적합성, 적응도
□ frequently 빈번히
□ standpoint 관점, 견지
□ class 부류, 종류
□ underlie (~의) 기초가 되다
□ superior 우월한
□ offspring 자녀, (동물의) 새끼
□ parental care (부모의) 자녀 돌보기

21

□ immigrant 이민자
□ derived 출신의
□ postmodernity 포스트모더니티, 탈근대성
□ mobility 이동성
□ migration 이주
□ refugee 난민
□ incorporation 유입, 편입, 합체
□ migrant 이주의
□ norm 규범
□ melting pot 용광로
□ telling 현저한
□ hybridize 혼합하다
□ marginalize 주변적 지위로 내쫓다

22

□ commercial 상업적인
□ geological 지질의, 지질학(상)의
□ extraction 채취
□ windmill farm 풍력 발전 단지
□ abundant 많은, 풍부한
□ inhabit (~에) 거주하다
□ disturbing 교란하는, 방해하는

23

□ conduct 수행하다
□ persuasive 설득력 있는
□ frequent 자주 있는
□ attitude 태도
□ needless to say 말할 필요도 없이
□ recall 기억하다, 회상하다
□ deceive 속이다
□ behave 행동하다

- □ sensible 분별 있는

24~25

- □ by default 자동적으로
- □ by extension 더 나아가
- □ institution 기관
- □ seek out ~을 찾다, ~을 추구하다
- □ to the contrary 반대되는
- □ match up with ~에 필적하다
- □ assumption 가정
- □ urban legend 도시 괴담
- □ folklore 민담
- □ superstition 미신
- □ strong suit 장점
- □ corporation 기업
- □ set aside ~을 따로 두다
- □ division 부서
- □ task 업무를 담당하다
- □ agency 기관
- □ undertaking 사업, 일
- □ devoted to ~에 전념하는
- □ operation 운영
- □ mistaken 틀린, 잘못된
- □ beat 능가하다
- □ constantly 끊임없이
- □ browse 검색하다
- □ stupidity 어리석음
- □ enterprise (중요하거나 어려운) 일[사업], 기획, 계획

26~28

- □ ballroom 무도회장
- □ obey 따르다, 순종하다
- □ instruction (보통 복수로) 지시
- □ grip 꽉 잡다, 움켜쥐다
- □ thrilling 흥분되는
- □ barely 거의 ~ 않다
- □ extremely 몹시, 극도로
- □ get carried away 도취되다, 들뜨다
- □ clap 박수를 치다
- □ firmly 단호하게
- □ rest 얹다, 놓다
- □ steady 균형을 잡다
- □ explore 살펴보다, 탐구하다
- □ lyrical 서정적인
- □ regard 존경하다

memo
www.ebsi.co.kr

memo

memo

고2~N수 수능 집중 로드맵

수능 입문 → **기출 / 연습** → **연계+연계 보완** → **심화 / 발전** → **모의고사**

수능 입문
- 윤혜정의 개념/패턴의 나비효과
- 하루 6개 1등급 영어독해
- 수능 감(感)잡기
- 수능특강 Light
- 강의노트 수능개념

기출 / 연습
- 윤혜정의 기출의 나비효과
- 수능 기출의 미래
- 수능 기출의 미래 미니모의고사
- 수능특강Q 미니모의고사

연계+연계 보완
- 수능연계교재의 VOCA 1800
- 수능연계 기출 Vaccine VOCA 2200
- 연계: 수능특강, 수능완성
- 수능특강 사용설명서
- 수능특강 연계 기출
- 수능 영어 간접연계 서치라이트
- 수능완성 사용설명서

심화 / 발전
- 수능연계완성 3주 특강
- 박봄의 사회 · 문화 표 분석의 패턴

모의고사
- FINAL 실전모의고사
- 만점마무리 봉투모의고사
- 만점마무리 봉투모의고사 시즌2

구분	시리즈명	특징	수준	영역
수능 입문	윤혜정의 개념/패턴의 나비효과	윤혜정 선생님과 함께하는 수능 국어 개념/패턴 학습		국어
	하루 6개 1등급 영어독해	매일 꾸준한 기출문제 학습으로 완성하는 1등급 영어 독해		영어
	수능 감(感) 잡기	동일 소재 · 유형의 내신과 수능 문항 비교로 수능 입문		국/수/영
	수능특강 Light	수능 연계교재 학습 전 연계교재 입문서		영어
	수능개념	EBSi 대표 강사들과 함께하는 수능 개념 다지기		전 영역
기출/연습	윤혜정의 기출의 나비효과	윤혜정 선생님과 함께하는 까다로운 국어 기출 완전 정복		국어
	수능 기출의 미래	올해 수능에 딱 필요한 문제만 선별한 기출문제집		전 영역
	수능 기출의 미래 미니모의고사	부담없는 실전 훈련, 고품질 기출 미니모의고사		국/수/영
	수능특강Q 미니모의고사	매일 15분으로 연습하는 고품격 미니모의고사		전 영역
연계 + 연계 보완	수능특강	최신 수능 경향과 기출 유형을 분석한 종합 개념서		전 영역
	수능특강 사용설명서	수능 연계교재 수능특강의 지문 · 자료 · 문항 분석		국/영
	수능특강 연계 기출	수능특강 수록 작품 · 지문과 연결된 기출문제 학습		국어
	수능완성	유형 분석과 실전모의고사로 단련하는 문항 연습		전 영역
	수능완성 사용설명서	수능 연계교재 수능완성의 국어 · 영어 지문 분석		국/영
	수능 영어 간접연계 서치라이트	출제 가능성이 높은 핵심만 모아 구성한 간접연계 대비 교재		영어
	수능연계교재의 VOCA 1800	수능특강과 수능완성의 필수 중요 어휘 1800개 수록		영어
	수능연계 기출 Vaccine VOCA 2200	수능-EBS 연계 및 평가원 최다 빈출 어휘 선별 수록		영어
심화/발전	수능연계완성 3주 특강	단기간에 끝내는 수능 1등급 변별 문항 대비서		국/수/영
	박봄의 사회 · 문화 표 분석의 패턴	박봄 선생님과 사회 · 문화 표 분석 문항의 패턴 연습		사회탐구
모의고사	FINAL 실전모의고사	EBS 모의고사 중 최다 분량, 최다 과목 모의고사		전 영역
	만점마무리 봉투모의고사	실제 시험지 형태와 OMR 카드로 실전 훈련 모의고사		전 영역
	만점마무리 봉투모의고사 시즌2	수능 완벽대비 최종 봉투모의고사		국/수/영

FROM
KSU
경성은 특별해!
꿈이 있는 경성!
미래를 향해 가는 대학
김서현_23 경영학과
이승민_23 토목공학과

국립 강릉원주대학교
국립
강릉원주
대학교

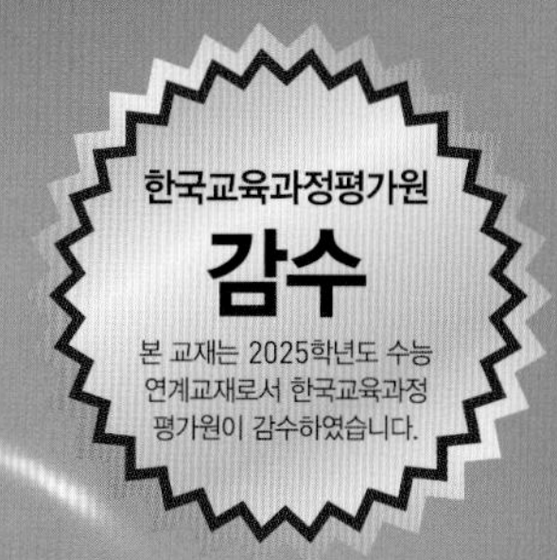

문제를 사진 찍고
해설 강의 보기
Google Play | App Store

EBS*i* 사이트
무료 강의 제공

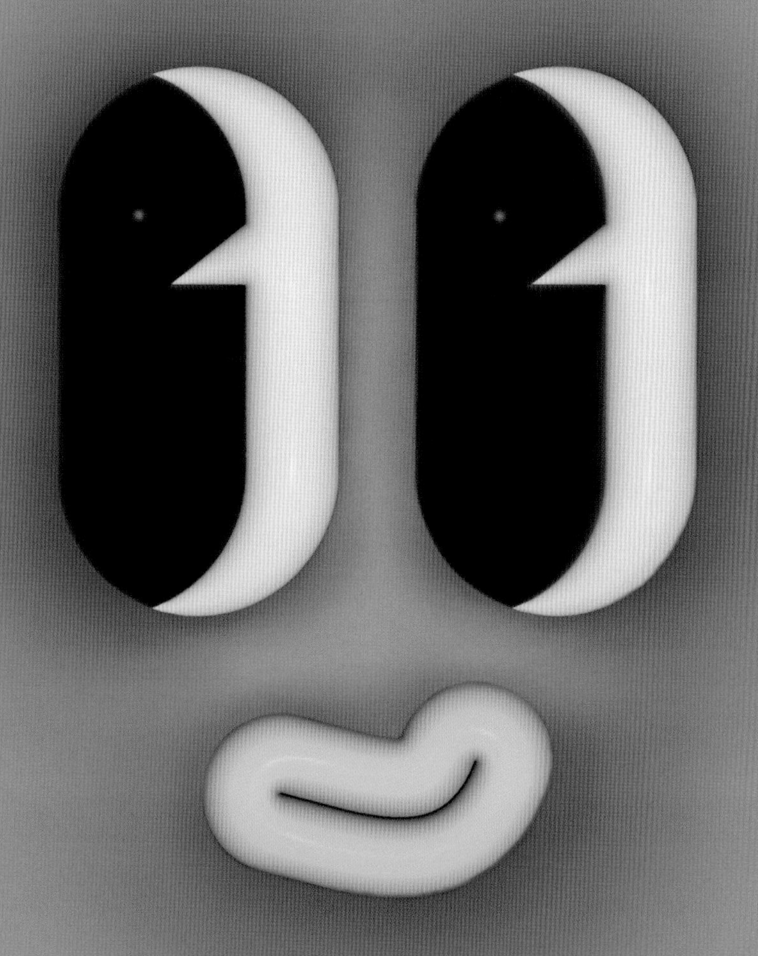

정답과 해설

수능특강

영어영역
영어

2025학년도 수능 연계교재

본 교재는 대학수학능력시험을 준비하는 데 도움을 드리고자 영어과 교육과정을 토대로 제작된 교재입니다.
학교에서 선생님과 함께 교과서의 기본 개념을 충분히 익힌 후 활용하시면 더 큰 학습 효과를 얻을 수 있습니다.

수능특강

영어영역 **영어**

정답과 해설

01 글의 목적 파악

Gateway ①
Exercises 01 ④ 02 ④ 03 ② 04 ③

Gateway

본문 10쪽

정답 ①

소재 웹툰 제작 온라인 강좌

해석 저는 Charlie Reeves이고 Toon Skills Company의 경영자입니다. 여러분이 새로운 웹툰 제작 기술과 기법에 관심이 있으시다면, 이 게시물은 여러분을 위한 것입니다. 올해, 저희는 특별 온라인 강좌를 시작했는데, 웹툰 제작에 관한 다양한 콘텐츠가 담겨 있습니다. 각 강좌는 여러분의 그리기와 스토리텔링 기술을 향상하는 데 도움을 주는 10차시로 설계되어 있습니다. 게다가, 이 강좌들은 초급에서 고급까지 어떤 수준에도 맞게 구성되어 있습니다. 비용은 한 강좌당 45달러이며 여러분은 여러분의 강좌를 6개월 동안 원하는 만큼 여러 번 보실 수 있습니다. 재능이 있고 노련한 강사들이 담당하는 저희 강좌는 여러분에게 창의력의 새로운 세계를 열어 줄 것입니다. 이제 https://webtoonskills.com에서 여러분의 웹툰 세계를 창조하기 시작할 때입니다.

Structure in Focus

- This year, we've launched special online courses, [which contain a variety of contents about webtoon production].
  [ ]는 special online courses를 부가적으로 설명하는 관계절이다.
- Each course consists of ten units [that help improve your drawing and story-telling skills].
  [ ]는 ten units를 수식하는 관계절이다.

Exercises

본문 12~15쪽

01

정답 ④

소재 별장 사용 불가 통보

해석 Dave와 Gretchen에게

너와 너희 가족에게 모든 일이 잘 풀리기를 바라. 마침내, 봄의 기운이 감돌고 있는데, 이는 여름이 그리 멀지 않았다는 것을 뜻하지. 지난 몇 년 동안 Mirror Pond에 있는 우리 별장을 너희와, 그리고 다른 몇몇 친한 친구들과 함께 쓰며 많은 기쁨을 누려 왔어. 하지만 올해는 조금 다르게 운영해야 할 것 같아. 그 집을 유지하는 데 드는 비용이 꽤 많이 올라서, 우리는 적어도 이번 여름에는 별장을 임대 부동산으로 시장에 내놓기로 했거든. 우리는 여름 대부분이나 여름 내내 별장 임차를 고려하고 있는 사람들로부터 이미 몇 가지 좋은 제의를 받고 있어. 우리는 너희가 이해해 주기 바라. 그리고 가을에 예약이 없는 시간이 생기게 되면 알려 줄게.

Sandy Webb 보냄

Solution Guide

지난 몇 년과는 달리, 별장 유지 비용이 꽤 많이 올라 이번 여름에는 별장을 임대 부동산으로 시장에 내놓기로 해 함께 쓸 수 없다는 것을 알리고 있는 내용이다. 따라서 글의 목적으로 가장 적절한 것은 ④이다.

Structure in Focus

- [The expense of maintaining the house has gone up quite a bit], and [for at least the coming summer we have decided to put the cottage on the market as a rental property].
  두 개의 [ ]가 and로 연결되어 한 문장을 이루고 있다.
- We already have several leads from people [who are considering taking the cottage for most or all of the summer].
  [ ]는 people을 수식하는 관계절이다.

02

정답 ④

소재 체스 동아리 물품 마련을 위한 기부 부탁

해석 Butler 씨께

저는 Grandview 고등학교 교장 James Franklin입니다. 매년 저희는 학교 공동체를 결속하기 위한 재미있는 행사를 제공합니다. 올해는 체스 대회를 개최하려고 합니다. 저희는 그것이 건전한 경쟁 분위기를 조성하고 학생들이 새로운 친구를 사귀는 데 도움이 될 것으로 생각합니다. 그리고 저희 학교 체스 동아리 학생 중 일부는 매우 전도유망한 성과를 보여 주고 있고, 시 체스 대회에 참가하는 것을 목표로 하고 있습니다. 그들은 대회를 위해 열심히 연습하고 있습니다. 하지만 학교의 예산상 제약으로 인해 저희는 교육용 물품을 줄여야 했습니다. 저희 학생들에게 가능한 최상의 교육을 제공하기 위해서는 체스 동아리를 계속 운영할 수 있는 물품이 필요합니다. 돈을 기부함으로써 체스 동아리가 계속 운영될 수 있도록 도와주시길 부탁드리고자 합니다. 귀하께서 저희 학교에 기부해 주시면 귀하는 체스 선수가 되는 꿈을 추구하고 있는 학생들에게 영웅이 되실 것입니다.

James Franklin 드림

Solution Guide

학교의 예산상 제약으로 교육용 물품을 줄여야 했다고 하면서 체스 동아리를 계속 운영할 수 있는 물품이 필요하니 돈을 기부해 달라고 부탁하는 내용이므로, 글의 목적으로 가장 적절한 것은 ④이다.

Structure in Focus

- We think [that it will {create a healthy competitive atmosphere} and {help students make new friends}].
  [ ]는 think의 목적어 역할을 하는 명사절이고, 그 안에서 두 개의 { }가 and로 연결되어 will에 이어진다.
- If you contribute to our school, you'll be a hero to the students [who are pursuing their dream of becoming chess players].
  [ ]는 the students를 수식하는 관계절이다.

03

정답 ②

소재 교체 상품 배송 요청

해석 관계자분께

저는 저의 최근 휴대 전화 주문과 관련한 문제에 대해 귀하께 편지를 드립니다. 저는 은색 모델을 주문했지만, 검은색 모델을 받았습니다. 그러나 저는 어쨌든 그것을 사용하기로 마음먹었습니다. 그럼에도 불구하고 저는 그것에 번호를 저장할 수 없었고, 배터리는 완전 충전 상태에서 하루도 가지 않았습니다. 제가 고객 서비스에 연락했을 때 담당자는 저에게 그 전화기를 반품할 것을 요청하면서 교체 상품을 보내 주겠다고 약속했습니다. 그것이 2주 전이었는데, 저는 아직도 새 전화기를 받지 못했습니다. 가능한 한 빨리 저에게 은색이고 배터리가 정상인 교체 전화기를 보내 주시면 대단히 감사하겠습니다.
제 요청에 대한 신속한 조치를 고대합니다.
John Smith 드림

Solution Guide

주문했던 색상과 다른 휴대 전화를 받았을 뿐 아니라 그 상품의 성능에 문제가 있어 교체를 요청했으나 아직도 교체 전화기를 받지 못한 필자가 교체 상품의 빠른 배송을 요청하고 있는 글이다. 따라서 글의 목적으로 가장 적절한 것은 ②이다.

Structure in Focus

- When I contacted customer service, the representative [asked me {to return the phone}] and [promised to send a replacement].
  두 개의 [ ]는 and로 연결되어 주절의 술어 역할을 한다. 첫 번째 [ ] 안의 { }는 asked의 목적격 보어 역할을 하는 to부정사구이다.

04

정답 ③

소재 복사기 유지 관리 서비스 광고

해석 Scott 씨께

귀하께서 귀하의 행정 직원들에게 물어보면, 그들은 아마 복사기의 유지 관리가 성공적인 사무실에 매우 중요하다는 것에 동의할 것입니다. 저희가 조사한 바에 따르면 일반 기업은 복사 장비를 수리하거나 교체하기 전에 약 6개월 정도 사용하는 것으로 나타났습니다. 과거에는, 귀하가 서비스가 필요했을 때 선택할 수 있는 유일한 것은 매우 높은 비용에 수리 기사를 부르는 것이었습니다. 다행히도, 이제 귀하의 복사기 수명을 연장하고 다음 한 해 동안 귀사가 수천 달러를 절약할 수 있게 해 주는 서비스가 있습니다. Lake Paperworx는 복사기 유지 관리를 전문으로 하며 미국 전역의 기업 및 법률 회사에 성공적으로 서비스를 제공하고 있습니다. 저희는 귀하의 유지 관리 비용과 (고장으로 인한) 작업 중단 시간을 크게 줄일 수 있습니다. 동봉된 소책자에 저희 서비스의 개요가 기술되어 있습니다. 저희 서비스를 이용하는 데 관심이 있으시면, 920-4848-1212로 저에게 바로 전화해 주십시오.
Lake Paperworx 영업부장 James Palmer 드림

Solution Guide

복사기 유지 관리 전문 업체 직원이 복사기 수명 연장, 유지 관리비 절약 등 자신들이 제공하는 서비스의 장점을 언급하면서 이를 이용하도록 광고하기 위해 쓴 글이므로, 글의 목적으로 가장 적절한 것은 ③이다.

Structure in Focus

- [If you ask your administrative employees], they will probably agree [that copier maintenance is critical to a successful office].
  첫 번째 [ ]는 조건을 나타내는 부사절이고, 두 번째 [ ]는 agree의 목적어 역할을 하는 명사절이다.
- Fortunately, there is now a service [that can {extend the life of your copier} and {save your company thousands of dollars during the next year}].
  [ ]는 a service를 수식하는 관계절이고, 그 안에서 두 개의 { }가 and로 연결되어 can에 이어지면서 관계절의 술어 역할을 한다.

PART I 유형편

02 심경·분위기 파악

Gateway ①
Exercises 01 ④ 02 ⑤ 03 ③ 04 ①

Gateway

본문 16쪽

정답 ①

소재 출근 첫날 버스 기다리기

해석 David는 밴쿠버에서 새로운 일을 시작하게 되었고, 자신이 탈 버스를 기다리고 있었다. 그는 계속 자신의 시계와 버스가 올 방향을 번갈아 보았다. 그는 "내가 탈 버스가 아직 오지 않아. 내가 첫날 지각할 수는 없어."라고 생각했다. David는 마음을 놓을 수가 없었다. 그가 다시 고개를 들어 보았을 때, 그는 바로 자신의 직장으로 가는 다른 버스가 오고 있는 것을 보았다. 그 버스는 그의 앞에 섰고 문을 열었다. 그는 버스에 오르며, "휴! 다행히도 내가 지각하지 않도록 이 버스가 딱 맞춰 왔네."라고 생각했다. 그는 버스의 비어 있는 좌석에 등을 기대며 숨을 깊이 들이쉬었고, 마침내 긴장을 풀 수 있었다.

Structure in Focus

- When he looked up again, he saw a different bus coming [that was going right to his work].
  [ ]는 a different bus를 수식하는 관계절로, saw의 목적격 보어인 coming 뒤에 위치하였다.
- He [leaned back on an unoccupied seat in the bus] and [took a deep breath, finally able to relax].
  두 개의 [ ]는 and로 연결되어 문장의 술어 역할을 한다.

Exercises

본문 18~19쪽

01

정답 ④

소재 원하는 옷감의 구매 실패

해석 Olivia는 진열대로부터 샛노란 비단 천 조각을 끌어당겼다. 그녀는 빈손에 구슬이 달린 레이스의 견본을 들고는 춤을 출 때 그것이 발목 주위에서 살랑거리며 낼 소리를 상상하려 했다. 전쟁이 끝났으므로 댄스파티가 많으리라. 기대가 그녀의 가슴 속에서 부풀었다. 이번 사교 시즌에, 그녀는 진짜 신사를 만날 것이고, 그리고 누가 알겠는가? 어쩌면 그녀는 결혼할지도 모른다. "도와드릴까요?" 가게 점원이 그녀의 옆에 서 있었다. "이 비단 5야드와 이 레이스 한 두루마리를 주세요."라고 Olivia가 말했다. "정말 죄송합니다, 손님. 그것들은 이미 예약되어 있습니다." 정말 낙담스러웠다! 다른 어떤 직물도 그 노란 비단만큼 그녀를 아름답게 만들지 않을 것이고, 다른 어떤 진주도 그토록 매력적인 살랑거리는 소리를 내지 않을 것이다. 한숨을 쉬면서, 그녀는 그 상품들을 다시 진열대에 갖다 놓았다.

Solution Guide

Olivia는 노란색 비단과 레이스를 보며 파티에서 그것들로 만들어진 옷을 입고 춤을 출 기대감에 부풀어 있다가 그것들이 모두 예약되어 살 수 없음을 알고 낙담했다고 했으므로, 글에 드러난 Olivia의 심경 변화로 가장 적절한 것은 ④ '기대하는 → 실망한'이다.

① 감사하는 → 좌절한
② 호기심이 나는 → 기쁜
③ 걱정하는 → 질투심을 느끼는
⑤ 긴장한 → 확신하는

Structure in Focus

- In her free hand she held a sample of beaded lace and tried to imagine the sound [it would make whispering around her ankles {as she danced}].
  [ ]는 the sound를 수식하는 관계절이고, 그 안의 { }는 시간을 나타내는 부사절이다.

02

정답 ⑤

소재 Garcia 씨의 트럼펫 연주

해석 Garcia 씨는 자신의 벽장으로 걸어가 케이스에서 트럼펫을 꺼냈다. 그는 그러니까, 다 비워 내듯이 트럼펫을 불었다. 그는 밸브를 따라 손가락을 움직이며 음계를 연주했다. 그러고는 "자, Zach, 준비됐어?"라고 그가 말했다. 그런 다음 그는 연주를 시작했다. 내 말은 그가 연주할 줄 알았다는 것이다. 그는 정말 부드럽고 아름다운 이 곡을 연주했다. 나는 트럼펫이 속삭이듯 소리 낼 수 있다는 것을 전혀 알지 못했다. 나는 그의 손가락을 계속 바라봤다. 나는 그가 끝없이 연주를 계속하기를 바랐다. 그것은 그가 수업 시간에 우리에게 읽어 주었던 그 어떤 시보다 좋았다. 시끄러운 온 세상이 정말, 정말 조용해진 것 같았고, 이 노래 한 곡만, 나뭇잎 사이로 부는 산들바람처럼 은은한 이 감미롭고 부드러우며 아주 멋진 노래 한 곡만 남은 것 같았다. 세상이 그저 사라져 버렸다. 나는 그 고요함 속에서 영원히 살고 싶었다. 나는 박수를 치고 싶었다. 그러고 나서 나는 무엇을 해야 할지, 무슨 말을 해야 할지 전혀 몰랐다.

Solution Guide

'I'는 Garcia 씨의 트럼펫 연주를 들으며 고요한 세상에 그의 연주만 남아 있는 느낌이었고 그 고요함 속에서 영원히 살고 싶다고 했다. 또한, 그의 연주에 크게 감동하여 무엇을 하고 무슨 말을 해야 할지 전혀 알지 못했다고 했으므로, 'I'의 심경으로 가장 적절한 것은 ⑤ '감동하고 압도된'이다.

① 자랑스럽고 자신감 있는
② 지루하고 무관심한
③ 무섭고 겁먹은
④ 실망하고 화가 난

Structure in Focus

- It was better than any of the poems [he'd read to us in class].
  [ ]는 the poems를 수식하는 관계절이다.
- It was like [the whole loud world had gone really, really quiet] and [there was nothing but this one song, {this one sweet and gentle and brilliant song that was as soft as a breeze blowing through the leaves of a tree}].
  두 개의 [ ]는 and로 연결되어 It was like에 이어진다. { }는 this one song을 구체적으로 설명하는 명사구이다.

03

정답 ③

소재 처벌받을 위기에서 벗어남

해석 덩치가 매우 큰 한 전사가 다가와 Benny 앞에 섰다. 그 전사가 그의 팔을 붙잡았고 Benny는 자신이 처벌받게 될 것이라고 확신했다. 그는 끌려가는 동안 두려움에 떨었다. 그 전사는 Benny를 마을의 공터로 데려갔다. 거기에는 한 노인이 앉아 있었다. 그는 모든 전사에게 엄청난 존경을 받는 듯 보였다. 그는 자신을 '대추장'이라는 뜻의 Ailani라고 소개했고 매우 놀랍게도 영어로 말을 했다. 그는 Benny에게 "나는 우리가 당신을 처벌하지 않기로 결정했습니다. 우리는 선량한 사람을 처벌하지 않으니 안심해도 됩니다."라고 말했다. 그 추장은 계속 말했다. "당신이 우리를 위해 한 일을 들었습니다. 당신의 친절함은 내게 환영의 말을 전하게 하는군요. Life Island에 온 걸 환영합니다." 안도의 눈물이 쏟아져 Benny의 얼굴을 타고 흘러내렸다.

Solution Guide

덩치가 매우 큰 전사에게 끌려가면서 자신이 처벌받게 될 것이라고 확신하며 두려움에 떨었던 Benny가 추장으로부터 자신을 처벌하지 않을 것이며 오히려 환영한다는 말을 듣고 안도의 눈물을 흘렸다는 내용이므로, Benny의 심경 변화로 가장 적절한 것은 ③ '공포에 질린 → 안도하는'이다.

① 만족한 → 좌절한
② 기쁜 → 화가 난
④ 후회하는 → 감동한
⑤ 차분한 → 신이 난

Structure in Focus

- The warrior took him by the arm, and Benny was convinced [that he was going to be punished].
  [ ]는 convinced의 의미를 보충한다.

04

정답 ①

소재 Charlotte이 준비한 추수 감사절 파티

해석 "이제 모두 모인 것 같네요! 우리 모두 앉을까요?" 모든 이들이 더할 나위 없이 기쁘게 응했고 곧 모인 사람 모두가 식당의 긴 식탁을 둘러서 자리를 잡았고, Charlotte의 요리가 가득 담긴 접시를 전달했다. 곧 모두가 접시를 가득 채웠고, 음식을 먹는 사이에 식탁 주위에서 바쁘게 대화가 오갔다. Charlotte은 자신이 만든 음식의 소를 조심스럽게 한입 베어 물었고 양념이 모두 기막히게 어우러져 풍미 가득한 경험을 만들어 낸다는 것을 알게 되었다. Charlotte은 자신의 접시에 담긴 요리를 맛보고 모든 음식이 맛있다는 것을 알게 되어 조금 더 긴장을 풀었다. 아니면 적어도 그녀는 그렇게 생각했다. 그녀는 그저 다른 사람들도 모두 같은 생각을 하길 바랐다. 그녀의 마음을 읽은 듯 Addison이 그녀 쪽으로 몸을 기울였다. "모든 것이 너무 맛있어요." 그녀는 자신의 배를 두드리며 이미 반쯤 먹은 접시를 가리키면서 조용히 말했다. "결국 날 굴려서 여기 밖으로 데리고 나가야 할 거예요." Charlotte은 웃으며 "마음껏 먹어요."라고 대답했다. "흉볼 사람 없어요, 특히 추수 감사절에는요!"

Solution Guide

Charlotte은 추수 감사절 파티를 위해 자신이 준비한 음식을 맛보고 모든 음식이 맛있다는 사실에 안도하면서 흡족해하고 있고, 파티에 참석한 Addison도 Charlotte에게 음식이 맛있다고 말하고 있으므로, Charlotte의 심경으로 가장 적절한 것은 ① '안도하고 기쁜'이다.

② 긴장하고 짜증 나는
③ 차분하고 단호한
④ 부끄럽고 후회하는
⑤ 혼란스럽고 전전긍긍하는

Structure in Focus

- Charlotte took a careful bite of her stuffing and found

[that the seasonings had all blended together beautifully {to create a flavorful experience}].
[ ]는 found의 목적어 역할을 하는 명사절이고, 그 안의 { }는 결과를 나타내는 to부정사구이다.

- "Everything tastes so delicious," she said quietly, [patting her belly] and [indicating her already half-eaten plate].
and로 연결된 두 개의 [ ]는 주절이 기술하는 상황에 부수하는 상황을 나타내는 분사구문이다.

03 요지 파악

Gateway ①
Exercises 01 ⑤ 02 ③ 03 ⑤ 04 ⑤

Gateway

본문 20쪽

정답 ①

소재 고객의 칭찬에 대한 응답

해석 여러분의 응답에 우선순위를 매길 수 있는 것은, 그것이 특별히 즐겁거나 화가 나는 경험에 관한 일회성 상호 작용이든, 여러분의 고객 기반 내에서 상당히 영향력 있는 개인과의 장기적 관계의 발전이든 간에, 여러분이 개별 고객들과 더 깊은 관계를 맺을 수 있게 해 준다. 만약 여러분이 어떤 브랜드, 제품 또는 서비스에 관해 호의적인 의견이나 혹은 그 문제에 대해서 어떠한 의견이라도 올려 본 적이 있다면, 그 결과로서, 예컨대 그 브랜드 관리자로부터 개인적으로 인정의 반응을 얻는다면 기분이 어떨지 생각해 보라. 일반적으로, 사람들은 할 말이 있기 때문에, 그리고 그것을 말한 것에 대해 인정받기를 원하기 때문에 글을 올린다. 특히, 사람들이 긍정적인 의견을 게시할 때 그것은 그 게시물을 작성하게 만든 경험에 대한 감사의 표현이다. 여러분 옆에 서 있는 사람에 대한 칭찬은 보통 '감사합니다'와 같은 응답을 받는 반면, 슬픈 사실은 대부분의 브랜드 칭찬은 응답 없이 지나간다는 것이다. 이것은 무엇이 칭찬을 이끌어 냈는지 이해하고 그 칭찬을 바탕으로 확고한 팬을 만들어 낼 기회를 잃은 것이다.

Structure in Focus

- [Being able to prioritize your responses] allows you to connect more deeply with individual customers, [be it {a one-off interaction around a particularly delightful or upsetting experience}, or {the development of a longer-term relationship with a significantly influential individual within your customer base}].
첫 번째 [ ]는 주어 역할을 하는 동명사구이다. 두 번째 [ ]는 '~이든, …이든 간에'라는 의미를 나타내는 부사절이고, 그 안의 두 개의 { }는 or로 연결되어 be의 주격 보어 역할을 한다.
- While [a compliment to the person standing next to you] is typically answered with a response like "Thank You," the sad fact is [that most brand compliments go unanswered].
첫 번째 [ ]는 부사절의 주어 역할을 하는 명사구이고, 두 번째 [ ]는 is의 주격 보어 역할을 하는 명사절이다.

Exercises

본문 22~23쪽

01

정답 ⑤

소재 창의력에 관한 오해

해석 창의력에 대한 가장 큰 오해 중 하나는 복잡한 문제를 해결하는 데 한 개의 기발한 아이디어가 필요하다는 것이다. 순수 과학에서는 이것이 맞을 수도 있지만, 대부분의 상업적 상황에서는, 혹은 심지어 일상생활에서도, 마법을 부리는 것은 결코 한 가지 묘책이 아니다. 사실, 중요한 것은 바로 단순해 보이는 일련의 아이디어이다. 핵심은 전체 문제의 특정 부분을 해결하는 충분한 아이디어를 갖는 것이며, 그러면 골치 아픈 과업이 많이 참아 낼 수 있는 것으로 보인다. 창의성은 개념을 독특한 방식으로 결합하는 것에서 나오며, 또 아이디어의 근원을 추적하는 것은 매우 어렵기 때문에 여러분은 아이디어 중 일부가 성공하기를 바라면서 가능한 한 많은 아이디어를 만들어 낸다면 더 유리할 것이다. 이것이 바로 위대한 과학자와 예술가가 하는 일이다. 작가 Walter Isaacson이 말한 대로, '(창의력의) 불꽃은 예상치 못하게 (난데없이) 발생하는 것이 아니라 아이디어가 서로 마찰하며 생겨난다'.

Solution Guide

하나의 기발한 아이디어가 복잡한 문제를 해결한다는 잘못된 통념을 반박하며 창의성에 관해 설명하고 있는 글이다. 여러 단순한 아이디어가 중요하고, 가능한 많은 아이디어를 만들어 내면 창의적으로 문제를 해결할 수 있다는 내용의 글이므로, 글의 요지로 가장 적절한 것은 ⑤이다.

Structure in Focus

- **It is**, in fact, [a series of seemingly simple ideas] **that** counts.
  [ ]는 It is와 that 사이에 놓여 그 의미가 강조되고 있다.
- The key is [to have enough ideas {that solve specific parts of the overall problem}], ~.
  [ ]는 is의 주격 보어 역할을 하는 to부정사구이고, 그 안의 { }는 enough ideas를 수식하는 관계절이다.

02

정답 ③

소재 환경을 위한 선택

해석 가끔은 지구를 위해 할 적절한 일을 아는 것이 어렵다. 좋게 들리는 것이 반드시 그렇지는 않을 수도 있다. 예를 들어 지붕에 설치하는 태양 전지판은 환경을 돕는 가장 비싸고 가장 효과적이지 않은 방법의 하나다. 지역 농산물을 구매하는 것이 실제로는 수질 오염과 쓰레기를 증가시킬 수도 있다. 덴마크와 영국 정부의 연구에 의하면, 식료품용 비닐봉지가 사실상 기후와 물을 위해 면 가방보다 더 나을 수도 있다. 여러분은 그러한 주장 전부나 일부에 동의하지 않을 수도 있고, 여러분이 맞을 수도 있다. 그것은 여러분의 개인적인 상황에 달려 있다. 예를 들어 여러분이 애리조나 주의 Phoenix에 산다면, 태양 전지판은 현명한 선택이 될 수 있다. 몇 년 동안 장을 보기 위해 자신의 면 가방을 예외 없이 계속 사용하는 것은 대안들보다 아마 환경에 더 좋을 것이다. 이러한 선택 각각은 개인적인 상황과 행동에 달려 있다. 환경을 위한 최선의 해결책은 개인적이다.

Solution Guide

태양 전지판, 식료품용 비닐봉지, 면 가방의 사례를 들어, 개인적인 상황과 하는 행동에 따라 지구 환경을 위해 무엇이 더 나은지가 달라질 수 있다는 점을 설명하는 내용의 글이므로, 글의 요지로 가장 적절한 것은 ③이다.

Structure in Focus

- Sometimes **it** is hard [to know the right thing to do for the planet].
  it은 문장의 형식상의 주어이고, [ ]는 내용상의 주어이다.
- [Using your own cotton bags continuously and without exception for shopping for several years] **is** probably better for the environment than the alternatives.
  [ ]는 문장의 주어 역할을 하는 동명사구이고, 문장의 술어동사는 is이다.

03

정답 ⑤

소재 장애인에 대한 편견

해석 장애가 있는 사람을 생각해 보라. 흔히 그들은 비장애인에게 유리하게 '편향된' 능력 기준을 사용하여 평가받는다. 예를 들어 보통의 시각 장애인과 보통의 앞을 볼 수 있는 사람을 비교해 보라. 한 장소에서 다른 장소로 걸어 갈 때 누가 더 유능할까? 여러분은 앞을 볼 수 있는 사람이 자신이 어디로 가고 있는지를 볼 수 있으므로 더 유능할 것으로 생각할 수도 있지만, 이는 불공정한 기준을 사용하고 있다. 만약 여러분이 누가 눈을 감고 가장 잘 걸을 수 있느냐는 더 공정한 기준에 근거하여 능력에 대해 생각한다면, 시각 장애인이 분명히 더 유능할 것이다. 시각 장애인, 더 나아가 다른 사회 소외 계층에 관한 이러한 지식은 우리의 인습적이고 편견에 찬 상상이 꾸며 낸 것인 것을 제외하면 실재하지 않는 무능함을 이유로 그들을 차별하거나, 동정하거나, 아니면 깔보는 듯한 태도로 대하는 것이 아니라 그들의 가치를 인정하고 그들의 고유한 능력을 있는 그대로 기념할 수 있게 한다.

Solution Guide

장애인의 능력에 대한 평가 기준이 비장애인에게 유리하도록 편향되어 있다는 것을 알아야, 즉 장애인에 대한 편견이 없어야 그들의 능력을 제대로 평가할 수 있다는 내용의 글이다. 따라서 글의 요지로 가장 적절한 것은 ⑤이다.

Structure in Focus

- [If you think about competence based on the fairer criterion of {who can best walk with the eyes closed}], then the blind person will definitely be more competent.
  [ ]는 조건을 나타내는 부사절이고, 그 안의 { }는 전치사 of의 목적어 역할을 하는 명사절이다.
- [Such knowledge about people who are blind and, by extension, other socially marginalized people], can make us [appreciate them and celebrate their unique abilities as they really are, {rather than discriminate against, pity, or patronize them for some incompetence 〈that does not exist except as a figment of our traditional, prejudiced imaginations〉}].
  첫 번째 [ ]는 문장의 주어이고, 두 번째 [ ]는 make의 목적격 보어이다. 두 번째 [ ] 안의 { }는 전치사구이고, 그 안의 〈 〉는 some incompetence를 수식하는 관계절이다.

04

정답 ⑤

소재 상상의 본질

해석 여러분이 생각할 때는 상상력을 이용하여 실제적인 것이 아닌 사건에 대한 이미지나 그림을 마음속에 만들고 있는 것이다. 여러분이 축구 경기를 마치고 차를 몰고 집에 돌아오는 길에 마음속으로 경기를 복기하고 있다면, 그 경기가 어땠는지 그저 상상하고 있는 것이다. 그 경기는 더는 현실이 아니며, 그것은 이제 여러분의 마음속에만, 즉 여러분의 기억 속에만 있다. 그것은 한때는 현실이었지만 더는 그렇지 않다. 마찬가지로, 여러분이 여러분의 결혼 생활이 얼마나 안 좋은지 생각하고 있다면, 여러분은 그것을 여러분의 마음속으로 생각하고 있는 것이다. '그 모든 것은 상상 속에 있는 것이다.' 여러분은 말 그대로 여러분의 관계를 '만들어 내고' 있는 것이다. 여러분이 여러분의 관계에 관해 가지고 있는 생각은 단지 생각일 뿐이다. 그렇기 때문에 '상황이 보이는 것만큼 나쁘지는 않다'라는 옛말은 거의 항상 사실이다. 상황이 '그렇게 나빠 보이는' 이유는 실제로는 그렇지 않지만 그 순간 거의 마치 바로 눈앞에서 일어나고 있는 것처럼, 여러분의 마음이 과거의 사건을 재현하고, 다가오는 사건을 미리 볼 수 있기 때문이다. 설상가상으로, 여러분의 마음은 어떤 사건에든 여분의 드라마를 추가하여 그 사건이 실제로 현재에 그러하거나, 과거에 그러했거나, 미래에 그러할 것보다 훨씬 더 나빠 보이게 만들 수 있다.

Solution Guide

상상은 더는 현실이 아닌 것에 대한 이미지나 그림을 마음속에 만들어 상황을 더 나쁘게 보이게 할 수 있는 생각일 뿐이라는 내용의 글이다. 따라서 글의 요지로 가장 적절한 것은 ⑤이다.

Structure in Focus

- If you are driving home from a football match, [reviewing the game in your mind], you are merely imagining [what the game was like].
  첫 번째 [ ]는 앞에서 기술한 상황과 동시에 일어나는 동작을 나타내는 분사구문이고, 두 번째 [ ]는 imagining의 목적어 역할을 하는 명사절이다.
- The reason [things 'seem so bad'] is [because your mind is able to {recreate past events}, and {preview upcoming events}, almost as though they were happening right in front of you, at that moment — even though they're not].
  첫 번째 [ ]는 The reason을 수식하는 관계절이고, 두 번째 [ ]는 is의 보어 역할을 하는 명사절이다. 두 번째 [ ] 안의 두 개의 { }는 and로 연결되어 to에 이어진다.

04 주장 파악

Gateway ⑤
Exercises 01 ③ 02 ① 03 ③ 04 ②

Gateway

본문 24쪽

정답 ⑤

소재 조직의 문화 형성의 조건

해석 가치만으로는 문화가 창조되고 구축되지 않는다. 일정 시간에만 가치에 따라 생활하는 것은 문화의 창조와 유지에 기여하지 않는다. 가치를 행동으로 바꾸는 것은 전투의 절반에 불과하다. 물론, 이것은 올바른 방향으로 나아가는 한 단계이지만, 그다음에 그러한 행동은 기대되는 것에 대한 명확하고 간결한 설명과 함께 조직 전체에 널리 공유되고 퍼져 나가야 한다. 단순히 그것에 관해 이야기하는 것만으로는 충분하지 않다. 리더와 모든 인력 관리자가 자기 사람들을 지도하는 데 사용할 수 있는, 구체적 행동을 시각적으로 표현한 것을 갖는 것이 중요하다. 스포츠 팀이 좋은 성과를 내고 승리하는 데 도움이 되도록 고안된, 특정 플레이를 담고 있는 플레이북을 갖고 있는 것과 마찬가지로, 여러분의 회사는 여러분의 문화를 행동으로 바꾸고 여러분의 가치를 승리하는 행동으로 바꾸는 데 필요한 핵심적인 변화를 담은 플레이북을 갖고 있어야 한다.

Structure in Focus

- **It** is critical [to have a visual representation of the specific behaviors {that leaders and all people managers can use to coach their people}].
  It은 형식상의 주어이고, [ ]는 내용상의 주어이다. { }는 a visual representation of the specific behaviors를 수식하는 관계절이다.
- Just like a sports team has a playbook with specific plays [designed to help them perform well and win], your company should have a playbook with the key shifts [needed to {transform your culture into action} and {turn your values into winning behaviors}].
  첫 번째 [ ]는 a playbook with specific plays를 수식하는 분사구이다. 두 번째 [ ]는 a playbook with the key shifts를 수식하는 분사구이고, 그 안의 두 개의 { }는 and로 연결되어 to에 이어진다.

Exercises

본문 26~27쪽

01

정답 ③

소재 성과에 대한 긍정적이고 구체적인 인정

해석 대부분 사람은 침묵과 인정을 동일시하지 않는다. 업무가 항상 훌륭한 사람들도 여전히 가끔은 여러분으로부터 그것을 들을 필요가 있다. 그들이 목표를 달성하고 있음을 여러분이 알아차렸다는 사실을 그들에게 알게 하라. 감사와 인정은 서로를 지지하는 업무 환경을 조성하고 의욕을 계속 유지시킨다. 무엇이 잘되었고 그것이 왜 중요한지를 언급함으로써 여러분의 인정 표현이 구체적이고 긍정적이 되도록 하라. 이렇게 하면 사람들이 기분이 좋아지고, 그것은 또한 여러분이 확인하는 행동이 반복되는 것을 보장한다. 그러니 그냥 "그것은 좋았어요!"라고 말하지 말라. "그것은 …이라서 좋았어요."라고 말하라. 팀과 개인 둘 다 자신의 성과에 대한 긍정적이고 구체적인 정보가 필요하다. 상상력을 발휘하여 팀이 달성한 것을 보여 주는 그래프를 게시하고, 모두가 나눠 먹을 점심 식사로 샌드위치를 가져오거나 풍선을 달아 주요 획기적인 일이나 목표 달성을 축하하고, 감사 메모를 보내라. 여러분이 성공을 무시할 때, 사람들은 그것이 중요하지 않다고 생각하고 노력을 멈춘다.

Solution Guide

팀이건 개인이건 업무에 대해 잘한 점과 그것이 중요한 이유를 긍정적이면서도 구체적으로 언급함으로써 성과를 인정해 주라는 것이 글의 중심 내용이므로, 필자가 주장하는 바로 가장 적절한 것은 ③이다.

Structure in Focus

- Make your appreciation specific and positive by noting [what was done well and why it matters].
  [ ]는 noting의 목적어 역할을 하는 명사절이다.
- Use your imagination: [post graphs showing {what the team has achieved}]; [mark the achievement of major milestones or goals by {bringing in sandwiches for lunch for everyone to share} or {putting up balloons}]; [send thank you notes].
  세 개의 [ ]는 Use your imagination의 구체적 예시를 보여 준다. 첫 번째 [ ] 안에서 { }는 showing의 목적어 역할을 하는 명사절이다. 두 번째 [ ] 안에서 두 개의 { }는 or로 연결되어 전치사 by의 목적어 역할을 하는 동명사구이다.

02

정답 ①

소재 뉴스의 질을 판단하는 기준

해석 뉴스의 질은 판단하기 어려운데, 고품질에 관한 모든 사람의 정의를 충족하는 합의된 기준이 없기 때문이다. '질'이라는 용어는 일반적으로 한 집단이나 공동체 내에서 높은 평가를 받는 어떤 속성, 서비스 또는 성과를 일컫는다. 따라서 질을 정의하는 것은 상황에 따라 다르고, 분야에 국한되며, 개인의 선호와 취향에 영향받는다. 그러나 음악과 그림 같은 다른 문화적 산물과 비교하여 저널리즘 콘텐츠는 시민적이고 민주적인 요소가 강하기 때문에 그것이 독특하다는 것에 주목하는 것이 중요하다. 언론을 '제4의 자산'이라고 보는 생각은 고품질 저널리즘이 감시자 역할을 하고, 대중 공론의 장을 제공하며, 신뢰할 수 있는 정보 제공자 역할을 함으로써 민주주의의 이상을 증진한다는 기대에서 비롯된다. 그러므로 뉴스의 질을 논할 때 규범적인 측면은 아무리 강조해도 지나치지 않다.

Solution Guide

음악, 그림 같은 문화적 산물과 다르게 저널리즘 콘텐츠는 시민적이고 민주적인 요소가 강하며 민주주의의 이상을 증진하는 역할을 하도록 기대되므로 뉴스의 질을 논할 때는 규범적인 측면을 강조해야 한다고 말하고 있으므로, 필자가 주장하는 바로 가장 적절한 것은 ①이다.

Structure in Focus

- **It** is important [to note, however, {that compared to other cultural products such as music and paintings, journalistic content is unique because it has a strong civic and democratic component}].
  It은 형식상의 주어이고, [ ]는 내용상의 주어이다. [ ] 안의 { }는 note의 목적어 역할을 하는 명사절이다.
- The idea of the press as the "fourth estate" stems from the expectation [that high-quality journalism promotes democratic ideals by {playing the role of a watchdog}, {providing a public forum}, and {serving as a reliable information provider}].
  [ ]는 the expectation과 동격 관계인데, 그 안에서 세 개의 { }는 and로 연결되어 전치사 by의 목적어 역할을 하는 동명사구이다.

03

정답 ③

소재 적과 반대자

해석 경영자가 명심해야 할 한 가지는 어떤 말다툼이라도 하고 나서는 울타리를 고쳐야 한다는 것이다. 반대자가 반드시 적은 아니다. 물론 반대자는 쟁점에 관해 여러분과 의견이 다르지만, 적은 여러분이 부정적인 관계도 또한 맺고 있는 사람이다. 그 점은 그것을 개인적으로 만든다. 여러분은 흔히 반대자와 함께 일하고 서로에게 성공적인 결과를 향해 전략을 세울 수 있지만, 적은 훨씬 더 어렵고 따라서 훨씬 더 위험하다. 반대자가 적이 되지 않게 노력하고 적을 단순한 반대자로 바꾸기 위해 노력하라. 합의점을 찾고 반대자였던 사람들을 여러분이 정당하게 옹호할 수 있는 방법을 찾아라. 말다툼의 주제는 결국 희미해지겠지만, 여러분은 여전히 관계가 필요하다.

Solution Guide

경영자는 어떤 말다툼이라도 하고 나서는 울타리를 고쳐야 하고, 반대자를 적으로 만들지 않으며, 적은 단순한 반대자로 만들기 위해 노력해야 한다는 내용이므로, 필자가 주장하는 바로 가장 적절한 것은 ③이다.

Structure in Focus

- An opponent disagrees with you on the issue, of course, but enemies are ones [with whom you also have a negative relationship].
  [ ]는 ones를 수식하는 관계절이다.
- Find points of agreement, and find ways [you can legitimately support those {who were your opponents}].
  [ ]는 ways를 수식하는 관계절이고, 그 안의 { }는 those를 수식하는 관계절이다.

04

정답 ②

소재 끊임없는 경제 성장 추구의 문제점

해석 어떤 특정한 종이라도 그것을 얼마나 많이 수확할 수 있는지에 대한 정치적 결정과 관리 결정은 흔히 벌어들일 수 있는 금액에 근거한다. 이윤은 경제 성장으로 이어지며, 이는 많은 정치인과 기업 리더의 목표이다. 하지만 지속적인 경제 성장을 추구할 때 발생하는 문제는 우리의 경제가 우리의 환경과 분리되어 있지 않다는 것이다. 우리 경제의 모든 것은 우리 환경에서 나온다. 우리는 주변 세계에서 자원을 채취하여, 우리가 먹거나 사용하는 제품으로 그것을 소비한 다음, 그 폐기물을 다시 지구에 버린다. 우리 지구는 유한한 생태계인데, 이것은 자연 과정이 제대로 기능하는 것을 멈추기까지, 우리가 우리 경제를 먹여 살리기 위해 자연계에서 단지 제한된 양만 채취할 수 있고, 지구는 단지 제한된 양의 폐기물만 흡수할 수 있다는 것을 의미한다. 점점 더 많은 자원을 채취하려는 끊임없는 노력은 사실 장기적으로 볼 때 생태학적으로 불가능하다. 우리의 생존은 생태계의 한계 내에서 살아가는 법을 배우는 데 달려 있다.

Solution Guide

우리의 경제가 우리의 환경과 분리되어 있지 않다는 것, 즉 생태계에 한계가 있다는 것을 고려하지 않고 지속적인 경제 성장을 추구하는 것은 문제를 일으킨다는 내용의 글이다. 따라서 필자가 주장하는 바로 가장 적절한 것은 ②이다.

Structure in Focus

- But [the problem with seeking continuous economic growth] is [that our economy is not separate from our environment].
  첫 번째 [ ]는 문장의 주어 역할을 하는 명사구이다. 두 번째 [ ]는 is의 주격 보어 역할을 하는 명사절이다.
- Our Earth is a finite ecosystem, [which means {there is only so much 〈that we can take from the natural world to feed our economy〉, and only so much waste 〈that the Earth can absorb〉, before natural processes stop functioning properly}].
  [ ]는 주절의 내용을 부가적으로 설명하는 관계절이고, 그 안의 { }는 means의 목적어 역할을 하는 명사절이다. 첫 번째 〈 〉는 only so much를 수식하는 관계절이고, 두 번째 〈 〉는 only so much waste를 수식하는 관계절이다.

05 함축적 의미 파악

Gateway ④
Exercises 01 ⑤ 02 ④ 03 ② 04 ②

Gateway

본문 28쪽

정답 ④

소재 스트레스에 대처하는 자세

해석 여러분이 여러분의 주의를 집중하는 방식은 여러분이 스트레스에 대처하는 방식에 중요한 역할을 한다. 주의가 분산되면 스트레스를 해소하는 여러분의 능력이 손상되는데, 왜냐하면 여러분의 주의가 분산되더라도, 그것이 좁게 집중되기 때문인데, 여러분이 여러분의 경험 중 스트레스가 많은 부분에만 집착할 수 있다는 이유로 인해서이다. 여러분의 주의의 초점이 넓어지면, 여러분은 스트레스를 더 쉽게 해소할 수 있다. 여러분은 어떤 상황이라도 그 상황의 더 많은 측면을 균형 있는 시각으로 볼 수 있으며, 피상적이고 불안을 유발하는 수준의 주의로 여러분을 옭아매는 한 부분에 갇히지 않을 수 있다. 초점이 좁으면 각 경험의 스트레스 수준이 높아지지만, 초점이 넓으면 여러분은 각 상황을 더 넓은 시각으로 더 잘 볼 수 있으므로 스트레스 수준이 낮아진다. 불안감을 유발하는 하나의 세부 사항은 더 큰 전체적인 상황보다 덜 중요하다. 그것은 여러분 자신이 눌어붙지 않는 프라이팬으로 탈바꿈하는 것과 같다. 여러분은 여전히 달걀을 부칠 수 있지만, 그 달걀이 팬에 눌어붙지 않을 것이다.

Structure in Focus

- Scattered attention harms your ability to let go of stress, [because {even though your attention is scattered}, {it is narrowly focused}, {for you are able to fixate only on the stressful parts of your experience}].
  [ ]는 because로 유도되는 부사절인데, 그 안에 세 개의 { }가 차례대로 양보의 부사절, 주절, 이유의 등위절로 쓰였다.
- You can [put in perspective many more aspects of any situation] and [not get locked into one part {that ties you down to superficial and anxiety-provoking levels of attention}].
  두 개의 [ ]는 and로 연결되어 can에 이어져 문장의 술어를 이룬다. 두 번째 [ ] 안의 { }는 one part를 수식하는 관계절이다.

Exercises

본문 30~33쪽

01

정답 ⑤

소재 지속 가능성을 추구하는 것의 엄중함

해석 삶에서 흑백 논리의 문제는 없다. 단정적인 답은 없다. 모든 것이 끊임없는 토의와 타협의 사안이다. 이것은 현재 우리 사회의 핵심 원칙 중 하나이다. 그 핵심 원칙이 틀렸기 때문에 결국 사회는 지속 가능성에 관해서 많은 문제를 유발하고 있다. 흑백 논리인 몇몇 문제가 '있다.' 정말로 넘어서는 안 되는 지구적이고 사회적인 경계가 있다. 예를 들어, 우리는 우리 사회가 다소 더 혹은 다소 덜 지속 가능할 수도 있다고 생각한다. 그러나 장기적으로 여러분은 다소 지속 가능할 수는 없으며, 여러분은 지속 가능하거나 지속 가능하지 않거나이다. 그것은 살얼음판 위를 걷는 것과 같은데, 그것이 여러분의 체중을 지탱하거나 그러지 못하거나이다. 여러분은 기슭에 도달하거나 깊고 어둡고 차가운 물속으로 빠지거나이다. 그리고 만일 그것이 우리에게 일어나기라도 한다면, 우리를 구조하러 올 근처의 행성은 전혀 없을 것이다. 우리는 전적으로 혼자인 것이다.

Solution Guide

지속 가능성의 문제는 흑백 논리이고, 지속 가능하거나 아니거나 둘 중의 하나일 뿐이며, 우리가 위태로운 상황을 벗어나 생존의 길로 가거나 아니거나 둘 중의 하나의 결과가 있을 뿐이라는 내용이므로, 밑줄 친 부분이 글에서 의미하는 바로 가장 적절한 것은 ⑤ '지속 가능성은 실패가 지구상의 생명체의 끝을 의미하는 매우 중요한 상황이다.'이다.

① 지속 가능성을 유지하려면 극단 사이의 균형이 필요하다.
② 우리는 기술을 득이 되거나 해로운 것으로 생각해서는 안 된다.
③ 우리의 생존은 세계적인 문제에 대해 개방적인 태도를 유지하는 데 달렸다.
④ 기후 변화 논쟁에서 실용적인 시각을 유지하는 것이 매우 중요하다.

Structure in Focus

- There are indeed planetary and societal boundaries [that must not be crossed].
  [ ]는 planetary and societal boundaries를 수식하는 관계절이다.
- And [if that **should happen** to us], there will not be any nearby planet [coming to our rescue].
  첫 번째 [ ]는 「should+동사원형」이 사용되어 미래에 대한 불확실한 추측을 나타내는 가정의 부사절이고, 두 번째 [ ]는 any nearby planet을 수식하는 분사구이다.

02

정답 ④

소재 19세기 시장 사회의 철학

해석 자유방임 경제와 시장 사회의 산물인 현대 기업은 사회에서 개인의 신분과 기능에 대한 필요성을 보지 못하는 것이 가장 큰 약점인 신조에 기반을 두고 있다. 시장 사회의 철학에는 경제적 보상 외에 다른 사회적 기준은 없다. 현대사의 흐름이 신분에서 계약으로 이어졌다는 Henry Maine의 유명한 경구는 사회적 신분과 기능이 전적으로 경제적 성공의 결과이어야 한다는 19세기의 신념을 깔끔하게 요약한다. 이러한 강조는 인간의 지위를 오로지 정치적으로 결정된 신분의 관점에서만 정의하고 따라서 기회의 평등을 부정하는 사회 개념에 대한 반란의 결과였다. 그러나 그 반란은 너무 멀리 나갔다. 정의를 확립하기 위해 그것은 좋은 사회는 정의와 신분을 모두 부여해야 한다는 것을 깨닫는 대신, (경제적으로) 성공하지 못하는 사람들, 즉 다수에게 의미와 성취감을 허용하지 않고 말았다.

Solution Guide

19세기 시장 사회의 철학은 사회적 신분이 정치적으로 결정되는 기존 질서를 바로잡기 위해 사회적 신분을 부여하는 기준으로 경제적 보상에만 집중한 결과, 경제적으로 성공하지 못하는 다수에게는 의미와 성취감을 부여하는 사회적 신분을 허용하지 않았다는 내용의 글이므로, 밑줄 친 부분이 글에서 의미하는 바로 가장 적절한 것은 ④ '(인간으로서의 사회적) 신분은 경제적 성공에 의해 가려졌다.'이다.

① 어떤 경제적인 보상도 실제로 이루어지지 않았다.
② 대중의 사회적 신분은 너무 많이 성장했다.
③ 사회는 개인을 오로지 사회적 존재로서만 규정했다.
⑤ 새로운 질서는 집단보다는 개인을 지나치게 강조했다.

Structure in Focus

- [The modern corporation as a child of laissez-faire economics and of the market society] is based on a creed [whose greatest weakness is the inability {to see the need for status and function of the individual in society}].
  첫 번째 [ ]는 문장의 주어 역할을 하는 명사구이다. 두 번째 [ ]는 a creed를 수식하는 관계절이고, 그 안의 { }는 the inability를 구체적으로 설명하는 to부정사구이다.
- Henry Maine's famous epigram [that the course of modern history has been from status to contract] neatly summarizes the belief of the nineteenth century, [that social status and function should be exclusively the result of economic advancement].

첫 번째 [ ]는 Henry Maine's famous epigram과 동격 관계이고, 두 번째 [ ]는 the belief of the nineteenth century와 동격 관계이다.

03

정답 ②

소재 섬유 재활용의 비현실성

해석 재료가 몇 번이고 다시 사용되고 재사용되면서 지속적으로 순환되는 '순환 경제'라는 개념은 매력적인 비전이다. 그러나 현재 우리가 그 목표로부터 그저 얼마나 멀리 있는지를 강조하는 것이 매우 중요하다. 비록 직물 대부분은 완전히 재활용할 수 있지만, 2015년에 전 세계적으로 폐의류의 73퍼센트가 소각되거나 매립되었다. 불과 12퍼센트만이 매트리스 충전재와 같은 저가치 직물 활용으로 재활용되었고 1퍼센트 미만이 의류로 다시 재활용되었다. 혹자는 '루프 닫기'라는 아이디어가 얼마나 현실적일 수 있는지 의문을 제기할 것인데, 의류업계의 복잡성은 재사용 순환에서 재료가 '누출'될 기회가 많다는 것을 의미한다는 것이다. 더욱이 섬유 재활용이 그 자체의 환경 발자국이 없는 것은 아니라는 점에 주목해야 한다. 중고 의류의 재사용조차도 자원 사용과 폐기물 측면에서 영향이 있는데, 특히 제품이 장거리로 운송되고, 드라이클리닝되고, 재포장되는 경우에 그렇다.

Solution Guide

폐의류가 실제로 재활용되는 비율이 상당히 낮고 이를 재사용하는 순환 과정에서도 환경 발자국을 남긴다는 점에서, '순환 경제'라는 매력적인 목표가 현실적으로 달성하기 어렵다는 내용의 글이다. 따라서 밑줄 친 부분이 글에서 의미하는 바로 가장 적절한 것은 ② '폐기물이 전혀 발생하지 않는 지속 가능한 직물 재활용'이다.

① 매 시즌 새로운 패션 제품 생산
③ 재활용 가능한 재료를 개발하기 위한 지속적인 노력
④ 수요를 맞출 수 있을 만큼만의 제작과 공급
⑤ 특정 패션 상품을 독점적으로 생산하는 것의 종말

Structure in Focus

- However, **it** is crucial [to highlight just how far we are from that goal at present].
  it은 형식상의 주어이고, [ ]는 내용상의 주어이다.
- Some would question [how realistic the idea of "closing the loop" can be]; the complexity of the fashion system means [that there are multiple opportunities {**for materials** to "leak" from the reuse cycle}].
  첫 번째 [ ]는 question의 목적어 역할을 하는 명사절이고, 두 번째 [ ]는 means의 목적어 역할을 하는 명사절이다. 두 번째 [ ] 안의 { }는 opportunities를 구체적으로 설명하는 to부정사구인데, for materials는 to부정사의 의미상의 주어를 나타낸다.

04

정답 ②

소재 시간의 영향

해석 시간의 영향을 예견할 때, 우리는 그것이 무엇일지를 마음속에서 예측해야 하며, 시간만이 이행할 수 있는 약속의 즉각적인 성과를 요구함으로써 그것이 일어나는 것을 실제로 막아서는 안 된다. 그런 요구를 하는 사람은 '시간'보다 더 나쁘거나 더 가혹한 고리대금업자가 없다는 것을 알게 될 것이며, 여러분이 '시간'에게 미리 돈을 줄 것을 강요한다면, 그 어느 고리대금업자가 요구하는 것보다 훨씬 더 높은 금리의 이자를 내야 하리라는 것을 알게 될 것이다. 예를 들어, 생석회를 쓰고 인공적인 열을 가해서 며칠 만에 갑자기 나무에 잎이 돋고 꽃이 피고 심지어 열매를 맺게 하는 것이 가능하지만, 그 후에 그 나무는 시들어 죽을 것이다. 따라서 젊은이는 단 몇 주 동안일 수도 있지만, 자신이 서른 살에 쉽게 할 수 있는 일을 열아홉 살에 하려고 시도함으로써 자신의 힘을 남용할 수도 있고, '시간'은 그가 요구하는 대출금을 줄 수도 있지만, 그가 내야 할 이자는 그 자신의 노년의 힘에서 나오는데, 진정 그것은 바로 그의 생명 자체의 일부이다.

Solution Guide

시간이 지나야 이루어질 수 있는 성과를 미리 얻으려고 하면, 어느 정도의 성과는 얻을 수 있지만, 그것에 대한 대가를 내야 한다는 내용의 글이므로, 밑줄 친 부분이 글에서 의미하는 바로 가장 적절한 것은 ② '적절한 시기가 오기 전에 시기상조의 결과를 얻으려고 한다'이다.

① 자신의 책임을 다른 사람에게 떠넘긴다
③ 일의 성공이나 실패를 예측하는 것을 목표로 한다
④ 일을 성공적으로 마치기 위해 충분한 시간을 요구한다
⑤ 예정보다 일찍 완료한 일에 대한 대가를 받기 원한다

Structure in Focus

- The man [who makes his demand] will find out [that there is no worse or stricter usurer than Time]; and [that, if you compel Time to give money in advance, you will have to pay a rate of interest much higher than any usurer would require].
  첫 번째 [ ]는 The man을 수식하는 관계절이고, 두 번째와 세 번째 [ ]는 find out의 목적어 역할을 하는 명사절이다.
- So a young man may abuse his strength — it may be only for a few weeks — by trying to do at nineteen

[what he could easily manage at thirty], and Time may give him the loan [for which he asks]; but the interest [he will have to pay] comes out of the strength of his later years; indeed, it is part of his very life itself.
첫 번째 [ ]는 do의 목적어 역할을 하는 명사절이다. 두 번째와 세 번째 [ ]는 각각 the loan과 the interest를 수식하는 관계절이다.

06 주제 파악

Gateway ②
Exercises 01 ④ 02 ⑤ 03 ⑤ 04 ⑤

Gateway

본문 34쪽

정답 ②

소재 삼림지가 제공하는 생태계 서비스의 비시장적 가치

해석 천연자원 관리자들은 일반적으로 이용에 대한 재정적 보상을 제공하는 시장 인센티브에 직면한다. 예를 들어, 삼림지 소유자들은 탄소 포집, 야생 생물 서식지, 범람 방지 및 다른 생태계 서비스를 위해 숲을 관리하기보다는 벌목을 위한 시장 인센티브를 가지고 있다. 이러한 (생태계) 서비스는 소유자에게 아무런 재정적 이익도 제공하지 않으므로, 관리 결정에 영향을 미치지 않을 것이다. 그러나 이러한 서비스가 그것들의 비시장적 가치에 근거하여 제공하는 경제적 이익은 목재의 경제적 가치를 초과할 수도 있다. 예를 들어, 유엔의 한 계획은 기후 조절, 수질 정화 및 침식 방지를 포함하여 열대림이 제공하는 생태계 서비스의 경제적 이익이 시장 이익보다 헥타르당 3배 넘게 크다고 추정했다. 따라서 벌목하는 것은 경제적으로 비효율적이며, 시장은 채취 이용보다 생태계 서비스를 선호하라는 올바른 '신호'를 보내지 않고 있다.

Structure in Focus

- For example, a United Nations initiative has estimated [that the economic benefits of ecosystem services {provided by tropical forests, including climate regulation, water purification, and erosion prevention}, are over three times greater per hectare than the market benefits].
  [ ]는 estimated의 목적어 역할을 하는 명사절이고, 그 안의 { }는 ecosystem services를 수식하는 분사구이다.
- Thus [cutting down the trees] is economically inefficient, and markets are not sending the correct "signal" [to favor ecosystem services over extractive uses].
  첫 번째 [ ]는 주어 역할을 하는 동명사구이고, 두 번째 [ ]는 the correct "signal"의 구체적인 내용을 설명하는 to부정사구이다.

Exercises

본문 36~37쪽

01

정답 ④

소재 표준화 시험 위주 교육의 문제점

해석 오늘날의 학교 체제에 불안한 변화가 진행 중이다. 재정 지원은 흔히 표준화 시험에서 얻는 점수와 결부되는데, 이 시험은 주로 기계적 암기를 평가한다. 이와 같은 시험에 '맞춰' 가르치는 것은 필연적으로 자원과 교육 과정을 점수가 낮은 학생에게 집중하게 한다. 이 힘겨워하는 학생들의 시험 점수를 끌어올려야 한다는 압박감은 모든 학생이 자신의 잠재력을 최대한 발휘할 수 있도록 장려하는 개별화된 학습 형태를 위한 시간을 제한하며, 교사는 창의적 사고를 장려하고 체험 활동을 포함할 기회가 줄어든다. 교육이 탐구, 발견, 문제 해결, 그리고 창의적 사고로 풍성해지지 않으면 학생은 자신의 학습에 진정으로 참여하지 않는다. 교사는 흥미를 주지 않는 워크북과 반복 학습을 강조해야 하므로, 점점 더 많은 학생에게 수학, 과학, 역사, 문법, 작문에 대해 부정적인 감정이 생기고 있다. 진정으로 지식을 배우고 기억할 수 있는 기회가 '시험에 맞춰' 가르치는 교육으로 바뀌고 있다.

Solution Guide

오늘날의 학교 체제는 학생을 표준화 시험을 준비시키는 데 집중하고 있는데, 이와 같은 방식으로 진행될 경우 학생과 교사에게 발생하는 여러 문제점을 나열하는 내용의 글이다. 따라서 글의 주제로 가장 적절한 것은 ④ '학생을 표준화 시험 준비에 집중시키는 것의 문제점'이다.

① 학생들이 시험을 치르는 동안 집중력을 유지하도록 도와주는 방법
② 학생들의 창의력 발달에 도움을 주기 위한 교육 접근 방식
③ 학생의 시험 점수를 성격과 연관 짓는 것의 위험
⑤ 체험 활동이 학생들의 학업 성취도에 미치는 영향

Structure in Focus

- Funding is frequently tied to scores [achieved on standardized tests], [which primarily evaluate rote memory].
  첫 번째 [ ]는 scores를 수식하는 분사구이고, 두 번째 [ ]는 standardized tests에 대해 부가적으로 설명하는 관계절이다.
- Opportunities [to authentically learn and retain knowledge] are being replaced by instruction [that teaches "to the tests]."
  첫 번째 [ ]는 Opportunities의 구체적인 내용을 설명하는 to부정사구이고, 두 번째 [ ]는 instruction을 수식하는 관계절이다.

02

정답 ⑤

소재 성인 뇌의 적응성

해석 오랫동안 성인의 뇌는 우리가 필요로 할 모든 뉴런과 주요 연결부를 가진 본질적으로 '고정된' 것으로 실제로 널리 믿어졌다. 물론 우리는 항상 새로운 것을 배우고 사물에 대한 이해를 업데이트하는데 이는 학습과 기억을 관장하는 네트워크에서 새로운 연결이 정기적으로 형성되고 교체되고 있다는 것을 뜻한다. 하지만 전체적인 물리적 구조와 주요 연결부, 즉 우리를 '지금의 우리'로 만드는 것의 측면에서 보면, 성인의 뇌는 '완성된' 것으로 오랫동안 여겨져 왔다. 하지만 최근 몇 년 동안 성인의 뇌는 변화하고 적응'할 수' 있고, 심지어 새로운 뉴런을 생성'할 수'도 있으며, 경험이 뇌를 여전히 재구성할 수 있는데, 우리가 황혼기에 접어들 때조차도 그러하다는 것을 보여 주는 증거가 꾸준히 이어져 왔다. 혼잡한 런던 거리를 계속 운전하고 주행하는 것이 해마 크기의 증가를 가져오고 이는 성인의 뇌 구조가 어느 정도 적응성이 있다는 사실을 밝히고 있는 택시 운전사를 대상으로 한 연구를 생각해 보라.

Solution Guide

성인의 뇌는 완성된 것으로 오랫동안 여겨져 왔지만, 최근 몇 년 동안 성인의 뇌가 변화하고 적응할 수 있으며 경험이 뇌를 여전히 재구성할 수 있다는 것을 보여 주는 증거가 꾸준히 있었다고 했으므로, 글의 주제로 가장 적절한 것은 ⑤ '새로운 경험에 적응하는 성인 뇌의 유연성'이다.

① 부정적인 삶의 경험이 두뇌 활동에 미치는 영향
② 뇌에서 신경 통로의 견고한 연결성
③ 성인의 뇌와 아이의 뇌 사이의 차이
④ 분석적이고 창의적인 사고를 위해 사용되는 뇌 부위

Structure in Focus

- For many years, **it** was indeed widely believed [that the adult brain was essentially 'set', with all the neurons and major connections {we'd need}].
  it은 형식상의 주어이고 [ ]는 내용상의 주어이며, 그 안의 { }는 all the neurons and major connections를 수식하는 관계절이다.
- Consider the taxi driver study, [where constant driving and navigation of chaotic London streets leads to increased hippocampus size, {revealing the adult brain structure is somewhat malleable}].
  [ ]는 the taxi driver study의 구체적 내용을 설명하는 관계절이다. 그 안의 { }는 앞에 기술된 내용을 부가적으로 설명하는 분사구문이다.

03

정답 ⑤

소재 이념적 원칙에 맞춰 창의적으로 거래 성사시키기

해석 흔히 이념적 원칙은 거래를 막겠다고 위협하는 법, 규칙 및 제도에서 구체화된다. 내셔널리즘은 모든 자원이 국가에 속하며 그 외에 누구도 그것을 소유할 수 없도록 요구한다. 이슬람 근본주의는 대출에 대한 이자 지불금을 금지한다. 이집트 사회주의는 노동자가 기업의 경영과 이익에 모두 참여할 것을 요구한다. 이러한 원칙 각각은 특정 사례에서 거래 성사에 걸림돌이 될 수 있다. 하지만 창의력을 조금 발휘하면 이념적 원칙을 존중하면서도 사업이 진행되는 방식으로 거래를 구성할 수 있다. 예를 들어, 노동자의 경영 참여는 회사 이사회의 자리를 의미할 필요는 없으며, 그저 회사 임원과 정기적으로 만나는 자문 위원회를 의미할 뿐이다. 그리고 석유 개발 계약서는 기름이 땅속에 있을 때가 아니라 그것이 유정(油井)의 철관 끝 테두리를 떠나는 시점에서 기름 소유권이 이전되는 방식으로 작성될 수 있다.

Solution Guide

이념적 원칙이 거래의 걸림돌이 될 수 있지만, 조금만 창의력을 발휘하면 이념적 원칙을 존중하면서도 사업이 진행되는 방식으로 거래를 구성할 수 있다는 내용의 글이다. 따라서 글의 주제로 가장 적절한 것은 ⑤ '이념적 장애물을 뚫고 나가기 위해 창의적으로 거래를 설계할 필요성'이다.

① 원래의 협상 원칙을 고수할 때의 문제점
② 보편적으로 받아들여지는 합의에 대한 이념적 장벽
③ 이념적 원리를 보편적으로 적용하는 것의 불가능성
④ 사업이 이념적 편견을 타파하는 데서 하는 중요한 역할

Structure in Focus

- Nationalism requires [that all resources belong to the state] and [that no one else may own them].
  두 개의 [ ]는 and로 연결되어 requires의 목적어 역할을 하는 명사절이다.
- And a petroleum development contract could be written in [**such a way that** the ownership of oil is transferred **not** {when the oil is in the ground} **but** {at the point 〈that it leaves the flange of the well〉}].
  [ ]에서 「such a way that ~」은 '~과 같은 방식'이라는 의미이며 that 이하는 a way를 수식하는 관계절이다. [ ] 안의 두 개의 { }는 「not ~ but ...」에 의해 연결되어 있고, 두 번째 { } 안의 〈 〉는 the point를 수식하는 관계절이다.

04

정답 ⑤

소재 지속 가능성에 대한 과학의 기여도

해석 모든 과학 지식과 관련 기술이 지속 가능성에 기여한다는 의심의 여지가 없는 가정은 지구의 문제들을 해결하기 위한 객관적 지식의 중요성에 대한 믿음에서 비롯된다. 과학자는 그러한 놀라운 일을 하는 데 이용될 수 있는 특별한 형태의 지식을 제공한다는 점에서 권력을 얻고 우리 시대의 사제가 된다. 그리고 우리는 흔히 그것을 과학적 지식에 대한 최종 시험으로 여기는데, 우리가 그것의 결과를 가지고 일을 '실행할' 수 있다는, 이를테면 멸종 위기종의 감소를 되돌리기 위해 그것을 적용하는 것이다. 그럼에도 불구하고, 우리는 이제 과학과 사회적 결과 사이의 관계에 대한 선형적 관점에 결함이 있다는 것을 알고 있다. 과학은 우리가 무언가를 할 수 있게 할지 모르지만, 더 광범위한 맥락적, 사회 생태학적 문제를 통합해야만 우리는 지속 가능성에 대한 그것의 기여도를 평가할 수 있다. 실제로는 우리가 문제를 설정하는 방식을 먼저 재평가해야 할지도 모르는데도 불구하고, 우리는 보통 지속 가능성을 현실 세계에서 무언가를 하는 것으로 생각한다.

Solution Guide

과학적 지식은 지속 가능성에 기여한다는 믿음이 있으나, 과학이 더 광범위한 맥락적, 사회 생태학적 문제를 통합해야만 지속 가능성에 대한 과학의 기여도를 평가할 수 있다는 내용의 글이므로, 글의 주제로 가장 적절한 것은 ⑤ '지속 가능성을 달성하기 위해 과학에 사회 환경적 요소를 통합해야 할 필요성'이다.

① 생물 다양성 손실과 그것이 인류에 미치는 영향에 대한 우려
② 모두를 위한 지속 가능한 미래의 중심이 되는 지속적인 과학적 진보
③ 경제 발전 문제를 해결하기 위한 과학에 대한 요구 사항
④ 기술 혁신의 유용성을 정당화하기 위한 다양한 과학적 방법

Structure in Focus

- The unquestioned assumption [that any and all scientific knowledge — and associated technology — contributes to sustainability] derives from faith in the importance of objective knowledge for solving global problems.
  [ ]는 The unquestioned assumption과 동격 관계이다.
- Regardless, we know now [that {the linear view of the relation between science and social outcomes} **is** flawed].
  [ ]는 know의 목적어 역할을 하는 명사절이고, 그 안의 { }는 that절의 주어 역할을 하는 명사구이며, 술어동사는 is이다.

07 제목 파악

Gateway ⑤
Exercises 01 ⑤ 02 ④ 03 ② 04 ⑤

Gateway

본문 38쪽

정답 ⑤

소재 단순하지 않은 과잉 관광의 개념

해석 과잉 관광의 개념은 관광학과 사회 과학 전반에서 흔히 볼 수 있는 사람과 장소에 관한 특정한 가정에 기초한다. 그 둘은 모두 명확하게 정의되고 경계가 정해진 것으로 여겨진다. 사람들은 주인 혹은 손님 역할을 하는 경계가 확실한 사회적 행위자로 표현된다. 마찬가지로, 장소는 명확한 경계가 있는 안정적인 용기로 취급된다. 그리하여, 장소는 관광객으로 가득 찰 수 있고, 따라서 과잉 관광으로 고통받을 수 있다. 하지만 어떤 장소가 사람으로 가득 차 있다는 것은 무엇을 의미하는가? 사실, 수용력이 제한적이며 사실상 더 많은 방문객을 수용할 공간이 없는 특정 명소의 예가 있다. 이것은 특히 에펠탑과 같은 일부 인공 건축물의 경우이다. 그러나 도시, 지역 또는 심지어 국가 전체와 같은 장소가 목적지로 홍보되고 과잉 관광의 피해지로 묘사되는 상황에서, 사정은 더 복잡해진다. 과도하거나 균형이 안 맞는 것은 매우 상대적이며, 물리적 수용력 이외에 (정치 및 지방 권력 역학은 말할 것도 없이) 자연의 질적 저하와 경제적 유출 같은 다른 측면과 더 관련이 있을 수도 있다.

Structure in Focus

- Indeed, there are examples of particular attractions [that have limited capacity] and [where there is actually no room for more visitors].
  두 개의 [ ]는 and로 연결되어 particular attractions를 수식하는 관계절이다.
- [What is excessive or out of proportion] is highly relative and might be more related to other aspects than physical capacity, [such as natural degradation and economic leakages (not to mention politics and local power dynamics)].
  첫 번째 [ ]는 주어 역할을 하는 명사절이고, 두 번째 [ ]는 other aspects의 구체적인 예를 열거하는 형용사구이다.

Exercises

본문 40~43쪽

01

정답 ⑤

소재 낭비되는 식품을 줄이는 방안

해석 애리조나 대학교 인류학 응용 연구국의 연구에 따르면, 일반 가정에서는 사용하지 않거나 상한 음식을 버려 식료품 지출의 평균 14퍼센트를 결국 낭비하게 된다. 훨씬 더 심각한 것은 이러한 낭비 중 15퍼센트는 개봉하지 않았고 아직 유통 기한 내에 있었던 제품을 포함한다는 것이다! (이 통계는 나를 정말 움찔하게 하는데, 기왕 말 나온 김에 그냥 달러 지폐를 불태우면 어떨까?) 이 연구는 또한 4인 가족이 육류, 농산물, 유제품, 곡물 제품 등 상하기 쉬운 식료품을 연간 평균 590달러어치 버린다는 것도 발견했다. 여러분은 상하기 쉬운 식품을 과도하게 사지 않음으로써 매달 평균 50달러를 절약할 수 있다. 쇼핑하기 전에 생필품을 점검하고 다음 주를 위해 사야 할 정확한 양을 추정하라. 이때는 또한 오래된 남은 음식은 버리고, 상하기 쉬운 품목은 틀림없이 눈에 잘 띄는 곳에 보관하며, 상태가 좋은 남은 음식은 그날의 식사로 다 먹어 치울 수 있는 좋은 시간이다.

Solution Guide

상하기 쉬운 식품을 과도하게 사지 않고, 쇼핑하기 전에 생필품을 점검하며, 식사를 위해 식품을 상태에 따라 정리함으로써 낭비되는 식품을 줄일 수 있다는 내용의 글이므로, 글의 제목으로 가장 적절한 것은 ⑤ '신중한 쇼핑과 식사 계획으로 식품 낭비를 줄이라'이다.

① 인내심은 전략적 쇼핑 덕목이다
② 싼 식품 가격에 현혹되지 말라
③ 건강과 영양을 위한 쇼핑 목록 만들기
④ (사야 할) 식료품 목록을 고수하고 가능한 한 빠르게 쇼핑하라

Structure in Focus

- Even worse, 15 percent of that waste includes products [that {were never opened} and {were still within their expiration date}]!
  [ ]는 products를 수식하는 관계절이다. 두 개의 { }는 and로 연결되어 that에 이어진다.
- This is also a good time [to {throw away outdated leftovers}, {make sure perishable items are in view}, and {use up good leftovers for that day's meals}].
  [ ]는 a good time을 수식하는 to부정사구이다. 세 개의 { }는 and로 연결되어 to에 이어진다.

02

정답 ④

소재 근거 없는 믿음이 되는 오래된 오류

해석 역사 내내, 인간의 상상력은 양날의 검이었다. 한편으로, 그것은 새로운 발견을 촉진하지만, 모든 새롭게 확립된 과학적인 사실마다, 흔히 다수의 부정확한 가설이 있고, 그것들은 도중에 수정되어야 하며 그러지 않으면 근거 없는 믿음이 되는 위험에 놓이게 된다. "나는 실패하지 않았다. 나는 작동하지 않을 1만 개의 방식을 찾았을 뿐이다."라고 말하여 오류가 발명의 한 부분이라고 암시한 사람은 Thomas Edison이라고 한다. 유감스럽게도, 오류나 부분적인 진실이 상당히 오래 유통되면, 그것들은 반복의 잘못된 메아리 방으로 이어지고 진실이 전혀 존재하지 않는데도 '진실'을 암시할 수 있다. 예를 들어, 여러 세기 동안 '체액'은 신빙성이 떨어졌음에도 불구하고 일부 사람들은 여전히 (혈액은 네 가지 '체액'의 하나여서) 혈액형이 성격을 결정할 수 있다는 근거 없는 믿음을 믿는다. 빠르게 인터넷 검색을 해 보면 이 주제와 관련된 5백만 개가 넘는 웹사이트가 발견되는데, 그것은 이 근거 없는 믿음이 없어지는 데 오래 걸린다는 것을 의미한다.

Solution Guide

새롭게 확립된 과학적인 사실에는 부정확한 다수의 가설이 있고, 그것은 오래 유통되면 근거 없는 믿음이 될 가능성이 있으며, 체액에 대한 근거 없는 믿음이 그 사례라는 내용의 글이다. 따라서 글의 제목으로 가장 적절한 것은 ④ '오래 지속된 오류에서 비롯된 쉽게 사라지지 않는 근거 없는 믿음'이다.

① 해가 되는 근거 없는 믿음과 싸우는 과학적 노력
② 과학적인 진실은 증명된 것인가 아니면 그냥 믿어진 것인가?
③ 왜 우리는 성격이 타고났다고 믿는가?
⑤ 성격 결정 요인으로서의 혈액형: 명백한 거짓말

Structure in Focus

- On one hand, it pushes new discoveries, but for every newly established scientific fact, there are often multiple incorrect hypotheses, [which {must be corrected along the way} or {risk becoming myths}].
  [ ]는 multiple incorrect hypotheses를 부가적으로 설명하는 관계절인데, 그 안에서 두 개의 { }가 or로 연결되어 which에 이어진다.
- For example, [even though the *humors* have been discredited for centuries], some still believe in the myth [that blood types (blood being one of the four *humors*) can determine personalities].
  첫 번째 [ ]는 양보의 의미를 나타내는 부사절이며, 두 번째 [ ]는 the myth와 동격 관계이다.

03

정답 ②

소재 혼자 하는 예술 활동의 이점

해석 이상적으로, 우리가 혼자 예술을 창작하거나 어떤 창의적인 활동이든 할 때, 우리는 그것의 가치를 인정하고 우리 삶에서 그것을 위한 시간과 공간을 할애한다. 지난 몇 년 동안 컬러링(색칠하기) 북과 컬러링 페이지의 인기가 그러한 사례의 하나이다. 그것은 시각 예술 창작과 기술의 어려운 부분을 없애고 비교적 쉽고 감당할 만한 수준의 도전을 제공한다. 암 환자와 간병인을 대상으로 한 우리의 연구는 색칠하기와 같은 혼자 하는 활동이 우리를 일상적인 걱정에서 벗어날 수 있는 공간으로 데려감으로써 명상적, 성찰적 방식으로 도움이 됨을 보여 주었다. 이러한 활동이 우리가 우리의 문제를 해결하는 것에 꼭 도움이 되는 것은 아니지만, 그보다는 우리가 그것들을 직접적으로 해결할 수 있는 그런 시간이 생길 때까지 휴식하는 시간과 다른 곳에 주의를 집중하는 방법을 제공한다. 우리가 혼자서 예술을 창작하면, 그것은 우리가 우리 자신을 통제하는 데, 우리 삶에 대한 숙달감, 통제감, 주체성을 느끼는 데, 그리고 성찰, 검증, 사색 또는 명상 수행을 하는 데 도움이 될 수 있다.

Solution Guide

혼자 예술을 창작하는 활동이 우리가 겪고 있는 문제의 직접적인 해결법이 될 수는 없겠지만 그 문제에서 벗어나 잠시 휴식할 시간과 삶에 대한 주체성, 그리고 사색이나 명상 수행 등의 기회를 제공한다는 점에서 정신적인 이점을 갖고 있다는 내용의 글이다. 따라서 글의 제목으로 가장 적절한 것은 ② '혼자 하는 창작 활동: 정신적 도구 상자'이다.

① 협동해서 예술을 창작하는 것의 치유 효과
③ 컬러링(색칠하기) 북: 간병인을 위한 새롭게 떠오르는 취미 활동
④ 감당할 만한 과업보다 어려운 과업이 더 재미있다
⑤ 명상에 대한 근거 없는 믿음: 정말 그것이 집중력을 향상하는가?

Structure in Focus

- [The boom in coloring books and coloring pages in the past few years] **is** one such example.
  [ ]는 문장의 주어 역할을 하는 명사구이고, 술어동사는 is이다.
- It [takes away the challenging part of visual art-making and skills] and [provides us with a level of challenge {that is relatively easy and manageable}].
  두 개의 [ ]는 and로 연결되어 문장의 술어 역할을 한다. 두 번째 [ ] 안의 { }는 a level of challenge를 수식하는 관계절이다.

04

정답 ⑤

소재 과학에서 중요한 것

해석 갈릴레오가 경사면에서 공을 굴렸을 때, 무슨 일이 일어나는지 그저 쳐다보며 보기만 한 것은 아니었다. 그는 이동 거리와 그 거리를 이동하는 데 걸린 시간을 매우 주의 깊게 측정했다. 이러한 측정으로부터 그는 이동 속도를 계산했다. 그가 생각해 낸 것은 수량과 관련한 수학 방정식이었다. 우리는 그가 목성의 위성을 관찰했을 때 밤마다 여러 다른 장소에서 몇 개의 점들을 그저 보기만 한 것이 아니라, 그 점들이 어디에 있는지 추적하고, 밤마다 그것들의 위치를 비교하였으며, 아마 그것들이 어떤 경로로 이동하고 있는지 산출하려는 의도가 있는 몇 가지 계산을 수행하여, 그것들의 시위치 변화가 그것들이 목성 주위를 도는 천체라는 것과 일치한다는 것을 알아냈다고 상상할 수 있다. 마찬가지로, 내가 하는 가상의 새 실험에서 나는 내 자신을 새장에 넣은 먹이의 무게를 재고 새가 먹은 것의 무게로 비율을 계산하는 초보 신예 과학자라고 상상했다. 분명한 것은, 과학에는 숫자가 중요하다는 것이다. 과학자는 측정하고 계산하며, 단지 관찰만 하는 것이 아니다.

Solution Guide

갈릴레오가 어떤 현상에 대해 단지 보기만 한 것이 아니라 계산도 했듯이, 과학은 단지 관찰만 하는 것이 아니라 측정하고 계산하는 것도 중요하다는 내용의 글이다. 따라서 글의 제목으로 가장 적절한 것은 ⑤ '진정한 과학 활동: 측정과 관찰을 결합하는 것'이다.

① 일반적이지 않다: 과학 측정의 불확실성
② 과학 연구에서 정확한 계산이라는 환상
③ 과학자의 연구가 해를 끼치는 데 사용되면 누가 책임을 지는가?
④ 과학에서 실험과 이론 중 무엇이 더 중요한가?

Structure in Focus

- He very carefully measured [the distance {traveled}] and [the time {it took to travel that distance}].
  두 개의 [ ]는 and로 연결되어 measured의 목적어 역할을 한다. 첫 번째 [ ] 안의 { }는 the distance를 수식하는 과거분사이고, 두 번째 [ ] 안의 { }는 the time을 수식하는 관계절이다.
- Similarly, in my hypothetical bird experiment I imagined myself as a budding junior scientist [weighing the stuff {I put into the cage}] and [calculating percentages by weight of {what was eaten}].
  and로 연결된 두 개의 [ ]는 a budding junior scientist를 수식하는 분사구이다. 첫 번째 [ ] 안의 { }는 the stuff을 수식하는 관계절이고, 두 번째 [ ] 안의 { }는 전치사 of의 목적어 역할을 하는 명사절이다.

08 도표 정보 파악

Gateway ④
Exercises 01 ⑤ 02 ⑤ 03 ⑤ 04 ④

Gateway

본문 44쪽

정답 ④

소재 때때로 또는 자주 적극적으로 뉴스를 회피한 응답자 비율

해석 위 도표는 2017년, 2019년, 그리고 2022년에 때때로 또는 자주 적극적으로 뉴스를 회피한 다섯 개 국가의 응답자 비율을 보여 준다. 세 해 각각에 대해, 아일랜드가 도표상의 국가 중, 때때로 또는 자주 적극적으로 뉴스를 회피한 응답자의 가장 높은 비율을 보여 주었다. 독일의 경우, 때때로 또는 자주 적극적으로 뉴스를 회피한 응답자 비율이 세 해 각각 30퍼센트를 밑돌았다. 덴마크의 경우, 2019년에 때때로 또는 자주 적극적으로 뉴스를 회피한 응답자 비율이 2017년의 비율보다는 더 높았으나 2022년의 비율보다는 더 낮았다. 핀란드의 경우, 2019년에 때때로 또는 자주 적극적으로 뉴스를 회피한 응답자 비율이 2017년의 비율보다 더 낮았으며, 이는 일본도 마찬가지였다. 일본의 경우, 때때로 또는 자주 적극적으로 뉴스를 회피한 응답자 비율이 세 해 각각 15퍼센트를 넘지 않았다.

Structure in Focus

- For each of the three years, Ireland showed [the highest percentage of the respondents {who sometimes or often actively avoided news}], among the countries in the graph.
  [ ]는 showed의 목적어 역할을 하는 명사구이고, 그 안의 { }는 the respondents를 수식하는 관계절이다.
- In Denmark, the percentage of the respondents [who sometimes or often actively avoided news in 2019] was higher than **that** in 2017 but lower than **that** in 2022.
  [ ]는 the respondents를 수식하는 관계절이고, 두 개의 that은 모두 the percentage of the respondents who sometimes or often actively avoided news를 대신한다.

Exercises

본문 46~49쪽

01

정답 ⑤

소재 국가별 1인당 연간 음식물 쓰레기 양

해석 위 도표는 선정된 9개 국가에 대한 소매 및 가정 단계에서의 1인당 연간 음식물 쓰레기 총량을 보여 준다. 그 국가들 중 사우디아라비아가 1인당 연간 음식물 쓰레기 총량이 가장 많았고, 호주와 덴마크가 바로 그 뒤를 이었다. 오스트리아는 1인당 연간 음식물 쓰레기 총량이 50kg 미만인 유일한 국가였다. 소매 단계에서의 1인당 연간 음식물 쓰레기 면에서는 덴마크가 25kg을 넘어서 1위를 차지했다. 독일은 영국과 1인당 연간 음식물 쓰레기 총량이 거의 같았다. 가정 단계에서는 미국이 거의 뉴질랜드만큼 낭비했고, 게다가 소매 단계에서는 전자가 후자보다 훨씬 더 적게 낭비했다.

Solution Guide

소매 단계에서 더 적은 음식물을 낭비한 국가는 미국이 아니라 뉴질랜드였으므로, 도표의 내용과 일치하지 않는 것은 ⑤이다.

Structure in Focus

- Among the countries, Saudi Arabia had the largest amount of total annual food waste per capita, [immediately followed by Australia and Denmark].
  [ ]는 주절이 기술하는 상황에 부수하는 상황을 나타내는 분사 구문이다.
- Austria was the only country [whose total annual food waste per capita was less than 50 kg].
  [ ]는 the only country를 수식하는 관계절이다.

02

정답 ⑤

소재 세계 스키 핫스팟의 시즌별 평균 스키어 방문 수

해석 위 도표는 2022년 4월 현재, 세계 스키 핫스팟의 시즌별 최근 5년 평균 스키어 방문 수를 보여 준다. 미국은 10개국 중 시즌별 평균 스키어 방문 수가 가장 많았는데, 내국인 스키어의 수가 5천만 명을 넘었다. 오스트리아는 10개국 중 두 번째로 시즌별 평균 스키어 방문 수가 많았고, 가장 많은 외국인 스키어 방문 수를 기록했다. 일본의 시즌별 평균 내국인 스키어 방문 수는 이탈리아의 시즌별 평균 내국인 스키어 방문 수와 외국인 스키어 방문 수를 합친 수보다 많았다. 이탈리아의 시즌별 평균 스키어 방문 수는 스위스의 시즌별 평균 스키어 방문 수보다 많았는데, 그 차이는 30만 명이었다. 시즌별 평균 스키어 방문 수가 1,000만 명 미만인 두 국가는 스웨덴과 독일이었는데, 후자가 전자보다 스키어의 수가 더 많았다.

Solution Guide

시즌별 평균 스키어 방문 수가 1,000만 명 미만인 두 국가는 스웨덴과 독일이었는데, 후자(독일)의 방문 수 700만 명으로 전자(스웨덴)의 방문 수 920만 명보다 더 적었으므로, 도표의 내용과 일치하지 않는 것은 ⑤이다.

Structure in Focus

- The average number of domestic skier visits per season in Japan was more than **that** of domestic and foreign skier visits per season combined in Italy.
  that은 the average number를 대신한다.

03

정답 ⑤

소재 미국 학생들이 재미로 책을 읽는 빈도

해석 위 도표는 1984년부터 2020년까지 9세와 13세의 미국 학생들이 재미로 책을 읽는 빈도에 대한 설문 조사 결과를 보여 준다. 1984년에는 9세의 절반 이상이 거의 매일 재미로 책을 읽는다고 답했지만, 2020년에는 그 비율이 재미로 책을 읽는 빈도가 낮다고 답한 9세의 비율과 같은 수준으로 떨어졌다. 2020년에는 재미로 책을 전혀 읽지 않거나 거의 읽지 않는다고 답한 9세의 비율이 설문 기간 중 가장 높은 수준이었다. 2020년 설문에 참여한 13세 중 거의 매일 재미로 책을 읽는다고 답한 비율은 17퍼센트로, 1984년에 그렇다고 말한 비율의 절반보다 더 작았다. 2020년에는 이 연령대의 학생 10명 중 약 3명이 자신은 재미로 책을 전혀 읽지 않거나 거의 읽지 않는다고 답했으며, 이것은 1984년과 비교해서 21퍼센트포인트 증가한 것이다. 2020년에 재미로 책을 읽는 빈도가 낮다고 답한 13세의 비율은 똑같이 답한 9세의 비율보다 12퍼센트포인트 더 낮았다.

Solution Guide

2020년에 재미로 책을 읽는 빈도가 낮다고 답한 13세의 비율은 54퍼센트로, 똑같이 답한 9세의 비율인 42퍼센트보다 12퍼센트포인트 더 높았으므로, 도표의 내용과 일치하지 않는 것은 ⑤이다.

Structure in Focus

- In 2020, the proportion of 9-year-olds [who said {they never or hardly ever read for fun}] was at its highest level in the survey period.
  [ ]는 9-year-olds를 수식하는 관계절이고, 그 안의 { }는 said의 목적어 역할을 하는 명사절이다.

04

정답 ④

소재 미국 성인의 온라인 쇼핑 기기

해석 위 도표는 연령 및 소득에 따른 기기별 분포를 포함하여 2022년 미국 성인이 온라인 쇼핑에 사용한 기기를 보여 준다. 2022년에 대부분의 미국인이 온라인 쇼핑을 할 때 가장 선호하는 방식은 스마트폰이었고, 약 4분의 3이 온라인 구매 시 스마트폰을 사용한다고 말했다. 이에 비해, 69퍼센트는 온라인 쇼핑 시 데스크톱 또는 노트북 컴퓨터를 사용한다고 답했고, 반면에 태블릿을 사용한다는 응답은 28퍼센트에 불과했다. 온라인 쇼핑 시 스마트폰 사용은 50세 미만의 성인에서 더 많이 나타났는데, 특히 30~49세의 92퍼센트가 스마트폰을 사용하여 온라인 쇼핑을 한다고 응답했다. 한편, 태블릿을 이용한 온라인 쇼핑의 연령별 차이를 살펴보면, 18~29세가 30세 이상보다 온라인 쇼핑 시 태블릿을 사용할 가능성이 더 컸다. 온라인 쇼핑을 위한 기기 형태는 또한 가구 소득에 따라 달랐는데, 소득이 높을수록 온라인 구매 시 각각의 기기를 사용할 가능성이 더 컸다.

Solution Guide

30세 이상의 연령층은 모두 18~29세의 연령층보다 온라인 쇼핑 시 태블릿을 사용하는 비율이 더 높았다. 따라서 도표의 내용과 일치하지 않는 것은 ④이다.

Structure in Focus

- In comparison, 69% reported using a desktop or laptop computer for online shopping, [while only 28% said they used a tablet].
  [ ]는 대조를 나타내는 부사절이다.
- The use of smartphones for online shopping was more common among adults under 50 years old, especially [with 92% of those aged 30 to 49 reporting that they shopped online using a smartphone].
  [ ]는 「with + 명사구(92% of those aged 30 to 49) + 분사구(reporting that they shopped online using a smartphone)」의 구조로 주절이 기술하는 상황에 부수하는 상황을 나타낸다.

09 내용 일치·불일치(설명문)

Gateway ②

Exercises 01 ⑤ 02 ⑤ 03 ④ 04 ④

Gateway

본문 50쪽

정답 ②

소재 미국의 물리학자 Charles H. Townes

해석 가장 영향력 있는 미국의 물리학자 중 한 명인 Charles H. Townes는 사우스캐롤라이나주에서 태어났다. 어린 시절에 그는 농장에서 성장하며 하늘에 있는 별을 연구했다. 1939년에 그는 California Institute of Technology에서 박사 학위를 받았고, 그 후 뉴욕시에 있는 Bell Labs에서 일자리를 얻었다. 제2차 세계 대전 후에 그는 Columbia 대학교의 물리학 부교수가 되었다. 1958년에 Townes와 그의 동료 연구자는 레이저의 개념을 제안했다. 레이저 기술은 산업과 연구에서 빠르게 인정받았다. 1964년에 그는 노벨 물리학상을 받았다. 그는 또한 달 착륙 프로젝트인 아폴로 프로젝트에 관여했다. 인터넷과 모든 디지털 미디어는 레이저 없이는 상상할 수 없을 것이므로, 그의 공헌은 값을 매길 수 없을 정도이다.

Structure in Focus

- In his childhood, he grew up on a farm, [studying the stars in the sky].
  [ ]는 주어 he를 부가적으로 설명하는 분사구문이다.
- His contribution is priceless [because the Internet and all digital media would be unimaginable without the laser].
  [ ]는 이유의 부사절이다.

Exercises

본문 52~53쪽

01

정답 ⑤

소재 Gladys West의 생애

해석 Gladys West는 미국의 수학자이다. 그녀는 1930년에 버지니아주의 시골에서 태어났다. 그녀는 가족의 작은 농장에서 성장했고 좋은 교육을 받을 것을 꿈꿨다. 그녀는 열심히 공부했고 역사적으로 흑인 대학이었던 Virginia State College(오늘날

Virginia State University)에 갈 장학금을 받았다. 1956년 그녀는 버지니아주 Dahlgren에 있는 해군 기지에 수학자로 고용되었다. 그녀는 그 기지에 고용된 두 번째 흑인 여성이자 단 네 명의 흑인 직원 중 한 명이었다. 그곳에서, West는 지구의 크기, 모양, 중력장의 측정을 다루는 응용 수학에 중요한 기여를 했다. West와 그녀의 팀은 GPS 시스템이 지구상의 어느 장소에 대해서도 정확한 계산을 할 수 있게 하는 모델을 만들었다. West는 1998년 68세로 그 기지에서 퇴직했지만, 자신의 교육을 계속했다. 그녀는 나중에 원격 교육으로 Virginia Tech에서 행정학 박사 학위를 마쳤다.

Solution Guide

68세로 해군 기지에서 퇴직했지만, 자신의 교육을 계속했다(West retired from the base in 1998 at the age of 68 but continued her education.)는 내용이 있으므로, 글의 내용과 일치하지 않는 것은 ⑤이다.

Structure in Focus

- She [was the second black woman {to be hired at the base}] and [was one of only four black employees].
  두 개의 [ ]는 and로 연결되어 문장의 술어 역할을 한다. 첫 번째 [ ] 안의 { }는 the second black woman을 수식하는 to부정사구이다.
- There, West made significant contributions to the applied mathematics [that deals with the measurement of the Earth's size, shape, and gravitational field].
  [ ]는 the applied mathematics를 수식하는 관계절이다.

02

정답 ⑤

소재 포르투갈 전통 음악 fado

해석 fado는 포르투갈어로 '운명'이라는 뜻이지만, 리스본에서 유래한 음악의 한 형태의 이름이기도 하다. 그것은 보통 한 명의 가수에 의해 공연되는데, 두 대의 *guitarras*(만돌린 모양의 12현 기타)와 한 대의 *viola*(스페인 기타)로 반주된다. fado 가사는 흔히 일상생활의 고단한 현실이나 사랑의 시련에 중점을 둔다. fado는 또한 이룰 수 없는 것에 대한 갈망인 *saudade*라는 개념과 관련이 있다. fado 가수로 알려진 *fadistas*는 종종 검은색 애도의 숄을 착용하지만, 노래는 경쾌할 수도 있다. 19세기 이후, fado는 리스본의 노동자 계층 구역에 있는 바와 클럽에서 공연되었다. 그것은 Salazar 시대에 번성하다가, 1974년 혁명 이후 인기가 떨어졌다. 최근에 이 장르가 부활하여 리스본 곳곳의 *casas de fado*에서 새로운 세대의 음악가들과 가수들이 노래하는 것을 들을 수 있다.

Solution Guide

Salazar 시대에 번성하다가, 1974년 혁명 이후 인기가 떨어졌다(It flourished during the Salazar years, before falling out of favour after the 1974 Revolution.)고 했으므로, 글의 내용과 일치하지 않는 것은 ⑤이다.

Structure in Focus

- It is usually performed by one singer, [accompanied by dual *guitarras* (mandolin-shaped 12-string guitars) and a *viola* (Spanish guitar)].
  [ ]는 주절이 기술하는 상황에 부수하는 상황을 나타내는 분사구문이다.
- Fado is also linked with the notion of *saudade*, [which is a longing for something {impossible to attain}].
  [ ]는 *saudade*를 부가적으로 설명하는 관계절이고, 그 안의 { }는 something을 수식하는 형용사구이다.

03

정답 ④

소재 마야의 구기 경기

해석 마야의 구기 경기는 마야 문화의 매우 중요한 부분이었다. 그 구기 경기는 두 명의 선수나 두 팀의 선수들에 의해 행해졌다. 경기의 목표는 상대 팀이 다른 돌 고리에 공을 넣지 못하게 하는 동안, 공을 돌 고리 중 하나에 넣는 것이었다. 공은 농구공보다 조금 더 컸고 단단한 고무로 만들어졌다. 보호를 위해 선수들은 단단한 가죽 장갑, 팔꿈치 및 무릎 보호대, 마스크, 그리고 나무나 돌로 만들어진 벨트를 착용했다. 비록 모든 역사가가 동의하는 것은 아니지만, 몇몇 역사가들은 규칙상 선수들이 자신의 손이나 발로 공을 건드리는 것이 허용되지 않았다고 생각한다. 그들은 오로지 자신의 팔꿈치, 골반 부위, 무릎만 사용하여 공을 쳤고, 공이 땅에 닿지 않도록 해야 했다. 모든 계층의 관중들이 경기를 보며 내기하기를 좋아했다.

Solution Guide

공이 땅에 닿지 않도록 해야 했다(had to keep the ball from touching the ground)고 했으므로, 글의 내용과 일치하지 않는 것은 ④이다.

Structure in Focus

- For protection, players wore [hard leather gloves, elbow and knee pads, masks, and belts {that were made of wood or stone}].
  [ ]는 wore의 목적어 역할을 하는 명사구이고, 그 안의 { }는 belts를 수식하는 관계절이다.

- [Although not all historians agree], some think [the rules did not allow players to touch the ball with their hands or feet].
  첫 번째 [ ]는 양보를 나타내는 부사절이고, 두 번째 [ ]는 think의 목적어 역할을 하는 명사절이다.

04

정답 ④

소재 조각가 Lysippus

해석 Lysippus는 기원전 4세기의 위대한 조각가 중 가장 저명하고, 다작을 하였으며, 장수했다. 그는 1,500개의 작품을 제작한 것으로 전해질 정도로 활발하게 활동했는데, 그것들 모두 청동으로 만들어졌다. 당대 가장 뛰어난 예술가로 여겨진 Lysippus는 당연히 알렉산더 대왕의 총신, 실은 궁정 조각가가 되었다. 그 세계 정복자는 거의 다른 어느 누구에게도 자신을 조각하는 것을 허용하지 않았다. Lysippus는 Cassander와 Seleucus 1세 등 알렉산더 대왕의 서로 싸우는 많은 후계자의 초상 흉상을 계속해서 만들었다. Peloponnese의 Sicyon 출신으로 Lysippus는 그의 아들들이 그의 사후에도 이어 나갔던 거의 산업적인 규모의 작업장을 운영했다. Pliny와 같은 고대 작가들은 Lysippus가 완전히 새로운 규범, 즉 수학적으로 계산된 이상적인 미를 만들어 내어 Polyclitus의 규범을 거의 대체했다고 말한다.

Solution Guide

거의 산업적인 규모의 작업장을 운영했으며, 그의 아들들이 Lysippus 사후에도 그것을 이어 나갔다고 했으므로, 글의 내용과 일치하지 않는 것은 ④이다.

Structure in Focus

- [A native of Sicyon in the Peloponnese], Lysippus ran a workshop of almost industrial size [that was continued after his death by his sons].
  첫 번째 [ ]는 주절의 주어인 Lysippus와 동격 관계이고, 두 번째 [ ]는 a workshop of almost industrial size를 수식하는 관계절이다.
- Ancient writers such as Pliny relate [that Lysippus invented {an entirely new canon}, or {mathematically calculated ideal beauty}, almost displacing **that** of Polyclitus].
  [ ]는 relate의 목적어 역할을 하는 명사절이고, 그 안의 두 개의 { }는 동격 관계이다. that은 the canon을 대신한다.

10 내용 일치·불일치(실용문)

Gateway ③

Exercises 01 ④ 02 ④ 03 ③ 04 ④

Gateway

본문 54쪽

정답 ③

소재 Turtle Island 보트 투어

해석 **Turtle Island 보트 투어**

환상적인 Turtle Island 보트 투어가 아름다운 바다 세계로 여러분을 초대합니다.

날짜: 2024년 6월 1일부터 8월 31일까지

투어 시간

주중	오후 1시~오후 5시
주말	오전 9시~오후 1시
	오후 1시~오후 5시

※ 각각의 투어는 네 시간 동안 진행됩니다.

표와 예약

- 투어별로 1인당 50달러
  (17세 이상만 참가할 수 있습니다.)
- 예약은 늦어도 투어 당일 이틀 전에 완료되어야 합니다.
- 출발 시간 이후에는 환불 불가
- 각각의 투어 그룹 규모는 10명의 참가자로 제한됩니다.

활동

- 전문 다이버와 함께 하는 스노클링
- 열대어에게 먹이 주기

※ 저희 웹사이트인 www.snorkelingti.com을 마음껏 탐색하세요.

Structure in Focus

- [The fantastic Turtle Island Boat Tour] invites you to the beautiful sea world.
  [ ]는 문장의 주어 역할을 하는 명사구이다.
- Only those [aged 17 and over] can participate.
  [ ]는 those를 수식하는 분사구이다.

Exercises

본문 56~59쪽

01

정답 ④

소재 미술관 보수 공사 공지

해석 **Sunflower 미술관 보수 공사 공지**

보수 공사: 2024년 3월 1일~31일

미술관은 보수 공사 기간 동안 휴관할 것입니다.

성대한 재개관 전시회(4월 1일~30일): '봄의 꽃'

미술관 회원권 변경	상품권 변경
생일 입장권 20퍼센트 할인 3월 생일은 4월에 생일 할인을 받을 수 있습니다. **미술관 포인트 만료일** 3월에 만료되는 모든 미술관 포인트의 만료일은 두 달 연장될 것입니다.	사용 기간에 3월이 포함된 모든 상품권은 한 달 더 유효할 것입니다. (예: 2023년 12월~2024년 6월은 2024년 7월까지 유효할 것입니다.)

• 보수 공사 기간 동안에 미술관 안내 데스크는 열려 있을 것입니다.

• 언제나 그렇듯, 우리 디지털 미술관은 연중무휴로 열립니다!

Solution Guide

3월이 사용 기간에 포함된 모든 상품권은 한 달 더 유효할 것이다(All vouchers with March included in the term will be valid for an additional month.)라는 언급이 있으므로, 안내문의 내용과 일치하지 않는 것은 ④이다.

Structure in Focus

■ [All vouchers {with March included in the term}] will be valid for an additional month.

[ ]는 문장의 주어 역할을 하는 명사구이며, 그 안의 { }는 「with+명사(구)+분사구」의 구조로 All vouchers를 수식한다.

02

정답 ④

소재 Kids' Night Out

해석 **Kids' Night Out**

Kids' Night Out은 5~12세 사이의 어린이들이 Chester 대학교의 레크리에이션 센터에 와서 놀고, 공예 활동을 하고, 영화 보고, 다른 어린이들과 교류하고, 피자 파티를 즐길 수 있는 기회입니다.

행사 날짜

– 5월부터 8월까지 매월 둘째 주 금요일

일정

오후 5:00~6:15: 공예

오후 6:15~6:50: 피자 파티

오후 6:50~7:55: 영화 보기

오후 7:55~9:00: 기타 활동

* 픽업은 프로그램이 끝나기 30분 전인 오후 8시 30분부터 시작됩니다.

등록

– 등록은 www.curc.edu에서 온라인으로 하며, 비용은 어린이 당 30달러입니다.

– 등록은 각 행사 당일 전날 오후 5시까지 해야 합니다.

– 대학교의 교직원인 경우, 대학교 ID와 비밀번호를 사용하여 로그인하세요.

– 현재 대학교의 교직원이 아닌 경우, '등록'을 선택하여 손님 계정을 만드세요.

Solution Guide

등록은 각 행사 당일 전날 오후 5시까지 해야 한다(Registration is required by 5 p.m. the day prior to each event day.)고 했으므로, 안내문의 내용과 일치하는 것은 ④이다.

Structure in Focus

■ Kids' Night Out is an opportunity [**for children ages 5–12** to come to the Chester University Recreation Center to play, do crafts, watch a movie, interact with other children, and enjoy a pizza party].

[ ]는 an opportunity를 구체적으로 설명하는 to부정사구이고, for children ages 5–12는 to부정사의 의미상의 주어를 나타낸다.

03

정답 ③

소재 2024 Sunrise 동물원 봄 캠프

해석 **2024 Sunrise 동물원 봄 캠프**

Sunrise 동물원 봄 캠프에서 새로운 계절을 맞이하고 자연의 경이로움을 발견하세요! 참가자는 Sunrise 동물원을 탐험하고 봄에 돌아오는 식물, 꽃가루받이 매개자, 동물에 대해 배우게 될 것입니다.

■ 모든 캠프는 3일(3월 6일~8일) 일정으로 오전 9시부터 오후 3시까지 진행됩니다.

■ 참가자는 편안한 신발을 포함한 야외용 복장을 착용해야 합니다.

- 참가자는 점심 도시락과 마실 것을 지참해야 합니다. 간식은 제공될 것입니다.
- 비용: 120달러
- 캠프: 4개의 캠프가 학년에 따라 운영됩니다.
  - 동물원 어린아이(어린이집 및 유치원)
  - 동물원 친구들(1학년 및 2학년)
  - 동물원 탐험가(3학년 및 4학년)
  - 동물원 조사관(5학년 및 6학년)

등록 세부 사항

- 등록하고 전체 프로그램 세부 정보를 보려면 www.sunrisezoo.org를 방문하세요.
- 전화 등록은 받지 않습니다.
- 궁금한 점이 있으시면, education@sunrisezoo.org로 저희에게 이메일로 연락하시기를 바랍니다.

Solution Guide

간식은 제공된다(Snacks will be provided.)고 했으므로, 안내문의 내용과 일치하지 않는 것은 ③이다.

Structure in Focus

- Participants will [explore the Sunrise Zoo] and [learn about the plants, pollinators, and animals {that return in the spring}].
  두 개의 [ ]는 and로 연결되어 will에 이어지며 문장의 술어 역할을 한다. { }는 the plants, pollinators, and animals를 수식하는 관계절이다.

04

정답 ④

소재 철자 맞히기 경연 대회

해석 **Homer 초등학교 철자 맞히기 경연 대회**

철자 맞히기를 잘하나요? 경쟁하는 것을 좋아하나요?
그렇다면 철자 맞히기 학교 경연 대회에 참가하세요!

누가: 1학년에서 4학년까지의 모든 학생이 참가할 수 있음
언제: 3월 20일 수요일 오후 4시 30분
어디서: Homer 초등학교 강당

참가 방법

- 영어 선생님에게 신청하거나 학교 웹사이트에 신청서를 (직접) 올릴 수 있습니다.

※ 준비하는 것을 돕기를 원한다면 영어 교사실로 와서 신청하세요.

형식

- 다섯 판의 철자 맞히기 도전이 있습니다.
- 마지막 판을 통과한 모든 학생이 수상자가 됩니다!

상품

- 티셔츠, USB 드라이브, 피자 쿠폰, 메달

질문이나 신청을 위해서는 www.homeressb.ac.au나 영어 교사실을 방문하세요.

Solution Guide

다섯 판의 철자 맞히기 도전이 있다(There will be 5 rounds of spelling challenges.)는 내용이 언급되어 있으므로, 안내문의 내용과 일치하는 것은 ④이다.

Structure in Focus

- You can [sign up with your English teacher] or [post your application on the school website].
  두 개의 [ ]가 or로 연결되어 can에 이어져 문장의 술어 역할을 한다.

11 어법 정확성 파악

Gateway ②
Exercises 01 ④ 02 ⑤ 03 ② 04 ②

Gateway

본문 60쪽

정답 ②

소재 타인을 모방하려는 인간의 타고난 성향

해석 많은 연구가 사회적 자극에 구별하여 반응하는 인간의 타고난 성향에 대한 상당한 증거를 제시한다. 태어날 때부터, 아기는 사람의 얼굴과 목소리 쪽으로 우선하여 향하며, 그러한 자극이 특히 자신에게 의미가 있다는 것을 알고 있는 듯하다. 게다가, 아기는 혀 내밀기, 입술을 꽉 다물기, 입 벌리기처럼 자신에게 보이는 다양한 얼굴 제스처를 따라 하면서 이러한 친밀함(관계)을 적극적으로 표현한다. 심지어 그들은 자신들이 다소 어려움을 겪는 제스처와 일치하게 하려고, 성공할 때까지 자기 자신의 얼굴로 실험한다. 그들은 실제로 성공하면 눈을 반짝이면서 기쁨을 보여 주고, 실패할 때는 불편함을 나타낸다. 다시 말해, 그들은 운동감각적으로 경험한 그들 자신의 신체적 움직임과 시각적으로 지각되는 다른 사람의 그것을 일치시키는 타고난 능력을 지니고 있을 뿐만 아니라, 그렇게 하려는 타고난 욕구도 가지고 있다. 즉, 그들에게는 '나와 비슷하다'라고 판단하는 타인을 모방하려는 타고난 욕구가 있는 것처럼 보인다.

Structure in Focus

- A number of studies provide substantial evidence of an innate human disposition [to respond differentially to social stimuli].
  [ ]는 an innate human disposition을 수식하는 to부정사구이다.
- Moreover, they register this connection actively, [imitating a variety of facial gestures {that are presented to them} — tongue protrusions, lip tightenings, mouth openings].
  [ ]는 they를 부가적으로 설명하는 분사구문이고, 그 안의 { }는 a variety of facial gestures를 수식하는 관계절이다.

Exercises

본문 62~63쪽

01

정답 ④

소재 컴퓨터 은유

해석 인간과 기계의 상호 작용을 더 자연스럽게 만드는 좋은 방법은 더 나은 은유를 개발하는 것일 것이다. 컴퓨터 은유란 컴퓨터가 그것의 명령어, 디스플레이 배열 및 동작을 통해 모방하는 친숙한 사물이나 행동이다. 오늘날 우리가 가진 두 가지 주요 은유는 데스크톱과 브라우저이다. 데스크톱 은유에서 디스플레이 화면은 일반적인 책상을 모방하는데, 정보는 폴더 안에 보관되며, 폴더를 여닫고 다른 폴더에 넣을 수 있다. 웹 브라우징에서 은유는 번화가 윈도쇼핑인데, 여러분은 다양한 '상점'을 응시하다가 마음에 드는 곳을 보고 (클릭하여) 들어간다. 그 안에는 탐색할 더 많은 선택 사항이 있고, 또 하나의 선택 사항을 선택한 다음 다시 들어간다. 언어적 은유처럼, 좋은 컴퓨터 은유의 힘은 그것이 여러분이 모르는 새로운 시스템을 여러분이 친숙한 기존 '시스템'처럼 행동하게 만든다는 것이다. 여러분이 새로운 개념과 명령어를 배우느라 애쓸 필요가 없으므로 이것은 여러분이 새로운 시스템을 사용하여 그것으로부터 유용한 결과를 쉽게 얻을 수 있게 해 준다.

Solution Guide

④ an old "system"을 수식하는 관계절에서 '~에 친숙하다'의 의미로 쓰이는 be familiar with에서 with가 있어야 한다. 따라서 which를 with which로 고쳐야 한다.

① your computer를 가리키는 소유격 대명사이므로 단수형 its는 어법상 적절하다.

② 주어인 information이 보관되는 대상이므로 수동형 is kept는 어법상 적절하다.

③ a storefront를 대신하는 대명사이므로 one은 어법상 적절하다.

⑤ use the new system과 함께 동사 lets의 목적격 보어를 이루는 원형부정사구를 이끄는 get은 어법상 적절하다.

Structure in Focus

- In the desktop metaphor, the display screen mimics a typical desk; information is kept inside folders, [which can be {opened}, {closed}, and {slipped into other folders}].
  [ ]는 folders를 부가적으로 설명하는 관계절로 그 안에서 세 개의 { }가 and로 연결되어 be에 이어진다.
- Like a linguistic metaphor, the power of a good computer metaphor is [that it makes a new system

{you don't know} **behave** like an old "system" {with which you are familiar}].
[ ]는 is의 주격 보어 역할을 하는 명사절이고, 그 안의 첫 번째 { }는 a new system을 수식하는 관계절이며, 두 번째 { }는 an old "system"을 수식하는 관계절이다. behave는 명사절 안에서 동사 makes의 목적격 보어를 이끄는 원형부정사이다.

02

정답 ⑤

소재 토양 침식의 원인이 되는 인간 활동

해석 자연 경관에 가해지는 인간 활동은 토양 침식의 커다란 원인이 될 수 있다. 자연 상태에서 초목은 뿌리 연결망이 바람과 물 같은 다양한 침식력에 대항하여 토양을 제자리에 고정하는 데 도움이 되기 때문에 침식에 대한 자연적인 보호 역할을 한다. 과학자들은 미국에서 침식의 30퍼센트는 자연력에 의한 것이고 70퍼센트는 인간의 영향에 의한 것으로 추정한다. 흔히, 사람들이 토지를 농사를 위해 사용할 때, 자연 초목의 보호막은 파괴되고 침식 과정은 가속화된다. 실제로, 연구에 따르면 인위적으로 만들어진 침식이 많은 초기 문명의 몰락에 큰 역할을 한 것으로 나타났다. 잘못된 토지 관리 관행은 그 지역에 거주하는 인구를 더 이상 부양할 수 없을 정도로 생산성이 떨어질 때까지 토양을 악화시켰다. 침식의 재앙적인 영향을 인식한 초기 문명은 물이 비옥한 토양을 휩쓸어 갈 수 있는 산비탈 경사면에서 쟁기질, (작물) 심기, 관개 작업을 못하게 하기 위해 토지를 계단식으로 만드는 것과 같은 방법을 이용했다.

Solution Guide

⑤ hillside slopes를 수식하는 관계절이 주어와 목적어를 모두 갖추고 있으므로, 관계대명사 which는 관계부사 where로 고쳐야 한다.

① because가 이끄는 부사절 안에서 주어의 핵은 network이므로, 단수 동사 helps는 어법상 적절하다.

② estimate의 목적어 역할을 하는 명사절을 이끄는 접속사 that은 어법상 적절하다.

③ 과거분사 created를 수식하는 부사 artificially는 어법상 적절하다.

④ the population을 수식하는 분사구가 필요한데, the population은 live라는 행위의 주체이므로, 현재분사 living은 어법상 적절하다.

Structure in Focus

- Early civilizations [that recognized the disastrous effects of erosion] **used** devices such as terracing the land to keep from plowing, planting, and irrigating on hillside slopes where water could wash the fertile soil away.
[ ]는 문장의 주어인 Early civilizations를 수식하는 관계절이고, 술어동사는 used이다.

03

정답 ②

소재 네안데르탈인의 특징

해석 네안데르탈인은 털로 완전히 뒤덮인 우둔하고 구부정한 원시인이라고 여겨졌었다. 하지만 이러한 평판은 단 하나의 화석에 근거한 것인데, 이 화석은, 현대 학문이 입증하기를, 우연히도 늙고 병들고 다친 한 남성의 것이었다. 그는 죽었을 때 대략 마흔 살 또는 마흔다섯 살이었으며, 그 당시로는 매우 나이가 많은 사람이었다. 건강한 네안데르탈인은 직립 보행을 했을 것이다. 네안데르탈인 유적지에서 발견된 물건들은 네안데르탈인이 복잡한 도구를 만들 수 있었음을 보여 준다. 그들의 두개골 특징은 현대인이 내는 소리의 전체 범위는 아니겠지만, 그들이 아마도 말을 할 수 있었음을 시사한다. 유적지는 또한 그들이 반드시 동굴에서 살지는 않았지만, 그랬다면, 아마도 동굴을 더 살기 좋게 개조했으리라는 것을 보여 준다. 그들은 때로 동굴에 자리를 잡기보다는 주거지를 만들었다. 1996년 슬로베니아의 네안데르탈인 유적지를 발굴하던 과학자들은 곰 뼈로 만든 피리인 악기로 보이는 것을 발견했다고 발표했다.

Solution Guide

② 문장의 전체 구조를 보면 show를 술어동사로, 그 뒤에 이어지는 that절을 목적어로 보는 것이 타당하므로 Objects ~ sites는 주어 역할을 해야 한다. 따라서 술어동사의 형태를 한 were found는 Objects를 수식하는 분사구를 이끄는 분사가 되어야 하므로 were found를 found로 고쳐야 한다.

① the fossil을 대신하여 쓰인 대명사 that은 어법상 적절하다.

③ make의 목적격 보어 역할을 하는 형용사 livable은 어법상 적절하다.

④ built shelters와 rather than으로 연결되면서 술어를 이끄는 settled는 어법상 적절하다.

⑤ found의 목적어 역할을 하는 명사절을 이끌면서 그 절 안의 동사 appeared의 주어 역할도 하는 관계대명사 what은 어법상 적절하다.

Structure in Focus

- But this reputation is based on just one fossil, [which {modern scholarship has proved} happens to be that of an old, diseased, and injured man].

[ ]는 just one fossil을 부가적으로 설명하는 관계절이고, 그 안의 { }는 which와 happens 사이에 삽입된 절이다.

- In 1996, scientists [digging at a Neanderthal site in Slovenia] announced [they had found {what appeared to be a musical instrument, a flute made from a bear bone}].
  첫 번째 [ ]는 scientists를 수식하는 분사구이다. 두 번째 [ ]는 announced의 목적어 역할을 하는 명사절이고, 그 안의 { }는 found의 목적어 역할을 하는 명사절이다.

04

정답 ②

소재 제도적 차별과 개인적 차별

해석 차별은 두 가지 차원, 즉 제도적 차원과 개인적 차원에서 발생한다. 제도적 차원에서는, 차별적 관행이 한 사회의 사회 구조 안에 묻혀 있는 반면, 개인적 차원에서는 차별이 개인 또는 집단 간의 직접적인 상호 작용 중에 발생한다. 공공연하고 의도적이며 직접적인 경향이 있는 개인적 차별과 달리 제도적 차별은 은밀하고 의도적이지 않은 경우가 많으며, 이러한 보이지 않는 특성 때문에 그것을 감지하기가 훨씬 더 어렵다. 예를 들어, 학교에서의 표준화된 시험은 학업 환경에서 성공하는 것에서 역사적으로 소외된 특정 집단을 차단할 수도 있다. 정부가 의도적으로 문화적으로나 계층적으로 편향된 시험 기준을 정하지는 않았을지라도, 실제로 이러한 기준은 소수 민족 학생에게 균형이 맞지 않는 부정적인 영향을 미치는 경향이 있다. 게다가 제도적 차별은 흔히 특정 소수 민족 집단에 세대 전체에 또는 순환적으로 영향을 미치기 때문에 그 결과는 개인적 차별을 겪는 사람들에게만큼이나, 어쩌면 그보다 더 혹독할 수도 있다.

Solution Guide

② institutional discrimination을 대신하는 대명사이므로 복수형 대명사 them을 단수형인 it으로 고쳐야 한다.
① 명사구 direct interactions among individuals or groups를 목적어로 취해야 하므로 전치사 during은 적절하다.
③ 과거분사 marginalized를 수식해야 하므로 부사 historically는 적절하다.
④ testing standards를 선행사로 하는 관계사 that이 술어동사 are의 주어이므로 주어-술어 일치에 따라 are는 적절하다.
⑤ those를 수식하는 분사구가 필요한데, those가 suffer라는 행위의 주체이므로 현재분사 suffering은 적절하다.

Structure in Focus

- On the institutional level, discriminatory practices are embedded in the social structures of a society, [whereas on the individual level, discrimination takes place during direct interactions among individuals or groups].
  [ ]는 대조를 나타내는 부사절이다.
- Unlike individual discrimination, [which tends to be overt, intentional, and direct], [institutional discrimination is often covert and unintentional], and [this invisibility makes it much harder to detect].
  첫 번째 [ ]는 individual discrimination을 부가적으로 설명하는 관계절이다. 두 번째와 세 번째 [ ]는 and로 연결된다.

12 어휘 적절성 파악

Gateway ④
Exercises 01 ⑤ 02 ④ 03 ⑤ 04 ⑤

Gateway

본문 64쪽

정답 ④
소재 바자 경제
해석 바자(상점가) 경제는 공유 문화라는 더 지속적인 유대관계 위에 자리 잡은, 겉으로 보기에 유연한 가격 설정 메커니즘을 특징으로 한다. 구매자와 판매자 둘 다 서로가 가진 제약을 알고 있다. 델리의 바자에서, 구매자와 판매자는 대체로 일상 생활에서 다른 관계자가 가지는 재정적인 압박을 판단할 수 있다. 특정 경제 계층에 속하는 각 관계자는 상대방이 무엇을 필수품으로 여기고 무엇을 사치품으로 여기는지를 안다. 비디오 게임과 같은 전자 제품의 경우, 그것들은 식료품과 같은 다른 가정용 구매품과 동일한 수준의 필수품이 아니다. 따라서 델리의 바자에서 판매자는 비디오 게임에 대해 곧장 매우 낮은(→ 높은) 가격을 요구하지 않으려 주의하는데, 구매자가 비디오 게임의 소유를 절대적인 필수 사항으로 볼 이유가 전혀 없기 때문이다. 이러한 유형의 지식에 대한 접근은 비슷한 문화적 경제적 세계에 속함으로써 비롯된 서로의 선호와 한계를 결부시킴으로써 가격 일치를 형성한다.

Structure in Focus

- Bazaar economies feature an apparently flexible price-setting mechanism [that sits atop more enduring ties of shared culture].
  [ ]는 an apparently flexible price-setting mechanism을 수식하는 관계절이다.
- [Access to this type of knowledge] establishes a price consensus by [relating to each other's preferences and limitations of belonging to a similar cultural and economic universe].
  첫 번째 [ ]는 문장의 주어이고, 두 번째 [ ]는 전치사 by의 목적어인 동명사구이다.

Exercises

본문 66~67쪽

01

정답 ⑤
소재 익숙함에 대한 선호
해석 왜 매우 단순한 동물조차 익숙한 자극이나 익숙한 다른 동물들을 선호하는지 아마도 질문해 봐야 할 것이다. 익숙한 것이 좋아지는 경향은 (동물이 자신의 집을 좋아하는 것을 배울 수 있도록) 안정된 환경에 대한 선호를 새겨 넣는 것에 도움이 될 것이다. 그것은 틀림없이 안정적인 사회적 유대를 촉진할 것이다. 예를 들어, 자연이 정반대의 방식으로 동물을 길들여서 익숙함이 경멸이나 다른 형태의 혐오를 낳도록 했다고 상상해 보라. 가족은 어떻게 함께 지낼 것인가? 우정, 동맹 또는 다른 동반자 관계는 어떻게 살아남을 수 있을 것인가? 여러분이 항상 아는 사람보다 낯선 사람을 선호한다면, 사회생활은 끊임없는 혼란과 전복에 놓일 것이다. 반대로 여러분이 정기적으로 만나는 사람들을 자연히 좋아하게 된다면, 여러분은 곧 낯선 사람보다 그들을 선호하게 될 것이고, 집단이 쉽게 형성되고 안정화될 것이다. 안정된 집단의 장점(예를 들면, 사람들은 서로를 알고, 함께 일하는 방법을 알고, 함께 의사를 결정하는 방법을 알고, 서로에게 적응하는 방법을 안다)을 고려해 볼 때, 자연이 익숙함을 기반으로 서로를 (싫어하는 대신에) 좋아하게 된 동물을 없앤(→ 선호한) 것은 놀라운 일이 아니다.

Solution Guide

동물은 익숙한 자극이나 익숙한 다른 동물을 선호하는 경향이 있는데, 이것은 안정적인 사회적 유대를 촉진해서 집단이 쉽게 형성되고 안정화되게 한다는 내용의 글이다. 따라서 자연은 익숙함을 기반으로 서로를 좋아하게 된 동물을 선호한다는 내용이 되어야 하므로 ⑤의 removed를 favored와 같은 낱말로 바꾸어야 한다.

Structure in Focus

- In contrast, [if you automatically grew to like the people {you saw regularly}], you would soon prefer them over strangers, and groups would form and stabilize easily.
  [ ]는 조건을 나타내는 부사절이고, 그 안의 { }는 the people을 수식하는 관계절이다.
- [Given the advantages of stable groups (e.g., people know each other, know how to work together, know how to make decisions together, know how to adjust to each other)], **it** is not surprising [that nature favored animals {that grew to like (rather than dislike) each other on the basis of familiarity}].

첫 번째 [ ]는 '~을 고려할 때'라는 뜻을 나타내는 전치사구이다. it은 형식상의 주어이고, 두 번째 [ ]는 내용상의 주어이며, 그 안의 { }는 animals를 수식하는 관계절이다.

첫 번째 [ ]는 전치사 to의 목적어 역할을 하는 동명사구이고, 두 번째 [ ]는 문장의 주어 역할을 하는 동명사구이다. 세 번째 [ ]는 the state of groupthink를 부가적으로 설명하는 관계절이다.

02

정답 ④

소재 집단 순응 사고

해석 사회 심리학자 Irving Janis는 집단 순응 사고의 문제점을 인식했지만, 그것을 피할 수 있다고 생각했다. 그것은 개별 구성원의 의견보다 팀 정신이 더 중요해질 때 생겨날 가능성이 매우 크다. 또한 집단이 처음부터 생각이 비슷한 사람들로 구성되어 있고 그들이 어려운 결정에 직면했을 때 형성될 가능성이 있다. 집단 순응 사고를 방지하기 위해 Janis는 독립적인 사고를 장려하는 조직 체계를 제안했다. 집단의 지도자는 구성원들이 복종해야 한다는 어떤 압박감도 느끼지 않도록 공정한 모습을 보여야 한다. 그뿐만 아니라, 그 지도자는 집단이 모든 선택 사항을 검토하고 집단 외부의 사람들과 상의도 하도록 해야 한다. Janis는 의견 일치(→ 의견 불일치)는 실제로 좋은 것이라고 주장하며, 구성원들은 토론을 일으키기 위해 대안의 관점을 소개하는 '악마의 변호인' 역할을 하도록 요구받아야 한다고 제안했다. 집단이 더 합리적이고 공정한 결정을 내리게 보장할 뿐만 아니라, 구성원들이 자신의 개성을 유지할 수 있게 하는 것은 순응과 복종에서 비롯되는 집단 순응 사고의 상태보다 더 건강한 팀 정신을 만들어 낸다.

Solution Guide

집단 순응 사고를 피하거나 방지하기 위해 Irving Janis가 제안한 독립적인 사고를 장려하는 조직 체계에 관해 설명하는 내용의 글이다. 그 조직 체계에서는 '악마의 변호인' 역할을 구성원들에게 요구할 정도로 토론이 중요하다고 했으므로, Janis가 좋다고 주장한 것은 의견 일치가 아니라 의견 불일치일 것이다. 따라서 ④의 Agreement를 Disagreement와 같은 낱말로 바꾸어야 한다.

Structure in Focus

- It's also likely to form [if the group is made up of like-minded people to begin with], and [if they are faced with a difficult decision].
  두 개의 [ ]는 조건을 나타내는 부사절로 and에 의해 연결되어 있다.
- In addition to [ensuring that the group comes to more rational and fair decisions], [allowing members to retain their individuality] creates a healthier team spirit than the state of groupthink, [which results from conformity and obedience].

03

정답 ⑤

소재 사이버공간에서의 프라이버시

해석 사이버공간에 의해 제공되는 새로운 세상은 본질적으로 각자가 드러나는 정보를 통제하는 이상적인 사적인 세상이다. 이 세상에서, 사람의 신분 전체가 드러나는 것은 아니고, 두 사람은 물리적으로 서로 멀리 떨어져 있다. 따라서 참가자가 사적으로 유지하고 싶은 어떤 영역이든 그렇게 하는 것이 훨씬 쉽다. 이러한 상황은 참가자들이 완전히 비밀스러운 존재로 남도록 이끄는 것은 아니며, 반대로 많은 경우 그것은 참가자들이 보통 그러할 것보다 자신에 대해 훨씬 더 드러내도록 이끈다. 우리가 자신을 위협할 것 같은 것을 비공개로 유지할 수 있다면, 우리는 다른 일에 관해서는 더욱 개방적이 될 수 있다. 더 높은 정도의 개방성은 또한 더 높은 수준의 감정적인 친밀감도 만들어 낸다. 따라서, 온라인 관계에서 우리는 더 많은 프라이버시와 더 큰 친밀감과 개방성 둘 다를 발견할 수 있으며, 이것은 개방성과 프라이버시 사이의 흔한 갈등을 상당히 극대화한다(→ 줄인다).

Solution Guide

사이버 공간은 각자가 드러나는 정보를 통제하는 이상적인 세상이며, 우리는 위협적인 것은 비공개로 유지할 수 있다면 다른 일에 관해서는 더욱 개방적이 될 수 있고, 온라인 관계에서 더 많은 프라이버시 보호와 더 큰 친밀감과 개방성이 모두 나타나므로 개방성과 프라이버시 사이에서의 갈등은 줄어들게 될 것이다. 따라서 ⑤의 maximizes를 reduces와 같은 낱말로 바꾸어야 한다.

Structure in Focus

- The alternative world [provided by cyberspace] is essentially an ideal private world [in which each person controls the information {that is revealed}].
  첫 번째 [ ]는 The alternative world를 수식하는 분사구이고, 두 번째 [ ]는 an ideal private world를 수식하는 관계절이며, 그 안의 { }는 the information을 수식하는 관계절이다.
- These circumstances do not lead the participants [to remain completely mysterious] — on the contrary, in many cases it leads the participants [to reveal much more about themselves than they would usually **do**].

두 개의 [ ]는 각각 lead와 leads의 목적격 보어 역할을 하는 to부정사구이다. do는 앞 절에 언급된 reveal about themselves를 대신한다.

04

정답 ⑤

소재 은행식 교육 모델

해석 사람들은 흔히 교육에 대해 서로 다른 정의를 내리는데, 그 이유는 교육의 본질이 다소 유동적이기 때문이다. 거의 600년 전 인쇄기는 교육의 많은 부분이 일어나는 방식을 변화시켰다. 학생들은 정보를 읽기 시작했는데, (여기에) 교사가 공유하려 하는 정보가 더해졌다. 학생이 정보를 기억했다는 것을 확실히 하기 위해, 흔히 그 기억을 평가할 시험이나 보고서가 필요했다. 이러한 정보의 내려받기는 은행식 모델이라고 알려져 있으며, 은행식 모델이 하는 것은 그것이 학생을 비판적이고 독립적으로 사고하는 사람에서 사실을 담는 용기로 전락시키는 일이다. 은행식 모델의 과정은 교사의 권력과 통제력을 높이는 동시에 학생이 단순히 생각하지 않는 백지상태 이상의 존재라고 인식하지 못한다. 따라서 이 개념은 학생들의 생각 속에 분명하게 자리 잡게 되고, 학생들은 자신이 정보 보유자에게 부차적인 역할을 하며 신세를 지고 있다고 배운다. 그 결과, 학생들은 자기 자신의 사고와 자기 자신의 교육에 대한 상당한 통제력을 갖게 된다(→ 통제력을 거의 갖지 못하게 된다).

Solution Guide

인쇄기 등장으로 나타나게 된 교육의 여러 변화 중 하나인 은행식 모델을 설명하는 글로, 교사가 지식을 전달하고 학생들은 수동적으로 그 지식을 수용하여 암기한다고 했으므로 교사 중심의 교육 방식임을 알 수 있다. 따라서 교사의 통제력이 높고 학생은 자기 자신의 사고와 교육에 대한 통제력을 거의 갖지 못하게 된다고 추론할 수 있으므로, ⑤의 considerable을 little과 같은 낱말로 바꾸어야 한다.

Structure in Focus

- ~, and [what the banking model does] is [it reduces the student from being a critical and independent thinker to being a receptacle for facts].
  첫 번째 [ ]는 문장의 주어 역할을 하는 명사절이고, 두 번째 [ ]는 is의 주격 보어 역할을 하는 명사절이다.
- The concept, then, is placed squarely into the minds of students, [who are taught {that they are subservient and beholden to the keeper of information}].
  [ ]는 students를 부가적으로 설명하는 관계절이고, 그 안의 { }는 are taught의 직접목적어 역할을 하는 명사절이다.

13 빈칸 내용 추론

Gateway ②

Exercises 01 ② 02 ① 03 ④ 04 ① 05 ③ 06 ② 07 ③ 08 ③ 09 ⑤ 10 ② 11 ② 12 ③

Gateway

본문 68쪽

정답 ②

소재 영화에서 친숙한 악보가 하는 역할

해석 어떤 영화에서든 악보는 영화 텍스트에 추가적인 층을 더할 수 있는데, 그것은 보이는 연기를 단순히 흉내 내는 것을 넘어선다. 미래 세계에 관해 말하는 영화에서, 작곡가는 사운드 디자이너와 꼭 마찬가지로, 관객에게 알려지지 않은 새로운 세계를 창조할 수 있는 추가적인 자유를 가진다. 그러나 사운드 디자이너와 달리, 작곡가는 흔히 이러한 새로운 세계를 반영하는 독특한 악곡을 만들어 내는 것을 피하고, 흔히 친숙한 구조와 박자가 있는 악보를 내놓는다. 아마도 이것이 창의성과 시간 및 공간 감각을 방해할 수도 있지만, 사실 그것은 관객이 영화에 다가가는 데 도움이 된다. 쉽게 인식할 수 있는 악보를 통해 미래나 머나먼 은하계에 대한 상상은 쉽게 인식할 수 있는 맥락 안에 놓일 수 있다. 그러한 친숙함을 통해 관객은 편안한 공간에 놓일 수 있게 되고, 그러면 영화는 관객을 낯설지만 받아들일 수 있는, 그들 자신의 세계와는 다른 세계에 대한 상상으로 이끌 수도 있다.

Structure in Focus

- In films [that tell of futuristic worlds], composers, much like sound designers, have added freedom to create a world [that is unknown and new to the viewer].
  첫 번째 [ ]는 films를 수식하는 관계절이고, 두 번째 [ ]는 a world를 수식하는 관계절이다.
- Such familiarity allows the viewer to be placed in a comfortable space so that the film may then lead the viewer to [what is an unfamiliar, but acceptable vision of a world {different from their own}].
  [ ]는 전치사 to의 목적어 역할을 하는 명사절이고, 그 안의 { }는 a world를 수식하는 형용사구이다.

Exercises

본문 70~79쪽

01

정답 ②

소재 부모의 문제 상황 대처가 자녀의 자존감 형성에 주는 영향

해석 Coopersmith는 자신의 1967년 저서에서 최초로 어머니와 자녀의 자존감 수준 사이에 정적 상관관계가 있음을 언급했다. 그러나 Bednar, Wells 및 Peterson은 부모가 실제로 자신의 어려운 과제, 갈등 및 쟁점을 처리하는 방식을 통해 자녀에게 자존감에 이르는 길을 '보여 준다'는 점을 지적함으로써 이 요소를 상당히 활용했다. 부모의 행동이 자녀의 자존감에 미치는 영향은 부인할 수 없지만, 아이들의 미성숙함을 감안할 때, 자존감 문제에 대한 부모 자신의 해답을 표현하는 것은 그들이 말로 가르치는 것보다 훨씬 더 영향력이 있다. 인생의 어려운 과제를 솔직하게 드러내 놓고 직시하고, 어려움을 피하는 대신 대처하려고 시도하는 부모는 그렇게 함으로써 자녀가 자존감 친화적인 문제 해결 전략을 일찍 접하게 한다. 어려운 일을 처리하는 것을 피하는 사람들은 삶의 어려운 과제와 문제를 다루는 데 부정적인 길을 드러내 보인다. 어느 쪽이든, 모델이 되는 것은 건강한 자존감 혹은 그것에 관한 문제를 위한 장을 마련하는 것을 돕는다는 것을 기억하는 것이 중요하다.

Solution Guide

부모가 자신이 처한 문제 상황을 어떻게 처리하는지가 자녀의 자존감 형성에 영향을 미친다는 내용의 글로, 삶에서 당면할 수 있는 여러 어려움을 피하지 않고 대처하는 모습을 부모가 보여 줌으로써 자녀가 이를 본받아 자존감 친화적인 문제 해결 전략을 조기에 접할 수 있음을 설명하고 있다. 따라서 빈칸에 들어갈 말로 가장 적절한 것은 ②이다.

① 계획하는 것
③ 미루는 것
④ 토론하는 것
⑤ 지원하는 것

Structure in Focus

- But Bednar, Wells, and Peterson made considerable use of this factor by pointing out [that parents actually *show* their children the route to self-esteem by {how they handle their own challenges, conflicts, and issues}].

  [ ]는 pointing out의 목적어 역할을 하는 명사절이고, 그 안의 { }는 수단을 나타내는 전치사 by의 목적어 역할을 하는 명사절이다.

- Parents [who face life's challenges honestly and openly] and [who attempt to cope with difficulties instead of avoiding them] thereby expose their children early to a pro–self-esteem problem-solving strategy.

  [ ]로 표시된 두 개의 관계절은 and로 연결되어 Parents를 수식한다.

02

정답 ①

소재 판매 촉진을 위한 새로운 용도 제공

해석 우리가 구매하도록 하기 위해 여러 다양한 전략이 사용될 것이다. 신제품의 경우 마케터는 우리에게 자기 제품을 사용해 보도록 유도하고 싶으므로, 해야 할 일은 그것을 가능한 한 많이 광고하여 입소문을 퍼뜨리는 것이다. 자리를 잡은 제품의 경우 마케터는 우리가 그것을 다시 사용해 보길 원하거나(리마인더 광고), 우리가 자기 제품을 더 많이 소비하게 하려고 애쓸 수 있다. 이를 위한 좋은 방법은 새로운 용도를 제공하는 것이다. 한 베이킹 소다 브랜드가 좋은 예이다. 1960년대에 여성들이 취업 시장에 대거 진출하면서 빵 굽는 시간이 줄어들자, 그 회사는 그 제품을 사용하여 냉동고와 냉장고를 냄새 없는 청결한 상태로 유지하고 3개월마다 베이킹 소다 상자를 바꾸라고 홍보했다. 또는 여성들이 상당한 액수의 급여를 받고 더 늦게 결혼하는 양상이 나타나기 시작하자 다이아몬드 업계는 왼손은 '우리'를 위한 것이고 오른손은 '나'를 위한 것이라고 주장하면서 여성들에게 다이아몬드 반지를 판매하기 시작했다.

Solution Guide

빈칸이 있는 문장 이후에 자리를 잡은 제품들이 새로운 용도로 쓰일 수 있다고 광고하는 내용이 이어지고 있으므로, 빈칸에 들어갈 말로 가장 적절한 것은 ①이다.

② 포장 상자
③ 명칭
④ 디자인
⑤ 도구

Structure in Focus

- With an established product, [marketers will either want us to try it again (reminder advertising)], or [they may try to get us {to consume more of their product}].

  두 개의 [ ]가 or로 연결되어 있다. 두 번째 [ ] 안의 { }는 get의 목적격 보어 역할을 하는 to부정사구이다.

- Or when women started earning significant salaries and getting married later, the diamond industry started selling diamond rings to women, [claiming {that the

left hand is for "we" and the right is for "me}]."
[ ]는 주절이 기술하는 상황에 부수하는 상황을 나타내는 분사 구문이고, 그 안의 { }는 claiming의 목적어 역할을 하는 명사절이다.

03

정답 ④

소재 통제하는 부모를 둔 아기들의 성향

해석 아이들이 어떤 일을 하도록 강요당한다고 느끼거나 그들이 어떤 일을 하는 '방식'이 너무 엄격하게 통제되면, 그들은 자신이 하는 일에 흥미를 덜 느낄 가능성이 있고 도전적인 일을 계속할 가능성이 더 작아질 것이다. 아주 흥미로운 한 실험에서, 부모들이 요청을 받아 장난감을 가지고 놀고 있는, 심지어 두 살도 안 된 아주 어린 자녀들 바로 옆 바닥에 앉았다. 부모 중 일부는 즉시 과제를 인계받거나 지시 사항을 큰 소리로 외쳤다("블록을 안에 넣어. 아니, 거기가 아니고, '저기!'"). 다른 부모들은 아이가 탐색하도록 그냥 놔두는 데 만족하며, 격려하고 필요할 때만 도움을 제공했다. 나중에, 아기들에게 가지고 놀 수 있는 다른 것을 주었는데, 이번에는 부모가 함께 있지 않았다. 일단 혼자 있게 되자, 통제하는 부모를 가진 아기들은 새로운 장난감이 어떻게 움직이는지 알아내려고 노력하기보다 더 쉽게 포기하는 경향이 있음이 드러났다.

Solution Guide

아이들이 어떤 일을 하도록 강요당한다고 느끼거나 어떤 일을 하는 그들의 방식이 너무 엄격하게 통제되면, 그들은 자신이 하는 일에 흥미를 덜 느끼고 더 쉽게 포기하는 경향이 생겨, 도전적인 일을 계속할 가능성이 더 작아질 것이라는 내용의 글이다. 따라서 빈칸에 들어갈 말로 가장 적절한 것은 ④이다.

① 놀기 좋아하는
② 민주적인
③ 공손한
⑤ 신경 쓰지 않는

Structure in Focus

- When kids [feel forced to do things] — or [are too tightly regulated in the *way* {they do things}] — they're likely to become [less interested in what they're doing] and [less likely to stick with something challenging].
첫 번째와 두 번째 [ ]는 or로 연결되어 When으로 유도되는 절의 술어 역할을 하고, 두 번째 [ ] 안의 { }는 the *way*를 수식하는 관계절이다. 세 번째와 네 번째 [ ]는 and로 연결되어 become의 보어 역할을 한다.
- Others were content to let their kids explore, [providing encouragement and offering help only when it was needed].
[ ]는 주절이 기술하는 상황에 부수하는 상황을 나타내는 분사 구문이다.

04

정답 ①

소재 필요와 욕구 사이의 경계

해석 우리가 지속 가능한 형태로 상호 공급을 재창조할 때, 필요와 욕구 사이의 경계를 파악하는 것이 중요하다. 지구가 사람들이 영구적으로 살 수 있는 곳이 되려면 우리의 필요를 충족해야 하지만, 다른 사람들은 음식과 거처가 부족한데도, 불필요한 재화를 대량으로 욕심껏 모아 두는 사람들은 영속성 있는 체제의 일부가 될 수 없다. 자신의 배를 불리려고 다른 사람을 억압하는 사회는 외국에 해를 끼치는 데 그치지 않을 것이다. 그 윤리는 국내에서의 착취로 모습을 드러낼 것이다. 사회가 지역의 자원을 점점 더 효과적으로 사용함에 따라, 창의력과 노력을 통해 상황은 여전히 개선되겠지만, 자신이 이룬 부유함이 다른 사람의 희생으로 이루어진다면 많은 선의와 노력, 자원이 분노와 반란, 억압으로 사라지게 될 것이다. 개발의 초점이 모두의 삶의 질을 확보하고 개선하는 것이 될 때 모두에게 큰 보너스가 주어진다.

Solution Guide

지구가 사람들이 영구적으로 살 수 있는 곳이 되려면 우리의 필요를 충족해야 하지만, 자신의 풍요함이 다른 사람의 희생을 바탕으로 이루어진다면 많은 선의와 노력 및 자원이 사라지게 될 것이므로, 필요와 욕구 사이의 경계를 아는 것이 중요하다는 내용의 글이다. 따라서 빈칸에 들어갈 말로 가장 적절한 것은 ①이다.

② 지역 사회에 도움이 되는 기술을 개인에게 가르치는 것
③ 불평등을 감수하면서 경제적 번영을 추구하는 것
④ 지속적인 노력을 통해 성공적인 사람이 되는 것
⑤ 자원 보존을 위해 제품 소비를 줄이도록 장려하는 것

Structure in Focus

- **It** is critical, [as we recreate mutual provision in a sustainable form], [that we keep track of the line between needs and wants].
첫 번째 [ ]는 시간을 나타내는 부사절이다. It은 형식상의 주어이고, 두 번째 [ ]는 내용상의 주어이다.
- While a permanent place for people on Earth requires [that our needs be met], [people {gathering about themselves quantities of unnecessary goods}], while others lack food and shelter, cannot be part of a

durable order.

첫 번째 [ ]는 requires의 목적어 역할을 하는 명사절이다. 두 번째 [ ]는 주절의 주어 역할을 하는 명사구이고, 그 안의 { }는 people을 수식하는 분사구이다.

content of the technology **that** we neglect to notice the influence of the technology itself on people].

[ ]는 asserts의 목적어 역할을 하는 명사절이다. 그 안에서 「so ~ that ...」은 '매우 ~해서 …하다'라는 의미를 나타낸다.

05

정답 ③

소재 매체와 기술 자체에 대한 주목

해석 1964년 Marshall McLuhan이 참으로 예지력 있게 말했듯이, "매체는 메시지인"데, 이는 전달되는 콘텐츠를 넘어 매체 자체가 그것의 본질과 고유한 특성으로 영향력을 갖는다는 것을 의미한다. 예를 들어, 소셜 미디어를 사용한다는 것은 다른 사람들과 직접 상호 작용을 할 필요성이 줄어든다는 것을 의미한다. 이러한 소통의 거리 두기는 아이들의 발달에 실질적인 영향을 미친다. 다른 사람과 소통하는 법을 배우는 것이 연습을 통해 발달하는 기술이라면, 아이들이 소셜 미디어를 끊임없이 사용하면 사회적 기술을 배울 수 있는 그들이 가지는 경험은 줄어든다. McLuhan은 우리가 기술의 콘텐츠에 너무 집중한 나머지 기술 자체가 사람들에게 미치는 영향에 대한 주목을 게을리한다고 주장한다. 이러한 소견은 오늘날 분명 사실인데, 우리는 기술이 제공하는 것(예를 들어, 영상, 문자 메시지, 소셜 미디어)에는 집중하지만, 이러한 발전된 기술을 사용하는 행위 자체가 우리에게 어떻게 영향을 미치는지는 고려하지 않는다.

Solution Guide

기술이 전달하는 콘텐츠뿐만 아니라 기술 자체가 사람들에게 미치는 영향에 주목해야 한다는 내용의 글이다. 따라서 빈칸에 들어갈 말로 가장 적절한 것은 ③이다.

① 이 기술이 얼마나 많이 우리를 이롭게 하는지는
② 기술이 단순히 생각을 담는 그릇이라는 것을
④ 왜 우리가 기술 발전에 적응하는 것이 어려운지는
⑤ 새로운 기술이 다양한 방식으로 아이들의 성장을 돕는다는 것을

Structure in Focus

- [If {learning to communicate with others} is a skill that develops with practice], children's constant use of social media reduces the experiences they have [with which to learn social skills].
  첫 번째 [ ]는 조건을 나타내는 부사절이고, 그 안의 { }는 부사절의 주어 역할을 하는 동명사구이다. 두 번째 [ ]는 with which they can learn social skills로 풀어서 이해할 수 있다.
- McLuhan asserts [that we are **so** focused on the

06

정답 ②

소재 도시의 지속적인 재창조

해석 도시는 계속해서 스스로를 재창조하고 있다. 지난 수십 년 동안 많은 도시가 공해 유발 차량을 제한하고, 에너지 효율이 높은 건물을 장려하며, 나무를 심어 오염을 줄이고 매력적인 현대적 공간을 만들기 위해 노력해 왔다. 2020년에는, COVID-19라는 모습으로 변화의 또 다른 원동력이 나타났는데, 이것은 소매점이 텅 비었고 기업은 직원을 집으로 돌려보냈으며 일부 사람들은 혼잡한 도시가 안전한 환경인지에 대해 의문을 제기하는 것을 목격했다. 그러나 도시는 지금까지 변화하는 상황에 적절히 대응해 왔다. 메소포타미아 최초의 왕국, 전 세계적 팽창, 그리고 산업 혁명을 거치면서, 도시는 발전하여 여전히 정치, 경제, 문화의 중심지로 남아 있다. 세계의 역사는 곧 위대한 도시의 역사이며, 우리가 어떤 미래를 건설하든 이 교역, 창의성, 변혁의 장은 그것의 중심부에 있을 것이다.

Solution Guide

역사적으로 도시는 다양한 변화 상황에 적절히 대응했고 그 변화에 적응하는 방식으로 발전해 왔다는 내용의 글이므로, 빈칸에 들어갈 말로 가장 적절한 것은 ②이다.

① 계속 문화적 갈등을 초래한다
③ 각계각층의 사람들을 끌어들인다
④ 경제 발전의 원동력 역할을 한다
⑤ 시민들의 요구에 따라 변화한다

Structure in Focus

- In the last few decades, many have worked to reduce pollution and create appealing modern spaces by [restricting polluting vehicles], [encouraging energy-efficient buildings], and [planting trees].
  and로 연결된 세 개의 [ ]는 전치사 by의 목적어 역할을 하는 동명사구이다.
- In 2020, another impetus for change came in the form of COVID-19, which saw retail centres [empty], businesses [send workers home], and some [question {whether crowded cities were a safe environment}].
  세 개의 [ ]는 saw의 목적격 보어 역할을 하고 있는데, 두 번째와 세 번째 [ ]는 목적격 보어 역할을 하는 원형부정사구이

다. 세 번째 [ ] 안의 { }는 question의 목적어 역할을 하는 명사절이다.

07

정답 ③

소재 문화적 특수성과 보편성

해석 인간의 문화는 무한히 가변적인 것처럼 보이지만, 사실 그 가변성은 신체적, 정신적 능력에 의해 만들어진 한계 내에서 발생한다. 예를 들어, 인간의 언어는 엄청나게 다양하여, 음, 문법, 의미에 있어 차이가 있다. 하지만 모든 것은 언어 학습을 위한 인간의 고유한 능력과 성향으로 보이는 것에 달려 있다. 인간의 언어에서 사용되는 음의 범위는 흡착음과 파열음부터 후두 폐쇄음까지 펼쳐져 있지만, 전 세계 모든 언어에서 의미 있는 특유의 말소리는 인간이 낼 수 있는 음의 일부에 불과하다. 문화적 특수성과 보편성 사이의 복잡한 관계를 알 수 있는 또 다른 방법은 한 미국인 소년과 그의 Mixtec 족(멕시코의 아메리칸 인디언) 친구들이 벌 애벌레와 양파 수프에 감정적으로, 심지어 본능적으로 반응하는 방식인데, 그들이 기쁨을 느끼는지 아니면 혐오를 느끼는지는 그들이 음식을 인식하는 법을 배우는 방식에 의해 결정되지만, 기쁨과 혐오감은 음식에 대한 인간의 기본적이고 보편적인 반응인 것처럼 보인다.

Solution Guide

인간 문화의 가변성과 그 한계를 인간 언어의 말소리, 그리고 미국인 소년과 Mixtec 족 친구들이 벌 애벌레와 양파 수프에 감정적으로 반응하는 방식을 예로 들어 설명하고 있는 글이다. 두 경우 모두 문화적으로 다르게 나타나지만, 그 차이는 인간의 고유하고 기본적이며 보편적인 능력, 성향, 반응을 전제로 한다고 설명하고 있으므로, 빈칸에 들어갈 말로 가장 적절한 것은 ③이다.

① 집단의 크기와 순응
② 개인적 선택과 집단적 결정
④ 문화적 행동과 환경
⑤ 주관적 해석과 객관적 현실

Structure in Focus

- [While the range of sounds used in human languages extends from clicks and pops to guttural stops], the distinctive speech sounds [that are meaningful in all the languages of the world] are but a fraction of the sounds [it is possible for humans to make].
  첫 번째 [ ]는 양보를 나타내는 부사절이다. 두 번째 [ ]는 the distinctive speech sounds를 수식하는 관계절이다. 세 번째 [ ]는 the sounds를 수식하는 관계절이다.
- ~: [whether they feel delight or disgust] is determined by the way [they learn to perceive food], but delight and disgust seem to be basic and universal human reactions to food.
  첫 번째 [ ]는 문장의 주어 역할을 하는 명사절이다. 두 번째 [ ]는 the way를 수식하는 관계절이다.

08

정답 ③

소재 실험에서 중요 요인 분리하기

해석 특정 세탁 세제가 표백하는 방식을 알아내기 위한 표준 과학 실험에서 일어나는 일에 대해 생각해 보라. 정상적인 사용 시, 세제가 특정 방식으로 작용하게 할 수 있을 몇 가지 요인이 있다. 이것에는 세제의 유효 성분, 성분이 섞이는 물의 유형과 온도, 세탁되고 있는 소재, 그리고 만약 있다면, 세탁하는 데 사용되는 기계가 포함될 것이다. 무엇이 표백이 '일어나게 했는지' 알아내기를 바랄 수 있는 어떤 실험이든 중요한 요인이 다른 변수와 정확하게 분리되는 것을 확실히 하는 방식으로 고안되어야 할 것이다. 따라서, 예를 들어, 표백 작용을 하는 것은 바로 염소라는 것이 가설이라면, 그 실험은 '다른 모든 요인이 동일하게 유지될 경우에' 염소의 존재나 부재가 세탁 세제가 표백하는지를 결정할 것임을 보여줄 필요가 있다.

Solution Guide

표준 과학 실험에서 특정 세탁 세제가 표백이 일어나게 하는 요인을 알아내기 위해서는 다른 변수를 동일하게 유지한 상태로 특정 요인의 유무에 따른 그 결과를 보고, 그것이 중요한 요인임을 결정할 수 있다는 내용의 글이다. 따라서 빈칸에 들어갈 말로 가장 적절한 것은 ③이다.

① 그 가설이 예상치 못한 변수에 의해 거부될 수 있다는
② 그 실험은 연구자들이 이전에 시도한 적이 없었던 실험이라는
④ 사용되고 있는 그 세제가 어떤 기계라도 세탁을 잘하는 데 도움이 될 수 있는
⑤ 실험 속 요인이 모두 서로 밀접하게 연결되어 있는

Structure in Focus

- Any experiment [that could hope to discover {what *caused* bleaching}] would have to be devised in such a way as to ensure [that the crucial factors were properly isolated from the other variables].
  첫 번째 [ ]는 Any experiment를 수식하는 관계절이고, 그 안의 { }는 discover의 목적어 역할을 하는 명사절이다. 두 번째 [ ]는 ensure의 목적어 역할을 하는 명사절이다.
- So if, for example, the hypothesis is [that **it is** {the chlorine} **that** does the bleaching], the experiment

needs to show [that *if all the other factors remain the same*, the presence or absence of the chlorine will determine {whether the laundry detergent bleaches}].
첫 번째 [ ]는 is의 주격 보어 역할을 하는 명사절이고, 그 안의 { }는 it is와 that 사이에 놓여 그 의미가 강조되고 있다. 두 번째 [ ]는 show의 목적어 역할을 하는 명사절이고, 그 안의 { }는 determine의 목적어 역할을 하는 명사절이다.

09

정답 ⑤

소재 AI가 인간 지식에 미치는 영향

해석 AI가 인간 지식에 미치는 영향은 역설적이다. 한편으로는, AI 중개자는 도움을 받지 않은 인간이 이전에 상상할 수 있었던 것보다 더 방대한 양의 데이터를 탐색하고 분석할 수 있다. 다른 한편으로는 이 힘, 즉 방대한 양의 데이터를 다룰 수 있는 능력은 또한 여러 형태의 조작과 오류를 두드러지게 할 수도 있다. AI는 전통적인 선전보다 인간의 열망을 더 효과적으로 이용할 수 있다. AI는 자신을 개인의 선호도와 본능에 맞춰 가면서 제작자나 사용자가 원하는 반응을 끌어낸다. 마찬가지로, AI 중개자를 배치하면 이 AI 중개자가 기술적으로 인간의 통제하에 있더라도 내재한 편견을 또한 증폭시킬 수도 있다. 시장 경쟁의 역학 관계는 소셜 미디어 플랫폼과 검색 엔진이 사용자가 가장 흥미롭다고 생각하는 정보를 제시하도록 자극한다. 그 결과, 사용자가 보고 싶어 하는 것으로 여겨지는 정보가 우선순위를 차지하게 되어 현실의 전형적인 모습을 왜곡한다. 19세기와 20세기에는 기술이 정보 생산과 전파 속도를 가속했지만, 이 시대에는 AI를 전파 과정에 배치하면서 정보가 바뀌고 있다.

Solution Guide

AI는 방대한 양의 데이터를 탐색하고 분석할 수 있지만, 자신을 개인의 선호도와 본능에 맞춰 가면서 제작자나 사용자가 원하는 반응을 끌어내고 내재한 편견을 또한 증폭시킬 수 있으며, 그 결과 사용자가 보고 싶어 하는 것으로 여겨지는 정보가 우선순위를 차지하게 되어 현실의 전형적인 모습을 왜곡한다고 했으므로, 빈칸에 들어갈 말로 가장 적절한 것은 ⑤이다.
① 사람들이 따를 기준을 설정할
② 사람들이 창의적으로 생각하지 못하게 할
③ 사람들의 요구를 더 철저히 무시할
④ 현대인들에게 무관한 데이터를 생산할

Structure in Focus

- [The dynamics of market competition] prompt social media platforms and search engines [to present information {that users find most compelling}].
첫 번째 [ ]는 문장의 주어 역할을 하는 명사구이고, 두 번째 [ ]는 prompt의 목적격 보어 역할을 하는 to부정사구이며, 그 안의 { }는 information을 수식하는 관계절이다.
- As a result, [information {that users are believed to want to see}] is prioritized, [distorting a representative picture of reality].
첫 번째 [ ]는 문장의 주어 역할을 하는 명사구이고, 그 안의 { }는 information을 수식하는 관계절이다. 두 번째 [ ]는 주절이 기술하는 상황에 부수하는 상황을 나타내는 분사구문이다.

10

정답 ②

소재 존경하는 사람을 모방하여 닮아 가는 경향

해석 자녀가 부모처럼 된다는 것은 우연이 아니다. 세상에 태어나는 순간부터 어머니와 아버지는 여러분의 역할 모델이다. 여자아이들은 자라면서 엄마 옷을 입어 보고 엄마의 화장품을 바르고 엄마인 척한다. 남자아이들은 성년이 되면 아버지의 도구를 가지고 놀며 진짜인 무언가를 만들거나 고치려고 한다. 사실 아이들은 부모를 멘토로 존경한다. 그들은 부모를 칭송하고 깊이 존경한다. 자라면서 그들이 부모에게 줄 수 있는 가장 큰 찬사는 부모를 똑같이 닮아 가는 것이다. 잠시 멈추고 자신을 성찰해 보면, 여러분은 자신이 모방하는 사람들과 많이 닮아 있다는 것을 발견할 수도 있을 것이다. 부모, 코치, 교사 또는 지도자는 모두 여러분의 이름이 적힌 최종 꾸러미에 자신들의 흔적을 남긴다. 거울을 보면, 여러분은 거울에 비친 상에서 그들 중 하나 또는 모두를 볼 수도 있을 것이다.

Solution Guide

세상에 태어나는 순간부터 아이는 어머니와 아버지를 역할 모델로 하여 그들을 모방하고, 부모, 코치, 교사 또는 지도자는 모두 아이들의 이름이 적힌 최종 꾸러미에 자신들의 흔적을 남긴다고 했으므로, 거울을 보면 거울에 비친 모습에 존경하여 모방하는 사람의 모습이 보일 것임을 추론할 수 있다. 따라서 빈칸에 들어갈 말로 가장 적절한 것은 ②이다.
① 친숙함을 기준으로 그들을 판단할
③ 그들의 어떤 약점이든 외면할
④ 거울 안에 있는 그 사람을 불편하게 느낄
⑤ 그들과는 다른 여러분 자신의 이미지에 실망할

Structure in Focus

- **It** is not a coincidence [that children turn out like their parents].

It은 형식상의 주어이고 [ ]는 내용상의 주어이다.

- The greatest compliment [they can give their parents as they grow] is [to turn out just like them].
첫 번째 [ ]는 The greatest compliment를 수식하는 관계절이고, 두 번째 [ ]는 is의 보어 역할을 하는 to부정사구이다.

11

정답 ②

소재 이성과 욕망 사이의 싸움

해석 우리는 모두 이성과 욕망 사이의 싸움을 잘 알고 있다. 소크라테스는 목이 마른데 마시고 싶어 하지 않는 사람이 있는지 묻는다. 실제로 있다. (수도꼭지에 "마실 수 없는 물, 마시지 마시오."라고 적힌 표지판이 누군가의 목마름을 없애지는 않겠지만, 그 사람은 거기에서 물을 마시고 싶지 않을 것이다.) 그러나 여기에는 역설적인 것이 있는데, 즉 '목마른'이라는 단어는 '마시고 싶다'라는 의미이다. 그렇다면 우리는 마시고 싶지만 마시고 싶어 하지 않는 사람을 상상하고 있다. 어떻게 그럴 수 있는가? "동일한 것이 그것 자체의 동일한 부분에서 동일한 것과 관련하여 동시에 정반대의 일을 하려 하거나 겪지 않으려 할 것이라는 것은 분명하다. 따라서 정신에 이런 일이 일어나는 것을 한 번이라도 발견하면, 우리는 우리가 한 가지가 아니라 여러 가지를 처리하고 있다는 것을 알게 될 것이다." 다시 말해, 어떠한 것도 (동시에 같은 방식으로) 마시고 싶어 하기도 하고 마시고 싶어 하지 않기도 할 수 없으므로, 어떠한 것도 그러한 두 가지 특성을 모두 가질 수는 없기에, 우리는 하나보다 더 많은 존재가 되는 것으로, 즉 정신의 한 부분은 마시고 싶어 하고, 다른 부분은 마시고 싶어 하지 않음으로써 이것을 감당한다.

Solution Guide

우리는 이성과 욕망 사이에서 서로 반대되는 일을 동시에 처리해야 할 경우가 있는데, 목이 마른 상황에서 앞에 놓인 물이 마실 수 없는 물이라는 것을 알게 되면 우리 정신의 한 부분은 물을 마시고 싶다는 욕망이 담당하고, 다른 한 부분은 마시고 싶지 않다는 이성이 담당하는, 한 가지 이상의 존재가 된다는 내용의 글이다. 따라서 빈칸에 들어갈 말로 가장 적절한 것은 ②이다.

① 우리가 결국 하는 일이 더 나은 행동이라는
③ 우리의 행동은 이성에 의한 경우가 거의 없다는
④ 한 가지 일을 하는 것이 다른 일을 하도록 만든다는
⑤ 생각과 행동은 조화롭게 함께 작용할 수 있다는

Structure in Focus

- [A sign on a faucet {that reads "nonpotable water, do not drink"}] won't take away a person's thirst, but she won't want to drink there.
[ ]는 문장의 주어 역할을 하는 명사구이고, 그 안의 { }는 A sign on a faucet을 수식하는 관계절이다.
- In other words, [since no one thing can **both** {wish to drink} **and** {not wish to drink} (in the same way at the same time)], no one thing can have both of those two characteristics; ~.
[ ]는 이유를 나타내는 부사절인데, 그 안에서 두 개의 { }가 「both ~ and ...」으로 연결되어 can에 이어져 술어 역할을 한다.

12

정답 ③

소재 미디어 경영진의 목표 고객층

해석 미디어 경영진은 고객을 자신들의 제품을 구매하거나 자신들이 광고주에게 판매하는 소비자로 생각해야 한다는 것을 알고 있다. 불만을 제기하는 사람이 미디어 경영진에게 그들이 콘텐츠를 변경하거나 심지어 삭제하지 않으면 목표 시장의 상당 부분을 잃을 수도 있다고 설득하면, 그 사람은 그렇게 하게 하는 데 성공할 수도 있다. 그러나 한 개인이 목표 고객층에 속하지 않는 것이 분명하다면, 그 사람의 우려는 관심을 거의 받지 못할 것이다. 예를 들어, 20대 미혼 여성을 대상으로 하는 *Cosmopolitan* 잡지의 편집자들은 슈퍼마켓에서 보는 잡지 표지에서 여성을 비하하는 듯한 묘사라고 느끼는 부분에 대해 항의하고자 전화한 캔자스주 시골에 사는, 목소리로 보아 나이가 지긋한 듯한 여성의 조언을 따르지 않을 것이다. 그러나 그 잡지사 직원들은 한 *Cosmopolitan* 구독자가 자신들이 독자로 원하는 고소득 미혼 여성들을 더 많이 끌어들일 새로운 칼럼을 제안하는 글을 쓰면 당연히 호의적으로 반응할 것이다.

Solution Guide

불만이 있는 고객은 미디어 경영진을 설득하여 자신의 불만을 해결하는 데 성공할 수 있다는 내용이 빈칸이 있는 문장 앞에 전개된다. 빈칸에는 불만이 있는 고객이라도 미디어 경영진의 관심을 얻지 못하는 조건이 들어가야 하는데, 이후의 사례는 목표 구독자인지 아닌지에 따라 달라지는 미디어의 대응 방식을 설명하고 있으므로, 빈칸에 들어갈 말로 가장 적절한 것은 ③이다.

① 그 문제가 미디어 매체의 통제를 벗어나는
② 다른 소비자들이 그 사람에게 동의하지 않는
④ 그 우려가 이미 다른 사람들에 의해 다뤄진
⑤ 광고주들이 고객 불만의 가치를 알지 못한다는

Structure in Focus

- The complaining individual might be successful in getting the content changed or even removed [if he or she convinces the media executives {that they might

otherwise lose a substantial portion of their target market}].
[ ]는 조건을 나타내는 부사절이고, 그 안의 { }는 convinces의 직접목적어 역할을 하는 명사절이다.

- The editors from *Cosmopolitan* magazine, [which aims at 20-something single women], for example, are not likely to follow the advice of an elderly-sounding woman from rural Kansas [who phones to protest {what she feels are demeaning portrayals of women on covers of the magazine that she sees in the supermarket}].
첫 번째 [ ]는 *Cosmopolitan* magazine을 부가적으로 설명하는 관계절이다. 두 번째 [ ]는 an elderly-sounding woman from rural Kansas를 수식하는 관계절이고, 그 안의 { }는 protest의 목적어 역할을 하는 명사절이다.

14 흐름에 무관한 문장 찾기

Gateway ③
Exercises 01 ④ 02 ③ 03 ③ 04 ③

Gateway

본문 80쪽

정답 ③

소재 빠르게 말하는 것의 위험 부담

해석 빠르게 말하는 것은 위험 부담이 큰 일이다. 입이 제한 속도를 훨씬 초과하여 움직일 때 설득력 있고, 말을 정확하게 하고, 효과적이기 위한 이상적인 상태를 유지하는 것이 거의 불가능하다. 우리는 우리의 정신이 항상 최대의 효율로 훌륭한 결정을 내릴 수 있을 정도로 예리하다고 생각하고 싶겠지만, 그것이 꼭 그렇지는 않다. 실제로 뇌는 말할 가능성이 있는 것들 네다섯 가지가 교차하는 지점에 도달하고, 몇 초간 선택 가능한 것들을 고려하면서 아무것도 하지 않은 채로 있는다. (훌륭한 결정을 내리면 여러분이 더 빠르게 말할 수 있도록 하는데, 이는 그것이 여러분에게 반응을 생각해 낼 시간을 더 많이 주기 때문이다.) 뇌가 입으로 조종 지시를 다시 보내는 것을 멈추고 입이 너무 빠르게 움직여 멈추지 못할 때, 이때가 바로 여러분이 가벼운 언어적 충돌, 또 다르게는 필러라고 불리는 것을 겪게 되는 때이다. '음', '아', '저기', '있잖아'는 입이 갈 곳이 없을 때 하는 행동이다.

Structure in Focus

- **It**'s nearly impossible [to maintain the ideal conditions to be persuasive, well-spoken, and effective {when the mouth is traveling well over the speed limit}].
It은 형식상의 주어이고, [ ]는 내용상의 주어이며, 그 안의 { }는 시간을 나타내는 부사절이다.
- [Although we'd like to think {that our minds are sharp enough to always make good decisions with the greatest efficiency}], they just aren't.
[ ]는 양보를 나타내는 부사절이고, 그 안의 { }는 think의 목적어 역할을 하는 명사절이다.

Exercises

본문 82～83쪽

01

정답 ④

소재 인상주의 미술

해석 모네와 다른 인상파 화가들은 자신들이 경험한 그 어떤 아카데미 훈련도 거부하고 눈앞에 보이는 것을 그리는 객관적인 방법을 갖춘 자신들의 예술이 그 어떤 아카데미 예술보다 더 진실하다고 믿었다. 이들은 모두 자신의 '감각', 즉 그림을 그리면서 그들이 볼 수 있는 것을 포착하는 것을 목표로 삼는 데 동의했다. 이러한 감각에는 사물을 응시할 때 눈이 포착하는 빛의 깜빡거리는 효과가 포함되었다. 아카데미(프랑스의 미술 교육 기관)와는 완전히 대조적으로 인상파 화가들은 일상적이고 현대적인 배경의 평범한 현대인을 그렸으며, 자신들의 그림 기법을 숨기려 하지 않았다. (원래 아카데미 제도는 육체 노동자로 여겨지던 장인보다 예술가의 지위를 높이기 위해 시작되었기 때문에 예술의 지적인 측면이 강조되었다.) 그들은 상징이나 그 어떤 서사적인 내용도 피했고, 보는 사람들이 그림을 '읽지' 못하게 했지만 자신들의 그림을 시간상의 한 고립된 순간으로 경험하게 했다.

Solution Guide

모네를 비롯한 인상파 화가들이 아카데미의 훈련을 거부하고 자신만의 예술을 확립하려 하기 위해 시도한 노력에 관한 내용이므로, 아카데미 제도가 예술가의 지위를 높이기 위해 시작되었다는 내용의 ④는 글의 전체 흐름과 관계가 없다.

Structure in Focus

- ~, Monet and the other Impressionists believed [that their art, with its objective methods of painting {what they saw before them}, was more sincere than any academic art].
  [ ]는 believed의 목적어 역할을 하는 명사절이고, 그 안의 { }는 painting의 목적어 역할을 하는 명사절이다.
- They avoided symbols or any narrative content, [preventing viewers from "reading" a picture], but [making them {experience their paintings as an isolated moment in time}].
  두 개의 [ ]는 주절을 부가적으로 설명하는 분사구문이고, 두 번째 [ ] 안의 { }는 making의 목적격 보어 역할을 하는 원형부정사구이다.

02

정답 ③

소재 생존을 위한 식물의 경쟁

해석 식물은 언제 경쟁이 필요한지, 언제 협력하는 것이 더 현명한지 가늠한다. 이러한 종류의 결정을 내리기 위해 그것은 성장 및 지속성 향상에 따른 이익과 비교하여 에너지 비용을 따져 본다. 예를 들어 일반적으로 식물은 햇빛을 우선적으로 이용하기 위해 가까운 곳에 있는 이웃의 식물보다 더 크게 자라려 하지만, 이웃 식물이 이미 키가 상당히 더 커서 경쟁에서 질 것 같으면, 그 식물은 자신의 경쟁 본능을 누그러뜨릴 것이다. 즉, 식물은 자신의 성장과 번식을 유지할 능력을 향상하기 위해 경쟁이 필요하고 성공 가능성이 어느 정도 있을 경우에만 경쟁한다. (모든 유기체에서와 마찬가지로, 식물의 진화, 발달 및 성장은 끊임없고 치열한 경쟁에 달려 있다.) 일단 경쟁이 필요한 결과를 산출하면, 식물은 경쟁을 중단하고 에너지를 생존하는 데로 돌린다. 식물에게 경쟁은 승리의 짜릿함이 아니라 생존에 관한 것이다.

Solution Guide

식물은 성장과 번식에 필요하고 성공할 가능성이 있을 경우에만 경쟁한다는 내용의 글이므로, 모든 유기체와 마찬가지로 식물의 진화, 발달 및 성장은 끊임없고 치열한 경쟁에 달려 있다는 내용의 ③은 글의 전체 흐름과 관계가 없다.

Structure in Focus

- Plants assess [when they need to be competitive] and [when **it** is more prudent {to be collaborative}].
  두 개의 [ ]는 and로 연결되어 assess의 목적어 역할을 하는 명사절이다. 두 번째 [ ] 안의 it은 형식상의 주어이고, { }는 내용상의 주어이다.
- That is, plants compete only when competition [is needed to improve their ability to support their own growth and reproduction] and [has some likelihood of success].
  두 개의 [ ]는 when이 이끄는 부사절에서 and로 연결되어 술어 역할을 한다.

03

정답 ③

소재 수직 이동의 속도를 높인 기계화

해석 기계화는 수직 이동의 속도를 높였다. 계단과 램프가 전통적으로 오르내리는 방식이었기 때문에, 흔히 사용되는 건물은 5층을 넘는 것이 거의 없었다. 1853년에 뉴욕에서 설립된 Otis Company는 더 높은 건물을 가능하게 한 (케이블이 고장 나면 그것이 (엘리베이터의) 타는 칸을 제자리에 고정시키기 때문에 안전한) 안전 엘리베이터를 발명하면서 그 모든 것을 바꾸어 놓았다. 에스컬레이터가 이후에 등장해 더 많은 사람을 더 짧은 수직 거리로 이동시킬 수 있는 더 큰 능력을 제공해 주었는데, 그것은 1900년 파리 박람회에서 첫선을 보여 돌풍을 일으켰다. (세계 박람회는 기업, 국가, 혁신가들이 서로로부터 배우고 서로에 의해 영감을 받을 수 있는 기회였다.) 엘리베이터와 에스컬레이터로 인해 도시는 이제 외곽으로뿐만 아니라 깊은 지하층, 지하철, 터널과 함께 지하로, 그리고 고층 건물과 함께 위로도 또한 뻗어 나갈 수 있게 되었다. 맨해튼이 여전히 상징적인 전형으로 꼽히는 현대 도시 경관이 생겨났다.

Solution Guide

엘리베이터와 에스컬레이터 같은 기계화가 수직 이동의 속도를 높여 지하 구조물과 고층 건물의 건설을 가능하게 했다는 내용의 글이다. 따라서 기업, 국가, 혁신가들이 세계 박람회를 통해 서로로부터 배우고 서로에 의해 영감을 받을 수 있었다는 내용의 ③은 글의 전체 흐름과 관계가 없다.

Structure in Focus

- The Otis Company, [founded in 1853 in New York], changed all that with the invention of the safety elevator (safe because it locked the car in place [should the cables fail]) [that made taller buildings possible].
  첫 번째 [ ]는 The Otis Company를 부가적으로 설명하는 분사구이다. 두 번째 [ ]는 if the cables should fail에서 if가 생략되어 should가 the cables 앞으로 도치된 것으로 이해할 수 있다. 세 번째 [ ]는 the safety elevator를 수식하는 관계절이다.
- World Expositions were a chance [**for companies, countries and innovators** to learn from each other and to be inspired by each other].
  [ ]는 a chance의 구체적인 내용을 설명하는 to부정사구이고, for companies, countries and innovators는 to부정사의 의미상의 주어를 나타낸다.

04

정답 ③

소재 19세기 이전의 극장 관객

해석 만약 여러분이 19세기 이전에 극장에서 (공연을) 즐기고 싶었다면 동료 관객이나 배우와 어느 정도 다이얼로그, 즉 대화에 참여하게 된다는 사실을 피할 수 없었을 것이다. 관객이 어둠 속에 앉아 조용히 무대를 지켜본다는 개념은 새로운 것이다. 19세기 이전의 관객은 조명 빛을 받았고 흔히 매우 말이 많고 활동적이었으며, 심지어 무대 위로 뛰어올라 출연진과 싸우기도 했다. (19세기에는 많은 노동자가 돌봐야 할 가족과 자녀가 있었기 때문에 그들은 가난했고 극장에 갈 여유가 없거나 사교 집단에 참여할 시간이 없었다.) 관객이 입을 다물고 경청해야 한다는 개념을 주창한 것은 18세기 배우 David Garrick이었다. 오늘날의 배우들이 만끽할 수 있는 수동적이고 경건한 침묵은 새로운 현상이며, 물론 영화관도 마찬가지인데, 그곳에서는 스크린 속 우리의 대리인들이 우리의 반응을 의식하지 않고 자신의 이야기를 펼칠 수 있다.

Solution Guide

19세기 이전의 극장에서는 관객이 무대를 조용히 지켜보는 것이 아니라 다른 관객이나 배우와 대화에 참여했으며 오늘날의 수동적이고 경건한 침묵은 새로운 현상이라는 내용의 글인데 ③은 19세기의 많은 노동자가 극장에 갈 여유가 없거나 사교 집단에 참여할 시간이 없었던 이유를 설명하는 문장이므로 글의 전체 흐름과 관계가 없다.

Structure in Focus

- If you wanted to be entertained in a theater before the nineteenth century, you could not avoid the fact [that you were at some level participating in a dialog, a conversation, **either** {with your fellow members of the audience}, **or** {with the actors}].
  [ ]는 the fact와 동격 관계이고, 그 안의 두 개의 { }는 「either ~ or ...」로 연결되어 있다.
- The passive and reverential silence [in which today's actors can indulge themselves] is a new phenomenon, as, of course, is the cinema, [where our surrogates on the screen can unfold their stories {unaware of our responses}].
  첫 번째 [ ]는 The passive and reverential silence를 수식하는 관계절이고, 두 번째 [ ]는 the cinema를 부가적으로 설명하는 관계절이다. 두 번째 [ ] 안의 { }는 두 번째 관계절의 주어인 our surrogates on the screen의 부수적인 상황을 설명하는, 앞에 being이 생략된 분사구문이다.

15 문단 내의 글의 순서 파악하기

Gateway ④
Exercises 01 ⑤ 02 ③ 03 ① 04 ③ 05 ②
06 ⑤

Gateway

본문 84쪽

정답 ④

소재 규범 발생 과정

해석 규범은 사람들이 다른 사람들의 행동을 따르는 결과로 집단에서 생겨난다. 따라서 규범의 시작은 한 사람이 자신이 그래야만 한다고 생각하기 때문에 특정한 상황에서 특정한 방식으로 행동할 때 생겨난다. (C) 그런 다음 다른 사람들은 여러 가지 이유로 이 행동에 따를 수도 있다. 그 행동을 처음 한 사람은 이런 종류의 상황에서는 다른 사람들이 자신이 행동하는 것처럼 행동해야 한다고 생각할 수도 있다. (A) 따라서 그 사람은 지시하는 방식으로 규범 진술을 말함으로써 그들에게 행동을 지시할 수도 있다. 다른 방법으로는, 그 사람이 몸짓에 의한 것과 같은 다른 방식으로 따름이 바람직하다는 것을 전달할 수도 있다. 게다가 자신이 원하는 대로 행동하지 않으면 그들에게 제재를 가하겠다고 위협할 수도 있다. 이렇게 하면 일부 사람들은 그 사람의 바람을 따르고 그 사람이 행동하는 대로 행동하게 될 것이다. (B) 그러나 다른 일부 사람들에게는 그 행동이 자신에게 지시되게 할 필요가 없을 것이다. 그들은 행동의 규칙성을 관찰하고 자신이 따라야 한다고 스스로 결정할 것이다. 그들은 이성적 또는 도덕적 이유로 그렇게 할 수도 있다.

Structure in Focus

- This will cause some [to {conform to her wishes} and {act as she acts}].
  [ ]는 cause의 목적격 보어 역할을 하는 to부정사구이고, 그 안의 두 개의 { }는 and로 연결되어 to에 이어진다.
- The person [who performed the initial action] may think [that others ought to behave {as she behaves} in situations of this sort].
  첫 번째 [ ]는 The person을 수식하는 관계절이고, 두 번째 [ ]는 think의 목적어 역할을 하는 명사절이다. 두 번째 [ ] 안의 { }는 부사절로 as는 '~처럼, ~ 대로'의 뜻을 나타낸다.

Exercises

본문 86~91쪽

01

정답 ⑤

소재 세계화에 대한 대안적 개념의 필요성

해석 세계화는 흔히 거시적인 현상으로 연구되었다. 그러나 세계화 과정이 개인의 삶에 확실히 영향을 미치면서, 대안적인 개념의 필요성이 대두했다. (C) 따라서 '세계주의' 및 '세계 시민권' 같은 개념은 개인을 분석 대상으로 삼아, 세계화가 어떻게 '아래로부터' 경험되는지를 포착하는 데 빈번하게 사용되었다. 여기서 세계주의는 세계 시민권과 많은 유사성을 갖는 것으로 해석된다. (B) 예를 들어, 문화사회학자 John Tomlinson은 세계주의자가 된다는 것은 '더 넓은 세계에 속해 있다'는 능동적인 경험을 가진다는 것을 의미한다고 주장한다. 따라서 세계주의는 정체성과 밀접하게 연결되어 있으며, 세계주의자는 우리를 인간으로 결속시키는 특징에 대한 성찰적 인식을 얻게 된다. (A) 여기에는 자기 자신의 가정과 편견에 의문을 제기할 수 있는 능력이 필요하다. 정체성은 이러한 맥락에서 본질주의적이거나 안정된 것이 아니며, 오히려 그것은 개인이 참여하는 각기 다른 관행과 입장 전반에서 분해되고 구성되고 재구성된다.

Solution Guide

세계화는 흔히 거시적인 현상으로 연구되었지만, 이것이 개인의 삶에 영향을 미친다는 점이 확인되면서 대안적인 개념의 필요성이 대두되었다는 내용의 주어진 글 다음에는 therefore와 함께 그래서 '세계주의' 및 '세계 시민권' 같은 개념이 대안으로 제시되어 세계화와 개인의 관계를 조망하는 데 사용되었다는 내용의 (C)가 이어져야 한다. 그다음에는 (C)에 언급한 내용에 대한 예를 For instance로 제시하는 (B)가 이어지고, 세계주의는 정체성과 밀접하게 연결되어 있으며, 세계주의자는 우리를 인간으로 결속시키는 특징을 성찰적 인식을 통해 알게 된다는 내용을 This로 지칭하여 여기에는 자기 자신의 가정과 편견에 의문을 제기할 수 있는 능력이 필요하다는 내용의 (A)가 그 뒤를 잇는 것이 글의 순서로 가장 적절하다.

Structure in Focus

- For instance, cultural sociologist John Tomlinson claims [that {being a cosmopolitan} means {that one has an active experience of "belonging to the wider world}]."
  [ ]는 claims의 목적어 역할을 하는 명사절이고, 그 안의 첫 번째 { }는 명사절 안의 주어 역할을 하는 동명사구이며, 두 번째 { }는 means의 목적어 역할을 하는 명사절이다.
- As such, cosmopolitanism is closely connected to

identity; a cosmopolitan obtains a reflexive awareness of the features [that unite us as human beings].
[ ]는 the features를 수식하는 관계절이다.

02

정답 ③

소재 원폭 피해자들을 만난 Roosevelt 여사

해석 1953년 6월 17일, Roosevelt 여사는 히로시마에 가서 그곳에서 피폭 생존자에 끼친 핵 공격의 영향을 연구하는 미국 연구 단체인 원폭 피해자 위원회를 방문했다. 많은 사람이 원자 폭탄으로 인한 화재로 다쳤다. (B) 공식 모임이 끝난 후, 몇 명의 소녀가 그녀를 만나기 위해 기다리고 있었다. 소녀들은 원자 폭탄에 대해 그녀를 비난하는 것이 아님을 분명히 하였는데, 그들은 원자 폭탄의 영향을 고려할 때 다시는 인간에게 이러한 무기가 사용되지 않도록 해야 한다는 것을 분명히 할 필요를 그녀에게 이해시키기를 원했을 뿐이었다. (C) 그녀가 직접적으로 그렇게 말하지는 않았지만, 소녀들은 그 공격으로 인해 얼굴이 영구적으로 흉하게 된 사람 중에 속했을 것이었다. Roosevelt 여사가 그것을 '비극적인 순간'이라고 불렀기 때문에 이것은 강렬한 만남이었음이 분명하다. (A) 그것으로 인해 그녀는 (피폭 희생자들에게) 도움을 주기 위해 더 많은 것을 하도록 미국인들에게 촉구했다. 그녀는 그들이 미국이 직접 책임져야 할 대상은 아니라고 주장했지만, '이 지난 전쟁의 희생자들에 대한 선의의 제스처로서 그러한 도움은 매우 귀중할 것이었다.'

Solution Guide

주어진 글에서 Roosevelt 여사가 히로시마에서 원폭 피해자 위원회를 방문하는 내용이 나오므로, 공식 모임이 끝난 후 자신을 기다리는 몇 명의 소녀를 만나는 (B)가 그 뒤에 이어져야 한다. 그다음에는 원자 폭탄 공격으로 인해 얼굴이 영구적으로 흉하게 된 것으로 추측되는 소녀들과의 만남을 Roosevelt 여사가 강렬하게 받아들였다는 내용의 (C)가 이어지고, 이 만남을 It으로 지칭하면서 그 만남으로 인해 도움을 주기 위해 더 많은 것을 하도록 미국인들에게 촉구했다는 내용의 (A)가 이어지는 것이 글의 순서로 가장 적절하다.

Structure in Focus

- On June 17, 1953, Mrs. Roosevelt traveled to Hiroshima, [where she visited the Atomic Bomb Casualty Commission], [an American research group {that studied the effects of the nuclear attacks on bomb survivors}].
  첫 번째 [ ]는 Hiroshima를 부가적으로 설명하는 관계절이고, 두 번째 [ ]는 the Atomic Bomb Casualty Commission과 동격 관계이며, 그 안의 { }는 an American research group을 수식하는 관계절이다.
- The girls explained [that they did not blame her for the atomic bomb]; they only wanted to impress on her the need [to ensure {that these weapons were never used again on human beings, given their effects}].
  첫 번째 [ ]는 explained의 목적어 역할을 하는 명사절이다. 두 번째 [ ]는 the need의 구체적 내용을 설명하는 to부정사구이고, 그 안의 { }는 ensure의 목적어 역할을 하는 명사절이다.

03

정답 ①

소재 Gettier 문제

해석 대부분의 철학자는 1960년대 Edmund Gettier가 플라톤의 지식에 관한 정의가 항상 만족스러운 설명을 제공하지는 않는다는 것을 보여 주기 전까지는 그것을 정당화된 참인 믿음으로 받아들였다. (A) 그는 어떤 사람의 믿음이 참이고 정당화된다고 해도 그 사람이 무언가를 정말로 알지는 못한다는 것을 우리가 본능적으로 깨닫는 몇 가지 사례를 제시했다. 예를 들어, 나는 내 친구 Sue를 그녀의 집에서 만나기로 약속했는데, 나는 도착해서 창문을 통해 그녀가 부엌에 앉아 있는 것을 본다. (C) 사실 내가 보는 것은 Sue가 아니라 그녀의 일란성 쌍둥이 자매이고, Sue는 실제로 다른 방에 있다. Sue가 집에 있다는 나의 믿음은 참이고, 내가 그녀를 본 것을 확신하기 때문에 그것을 믿을 만한 타당한 이유가 있지만, 내가 그녀가 집에 있다는 것을 알았다고 말하는 것은 잘못된 것인데, 왜냐하면 나는 알지 못했기 때문이다. (B) 이러한 사례는 'Gettier 문제'로 알려지게 되었고, 철학자들이 믿음, 참, 정당화 외에 지식에 대한 네 번째 기준이 있는지를 묻도록 유도했다. Gettier는 플라톤의 정의뿐만 아니라 지식이 무엇인지 완벽하게 정의할 수 있는지 여부에 대해서도 의문을 제기했다.

Solution Guide

Edmund Gettier 이전에는 대부분의 철학자가 플라톤의 지식에 관한 정의를 참이고 정당화된 믿음으로 받아들였다는 내용의 주어진 글 다음에는, 플라톤의 정의와는 달리 어떤 사람의 믿음이 참으로 여겨지고 그럴 만한 정당한 이유가 있어도 그 사람이 무언가를 정말로 알지 못할 수 있다는 Edmund Gettier의 통찰 내용을 언급하고 그 사례를 도입하는 (A)가 이어져야 한다. 그다음에는 (A)에서 도입한 사례의 내용을 구체적으로 설명하는 내용인 (C)가 온 후, (C)에서 제시한 사례가 철학자들에게 던진 과제와 Gettier가 추가로 제기한 의문으로 글을 마무리하는 (B)가 이어지는 것이 글의 순서로 가장 적절하다.

Structure in Focus

- Most philosophers accepted Plato's definition of knowledge as justified true belief until the 1960s, [when Edmund Gettier showed {that it didn't always provide a satisfactory explanation}].
  [ ]는 the 1960s를 부가적으로 설명하는 관계절이고, 그 안의 { }는 showed의 목적어 역할을 하는 명사절이다.
- He came up with several instances [where we instinctively realize {that someone doesn't really know something, even though that person's belief is both true and justified}].
  [ ]는 several instances를 수식하는 관계절이고, 그 안의 { }는 realize의 목적어 역할을 하는 명사절이다.

04

정답 ③

소재 이마누엘 칸트의 도덕관

해석 어떤 면에서는, 자신이 어떤 종류의 윤리 체계를 가졌는지와 어떤 종류를 자신이 높이 평가하는지를 파악하는 것이 개인에게 도움이 된다. (B) 이마누엘 칸트는 이것을 한 단계 더 발전시켜, 의무론자에게는 흔치 않은 규칙을 추가한다. 그는 도덕적 윤리적 건전성을 위해 사람들이 자신의 결정을 검증할 수 있고 검증해야 한다고 믿었으며, 사람들이 바로 그것을 하도록 돕기 위해 자신이 '정언 명령'이라 부른 사고 실험의 개요를 설명했다. (C) 어떤 행동 방침을 고려할 때, "다른 모든 사람이 내 입장에 놓인다면 같은 행동을 하기를 바라겠는가?"라고 자문해 보라. 만일 대답이 '그렇다'라면 여러분은 올바른 길을 가고 있는 것이다. (A) 만일 대답이 '아니다'라면 여러분 자신은 그것을 하지 말라. 예를 들어, 거짓말을 하는 것이 자신에게 유리할 수도 있는 상황을 쉽게 상상할 수 있지만, 여러분은 모든 사람이 거짓말하는 것을 원하지는 않을 것이므로, 여러분 자신도 거짓말을 해서는 안 된다.

Culture Note

Categorical Imperative(정언 명령) 칸트 철학의 개념으로, 행위 자체가 선이므로 무조건 그것을 하도록 요구되는 도덕적 명령을 의미한다.

Solution Guide

자신이 가진 윤리 체계를 파악하는 것은 개인에게 도움이 된다고 언급한 주어진 글의 내용에 이어, 그것을 it으로 지칭하면서 칸트가 이를 발전시켜 도덕적 윤리적 건전성을 위해 자신의 결정을 검증하도록 돕기 위해 정언 명령이라는 사고 실험의 개요를 설명했다는 (B)가 이어지고, 그런 다음 사고 실험의 구체적인 내용으로, 다른 모든 사람이 자신의 입장이라면 같은 행동을 하기를 바라겠는지 자문해 보라는 내용의 (C)가 이어지고, 마지막으로 If the answer is no로 그 자문에 대한 답을 언급하며, 답이 '아니다'라면 그것을 하면 안 된다고 결론을 내리는 (A)가 이어지는 것이 글의 순서로 가장 적절하다.

Structure in Focus

- On one level, **it** is helpful [for individuals to identify {which kind of ethical system they have} and {which kind they admire}].
  it은 형식상의 주어이고, [ ]는 내용상의 주어이며, [ ] 안의 두 개의 { }는 identify의 목적어 역할을 하는 명사절이다.
- He [believed {that you can and should test your decisions for moral and ethical soundness}] and [outlined a thought experiment {he called the Categorical Imperative} {to help you do just that}].
  두 개의 [ ]는 and로 연결되어 문장의 술어 역할을 한다. 첫 번째 [ ] 안의 { }는 believed의 목적어 역할을 하는 명사절이다. 두 번째 [ ] 안의 첫 번째 { }는 a thought experiment를 수식하는 관계절이고, 두 번째 { }는 목적을 나타내는 to부정사구이다.

05

정답 ②

소재 컴퓨터의 생존 전략

해석 생명체는 생존 전략을 진화시키기 위해 노력하지만, 그 과정을 반드시 의식하지는 않는다. 의식이 어쩌다가 그것을 가지게 된 유기체에 대해 많은 것을 말해 주기는 하지만, 생명의 필수 조건은 아니다. (B) 대부분의 생물 종은 생존을 위한 기술과 기제를 진화시킨다는 사실을 숙고하지 않고 그렇게 해 왔으며, 이것이 지금까지 컴퓨터 생명체에 일어났던 일이다. 우리는 컴퓨터가 자신의 생존에 대해 어떻게 숙고할지 짐작해 볼 수 있지만, 이것은 본질적으로 미래의 문제이다. (A) 현재 우리는 컴퓨터에서 다수의 원시적인 생존 기제를 보는데, 우리는 이것이 발전하고 새로운 것이 등장할 것으로 예상할 수 있을 것이다. 발전의 현재 단계에서는 컴퓨터의 생존 전략이 컴퓨터 설계에서의 인간 개입에 거의 모든 것을 신세진다는 것은 불가피한 것이다. (C) 그러나, 기계의 자율성이 발전함에 따라, 컴퓨터 진화에 대한 인간의 영향력 범위는 점차 줄어들 것이다. 컴퓨터는 세상에서 자기 자신의 위치에 대해 생각하게 되고 자신의 안전을 강화하는 조치를 취할 것이다.

Solution Guide

대부분의 생명체는 자신의 생존 전략을 진화시키기 위해 노력해 왔지만, 그 과정은 의식하지 못하고 있다는 내용의 주어진 글 다음에, 컴퓨터도 자신의 생존에 관해 숙고하지 않은 채 생존 기술과 기제를 진화시켜 왔으며 컴퓨터가 자신의 생존에 관해 어떻게 숙고할지는 미래의 문제라는 내용의 (B)가 이어진다. 그다음에는 (B)에 언급된 미래의 문제와 대비되는 현 단계에서의 컴퓨터의 생존 전략이 인간의 개입에 신세지고 있다는 내용의 (A)가 이어지고, However로 (A)의 마지막 문장에서 언급한 현재 인간의 영향력과 대비되는 미래의 기계의 자율성을 언급하는 내용의 (C)가 그 뒤를 잇는 것이 글의 순서로 가장 적절하다.

Structure in Focus

- At present we see a host of rudimentary survival mechanisms in computers: we may expect these [to develop] and new ones [to emerge].
  두 개의 [ ]는 expect의 목적격 보어 역할을 하는 to부정사구이다.

06

정답 ⑤

소재 도시화와 도시 계획

해석 적어도 19세기 후반 산업 도시가 부상한 이후로, 도시화와 도시 계획의 역사는 정치적, 행정적, 기술 관료적 전문 지식의 역사였다. (C) 도시는 사회가 경제적, 사회적, 정치적으로 더 복잡해짐에 따라 부, 건강, 안전, 기회, 개인 발전에 대한 수요의 해결책으로 여겨지게 되었다. 도시는 또한 새로운 문제들을 제기하는 것으로도 여겨지게 되었는데, 그것들은 흔히 더 이전의 사회적 수요를 충족시키는 데 성공하면서 야기된 것들이었다. (B) 그러한 문제/해결 구조에 의해 자극받기도 하고 그것을 자극하기도 하면서 20세기 초의 진보주의 정치 운동은 훈련되고 신뢰할 수 있는 전문가, 특히 경제학자 및 기타 사회과학자에게 크게 의존했다. 그러한 전문가는 새로 형성된 직업 분야와 전문학교에서 교육받은 경우가 많았다. (A) 학위를 손에 쥐고, 그들은 정부와 기업 둘 다를 자유방임주의의 시대에서 벗어나 자기 자신, 노동자, 시민을 위한 더 나은 결과를 향하도록 이끌 준비가 되어 있었다. 그것은 더 안전한 식품, 더 안전한 물, 더 나은 근무 여건, 더 안전하고 덜 비싼 자동차, 그리고 교육, 여가, 개인적 성취를 위한 기회 확대 등을 의미했다.

Solution Guide

적어도 19세기 후반 산업 도시가 부상한 이후 도시화와 도시 계획의 역사는 전문 지식의 역사였다는 주어진 글에 이어, 전문 지식의 역사에 관한 부연으로 도시가 부, 건강, 안전, 기회, 개인 발전에 대한 수요의 해결책으로 여겨지게 된 것과 동시에 새로운 문제를 제기한다는 (C)가 이어진다. 그다음에는 (C)의 solutions와 new problems를 that problem/solution framework로 받아 내용을 전개하는 (B)가 이어지고, (B)의 Those experts를 they로 지칭하며 이들에 대해 부연하는 내용의 (A)가 이어지는 것이 글의 순서로 가장 적절하다.

Structure in Focus

- [Both fueled by and fueling {that problem/solution framework}], [the Progressive political movement of the early twentieth century] relied heavily on trained and trusted experts, especially economists and other social scientists.
  첫 번째 [ ]는 주어인 두 번째 [ ]를 부가적으로 설명하는 분사구문이고, 첫 번째 [ ] 안의 { }는 fueled by와 fueling의 공통 목적어이다.
- Cities also came to be seen as posing new problems, [often caused by their successes in meeting earlier social demands].
  [ ]는 new problems를 부가적으로 설명하는 분사구문이다.

16 주어진 문장의 적합한 위치 찾기

Gateway ③
Exercises 01 ⑤ 02 ⑤ 03 ④ 04 ⑤ 05 ④ 06 ④

Gateway

본문 92쪽

정답 ③

소재 승자 독식의 경쟁으로 잘못 이해되는 과학

해석 과학은 때때로 승자 독식의 경쟁으로 묘사되는데, 이는 2등이나 3등인 것에 대한 보상이 없다는 것을 의미한다. 이는 과학 분야의 경쟁의 본질에 대한 극단적인 견해이다. 과학 분야의 경쟁을 그런 식으로 설명하는 사람들조차도 반복과 입증이 사회적 가치를 지니고 있으며 과학에서 일반적이라는 점을 고려할 때, 이는 다소 부정확한 설명이라고 말한다. 그것은 또한 소수의 경쟁만 존재한다고 시사하는 정도로 부정확하다. 물론, 힉스 입자 규명이나 고온 초전도체 개발과 같은 몇몇 경쟁은 세계적인 수준으로 여겨진다. 하지만 그 밖의 많은 다른 경쟁은 다양한 측면을 가지고 있고, 그런 경쟁의 수는 증가하고 있을 수도 있다. 예를 들어, 여러 해 동안 암에 대해 '하나'의 치료법만 있다고 생각되었지만, 이제는 암은 여러 가지 형태를 가지며 치료를 제공하기 위해 다양한 접근 방식이 필요하다고 인식된다. 승자는 한 명이 아니라 여러 명이 있을 것이다.

Structure in Focus

- Even those [who describe scientific contests in such a way] note [that it is a somewhat inaccurate description, given that replication and verification {have social value} and {are common in science}].
  첫 번째 [ ]는 those를 수식하는 관계절이고, 두 번째 [ ]는 note의 목적어 역할을 하는 명사절이다. 두 번째 [ ] 안의 두 개의 { }는 and로 연결되어 that절의 술어 역할을 한다.
- By way of example, for many years **it** was thought [that there would be "one" cure for cancer], but **it** is now realized [that cancer takes multiple forms] and [that multiple approaches are needed to provide a cure].
  두 개의 it은 모두 형식상의 주어이고, 세 개의 [ ]는 모두 내용상의 주어이다.

Exercises

본문 94~97쪽

01

정답 ⑤

소재 기자의 정보 습득

해석 기자는 한 전문적인 구역에 배정되는 즉시 그 구역이 어떻게 작동하는지에 대해 전반적으로 친숙해지기 위해 그 주제에 관한 기본 서적을 여러 권 읽어야 한다. 예를 들어, 주의회나 법원 시스템과 같은 정부 영역이 관련된 경우, 기자는 그 특정 기관이 어떻게 운영되는지 알지 못한 채 첫 임무[취재]를 나가서는 안 된다. 도서관에 그런 책이 비치되어 있는데, 나중에 참조할 수 있도록 기자가 자기 소유의 책을 구매하는 것이 더 좋기는 하다. 예를 들어 어떤 의학 기자도 좋은 의학 사전 없이는 성공적으로 일할 수 없다. 또한 비즈니스 담당 기자가 기본적인 경제서가 없어서도 안 된다. 기자의 취재 구역 내 모든 도시의 도시 명부와 전화번호부는 귀중한 도구이며, 기자가 그 구역에서 마주치게 될 기관의 내부 명부 또한 그렇다. 흔히 공식적으로 얻을 수 없는 이런 번호를 가지고 있으면 기자는 장애물을 우회하여 잠재적인 취재원에 빠르게 도달할 수 있게 된다.

Culture Note

city directory(도시 명부) 도시 내 거주자, 거리, 사업체, 조직 또는 기관의 연락처 및 주소 목록이며, 책으로 출간되거나 인터넷으로 검색 가능한 페이지로 제공되기도 한다. 명부는 알파벳 순이나 지리적으로 또는 다른 방식으로 배열된다.

Solution Guide

전문적인 구역에 배정을 받으면 기자는 그 구역의 작동 방식에 관한 정보를 구해야 한다는 내용의 글로, 주어진 문장이 ⑤에 들어가면, 주어진 문장에서 언급한 명부와 전화번호부의 내용을 ⑤ 뒤의 such numbers가 받게 되어 글의 흐름이 자연스럽게 연결될 수 있다. 따라서 주어진 문장이 들어가기에 가장 적절한 곳은 ⑤이다.

Structure in Focus

- [City directories and telephone books from all cities in a reporter's area of coverage] are valuable tools, as are [internal directories of the organizations {he or she will encounter on the beat}].
  첫 번째 [ ]는 문장의 주어 역할을 하는 명사구이고, 두 번째 [ ]는 as가 이끄는 절의 주어로, 술어동사 are 다음에 쓰였다. { }는 the organizations를 수식하는 관계절이다.
- **Nor should** a business reporter **be** without a basic economics text.
  부정어인 Nor로 문장이 시작되면서 「조동사(should)+주어

(a business reporter) + 본동사(be)」의 어순이 되었다.

02

정답 ⑤

소재 문화적 다양성과 인간의 선천적 능력

해석 문화적 다양성과 행동의 다양성은 환경에 유연하게 대응하고, 사회적 학습에 참여하며, 문화를 만드는 인간의 타고난 능력(그 자체가 사회성 모둠의 일부인 능력)에서 비롯될 수 있다. 그 다양성은 역설적으로 문화적 필요성보다는 우리의 유전자와 더 관련이 있을 수 있는 근본적인 보편성을 숨기고 있을 수도 있다. 진화 심리학자 John Tooby와 Leda Cosmides는 이 생각에 대한 기발한 예를 제공한다. 그들은 외계인이 인간을 주크박스로 대체하는데, 각각의 주크박스가 수천 곡의 레퍼토리를 가지고 있고 그것이 있는 장소와 시간에 따라 특정 곡을 재생할 수 있는 능력을 가지고 있다는 사고 실험을 제안한다. 그렇게 되면 우리는 세계 각지의 주크박스가 서로 다른 시간에 서로 다른 노래를 재생하는 것을 알게 될 것인데, 노래는 근처 주크박스에 있는 노래와 비슷한 노래일 것이다. 그러나 이러한 집단 간 차이와 집단 내 공통성 어느 것도 문화의 작용과 아무런 관련이 없을 것이다. 이것은 인간이 환경에 유연하면서도 예측 가능하게 반응할 수 있는 선천적 능력을 가지고 있을 수 있다는 것을 보여 주는 하나의 방식이다.

Culture Note

social suite(사회성 모둠) 예일대 사회학과 교수인 Nicholas Christakis가 말한 우리 유전자에 새겨진 진화적으로 계승된 보편적 특징의 8가지 목록으로, 개인 정체성 소유와 식별, 짝과 자녀를 향한 사랑, 우정, 사회 연결망, 협력, 내집단 편애, 온건한 계층 구조, 사회 학습과 사회 교육을 일컫는다.

Solution Guide

주어진 문장의 this intergroup variation and intragroup commonality는 ⑤ 앞의 문장에서 언급한 세계 각지의 주크박스가 서로 다른 시간에 서로 다른 노래를 재생하는 집단 간 차이와, 가까운 곳에 있는 주크박스에 있는 노래와 비슷한 노래를 재생하는 집단 내 공통성을 나타내므로, 주어진 문장이 들어가기에 가장 적절한 곳은 ⑤이다.

Structure in Focus

- Cultural and behavioral diversity can result from humans' innate ability [to flexibly respond to their environments], [to engage in social learning], and [to make culture] (an ability which is itself a part of the social suite).

  세 개의 [ ]는 and로 연결되어 humans' innate ability의 구체적 내용을 설명하는 to부정사구이다.

- We would then observe [that jukeboxes in different parts of the world played different songs at different times, songs {that were similar to **those** on the jukeboxes near them}].

  [ ]는 동사 observe의 목적어 역할을 하는 명사절이고, 그 안의 { }는 songs를 수식하는 관계절이다. those는 songs를 대신한다.

03

정답 ④

소재 오늘날 리더의 자질

해석 기업이 리더를 선발할 때, 그들이 묻는 첫 질문 두 가지는 "그가 전에 이런 일을 해 본 적이 있는가?" "그의 실적은 어떤가?"이다. 우리는 만약 그 사람이 전에 그 일을 해 본 적이 있다면(그리고 그것을 잘 해냈다면), 그는 다시 그 일을 할 수 있다고 가정한다. 리더에게 경험은 여전히 중요하며, 그것이 미래의 성공을 가장 효과적으로 예측하는 변수일 때가 있다. 그러나 문제는 끊임없이 변화하고 성공의 기준이 계속 재정의되고 있는 세상에서 끊임없이 개선되는 기술, 과정, 모범 사례로 인해 경험이 불리한 조건이 될 수 있다는 것이다. 오늘날, 리더는 새로운 시각으로 문제와 기회를 바라볼 수 있도록 스스로를 단련해야 한다. 이것은 어려운 일인데, 사람들은 비슷한 상황에서 효과적이었던 접근 방식을 반복하기를 당연히 원하기 때문이다. 과거에 성공을 가져다준 것이나 현재 여러분의 현 위치에 대한 대안을 고려하는 것은 힘든 일이다.

Solution Guide

경험이 불리한 조건이 될 수 있는 오늘날에는, 리더가 과거의 성공 사례와는 다른 시각으로 문제와 기회를 바라봐야 한다는 내용의 글이다. 주어진 문장은 오늘날, 리더는 새로운 시각으로 문제와 기회를 바라볼 수 있도록 스스로를 단련해야 한다는 내용이므로, 이 일이 어려운 이유를 This is difficult because ~로 기술하는 문장 앞에 들어가야 한다. 따라서 주어진 문장이 들어가기에 가장 적절한 곳은 ④이다.

Structure in Focus

- The problem, however, is [that because of constantly improving technology, processes, and best practices in a world {that is constantly changing} and {where success is being continually redefined}, experience can be a handicap].

  [ ]는 is의 보어 역할을 하는 명사절이고, 그 안의 두 개의 { }

는 and로 연결되어 a world를 수식하는 관계절이다.

- **It** is a challenge [to consider an alternative {to what brought you success in the past} or {to your current position in the present}].
  It은 형식상의 주어이고, [ ]는 내용상의 주어이다. 두 개의 { }는 or로 연결되어 an alternative에 이어진다.

04

정답 ⑤

소재 후각의 힘

해석 후각은 맛을 판단하는 감각일 뿐만 아니라, 욕구를 자극하고 다른 감각을 압도할 수도 있는 강력한 힘이기도 하다. 지난 10년 동안 방향 요법은 대체 치유법으로, 그리고 또한 소비자에게 광고할 수 있는 새로운 상품으로 부상했다. 일부 매장은 갓 구운 빵이나 사과파이의 향을 퍼뜨려 고객이 더 오래 머무르고 더 많이 구매하도록 유도한다. 냄새는 또한 먹을 수 있는 음식과 먹기에 적합하지 않은 음식을 구분하는 데 중요하다. 한약재 매장에는 흔히 다양한 자극적인 냄새가 있다. 한약 제조에는 식물을 액체 형태로 조리하거나 알코올로 진액을 증류하는 것이 포함될 수도 있는데, 이 과정에서 흔히 냄새가 유발된다. 그러나 생의학 알약 및 정제는 더 맛있다고 여겨지는 냄새를 강조하지 않는 방식으로 준비된다. 냄새가 없으면 약과 음식의 거리가 더 멀어진다.

Solution Guide

후각은 욕구를 자극하고 다른 감각을 압도할 수 있는 강력한 힘이며, 음식의 냄새로 고객의 구매를 유도할 수 있고, 먹을 수 있는 음식과 먹기에 적합하지 않은 음식을 구분하는 데에도 중요한 역할을 한다는 내용의 글이다. 주어진 문장은 Yet으로 시작해서 생의학 알약 및 정제는 냄새를 강조하지 않는 방식으로 준비된다고 했으며, 이것은 ⑤의 앞 문장에서 언급된 자극적인 냄새를 풍기는 한약의 제조와는 다른 점을 설명하고 있고, ⑤ 바로 다음 문장의 The absence of smells는 주어진 문장에서 언급된 생의학 알약 및 정제의 특징이라고 볼 수 있으므로, 주어진 문장이 들어가기에 가장 적절한 곳은 ⑤이다.

Structure in Focus

- Some stores spread scents of freshly baked bread or apple pie to encourage shoppers [to stay longer and buy more].
  [ ]는 encourage의 목적격 보어 역할을 하는 to부정사구이다.
- The preparation of herbal medicines may include [cooking plants into liquid form] or [distilling essences with alcohol], which often creates an odor.
  두 개의 [ ]는 or로 연결되어 include의 목적어 역할을 하는 동명사구이다.

05

정답 ④

소재 부모와 또래 집단의 차이

해석 부모와 또래의 가치 사이의 차이가 부모와 십 대가 반드시 적대적으로 대립하는 것으로 이어지는 것은 아니다. 사실 대부분의 청소년은 또래만큼이나 부모와도 친근하게 지낸다. 그들은 단지 서로 다른 유형의 활동, 즉 부모와는 일과 과제 활동을, 또래와는 놀이와 여가 활동을 함께 할 뿐이다. 돈을 어디에 쓸지, 어떤 직업을 선택할지 등 재정, 교육, 진로 및 기타 진지한 문제와 관련하여 청소년은 부모에게 조언을 구하는 경향이 있다. 누구와 데이트할지, 어떤 동아리에 가입할지 등 사교 활동과 관련해서는 그들은 그것을 또래와 상의할 가능성이 더 크다. 이는 또래 집단이 '타인지향형 행동', 즉 개인적 신념과 전통적 가치에의 의존이 아닌 승인과 지지를 타인에게 기대하는 것을 매우 중요시함을 반영한다. 사실 또래 집단은 독립성과 개성을 희생하면서 순응을 요구한다.

Solution Guide

글의 서두에서 십 대는 부모 및 또래 집단과 서로 다른 유형의 활동을 함께 한다고 전제한 다음, 주어진 문장에서는 십 대가 사교 활동과 관련해서는 또래 집단과 상의할 가능성이 더 크다는 것을 설명한다. 따라서 이 문장 바로 뒤에는 이런 경향성의 이유를 또래 집단의 특징에 기반하여 제시하는 것이 자연스러운데, ④ 다음 문장이 그 이유에 해당한다. 또한, 주어진 문장 앞에는 십 대가 부모의 조언을 구하는 활동에 대한 설명이 대조적으로 제시되는 것이 자연스럽다. 따라서 주어진 문장이 들어가기에 가장 적절한 곳은 ④이다.

Structure in Focus

- Concerning [financial, educational, career, and other serious matters, such as what to spend money on and what occupation to choose], youths are inclined to seek advice from parents.
  [ ]는 전치사 Concerning의 목적어 역할을 하는 명사구이다.
- This reflects the great importance [placed by the peer group on *other-directed behavior*, {looking to others for approval and support as opposed to reliance on personal beliefs and traditional values}].
  [ ]는 the great importance를 수식하는 분사구이고, 그 안의 { }는 *other-directed behavior*를 구체적으로 설명하는 동명사구이다.

06

정답 ④

소재 고통스러운 자극의 재현

해석 가상이나 기계로 매개되는 환경에서 믿을 만한 촉감을 재현할 수 있는 가능성과 관련된 한 가지 중요한 점은 '고통'의 역할에 있다. 확실히, 고통스러운 자극이 없다면 수많은 실제 상호 작용은 완전히 믿을 만하지는 않을 것이다. 그러나 가상 또는 매개되는 상호 작용 내에 그러한 종류의 자극을 재현하는 것이 과연 유용할지 의문이 들 수도 있다. '가상의' 세계는 어떤 의미에서 고통이 없는 것이 '더 나은' 것이 아닐까? 즉각적으로 직관적이지는 않더라도, 고통스러운 자극을 전달하는 능력이 매개되는 환경 내에서 유용할 수 있는 상황은 (물론 소수이기는 하지만) 꽤 있다. 사실, 지난 몇 년 동안 우리 지각의 이러한 측면을 재현하기 위한 수많은 시도 또한 있어 왔다. 이것(이러한 시도)은 시뮬레이션의 사실감을 높이기 위해 비디오 게임에서 혹은 훨씬 더 중요하게는 고통이 직업적 위험 요소이며 이를(고통을) 처리해야 하는 군인을 위한 훈련 프로그램에서 있을 수 있다.

Solution Guide

가상이나 기계로 매개되는 환경에서 촉감의 중요성에 관한 글이다. ④ 바로 앞의 문장은 가상의 세계는 고통이 없는 것이 더 나은 것이 아닌가라는 질문을 제시하고 있으므로, 주어진 문장이 ④에 들어가면 그 대답으로 고통스러운 자극이 유용한 상황이 꽤 있다는 내용을 제시한 다음 그 사례로 ④ 뒤에서 이러한 측면의 재현을 위한 시도가 있었고, 비디오 게임이나 군인을 위한 훈련 프로그램과 같은 상황에서 고통스러운 자극이 유용하게 쓰일 수 있다고 언급하는 것이 자연스럽다. 따라서 주어진 문장이 들어가기에 가장 적절한 곳은 ④이다.

Structure in Focus

- Even if not immediately intuitive, there are a (admittedly small) number of situations [in which {the ability to deliver painful stimulation} comes in handy within mediated environments].
  [ ]는 a (admittedly small) number of situations를 수식하는 관계절이고, 그 안의 { }는 관계절의 주어 역할을 하는 명사구이다.
- This may occur [in video games to increase the realism of the simulation] or even more importantly [in training programs for soldiers {where pain is an occupational hazard and will need to be dealt with}].
  두 개의 [ ]는 or로 연결되어 occur를 수식하는 전치사구이고, 두 번째 [ ] 안의 { }는 training programs for soldiers를 수식하는 관계절이다.

17 문단 요약하기

Gateway ①

Exercises 01 ① 02 ① 03 ② 04 ④

Gateway

본문 98쪽

정답 ①

소재 다양한 과학 분야에서 성과를 낼 수 있는 탐구 방법

해석 평균적인 재능을 가진 사람이라도 다양한 과학 분야에서 주목할 만한 성과를 낼 수 있는데, 그것들(다양한 과학 분야)을 한꺼번에 모두 포괄하려고 하지만 않는다면 가능하다. 대신에 그들은 한 주제 다음에 다른 주제에(즉, 다른 기간에) 집중해야 하는데, 비록 나중의 성과가 다른 영역에서의 더 이전의 성취를 약화시킬 수 있지만 말이다. 이는 뇌가 '공간' 안에서가 아닌, '시간' 안에서 과학적 보편성에 적응한다고 말하는 것과 같다. 사실, 뛰어난 능력을 가진 사람들도 이런 식으로 나아간다. 따라서, 우리가 서로 다른 과학 분야에 출판물을 가진 사람에게 놀랄 때, 각 주제가 특정 기간 동안 탐구되었다는 것을 인식하라. 더 이전에 얻은 지식은 확실히 저자의 머리에서 사라지지 않았을 것이지만 그것은 공식이나 크게 축약된 기호로 응축되어 단순화되어 있을 것이다. 따라서 대뇌 칠판에 새로운 이미지를 인식하고 학습할 수 있는 충분한 공간이 남아 있다.

→ 하나의 과학 주제를 탐구한 다음에 다른 주제를 탐구하는 것은 과학 전반에 걸친 주목할 만한 성과를 가능하게 하는데, 이전에 습득된 지식은 뇌 안에서 단순화된 형태로 유지되며 이는 새로운 학습을 위한 공간을 남겨 두기 때문이다.

Structure in Focus

- Thus, when we are astonished by someone [with publications in different scientific fields], realize [that each topic was explored during a specific period of time].
  첫 번째 [ ]는 someone을 수식하는 전치사구이고, 두 번째 [ ]는 realize의 목적어 역할을 하는 명사절이다.
- Knowledge [gained earlier] certainly will not have disappeared from the mind of the author, but it will have become simplified by [condensing into {formulas} or {greatly abbreviated symbols}].
  첫 번째 [ ]는 Knowledge를 수식하는 분사구이다. 두 번째 [ ]는 전치사 by의 목적어 역할을 하는 동명사구이고, 그 안에서 두 개의 { }가 or로 연결되어 into의 목적어 역할을 한다.

Exercises 본문 100~103쪽

01

정답 ①

소재 일상 제품도 가질 수 있는 상징적 의미

해석 손과 얼굴을 씻기 위해 욕실 세면대 옆에 두는 물건인, 비누 한 개를 생각해 보라. 이런 눈에 띄지 않는 물건이 얼마나 많은 의미를 담을 수 있을까? '큰 의미 없어' 또는 심지어 '아무 의미 없어'라고 대답하고 싶은 마음이 들 수도 있지만, 사실 비누조차도 일련의 다양한 상징을 담을 수 있다. 특정 브랜드의 비누를 생각해 보라. 그 자체로 그 비누는 다른 어떤 비누와 마찬가지로 깨끗하게 씻어 준다. 하지만 그 브랜드는 어떤 영리한 마케팅, 포장, 광고를 통해 자기네 비누를 환경, 개인의 자율권, 진보 정치에 대한 일련의 복합적인 메시지 속에 담근다. 그 브랜드 웹사이트에는 심지어 "우리는 동물 보호, 환경 보호 및 인권 존중에 매진합니다."라는 말도 있다. 이러한 의미로 인해 그 브랜드의 고객은 그 비누로 단지 자신의 얼굴을 씻는 것 이상의 일을 할 수 있는데, 이러한 제품을 사용함으로써 고객은 자신이 어떤 종류의 사람인지, 자신이 어떤 종류의 정치적 견해를 수용하는지에 대해 자신의 생각을 표현할 수 있는 것이다.

→ 흔한 일상 제품이 영리한 마케팅, 포장, 광고를 통해 상징적인 의미를 가질 수 있으며, 그 제품을 사용함으로써 소비자는 자신의 개인적, 정치적 정체성을 표현할 수 있다.

Solution Guide

비누와 같은 흔한 일상 제품이 영리한 마케팅, 포장, 광고 등을 통해 다양한 상징을 담을 수 있으며, 소비자들은 이러한 제품을 사용함으로써 자신의 개인적, 정치적 정체성을 표현할 수 있다는 내용의 글이므로, 빈칸 (A), (B)에 들어갈 말로 가장 적절한 것은 ① '상징적인 – 표현하다'이다.

② 영적인 – 숨기다
③ 혁신적인 – 탐구하다
④ 문화적인 – 바꾸다
⑤ 사회적인 – 거부하다

Structure in Focus

- [While **it** may be tempting {to answer "not much," or even "none}]," in fact, even soap can embody a rich set of symbols.
  [ ]는 양보를 나타내는 부사절이다. 그 안의 it은 형식상의 주어이고, { }는 내용상의 주어이다.
- ~: By using these products, they can make a statement about [what kind of person they are] and [what kind of politics they embrace].
  두 개의 [ ]는 and로 연결되어 about의 목적어 역할을 하는 명사절이다.

02

정답 ①

소재 인간에게 유일한 가리키기

해석 비교 심리학에 따르면 (완전한 형태의) 가리키기는 우리 종에 유일하다. 가리키기를 이해할 수 있는 것처럼 보이는 비인간 종은 거의 없으며(특히 집에서 기르는 개는 가리키는 곳으로 갈 수 있지만, 대형 유인원 중 우리와 가장 가까운 동류는 할 수 없다), 인간 이외의 다른 어떠한 종의 구성원 간에 가리키기가 자발적으로 발생한다는 증거는 거의 없다. 가리키는 제스처가 전제로 하는 협동적이고 친사회적인 종류의 동기를 지원하는 데 필요한 사회 인지적 토대가 인간에게만 있음이 분명한 것 같다. 이는 인간 언어의 출발점을 찾을 수 있는 새로운 기회를 제시한다. 인지과학에서 언어에 관한 연구는 오랫동안 그것(언어)의 논리적 구조에 초점을 맞춰 왔지만, 가리키기에 관한 정보는 대안을 제시하는데, 그것은 언어의 본질이 지향점 공유를 통한 우리의 마음 교감 능력에서 찾아진다는 것이다. 그 중심에는 언어를 조금이라도 배울 수 있기 전에 익혀야 하는 행위인, 놀랄 정도로 단순한 가리키기라는 행위가 있다.

→ 협동적이고 친사회적인 동기를 나타내는 가리키기는 인간에게 유일하며, 언어의 특성상 지향점 공유를 요하므로 가리키기를 숙달하는 것은 언어 학습에 선행해야 한다.

Solution Guide

가리키기는 우리 종에 유일한데 가리키기에 관한 정보는 언어의 본질을 지향점 공유를 통한 마음의 교감 능력에서 찾을 수 있다는 대안을 제시하며, 언어를 조금이라도 배울 수 있기 전에 가리키기를 익혀야 한다는 것이 글의 중심 내용이다. 따라서 빈칸 (A), (B)에 들어갈 말로 가장 적절한 것은 ① '유일한 – 선행하다'이다.

② 유일한 – 따르다
③ 적합한 – 따르다
④ 적합한 – 야기하다
⑤ 유익한 – 선행하다

Structure in Focus

- Apparently only humans have the social-cognitive infrastructure [needed to support the kind of cooperative and prosocial motivations {that pointing gestures presuppose}].
  [ ]는 the social-cognitive infrastructure를 수식하는 분사구이고, 그 안의 { }는 the kind of cooperative and

prosocial motivations를 수식하는 관계절이다.

- While [research on language in cognitive science] has long focused on its logical structure, the news about pointing suggests an alternative: [that the essence of language is found in our capacity for the communion of minds through shared intentionality].
첫 번째 [ ]는 While이 이끄는 부사절의 주어이다. 두 번째 [ ]는 an alternative와 동격 관계이다.

03

정답 ②

소재 협력 과업에 대한 어린 침팬지와 인간의 차이

해석 우리는 관계를 시작할 준비가 된 채로 세상에 태어나고, 신체에 대한 통제력을 얻게 되면서 다른 사람과의 협력이 수반되는 게임과 과제에 참여하기를 열망한다. 이런 점에서, 우리는 어린 침팬지와 매우 다르다. 실험에 따르면, 침팬지는 협력 과제를 완벽하게 잘 이해할 수 있지만, 그로 인해 과일 한 조각이나 어떤 다른 보상을 어떻게 얻게 될 것인지 알 수 있을 경우에만 참여하려 애쓰는 것으로 나타났다. 이와 대조적으로, 인간은 단지 일하는 즐거움을 위해 함께 일하는 경우가 많다. 실험에 따르면 다른 사람과 함께 일하는 것이 아이들의 행동에 영향을 미치는 것으로 나타났다. 그 후에 그들은 마치 다른 사람들과 함께 일함으로써 기분이 더 좋아진 것처럼, 실험자가 그들에게 준 간식을 더 관대하게 나눠 준다. 아이들의 나눔에 대한 더 큰 의지는 단순히 함께 일하는 것에 대해 사람에게 대가를 지불해야 한다는 것을 학습한 결과일 것 같지는 않지만, 우리가 모든 것에 대해 느끼는 방식은 뇌의 발달에 영향을 준 경험에 의해 크게 영향을 받는다. 어린 시절 타인을 관찰한 경험은 우리가 행동하는 방법을 배우는 데 도움이 될 뿐만 아니라, 우리가 어떻게 '느껴야' 하는지를 이해하는 데도 도움이 된다.

→ 어린 침팬지는 자신의 이익을 위해서만 협력하지만, 인간은 다른 사람과 함께 일하는 것에서 즐거움을 얻고, 그런 경험을 통해 그들은 더 기분 좋게 느끼고 더 자비롭게 된다.

Solution Guide

어린 침팬지는 보상을 얻을 수 있는 경우에만 협력 과제에 참여하는 반면에, 인간은 단지 즐거움을 위해 함께 일하는 경우가 많으며, 실험을 통해 인간이 다른 사람과 함께 일하게 되면 더 기분 좋게 느끼고 더 관대해진다는 내용의 글이다. 따라서 빈칸 (A), (B)에 들어갈 말로 가장 적절한 것은 ② '이익 – 자비로운'이다.

① 이익 – 생산적인
③ 학습 – 안전한
④ 학습 – 희망에 찬
⑤ 상호 작용 – 정의로운

Structure in Focus

- Experiments have shown [chimps can understand collaborative tasks perfectly well, but they only bother to take part if they can see {how it will result in 〈**their** getting a piece of fruit or some other reward〉}].
[ ]는 shown의 목적어 역할을 하는 명사절이고, 그 안의 { }는 see의 목적어 역할을 하는 명사절이다. 〈 〉는 result in의 목적어 역할을 하는 동명사구인데, their가 이 동명사구 안에서 의미상의 주어이다.
- It seems unlikely that children's greater willingness to share is simply the result of learning [that they should pay people for working with them], but the way [we feel about everything] is strongly influenced by the experiences [that shaped the development of our brain].
첫 번째 [ ]는 learning의 목적어 역할을 하는 명사절이고, 두 번째 [ ]는 the way를 수식하는 관계절이며, 세 번째 [ ]는 the experiences를 수식하는 관계절이다.

04

정답 ④

소재 합리적 행위 이론

해석 합리적 행위 이론은 의도적인 행동에 참여하겠다는 누군가의 결정은 여러 가지 요인에 따라 달라지며, 그중 일부는 상황적이고 일부는 개인적 성향이나 특성에 의해 조정된다고 주장한다. 이 이론의 핵심은 사람들이 특정 행동을 할 때, 그렇게 하려는 의도를 형성했고, 자신의 의도를 실현하기로 한 결정에 대한 이유가 있기 때문이라는 생각이다. 이러한 이유로, 우리의 행동 대부분은 '합리적 행위'로 특징지어질 수 있다. Fishbein과 Ajzen은 행동의 의도는 행위에 대한 태도와 규범적 요소라는 두 가지 요인에 의해 통제된다고 했다. 행위에 대한 태도는 사람들이 어떤 행위를 했을 때의 결과에 대해 가지는 믿음에 의해 영향을 받는다. 규범적 요소는 소중한 타인(즉, 우리 삶에서 중요한 사람들)이 우리가 무엇을 하기를 기대하는지에 대한 우리의 믿음에 의해 통제된다. 어떤 행동의 경우 우리는 행위에 대한 우리의 태도에 더 많이 의존하는 반면, 다른 행동의 경우 우리는 어떻게 행동해야 할지에 대한 지침을 얻기 위해 규범적 요소에 더 많이 의존할 수도 있다.

→ 합리적 행위 이론에 따르면 우리의 행동은 미리 형성된 행동 의도를 실현하려는 합리적인 결정에서 비롯되는데, 미리 형성된 행동 의도는 행동의 결과에 대한 믿음과 소중한 타인의 기대에 의해 영향을 받는다.

Solution Guide
합리적 행위 이론에 따르면 행동은 의도가 형성되고 그러한 의도를 실현하려는 결정에 영향을 받는데, 의도는 행동의 결과에 대한 믿음과 소중한 사람의 기대에 의존한다는 내용의 글이므로, 빈칸 (A), (B)에 들어갈 말로 가장 적절한 것은 ④ '실현하다 – 결과'이다.

① 평가하다 – 목적
② 수정하다 – 목적
③ 수정하다 – 결과
⑤ 실현하다 – 상황

Structure in Focus
- The theory of reasoned action maintains [that {a person's decision to engage in a purposeful activity} depends on several factors, {of which some are situational and some are mediated by personal dispositions or characteristics}].
  [ ]는 maintains의 목적어 역할을 하는 명사절이다. 그 안의 첫 번째 { }는 that절의 주어 역할을 하는 명사구이고, 두 번째 { }는 several factors를 부가적으로 설명하는 관계절이다.
- At the core of the theory is the idea [that {when people engage in a given behavior} it is because they {formed an intention to do so} and {have reasons for their decision to actualize their intentions}].
  전치사구로 문장이 시작되어 주어인 the idea that ~이 술어동사인 is 다음에 쓰였다. [ ]는 the idea와 동격 관계이고, 그 안의 첫 번째 { }는 시간을 나타내는 부사절이며, 두 번째와 세 번째 { }는 and로 연결되어 because로 유도되는 절의 술어 역할을 한다.

18 장문 독해 (1)

Gateway 01 ② 02 ⑤
Exercises 01 ④ 02 ⑤ 03 ③ 04 ④ 05 ②
06 ③ 07 ① 08 ②

PART I 유형편

Gateway

본문 104쪽

정답 01 ② 02 ⑤

소재 과학자의 미디어 접촉

해석 이야기를 과대광고하는 데 기여하는 것을 피하는 한 가지 방법은 아무 말도 하지 않는 것일 것이다. 그러나 그것은 대중과 정책 입안자에게 정보를 전하고/전하거나 제안을 제공해야 한다는 강한 책임감을 느끼는 과학자들에게는 현실적인 선택이 아니다. 미디어 구성원들과의 대화는 메시지를 알려지게 하고 아마 호의적인 인정을 받는 데는 이점이 있지만, 오해가 발생하고 반복적인 해명이 필요하며 끝없는 논란에 얽힐 위험이 있다. 따라서 미디어와 대화를 해야 하는지에 관한 결정은 아주 개별화되는 경향이 있다. 수십 년 전에 지구 과학자들이 미디어의 흥미를 끄는 결과를 얻는 것은 흔치 않은 일이었고, 그 결과 미디어와의 접촉이 기대되거나 권장되는 경우는 거의 없었다. 1970년대에는, 미디어와 자주 대화했던 소수의 과학자는 그렇게 한 것에 대해 흔히 동료 과학자들의 비난을 받았다. 이제 상황은 꽤 다른데, 왜냐하면 많은 과학자가 지구 온난화와 관련 문제의 중요성 때문에 공개적으로 말해야 한다는 책임감을 느끼고 있고 많은 기자도 이런 감정을 공유하고 있기 때문이다. 게다가, 많은 과학자는 자신들이 미디어의 주목과 그에 따른 대중의 인정을 즐긴다고 생각하고 있다. 그와 동시에, 다른 과학자들은 기자들과의 대화를 계속 거부하고, 그렇게 함으로써 자신의 과학을 위해 더 많은 시간을 남겨두고, 잘못 인용되는 위험과 미디어 보도와 연관된 다른 불쾌한 상황을 감수한다(→ 피한다).

Structure in Focus
- ~, but it runs the risk of [misinterpretations], [the need for repeated clarifications], and [entanglement in never-ending controversy].
  세 개의 [ ]는 and로 연결되어 전치사 of의 목적어 역할을 한다.
- The situation now is quite different, [as {many scientists feel a responsibility to speak out because of the importance of global warming and related issues}, and {many reporters share these feelings}].

[ ]는 이유를 나타내는 부사절이다. 그 안의 두 개의 { }는 and로 연결되어 있다.

Exercises

본문 106~109쪽

01~02

정답 01 ④ 02 ⑤

소재 세상에 대한 우리의 인식

해석 우리는 대체로 우리가 세상을 바로 있는 그대로 본다는 믿음인 '소박실재론'에 빠지는 경향이 있기 때문에 우리의 상식을 신뢰한다. 우리는 '보는 것이 믿는 것이다'라고 가정하고 세상과 우리 자신에 대한 직관적인 인식을 신뢰한다. 일상생활에서 소박실재론은 자주 우리에게 도움이 된다. 만약 여러분이 편도 1차선 도로를 운전하고 있는데 트랙터 트레일러 한 대가 시속 120킬로미터로 여러분을 향해 통제할 수 없이 다가오고 있는 것을 본다면, 피하는 것이 현명한 생각이다. 대부분의 경우 우리는 우리의 지각을 신뢰'해야 한다'. 하지만 겉모습은 때때로 판단을 그르치게 할 수 있다. 지구는 평평해 보인다. 태양은 지구 주위를 도는 것처럼 보인다. 하지만 두 경우 모두 우리의 직관이 틀렸다. 때로는 명백해 보이는 것이 우리 자신과 타인의 평가에 관한 한 우리를 잘못 인도할 수 있다. 과학적 연구는 그렇지 않다는 것을 보여 주는데도, 우리의 상식은 우리의 기억이 우리가 본 거의 모든 것을 정확하게 포착한다고 우리에게 말한다. 우리의 상식은 또한 우리의 정치적 견해를 공유하지 않는 사람들은 편향되어 있지만, 우리는 객관적이라고 확신시킨다. 그러나 심리학 연구는 우리가 모두 편향된 방식으로 정치적 문제를 평가하기 쉽다는 것을 보여 준다. 따라서 겉모습을 믿는 경향으로 인해 우리는 인간 본성에 대해 신뢰할 수 있는(→ 잘못된) 결론을 내리게 될 수 있다. 많은 경우, 그 반대가 아니라 '믿는 것이 보는 것이다.' 즉 우리의 믿음이 세상에 대한 우리의 인식을 형성한다.

Culture Note

naive realism(소박실재론) 시간적 · 공간적인 규정은 물론 감각적 성질까지도 객관적으로 존재하는 사물의 구성 요소로 보는 학설로서, 사물은 우리가 지각하는 그대로 존재한다고 보며 그 사물은 우리가 지각하든지 않든지 간에 독립적으로 존재한다고 믿는 이론이다.

Solution Guide

01 우리는 소박실재론에 따라 세상에 대한 우리의 직관적인 인식을 신뢰하지만, 때로는 겉모습이 판단을 그르치게 할 수 있어서 우리의 직관이 틀릴 수 있고, 명백해 보이는 것이 우리를 실수하게 만들 수도 있다는 내용의 글이므로, 글의 제목으로 가장 적절한 것은 ④ '소박실재론을 넘어서: 현실에 대한 우리의 인식은 신뢰할 수 있는가?'이다.

① 과학은 지구가 둥글다는 것을 어떻게 증명했는가?
② 상식과 과학적 해석의 비교
③ 보는 것이 믿는 것이다: 더 나은 결정을 내리기 위한 직관의 사용
⑤ 위험 부담에 관한 한, 여러분의 본능을 믿는 것은 위험하다

02 우리는 자신을 객관적이라고 장담하지만, 심리학 연구에 따르면 우리는 모두 편향된 방식으로 정치적 문제를 평가하기 쉽다고 했으므로, 겉모습을 믿는 우리의 경향은 잘못된 결론을 내릴 수 있다는 내용이 되어야 한다. 따라서 (e)의 reliable을 erroneous와 같은 낱말로 바꾸어야 한다.

Structure in Focus

- [If you {are driving down a one-lane road} and {see a tractor-trailer moving uncontrollably towards you at 120 kilometres per hour}], **it** is a wise idea [to get out of the way].
  첫 번째 [ ]는 조건을 나타내는 부사절이고, 그 안에서 두 개의 { }가 and로 연결되어 술어 역할을 한다. it은 형식상의 주어이고, 두 번째 [ ]는 내용상의 주어이다.
- Our common sense also assures us [that people {who do not share our political views} are biased], but [that we are objective].
  두 개의 [ ]가 but으로 연결되어 assures의 직접목적어 역할을 한다. { }는 people을 수식하는 관계절이다.

03~04

정답 03 ③ 04 ④

소재 감사가 갖는 긍정적 감정과 부정적 감정

해석 어떤 사람들은 감사하는 마음은 좋은 생각을 하고 좋은 일을 기대하는 것과만 관련이 있어서, 삶에서 부정적인 것, 고통, 괴로움은 무시한다고 주장한다. 그런데, 그들은 틀렸다. 감사란 혜택을 받고 그 혜택에 대해 자신 외에 다른 사람에게 공로를 돌리는 것에 대한 특정한 사고방식이라는 우리의 정의를 생각해 보라. 사실, 감사는 다른 사람에 대한 의존성을 인정해야 하고 그것이 항상 긍정적인 것은 아니기 때문에 매우 어려울 수 있다. 여러분은 다른 사람의 지원과 관대함을 잘 받아들여야 한다는 의미에서 자신을 낮춰야 한다. 그것은 매우 어려울 수 있는데, 사람들 대부분이 받는 것보다는 주는 것을 더 잘한다.

게다가, 감사의 감정은 가끔 부채감과 의무감이라는 관련 감정을 불러일으킬 수 있는데, 그것은 전혀 긍정적인 생각으로 들리지 않는다. '여러분이 나에게 준 것에 대해 감사한다면, 나는 그것을 신경 써야 하고, 심지어 미래에 적절한 시점에 보답해야 할 수도 있다.' 그러한 종류의 부채나 의무는 매우 부정적으로 인식될 수 있으며, Jill Suttie가 자신의 에세이 '빚을 진 느낌을 받지 않고 감사하다고 말하는 법'에서 살펴보듯이 사람들에게 실질적 편안함(→ 불편함)을 야기할 수 있다.
데이터는 이것을 실증한다. 감사할 때, 사람들이 반드시 부정적인 감정이 없는 것은 아니며, 불안, 긴장, 혹은 불행을 반드시 덜 느낀다는 것도 발견되지 않는다. 감사를 실천하면 부정적인 감정이 줄어들기보다는 긍정적인 감정이 더 커진다. 만일 감사가 긍정적인 생각이거나 부인의 한 형태에 불과하다면, 예를 들어 감사 일기를 쓰고 있을 때는 부정적인 생각이나 감정을 전혀 경험하지 못할 것이다. 그러나 실제로 사람들은 경험한다.

Solution Guide

03 감사는 매우 어려울 수 있어 수혜자가 되면 부채감과 의무감이라는 부정적인 감정도 경험해야 해서 감사하는 것이 완전히 긍정적인 감정만으로 이어지는 것은 아니라는 내용이므로, 글의 제목으로 가장 적절한 것은 ③ '감사: 긍정적인 사고의 절대적인 형태가 결코 아니다'이다.
① 진정한 감사: 부채와는 다른 어떤 것
② 다른 사람의 감사는 정말 여러분을 만족시키는가?
④ 더 많이 감사할수록, 더 많은 혜택을 얻는다
⑤ 여러분에게 의미 있는 사람들을 기쁘게 하기 위해 감사를 실천하라

04 받은 것에 대해 감사한다면 그것을 신경 써야 하고, 심지어 보답해야 할 수도 있다고 느끼기 마련이라는 맥락이므로, 이러한 부채감이나 의무감은 사람들에게 실질적 불편함을 야기할 수 있을 것이다. 따라서 (d)의 comfort를 discomfort와 같은 낱말로 바꾸어야 한다.

Structure in Focus

- Consider our definition of gratitude, as a specific way of thinking about [receiving a benefit] and [giving credit to others besides yourself for that benefit].
  두 개의 [ ]는 and로 연결되어 전치사 about의 목적어 역할을 하는 동명사구이다.
- In fact, gratitude can be very difficult, because [it requires {that you recognize your dependence on others}], and [that's not always positive].
  두 개의 [ ]는 and로 연결되어 because로 유도되는 절을 이룬다. 첫 번째 [ ] 안의 { }는 requires의 목적어 역할을 하는 명사절이다.

05~06

정답 05 ② 06 ③

소재 문화와 학습의 산물인 행동 규범

해석 모든 사회 체계에서, 사람들의 행동은 사회적 규칙의 영향을 받으며 그들이 놀라울 정도로 적응력이 뛰어나다는 것은 사실이다. 개코원숭이를 대상으로 하는 한 가지 자연 실험은 시사하는 바가 크다. 2004년의 한 연구는 덩치가 크고 공격적인 수컷들이 지배하는 개코원숭이 무리가 지배적인 그 수컷들이 모두 질병에 걸려 죽은 후 어떻게 변했는지 조사했다. 더 작고 더 온순한 수컷들만 남게 되자, 그 무리의 문화는 극적인 변화를 겪었는데, 만연한 괴롭힘과 싸움이 특징이었던 사회 구조에서 훨씬 더 평화롭게 서로 털 손질을 해 주는 사회 구조로 바뀌었다. 물론 갈등은 여전히 있었지만, 그것은 평화적인 방법으로 해결되는 경향이 있었고, 실제로 싸움이 일어나더라도 큰 것이 작은 것을 괴롭히는 것이 아니라 오히려 동등하게 맞먹는 개코원숭이들 사이에서 더 일어났다. 놀랍게도 그 무리의 문화는 심지어 원래의 수컷들이 모두 죽고 외부에서 들어온 다른 수컷들로 대체된 후에도 지속되었다. 새로운 수컷들은 그 집단 규범에 동화되었고, 덜 관대하게(→ 공격적으로) 행동하는 법을 배웠다.
분명 인간은 개코원숭이가 아니다. 그러나 이 점은 다양한 인간 사회가 대단히 다른 행동 규범을 가질 수 있는 이유와 근본적으로 유사할 가능성이 매우 높아 보인다. 자신들의 조상을 숭배하고 음식을 공동으로 나누던 전근대 부족, 왕의 신성한 권리를 인정하고 봉건 영주를 위해 무급 노동을 수행하던 중세 농민, 그리고 민주주의와 기업 고용 계약을 믿는 오늘날의 사람들을 생각해 보라. 인간 사회는 개코원숭이 사회보다 훨씬 더 많은 복잡성과 선택을 가지지만, 중요한 점은 행동 규범은 대부분 문화와 학습의 산물이지 그 반대가 아니라는 것이다.

Solution Guide

05 무리의 문화에 따라 행동 방식이 바뀐 개코원숭이 실험을 사례로 들어, 사람의 행동은 적응력이 뛰어나기에 사회 체계에 영향을 받는다는 내용의 글이다. 역사적으로 다양한 인간 사회가 다른 행동 규범을 가졌던 이유도 바로 행동 규범이 문화와 학습의 산물이기 때문이라고 말하고 있다. 따라서 글의 제목으로 가장 적절한 것은 ② '인간 행동의 가변성: 사회적으로 구성된'이다.
① 의사 결정에서 사회적 압력의 힘
③ 다양한 문화를 배워서 여러분의 시야를 넓혀라!
④ 가장 다정한 자의 생존: 모든 사회의 보편적 특징
⑤ 개코원숭이 실험의 맹점: 동물의 권리 보호

06 덩치가 크고 공격적인 수컷들이 질병으로 죽은 후, 개코원숭이 무리는 서로 털 손질을 해 주는 평화로운 사회 구조로 바뀌었으며, 외부에서 들어온 새로운 수컷들도 이렇게 바뀐 집단 규범에 동화되었다고 했으므로, (c)의 generously를 aggressively와

같은 낱말로 바꾸어야 한다.

Structure in Focus

- A study in 2004 examined [how a troop of baboons {dominated by large and aggressive males} changed after all those dominant males caught a disease and died].
  [ ]는 examined의 목적어 역할을 하는 명사절이다. 그 안의 { }는 a troop of baboons를 수식하는 분사구이다.
- With only smaller, gentler males remaining, the culture of that troop underwent a dramatic shift, [moving from a social structure {characterized by widespread bullying and fighting} to **one** with much more peaceful grooming].
  [ ]는 주절이 기술하는 상황에 부수하는 상황을 나타내는 분사구문이다. 그 안의 { }는 a social structure를 수식하는 분사구이고, one은 a social structure를 대신한다.
- But **it** seems highly possible [that this is basically similar to {why different human societies can have much different behavioral norms}] ~.
  it은 형식상의 주어이고, [ ]는 내용상의 주어이다. 그 안의 { }는 전치사 to의 목적어 역할을 하는 명사절이다.

07~08

정답 07 ① 08 ②

소재 소프트웨어 오작동의 원인

해석 놀랄 것도 없이, 안전하지 않게 설계되고 불안정하게 구현된 소프트웨어의 사용은 몇 가지 위험 요소를 야기한다. 유통된 소프트웨어가 사용자 측에 도달한 후, 시스템 및 응용 소프트웨어의 설치 및 관리가 부적절하게 수행되면 그런 소프트웨어의 성능과 올바른 작동에 악영향을 미칠 수도 있다. 이러한 시스템의 부적절한 문서화로 인해서뿐만 아니라 복잡성으로 인해, 사용자는 그런 시스템을 '올바르게' 사용하려는 자신의 노력이 미치는 영향을 거의 이해하지 못한다. 따라서 사용자는 어떤 기능이 어떤 영향을 미칠 수 있는지, 그리고 원치 않는 부작용을 피하기 위해 어떤 예방 조치를 취해야 하는지 방법론적으로 이해하려고 노력하기보다는 새로운 기능을 작동하는 방식을 배우는 데 '시행착오' 방식을 무시한다(→ 적용한다). 이러한 다소 '탐색적인' 시스템 사용 방식은, 예컨대 알지 못하는 첨부 파일을 적절한 주의 없이 클릭함으로써, 잠재적으로 해로운 영향이 있는 위험한 태도를 야기하는 경우가 꽤 많다.
소프트웨어 제조업체는 흔히 소프트웨어의 오작동이 주로 사용자의 부적절한 행동으로 인해 발생한다고 주장한다. 그러나 대부분은 아니라도 많은 경우, 인간-컴퓨터 인터페이스(예를 들어, 화면에 있는 기능 및 작업 표시나 마우스 및 키보드와 같은 입력 장치의 조작)가 부적절하게 설계되어 있으며 사용자는 도움말 기능의 지원을 제대로 받지 못한다(많은 경우, 도움말 기능이 있다 하더라도 너무 복잡하여 사용자를 더 오도한다). 사용자는 주로 자신의 업무를 수행하는 데 관심이 있지만, 자신의 업무 수행 능력이 저하된다고 생각하게 되면 예방 조치는 다 잊어버리고, 심지어 때로는 보안 조치까지 건너뛰는 경향이 꽤 자주 있다는 사실을 우리는 인정해야 한다.

Solution Guide

07 안전하지 않게 설계되고 불안정하게 구현된 소프트웨어를 사용할 경우 사용자가 잘못 사용하는 경우가 많으며, 소프트웨어 제조업체는 오작동의 원인을 주로 사용자에게 돌리지만, 그것이 부적절하게 설계된 경우가 많고, 사용자 또한 잘못 사용하는 경향이 있다는 내용의 글이다. 따라서 글의 제목으로 가장 적절한 것은 ① '소프트웨어 오작동의 진짜 원인은 무엇인가?'이다.
② 성공적이지 못한 소프트웨어 구현을 피하는 법
③ 사이버 보안: 제조업체의 디지털 딜레마
④ 새로운 소프트웨어 개발로 우리는 무엇을 기대할 수 있는가?
⑤ 사회적 책임은 소프트웨어 개발 과정에 영향을 준다

08 알지 못하는 첨부 파일을 적절한 주의 없이 클릭함으로써 위험을 초래할 수 있는 다소 '탐색적인' 사용 방식, 즉 위험한 태도를 야기하는 경우가 꽤 많다고 했으므로, '시행착오' 방식을 적용한다고 해야 할 것이다. 따라서 (b)의 disregard를 apply와 같은 낱말로 바꾸어야 한다.

Structure in Focus

- Software manufacturers often argue [that failure of software is mainly caused by improper actions of users].
  [ ]는 argue의 목적어 역할을 하는 명사절이다.
- While users are primarily interested in doing their work, one must admit [that they rather often tend to forget about any precaution and even sometimes bypass security measures **when thinking** that their work performance is reduced].
  [ ]는 admit의 목적어 역할을 하는 명사절이고, when thinking은 when they think로 풀어서 이해할 수 있다.

19 장문 독해 (2)

Gateway 01 ⑤ 02 ③ 03 ③
Exercises 01 ② 02 ③ 03 ④ 04 ④ 05 ③
06 ④ 07 ③ 08 ③ 09 ⑤ 10 ④
11 ⑤ 12 ④

Gateway

본문 110~111쪽

정답 01 ⑤ 02 ③ 03 ③

소재 인생의 어려움으로부터의 회복

해석 (A) Emma와 Clara는 끝없이 펼쳐진 바다에 시선을 고정한 채로 해변 도로에 나란히 서 있었다. 그들을 둘러싸고 있는 숨 막히는 풍경은 말로 표현할 수 없을 정도였다. 일출 직후에, 그들은 해변 도로를 따라 자전거를 탈 준비를 마쳤다. Emma는 Clara를 보며, "이것이 네 인생 최고의 라이딩이 될 것 같니?"라고 물었다. Clara가 고개를 끄덕일 때 그녀의 얼굴이 환한 미소로 밝아졌다. "물론이지! 나는 어서 저 아름다운 파도를 보며 자전거를 타고 싶어!"

(D) Emma와 Clara는 자전거에 올라타서 해변 도로가 끝나는 하얀 절벽을 향해 페달을 밟기 시작했다. 속도를 내고 넓고 푸른 바다를 즐기면서, Emma는 자신의 흥분을 감추지 못하고 "Clara, 경치가 정말 멋져!"라고 외쳤다. 하지만, Clara의 침묵은 그녀가 생각에 빠져 있다는 것을 말하는 것 같았다. Emma는 그녀의 침묵의 의미를 알고 있었다. 자기 옆에서 자전거를 타고 있는 Clara를 지켜보며, Emma는 지금은 그녀가 극복한 것처럼 보이는, Clara의 과거의 비극적 사건에 대해 생각했다.

(C) Clara는 재능 있는 수영 선수였지만, 어깨 부상으로 인해 올림픽 수영 메달리스트가 되겠다는 자신의 꿈을 포기해야만 했다. 하지만 그녀는 그 고난에 적극적인 방식으로 대응했다. 수년간의 고된 훈련 끝에, 그녀는 놀라운 회복을 이뤄 냈고 자전거 라이딩에 대한 새로운 열정을 발견했다. Emma는 고통스러운 과거가 그녀를 어떻게 더 성숙하게 만들어 주었고, 그리고 그것이 결국에는 그녀를 어떻게 더 강하게 만들어 주었는지를 보았다. 한 시간 후에, Emma보다 앞서 가던 Clara가 뒤를 돌아보며 "저 하얀 절벽을 봐!"라고 외쳤다.

(B) 그들의 목적지에 도착했을 때, Emma와 Clara는 자전거를 멈췄다. Emma는 Clara에게 다가가 "자전거 라이딩은 수영과는 다르지, 그렇지 않니?"라고 물었다. Clara는 미소를 지으며 "사실은, 상당히 비슷해. 수영과 꼭 마찬가지로 라이딩은 나에게 정말 살아 있다는 느낌이 들게 해 줘."라고 대답했다. "그것은 나에게 인생의 힘든 도전에 직면하면서 산다는 것이 어떤 의미인지 보여 줘."라고 그녀는 덧붙였다. Emma는 동의하면서 고개를 끄덕이고, "너의 첫 번째 해변 자전거 라이딩은 정말 대성공이었어. 내년 여름에 다시 오는 건 어때?"라고 제안했다. Clara는 "너와 함께라면, 물론이지!"라고 기뻐하면서 대답했다.

Structure in Focus

- Emma saw [how the painful past made her maturer] and [how it made her stronger in the end].
  명사절인 두 개의 [ ]는 saw의 목적어 역할을 한다.
- [Speeding up] and [enjoying the wide blue sea], Emma couldn't hide her excitement and exclaimed, "Clara, the view is amazing!"
  분사구문인 두 개의 [ ]는 and로 연결되어 주어인 Emma의 상태를 부가적으로 설명한다.

Exercises

본문 112~119쪽

01~03

정답 01 ② 02 ③ 03 ④

소재 인기 팟캐스트를 탄생시킨 Monica Padman

해석 (A) Monica Padman은 2009년 연극과 홍보학 두 분야의 학위를 받으며 대학을 졸업했다. 그녀는 배우이자 코미디언이 되겠다는 자신의 꿈을 좇기 위해 할리우드로 이사했다. 대부분의 노력하는 배우들처럼 그녀는 오디션을 하고 작은 배역을 맡는 중간중간에 다양한 아르바이트를 했다. Padman은 Showtime의 *House of Lies*에서 작은 배역을 얻었고, 거기서 배우 Kristen Bell의 배역상의 보조자 역을 맡았다. 그들은 친해졌고, Padman이 Bell에게 어린 딸이 있다는 것을 알게 되었을 때 그녀는 자신이 아이를 봐 주는 일도 좀 한다고 말했다.

(C) Bell과 그녀의 남편인 배우 Dax Shepard는 그녀의 제안을 수락했다. Bell이 다수의 역할을 동시에 수행하고 프로젝트를 제작하면서 겪는 어려움을 보았을 때, 그녀는 그녀에게 일정 관리를 도와주겠다고 제안했다. 배우 지망생이 할리우드 특급 배우에게 자신이 영화 배역을 따내도록 도와 달라고 요청하고 싶은 유혹을 느낄 수도 있었겠지만, Padman은 아이러니하게도 Bell의 영화 밖 보조자로서 자신을 필요로 하는 곳에서 일했다. Bell과 Shepard가 그녀에게 자신들을 위해 풀타임으로 일해 달라고 요청했을 때, Padman이 주저한 것은 이해할 만했다. 그녀가 오디션 볼 시간을 어떻게 낼 수 있겠는가?

(B) 그 일은 돌아가는 길일 수 있었다. 하지만 Padman은 그것을 받아들이기로 결정했다. 시간이 지나면서, 그녀는 Bell의 친구이자 창의적인 파트너가 되었다. 그녀는 도움이 필요한 곳이면

어디서든 열정적으로 일했다. Bell은 Padman에 대해 "그녀가 하는 모든 일은 110퍼센트에 달합니다."라고 말했다. 얼마 지나지 않아, Padman은 매우 없어서는 안 될 존재가 되어 Bell은 "그녀가 없었으면 이 모든 일을 내가 어떻게 했을까?"라고 큰 소리로 자문했다. 그녀의 가족을 위해 일하는 동안 Padman은 테라스에 앉아 Bell의 남편과 토론하며 많은 시간을 보냈다.

(D) 그들의 토론은 치열한 만큼 재미도 있었기 때문에 Bell이 그들의 재치 있는 농담을 팟캐스트로 발전시키자고 제안했을 때 Padman도 그것에 흔쾌히 동의했다. 그렇게 *Armchair Expert*가 탄생했다. 그 팟캐스트는 2018년 가장 많이 다운로드된 신규 팟캐스트가 되었으며 계속해서 인기가 높아져 왔다. Padman은 자신의 열정으로 가는 직통 경로를 추구할 수도 있었을 것이다. 대신에 그녀는 자신이 가장 유용하게 쓰일 수 있는 곳에서 진심으로 일했다. Bell의 집에서 열정적으로 일하면서 그녀는 더 큰 기회와 어쩌면 자신의 진정한 목적을 찾았다.

Solution Guide

01 Monica Padman이 대학을 졸업하고 할리우드에서 배우 Kristen Bell과 친해져 Bell의 아이를 봐 주겠다고 제안하는 내용의 (A)에 이어, Bell과 그녀의 남편인 배우 Dax Shepard가 그녀의 제안을 수락하는 (C)가 이어진다. 그다음에는 Bell과 Shepard가 Padman에게 자신들을 위해 풀타임으로 일해 달라는 요청을 하자 그 일이 자신의 꿈을 이루는 데 있어 돌아가는 길일 수 있으나 수락하는 (B)가 오고, 그녀가 Bell의 남편과 토론을 즐겨 했다는 내용에 이어, 그 내용을 팟캐스트로 발전시키자는 Bell의 제안을 받아들여 *Armchair Expert*라는 팟캐스트가 탄생했다는 내용의 (D)로 이어지는 것이 가장 적절한 글의 순서이다.

02 (a), (b), (d), (e)는 모두 Padman을 가리키지만, (c)는 Bell을 가리킨다.

03 할리우드 특급 배우인 Bell에게 자신이 영화 배역을 따내도록 도와 달라고 요청하고 싶은 유혹을 느낄 수도 있었겠지만, 자신이 필요한 곳에서 일했다고 했으므로, Padman에 관한 내용으로 적절하지 않은 것은 ④이다.

Structure in Focus

- Though **it** might have been tempting [**for the aspiring actress** to ask the Hollywood A-lister to help her get on-screen roles], Padman worked where she was needed — ironically, as Bell's off-screen assistant.
  it은 형식상의 주어이고, to부정사구인 [ ]가 내용상의 주어이며, for the aspiring actress는 to부정사의 의미상의 주어를 나타낸다.
- The podcast [became 2018's most downloaded new podcast] and [has continued to grow in popularity].
  두 개의 [ ]는 and로 연결되어 문장의 술어 역할을 한다.

04~06

정답 04 ④ 05 ③ 06 ④

소재 바이올린 연주를 통한 자원봉사

해석 (A) 어느 날 저녁 Vienna의 Prater 공원에서 늙고 허약한 한 병사가 바이올린을 연주하고 있었다. 그의 충실한 개가 그의 모자를 물고 있었는데, 행인들이 길을 가면서 그곳에 동전 몇 개를 떨어뜨렸다. 그러나 문제의 그날 저녁에는 그 노병의 모자에 작은 동전을 넣으려고 멈추는 사람이 아무도 없었다. 모두 곧장 지나갔고, 군중의 즐거움은 노병의 마음에 슬픔을 더했는데, 그 슬픔은 그의 활기 없는 얼굴에 그대로 드러났다.

(D) 하지만, 갑자기, 잘 차려입은 신사 한 명이 노병이 서 있는 곳으로 다가와, 몇 분 동안 그의 연주를 듣고는 연민 어린 눈으로 그를 바라보았다. 얼마 지나지 않아, 노병의 피곤한 손은 더 이상 활을 잡을 힘이 없었다. 팔다리에 힘이 풀려 그는 더 이상 움직일 수 없었다. 그는 돌 위에 앉아 머리를 손에 얹고 소리 없이 울기 시작했다. 그 순간 신사가 다가와 노병에게 금화 한 닢을 내밀며 "당신의 바이올린을 제게 잠시 빌려주십시오."라고 말했다.

(B) 그러고는 바이올린을 조심스럽게 조율하고 난 후 신사가 말했다. "당신은 돈을 가지세요, 제가 연주하겠습니다." 그는 '정말로' 연주했다! 모든 행인이 길을 멈추고 연주를 들었는데, 그 음악가의 기품 있는 분위기에 감명 받고 그의 놀라운 천재성에 매혹되었다. 시시각각 (행인이 만드는) 원은 점점 더 커졌다. 동전만 아니라, 은화, 심지어 금화까지도 노병의 모자에 던져졌다. 개가 으르렁거리기 시작했는데, 모자는 그가 물고 있기에는 너무 무거워지고 있었기 때문이었다. 청중의 제안에 따라 노병은 모자 속에 든 것을 자기 가방에 비웠고 그들은 그것을 다시 채웠다.

(C) 그곳에 있던 모든 사람이 모자를 벗고 함께 부른 국가를 연주한 후에, 그 바이올린 연주가는 악기를 노병의 무릎 위에 올려놓고는 감사의 말을 받으려고 기다리지도 않고 사라졌다. "누구야?"라는 질문이 사방에서 쏟아졌다. "유명한 바이올린 연주자 Armand Boucher입니다."라고 군중 속 누군가가 대답했다. "그는 자신의 예술을 이용해 자선 봉사를 한 것입니다. 우리도 그의 본을 따릅시다." 그리고 말한 사람은 자기 모자도 돌려 새로 기부금을 받아 수익금을 노병에게 주고 "Boucher 만세!"라고 외쳤다. 깊이 감동한 노병은 주변의 모든 사람에게 감사를 표했다.

Solution Guide

04 Vienna의 Prater 공원에서 늙고 허약한 한 병사가 바이올린을 연주하고 있었지만, 노병의 개가 물고 있는 모자에 작은 동전을 넣으려고 멈추는 사람이 아무도 없었다는 내용의 주어진 글

(A) 다음에는, 잘 차려입은 신사 한 명이 노병에게 와서 바이올린을 잠시 자신에게 빌려 달라고 말한 (D)가 이어져야 한다. 그다음에는 신사의 천재적인 연주에 모든 행인이 멈춰 연주를 듣고 노병의 모자에 돈을 던졌다는 내용의 (B)가 이어지고, 마지막으로 신사는 사실 유명한 바이올린 연주자 Armand Boucher로 자신의 예술을 이용해 자선 봉사를 하고 있었던 것이 밝혀지는 내용의 (C)가 그 뒤를 잇는 것이 글의 순서로 가장 적절하다.

05 (a), (b), (d), (e)는 모두 늙고 허약한 노병을 가리키지만, (c)는 유명한 바이올린 연주자 Armand Boucher를 가리킨다.

06 (C)에서 바이올린 연주자는 공원에 있던 모든 사람이 함께 부른 국가를 연주한 후에 악기를 노병의 무릎 위에 올려놓고는 감사의 말을 받으려고 기다리지도 않고 사라졌다고 했다. 따라서 글에 관한 내용으로 적절하지 않은 것은 ④이다.

Structure in Focus

- All the passers-by stopped to listen — [struck with the distinguished air of the musician] and [fascinated by his marvelous genius].
  두 개의 [ ]는 and로 연결되어 주어 All the passers-by를 부가적으로 설명하는 분사구문이다.
- After a national melody, [in which everyone present joined, with uncovered heads], the violinist [placed the instrument upon the poor soldier's knees], and, [without waiting to be thanked, disappeared].
  첫 번째 [ ]는 a national melody를 부가적으로 설명하는 관계절이다. 두 번째와 세 번째 [ ]는 and로 연결되어 문장의 술어 역할을 한다.

07~09

정답 07 ③ 08 ③ 09 ⑤

소재 가족이 된 Say Say

해석 (A) 내가 어렸을 때 어느 날, 아버지가 Say Say가 어떻게 우리와 함께하게 되었는지에 대한 이야기를 해 주었다. 아버지는 자신이 막 돌아온, Kler Lwee Htu 지역에서의 자신의 일에 대해 어머니와 이야기하고 계셨다. 그곳은 우리와 멀리 떨어져 있었고, 버마 군대가 우리 마을들을 공격하고 있는 최전선과 훨씬 더 가까웠다. 버마 정권은 Karen 족을 탄압하기 위해 고안된 'Four Cuts'라는 악명 높은 정책을 시행하고 있었다. 그것은 지독히도 단순했는데, Karen 족 저항 운동에 대한 모든 보급품, 정보, 신병, 식량을 차단하는 것이었다.

(C) 아버지는 Four Cuts 정책이 사람들에게 끔찍한 상처를 주고 있었다고 설명했다. 어려서 나는 그가 우리에게 말한 모든 것을 이해할 수는 없었다. 나는 우리 민족 사람들이 굶어 죽고 있는 것을 알고 있었지만, 무서웠고 그것에 대해 생각하고 싶지 않았다. 나는 아버지가 고통스러워하는 것을 알 수 있었지만, 그 사실에 대해 외면하려고 애썼다. 이 시기에 우리는 모두 어머니와 더 가까웠는데, 그녀가 옆에 있다는 단순한 이유 때문이었다. 그가 우리와 있을 때는 나는 아버지와 가까워졌지만, 그가 떠났을 때, 상처받고 멀어졌다.

(D) Four Cuts 정책은 가족들을 더욱더 절망적인 한계로 몰았다. 어느 날 저항 운동을 위해 일하던 한 남자가 아버지에게 다가왔다. 함께 일한 시간 동안 그들은 서로를 좋아하고 존경하게 되었다. 그는 아이가 일곱 명인데 자신은 적어도 한 명은 제대로 된 교육을 받기를 원한다고 아버지에게 말했다. 하지만 Four Cuts 정책은 그 지역의 모든 학교를 파괴했다. 그는 아버지에게 그가 자신의 나이가 더 많은 아들 중 한 명인 Say Say를 데리고 가서 우리 마을에서 그를 교육시켜 줄 수 있는지 물었다.

(B) 당시 어머니와 아버지에게는 자녀가 한 명, 나의 누나인 Bwa Bwa만 있었고, 아버지는 자신의 친구에게 깊은 연민을 느꼈다. 그는 Say Say를 자신의 자녀 중 하나로 받아들이기로 동의했고, Say Say는 내 부모님의 양자가 되었다. Say Say의 아버지는 긴 여행을 할 시간의 여유가 생기면, 일 년에 한 번씩 방문하려 애썼다. 그가 그럴 때마다 그는 아들이 학교에서 공부를 잘하는 모습을 보고 매우 행복했고 자랑스러워했다.

Solution Guide

07 Say Say가 가족이 된 이야기를 시작하며 버마 정권이 Karen 족을 탄압하기 위해 시행한 Four Cuts 정책을 설명한 (A) 다음에, Four Cuts 정책이 사람들에게 준 상처가 컸고, 아버지가 고통스러워하는 모습을 외면할 수밖에 없었던 상황을 언급한 (C)가 이어져야 한다. Four Cuts 정책으로 인해 아이들을 제대로 교육을 받게 할 수 없었던 아버지의 동료가 자신의 아들인 Say Say를 우리 마을로 데려가 달라고 부탁하는 내용의 (D)가 온 다음, 아버지가 Say Say를 양자로 받아들여 Say Say가 학교에서 공부하게 된 모습을 보고 그의 아버지가 행복해했다는 내용의 (B)가 그 뒤를 잇는 것이 글의 순서로 가장 적절하다.

08 (a), (b), (d), (e)는 모두 'I'의 아버지를 가리키지만, (c)는 아버지의 동료를 가리킨다.

09 Say Say를 'I'의 마을에서 교육받게 해 달라고 부탁했다고 했으므로, 글에 관한 내용으로 적절하지 않은 것은 ⑤이다.

Structure in Focus

- [Whenever he did], he was so happy and proud to see [how well his son was doing in his studies at school].
  첫 번째 [ ]는 시간을 나타내는 부사절이고, 두 번째 [ ]는 see의 목적어 역할을 하는 명사절이다.

10~12

정답 10 ④ 11 ⑤ 12 ④

소재 Raymond의 내재적 동기 부여와 강화 이론

해석 (A) 오래전 New Orleans에 Raymond라는 노신사가 있었는데, 그는 매일 현관에 앉아 있곤 했다. Raymond는 야외에서 자연 및 이웃과 교감하고 햇볕을 쬐며 보내는 시간을 즐겼다. 매일 같은 시간, 한 아이가 학교에서 집으로 돌아오는 길에 그가 있는 거리를 걸어가곤 했다. Raymond는 그 동네 아이와 이야기하는 것을 즐겼고, 그 아이 또한 그와 이야기하는 것을 좋아했다. 둘은 서로를 살폈다. 하지만 이 아이에게 나쁜 버릇이 생겼다. 매일 거리를 지나갈 때면 그는 막대기로 금속 쓰레기통을 두드리곤 했다.

(D) Raymond는 이 행동이 매우 짜증 나서 아이에게 그만두라고 부탁하려고 했지만, 그는 현관에 있는 그 노인의 말을 들으려 하지 않았다. Raymond는 내재적 동기 부여와 강화 이론의 개념을 적용하기로 결심했다. 다음에 아이가 거리를 따라 올 때 그는 아이가 내는 소리에 대해 그를 칭찬하고 그가 매일 그렇게 하겠다고 약속하면 그에게 하루에 1달러를 주겠다고 말했다. 아이는 (이를) 수락하여 그다음 주 동안 매일 쓰레기통을 두드렸고, Raymond는 그에게 1달러를 주었다.

(B) 그다음 주에 Raymond는 그 아이에게 돈이 부족하다며(실제로는 그렇지 않았지만) 자신은 쓰레기통을 두드리는 대가로 그에게 하루에 50센트만 줄 수 있다고 말했다. 아이는 이 새로운 합의가 마음에 들지 않았지만, 어쨌든 동의하고 쓰레기통을 두드린 후 매일 50센트를 받았다. 그다음 주에 Raymond는 그 아이에게 돈이 훨씬 더 빠듯해져서 자신은 그에게 하루에 25센트만 줄 수 있다고 말했다. 이번에도 그 아이는 이 새로운 합의가 마음에 들지 않았지만, 어쨌든 동의하고 쓰레기통을 두드리며 매일 25센트를 받았다.

(C) 그 아이에게 하루에 25센트를 지급한 지 일주일이 지난 후, Raymond는 그 아이에게 다가가 자신은 그에게 더 이상 돈을 줄 수 없지만, 여전히 그가 쓰레기통을 계속 두드리기를 원한다고 말했다. 이번에는 그 아이가 동의하지 않았다. 그는 돈을 받지 못하는 것에 화가 났고 더 이상 쓰레기통을 두드리기를 거부했다. Raymond는 매일 현관에 앉아 자연과 이웃을 즐기며 햇볕을 쬐는 것을 계속하고 있다.

Solution Guide

10 글의 주요 인물인 Raymond와 소년이 등장하고 소년이 쓰레기통을 두드리는 행동이 문제가 되었다는 내용의 주어진 글 (A) 다음에, 소년의 그 행동을 멈추기 위해 Raymond가 내재적 동기 부여와 강화 이론 개념을 적용하기로 결심하고는 우선 그의 행동에 대해 1달러를 주었다는 내용의 (D)가 이어져야 한다. 그다음에는 보상의 정도를 1달러에서 50센트로, 다시 50센트에서 25센트까지 줄였다는 내용의 (B)가 이어지고, 돈을 주지 않기로 했을 때 소년이 더 이상 쓰레기통을 두드리는 행동을 하지 않게 되었다는 내용의 (C)가 그 뒤를 잇는 것이 글의 순서로 가장 적절하다.

11 밑줄 친 (a), (b), (c), (d)는 모두 소년을 가리키지만, (e)는 Raymond를 가리킨다.

12 글 (C)에서, 소년은 돈을 받지 못하는 것에 화가 나 더 이상 쓰레기통을 두드리기를 거부했다고 했으므로, 글에 관한 내용으로 적절하지 않은 것은 ④이다.

Structure in Focus

- The next week Raymond told the kid [that he was short on money (even though that wasn't really true)] and [that he could only pay him fifty cents a day for banging on cans].
  두 개의 [ ]는 and로 연결되어 told의 직접목적어 역할을 한다.
- After a week of paying the kid twenty-five cents a day, Raymond [approached the kid] and [told him {〈he couldn't pay him anymore〉 but 〈he still wanted him to continue to bang cans〉}].
  두 개의 [ ]는 and로 연결되어 문장의 술어 역할을 한다. 두 번째 [ ] 안에서 { }는 told의 직접목적어 역할을 하고, 그 안에서 두 개의 〈 〉는 but으로 연결되어 있다.
- The next time the kid came down the street he [complimented him on the sound he made] and [said {he would pay him a dollar a day 〈if he promised to do it every day〉}].
  두 개의 [ ]는 and로 연결되어 주절의 술어 역할을 한다. 두 번째 [ ] 안에서 { }는 said의 목적어 역할을 하는 명사절이고, 〈 〉는 조건의 부사절이다.

20 인물, 일화, 기담

Gateway ④
Exercises 01 ③ 02 ① 03 ⑤

Gateway

본문 122쪽

정답 ④

소재 프랑스 영화감독 Jean Renoir

해석 프랑스 영화감독 Jean Renoir(1894~1979)는 프랑스 파리에서 태어났다. 그는 유명 화가 Pierre-Auguste Renoir의 아들이었다. 그와 그 밖의 Renoir 가족은 그의 아버지의 많은 그림의 모델이었다. 제1차 세계대전이 발발했을 때, Jean Renoir는 프랑스 군에 복무 중이었는데, 다리에 부상을 입었다. 1937년에 그는 자신의 더 잘 알려진 영화 중 하나인 *La Grande Illusion*을 만들었다. 그것은 엄청나게 성공적이었지만 독일에서는 상영이 허용되지 않았다. 제2차 세계대전 중, 1940년에 나치가 프랑스를 침공했을 때 그는 미국 할리우드로 가서 그곳에서 경력을 이어갔다. 그는 영화계에서 평생의 업적을 인정받아 1975년에 Academy Honorary Award(아카데미 명예상)를 포함하여 이력 전반에 걸쳐 수많은 명예상과 상을 받았다. 전체적으로 보아, 영화 제작자이자 예술가로서 Jean Renoir의 영향력은 지속되고 있다.

Solution Guide

제2차 세계대전 중이던 1940년에 미국 할리우드로 갔다고 했으므로, Jean Renoir에 관한 글의 내용과 일치하지 않는 것은 ④이다.

Structure in Focus

- At the outbreak of World War I, Jean Renoir [was serving in the French army] but [was wounded in the leg].
  두 개의 [ ]는 but으로 연결되어 문장의 술어 역할을 한다.
- During World War II, when the Nazis invaded France in 1940, he [went to Hollywood in the United States] and [continued his career there].
  두 개의 [ ]는 and로 연결되어 문장의 술어 역할을 한다.

Quick Review

본문 123쪽

1. idol / 그 젊은 가수는 마침내 무대 뒤에서 자신의 우상을 만나자 눈물을 터뜨렸다.
2. reputation / 치아 건강에 관한 한, 초콜릿은 평판이 나쁘다.
3. adaptation / 사랑받는 동화책을 뮤지컬로 각색한 그 작품은 모든 연령대의 관객에게 즐거움을 선사했다.
4. transform / 기술 발전은 전쟁 무기를 변화시킬 것이다.
5. vigor / 연사는 활기차게 연설했고 열정으로 청중을 사로잡았다.

Exercises

본문 124~125쪽

01

정답 ③

소재 프랑스의 극작가이자 영화 제작자 Marcel Pagnol

해석 Marcel Pagnol은 1895년 Aubagne에서 태어나 1974년에 사망했다. 자신이 *Souvenirs d'enfance*(유년 시절의 추억)에서 매우 생생하게 묘사한, 한 초등학교 교사의 아들이었던 이 남부 프랑스인은 영어 교사로 직장 생활을 시작했다. 그러나 그는 1920년대 자신이 쓴 희곡으로 빠르게 명성을 얻었는데, 1927년 *Topaze*와 1928년 *Marius*가 놀라운 성공을 거두면서 극작가로서 입지를 다졌다. Marcel Pagnol은 오랫동안 영화에 관심이 있었지만, 대화체 작품 작가로서 자신의 넘치는 활력을 사용하기 위해서는 발성 영화 기법이 발전할 때까지 기다려야만 했다. 그의 첫 영화 몇 편은 자신의 연극 작품을 각색한 작품으로, 예를 들면 극찬을 받은 3부작 *Marius, Fanny, César*가 있었다. 국내적으로나 국제적으로나 대중적으로 엄청난 성공이었다. 이를 계기로 Marcel Pagnol은 오로지 영화에만 전념하기로 결심했다. 자신의 두 번째 영화를 위해 그는 자기 자신의 제작사 La societe des films Marcel Pagnol을 설립했다. 그는 과거의 극작가가 미래의 영화 제작자가 될 것이라고 확신했는데, 이는 *Les cahiers du film*이라는 제목의 단명한 비평지에서 그가 논쟁적으로 전개시킨 논제(論題)였다.

Solution Guide

Marcel Pagnol의 영화 첫 몇 편은 자신의 연극 작품을 각색한 작품으로, 국내와 국제적으로 대중적인 엄청난 성공을 이루었다고 했으므로, Marcel Pagnol에 관한 글의 내용과 일치하지 않는 것은 ③이다.

Structure in Focus

- The son of a primary school teacher, [whom he described so vividly in his *Souvenirs d'enfance* (childhood memories)], this southern Frenchman began his professional life as an English teacher.
  [ ]는 The son of a primary school teacher를 부가적으로 설명하는 관계절이다.

▪ He was certain that [the dramatist of the past would be the film-maker of the future], [a thesis {which he controversially developed in a short-lived critical review ⟨entitled *Les cahiers du film*⟩}].
두 번째 [ ]는 첫 번째 [ ]를 부가적으로 설명한 명사구이다. 그 안의 { }는 a thesis를 수식하는 관계절이고, ⟨ ⟩는 a short-lived critical review를 수식하는 분사구이다.

02

정답 ①

소재 첼리스트 Yo-Yo Ma

해석 하버드 재학 시절, 세계적으로 유명한 첼리스트 Yo-Yo Ma는 보스턴과 그 주변 지역 연주회에서 자주 연주했다. 그는 큰 인기를 얻었고, 어느 날 자신의 연주회 중 하나가 매진되자 표를 구하지 못한 사람들을 위해 무료 연주회를 열었는데, 극장 로비에 앉아 바흐의 첼로 모음곡을 연주했다. 그의 경력 말년에, 국제적인 성공을 이룬 사람이었을 때도, 그는 여전히 요구되는 것 이상을 주곤 했던 경우가 많았다. 예를 들어, 많은 객원 첼로 독주자는 연주회 전반부에 연주하면, 그것으로 일과를 끝낸다. 그러나 Mr. Ma는 때때로 연주회 후반에 오케스트라의 일원으로 연주하곤 했는데, 필라델피아 오케스트라와 이렇게 협연하는 것이 그에게는 특히 즐거운 일이었다. 그는 "필라델피아 오케스트라의 백스탠드에서[한 구성원으로서] 연주할 수 있어서 영광입니다. 그 연주자들이 경청하는 방식, 그들이 가지고 있는 지식은 대단합니다. 저는 그걸 정말로 높이 평가합니다. 그리고 저는 부분의 합보다 더 큰 무언가의 일부가 되는 것, 즉 팀의 일원으로 받아들여지는 것의 짜릿함을 느낍니다."라고 말한다.

Culture Note

play the back stands(백스탠드에서[한 구성원으로서] 연주하다)
대부분의 오케스트라에서 음악가는 무대에서 위계적인 방식으로 배열된다. 흔히 '퍼스트스탠드(first stands)'라고 불리는 앞쪽의 음악가는 일반적으로 수석 또는 리드 연주자이며 공연에서 더 두드러진 역할을 담당한다. '백스탠드(back stands)'라고 하는 뒤쪽의 연주자는 여전히 오케스트라의 중요한 일원이지만 보조 역할을 맡는다. 이 글에서 Yo-Yo Ma는 뒤쪽에서 오케스트라의 일원으로 연주하는 것이 영광이라고 말하고 있다.

Solution Guide

첼리스트 Yo-Yo Ma는 연주회가 매진되면 표를 구하지 못한 사람들을 위해 무료 연주회를 열었고, 객원 첼로 독주자로 활동할 때는 하지 않아도 되는 후반부를 연주하는 등, 해야 하는 일 이상을 하곤 했다는 내용의 글이다. 따라서 빈칸에 들어갈 말로 가장 적절한 것은 ①이다.

② 자신의 예상치 못한 실수를 바로잡곤
③ 자신의 연주에서의 자유를 추구하곤
④ 음악 연주의 기본에 집중하곤
⑤ 악기 연주법을 사람들에게 가르치곤

Structure in Focus

▪ However, Mr. Ma would sometimes play as part of the orchestra in the second half of the concert — [doing this with the Philadelphia Orchestra] was especially enjoyable for him.
[ ]는 주어 역할을 하는 동명사구이다.

▪ And I feel the thrill of [being part of something {that's greater than the sum of its parts}] — [being accepted as part of the team].
첫 번째 [ ]는 전치사 of의 목적어 역할을 하는 동명사구이고, 그 안의 { }는 something을 수식하는 관계절이다. 두 번째 [ ]는 첫 번째 [ ]의 내용에 대해 부가적으로 설명하는 동명사구이다.

03

정답 ⑤

소재 Hugo de Vries와 Darwin의 만남

해석 1878년 여름, Hugo de Vries라는 이름의 서른 살의 네덜란드 식물학자는 Darwin을 만나기 위해 잉글랜드로 갔다. 그것은 과학과 관련된 방문이라기보다는 영적인 여행에 가까웠다. (C) Darwin은 Dorking에 있는 누나의 저택에서 휴가를 보내고 있었지만, de Vries는 그를 찾아내어 그를 만나러 갔다. Darwin의 턱수염에 필적하는 턱수염을 가진, 마르고, 열성적이고, 흥분을 잘하는 de Vries는 이미 자신의 우상(Darwin)의 더 젊은 시절 모습처럼 보였다. (B) 그는 또한 Darwin이 가진 끈기를 가지고 있었다. 만남은 틀림없이 진을 빼는 일이었을 것인데, 왜냐하면 그것은 단지 두 시간 동안 진행되었고 Darwin은 휴식을 취하기 위해 도중에 자리를 떠야만 했기 때문이었다. 그러나 de Vries는 변화된 모습으로 잉글랜드를 떠났다. (A) 짧은 대화에 불과했지만, Darwin은 de Vries의 질주하는 마음속에 수문(水門)을 끼워 넣어, 영원히 새로운 방향으로 완전히 돌려놓았다. 암스테르담으로 돌아온 de Vries는 식물의 덩굴손의 움직임에 관한 이전 연구를 갑자기 종료하고 유전의 수수께끼를 푸는 데 몰두했다.

Solution Guide

1878년 여름, Hugo de Vries가 Darwin을 만나기 위해 잉글랜드로 갔다는 내용의 주어진 글 다음에는 de Vries가 누나의 저택에서 휴가를 보내고 있던 Darwin을 추적하여 그를 만나러 갔다는 내용의 (C)가 이어져야 한다. 그다음에는 de Vries와 Darwin의 외형적 유사성을 기술한 (C)의 마지막 문장에 이어 de Vries와 Darwin의 정신적 유사성을 He also had Darwin's persistence.로 기술하는 내용의 (B)가 이어져야 한다. 그다음에 짧은 대화에 불과했지만, de Vries가 변화된 모습으로 암스테르담으로 돌아와 유전의 수수께끼를 푸는 데 몰두했다는 내용의 (A)가 그 뒤를 잇는 것이 글의 순서로 가장 적절하다.

Structure in Focus

- In the summer of 1878, a thirty-year-old Dutch botanist [named Hugo de Vries] traveled to England [to see Darwin].
  첫 번째 [ ]는 a thirty-year-old Dutch botanist를 수식하는 분사구이고, 두 번째 [ ]는 목적의 의미를 나타내는 to부정사구이다.
- Back in Amsterdam, de Vries [suddenly terminated his prior work on the movement of tendrils in plants] and [threw himself into solving the mystery of heredity].
  두 개의 [ ]는 and로 연결되어 문장의 술어 역할을 한다.

21 철학, 종교, 역사, 풍습, 지리

Gateway ④
Exercises 01 ② 02 ④ 03 ⑤

Gateway

본문 126쪽

정답 ④
소재 여가의 사유화
해석 1945년 이후 제2차 세계 대전 전후(戰後)에, 유례없는 경제 성장은 건축 붐과 중심 도시에서 새로운 교외 지역으로의 대규모 이주를 부추겼다. 교외 지역은 자동차에 훨씬 더 많이 의존했고, 이는 대중교통에 대한 주된 의존에서 자가용으로의 전환을 알렸다. 이것은 곧 더 나은 고속 도로와 초고속 도로의 건설과 대중교통의 감소, 심지어 쇠퇴까지로 이어졌다. 이러한 모든 변화와 함께 여가의 사유화가 이루어졌다. 더 많은 사람이 내부 공간은 더 넓어지고 외부 정원은 더 아름다운 자신의 집을 소유함에 따라 그들의 휴양과 여가 시간은 점점 더 집이나 기껏해야 이웃에 집중되었다. 이러한 가정에 기반한 여가의 한 가지 주요 활동은 텔레비전을 시청하는 것이었다. 더 이상 영화를 보기 위해 전차를 타고 극장까지 갈 필요가 없었고, 유사한 오락(물)이 텔레비전을 통해 무료로 그리고 더 편리하게 이용 가능하게 되었다.

Solution Guide

주거 지역이 중심 도시에서 교외 지역으로 이동되고 사람들이 자신들이 원하는 형태의 집을 소유하면서 여가나 오락을 즐기는 양상도 집에서 누리는 형태로 바뀌었다는 내용이므로, 빈칸에 들어갈 말로 가장 적절한 것은 ④이다.
① 몰락
② 획일성
③ 회복
⑤ 맞춤화

Structure in Focus

- The suburbs were far more dependent on the automobile, [signaling the shift from primary dependence on public transportation to private cars].
  [ ]는 앞 절의 내용을 부가적으로 설명하는 분사구문이다.
- **No longer did one** have to ride the trolly to the theater to watch a movie; similar entertainment was available for free and more conveniently from television.
  부정어구 No longer로 문장이 시작되어 조동사 did가 주어 one 앞에 놓이는 어순이 되었다.

Quick Review

본문 127쪽

1. consensus / 과학자들 사이에서 기후 변화가 현실이라는 합의가 증가하고 있다.
2. wilderness / 우리는 미래 세대를 위해 황무지를 보호해야 할 책임이 있다.
3. fertile / 아마존의 비옥한 토양에는 다양한 동식물이 서식하고 있다.
4. Morality / 도덕성은 조화로운 사회에서 함께 사는 데 도움이 되기 때문에 중요하다.
5. relative / 아름다움의 개념은 상대적이며 사람마다 다르다.

Exercises

본문 128~129쪽

01

정답 ②

소재 도덕적 판단의 상대성

해석 서로 다른 사회의 사람들은 서로 다른 관습과 옳고 그름에 대한 서로 다른 생각을 가지고 있다는 것은 논란의 여지가 없는 사실이다. 어떤 행동이 옳고 그른지에 대한 견해는 상당 부분 겹치기는 하지만, 그것에 관한 전 세계적인 합의는 없다. 도덕적 견해가 지역에 따라서도 또한 시대에 따라서도 얼마나 많이 변해 왔는지 생각해 보면, 절대적인 도덕적 사실은 존재하지 않으며, 오히려 도덕성은 항상 여러분이 자라 온 사회에 따라 상대적이라고 생각하는 것이 솔깃한 일일 수 있다. 그러한 관점에 따르면, 노예 제도는 대부분의 고대 그리스인에게는 도덕적으로 용인되었지만, 오늘날 대부분의 유럽인에게는 그렇게 되지 않으므로, 노예 제도는 고대 그리스인에게는 옳았지만, 오늘날의 유럽인에게는 잘못된 것일 것이다. 도덕적 상대주의로 알려진 이 관점은 도덕성을 특정 시기에 특정 사회가 지닌 가치관에 대한 설명에 불과하게 만든다. 이는 도덕적 판단의 본질에 관한 메타 윤리적 관점이다. 도덕적 판단은 오로지 특정 사회와 관련하여 옳거나 그른 것으로 판단될 수 있을 뿐이다. 절대적인 도덕적 판단은 존재하지 않으며, 그것은 모두 상대적이다.

Solution Guide

서로 다른 사회 사이에 어떤 행동이 옳고 그른지에 대한 견해는 상당 부분 겹치기는 하지만, 그것에 관한 전 세계적인 합의는 없는 것처럼, 도덕성은 사람이 자라온 사회와 관련되어 있으며, 그렇기 때문에 절대적인 도덕적 판단은 존재하지 않으며, 그것은 모두 상대적이라는 내용의 글이다. 따라서 글의 주제로 가장 적절한 것은 ② '도덕적 판단의 상대적 본성'이다.

① 도덕적 상대주의의 해로운 영향
③ 도덕적 판단을 내릴 때의 고려 사항
④ 도덕적 판단이 항상 바람직한 것은 아닌 이유
⑤ 자기 향상의 수단으로서의 도덕적 행동

Structure in Focus

- If we consider [how much moral views have changed both from place to place and from age to age] **it** can be tempting [to think {that there are no absolute moral facts}, but rather {that morality is always relative to the society ⟨in which you have been brought up⟩}].
  첫 번째 [ ]는 consider의 목적어 역할을 하는 명사절이다. it은 형식상의 주어이고, 두 번째 [ ]는 내용상의 주어이다. 두 번째 [ ] 안의 두 개의 { }는 but으로 연결되어 think의 목적어 역할을 하는 명사절이고, 두 번째 { } 안의 ⟨ ⟩는 the society를 수식하는 관계절이다.
- This view, [known as moral relativism], makes morality [simply a description of the values {held by a particular society at a particular time}].
  첫 번째 [ ]는 This view를 부가적으로 설명하는 분사구이다. 두 번째 [ ]는 makes의 목적격 보어 역할을 하는 명사구이고, 그 안의 { }는 the values를 수식하는 분사구이다.

02

정답 ④

소재 멕시코의 지형과 지역적 단절

해석 미국이 개발하기 가장 쉬운 지형 중 한 곳을 가지고 있다면, 멕시코는 가장 어려운 지형 중 하나를 가지고 있다. 멕시코 전체는 본질적으로 로키산맥의 남쪽 연장 부분인데, 이는 미국의 최악의 땅이 멕시코의 최상의 땅과 눈에 띄게 유사하다는 것을 완곡하게 말하는 것이다. 산악 지대가 많은 지역에서 예상할 수 있듯이, 미국 중서부는 말할 것도 없고, 미국 남동부나 컬럼비아 계곡처럼 배가 다닐 수 있는 강이 없고 넓고 응집된 비옥한 땅도 없다. 각각의 산골짜기는 소수의 과두 정치 독재자가 지역의 경제 생활과 정치 생활을 통제하는 일종의 요새이다. 멕시코는 통일된 국가가 아니라, 대신에 지역의 실세들이 끊임없이 서로 손을 잡고, 서로 맞서는 수십 개의 작은 멕시코의 모음(그리고 흔히 헛된 노력으로 더 응집력 있는 무언가를 만들어 내려고 시도하는 정부)으로 여겨져야 한다. 지역적 단절로 인해 멕시코는 자본 집약적 사회 기반 시설이 가장 필요한 국가가 일반적으로 그 사회 기반 시설 구축에 필요한 자본을 창출하는 능력이 가장 낮은 국가인 교과서적인 사례이다.

Solution Guide

미국과 달리 멕시코는 개발하기 가장 어려운 지형 중 하나로, 항해할 수 있는 강이 없고 넓고 응집된 비옥한 땅도 없으며, 각각의 산골짜기는 소수의 과두 정치 독재자가 지역의 경제 생활과 정치 생활을 통제하면서 지역의 실세들이 끊임없이 서로 손을 잡고, 서로 맞선다는 내용의 글이다. 따라서 빈칸에 들어갈 말로 가장 적절한 것은 ④이다.

① 민주적 분위기
② 농업의 방대함
③ 노동 집약적인 구조
⑤ 광범위한 산업화

Structure in Focus

- Each mountain valley is a sort of fastness [where a small handful of oligarchs control local economic and political life].
  [ ]는 a sort of fastness를 수식하는 관계절이다.
- Mexico should**n't** be thought of [as a unified state], **but** instead [as {a collage of dozens of little Mexicos 〈where local power brokers constantly align with and against each other〉} (and {a national government 〈seeking — often in vain — to stitch together something more cohesive〉})].
  두 개의 [ ]는 「not ~ but ...」으로 연결되어 be thought of에 이어진다. 두 번째 [ ] 안의 두 개의 { }는 전치사 as에 이어지는 명사구이다. 첫 번째 { } 안의 〈 〉는 dozens of little Mexicos를 수식하는 관계절이고, 두 번째 { } 안의 〈 〉는 a national government를 수식하는 분사구이다.

03

정답 ⑤

소재 바닷물을 마시는 것의 위험성

해석 1798년 Samuel Taylor Coleridge가 *The Rime of the Ancient Mariner*에서 '물, 물은 어디에나 있지만, 마실 물은 한 방울도 없다'라는 시구절을 썼을 때, 바닷물을 마시는 것의 위험성은 수천 년 동안 알려져 왔다. 바닷물은 실제로 정말 사람을 미치게 한다. 역사적 증거는, 고대 이집트인들이 바닷물이 마시기에 적합하지 않다는 것을 알고 있었음을 나타내지만, 그것이 마시기에 적합하지 않다는 가장 이른 시기의 깨달음은 까마득한 태고 시대의 일이었다. 콜럼버스 이전 시대에는 육지에서 너무 멀리 나가서 바다로 모험을 떠나는 것에 대한 가장 큰 두려움은 지표면에서 아래로 떨어지는 것이 아니라 식수용 담수의 부족이었다. 인간의 관점에서 볼 때, 바다는 지표면의 70퍼센트를 차지하는데, 여전히 지구상에서 가장 광활하고 독특한 사막 같은 황량한 지역이다. 바닷물은 지구 물의 97퍼센트를 구성하며, 담수인 3퍼센트 중에서 3분의 2는 빙하와 극지방의 얼음으로 얼어 있다. 따라서 지구상의 모든 물 중 (호수와 강, 지하수, 대기에 있는) 단 1퍼센트만이 담수이면서 육상 동식물이 이용할 수 있다.

Solution Guide

바닷물을 마시는 것의 위험성에 관한 내용의 글이다. 주어진 문장은 바닷물은 지구 물의 97퍼센트를 구성하며, 나머지 3퍼센트가 담수인데, 그중 3분의 2는 빙하와 극지방의 얼음으로 얼어 있다는 내용으로, Thus에 의해 지구상의 모든 물 중 단 1퍼센트만이 담수이며 육상 동식물이 이용할 수 있다는 내용으로 이어져야 맥락상 단절이 일어나지 않는다. 따라서 주어진 문장이 들어가기에 가장 적절한 곳은 ⑤이다.

Structure in Focus

- Historical evidence indicates [the ancient Egyptians knew {seawater was not portable}], but the earliest realization [that it was unsafe to drink] has been lost to antiquity.
  첫 번째 [ ]는 indicates의 목적어 역할을 하는 명사절이고, 그 안의 { }는 knew의 목적어 역할을 하는 명사절이다. 두 번째 [ ]는 the earliest realization과 동격 관계이다.
- From a human perspective, the oceans, [which cover 70% of Earth's surface], are still the most extensive and unique desert wildernesses on the planet.
  [ ]는 the oceans를 부가적으로 설명하는 관계절이다.

22 환경, 자원, 재활용

Gateway ①
Exercises 01 ④ 02 ② 03 ④

Gateway

본문 130쪽

정답 ①

소재 배달용 운송 수단으로서의 자전거

해석 도시의 배달용 운송 수단은 도시의 (인구) 분포의 밀도에 더 잘 맞게 조정될 수 있는데, 그것은 흔히 자전거를 포함하여 밴과 같은 더 작은 운송 수단을 포함한다. 후자(자전거)는 선호되는 '최종 단계' 운송 수단이 될 잠재력이 있는데, 특히 밀도가 높고 혼잡한 지역에서 그러하다. 네덜란드와 같이 자전거 사용이 많은 지역에서는, 배달용 자전거가 개인의 짐(예를 들어 식료품)을 운반하기 위해 또한 사용된다. 인도네시아의 *becak*(바퀴가 세 개 달린 자전거)과 같은 짐 자전거는 매입 비용과 유지 비용이 낮기 때문에 선진국에서도 개발 도상국에서도 모두 많은 잠재력을 나타낸다. 배달용 전기 보조 세발자전거를 사용하는 서비스는 프랑스에서 성공적으로 시행되었고 소포 배달 및 음식 배달처럼 다양한 서비스를 위해 유럽 전역에서 점차 채택되고 있다. 도심이나 상업 지구와 같은 도시의 특정 지역에 자동차 접근을 제한하는 정책이나 자전거 전용 도로의 확장과 결합되는 경우에는, 자전거를 짐 운송 수단으로 사용하는 것이 특히 장려된다.

Solution Guide

밀도가 높고 혼잡한 지역에서 자전거가 배달용 운송 수단으로 많은 잠재력을 갖고 있으며, 실제 많은 나라에서 자전거를 운송 수단으로 사용하는 서비스가 점차 늘고 있다는 내용의 글이다. 따라서 글의 요지로 가장 적절한 것은 ①이다.

Structure in Focus

- Urban delivery vehicles can be adapted to better suit the density of urban distribution, [which often involves smaller vehicles such as vans, including bicycles].
  [ ]는 주절의 내용을 부가적으로 설명하는 관계절이다.
- Services [using electrically assisted delivery tricycles] [have been successfully implemented in France] and [are gradually being adopted across Europe for services {as varied as parcel and catering deliveries}].
  첫 번째 [ ]는 Services를 수식하는 분사구이고, 두 번째와 세 번째 [ ]는 and로 연결되어 문장의 술어를 이룬다. 세 번째 [ ] 안의 { }는 services를 수식하는 형용사구이다.

Quick Review

본문 131쪽

1. demographics / 도시 계획가들은 사회 기반 시설 개발에 대해 정보에 입각한 결정을 내리기 위해 그 도시의 인구 통계를 분석했다.
2. conservation / 지속 가능한 어업 관행과 해양 보존을 위해 친환경 고기잡이 도구 사용이 권장된다.
3. conscious / 그 다큐멘터리는 시청자들이 기후 변화의 결과를 더 많이 의식하도록 만드는 것을 목표로 했다.
4. endangered / 멸종 위기에 처한 바다거북을 구하기 위한 노력에는 고기잡이 도구에 의한 우발적 포획을 줄이기 위한 조치를 시행하는 것이 포함된다.
5. disproportionate / 그 행사에 대한 언론 보도는 그 행사의 전반적인 중요성보다는 사소한 세부 사항에 지나치게 초점을 맞추어 불균형적인 것처럼 보였다.

Exercises

본문 132~133쪽

01

정답 ④

소재 거주지 결정 시 선호되는 항목

해석 변화하는 인구 통계, 가구 구조, 생활 방식 선호도, 소비자 가치관은 30년 전과 비교해 향후 30년의 다른 건축 환경과 도시 구조를 시사한다. 점점 더 많은 미국인, 호주인, 유럽인이 대기 오염과 에너지 사용을 줄이는 것이 자신들에게 중요하기 때문에, 자동차에 덜 의존하는 환경에서 살기를 선택하고 있다. 2천 명이 넘는 미국 성인을 대상으로 실시한 2011년의 한 설문 조사에 따르면, 거주지를 결정할 때 집의 크기보다 집이 위치한 동네가 더 큰 고려 사항이라고 답한 사람이 일곱 배나 더 많았다. 식당, 상점, 학교 및 기타 생활 편의 시설까지 걸어 다닌다는 점이 많은 응답자에게 가장 매력적인 동네의 특징이었다. 많은 20~30대에게 걸어 다닐 수 있는 지역 사회는 환경 발자국 감소 및 에너지 효율성과 동일시되며, 일상 활동 중에 칼로리를 소모할 수 있다는 추가적인 이점이 있다. 친환경 건물과 태양 전지판이 경관과 옥상을 덮고 있다면 더욱더 좋다. Urban Land Institute의 한 경제학자는 "에너지 효율성이 새로운 화강암 조리대 상판이 되고 있다. 즉, 그것은 부동산을 팔기 위해 없어서는 안 될 장점이다."라고 말한다.

Solution Guide

사람들이 자동차에 덜 의존하는 환경에서 살기를 선택하면서 거주지를 결정할 때 생활 편의 시설까지 걸어 다닐 수 있는 것을 가장 매력적인 동네의 특징으로 본다는 것이 글의 중심 내용이므로,

글의 주제로 가장 적절한 것은 ④ '걸어 다닐 수 있는 동네에 있는 주택 입지에 대한 증가하는 선호도'이다.
① 도시에서 세대별 선호하는 주택 유형
② 젊은이를 끌어들이는 도시 근린 시설
③ 도시 지역과 교외 지역의 인구 통계 차이
⑤ 교외 지역에 대비하여 도심에서 집 구매 시 고려할 요소

Structure in Focus

- More and more Americans, Australians, and Europeans are choosing to live in settings [where they are less dependent on their cars] [because {reducing air pollution and energy use} matters to them].
  첫 번째 [ ]는 settings를 수식하는 관계절이고, 두 번째 [ ]는 because가 이끄는 부사절이며, 그 안의 { }는 부사절의 주어 역할을 하는 동명사구이다.
- [A 2011 survey of more than two thousand adult Americans] found [seven times more people said {the neighborhood 〈where a house is located〉 is a bigger consideration in deciding 〈where to live〉 than the size of the house}].
  첫 번째 [ ]는 문장의 주어이고, 두 번째 [ ]는 found의 목적어 역할을 하는 명사절이다. 두 번째 [ ] 안의 { }는 said의 목적어 역할을 하는 명사절이고, 그 안의 첫 번째 〈 〉는 the neighborhood를 수식하는 관계절이며, 두 번째 〈 〉는 deciding의 목적어 역할을 하는 명사구이다.

02

정답 ②

소재 환경 쇠퇴의 주요 원인으로서의 천연자원 소비

해석 최근 몇 년 동안 경제학자, 과학자, 정치인들이 생물 다양성 손실의 더 중요한 근본 원인으로 인구 증가에서 소비로 초점을 옮기는 경향이 증가해 왔다. 많은 사람에게, 소비에 맞춰진 초점은 인구 통제와 같은 정치적으로 격론을 불러일으킬 수 있는 주제를 피하는데, 대부분의 사람이 윤리적 또는 도덕적 이유로 그리고 그것이 외국인 혐오, 인종 차별, 우생학과 같은 분열을 초래하는 주제와 연관되어 있기 때문에 그것을 반대한다. 다른 사람들은 환경 쇠퇴의 주요 원인이 인구수 자체가 아니라 천연자원이 소비되는 방식이라고 강조한다. 실제로 부유한 사람들과 부유한 국가들은 전 세계 천연자원의 불균형적으로 많은 부분을 소비하기 때문에, 자연환경에 불균형적인 영향을 미친다. 한 가지 예를 들자면, 미국은 전 세계 인류의 5퍼센트만 수용하지만 매년 전 세계에서 채취되는 천연자원의 25퍼센트를 사용한다. 실제로 미국의 크리스마스 장식용 조명만 해도 에티오피아나 탄자니아 전체의 연간 에너지 사용량보다 더 많은 에너지를 사용한다. 하지만 평균적인 미국 시민은 카타르의 평균적인 시민이 사용하는 에너지의 절반 미만을 사용하는데, 카타르는 작지만 부유한 중동 국가이다.

Solution Guide

② 관계대명사 what이 이끄는 절은 명사절로 문장에서 주어, 보어, 목적어의 역할을 해야 하는데 are consumed가 수동태이므로 목적어 역할을 할 수 없다. 따라서 what은 「it is ~ that ...」 표현을 이루는 that이 되어야 한다.
① 앞 절의 population control을 선행사로 하여 부가적으로 설명하는 관계절을 이끄는 which는 어법상 적절하다.
③ natural resources가 harvest의 대상에 해당하므로 과거분사 harvested는 어법상 적절하다.
④ 주어가 decorative Christmas lights이므로 복수 동사 use는 어법상 적절하다.
⑤ 앞 절의 내용을 부가적으로 설명하는 분사구문이므로 being은 어법상 적절하다.

Structure in Focus

- Others highlight [that **it is** {not the number of people per se, but how natural resources are consumed} **that** is the main cause of environmental decline].
  [ ]는 highlight의 목적어 역할을 하는 명사절이고, 그 안의 { }는 it is와 that 사이에 놓여 그 의미가 강조되고 있다.
- And yet, the average USA citizen uses less than half of the energy [that an average citizen of Qatar uses], [**Qatar** being a small but wealthy Middle Eastern country].
  첫 번째 [ ]는 the energy를 수식하는 관계절이다. 두 번째 [ ]는 앞 절의 내용을 부가적으로 설명하는 분사구문인데 주절과 주어가 달라 주어 Qatar가 표시되었다.

03

정답 ④

소재 환경 문제에 대한 인식을 높이는 영화

해석 멋진 자연 경관과 카리스마 넘치는 야생 동물이 등장하는 영화는 흔히 이러한 풍경과 동물을 직접 볼 수 있는 자연 지역을 방문하고 싶어 하는 영화 관람객의 욕구를 증가시킨다. 하지만 그것(그런 영화)은 또한 새로운 관람객들에게 환경 문제에 대한 인식을 높일 수도 있다. 많은 다큐멘터리가 이러한 목적을 염두에 두고 제작되지만, 그러한 이익은 또한 더 많은 관람객을 대상으로 하는 블록버스터 영화에까지 확대될 수 있다. 예를 들어, 디즈니의 *Happy Feet*(2006)은 어류 남획과 플라스틱 오염이 펭귄에 미치는 위협을 강조했고, *The Jungle Book*(2016)은 관람객에

게 멸종 위기에 처한 천산갑을 경험하게 했다. 그런 경험은 환경을 의식하는 행동 변화를 가져올 수도 있다. 예를 들어, 종말론적인 영화 *The Day After Tomorrow*(2004)를 본 후 영화 관람객들은 기후 완화에 50퍼센트 더 많은 돈을 기꺼이 기부하려 했다. 아마도 부분적으로는 환경 보호를 지향하는 영화의 영향 때문인지, 점점 더 많은 영화배우(그리고 기타 유명인)가 자신의 스타덤을 아프리카의 생물 다양성 보존 노력을 홍보하는 플랫폼으로 활용하기 시작했다.

Solution Guide

빈칸 이후의 글에서 다큐멘터리뿐만 아니라 블록버스터 영화들도 환경 오염의 위협을 강조하여 환경을 의식하는 행동 변화를 관람객들에게 유발할 수 있고, 종말론적인 영화를 본 관람객들이 더 많은 돈을 기꺼이 기부하려 했으며, 영화배우가 자신의 스타덤을 생물 다양성 보존 노력을 홍보하는 플랫폼으로 활용하기 시작했다는 내용이 나오고 있으므로, 빈칸에 들어갈 말로 가장 적절한 것은 ④이다.

① 희귀 식물 종의 보존을 강조할
② 토착민들의 삶에 긍정적인 영향을 끼칠
③ 영화사들이 더 많은 블록버스터 영화를 제작하게 자극할
⑤ 영화 관람객이 야생에서 재미있는 활동에 참여하게 할

Structure in Focus

- Movies [featuring wonderful natural landscapes and charismatic wildlife] often increase the desire of moviegoers to visit natural areas [where they can see these landscapes and animals first-hand].
  첫 번째 [ ]는 Movies를 수식하는 분사구이고, 두 번째 [ ]는 natural areas를 수식하는 관계절이다.
- Perhaps, in part, due to the influence of environmentally-orientated movies, [an increasing number of movie stars (and other celebrities)] have started [using their stardom as a platform {from where they promote biodiversity conservation efforts in Africa}].
  첫 번째 [ ]는 문장의 주어로 쓰인 명사구이다. 두 번째 [ ]는 started의 목적어 역할을 하는 동명사구이고, 그 안의 { }는 a platform을 수식하는 관계절이다.

23 물리, 화학, 생명과학, 지구과학

Gateway ⑤
Exercises 01 ③ 02 ⑤ 03 ④

Gateway

본문 134쪽

정답 ⑤
소재 식물의 적응 반응 조정
해석 식물은 영양소가 제한적일 때 섬세하게 조정된 적응 반응을 보인다. 정원사가 노란 잎을 부족한 영양 공급과 비료의 필요성에 대한 신호로 인식할 수도 있다. (C) 그러나 식물에 보충 미네랄을 공급해 줄 관리자가 없다면, 그것은 더 멀리 떨어진 토양 구역에서 (영양분을) 구하러 다닐 수 있게 해 주기 위해 뿌리를 급증시키거나 연장하고 뿌리털을 발달시킬 수 있다. 식물은 또한 영양소나 자원의 획득 가능성의 시간상, 또는 공간상 변동의 역사에 대응하기 위해 자기 기억을 사용할 수 있다. (B) 이 분야의 연구는 식물이 시공간 모두의 측면에서 환경 속에서의 자기 위치를 항상 인식한다는 것을 보여 주었다. 지금까지 가변적인 영양소 획득 가능성을 경험한 식물은 잎 생산 대신에 뿌리 연장에 에너지를 쓰는 것과 같은 위험 감수 행동을 보이는 경향이 있다. (A) 그와 반대로, 영양소가 풍부했던 역사를 가진 식물은 위험을 회피하고 에너지를 절약한다. 모든 발달 단계에서 식물은 성장, 생존, 번식에는 에너지를 사용하면서 자기의 귀중한 에너지의 손상과 비생산적인 사용은 제한할 수 있도록 환경 변화나 불균등에 반응한다.

Solution Guide

식물이 영양소가 제한적일 때 보이는 적응 반응을 말하며, 정원사의 예를 드는 주어진 글 다음에는 (정원사와 같은) 관리자가 없으면 식물이 뿌리를 급증시키는 특성과 영양소나 자원 가용성의 시간적 또는 공간적 변화의 역사에 대응하기 위해 기억을 사용할 수 있다고 설명하는 (C)가 먼저 온다. 그다음에는 앞서 언급한 분야의 연구가 식물은 시공간 모두의 측면에서 환경에서 자신의 위치를 항상 인식한다는 것을 보여 준다는 내용인 (B)가 오고, 앞서 언급한 영양소가 제한적일 때와 반대로 영양소가 풍부했던 역사를 가진 식물의 특성을 설명하는 (A)가 이어져야 한다. 따라서 주어진 글 다음에 이어질 글의 순서로 가장 적절한 것은 ⑤이다.

Structure in Focus

- At all developmental stages, plants respond to environmental changes or unevenness [so as to be able to use their energy for growth, survival, and reproduction, {while limiting damage and

nonproductive uses of their valuable energy}].
[ ]는 목적의 의미를 나타내는 to부정사구이다. 그 안의 { }는 use their energy for growth, survival, and reproduction과 동시에 일어나는 상황을 나타내는 분사구문으로, 의미를 명확히 하기 위해 접속사를 명시했다.

- Plants [that have experienced variable nutrient availability in the past] **tend** to exhibit risk-taking behaviors, such as spending energy on root lengthening instead of leaf production.
[ ]는 Plants를 수식하는 관계절이고, tend는 술어동사이다.

Quick Review

본문 135쪽

1. inedible / 극심한 기온으로 인해 하룻밤 동안 차에 놓여있던 음식은 먹을 수 없게 되었다.
2. variation / 계절이 여름에서 가을로 바뀌면서 나뭇잎의 색깔에 눈에 띄는 변화가 있었다.
3. predator / 집고양이는 포식자의 특성을 많이 가지고 있어 본능적으로 작은 설치류와 새를 사냥한다.
4. adaptation / 종의 자기 환경에의 적응은 그것의 생존과 번식 성공에 매우 중요하다.
5. minute / 오래된 책이 펼쳐졌을 때 작고 미세한 먼지 입자가 공기 중에 떠다녔다.

Exercises

본문136～137쪽

01

정답 ③

소재 개미의 겉모습과 생활 방식

해석 이것이 어느 정도까지 사실인지는 그것의 신체 구조의 모든 측면에 대해 충분히 연구되지는 않았지만, 개미의 겉모습의 많은 양상은 아마도 특정한 생활 방식의 요구에 맞게 진화했을 것이다. 적응 형태는 환경, 이용 가능한 먹이, 또는 포식자 때문일 수 있을 것이다. 긴 다리와 큰 눈은 탁 트인 지면에서 포식자를 피하거나 먹이 자원을 가장 먼저 확보하기 위해 빠르게 움직여야 하는, 땅에서 먹이를 찾는 개미에게서 흔히 보여진다. 반면, 낙엽 속에서 먹이를 찾고 집을 짓는 개미는 작은 눈과 함께 더 짧은 다리와 더듬이를 가지고 있다. 이는 작은 몸 구조로 좁은 공간을 더 쉽게 이동할 수 있는 낙엽의 어두운 환경에서는 말이 된다. 몸 크기 치수의 고유한 조합에 근거해서 과학자들은 개미가 어디서 집을 짓고 먹이를 찾는지, 또는 심지어 그것이 어떤 종류의 먹이를 먹는지를 예측할 수 있다. 포식자는 더 길고 더 납작한 아래턱뼈를 가지고 있는 반면, 다양한 먹이를 먹는 잡식성 개미는 더 짧고 구부러진 아래턱뼈를 가지고 있다.

Solution Guide

환경, 먹이, 포식자 등에 의한 특정한 생활 방식의 영향으로 개미의 겉모습이 진화했다는 것이 글의 중심 내용이므로, 글의 주제로 가장 적절한 것은 ③ '특정한 생활 방식에 따른 개미의 겉모습 적응 형태'이다.
① 먹는 것에 따라 달라지는 개미의 행동
② 과학자가 개미의 번식 주기를 예측하는 방법
④ 어두운 환경에서 포식자를 피하는 개미의 전략
⑤ 개미의 겉모습과 움직임 간의 관계

Structure in Focus

- Long legs and large eyes are commonly seen in ground-foraging ants [that need to move quickly {to avoid predators in open ground or be the first to acquire a food resource}].
[ ]는 ground-foraging ants를 수식하는 관계절이고, 그 안의 { }는 목적을 나타내는 to부정사구이다.
- Based on the unique combination of body size measurements, scientists can predict [where an ant nests and forages] or [even what kind of food it eats].
두 개의 [ ]는 or로 연결되어 predict의 목적어 역할을 하는 명사절이다.

02

정답 ⑤

소재 대왕 문어

해석 세계에서 가장 큰 문어 종인 대왕 문어는 보통 길이가 약 3m까지 자라고, 무게가 272kg까지 나간다. 그것은 북태평양 가장자리에 서식하며, 그곳에서 빨판으로 덮인 긴 팔을 이용해 바닥을 이리저리 기어다닌다. 그것은 해저에서 돌로 된 굴을 찾으며, 어린 것들은 자주 모래 지대의 바위 밑에 굴을 파기도 한다. 이곳에서 문어는 물개, 상어, 기타 대형 물고기 같은 굴 입구를 통과하기에는 너무 큰 포식자로부터 피신할 수 있다. 주로 밤에 먹이를 찾는 이 대왕 문어는 특히 게와 바닷가재를 찾지만, 새우와 조개류, 더 작은 문어, 물고기도 잡는다. 자주 그것은 굴로 돌아와 먹이를 먹으며, 빈 조개껍데기와 기타 먹을 수 없는 먹이 조각을 무더기로 입구에 쌓아 두기도 한다. 그것의 동종과 마찬가지로 이 문어도 성체가 짝짓기를 위해 함께 있는 짧은 기간을 제외하고는 대부분 혼자 산다. 암컷은 굴에 알을 낳고 새끼가 나올 때까지 알을 돌본다. 암컷은 이 기간 내내 먹이를 먹지 않으며 새끼가 나오고 난 후 곧 죽는다.

Solution Guide

암컷은 새끼가 나오고 난 후 곧 죽는다고 했으므로, ⑤는 글의 내용과 일치하지 않는다.

Structure in Focus

- It lives on the rim of the North Pacific Ocean, [where it crawls about on the bottom, {using its long, sucker-covered arms}].
  [ ]는 the rim of the North Pacific Ocean을 부가적으로 설명하는 관계절이고, 그 안의 { }는 it의 동작을 부가적으로 설명하는 분사구문이다.
- Like its relatives, this octopus mostly lives alone, except for a brief period [when adults come together for mating].
  [ ]는 a brief period를 수식하는 관계절이다.

03

정답 ④

소재 볼링공의 각도 변화

해석 볼링 실력이 아무리 뛰어나더라도 볼링공을 손에서 놓는 각도에는 항상 미세한 변화가 있으며, 공이 레인 구간을 따라 이동하면서 그 변화는 커질 것이다. 볼링공이 치면서 첫 번째 볼링핀은 약간 오른쪽 또는 왼쪽 뒤로 넘어지고 볼링공은 반대 쪽으로 약간 방향이 바뀐다. 그다음부터는 순식간에 볼링핀이 여러 방향으로 넘어지기 시작하고, 때로는 넘어지면서 다른 볼링핀과 부딪치기도 한다. 볼링공이 볼링을 치는 사람의 손을 떠날 때 약간의 각도 변화로 인해 매번 볼링핀의 최종 배열의 차이를 예측하기 어렵다. (대부분의 스포츠는 참가자가 신체 상태가 양호하고 비슷한 연령대의 사람들과 함께 경기하는 것을 요구하는 반면, 볼링은 온갖 규모, 연령, 기술 수준의 혼합 그룹이 참여할 수 있다.) 연달아 스트라이크를 성공할 수 있는 사람이라도 실제로는 매번 다른 스트라이크를 성공하는 것인데, 이는 볼링핀이 정확히 똑같은 방식으로 두 번 넘어지지 않을 것이기 때문이다.

Solution Guide

볼링 실력이 아무리 뛰어나더라도 볼링공을 손에서 놓는 각도에 항상 미세한 변화가 있으며 볼링핀이 넘어지면서 다른 볼링핀과 부딪치기도 해서 연달아 스트라이크를 성공하더라도 실제로는 매번 다른 스트라이크를 성공하는 것이라는 것이 글의 중심 내용이므로, 대부분의 스포츠와 달리 볼링은 온갖 규모, 연령, 기술 수준의 혼합 그룹이 참여할 수 있다는 내용의 ④는 글의 전체 흐름과 관계가 없다.

Structure in Focus

- However skilled you may be at bowling, there will always be minute changes in the angle [at which you release the ball] [that will be magnified {as the ball travels the length of the lane}].
  첫 번째 [ ]는 the angle을 수식하는 관계절이고, 두 번째 [ ]는 minute changes in the angle을 수식하는 관계절이다. 두 번째 [ ] 안의 { }는 '~하면서'라는 의미의 as로 유도되는 부사절이다.
- Even those [who can achieve strike after strike] actually achieve a different strike every time, [for the skittles will never fall in exactly the same way twice].
  첫 번째 [ ]는 those를 수식하는 관계절이고, 두 번째 [ ]는 앞 절 내용의 이유를 나타내는 부사절이다.

24 스포츠, 레저, 취미, 여행

Gateway ④
Exercises 01 ④ 02 ⑤ 03 ③

Gateway

본문 138쪽

정답 ④

소재 2017년에 관광한 유럽 연합 28개국 인구의 점유율

해석 위 도표는 2017년에 관광한 유럽 연합 28개국 인구의 점유율을 연령대와 목적지 범주별로 보여 준다. '여행 안 함' 범주에 속한 사람의 비율은 다섯 개의 연령대 각각에서 30퍼센트가 넘었다. '국외 여행만 함' 범주에 속한 사람의 비율은 35~44세 연령대에서보다 25~34세 연령대에서 더 높았다. 35~44세 연령대에서 '국내 여행만 함' 범주에 속한 사람의 비율은 34.2퍼센트였다. '국내외 여행 함' 범주에 속한 사람의 비율은 55~64세 연령대에서보다 45~54세 연령대에서 더 낮았다. 65세 이상 연령대에서 '여행 안 함' 범주에 속한 사람의 비율은 50퍼센트가 넘었다.

Solution Guide

'국내외 여행 함' 범주에 속한 사람의 비율은 55~64세 연령대(22.5퍼센트)에서보다 45~54세 연령대(23.3퍼센트)에서 더 높았으므로, 도표의 내용과 일치하지 않는 것은 ④이다.

Structure in Focus

- The above graph shows the share of the EU-28 population [participating in tourism in 2017] by age group and destination category.
  [ ]는 the EU-28 population을 수식하는 분사구이다.
- [The share of people in the No Trips category] was over 30% in each of the five age groups.
  [ ]는 문장의 주어 역할을 하는 명사구이다.

Quick Review

본문 139쪽

1. athlete / Emma는 육상과 필드 종목에서 모두 성과를 거두며 뛰어난 운동선수로 인정받았다.
2. Nutrient / 신체의 영양소 불균형은 다양한 건강 문제를 일으킬 수 있으므로, 균형 잡힌 식단의 중요성이 강조된다.
3. physical / 충분한 수면은 정신적, 신체적 건강 모두에 중요하며 신체가 회복할 수 있도록 한다.
4. spectator / 영화제 관객으로서 그녀는 다양한 명작을 감상하며 즐거운 시간을 보냈다.
5. satisfaction / 일과 삶의 균형을 유지하는 것은 전반적인 행복과 직무 만족을 위해 필수적이다.

Exercises

본문 140~141쪽

01

정답 ④

소재 각성의 원천인 관중

해석 관중은 추동 각성의 원천으로 여겨진다. 이런 고조된 각성 상태는 잘 학습된 기술이나 간단한 기술의 수행을 용이하게 하는 것으로 추정된다. 그러나 기술이 잘 학습되지 않거나 복잡하다면, 각성 증가가 그것(기술)의 수행을 방해할 것이다. 기본 개념은 추동 각성의 증가는 선수의 지배적인 반응의 방출을 돕는다는 것이다. 숙련된 선수의 경우, 그 선수의 지배적 반응은 대체로 '적절한' 것으로 여겨진다. 그 선수의 수행은 관중이 있을 때 개선될 것이다. 선수가 기술을 습득하는 데 여전히 어려움을 겪고 있는 경우, 적절한(→ 적절하지 않은) 반응이 다수 나타나서 지배적인 반응으로 여겨진다. 결과적으로, 관중은 초보자의 수행을 악화시키기만 할 수 있다. 따라서 선수의 기술 수준과 기술 자체의 복잡성이 관중이 수행에 도움이 될지 방해가 될지를 결정할 것이다.

Culture Note

drive theory(추동 이론) C. Hull이 처음 제기한 추동 이론에 의하면 운동 수행은 각성 수준이 강할수록 향상되지만, 각성 수준의 증가가 곧 수행의 향상을 의미하는 것은 아니며, 각성과 수행의 관계는 기술이 습관화된 정도에 따라 달라진다고 한다.

Solution Guide

각성 상태는 잘 학습되거나 간단한 기술의 수행을 용이하게 하지만, 잘 학습되지 않거나 복잡한 기술의 수행에는 방해가 되는데, 관중은 이러한 각성의 원천으로 여겨지므로 선수의 기술 수준과 기술의 복잡성에 따라 관중의 영향이 다르게 나타난다는 내용의 글이다. 선수가 기술을 습득하는 데 어려움을 겪고 있는 경우에는 적절하지 않은 반응이 나타난다고 해야 하므로, ④의 correct를 incorrect와 같은 낱말로 바꾸어야 한다.

Structure in Focus

- In a case [where the performer is still struggling to master a skill], incorrect responses [are present in abundance] and [are thereby presumed to be dominant responses].

첫 번째 [ ]는 a case를 수식하는 관계절이다. 두 번째와 세 번째 [ ]는 and로 연결되어 문장의 술어 역할을 한다.

- Hence, [the performer's level of skill and the complexity of the skill itself] will determine [whether an audience helps or hinders a performance].
  첫 번째 [ ]는 문장의 주어 역할을 하는 명사구이고, 두 번째 [ ]는 determine의 목적어 역할을 하는 명사절이다.

02

정답 ⑤

소재 운동에 필요한 단백질의 양

해석 운동선수는 몸을 많이 움직이지 않는 사람보다 (모든 영양소와) 단백질이 정말 더 많이 필요하지만, 그들이 더 최적으로 수행하기 위해 그들의 식단에서 여타의 다량 영양소에 비해 더 높은 비율의 단백질을 필요로 한다는 증거는 없다. 달리 말하자면, 운동선수와 비운동선수를 막론하고, 대부분의 사람에게 10퍼센트의 단백질이 포함된 식단이면 충분하다. 보통의 성인 여성이 2,000칼로리를 섭취하면, 10퍼센트는 200칼로리의 단백질이다. 보통의 여성 운동선수가 3,000칼로리를 섭취하면, 10퍼센트는 300칼로리의 단백질인데, 그것은 단백질 섭취량이 50퍼센트 늘어난 것으로, 같은 음식을 더 많이 섭취하는 것만으로도 얻을 수 있다. 따라서 운동할 때 음식의 구성을 바꿀(즉, 단백질 농도가 더 높은 음식을 섭취하거나 단백질 파우더를 섭취하는 것) 필요는 없다. 같은 음식을 더 많이 섭취하기만 하면 된다. 운동 활동의 증가는 기아 욕구를 북돋울 것이다. 이에 대응하여, 여러분은 모든 유형의 영양소뿐만 아니라 더 많은 단백질을 섭취할 것이다. 신체 활동에는 단백질뿐만 아니라 모든 영양소가 더 많이 필요할 것이기 때문에, 이런 방식이 효과적이다.

Solution Guide

운동선수도 10퍼센트의 단백질을 포함한 식단이면 충분하며, 운동 활동이 늘어나면 음식을 더 많이 섭취하게 되고, 자연스럽게 다른 영양소와 함께 단백질의 섭취량도 늘어날 것이므로, 단백질 농도가 더 높은 음식을 따로 더 섭취할 필요가 없다는 내용의 글이다. 따라서 글의 요지로 가장 적절한 것은 ⑤이다.

Structure in Focus

- [Athletes do require more protein (and all nutrients) than sedentary people], but [there is no evidence {that they require a higher percentage of protein compared to other macronutrients in their diet to perform more optimally}].
  두 개의 [ ]가 but으로 연결되어 문장을 이루고 있다. { }는 evidence와 동격 관계이다.

03

정답 ③

소재 오래된 수작업 기술에서 얻는 즐거움

해석 생산이 산업화 방식으로 전환되면 여가 소비자는 마음껏 더 오래된 수작업 기술에서 즐거움을 추구한다. 일반적으로, 시장이 취미 수요를 인식함에 따라 그 기술 자체가 하나 이상의 즐거움의 길로 들어서는데, 도구와 재료는 편안함, 아름다움, 만족감을 위해 설계된다. 많은 가능한 사례 중 두 가지만 말한다면, 바느질 도구와 취미 목공 도구 모두 이러한 변화를 거쳤다. 필기를 위한 생산 기술로는 구식으로 여겨졌던 만년필은 그저 종이에 잉크로 단어를 형성하는 과정을 즐기고 그 즐거움에 기꺼이 웃돈을 지불하려는 사람들에게 네 자릿수 가격에 팔리고 있다. 1950년대에, 고인이 된 Shelby Foote는 전하는 바에 따르면 당시 지배적인 필기 기술이었던 수동 타자기와 만년필을 멀리하고 잉크를 찍어 쓰는 펜으로 150만 단어에 이르는 3권의 남북 전쟁사를 집필하여 '순수 문학적인 역사'라는 용어에 새로운 의미를 부여했다.

Solution Guide

생산이 산업화 방식으로 전환되고 시장이 취미 수요를 인식하게 되면서, 도구와 재료는 편안함, 아름다움, 만족감을 추구하게 되었고, 바느질 도구와 취미 목공 도구를 비롯해 구식으로 여겨질 수도 있는 만년필과 잉크로 찍어 쓰는 펜이 기술 발전에도 불구하고 여전히 사용되었다는 내용의 글이다. 따라서 빈칸에 들어갈 말로 가장 적절한 것은 ③이다.

① 제품의 교체 또는 수리를 선택한다
② 더 저렴한 가격으로 제품을 구매해 이익을 얻는다
④ 기술 발전의 속도를 조절하려고 노력한다
⑤ 저렴한 형태의 오락 활동을 선택한다

Structure in Focus

- [Both needlework tools and **those** of hobby woodworking] have undergone this transition, to name only two of many possible examples.
  [ ]는 주어 역할을 하는 명사구이고, those는 the tools를 대신한다.
- Fountain pens, [considered obsolete as a production technology for writing], are selling at four-figure prices to people [who simply enjoy the process of forming words with ink on paper and are willing to pay a premium for the pleasure].
  첫 번째 [ ]는 Fountain pens를 부가적으로 설명하는 분사구이고, 두 번째 [ ]는 people을 수식하는 관계절이다.

25 음악, 미술, 영화, 무용, 사진, 건축

Gateway ⑤
Exercises 01 ② 02 ② 03 ⑤

Gateway

본문 142쪽

정답 ⑤

소재 피아니스트이자 작가였던 Charles Rosen

해석 거장 피아니스트이자 저명한 작가인 Charles Rosen은 1927년에 뉴욕에서 태어났다. Rosen은 어려서부터 피아노에 주목할 만한 재능을 보였다. 프린스턴 대학교에서 프랑스 문학 박사 학위를 받은 해인 1951년에, Rosen은 뉴욕에서 피아노 데뷔도 했고 첫 번째 음반 녹음도 했다. 열렬한 찬사 속에, 그는 전 세계의 수많은 독주회와 오케스트라 연주회에 출연했다. Rosen의 연주는 20세기의 가장 유명한 작곡가들 중 몇몇에게 감명을 주었고, 그들은 그에게 자신들의 음악 작품을 연주해 달라고 요청했다. Rosen은 또한 널리 칭송받는 많은 음악 저서의 저자였다. 그의 가장 유명한 책 *The Classical Style*은 1971년에 처음 출판되었고 다음 해에 U.S. National Book Award를 수상했다. 이 저작은 1997년에 증보판으로 재판을 찍었고, 그 분야의 획기적인 저작으로 남아 있다. 폭넓게 글을 쓰면서, Rosen은 2012년 사망할 때까지 여생 동안 피아니스트로서 계속 공연했다.

Solution Guide

폭넓게 글을 쓰면서 사망할 때까지 피아니스트로서 계속 공연했다고 했으므로, 글의 내용과 일치하지 않는 것은 ⑤이다.

Structure in Focus

- In 1951, [the year {he earned his doctoral degree in French literature at Princeton University}], Rosen made both his New York piano debut and his first recordings.
  [ ]는 1951과 동격 관계이고, 그 안의 { }는 the year를 수식하는 관계절이다.
- [This work, {which was reprinted in an expanded edition in 1997}], remains a landmark in the field.
  [ ]는 문장의 주어 역할을 하는 명사구이고, 그 안의 { }는 This work를 부가적으로 설명하는 관계절이다.

Quick Review

본문 143쪽

1. aesthetics / 그 패션 디자이너는 잘 맞을 뿐만 아니라 우아하게 보이는 의류를 만드는 데 있어 미학의 중요성을 강조했다.
2. enormous / 그 회사는 혁신적인 제품으로 막대한 성공을 거두며 빠르게 시장을 장악했다.
3. component / 그 엔지니어는 문제의 원인을 찾기 위해 기계의 각 요소를 면밀히 조사했다.
4. architectural / 그 마을의 건축 계획은 모든 연령의 주민들에게 친근하고 접근하기 쉬운 동네를 만드는 데 중점을 둔다.
5. catalog / 그 소프트웨어 개발자는 내용에 따라 파일을 자동으로 분류하는 프로그램을 고안했다.

Exercises

본문 144~145쪽

01

정답 ②

소재 예술적 사고에 도움이 되는 스트레스

해석 기쁨과 슬픔으로 삶에 대응하는 것은 인간다움의 일부이다. 고통과 괴로움을 피할 수 없을 때, 이것이 우리가 지식을 습득하는 과정의 일부라는 것을 기억하는 것이 중요하다. 이것은 예술을 창작하려면 고통의 상태에 있어야 한다는 의미는 아니지만, 스트레스는 호기심과 변화에 대한 동기를 유발한다면 창의력으로 전환될 수 있다. 그림 그리기를 통한 사고에 의해 우리는 우리의 고통을 맥락 안에 둘 수 있다. 우리가 만드는 이미지는 그것(우리의 고통)의 근원을 이해하고, 그것의 영역을 분류하고, 그것의 존재에 우리 자신을 적응시키고, 그것을 통제할 방법을 고안하는 데 우리에게 도움이 될 수 있다. 우리 자신의 개인적인 여정을 만듦으로써 우리가 스스로 발견해야 하는, 한때 지혜라고 불렸던, 삶에 존재하는 것들이 있다. 스트레스는 그러지 않았다면 무시되었거나 간과되었거나 반박되었을 수도 있는, 지적이고 상상력이 풍부한 탐구와 해결책에 대한 가능성을 열도록 유도될 수 있다.

Solution Guide

② 문장의 주어 역할을 하는 명사구가 필요하므로, Think를 Thinking으로 고쳐야 한다.
① it은 형식상의 주어이고 내용상의 주어 역할을 하는 to부정사구의 형태는 어법상 적절하다.
③ 앞 문장의 our distress를 대신하는 대명사 it은 어법상 적절하다.
④ wisdom을 부가적으로 설명하는 관계절을 이끌며, 관계절에서 목적어 역할을 하므로 관계대명사 which는 어법상 적절하다.
⑤ 문장의 주어인 Stress가 direct의 동작을 행하는 주체가 아니라 동작을 당하는 대상이므로 수동태 형태인 be directed는 어법상 적절하다.

Structure in Focus

- At times when pain and suffering are inescapable, **it** is important [to remember that this is part of the process {by which we acquire knowledge}].
  it은 형식상의 주어이고, [ ]는 내용상의 주어이며, 그 안의 { }는 the process를 수식하는 관계절이다.
- The images [we make] can help us [understand its source], [catalog its scope], [adapt ourselves to its presence], and [devise ways to control it].
  첫 번째 [ ]는 The images를 수식하는 관계절이다. 두 번째부터 다섯 번째 [ ]는 and로 연결되어 help의 목적격 보어 역할을 하는 원형부정사구이다.

02

정답 ②

소재 공간을 정의하는 건축적 특성

해석 건축 공간은 그것을 정의하는 건축적 특성을 통해 기억에 남게 된다. 규모, 사람에 대한 적합성, 미학, 시각적 효과라는 특성은 장소에 개성과 느낌을 부여하는 여러 요소 중 하나이다. 공간의 목적은 그 공간을 하나의 장소로 만들 수 있다. 백악관의 (타원형인) 대통령 집무실은 엄청난 역사적 중요성을 지닌 장소의 좋은 예이다. 이 훌륭한 방의 독특한 타원형 모양은 그것을 기억에 남게 하고 대단히 호사스럽지 않으면서도 특별한 중요성을 그것에 부여한다. 덧붙여 말하자면, George Washington은 손님들이 자신을 둘러서 있을 때 중앙에 서서 그들에게 인사할 수 있도록 Mount Vernon의 방 두 개를 개조해서 양 끝을 굽은 형태로 만들었다. Thomas Jefferson은 버지니아 대학에 있는 Rotunda 건물의 1층에 두 개의 타원형 회의실을 설계했다. 타원형 회의실은 그 회의실에서 누구도 다른 사람보다 더 중요한 자리에 위치할 수 없기 때문에 민주적인 것으로 여겨졌다.

Solution Guide

건축적 특성에 따라 건축 공간에 개성과 느낌이 부여되고, 공간이 기억에 남는 장소가 될 수 있다는 내용의 글이다. 주어진 문장은 백악관의 대통령 집무실이 역사적 중요성을 지니고 있다는 내용이며, ② 바로 뒤 문장의 The unique oval shape of this splendid room은 대통령 집무실에 중요성을 부여한 건축적 특성을 설명한다고 볼 수 있다. 따라서 주어진 문장이 들어가기에 가장 적절한 곳은 ②이다.

Structure in Focus

- [Qualities of scale, appropriateness for people, aesthetics, and visual impact] are among the many components [that give a place its character and feel].
  첫 번째 [ ]는 문장의 주어 역할을 하는 명사구이고, 두 번째 [ ]는 the many components를 수식하는 관계절이다.

03

정답 ⑤

소재 큐레이터의 역할

해석 박물관 및 미술관 전시는 (다른 미술관에 의해) '임대'되거나 다른 미술관과 공동 제작되며, 전시회가 2년 또는 그 이상 '이리저리 옮겨 다니는' 경우도 드물지 않다. 보통 그것들은 한 명 또는 그 이상의 사람이 선별하여 구성하는데, 그들의 역할에는 전시 구상 탐구, 작품 선정 (또는 의뢰), 전시 공간 내 작품 게시 계획 및 함께 제공되는 모든 책이나 카탈로그의 중요 부분 집필이 포함된다. 지역적, 국가적 또는 국제적으로 작용하는 큐레이터의 권한에 대한 의문이 제기되어 왔다. 물론 큐레이터는 작품 전시에 기여하는 주도권을 행사한다. 그러나 그들은 또한 다른 예술가들이나 작품 유형들을 희생하면서 자주 특정한 예술가들이나 작품 유형들을 선호할 수도 있다. 그뿐만 아니라 큐레이터는 흔히 '창작자'의 역할을 더 많이 수행하며, 아무리 적절하고 흥미롭다고는 하더라도, 예술가의 작품을 소개하는 것만큼이나 자신이 출세하는 데 도움이 되는 주제의 전시회를 연다는 의견이 제시되어 왔다. 실제로 모든 전시와 전시 작품 모음은 특정 기관의 강령, 우선 사항 및 위임 사항뿐만 아니라 큐레이터와 기록 보관인의 특별한 관심사를 반영한다.

Solution Guide

큐레이터는 작품 전시 구상을 탐구하고, 작품을 선정하고 전시 공간에 작품 게시를 계획하는 등의 역할을 하며 작품 전시에 기여하는 바가 크지만, 특정 예술가나 작품 유형에 대한 큐레이터의 선호도나 관심사가 반영된 전시회를 준비하기도 한다는 내용의 글이므로, 글의 제목으로 가장 적절한 것은 ⑤ '큐레이터의 영향력: 큐레이터의 관심사가 전시회를 구성하는 방식'이다.
① 예술적 표현을 확대하기 위한 새로운 아이디어
② 예술가가 큐레이터의 역할을 맡을 때 일어나는 일
③ 예술가와 큐레이터 사이의 진정한 협업의 힘
④ 오늘날 예술계에서 유능한 큐레이터가 되는 방법

Structure in Focus

- Museum and gallery exhibitions are 'hired' by or co-produced with other galleries; **it** is not uncommon [**for shows** to be 'on the road' for two years or longer].
  it은 형식상의 주어이고, [ ]는 내용상의 주어이다. for shows는 to부정사의 의미상의 주어이다.
- Furthermore, **it** has been suggested [that curators often act more as 'creators', putting together themed

exhibitions {which, however relevant and interesting, serve as much to advance themselves as to showcase the work of artists}].
it은 형식상의 주어이고, [ ]는 내용상의 주어이다. { }는 themed exhibitions를 수식하는 관계절이다.

26 교육, 학교, 진로

Gateway ④
Exercises 01 ⑤ 02 ⑤ 03 ②

Gateway

본문 146쪽

정답 ④

소재 창의성의 영역 간 활용

해석 다면적인 창의적 활동에 대한 어떤 방해 요인은 너무 이른 전문화, 즉 인생의 너무 이른 시기에 교육 방향을 선택하거나 한 가지 능력 개발에 집중해야 하는 것에 있을 수 있다. 그러나 한 영역에서의 창의적 능력 개발은 비슷한 기술을 요구하는 다른 영역에서 유효성을 높일 수 있고, 일반성과 특수성 사이의 유연한 전환은 많은 영역에서 생산성에 도움이 된다. 과도한 특수성은 해당 영역의 외부에서 오는 정보가 과소평가되고 활용될 수 없게 되는 결과를 낳을 수 있어 사고의 고정성으로 이어지는 반면에, 과도한 일반성은 혼돈, 모호함, 얄팍함을 일으킨다. 두 가지 경향 모두 영역 간 지식과 기술의 이동에 위협이 된다. 따라서 영역 간 창의성 개발을 위해 응당 최선일 것은 특정 영역에서 창의적인 도전을 하기 시작할 때 젊은이들을 지원하고 그 지원을 다른 영역, 분야, 과업에서 유래했을 뿐만 아니라 그런 영역, 분야, 과업 내의 지식과 기술을 적용하도록 장려하는 것과 결합하는 것이다.

Solution Guide

한 영역에서 개발된 창의적 능력은 일반성과 특수성 사이의 유연한 전환을 통해 영역 간에 적용될 수 있도록 장려해야 한다는 내용의 글이다. 따라서 필자가 주장하는 바로 가장 적절한 것은 ④이다.

Structure in Focus

- Excessive specificity may result in [{information from outside the domain} being underestimated and unavailable], [which leads to fixedness of thinking], [whereas excessive generality causes chaos, vagueness, and shallowness].
  첫 번째 [ ]는 result in의 목적어 역할을 하는 동명사구이고, 그 안의 { }는 being underestimated and unavailable의 의미상의 주어이다. 두 번째 [ ]는 주절의 내용을 부가적으로 설명하는 관계절이다. 세 번째 [ ]는 대조를 나타내는 부사절이다.
- [What should therefore be optimal for the development of cross-domain creativity] is [support for young

PART Ⅱ 주제·소재편

people in taking up creative challenges in a specific domain] and [coupling it with encouragement to apply knowledge and skills in, as well as from, other domains, disciplines, and tasks].
첫 번째 [ ]는 문장의 주어 역할을 하는 명사절이다. 두 번째와 세 번째 [ ]는 and로 연결되어 is의 주격 보어 역할을 한다.

Quick Review

본문 147쪽

1. flexible / 요가는 유연한 신체와 평온한 정신을 촉진한다.
2. aptitude / 언어 적성을 계발하는 것은 의사소통 기술을 강화한다.
3. commitment / 그 학생은 학문적 성공에 대한 강한 헌신을 보여 주었다.
4. integrate / 그 예술가의 작업은 혁신적인 방식으로 예술과 기술을 통합하는 것을 목표로 한다.
5. Consistent / 일관성 있는 행동은 개인 관계와 직업상의 관계에서 신뢰를 구축한다.

Exercises

본문 148~149쪽

01

정답 ⑤

소재 적성의 다양성

해석 우리가 일반 적성 같은 것이 있는지 물을 때 중요한 문제가 발생한다. 많은 사람이 미적분은 아주 잘하지만, 자기 인생이 달려 있다 해도 훌륭한 에세이를 쓰거나 훌륭한 그림을 그릴 수 없을 것이다. 어떤 사람들은 낯선 사람들로 가득 찬 방에 들어가서 그들 사이의 관계와 감정을 즉시 파악할 수 있지만, 또 어떤 사람들은 이 기술을 전혀 배우지 못할 수도 있다. Will Rogers의 말처럼, "모든 사람이 무지한데, 단지 서로 다른 주제에 대해 그러할 뿐이다." 분명히 특정한 방식으로 가르쳐지는 특정 유형의 지식이나 기술을 배우는 데 대한 적성이 개인마다 다르다. 사전에 전혀 몰랐던 주제에 관한 강의에 참석한 100명의 학생은 모두 서로 다른 배움의 양과 종류를 가지고 돌아갈 것인데, 그 특정 내용과 그 특정 교수법에 대한 적성이 이러한 차이를 설명하는 데 중요한 한 요소이다. 하지만 이 수업에서 가장 많이 배운 학생이 그 강의가 다른 주제에 관한 것이거나 같은 내용이 실습 경험을 통해 또는 소집단에서 제공될 때도 가장 많이 배울까?

Solution Guide

특정한 방식으로 가르쳐지는 특정 유형의 지식이나 기술을 배우는 데 적성이 개인마다 다르다는 내용의 글이다. 즉, 일반 적성은 없는 것인데, 그것의 존재를 주장할 때 문제가 발생하게 된다. 따라서 빈칸에 들어갈 말로 가장 적절한 것은 ⑤이다.
① 지능이 유전자의 산물인
② 학습 유형이 갑자기 변할 수 있는
③ 적성이 지능과 관련이 있는
④ 학습이 상호 목적이 있는 활동인

Structure in Focus

- A hundred students [attending a lecture on a topic they knew nothing about beforehand] will all walk away with different amounts and kinds of learning, and aptitude [for that particular content and that particular teaching method] is one important factor in explaining these differences.
첫 번째 [ ]는 A hundred students를 수식하는 분사구이다. 두 번째 [ ]는 aptitude를 수식하는 전치사구이다.
- But would the students [who learned the most in this class] also learn the most [if the lecture were on a different topic] or [if the same material were presented through hands-on experiences or in small groups]?
첫 번째 [ ]는 the students를 수식하는 관계절이다. 두 번째 [ ]와 세 번째 [ ]는 or로 연결되어 가정을 나타내는 부사절이다.

02

정답 ⑤

소재 학생의 발전 노력에 대한 보상

해석 기대 이론의 한 가지 함의는 모든 학생이 최선을 다하면 보상받을 기회를 가져야 하지만, 어떤 학생도 쉽게 최대 보상을 얻어서는 안 된다는 것이다. 전통적인 채점 관행은 이 원칙에 위배되는데, 어떤 학생은 A 학점과 B 학점을 얻기가 쉽다고 여기지만, 어떤 학생은 자신이 무엇을 하든 학문적 성공의 가능성이 거의 없다고 믿기 때문이다. 이러한 상황에서는, 높은 성취도를 보이는 학생이나 낮은 성취도를 보이는 학생 모두 최선의 노력을 다하지 않을 가능성이 있다. 이것이 높은 점수를 받는 것에 대해서만이 아니라 노력에 대해, 과거보다 더 잘한 것에 대해, 또는 진전을 이룬 것에 대해 학생들을 보상하는 것이 중요한 한 가지 이유이다. 예를 들어, 학생은 작문, 프로젝트, 보고서 또는 기타 작업으로 구성된 포트폴리오를 만들 수 있고, 그런 다음 시간이 지나면서 자신의 작업이 어떻게 향상하고 있는지 확인할 수 있다. 모든 학생이 똑같이 높은 점수를 받을 수 있는 것은 아니지만, 모든 학생이 똑같이 노력을 다하거나 자신의 과거 성과를 뛰어넘거나 발전할 수 있으므로, 이것이 보상의 기반이 되어야 하는, 흔히 더 좋고 더 평등하게 사용할 수 있는 기준이다.

Culture Note

expectancy theory(기대 이론) 사람들이 노력, 성과, 결과 사이의 연관성에 대한 믿음에 따라 행동하도록 동기를 부여한다는 이론이다. 이 이론에 따르면 개인은 자신의 노력이 성공적인 성과로 이어지고 성공적인 성과가 원하는 결과나 보상을 가져올 것이라고 믿을 때 동기를 부여받는다.

Solution Guide

학생이 최선의 노력을 다할 수 있도록 높은 점수를 받는 것에 대해서만이 아니라 학생이 이룬 노력과 진전에 대해 보상해야 한다는 내용의 글이므로, 글의 요지로 가장 적절한 것은 ⑤이다.

Structure in Focus

- One implication of expectancy theory is [that {even though all students should have a chance to be rewarded if they do their best}, no student should have an easy time achieving the maximum reward].
  [ ]는 is의 주격 보어 역할을 하는 명사절이고, 그 안의 { }는 양보를 나타내는 부사절이다.
- This principle is violated by traditional grading practices, [because some students find **it** easy {to earn A's and B's}, {whereas others believe that they have little chance of academic success no matter what they do}].
  [ ]는 이유를 나타내는 부사절이고, 그 안의 it은 형식상의 목적어이며, 첫 번째 { }는 내용상의 목적어이다. 두 번째 { }는 대조를 나타내는 부사절이다.

03

정답 ②

소재 정체성을 형성하는 청소년기

해석 학생들은 청소년기에 접어들면서 추상적인 사고와 타인의 관점을 이해하는 능력을 발달시킨다. 학생들이 사춘기에 접어들면서 훨씬 더 큰 신체적 변화가 일어나게 된다. (B) 따라서 청소년들은 정신과 신체가 발달하면서 성인기를 위한 확고한 기반을 제공할 정체성을 구축해야 하는 중요한 문제에 틀림없이 직면하게 된다. 그들은 유아기부터 자아의식을 발달시켜 왔다. (A) 하지만 청소년기는 지금 당장 시급한 질문, 즉 "나는 누구인가?"에 답하기 위해 의식적인 노력이 이루어지는 첫 시기에 해당한다. 이 시기를 정의하는 갈등은 정체성 대 역할 혼란이다. 정체성이란 개인의 욕구, 능력, 신념, 이력이 일관성 있는 자아상으로 조직된 것을 말한다. (C) 그것은 특히 일, 가치, 이념, 사람과 관념에 대한 헌신에 관한 신중한 선택과 결정을 수반한다. 청소년이 이러한 모든 측면과 선택을 통합하지 못하거나 전혀 선택할 수 없다고 느끼면, 역할 혼란이 발생할 우려가 있다.

Solution Guide

학생들은 청소년기에 접어들면서 사고 능력이 발달하고 큰 신체 변화를 경험한다는 내용의 주어진 글 다음에, 그 정신과 신체의 발달과 함께 정체성을 구축해야 하는 문제에 직면하게 된다는 내용의 (B)가 이어져야 한다. 그다음에 정체성을 구축하는 과정에서 정체성 대 역할 혼란의 갈등이 나타날 수 있음을 도입하는 (A)가 온 후, 그 역할 혼란의 양상을 구체적으로 설명하는 (C)가 이어지는 것이 글의 순서로 가장 적절하다.

Structure in Focus

- So, with developing minds and bodies, young adolescents must confront the central issue [of constructing an identity {that will provide a firm basis for adulthood}].
  [ ]는 the central issue를 구체적으로 설명하는 전치사구이고, 그 안의 { }는 an identity를 수식하는 관계절이다.
- [If adolescents fail to integrate all these aspects and choices], or [if they feel unable to choose at all], role confusion threatens.
  두 개의 [ ]는 or에 의해 연결되어 조건을 나타내는 부사절이다.

27 언어, 문학, 문화

Gateway ①
Exercises 01 ④ 02 ③ 03 ②

Gateway

본문 150쪽

정답 ①

소재 이민자의 문화적 정체성 유지

해석 주류 문화의 가치와 생활 방식을 받아들여야 하는 필요성 때문에 갈등이 증가하게 되었다. 다문화주의자들은 이민자들이 자신의 관습, 신념, 언어 중 일부를 유지하게 되는 부분 동화 모델이 있어야 한다고 제안한다. 그러나 자신의 문화적 정체성을 유지하기보다는 순응해야 한다는 압력이 있고, 이러한 갈등은 대개 이민자가 이주해 가는 사회에 의해 결정된다. 이러한 경험은 새로운 것이 아닌데, 19세기와 20세기에 처음 두 차례 이민이 급증했을 때 많은 유럽인이 배척과 빈곤을 경험했다. 결국 이 이민자들은 계몽과 다양성의 수용을 포함한 중대한 변화로 이 나라를 변모시켰다. 하지만 유색 인종들은 받아들여지기 위해 계속 투쟁한다. 거듭 말하자면, 도전 과제는 다른 문화는 다르게 생각하고 행동한다고, 그리고 그들이 그렇게 할 권리를 지니고 있다고 인정하는 것이다. 아마도, 그리 머지않은 미래에, 이민자들은 우리 사이에서 더는 이방인이 아닐 것이다.

Solution Guide

주류 문화에 순응하도록 강요함으로써 발생한 갈등을 해소하기 위해서는 이민자들의 다른 생각과 행동, 즉 그들의 고유한 문화적 정체성을 인정해야 한다는 내용의 글이다. 따라서 글의 요지로 가장 적절한 것은 ①이다.

Structure in Focus

- Multiculturalists suggest [that there should be a model of partial assimilation {in which immigrants retain some of their customs, beliefs, and language}].
  [ ]는 suggest의 목적어 역할을 하는 명사절이고, 그 안의 { }는 a model of partial assimilation을 수식하는 관계절이다.
- Once again, the challenge is [to recognize {that other cultures think and act differently} and {that they have the right to do so}].
  [ ]는 is의 주격 보어 역할을 하는 to부정사구이고, 그 안의 두 개의 { }는 and로 연결되어 recognize의 목적어 역할을 한다.

Quick Review

본문 151쪽

1. interpretation / 문학적 분석은 텍스트에 대한 깊은 해석을 수반한다.
2. Relative / 상대적 행복은 인생에 관한 자신의 관점에 달려 있다.
3. assimilate / 그 위원회가 이 제안을 받아들이는 데 시간이 필요할 것이다.
4. reputation / 그 예술가의 혁신적인 작업은 그녀의 예술적 명성을 강화했다.
5. conform / 그 팀은 자신들의 코치가 마련한 지침을 따라야 했다.

Exercises

본문 152～153쪽

01

정답 ④

소재 언어마다 다른 공간 개념에 대한 인식

해석 공간(즉, 사건과 사물이 발생하고 상대적인 방향과 위치를 갖는 3차원 영역)에 대한 개념이 보편적이라는 일부 가정은 재검토되고 있다. Stephen Levinson은 '공간을 추정하고 설명하는 체계는 실제로 문화마다 꽤 다를 수 있고, 언어적 차이는 뚜렷이 다른 인지적 성향과 서로 연관되어 있다'는 것을 보여 주었다. 보다 구체적으로 말하면, 언어는 공간 개념의 사용에 있어 각기 다르고, 어떤 경우에는 공간 개념과 관련된 인지 범주를 결정하기도 하며, 또한 많은 언어의 사용자들은 전후좌우의 신체 좌표에 해당하는 공간 용어를 사용하지 않는다. 한 가지 예로 멕시코의 Tenejapa Tzeltal 족을 들 수 있는데, 그들의 언어는 어떤 상대적 준거틀도 사용하지 않으므로 '왼쪽', '오른쪽', '앞', 그리고 '뒤'에 해당할 공간 준거를 위한 어떤 용어도 없다. '왼손'과 '오른손'에 대한 용어는 존재하지만, 그것들은 신체의 다른 부분이나 그것(신체)의 외부 영역으로 확장되지는 않는다.

Solution Guide

공간 개념은 보편적이지 않고, 언어가 공간 개념과 관련된 인지 범주를 결정할 정도로 여러 언어에 걸친 공간 개념의 인식이 다르다는 내용의 글이다. 따라서 글의 주제로 가장 적절한 것은 ④ '언어에 따른 공간 개념 인식의 다양성'이다.
① 문화가 비즈니스 의사소통에 미치는 영향
② 시간과 공간 개념에 대한 보편적인 인식
③ 공간과 관련된 비언어적 신호의 문화적 차이
⑤ 언어의 한계를 넘어서는 온라인 의사소통의 본질

Structure in Focus

- Some assumptions [that notions of space (that is, a three-dimensional area {in which events and objects occur and have relative direction and position}) are universal] — are being reexamined.
  [ ]는 Some assumptions와 동격 관계이고, 그 안의 { }는 a three-dimensional area를 수식하는 관계절이다.
- More specifically, languages [vary in their use of spatial concepts] and, [in some instances, determine the cognitive categories relating to space concepts]; also, the speakers of a number of languages do not use spatial terms [corresponding to the bodily coordinates of left-right and front-back].
  첫 번째와 두 번째 [ ]는 and로 연결되어 문장의 술어 역할을 한다. 세 번째 [ ]는 spatial terms를 수식하는 분사구이다.

02

정답 ③

소재 언어의 보편성

해석 언어는 이전에 생각되던 것보다 훨씬 더 유사하며, 그 보편성은 인간의 뇌가 특정 방식으로 세상을 이해하도록 설계되어 있고, 이는 아마도 현실의 구조와도 부합할 것임을 보여 준다. 따라서 모든 언어에는 명사와 동사, 수식어(부사와 형용사), 이름과 대명사가 있다. 언어는 문장 내 단어의 순서에서 차이가 있을 수 있지만(예를 들어, 동사가 중간에 오는지 아니면 끝에 오는지처럼), 문장은 항상 사용된다. (따라서 특정 공동체에 속한 개인은 그 공동체의 언어 습관을 따르지 않을 수도 있다.) 심지어 단어의 순서도 가능한 만큼 크게 다르지 않은데, Steven Pinker는 문장 주성분의 순서는 128가지가 가능하지만, 대부분 언어는 그러한 가능성의 단 두 가지 중 하나만 사용한다고 말한다. 결정적으로, 대부분 언어는 거의 동일한 개념 목록을 가지고 있는 듯 보이고, 그 결과 거의 모든 단어와 문장은 한 언어에서 다른 언어로 효과적으로 번역될 수 있다.

Solution Guide

언어에는 보편성이 존재한다는 내용의 글이므로, 개인이 자신이 속한 공동체의 언어 습관을 따르지 않을 수도 있다는 내용의 ③은 글의 전체 흐름과 관계가 없다.

Structure in Focus

- Languages are far more similar than had previously been thought, and that universality suggests [that the human brain is designed to understand the world in certain ways, {which may also correspond to the structure of reality}].
  [ ]는 suggests의 목적어 역할을 하는 명사절이고, 그 안의 { }는 앞 절의 내용을 부가적으로 설명하는 관계절이다.
- Even the sequence of words does not vary as widely as it **could**: Steven Pinker says [that {there are 128 possible orderings of the main parts of a sentence}, but {most languages use one of only two of those possibilities}].
  could 다음에는 vary가 생략되었다. [ ]는 says의 목적어 역할을 하는 명사절이고, 그 안에서 두 개의 { }는 but으로 연결되어 있다.

03

정답 ②

소재 작품 양식과 비평

해석 몇몇 명인들은 비평가들의 주목하려는 동기를 바꾸기 위해 자신들의 작품 양식을 능숙하게 다룬다. Richard Posner는 Shakespeare, Nietzsche, Wittgenstein과 Kafka에 대하여 모호하고, 어쩌면 심지어 모순되는 그들 글의 본질 덕분에 명성의 일부를 얻은 인물들이라고 언급한다. 불명확한 작가들은 최소한 실체와 깊이가 있는 경우, 비평가들로부터 더 많은 주목을 받고 더 많은 텍스트 해석을 요구한다. 개별 비평가들은 그러한 작가를 연구하고 그 작가의 작품에 대한 한 가지 해석을 다른 해석보다 더 승격시킴으로써 자신의 명성을 확립할 수 있다. 바로 이들 비평가는 자기가 한 비평의 중요성을 증진하기 위해 그 작가를 주요 문헌 목록에 포함하는 것을 지지할 것이다. 사실, 심오하고도 모호한 작가들은 비평가들에게 더 폭이 넓은 작품의 공동 저자의 역할을 해 달라고 암묵적인 초청을 제안하는 것이다. 비평가들은 이러한 작품들을 더욱 면밀히 검토하고 자신들의 명성을 더욱 널리 폄으로써 응답한다.

Solution Guide

심오하고도 모호한 작가들은 비평가들이 자신들의 작품을 해석할 동기를 부여하고, 비평가들은 이 작가의 작품에 대한 자신의 해석과 작품 두 가지를 모두 지지하게 되는 상호 작용이 일어나 비평가들에 의한 더 많은 텍스트 해석과 면밀한 검토가 이루어지게 된다는 내용의 글이다. 따라서 빈칸에 들어갈 말로 가장 적절한 것은 ②이다.

① 더 나은 텍스트의 분석을 위해 독자를 무시해 달라고
③ 그들의 주장으로부터 역설적인 요점을 제외해 달라고
④ 자신들의 글쓰기 양식을 고전적인 작가와 비교해 달라고
⑤ 작가들이 서로의 양식을 베끼는 방식에 대한 비판에 협조해 달라고

Structure in Focus

- Richard Posner cites Shakespeare, Nietzsche, Wittgenstein, and Kafka as figures [who owe part of their reputation to {the puzzling and perhaps even contradictory nature of their writings}].
  [ ]는 figures를 수식하는 관계절이고, 그 안의 { }는 전치사 to의 목적어 역할을 하는 명사구이다.
- These same critics will support the inclusion of the writer in the canon, [to promote the importance of their own criticism].
  [ ]는 목적을 나타내는 to부정사구이다.

28 컴퓨터, 인터넷, 정보, 미디어, 교통

Gateway ④
Exercises 01 ⑤ 02 ④ 03 ④

Gateway

본문 154쪽

정답 ④

소재 소프트웨어 복잡성 증가의 영향

해석 컴퓨터 소프트웨어 복잡성의 증가는 전 세계의 안전과 보안에 직접적인 영향을 주는데, 우리가 의존하는 물리적 대상, 즉 자동차, 비행기, 교량, 터널, 이식형 의료 기기와 같은 것들이 컴퓨터 코드로 변해감에 따라 특히 그렇다. (C) 물리적 사물은 점점 더 정보 기술이 되어 가고 있다. 자동차는 '우리가 타는 컴퓨터'이고, 비행기는 '수많은 산업 제어 시스템에 부착된 비행 솔라리스(컴퓨터 운영 체계의 일종) 박스'에 불과하다. (A) 이러한 코드 전체가 크기와 복잡성이 증가함에 따라, 오류와 소프트웨어 버그 수 또한 증가한다. Carnegie Mellon 대학교의 연구에 따르면, 상용 소프트웨어에는 코드의 보통 매 1,000줄마다 20~30개의 버그가 있어서, 5천만 줄의 코드는 100만~150만 개의 잠재적 오류가 부당하게 활용될 수 있다는 것을 의미한다. (B) 이것이 코드가 원래 하도록 의도되지 않았던 것을 하도록 이 컴퓨터 버그를 이용하는 모든 악성 소프트웨어 공격의 근간이다. 컴퓨터 코드가 더 정교해짐에 따라, 소프트웨어 버그는 창궐하고 보안은 악화되어, 사회 전반에 미치는 영향이 커진다.

Solution Guide

컴퓨터 소프트웨어 복잡성의 증가는 우리가 의존하는 물리적 대상이 컴퓨터 코드로 변해감에 따라 전 세계의 안전과 보안에 직접적인 영향을 준다는 내용의 주어진 글 다음에는 자동차와 비행기를 예로 제시하면서 부연하는 내용의 (C)가 와야 한다. 그다음에는 앞서 언급한 코드에 어떤 문제점이 있는지를 제시하는 내용의 (A)가 오고, 마지막으로 (A)의 마지막 부분에 언급된 점을 This로 지칭하면서 그것이 모든 악성 소프트웨어 공격의 근간이라는 점을 설명하는 내용의 (B)가 와야 한다. 따라서 주어진 글 다음에 이어질 글의 순서로 가장 적절한 것은 ④이다.

Structure in Focus

- The growing complexity of computer software has direct implications for our global safety and security, particularly [as {the physical objects upon which we depend — things like cars, airplanes, bridges, tunnels, and implantable medical devices —} **transform**

themselves into computer code].
[ ]는 시간을 나타내는 부사절이고, 그 안의 { }는 부사절의 주어인 명사구이며, 술어동사는 transform이다.

- [As all this code grows in size and complexity], so too **do** the number of errors and software bugs.
[ ]는 추이를 나타내는 부사절이며, do는 grow in size and complexity를 대신한다.

Quick Review

본문 155쪽

1. currently / 그 용의자는 현재 경찰의 심문을 받고 있다.
2. optimize / 그 선수는 자신의 경기력을 최적화하기 위해 엄격한 훈련 프로그램을 따랐다.
3. statement / 그 과학자는 연구의 결과를 확인하는 진술을 발표했다.
4. transition / 정부는 재생 가능한 에너지원으로 전환하기 위해 노력하고 있다.
5. automated / 그 공장은 고도로 자동화되어 있으며 로봇이 대부분의 작업을 수행한다.

Exercises

본문 156~157쪽

01

정답 ⑤

소재 데이터와 알고리즘에 의한 편향된 정보

해석 데이터의 급증은 정보를 보도하는 것과 소비하는 것 모두에서 많은 어려움을 수반한다. 소셜 네트워크 자체는 그 구성원에 의해 편향되어 있는데, 그들은 전체 인구 집단을 결코 정확히 반영하지 못한다. 특정 민족이 과도하게 대표되는데, 그것은 균형추로서의 소셜 뉴스에 있어 상당한 어려움이다. 게다가 점점 증가하는 알고리즘이 사람들에게 어떤 내용을 읽도록 추천할지에 대한 자동화된 결정을 내린다. 알고리즘은 인기 뉴스 목록이나 인기 트렌드를 생성하고 독자를 위한 맞춤형 추천을 제공하고 있다. 알고리즘은 중립적이라는 인상을 주지만, 그렇지 않다. 알고리즘은 인간의 창조물이다. 알고리즘은 설계자의 정치적 선택을 부호화하고 문화적 가치를 내재하게 한다. 자동화된 시스템에 의해 (데이터의) 선정, 조직 및 제시의 힘이 강화되기 때문에 우리는 작동하고 있는 편견을 알아야 한다. 아마도 더 중요하게는, 우리는 제품 엔지니어와 설계자가 단순히 트래픽 증가가 아니라 원하는 결과, 즉 대중에게 정보를 제공하려는 일을 최적화하는 노력을 보장하기 위해 힘써야 한다.

Solution Guide

소셜 네트워크는 전체 인구 집단을 정확히 반영하지 못하고, 알고리즘은 설계자의 정치적 선택을 부호화하고 문화적 가치가 내재화된 자료를 선정 및 제시하므로, 설계자와 엔지니어가 대중에게 정보를 제공하려는 일을 최적화하는 노력을 보장하도록 노력하는 것이 중요하다는 내용이다. 그러므로 글의 주제로 가장 적절한 것은 ⑤ '데이터, 알고리즘, 알고리즘 생산자에 의한 편향 인식의 중요성'이다.

① 소셜 네트워크의 데이터 양에 반영된 불평등
② 문화적으로 편향된 알고리즘에 의해 생성된 가짜 뉴스의 위험
③ 개인적인 필요를 위한 뉴스 선정에서 알고리즘의 커지는 역할
④ 뉴스 알고리즘에 의해 전통적인 매체가 위협받는 최근의 추세

Structure in Focus

- In addition, a growing number of algorithms make automated decisions on [which content to recommend for people to read].
[ ]는 전치사 on의 목적어 역할을 하는 명사절이다.
- Perhaps more important, we should work to make sure [product engineers and designers are seeking to optimize {the wanted outcome — an informed public —} not just {heightened traffic}].
[ ]는 make sure의 목적어 역할을 하는 명사절이고, 그 안의 두 개의 { }는 optimize의 목적어 역할을 하는 명사구이다.

02

정답 ④

소재 인간의 정보망에의 종속

해석 우리는 그 단어의 아날로그적인 또는 실제 의미에 있어서 다른 사물이나 사람과 '진정으로' 연결되지 않은 채 얼마나 많은 시간을 보내고 있을까? 많지 않다. 우리는 우리의 기억, 환상, 그리고 의식을 클라우드에 업로드하기 위해 참을성 있게 기다리는 동안, 우리 자신을 전화기에 끊임없이 붙어 있는, 스마트 워치와 AI 보조 장치로부터의 추가적인 센서를 갖춘 인간 웨어러블 기기로 변화시켰다. 비교적 짧은 기간 안에 우리는 인터넷에서 사물인터넷으로, 그리고 이제는 우리 몸을 지각이 있는 거대한 디지털 네트워크 일부로, 우리 존재 전체를 우리의 스마트 TV와 냉장고의 지위로 격하된 것으로 보는 개념인 '인간 인터넷'으로 빠르게 전환했다. 우리 자아가 우리를 타인과 그리고 세상과 연결하는 수많은 기기 속에 캡처된 우리 평판의 디지털 파편으로 거의 격하되었기 때문에 '우리는 아무도 제대로 이해하지 못하는 거대한 데이터 처리 시스템 내부의 작은 칩이 되어 가고 있다'는 Yuval Harari의 주장에 반박하기 어렵다.

Solution Guide

우리는 여러 디지털 기기와 인공 지능 기술로 인해 일종의 인간 웨어러블 기기로 변화되었고, 다른 사람이나 기기와 연결되어 많은 시간을 보내게 되었고, 우리의 자아는 수많은 기기 속에 캡처된 평판의 디지털 파편으로 거의 격하되었다는 내용이므로, 빈칸에 들어갈 말로 가장 적절한 것은 ④이다.

① 디지털 네트워크의 작동자 수준으로 높여진
② 디지털 정보의 원천으로 유의미하기를 멈춘
③ 우월한 정보 처리 기기보다 더욱 빨리 잊혀진
⑤ 소셜 미디어에 제시된 우리의 평판과 분리된

Structure in Focus

- We have turned ourselves into human wearables, [attached to our phones nonstop, with additional sensors {from our smart watches and AI assistant devices}], [while we patiently await to upload our memories, fantasies, and consciousness to the cloud].
  첫 번째 [ ]는 human wearables를 부가적으로 설명하는 분사구이고, 그 안의 { }는 from이 이끄는 전치사구로 additional sensors를 수식한다. 두 번째 [ ]는 시간을 나타내는 부사절이다.
- [Since our selves have been largely reduced to the digital fragments of our reputation {captured in the many devices 〈that connect us to others and the world〉}], it is hard to disagree with Yuval Harari's argument [that "we are becoming tiny chips inside a giant data-processing system {that nobody really understands}]."
  첫 번째 [ ]는 이유를 나타내는 부사절이고, 그 안의 { }는 the digital fragments of our reputation을 수식하는 분사구이며, 그 안의 〈 〉는 the many devices를 수식하는 관계절이다. 두 번째 [ ]는 Yuval Harari's argument와 동격 관계이고, 그 안의 { }는 a giant data-processing system을 수식하는 관계절이다.

03

정답 ④

소재 인터넷의 발전으로 인한 정보 편식 해소

해석 인터넷은 여러분 자신을 정보 버블에 가두어 자신의 견해를 뒷받침하는 사실만을 보도록 해 준다는 생각에 많은 경고(불안감)와 손떨림(걱정)이 있어 왔다. (C) 나는 이런 일이 일어난다고 확신하지만, 다른 가능성을 기억하는 것이 우리에게 도움이 될 것이다. 예를 들어 1980년에 여러분은 지역 신문과 세 개의 네트워크 뉴스 프로그램 중 선택된 하나로부터 매일 그날 분의 정보를 얻었는데, 그 뉴스 프로그램은 한 시간 동안 진행되었고, 모두 같은 기본적인 기사를 다루었다. (A) 사정은 그러했다. 우리는 모두 극소수의 견해에 갇혀 있었다. 인터넷은 모든 진술에 대해 사실 확인을 할 수 있게 하고 모든 거짓에 대해 이의를 제기할 수 있게 한다. 여러분이 알고 싶은 것은 어떤 것이나 몇 번 자판 키를 누르고 몇 번 클릭만 하면 얻을 수 있다. (B) 매초 10만 건이 훨씬 넘는 웹 검색이 수행되며, 근본적으로 그것의 각각은 현재 모르는 어떤 것을 알고자 하는 한 사람을 나타낸다. 그것은 지식의 위대한 민주화이며, 이는 의심할 여지가 없이 좋은 일이다.

Solution Guide

인터넷은 정보 버블에 우리 스스로를 가둘 수 있다는 우려를 자아낼 수 있다는 내용의 주어진 글 다음에 (C)에서 this로 주어진 글을 받아, 이러한 일이 일어날 수 있지만, 좋은 대안도 있다고 언급하며 1980년대의 제한된 정보원을 제시하고 (A)에서 We were ~ people.로 (C)의 내용을 언급한 다음, 지금은 정보를 구하기 매우 쉬워진 점을 강조한 다음 (B)에서 Well over ~로 그 내용을 다시 언급하고, 그것은 지식의 민주화이며 좋은 일이라고 마무리해야 글의 흐름이 자연스럽게 연결될 수 있다.

Structure in Focus

- Much alarm and handwringing have occurred over the idea [that the Internet allows you **to** {lock yourself in an information bubble} and {see only facts that support your views}].
  [ ]는 the idea와 동격 관계이다. 두 개의 { }는 and로 연결되어 to에 이어져 allows의 목적격 보어 역할을 한다.
- Well over 100,000 web searches are performed each second, and at their heart, they each represent a person [who wants to know something {they don't currently know}].
  [ ]는 a person을 수식하는 관계절이고, 그 안의 { }는 something을 수식하는 관계절이다.

29 심리, 대인 관계

Gateway ③
Exercises 01 ⑤ 02 ③ 03 ④

Gateway

본문 158쪽

정답 ③

소재 자산으로서의 스트레스 반응

해석 스트레스 반응을 자산으로 보는 것은 두려움이라는 생리 기능을 용기라는 생명 작용으로 바꿀 수 있다. 그것은 위험을 도전으로 바꿀 수 있고, 여러분이 압박을 받으면서 최선을 다하도록 도울 수 있다. 불안감의 경우에서처럼 스트레스가 도움이 되지 않는다고 느껴질 때조차도, 그것을 기꺼이 받아들이는 것은 그것을 도움이 되는 것, 즉, 더 많은 에너지, 더 많은 자신감, 그리고 더 기꺼이 행동을 취하려는 마음으로 바꿀 수 있다. 여러분은 스트레스의 징후를 알아차릴 때마다 이 전략을 여러분 자신의 삶에 적용할 수 있다. 여러분의 심장이 고동치거나 호흡이 빨라지는 것을 느끼게 되면, 그것은 여러분에게 더 많은 에너지를 주려고 하는 여러분의 몸의 방식이라는 것을 깨달으라. 여러분이 몸에서 긴장감을 감지한다면, 그 스트레스 반응이 여러분에게 여러분의 힘을 이용할 기회를 준다는 점을 자신에게 상기시키라. 손바닥에 땀이 나는가? 첫 데이트에 나갈 때 어떤 기분이었는지를 기억하라. 즉, 여러분이 원하는 것에 아주 가까이 있을 때 손바닥에 땀이 나는 것이다.

Solution Guide

③ When이 이끄는 부사절에 이어지는 주절에서 that절을 목적어로 취하는 술어동사가 필요하므로 realizing을 realize로 고쳐야 한다.
① help의 목적격 보어로 쓰인 do는 어법상 적절하다.
② 의미상 the stress를 가리키는 대명사 it은 어법상 적절하다.
④ remind의 직접목적어인 명사절을 이끄는 접속사 that은 어법상 적절하다.
⑤ 형식상의 주어 it에 대응하는 내용상의 주어를 이끄는 to go는 어법상 적절하다.

Structure in Focus

- [Viewing the stress response as a resource] can transform the physiology of fear into the biology of courage.
  [ ]는 문장의 주어 역할을 하는 동명사구이다.

Quick Review

본문 159쪽

1. identity / 여러분의 정체성은 여러분의 경험, 믿음, 가치로 구성된다.
2. drain / 그녀의 업무의 요구는 그녀의 개인 생활에서 소모를 유발하고 있다.
3. absurd / 달이 치즈로 만들어졌다는 주장은 터무니없다.
4. potential / 그 연구는 치명적인 질병을 치료할 수 있는 잠재력을 가지고 있다.
5. indifferent / 그 아이는 새 장난감에 무관심했기 때문에 그의 부모는 실망했다.

Exercises

본문 160～161쪽

01

정답 ⑤

소재 성장을 위한 취약성의 필요성

해석 유감스럽게도, 나이를 먹어 감에 따라, 우리는 변화를 피함으로써 취약성을 피하는 경향이 있어서 우리의 학습 기회는 줄어들고 새로운 학습이 느려진다. 오랜 친구와 재회했을 때 우리는 그 친구가 어떻게 지냈는지 이야기를 듣다가 우리가 오래 전에 버렸던 오래된 신념을 그 친구가 여전히 붙잡고 있는 것을 발견한 경험이 모두 있을 것이다. 아마 그 친구는 오랫동안 자신을 취약한 개방성의 상태에 놓아두지 않았을 것이다. 개인적인 성장은 새로운 행동, 태도, 믿음을 시도해 보는 것을 포함한다. 뭔가를 시도해 보는 것은 우리가 실패와 조롱에 취약하게 만든다. 학습할 때, 우리는 실수를 저지르고 멍청하고, 심지어는 터무니없어 보이기도 한다. 누가 그것을 좋아하는가? 결과가 불확실할지라도, 삶에서 위험을 무릅쓰려는, 즉 새로운 경험이나 도전이나 활동을 해 보려는 자발성은 그렇게 하는 동안 취약한 상태에 있는 것을 필요로 한다. 개방적인 태도를 가지는 것은 우리가 의도적으로 해야 하는 그러한 활동 중 하나인데, 이는 우리가 그것이 수반하는 취약성을 태생적으로 피하는 경향이 있기 때문이다.

Solution Guide

우리는 나이를 먹어 감에 따라 변화를 피하여 취약성을 피하려고 하며, 이것은 학습과 성장을 가로막는다는 내용의 글이므로, 글의 제목으로 가장 적절한 것은 ⑤ '취약성 거부하기: 일생에 걸친 배움과 성장의 장벽'이다.
① 나이가 들수록 실패가 더욱 뼈아픈 이유
② 다른 사람에 대해 기분이 나쁠 때 자신을 돌아보라
③ 불확실성으로 뛰어들기: 아이디어를 입증할 방법
④ 좋은 오랜 친구: 새로운 관계로 가는 믿을 만한 다리

Structure in Focus

- [Willingness {to take chances in life}, {to try new experiences, challenges or activities — even though the outcome is unsure — }] **demands** being vulnerable while doing so.
  [ ]는 문장의 주어인 명사구이고, 술어동사는 demands이다. 두 개의 { }는 Willingness의 구체적 내용을 설명하는 to부정사구이다.
- Open-mindedness is one of those activities [that we must do deliberately], because we are naturally inclined to avoid the vulnerability [**it** entails].
  첫 번째 [ ]는 those activities를 수식하는 관계절이고, 두 번째 [ ]는 the vulnerability를 수식하는 관계절이다. it은 Open-mindedness를 대신한다.

02

정답 ③

소재 기대가 아이들의 행동에 미치는 영향

해석 기대는 아이들의 행동에 영향을 미친다. Richard Miller와 동료들은 세 교실에서 쓰레기의 양을 관찰한 후, 교사와 여러 다른 사람들이 한 학급에 깔끔하고 정돈되어 있어야 한다고 반복해서 말하도록 했다. 이러한 설득은 쓰레기통에 버려지는 쓰레기의 양을 15퍼센트에서 45퍼센트로 증가시켰지만, 단지 일시적으로만이었다. 다른 학급 역시 쓰레기의 15퍼센트만 쓰레기통에 넣었지만, 그들은 매우 깔끔하고 정돈되어 있다는 칭찬을 반복해서 들었다. 이 말을 8일 동안 들은 후에, 그리고 2주 후에도 여전히 이 아이들은 자신들의 쓰레기의 80퍼센트가 넘는 것을 쓰레기통에 넣으며 기대에 부응하고 있었다. 아이들에게 (게으르고 못됐다기보다) 근면하고 친절하다고 말하면, 아이들은 그 칭호에 부응하도록 행동할 수도 있다. 정체성을 자아와 연결하는 것이 중요한데, '도움 주는 이'가 되라는 요청을 받은 아이들은 '도와주라'고 요청받은 아이들보다 추후의 과업에서 도움을 베풀 가능성이 더 높았다. 자신이 정돈되고 도움이 된다고 생각하면, 아이들은 정돈되고 도움이 되는 사람이 된다.

Solution Guide

③ 문장의 주어는 Another class이고, 이와 연결되는 술어동사가 필요하므로, 분사인 being을 was로 고쳐야 한다.

① 사역동사 had의 목적격 보어를 이끌고 있으므로 원형부정사인 tell은 적절하다.

② 동사 increased를 수식하므로 부사 temporarily는 적절하다.

④ Children을 수식하는 관계절을 이끌며, 관계절에서 주어 역할을 하므로 관계대명사 who는 적절하다.

⑤ think of의 동작 주체와 대상이 모두 children이므로 동작 대상을 themselves로 쓰는 것은 적절하다.

Structure in Focus

- After observing the amount of litter in three classrooms, Richard Miller and colleagues had the teacher and others repeatedly [tell one class {that they should be neat and tidy}].
  [ ]는 had의 목적격 보어 역할을 하는 원형부정사구이고, 그 안의 { }는 tell의 직접목적어 역할을 하는 명사절이다.
- Tying the identity to the self is important: [Children {who were asked to be "a helper"}] **were** more likely to help in later tasks than those asked to "help."
  [ ]는 콜론 뒤에 오는 절의 주어이고, 술어동사는 were이다. { }는 Children을 수식하는 관계절이다.

03

정답 ④

소재 관계의 관리

해석 관계에서 균형을 유지하는 데 많은 노력이 필요하다면 굳이 중간 지점을 목표로 삼을 이유가 있을까? 관계의 멋진 점은 적절히 유지하면 전체가 부분의 합보다 더 커진다는 것이다. 이상적으로, 두 구성원 모두는 팀의 잠재력을 실현할 뿐 아니라 개인으로서 자신의 잠재력을 실현하도록 지원받는다. 상황이 잘못되면 회복할 수 없을 정도로 손상된 관계로 인해 엄청난 에너지가 소모되어 전체가 부분의 합보다 더 작아질 수 있다는 것을 또한 의미할 수도 있다. 공동의 예금 계좌에서처럼 자원을 한데 모으는 것은 자원을 최적으로 크도록 한다. 그러나 만일 한 사람은 예치하기만 하고 다른 사람은 인출하기만 하면, 수표는 부도 처리되기 시작할 것이다. 이와 비슷하게, 만일 관계에서 한 사람만 (관계) 유지를 수행하고 다른 한 사람은 무관심하다면, 그들의 공동 계좌도 또한 결국 자금이 불충분해질 것이다. 초과 인출 보호 장치가 일상적 필수품은 충당할 수도 있겠지만, 어떤 큰 일이 닥칠 때는 도움이 되지 않을 것이다.

Culture Note

- **bounce(수표가 부도 처리되다)** 발행된 수표가 예금 부족 등의 이유로 지급이 이루어지지 않은 것을 의미한다.
- **overdraft protection(초과 인출 보호 장치)** 지불할 만큼의 금액이 계좌에 없을 때, 승인된 한도 내에서 보유한 계좌 금액보다 더 인출될 수 있도록 돕는 장치이다.

Solution Guide

관계에서 균형의 유지가 필요함을 다룬 글로, 주어진 문장을 ④에 넣으면, 공동의 예금 계좌에서처럼 자원을 한데 모으는 것은 자원을 최적으로 크도록 만들게 되지만, 주어진 문장의 내용처럼 한 사람은 예치하기만 하고, 다른 사람은 인출하기만 하면 수표는 부도 처리되기 시작한다는 글의 흐름이 된다. ④ 뒤의 문장에서 Similarly로 이어 앞선 내용과 비슷한 상황이 관계에서도 일어날 수 있음을 언급해야 글의 흐름이 자연스럽게 연결될 수 있다. 따라서 주어진 문장이 들어가기에 가장 적절한 곳은 ④이다.

Structure in Focus

- [The wonderful thing about relationships] is [that with the proper maintenance, the whole is greater than the sum of its parts].
  첫 번째 [ ]는 문장의 주어 역할을 하는 명사구이고, 두 번째 [ ]는 is의 주격 보어 역할을 하는 명사절이다.
- If things go sour, [the tremendous energy drain of an irreparably damaged relationship] can also mean [that the whole is less than the sum of its parts].
  첫 번째 [ ]는 문장의 주어 역할을 하는 명사구이고, 두 번째 [ ]는 mean의 목적어 역할을 하는 명사절이다.

30 정치, 경제, 사회, 법

Gateway ④
Exercises 01 ① 02 ① 03 ③

Gateway

본문 162쪽

정답 ④

소재 패션 산업에서 '장소'가 갖는 가치의 중요성

해석 '장소'의 가치는 왜 그렇게 중요한가? 역사적 관점에서 볼 때, 1700년대까지 직물 생산은 특정한 지리적 지역 내에서 구할 수 있는 섬유, 예를 들면, 면, 양모, 실크, 아마 섬유를 사용하는 수작업 공정이었다. 지역 간 무역은 이들 섬유 및 섬유로 만들어진 관련 직물의 입수 가능성을 증가시켰다. 1차 산업혁명과 뒤이은 제조 섬유에서의 기술 발달은 섬유와 직물이 더 이상 '장소에 얽매이지' 않게 되었다는 사실을 더했다. 제품이 어디서, 어떻게, 또는 누구에 의해 만들어졌는지에 대해 거의 또는 전혀 관련되지 않고, 패션 업체는 직물 및 직물로 만들어진 제품을 창출했고 소비자는 그것들을 얻을 수 있었다. 이것은 소비자와 그들이 매일 사용하는 제품 간의 단절, 이들 제품을 만드는 데 필요한 기술과 자원에 대한 이해와 올바른 인식의 상실, 그리고 이와 연관된, 제품 창출에 필요한 인간과 천연자원에 대한 경시를 저지했다(→ 초래했다). 따라서 '장소'의 가치를 새롭게 하는 것은 회사와 소비자를 특정한 장소의 사람, 지리, 그리고 문화와 다시 연결한다.

Solution Guide

지역 간 무역, 1차 산업혁명, 제조 섬유에서의 기술 발달로 섬유와 직물이 더 이상 장소에 얽매이지 않게 되자, 소비자는 더 이상 섬유나 직물 제품의 제조 장소, 제조법, 제조자에 관한 관련성을 갖지 못하게 되어 소비자는 자신이 사용하는 제품과 단절되었다는 내용의 글이다. 소비자는 제품 생산에 필요한 기술과 자원을 제대로 이해하지 못하게 되었다고 했으므로, 제품 창출에 필요한 인간과 천연자원을 올바로 인식하지 못하고 경시하게 되었을 것이다. 따라서 ④ countered(저지했다)를 resulted in(초래했다)과 같은 낱말로 바꾸어야 한다.

Structure in Focus

- [The First Industrial Revolution] and [subsequent technological advancements in manufactured fibers] added to the fact [that fibers and textiles were no longer "place-bound]."
  첫 번째와 두 번째 [ ]는 and로 연결되어 문장의 주어 역할을 하는 명사구이고, 세 번째 [ ]는 the fact와 동격 관계이다.

■ This resulted in [a disconnect between consumers and the products {they use on a daily basis}], [a loss of understanding and appreciation in the skills and resources {necessary to create these products}], and [an associated disregard for the human and natural resources {necessary for the products' creation}].
세 개의 [ ]는 and로 연결되어 resulted in의 목적어 역할을 하는 명사구이다. 첫 번째 [ ] 안의 { }는 the products를 수식하는 관계절이고, 두 번째와 세 번째 [ ] 안의 { }는 각각 the skills and resources와 the human and natural resources를 수식하는 형용사구이다.

Quick Review

본문 163쪽

1. ownership / 예술가는 원작의 소유권을 보유했지만 대중이 즐길 수 있도록 제한된 복제를 허용했다.
2. promote / 정부는 재생 가능한 에너지원을 장려하는 정책을 도입하여, 화석 연료에 대한 의존도를 낮추는 것을 목표로 했다.
3. inspector / 품질 관리 검사관은 제품 수준을 유지하기 위해 제조 결함을 찾아내고 처리했다.
4. financial / 사람들은 미래 목표를 위한 예산 편성, 저축, 투자를 포함하는 재정 계획을 세우도록 권고받는다.
5. regulate / 시의회는 비닐봉지 사용을 규제하는 법을 통과시키고 환경에 미치는 영향을 줄이기 위해 노력했다.

Exercises

본문 164~165쪽

01

정답 ①

소재 인간의 창조물인 색깔

해석 '색깔'을 뜻하는 고대 이집트 용어는 *iwn*이었는데, 그것은 또한 '피부', '본성', '성격' 그리고 '존재'를 뜻하는 단어였으며, 부분적으로는 인간의 머리카락을 나타내는 상형 문자로 표현되었다. 그 문명의 구성원들은 색깔과 인간 간의 놀라운 유사성을 알아차렸다. 그들에게 색깔은 인간과 마찬가지로 생명력, 에너지, 힘, 개성이 가득한 존재였다. 이제 우리는, 이집트인들은 그저 느낄 수만 있었지만, 이 둘이 얼마나 밀접하게 관련되어 있는지 알고 있다. 어쨌든 간에 색깔은 결국 그것을 지각하는 사람에 의해 만들어진다. 우리가 우리 주변에서 보는 모든 색조는 실제로 우리 안에서, 다시 말해, 언어를 만들고, 기억을 저장하고, 감정을 불러일으키고, 생각을 형성하고, 의식을 불러일으키는 동일한 두뇌에서 만들어진다. 색깔은 우리가 온 세상에 칠하는 우리의 상상의 빛깔이다. (색깔은) 그 어떤 도시보다 더 크고, 그 어떤 기계보다 더 정교하며, 그 어떤 그림보다 더 아름다운데, 그것은 사실상 인간이 만든 가장 위대한 창조물일 수도 있다.

Solution Guide

고대 이집트인이 알아차린 것처럼 색깔과 인간이 생명력, 에너지, 힘, 개성이 가득한 존재라는 점에서 유사하고 서로 밀접하게 관련되어 있으며, 결국 색깔을 지각하는 인간에 의해 색깔이라는 창조물이 나왔다는 내용의 글이다. 따라서 글의 제목으로 가장 적절한 것은 ① '색깔이라는 씨앗: 인간 안에 심어짐'이다.
② 생생함: 화가를 위한 영감의 원천
③ 개성을 나타내는 지표로서의 색깔 선호도
④ 이집트 문명에서 색깔은 어떤 역할을 했는가?
⑤ 비슷하지만 다른: 다양한 문화권의 색상 상징주의

Structure in Focus

■ We now understand, as the Egyptians could only sense, [how thoroughly the two are connected].
[ ]는 understand와 sense의 목적어 역할을 하는 명사절이다.

■ Every hue [we see around us] is actually manufactured within us — in the same grey matter [that forms language, stores memories, triggers emotions, shapes thoughts and gives rise to consciousness].
첫 번째 [ ]는 Every hue를 수식하는 관계절이고, 두 번째 [ ]는 the same grey matter를 수식하는 관계절이다.

02

정답 ①

소재 Bentham의 팬옵티콘

해석 대중 감시의 사회적 이점을 장려한 18세기 공리주의 철학자 Bentham은 팬옵티콘, 즉 감시당하는 사람이 죄수든, 노동자든, 환자든, 학생이든, 그들을 외벽을 따라 줄지어 있는 감방이나 방에 배치하는 원형 건물을 설계했다. 한 '감시자'가 그 원형 건물 중앙에 있는 부스(칸막이를 한 작은 공간)에 앉아 있고, 감시당하고 있는 사람에게는 보이지 않지만, (감시자는) 그들을 볼 수 있었다. Bentham에 따르면, 비록 이 감시자가 건물에 있는 모든 사람을 매 순간 관찰하지 못할 수도 있지만, 자신이 감시될 수도 있다는 사실을 아는 것만으로도 수감자가 바르게 행동하도록 만들고 노동자와 학생을 과업에 집중시키기에 충분할 것이었다. 팬옵티콘의 물리적 설계는 비현실적이라고 판명되었지만, 사생활을 없앰으로써 행동이 규제될 수 있다는 생각은 계속 이어졌다. 우리의 길거리에도 있고 공공의 공간과 사적 공간 내에도 있는 폐쇄

회로 TV는 그 최초의 건축물 팬옵티콘의 현대적이고, 영리하며, 더 실용적인 버전 2.0(중요한 두 번째 버전)이다.

Solution Guide

Bentham이 주장한 대중 감시 건물 팬옵티콘에 관한 글이다. 팬옵티콘 중앙에 있는 감시자는 실제로 팬옵티콘에 있는 모든 사람을 매 순간 감시하지 못할 수도 있지만, 그 사람들은 자신들이 감시될 수 있다는 사실을 알기에 함부로 행동하지 못한다. 팬옵티콘이 행동을 규제하는 이러한 방법은 계속 남아 있고, 이를 반영한 현대적 팬옵티콘의 사례로 길거리와 공공의 공간 및 사적 공간에 설치된 폐쇄 회로 TV가 제시되고 있다. 따라서 빈칸에 들어갈 말로 가장 적절한 것은 ①이다.

② 법적 강제력을 행사함
③ 재정적 인센티브를 제공함
④ 사람들이 서로를 지켜보도록 만듦
⑤ 건축의 실용성을 개선함

Structure in Focus

▪ Bentham, the eighteenth-century utilitarian philosopher [who promoted the social benefits of mass surveillance], designed a panopticon, a circular building [where those {to be observed}, whether prisoners, workers, patients, or students, were placed in cells or rooms {lined along an outside wall}].
첫 번째 [ ]는 the eighteenth-century utilitarian philosopher를 수식하는 관계절이다. 두 번째 [ ]는 a circular building을 수식하는 관계절이고, 그 안의 첫 번째 { }는 those를 수식하는 to부정사구이며, 두 번째 { }는 cells or rooms를 수식하는 분사구이다.

▪ According to Bentham, even though this inspector could not observe every resident at every moment, [simply knowing {that they could be seen}] would be enough to make prisoners behave and keep workers and students on task.
[ ]는 주절의 주어 역할을 하는 동명사구이고, 그 안의 { }는 knowing의 목적어 역할을 하는 명사절이다.

03

정답 ③

소재 공유 경제

해석 최근 몇 년간 소비자의 가치 인식 변화와 기술의 발전으로 인해 소비 방식이 소유에서 이용으로 변화하고 있다. 유형과 무형 자원을 무제한 이용할 수 있게 한 온라인 플랫폼의 등장으로 소비자의 마음에서 소유는 그 가치를 상실했다. 소비자는 자원의 이용이 소유보다 위험과 관련이 더 적다고 생각하는데, 예를 들어 그들은 상품을 무료나 유료로 이용할 때보다 상품을 구매할 때 잠재하는 재정적, 사회적 손실이 더 크다고 생각한다. (그러나, 대다수의 소비자는 실제 매장에 가서 한정된 상품 재고와 강요하려 드는 판매 직원을 마주하는 것보다 집이나 사무실에서 편안하게 자신의 휴대 전화나 태블릿으로 온라인 쇼핑을 하는 것을 선호한다.) 이러한 모든 새로운 변화와 믿음은 개인이 온라인 네트워크를 통해 자신의 자원을 다른 사람과 공유하고 협력적 소비문화를 촉진하는 '공유 경제'라는 공유 관행을 만들어 냈다. 다양한 분야에서 나타나는 공유 경제 관행이 매우 인기를 끌면서 전통적인 기업들을 와해시키기 시작했다.

Solution Guide

최근의 소비 방식이 소유에서 이용으로 변하면서 공유 경제라는 관행을 만들어 냈고, 이러한 새로운 변화 속에서 개인은 상품을 구매하는 것이 공유를 통해 상품을 이용하는 것보다 재정적, 사회적 손실이 더 크다고 여겨 자신의 자원을 다른 사람과 공유하는 새로운 소비 문화를 만들어 냈다는 것이 글의 요지이므로, 소비자가 실제 매장에서 쇼핑하는 것보다 온라인 쇼핑을 선호한다는 내용을 언급하고 있는 ③은 글의 전체 흐름과 관계가 없다.

Structure in Focus

▪ All these new changes and beliefs have created a sharing practice [named "sharing economy" {in which individuals share their resources with others through online networks and promote the culture of collaborative consumption}].
[ ]는 a sharing practice를 수식하는 분사구이고, 그 안의 { }는 "sharing economy"를 수식하는 관계절이다.

▪ Sharing economy practices, [which are seen in different sectors], have become very popular and started to disrupt traditional businesses.
[ ]는 Sharing economy practices를 부가적으로 설명하는 관계절이다.

31 의학, 건강, 영양, 식품

Gateway ⑤
Exercises 01 ⑤ 02 ② 03 ④

Gateway

본문 166쪽

정답 ⑤

소재 진화에서 잠이 하는 역할

해석 진화에서 잠이 하는 역할은 여전히 연구 중이다. 한 가지 가능성은, 더 이상 긴급한 활동이 없을 때는 그것(잠)이 동물에게 줄어든 신진대사의 유리한 적응 상태라는 것이다. 먹을 것이 거의 없고 적정한 체온을 유지하는 데 높은 신진대사 비용이 드는 겨울철의 겨울잠과 같은 더 깊은 비활동 상태의 경우에 이것은 사실인 것 같다. 그것은 또한 일상 상황에서도, 가령 어두워진 이후에 포식자를 피하려는 먹잇감 종의 경우에 사실일 수도 있다. 다른 한편으로는, 잠의 분명한 보편성, 그리고 고래목의 동물들과 같은 포유동물들이 적어도 한 번에 한쪽 뇌에서는 잠을 유지하는 매우 복잡한 기제를 발전시켰다는 관찰 결과는 잠이 생물체에게 생명 유지에 필수적인 어떤 도움(들)을 추가로 제공한다는 것을 보여 준다. 잠의 한 가지 측면이 환경에 대한 줄어든 반응성이기 때문에 이것은 특히 사실이다. 이러한 잠재적인 대가가 치러져야 할 때조차도 잠이 보편적이라면, 그 함의는 그것(잠)이 단지 조용하고, 깨어 있는 휴식만으로는 얻을 수 없는 중요한 기능을 갖고 있다는 것일 수도 있다.

Solution Guide

잠의 보편성으로 미루어 보아 주어진 문장에서 언급한 환경에 대한 줄어든 반응성이 잠으로 인해 치러야 할 대가이므로, 주어진 문장 앞에는 그런 대가가 있기 때문에 잠이 그 대가를 상쇄하는 기능이 있다는 내용이 있어야 하고, 주어진 문장 다음에는 치러야 할 대가가 있음에도 잠을 자는 것의 함의를 설명하는 내용이 와야 한다. 따라서 주어진 문장이 들어가기에 가장 적절한 곳은 ⑤이다.

Structure in Focus

- This seems true for deeper states of inactivity such as hibernation during the winter [when there are few food supplies, and a high metabolic cost to maintaining adequate temperature].
  [ ]는 deeper states of inactivity such as hibernation during the winter를 수식하는 관계절이다.
- On the other hand, the apparent universality of sleep, and the observation [that mammals such as cetaceans have developed such highly complex mechanisms to preserve sleep on at least one side of the brain at a time], suggests [that sleep additionally provides some vital service(s) for the organism].
  첫 번째 [ ]는 the observation과 동격 관계이고, 두 번째 [ ]는 suggests의 목적어 역할을 하는 명사절이다.

Quick Review

본문 167쪽

1. disorder / 그녀는 섭식 장애를 앓고 있다.
2. genetic / 검은 눈과 머리카락은 한국인의 유전적 특징이다.
3. nutrition / 이 음식은 여러분이 필요한 모든 영양을 공급할 것이다.
4. abuse / 그는 알코올 남용에 대한 치료법을 찾고 있었다.
5. adverse / 현대식 농법은 환경에 부정적인 영향을 미칠 수 있다.

Exercises

본문 168~169쪽

01

정답 ⑤

소재 환자의 감정적 영역에 대한 임상의의 관심

해석 숙련된 임상의는 질환과 치료법에 대한 자신의 지식에 자부심을 느낀다. 해부학 및 생리학, 약리학, 그리고 최신의 증거 기반의 획기적 연구들에 대해 폭넓은 지식을 갖는 것은 만족할 만한 치료를 제공하는 데 매우 중요하다. 하지만 그에 못지않게 중요한 것은 질병이 환자의 감정에 어떻게 영향을 미칠 수 있는지에 대한 지식이다. 또한 개인마다 차이가 있을 여지가 분명히 있지만, 전형적인 감정의 반응은 흔히 예상할 수 있다. 질병의 양상 및 단계에 수반하는 통상적인 감정을 이해하는 것은 임상의가 환자에 대한 진단과 치료 계획에 감정의 영역을 포함하는 방법에 대해 생각할 수 있게 해 준다. 이해하고 수용하는 입장에서 환자의 감정을 다루는 것은 임상의가 환자의 요구를 가장 잘 만족시키는 방식으로 능숙하게 감정을 다룰 수 있게 해 준다.

Solution Guide

임상의는 질환과 치료법에 대한 폭넓은 지식을 갖는 것도 중요하지만, 환자 진단과 치료 계획에 있어 감정적인 영역도 포함하는 것이 중요하다는 내용의 글이다. 따라서 필자가 주장하는 바로 가장 적절한 것은 ⑤이다.

Structure in Focus

- But **just as important** is [the knowledge of how illness can impact patient emotions].
  형용사구인 just as important가 문두에 오면서 동사 is가 주어인 [ ] 앞에 놓이는 어순이 되었다.
- [Working with patients' emotions, {from a place of understanding and acceptance}], allows the clinician to skillfully address the emotions in a manner [that best serves the patients' needs].
  첫 번째 [ ]는 문장의 주어인 동명사구이고, 그 안의 { }는 from이 이끄는 전치사구이다. 두 번째 [ ]는 a manner를 수식하는 관계절이다.

02

정답 ②

소재 질환에 대해 지나치게 광범위한 개념화를 하려는 경향

해석 의료 사회학에서 질환은, 질병이나 병과 비교하여, 한 개인 안의 생리적 기능 장애로 이루어진 좋지 않은 신체 상태로 간주된다. 실제의 업무에서, 질환이라는 용어는 그 정의에 정확히 부합하지 않는 매우 다양한 신체의 문제에 다소 자유롭게 적용된다. 더 논란이 많은 영역 중 하나는 정신적 질병과 관련이 있다. 대다수는 아닐지라도, 많은 정신적 장애가 위의 정의에 따라 질환으로 간주되지 않을 것이라고 주장될 수 있다. 다양한 경우에 '질환'으로 인정되었던 다른 신체의 문제에 대해서도 마찬가지라고 말할 수 있다. 예로는 알코올 중독과 약물 남용이 포함된다. 이러한 신체의 문제는 필수적인 명백한 병 증상과 기저 생물학적 건강 이상이 반드시 있는 것은 아니다. 그럼에도 불구하고 그것들은 마치 질환인 것처럼 취급되는 경우가 빈번하다. 이에 대한 한 가지 설명은 분명한데, 어떤 신체의 문제가 의료 제도에 의해 치료되려면 그것이 질환으로 인정되어야 한다는 것이다. 따라서 질환에 대해 지나치게 광범위한 개념화를 하려는 경향이 있다.

Solution Guide

질환이라는 용어가 정신적 질병의 예를 통해 알 수 있듯이, 의료 사회학에서 말하는 정의에 정확히 부합하지 않는 다양한 신체의 문제에 적용되어 온 경향이 있다는 내용의 글이다. 따라서 빈칸에 들어갈 말로 가장 적절한 것은 ②이다.

① 질환의 원인을 사회 문제로 돌림
③ 정신적 질병과 육체 질병의 구별
④ 의학에서의 학문적 업적에 대한 강조
⑤ 질환의 매우 복잡한 과정을 지나치게 단순화하는 것

Structure in Focus

- In medical sociology, a disease is considered an adverse physical state [consisting of a physiological dysfunction within an individual], as compared to illness or sickness.
  [ ]는 an adverse physical state를 수식하는 분사구이다.
- In actual practice, the term disease is applied rather liberally to [a wide variety of conditions {that do not precisely fit the definition}].
  [ ]는 전치사 to의 목적어 역할을 하는 명사구이고, 그 안의 { }는 a wide variety of conditions를 수식하는 관계절이다.

03

정답 ④

소재 지적 발전에 미치는 영양 및 건강의 영향

해석 지난 100년에 걸친 10년당 약 3점의 지능 지수 점수의 세계적인 상승은 지적 발전에 대한 잠재력을 여실히 보여 준다. 지능 지수 점수에서의 이러한 상승은 플린 효과로 알려져 있는데, 유전적 변화를 의미하기에는 너무 빠르게 일어났다. (C) 영양 및 기타 건강 요인의 개선이 아마도 그 변화의 일부를 설명할 것이다. 세계 보건 기구의 정보를 사용하여, 연구원들은 한 국가가 심각한 감염성 질병이 없는 것과 그 국가 시민들의 평균 지능 지수 점수 사이에 강력한 상관관계가 있음을 확인했다. (A) 국가가 더 부유해지고 질병과 싸우는 능력이 더 높아질수록, 그곳 시민들의 지능 지수 점수도 높아진다. 놀랍게도 그러한 검사 점수 향상은 레이븐 지능 검사 같은 문화가 배제된 것으로 추정되는 검사에서 가장 두드러진다. (B) 1990년 이후에 태어난 참가자들이 이러한 검사에서 1940년에 태어난 참가자들이 얻은 것보다 훨씬 더 좋은 점수를 얻었다. 이러한 변화는 현대 사회에서 살아가는 데 수반되는, 상이한 항목들을 관리하는 능력이 향상되었음을 반영하는 것일지도 모른다.

Culture Note

- **Flynn Effect(플린 효과)** 이전 세대보다 다음 세대의 평균 지능 지수(IQ)가 높아지는 현상으로, 뉴질랜드 통계학 교수 James Flynn이 발견하였다.
- **Raven's Progressive Matrices(레이븐 지능 검사)** 보통 교육 환경에서 사용되는 비언어적 그룹 테스트로서, 일반적으로 추상적 추론을 측정하는 데 사용되며 지능의 비언어적 추정으로 여겨지는 60개 항목으로 이루어진 테스트이다.

Solution Guide

지난 100년에 걸친 세계적인 지능 지수 점수의 상승은 유전적 변화의 결과로 볼 수 없다는 내용의 주어진 글 다음에는, 그러한 변화의 이유를 영양과 건강 요인으로 설명할 수 있다는 내용의

(C)가 이어져야 한다. 그다음에는 영양과 건강 요인이 지능 지수 상승에 미치는 영향을 구체적으로 언급하는 (A)가 이어지고, (A)의 supposed culture-free tests를 these tests로 대신하면서 점수 향상 이유를 분석하는 내용의 (B)로 이어지는 것이 글의 순서로 가장 적절하다.

Structure in Focus

- This increase in IQ scores, [known as the Flynn effect], has occurred far too quickly to represent genetic changes.
  [ ]는 This increase in IQ scores를 부가적으로 설명하는 분사구이다.
- This change might reflect [an improvement in the ability {to manage dissimilar items}] [that accompanies living in a modern society].
  두 번째 [ ]는 첫 번째 [ ]를 수식하는 관계절이고, 첫 번째 [ ] 안의 { }는 the ability의 구체적인 내용을 설명하는 to부정사구이다.

TEST 1

본문 172~191쪽

01 ⑤	02 ⑤	03 ③	04 ②	05 ④	06 ⑤	07 ②
08 ②	09 ⑤	10 ④	11 ④	12 ⑤	13 ⑤	14 ③
15 ④	16 ①	17 ⑤	18 ④	19 ②	20 ③	21 ②
22 ④	23 ③	24 ①	25 ⑤	26 ④	27 ⑤	28 ②

01

정답 ⑤

소재 업무 생산성 향상을 위한 작업 계획 수립 요청

해석 발신: FootCraft 신발 공장 수석 매니저 Michael Jones
수신: 시스템 관리팀장 Eric Donovan
현재 우리는 빠르게 발전하는 시장 환경에서 우리의 경쟁 우위를 유지하는 도전에 직면해 있습니다. 따라서 경영진과 저는 귀하가 이 도전을 다룰 방법을 모색해 주셨으면 합니다. 구체적으로, 우리는 향후 3개월 동안 귀하의 업무 그룹 내에서 관리 생산성을 25퍼센트 향상할 방법을 찾고 있습니다. 먼저 귀하의 팀과 만나 이 과제에 대해 논의해 주시기를 바랍니다. 논의 후에 귀하는 어떻게 진행할지에 대한 생각의 밑그림을 그리고 작업 계획을 만들어야 합니다. 저는 2주 후에 귀하의 계획을 보고 그것을 귀하와 함께 검토하고 싶습니다. 이것은 우리 부서와 회사에 매우 중요한 과제입니다. 경영진과 저는 귀하가 고안하는 혁신적인 해결책을 보기를 고대합니다. 귀하의 공헌은 우리의 성공에 매우 귀중합니다. 감사합니다.

Solution Guide

변화하는 시장 환경에서 경쟁력을 유지하기 위해 관리 생산성을 25퍼센트 향상할 방법을 찾고 있으며, 이를 위해 작업 계획을 만들어 달라고 요청하고 있으므로, 글의 목적으로 가장 적절한 것은 ⑤이다.

Structure in Focus

- We are currently facing the challenge of [maintaining our competitive edge in the rapidly evolving market environment].
  [ ]는 전치사 of의 목적어 역할을 하는 동명사구로, the challenge의 내용을 구체적으로 제시한다.
- Following the discussion, you should [outline your thoughts on {how to proceed}] and [create a work plan].
  두 개의 [ ]는 and로 연결되어 조동사 should에 이어져 문장의 술어 역할을 한다. 첫 번째 [ ] 안의 { }는 전치사 on의 목적어 역할을 한다.

02

정답 ⑤

소재 팔찌를 사게 된 Kira

해석 Kira는 인형을 가지고 놀다가 어떤 목소리가 노래 부르는 것을 들었다. "'츄리', '츄리', 꼬마 소녀들아, 와서 보거라." Kira는 창문으로 달려가 머리에 바구니를 인 팔찌 판매상을 보았다. 그는 Kira를 보고 "오너라, 꼬마 소녀야, 와서 '츄리' 좀 사 가렴."이라고 말했다. 그녀는 츄리를 몇 개 사고 싶었지만, 어머니가 지역 시장에 가셔서 그녀에게 돈을 줄 사람이 없었기 때문에 그럴 수 없었다. Kira는 팔찌를 살 수 없다는 생각에 의기소침했다. Kira가 팔찌 판매상에게 자신의 상황을 말하자, 그는 "어쨌든 와서 골라 보렴. 돈은 다른 날 받을게."라고 말했다. Kira는 잠시 생각한 후에 내려갔다. 팔찌 판매상은 "얘야, 어떤 색이 제일 마음에 드니?"라고 물었다. Kira는 "주황색이요."라고 말하며 팔찌를 몇 개 골랐다. 그때쯤 Kira의 어머니가 시장에서 돌아와 팔찌 판매상과 몇 마디 이야기를 나눈 뒤 팔찌 값을 지불했다. Kira는 너무 기뻤다. 팔찌가 서로 부딪히는 소리가 그녀에게 마치 음악처럼 들렸다. Kira는 콧노래를 흥얼거리며 자기 방으로 돌아갔다.

Solution Guide

Kira는 어머니가 지역 시장에 가셔서 그녀에게 돈을 줄 사람이 없었기 때문에 츄리를 살 수 없어서 실망했다가, 팔찌 판매상의 말대로 몇 개 고르는 동안 어머니가 시장에서 돌아와 판매자와 몇 마디 이야기를 나눈 뒤 팔찌 값을 지불하여 너무 기뻤다는 내용의 글이다. 따라서 Kira의 심경 변화로 가장 적절한 것은 ⑤ '실망한 → 매우 기쁜'이다.

① 지루해하는 → 궁금한
② 고마워하는 → 화난
③ 질투심을 느끼는 → 후회하는
④ 깜짝 놀란 → 안도하는

Structure in Focus

- Kira [ran to the window] and [saw a bangle seller with a basket on his head].
  두 개의 [ ]는 and로 연결되어 문장의 술어 역할을 한다.
- By then, Kira's mother [returned from the market] and [had a few words with the seller before paying for the bangles].
  두 개의 [ ]는 and로 연결되어 문장의 술어 역할을 한다.

03

정답 ③

소재 생태계 서비스의 상품화

해석 몇몇 경제학자에 의해 생태계 서비스를 상품화하려는 노력이 있어 왔는데, 생태계 서비스는 인간이 자연 생태계로부터 얻는 혜택과 자원을 가리킨다. 온실가스 폐기물 흡수 능력과 같이 일부 생태계 서비스는 경합성이 있으므로 배급이 필요하다. 배급을 가능하게 하려면 예를 들어 경매 가능한 배출권을 통한 배제성을 갖는 재산권이 필요하다. 배기가스를 흡수 능력에 한정해서 공평하게 배분한다면 상품화는 지속 가능하고 공정할 수 있다. 그러나 많은 생태계 서비스는 본질적으로 비배제성과 비경합성을 가지므로, 상품화할 수도 없고, 상품화해서도 안 된다. 그것들은 또한 무시되어서도 안 된다. 공공 서비스는 인류 공동체의 모든 구성원에게 도움이 되며, 경제학자들은 이러한 서비스가 상품화 및 시장을 통한 배분에 적합하지 않다는 점을 인식하고 있다. 생태계 서비스는 자연이 인간에게 주는 혜택으로 정의되어서는 안 되고, 오히려 단지 인간뿐만 아니라 생물 군집의 모든 구성원에게 혜택을 주는 기금 서비스로 정의되어야 한다. 일반적으로 생태계 서비스는 공공 서비스보다 상품화에 훨씬 더 적합하지 않다.

Solution Guide

몇몇 경제학자에 의해 생태계 서비스를 상품화하려는 노력이 있어 왔지만, 생태계 서비스는 인간뿐만 아니라 생물 군집의 모든 구성원을 위한 것이므로 상품화해서는 안 된다는 것이 글의 중심 내용이므로, 글의 요지로 가장 적절한 것은 ③이다.

Structure in Focus

- Public services serve all members of the human community; economists recognize [that these services are ill-suited to {commodification} and {market allocation}].
  [ ]는 recognize의 목적어 역할을 하는 명사절이고, 그 안에서 두 개의 { }는 and에 의해 연결되어 to에 이어진다.
- Ecosystem services should **not** be defined as nature's benefits to people, **but** rather as fund-services [that benefit all members of the biotic community, not simply humans].
  '~이 아니라 …'이라는 의미의 「not ~ but ...」이 쓰였다. [ ]는 fund-services를 수식하는 관계절이다.

04

정답 ②

소재 감정에 대처하는 방법

해석 우리의 감정이 우리의 '일부'이지만 우리 존재의 '전부'는 아니라고 생각한다면, 우리의 감정은 더 다루기 쉽다고 느껴질 수 있다. 이러한 생각은 여러분은 푸른 하늘이고 여러분의 감정은 날씨라는 이 은유에 잘 담겨 있다. 여러분이 푸른 하늘이고 여러분의 감정이 날씨라면, 최악의 허리케인이나 토네이도도 푸른 하늘을 해칠 수 없으며 그것이 결국 끝나는 것처럼, 여러분의 감정도 여러분을 해칠 수 없고, 그것도 결국 지나갈 것이다. 때때로 우리는 그저 폭풍이 끝나기를 기다려야 한다. 그것은 토네이도나 폭풍우를 겪어내는 것이 재미있다는 것을 의미하는가? 물론 아니다! 비가 오고 폭풍우가 몰아칠 때에 비해 날씨가 화창하고 화씨 80도일 때 여러분의 삶을 사는 것이 더 편할까? 물론이다! 하지만 날씨가 내가 할 수 있는 일을 결정하게 둔다면, 나는 영원히 내가 통제할 수 없는 무언가에 휘둘리게 될 것이다. 우리가 할 일은 우리의 감정에 대처하기 위해 건강하지 못한 습관적 행위를 하지 않아도 되고 우리에게 중요한 일을 계속할 수 있도록, 감정을 위한 공간을 마련하는 것, 푸른 하늘이 되는 것이다.

Solution Guide

우리 자신을 푸른 하늘, 우리의 감정을 날씨라고 비유했을 때, 허리케인이나 토네이도가 푸른 하늘을 해치지 않고 결국 끝나는 것처럼 우리의 감정 역시 우리를 해칠 수 없고 결국 지나갈 것이므로, 감정을 우리 존재의 일부로만 받아들여 그것에 휘둘려서는 안 된다는 내용의 글이다. 따라서 필자가 주장하는 바로 가장 적절한 것은 ②이다.

Structure in Focus

- Does that mean [**it**'s fun {to live through a tornado or a rainstorm}]?
  [ ]는 mean의 목적어 역할을 하는 명사절이다. it은 형식상의 주어이고, { }는 내용상의 주어이다.
- But if I let the weather determine [what I can get done], I'll forever be at the mercy of something [I can't control].
  첫 번째 [ ]는 determine의 목적어 역할을 하는 명사절이고, 두 번째 [ ]는 something을 수식하는 관계절이다.

05

정답 ④

소재 인종 간 차이에 대한 증거의 부재

해석 기억력에 관한 강의에서 나는 학생들에게 단어 목록을 기억해 보라고 한다. 그것은 '꿈', '침대'와 같은 단어를 포함한다. 그런 다음 나는 학생들에게 기억나는 단어를 적어 보라고 한다. 항상 그들은 내가 '잠'이라는 단어를 말한 적이 없는데도 '잠'이라는 단어를 들었다고 (잘못) 기억한다. 동일한 의미망에 있는 다른 단어들, 즉 끊임없는 반복을 통해 잠과 연관된 단어들도 또한 활성화되었기 때문에 '잠'이라는 개념이 뇌에서 활성화된다. '잠'이라는 단어가 그것이 마치 실제로 '들린' 것처럼 회상된다. 사람들이 '침대'를 들으면 그들은 '잠'을 들을 수밖에 없다. 사람들이 '유전자'

또는 '지능'을 들으면 그들은 '인종'을 들을 수밖에 없다. 따라서 이 주제를 처음 접하는 독자라면 유전학이 교육과 같은 결과에서 인종 간 차이를 설명한다는 증거가 전혀 없다는 것을 알고 놀랄 것이다. 현재는, 현대 산업화 경제에서 사회 불평등과 관련된 복잡한 인간 특성, 즉 끈기, 성실성, 창의성, 추상적 추론과 같은 특성에서의, 유전적 뿌리를 둔 인종 간 차이에 관한 이야기가 바로 그것이다. 그것들은 꾸며 낸 말이다.

Solution Guide

침대라는 단어를 들으면 잠이라는 개념이 뇌에서 활성화되는 것과 마찬가지로 유전자나 지능이라는 단어를 들으면 인종을 떠올리지만, 유전학이 인종 간 차이를 설명한다는 증거가 전혀 없다고 했으므로, 밑줄 친 부분이 의미하는 바로 가장 적절한 것은 ④ '인간의 특성에 관한 사람들의 인종적 편견은 유전적 근거가 없다.'이다.

① 사람들은 인종 간 평등에 관련된 이야기를 좋아한다.
② 동일한 의미망에 있는 단어들이 더 쉽게 활성화된다.
③ 사람들은 꿈과 사회 정의에 관한 이야기를 만드는 것을 즐긴다.
⑤ 인종과 관련된 단어들은 사람들 사이에 정서적 반응을 촉발한다.

Structure in Focus

- The idea of "sleep" is activated in the brain [because {other words in the same semantic network}, {words ⟨that have been associated with sleep through constant repetition⟩}, have also been activated].
  [ ]는 because로 유도되는 부사절이고, 그 안의 두 개의 { }는 동격 관계이다. 두 번째 { } 안의 ⟨ ⟩는 words를 수식하는 관계절이다.
- A reader [new to this topic] might therefore be surprised to learn [that there is zero evidence {that genetics explains racial differences in outcomes like education}].
  첫 번째 [ ]는 주어인 A reader를 수식하는 형용사구이다. 두 번째 [ ]는 learn의 목적어 역할을 하는 명사절이고, 그 안의 { }는 evidence와 동격 관계이다.

06

정답 ⑤

소재 수학적 모델과 생물학적 사실

해석 문제를 단순화하는 것은 그것을 수학적인 분석이 가능하도록 하는 것이므로, 불가피하게 일부 생물학적 세부 사항은 현실 세계에서 방정식으로 변환되는 중에 소실될 수밖에 없다. 그 결과, 수학을 사용하는 사람들은 그러한 세부 사항에 너무나 무관심하다고 자주 비판받는다. (현대 신경 과학의 아버지인) Santiago Ramón y Cajal은 자신의 1897년 책인 *Advice for a Young Investigator*에서 '의지의 질병'이라는 제목의 장에 이러한 현실 회피형의 이론가들에 관해 써 놓았다. 그는 그들의 증상을 '설명의 재능, 창의적이고 끊임 없는 상상력, 실험실에 대한 혐오감, 그리고 형이하학과 중요하지 않아 보이는 데이터에 대한 불굴의 반감'이라고 확인했다. Cajal은 또한 이론가가 사실보다 아름다움을 선호하는 것에 대해 불평했다. 생물학자들은 특정 형질과 어떤 규칙에도 있는 미묘한 예외가 풍부한 생물을 연구한다. 단순성, 우아함, 그리고 사물을 처리하기 쉽게 만들려는 욕구에 이끌리는 수학자들은 그 풍부함을 방정식으로 옮기면서 그것을 묵살한다.

Solution Guide

수학적 모델은 단순성, 우아함, 사물을 처리하기 쉽게 만드는 것을 추구하며, 수학자들은 이러한 욕구에 의해 움직이므로, 수학적 모델로의 변환은 생물학적인 풍부함을 잃는 결과로 이어질 수 있다는 내용이므로, 글의 주제로 가장 적절한 것은 ⑤ '생물학의 풍부함을 단순화하는 것에 대한 수학자를 향한 비판'이다.

① 수학적 모델에 의해 설명될 수 있는 생물학적인 패턴
② 생물학자와 수학자 사이의 역사적 갈등
③ 추상화하는 학문으로서의 수학에 대한 오해
④ 생물학 연구에서 이례적인 발견의 커지는 중요성

Structure in Focus

- He identified their symptoms as '[a facility for exposition], [a creative and restless imagination], [an aversion to the laboratory], and [an indomitable dislike for concrete science and seemingly unimportant data]'.
  네 개의 [ ]는 and로 연결되어 전치사 as의 목적어 역할을 하는 명사구이다.
- Biologists study living things [that are abundant with {specific traits} and {subtle exceptions to any rule}].
  [ ]는 living things를 수식하는 관계절이고, 그 안의 두 개의 { }는 and로 연결되어 with의 목적어 역할을 하는 명사구이다.

07

정답 ②

소재 인간 규범의 본질

해석 규범을 따를 때 인간이 하고 있는 행동과 다른 동물들이 관련된 행동 양식에서 하고 있는 행동을 구분하는 것이 중요하다. 싸우지 않기로 결정하는 동물은 대부분의 경우 단순히 다칠 위험

에 대해 걱정하는 것이지, 어떤 추상적인 '폭력에 반대하는 규범'에 대해 걱정하는 것이 아니다. 마찬가지로, 자신의 집단 밖의 동물과 먹이를 공유하는 동물은 일반적으로 단지 미래의 호혜를 얻으려 하고 있는 것이지, 어떤 '먹이 공유의 규범'을 따르고 있는 것이 아니다. 진정한 규범을 둘러싼 동기는 더 복잡하다. 우리가 '잘못된' 일을 할 때, 우리는 부당한 취급을 받은 당사자뿐만 아니라 제삼자로부터의 질책에 대해서도 걱정해야 한다. 흔히 이것은 우리 지역 집단의 (당사자를 제외한) 나머지 전체 또는 적어도 그것의 대다수를 의미한다. 덩치가 크고 힘이 센 Albert는 약한 Bob의 물건을 당사자인 Bob으로부터의 성가신 일을 걱정하지 않고 쉽게 훔칠 수 있지만, 인간 집단에서 Albert는 그럴 경우 공동체의 나머지 구성원이 내리는 처벌에 직면할 것이다. 따라서 '집단적 강제'는 규범의 본질이다. 이것이 바로 수렵 채집인 생활 방식에서 매우 특징적인 평등주의적 정치 질서를 가능하게 하는 것이다.

Solution Guide

동물과는 달리 인간은 잘못된 일을 할 때 부당한 취급을 받은 당사자뿐만 아니라 제삼자로부터의 질책에 대해서도 걱정해야 하며 집단적 강제가 인간 규범의 본질이라는 것이 글의 중심 내용이므로, 글의 제목으로 가장 적절한 것은 ② '사회적 압력: 인간이 규범을 따르는 이유'이다.

① 동물이 다른 동물과 먹이를 공유하게 하는 것
③ 집단의 크기가 사회적 규범의 발달에 영향을 미친다
④ 사회적 규범과 개인의 사고가 연관되어 있는 방식
⑤ 건강한 공동체를 위한 진정한 규범 확립의 어려움

Structure in Focus

- Likewise, an animal [that shares food with animals outside of its group] is typically just trying to get future reciprocity — not following some "norm of food-sharing."
  [ ]는 an animal을 수식하는 관계절이다.
- When we do something "wrong," we have to worry about reprisal **not just** [from the wronged party] **but also** [from third parties].
  두 개의 [ ]는 '~뿐 아니라 …도'라는 의미의 「not just ~ but also ...」로 연결되어 있다.

08

정답 ②

소재 Geoffrey Hinton의 신경망 연구

해석 Geoffrey Hinton은 1947년 잉글랜드에서 태어났다. 그는 신경망에 대한 자신의 커지는 관심을 탐구하고 싶어서 Cambridge 대학교에서 학부생으로 심리학을 공부하기로 했다. 그러나 그는 자신의 교수들이 신경 세포가 어떻게 학습하는지 또는 계산하는지를 실제로 이해하지 못한다는 것을 금방 깨달았다. 당시의 과학이 전기 신호가 하나의 신경 세포에서 또 다른 신경 세포로 전달되는 방식은 설명할 수 있었지만, 이런 수십억 개의 상호 작용에서 지능이 출현하는 것에 대한 설득력 있는 설명을 Hinton에게 제시할 수 있는 사람은 아무도 없었다. 그는 성장하는 인공 신경망 분야의 도구를 사용하면 뇌의 작동 방식을 더 잘 이해할 수 있다고 확신했고, 그래서 그는 이어서 1972년에 Edinburgh 대학교에서 인공 지능 박사 과정을 밟았다. 이후 연구에서 그는 인간의 뇌가 연결된 신경 세포의 촘촘한 그물망 곳곳에 정보를 퍼뜨리는 것처럼, 하드웨어와 소프트웨어를 사용하여 상호 연결된 정보의 층을 만들려고 했다. 경력 내내 Hinton은 Carnegie Mellon 대학교 및 Toronto 대학교를 포함하여 다양한 기관에서 근무했다.

Solution Guide

수십억 개의 신경 세포의 상호 작용을 통해 지능이 출현하는 것에 대한 설득력 있는 설명을 Hinton에게 제시할 수 있는 사람이 아무도 없었다고 했으므로, Geoffrey Hinton에 관한 글의 내용과 일치하지 않는 것은 ②이다.

Structure in Focus

- He quickly realized, however, [that his professors didn't actually understand {how neurons learned or computed}].
  [ ]는 realized의 목적어 역할을 하는 명사절이고, 그 안의 { }는 understand의 목적어 역할을 하는 명사절이다.
- While the science of the day could explain the mechanics of [electrical signals traveling from one neuron to another], no one could offer Hinton a compelling explanation for the emergence of intelligence from these billions of interactions.
  [ ]는 전치사 of의 목적어 역할을 하는 동명사구이고, electrical signals는 동명사 traveling의 의미상의 주어 역할을 한다.

09

정답 ⑤

소재 전 세계 플러그인 차량 판매량

해석 위 도표는 2020년 2월부터 2022년 12월까지 전 세계 플러그인 차량 판매량을 2개월 간격으로 나타낸 것이다. 3년 모두에서, 판매량은 2월에 가장 적었고 12월에 가장 많았다. 2020년의 같은 달과 비교했을 때 2021년의 각 달은 10만 대가 넘는 증가를 보였다. 2020년에는 6월에 전 세계 플러그인 차량의 판매량은 20만 대가 넘도록 증가했으며, 12월에 판매량은 약 60만 대에 도달했다. 2021년에는 전 세계 플러그인 차량 판매는 6월에 60만 대가 넘었다가 8월에 60만 대 미만으로 감소했지만, 그 후에 10월에는 60만 대가 넘도록 증가했다. 2022년에는 8월에 6월보다 판매량이 감소했지만, 10월에는 판매량이 증가하여 100만 대가 넘었다.

Solution Guide

2022년 8월의 판매량은 6월보다 적었다가 10월에는 약 94만 대로 증가했고, 100만 대에는 미치지 못했다. 따라서 도표의 내용과 일치하지 않는 것은 ⑤이다.

Structure in Focus

- The above graph shows global plug-in vehicle sales from February 2020 to December 2022, [represented by two-month intervals].
  [ ]는 global plug-in vehicle sales from February 2020 to December 2022를 부가적으로 설명하는 분사구이다.

10

정답 ④

소재 2024 파이썬 기초 캠프

해석

2024 파이썬 기초 캠프

11세~19세

파이썬을 이용하여 소프트웨어 개발, 애니메이션, 게임의 기초를 배워 보세요!

10시간 동안 진행되는 이 캠프에서 아이들은 다음을 배우게 됩니다:

- 21세기를 위한 상위 10대 STEM 기술 중 하나인 파이썬 문법 프로그래밍
- Turtle Race, Hangman 등과 같은 애니메이션과 게임을 만드는 법

세부 정보

- 학급당 최대 8명의 학생
- 캠프 참가비: 410달러(노트북 대여 포함) / 350달러(노트북 대여 미포함)
- 시간: 월, 수, 목, 금 매일 오후 1시 30분부터 오후 4시까지(화요일은 수업 없음)
- 시작 날짜: 3월 18일부터 4월 15일까지 매주 월요일
- 참가비는 환불되지 않습니다. 캠프 기간 중 자녀가 아플 경우 진료 기록을 제출해 주시면 대체 수업을 준비해 드리겠습니다.

Solution Guide

수업은 월, 수, 목, 금요일에 있고 화요일은 수업이 없다고 했으므로, ④는 안내문의 내용과 일치하지 않는다.

Structure in Focus

- [Python syntax programming], [one of the top 10 STEM skills for the 21st century]
  두 개의 [ ]는 동격 관계이다.

11

정답 ④

소재 2024 Forest Park 연례 도보 투어

해석

2024 Forest Park 연례 도보 투어

올해의 Forest Park 도보 투어는 10월 19일 토요일 오후 2시에 있습니다. 그것은 Albanios 역사 학회가 후원합니다. 그러니 운동화를 신고 나와 Forest Park의 역사와 전설에 대해 알아보세요!

도보 투어 정보:

- 예약이 필요합니다. 314-586-4023으로 역사 학회에 전화하거나 메시지를 남겨 예약을 할 수 있습니다.
- Forest Park는 오후 12시에 문을 열고, 주차는 공원 밖에 할 수 있습니다.
- Pinewoods Avenue나 인근의 다른 도로에는 주차가 금지됩니다.
- 이 행사는 무료이지만 Albanios Historical Society Forest Park 복원 프로젝트를 위해 어떤 액수의 기부금이든 환영합니다.

악천후 시에는 행사 당일 오후 1시에 Albanios Historical Society 웹사이트를 확인하여 행사 개최 여부를 알아보세요.

Solution Guide

행사는 무료이지만 Albanios Historical Society Forest Park 복원 프로젝트를 위해 어떤 액수의 기부금이든 환영한다고 했으므로, 안내문의 내용과 일치하는 것은 ④이다.

Structure in Focus

- In the event of bad weather, please check the Albanios Historical Society's website at 1:00 p.m. on the day of the event to know [if the event will be held or not].
  [ ]는 know의 목적어 역할을 하는 명사절이다.

12

정답 ⑤

소재 우주 이주의 난제

해석 진화론적 관점에서 볼 때, 우리 종(구체적으로 말하면, 우

리의 유전적 후손)의 지속을 보장하는 것은 생의 의미이자 목적이다. 그러나 생명 작용이 아닌 도덕성에 기반해 결정을 내릴 수 있는 지적인 동물로서, 우리는 우리의 게놈을 보존하는 것이 어떤 대가라도 치를 가치가 있는지에 대해 질문할 수 있다. 개개의 인간은 다른 인간이나 심지어 인간이 아닌 동물의 생명을 구하기 위해 자신의 생명을 희생하는 선택을 할 수 있고 때때로 정말 그렇게 한다. 그러나 포괄적인 수준에서 생명 작용과 도덕성 간의 그러한 선택을 살펴보자. 인간 종을 보존하는 것이 지구상의 다른 모든 생명을 말살하거나 버린다는 의미라면 어떨까? 그것이 인류가 영원히 황량하고 이질적인 환경 속에서 비참하고 궁핍한 상태로만 존재한다는 의미라면 어떨까? 이는 우주 정착이 반드시 이러한 최악의 시나리오를 초래할 것이라고 주장하는 것이 아니라, 오히려 인류의 멸종을 허용하거나 초래하는 것이 더 윤리적인 선택이 되는 상상 가능한 경우가 조금이라도 있는지를 묻는 것이다.

Solution Guide

⑤ 뒤에 이어지는 절이 문장의 필수 성분을 모두 갖추고 있으므로 관계대명사 what으로 유도되어서는 안 되고 what을 in which나 where로 바꾸어야 한다.

① 동명사구인 ensuring the continuation of our species (specifically, our genetic descendants)가 문장의 주어이고, 이와 이어지는 술어동사이므로 is는 적절하다.

② the choice의 구체적인 내용을 설명하는 to부정사구를 유도하므로 to sacrifice는 적절하다.

③ 동명사인 eliminating과 or로 연결되어 means의 목적어를 이루고 있으므로 동명사 abandoning은 적절하다.

④ 형용사구인 inhospitable and alien을 수식하므로 부사인 eternally는 적절하다.

Structure in Focus

- But as intelligent animals, [who can make decisions based on morality rather than biology], we could ask [whether preserving our genome is worth any cost].
  첫 번째 [ ]는 intelligent animals를 부가적으로 설명하는 관계절이고, 두 번째 [ ]는 ask의 목적어 역할을 하는 명사절이다.
- This is **not** [to argue {that space settlement will definitely result in these worst-case scenarios}], **but** rather [to ask {whether there is any imaginable case in which allowing or causing humans to become extinct is the more ethical choice}].
  두 개의 [ ]는 '~이 아니라 …'이라는 의미인 「not ~ but ...」으로 대등하게 연결되어 있다. 첫 번째 [ ] 안의 { }는 argue의 목적어 역할을 하는 명사절이고, 두 번째 [ ] 안의 { }는 ask의 목적어 역할을 하는 명사절이다.

13

정답 ⑤

소재 스포츠 팀 간의 건실한 경쟁상의 균형의 중요성

해석 대부분의 비즈니스 환경에서는 경쟁자를 폐업시키는 것이 바람직하다. 당연히 경쟁자가 더 적다는 것은 얻을 수 있는 고객이 더 많다는 것을 의미한다. 하지만 이것이 스포츠에서는 항상 사실인 것은 아니다. 사실 리그에서 경쟁하는 스포츠 조직은 조직 자체의 성공을 실제로 경쟁자의 상태에 의존한다. 예를 들어, 팬들은 흔히 박빙의 경쟁이 있고 승자를 미리 알 수 없는 경기에 더 큰 매력을 느낀다. 리그나 대회를 지배하는 것은 팬들의 관심이 서서히 사라질 수 있기 때문에 자멸적일 수 있다. 누가 경기에서 이길지 예측하기 어려울 때 스포츠 리그는 더 많은 관중과 시청자를 끌어들인다. 아이러니하게도, 계속 성공적이기 위해서 리그와 대회에서는 가능한 한 많은 클럽이 경쟁력을 갖출 필요가 있다. 경기 결과가 매우 예측 가능하면 경기는 많은 수의 관중을 끌어들이지 못하고 결국 그것은 입장권, 미디어, 후원 수익을 줄어들게 할 것이다. 스포츠에서는 팀 간에 건실한 경쟁상의 균형이 있는 것이 중요하다. 이것은 누가 경쟁에서 이길지에 대한 확실성(→ 불확실성)을 가져오고 팬들의 관람을 부추긴다.

Solution Guide

대부분의 비즈니스 환경에서와는 달리 스포츠에서는 팬들이 승자를 미리 알 수 없는 경기에 더 큰 매력을 느끼고, 팀 간에 건실한 경쟁상의 균형이 있는 것이 중요하다고 했으므로, 누가 경쟁에서 이길지에 대한 불확실성이 팬들의 관람을 부추길 것이다. 따라서 ⑤ certainty를 uncertainty와 같은 낱말로 바꾸어야 한다.

Structure in Focus

- For example, fans are often more attracted to a game [where {there is a close contest}, and {the winner is unknown in advance}].
  [ ]는 a game을 수식하는 관계절이고, 그 안의 두 개의 { }는 and로 연결되어 where에 이어진다.
- When **it** is difficult [to predict {who will win a match}], sport leagues attract higher attendances and viewers.
  When이 이끄는 부사절에서 it은 형식상의 주어이고, [ ]는 내용상의 주어이다. [ ] 안의 { }는 predict의 목적어 역할을 하는 명사절이다.

14

정답 ③

소재 어린아이에게 반복적으로 노출되는 광고

해석 어린아이의 뇌가 지속적인 흡수 상태에 있다는 사실은 우리를 잠시 멈추게 한다. 특정 유형의 기업이 어린이에게 직접 광고하지 못하게 막기 위한 규정이 마련되어 있다. 이것은 좋은 조치이지만, 또한 잘못된 안전감을 제공하기도 한다. 왜 그럴까? 언어 학습과 마찬가지로, 어린아이는 제품이나 일반적인 소비자 세계에 대해 배우기 위해 명확하게 자신을 대상으로 한 광고가 필요하지 않다. 웹사이트, 텔레비전, 모바일, 소셜 미디어, 비디오 게임에서의 광고를 생각해 보라. 아이들은 수백 개의 상표에 대한 수천 개 광고에의 반복된 노출 세례를 받고 있으며, 그들의 스펀지 같은, 영향을 잘 받는 뇌는 이러한 정보를 끊임없이 받아들이고 있다. 한 연구에서 연구원들은 아이들이 매우 많은 광고에 노출되어 10세가 되기 전에 이미 300~400개의 상표를 외우게 될 것이라는 것을 알아냈다. 오싹하게도, 아이들은 자라면서 여러분이 몰랐던 그들의 친구처럼, 정선된 수의 이러한 상표와 미래까지 오래 지속되는 관계를 형성한다.

Solution Guide

어린이에게 직접 광고하는 것을 금지하는 규정이 마련되어 있기는 하지만, 이것은 충분한 조치라고 할 수 없는데, 그 이유는 어린아이의 뇌는 스펀지와 같이 영향을 잘 받아서 광고에 지속적으로 노출되면 상당한 수의 상표를 외울 정도가 되기 때문이라는 내용의 글이다. 빈칸은 광고와 관련한 현실에 대해 다시 한번 생각해 보게 하는 뇌의 특성에 해당하므로, 빈칸에 들어갈 말로 가장 적절한 것은 ③이다.

① 변화
② 분석
④ 주의 산만
⑤ 다중 작업

Structure in Focus

■ [The fact {that the young brain is in a constant state of absorption}] should give us pause.
[ ]는 문장의 주어 역할을 하는 명사구이고, 그 안의 { }는 The fact와 동격 관계이다.

■ In a study, researchers discovered [that kids are exposed to **so** many ads **that** they will have memorized three hundred to four hundred brands before their tenth birthday].
[ ]는 discovered의 목적어 역할을 하는 명사절이고, 그 안에 '매우 ~해서 …하다'라는 의미의 「so ~ that ...」이 사용되었다.

15

정답 ④

소재 집단의 속성으로서의 협력하는 경향

해석 사람들은 흔히 친절함과 같은 성격 특성이 고정되어 있다고 생각한다. 하지만 집단을 대상으로 한 우리 연구는 매우 다른 것을 보여 주는데, 이타적인 성향이나 남을 이용해 먹는 성향은 사회 세계가 어떻게 구성되느냐에 따라 크게 좌우될 수 있다는 것이다. 따라서 '같은' 사람 집단을 선택하여 어떤 한 사회 세계에 그들을 배치하면 그들을 서로에게 매우 관대하게 만들 수 있고, 그들을 또 다른 종류의 세계에 두면 서로에게 매우 비열하거나 무관심하게 만들 수 있을 것이다. 아주 중요하게도, 이것은 협력하는 경향이 개인뿐만 아니라 집단의 속성이기도 하다는 것을 나타낸다. 협력은 우정 관계 형성을 지배하는 규칙에 따라 달라진다. 선량한 사람이 자신이 가지고 있는 신념이나 집단이 공유하는 신념과 관계없이 단지 자신이 속한 관계망의 구조 때문에 나쁜 일을 할 수 있다(그리고 그 반대의 경우도 마찬가지이다). 그것은 단지 '나쁜' 사람들과 관계를 맺는 문제가 아니라 사회적 관계의 수와 방식도 또한 중요하다. 협력과 사회 관계망 같은 사회성 모둠의 양상이 함께 작용한다.

Solution Guide

사람들의 성격이 사회 세계의 구성 방식에 따라 달라질 수 있다는 내용의 글이다. 이타적인 성향이나 남을 이용해 먹는 성향은 사회 세계가 어떻게 구성되느냐에 따라 크게 좌우될 수 있으며, 같은 사람 집단을 어떤 한 사회 세계에 배치하면 서로에게 매우 관대하게 만들 수 있고, 또 다른 종류의 세계에 두면 서로에게 매우 비열하거나 무관심하게 만들 수 있으며, 선량한 사람도 자신이 속한 관계망의 구조에 따라 나쁜 일을 할 수도 있다고 했으므로, 이것을 협력하는 경향과 관련지어 말하는 빈칸에 들어갈 말로 가장 적절한 것은 ④이다.

① 인간에게 고유한 기본적 욕구
② 공동체 번영을 위한 중요 필수 조건
③ 대대로 전해 내려오는 특성
⑤ 계속 변화하는 양상이 아니라 일종의 고정된 구조

Structure in Focus

■ But our research with groups suggests something quite different: [the tendency to be altruistic or exploitative may depend heavily on {how the social world is organized}].
[ ]는 something quite different의 구체적인 내용을 설명하고, 그 안의 { }는 전치사 on의 목적어 역할을 하는 명사절이다.

■ Good people can do bad things (and vice versa) simply as a result of the structure of the network [which they belong to], regardless of the convictions [they hold] or [that the group shares].
첫 번째 [ ]는 the network를 수식하는 관계절이고, 두 번째와 세 번째 [ ]는 or로 연결되어 the convictions를 수식하는

PART Ⅲ 테스트편

관계절이다.

16

정답 ①

소재 뜨거움과 차가움을 이용한 생리적 체계 강화

해석 우리의 타고난 생존 본능은 우리를 화씨 68에서 72도(섭씨 20~22.2도) 정도로 유지해 주는 온도 속에서 편안함을 찾는 것이다. 이러한 편안함의 영역에서 벗어나, 같은 기간에 뜨거움과 차가움을 이용하거나 한쪽의 극한 온도에 집중하여 신체의 세포 기능에 긴장을 줌으로써 우리는 우리의 생리적 체계를 강화한다. 우리는 우리의 일상적인 호흡 속도를 늦추고, 근육 조직을 개선하며, 스트레스 처리를 위한 역을 높인다. 증거에 따르면, 우리의 초기 조상들이 매일 노출되었던 것과 똑같은 불편함을 경험한 후에 우리는 최상의 상태가 되는데, 육체적으로 더 튼튼해지고, 정신적으로 더 강해지며, 영적으로 더 건전해진다. 실내 생활 방식과 자연과의 부정합으로 야기된 온도 변화의 결핍은 우리를 우리 조상들의 양육 방식에서 멀어지게 만들었고, 그것은 신경계를 계속 약화시킨다. 의도적으로 우리 자신을 뜨거움이나 차가움 속에 있게 함으로써, 우리는 육체적으로, 정신적으로 그리고 심지어 영적으로도 최상의 상태가 된다.

Solution Guide

우리의 생존 본능이 추구하는 화씨 68에서 72도(섭씨 20~22.2도) 정도의 편안함에서 벗어나 뜨거움과 차가움을 이용하여 우리 몸에 긴장과 불편함을 주면 육체적, 정신적, 그리고 영적으로도 최상의 상태가 된다는 내용의 글이다. 따라서 빈칸에 들어갈 말로 가장 적절한 것은 ①이다.

② 효과적인 호흡 역학이 무엇인지 이해함
③ 가끔 머리를 쓸 필요가 없고 반복적인 작업을 함
④ 우리를 편안하게 만들기 위해 실내 온도를 조절함
⑤ 개인별 맞춤 운동 루틴을 신중하게 설계함

Structure in Focus

- Our natural survival instinct is [to seek comfort in temperatures {that keep us around 68 to 72 degrees Fahrenheit (20–22.2 °C)}].
  [ ]는 is의 주격 보어 역할을 하는 to부정사구이고, 그 안의 { }는 temperatures를 수식하는 관계절이다.
- [The lack of temperature change {caused by indoor lifestyles and misalignment with nature}] **has** taken us far from our ancestorial upbringing, and it continues to weaken the nervous system.
  [ ]는 문장의 주어 역할을 하는 명사구이고, 술어동사는 has이다. [ ] 안의 { }는 The lack of temperature change를 수식하는 분사구이다.

17

정답 ⑤

소재 내적 모형과 불일치하는 가장(假裝) 놀이

해석 한 아이가 가장(假裝) 놀이를 한다고 가정하자. 그 아이는 짖고 네발로 기어다니며 "나는 강아지야!"라고 말한다. 그 주장을 하기 위해 그 아이의 뇌는 강아지는 짖고 네발로 걷는다는 정보를 포함해야 할 뿐만 아니라 "나는 강아지다."라는 핵심 명제를 구성해야 한다. 하지만 그 정보는 더 큰 맥락에서 존재한다. 그 아이의 뇌에는 "나는 실제로는 강아지가 아니다." "나는 게임을 하려고 그것을 꾸며 내고 있는 거다." "나는 어린 소녀다." 등을 포함하여 방대한 정보가 들어 있다. 그 정보 중 일부는 인지적, 언어적 수준에서 존재한다. 그것의 많은 부분은 더 깊은, 감각적 혹은 지각적 수준에 있다. 그 아이의 신체 도식은 상위 인지 아래에서 자동으로 구성되며, 그것은 강아지 몸이 아닌, 인간 신체의 육체적 구조를 기술한다. 그 아이는 자기 앞에 있는 자신의 인간 손을 보고, 그 시각 정보는 그 아이의 인간 정체성을 확인한다. 그 아이는 숟가락으로 아침 시리얼을 먹었고, 학교에 갔고, 책을 읽었던 것 등의 모든 인간 활동을 기억한다. "나는 강아지다."라는 주장은 그 아이의 가장 깊은 내적 모형과 불일치하는 피상적인 명제이다.

Solution Guide

가장(假裝) 놀이를 하는 아이는 자신이 강아지라고 주장하지만, 아이의 뇌에는 자신이 실제로는 강아지가 아니며, 게임을 하려고 그것을 꾸며내고 있다는 등의 방대한 정보가 존재하여, 자신이 인간의 정체성을 가지고 있다는 것을 확인하게 된다는 내용의 글이다. 따라서 빈칸에 들어갈 말로 가장 적절한 것은 ⑤이다.

① 그 아이의 개성과 취향을 밝히는
② 개에 대한 강한 애정을 보여 주는
③ 그 아이의 육체 건강과는 아무런 관련이 없는
④ 놀면서 학습하려는 그 아이의 성향과 모순되는

Structure in Focus

- In order to make the claim, her brain must [construct the key proposition "I'm a puppy"] **as well as** [contain the information {that puppies bark and walk on all fours}].
  두 개의 [ ]는 as well as로 연결되어 must에 이어져 문장의 술어 역할을 한다. 두 번째 [ ] 안의 { }는 the information과 동격 관계이다.
- The claim "I'm a puppy" is a superficial proposition [that is inconsistent with her deepest internal models].
  [ ]는 a superficial proposition을 수식하는 관계절이다.

18

정답 ④

소재 관계 형성의 기반이 되는 사회적 기본 값

해석 여러분의 자녀는 사회생활을 하는 여러분 자신을 관찰함으로써 그리고 자신이 겪는 사회적 경험을 통해 사회적 편안함과 사회적 기술을 생애에 일찍부터 확립한다. 이러한 최초의 사회적 경험은 평생의 (인간) 관계의 질과 양을 이끌고 형성할 기본 값이 된다. 유전적 특징은 이러한 기본 값에 분명히 영향을 미치는데, 연구는 아이들이 내향성에서 외향성으로의 연속체에서 어디에 놓이는지를 포함하여 특정 기질을 가지고 태어난다는 것을 보여 주었다. 하지만 격언이 말하듯이, "유전적 특징은 운명이 아닌"데, 여러분의 자녀가 다른 사람과 어떻게 상호 작용해야 하는지에 대해 생애에서 일찍이 여러분으로부터 받는 메시지는 유전적 성향이 발현되는 방식에 영향을 미친다. (예를 들어 아이가 텔레비전이나 영화를 보거나 비디오 게임을 하거나 인터넷 서핑을 할 때 하는 행동은 본인이나 다른 사람의 삶에 어떠한 직접적인 영향도 미치지 않는다.) 이러한 유전자와 양육의 상호 작용 안에서 여러분의 자녀는 사회적 편안함, 유대감, 건강한 관계를 촉진하거나 또는 사회적 불안, 외로움, 역기능적 관계를 유발하는 사회적 기본 값을 발달시키게 된다.

Solution Guide

아이들은 어렸을 때 부모와의 사회적 경험을 통해 평생을 지속하는 사회적 기본 값을 발달시킨다는 내용의 글이므로, 본인이나 다른 삶에 직접적인 영향을 미치지 않는 아이의 활동을 설명하는 내용의 ④는 글의 전체 흐름과 관계가 없다.

Structure in Focus

- ~; the messages [that your children get from you early in their lives about how they should interact with others] will influence [how their genetic predispositions will be expressed].
  첫 번째 [ ]는 the messages를 수식하는 관계절이고, 두 번째 [ ]는 influence의 목적어 역할을 하는 명사절이다.
- In this interaction of genes and upbringing, your children will develop social defaults [that trigger {social ease, connectedness, and healthy relationships}, or {social anxiety, loneliness, and dysfunctional relationships}].
  [ ]는 social defaults를 수식하는 관계절이다. 두 개의 { }는 or로 연결되어 trigger의 목적어 역할을 한다.

19

정답 ②

소재 서로 다른 문화의 충돌

해석 사회적 단계에서든 회사에서든 서로 다른 문화가 만나면 어떻게 일을 처리해야 하는지에 대한 생각이 충돌하는 경우가 많다. 그것을 해결하기 위해 우리는 일반적으로 다른 사람들이 우리와 더 비슷하게 변해야 한다는 가정을 한다. (B) 그리고 우리는 조직의 상사로서든 아니면 국가의 지배적인 문화로서든 힘을 가지고 있기 때문에 이러한 관점을 강요할 수 있다. 그러나 지배적인 위치에 있는 사람이나 국가가 올바른 규칙과 올바른 방식을 가지고 있다고 가정하는 것은 그 자체로 혁신이 아주 싫어하는 것이다. 자기만족에 빠진 사람은 좋은 혁신가가 아니다. (A) 그래서 사람들에게 자신의 문화적 배경과 일치하지 않는 어떤 일을 하라고 요구할 때는, 무엇이 가장 효과적인지에 대한 여러분의 가정을 재고해야 하는 것은 아닌지 자문해 보라. 예를 들어, 자유로운 대화는 일반적으로 좋은 회의의 특징으로 간주된다. 누구나 생각이 떠오를 때마다 그냥 (대화에) 끼어든다. (C) 그러나 어떤 문화에서는, 이것이 무례하고 강압적인 것으로 간주되어 훌륭한 아이디어를 가진 일부 사람들이 발언을 하지 않을 수도 있다. 한 가지 해결책은 그들의 집단 (협동) 능력을 강화하는 것일 수도 있지만, 다른 방법으로는 가끔 모든 사람에게 차례대로 의견을 말하도록 요청하거나, 서면으로 아이디어를 요청하거나, 아니면 다른 누군가를 대신하여 아이디어를 상정하는 것이 있다.

Solution Guide

서로 다른 문화가 만나 충돌할 경우의 해결책으로 우리는 다른 사람이 우리와 더 비슷하게 변해야 한다고 가정한다는 내용의 주어진 글 다음에는 그런 가정을 this view로 지칭하는 문장으로 시작하여 이런 가정의 위험성을 언급하는 (B)가 이어져야 한다. 그다음에는 문화 충돌의 바람직스러운 해결을 위해서 사람들에게 자신의 문화적 배경과 일치하지 않는 어떤 일을 하라고 요구할 때는 무엇이 가장 효과적인지에 대한 가정을 재고해야 하는 것은 아닌지 자문하라는 내용의 (A)가 이어져야 한다. 마지막으로 (A)에서 좋은 회의의 유형으로 예를 든 자유로운 대화가 어떤 문화에서는 적절하지 않을 수도 있다는 내용과 이에 대한 해결책을 제시하는 (C)가 그 뒤를 잇는 것이 글의 순서로 가장 적절하다.

Structure in Focus

- So when you ask people to do something [not consistent with their cultural background], ask yourself [whether you should be rethinking your assumptions about {what works best}].
  첫 번째 [ ]는 something을 수식하는 형용사구이고, 두 번째 [ ]는 ask의 직접목적어 역할을 하는 명사절이다. 두 번째

[ ] 안의 { }는 전치사 about의 목적어 역할을 하는 명사절이다.

- One solution might be [to strengthen their group skills] but other methods are [to {occasionally ask everyone to express an opinion in turn}, {ask for ideas in writing}, or {table an idea on someone else's behalf}].
  첫 번째 [ ]는 be의 보어 역할을 하는 to부정사구이고, 두 번째 [ ]는 are의 보어 역할을 하는 to부정사구인데, 그 안에서 세 개의 { }가 or로 연결되어 to에 이어진다.

20

정답 ③

소재 뉴런의 활동

해석 촉수를 뻗는 어떤 기이한 외계 생명체처럼 각 뉴런은 수천 개까지 다른 뉴런과 동시에 연결된다. 뉴런이 활성화되었는지 아닌지를 결정하는 것은 받아들여지는 정보 활동의 합이다. (B) 이러한 활동이 모두 모여 급변점에 도달하면 뉴런이 발화하여 그것의 연결부에서 작은 화학적 전기 신호를 방출하고 연쇄 반응을 일으킨다. 사실상, 각 뉴런은 자신과 연결된 모든 상대 뉴런의 활동의 합을 계산하기 때문에 마이크로프로세서와 다소 비슷하다. (C) 그것은 동네에서 소문을 퍼뜨리는 것과 다소 비슷하다. 여러분의 이웃 뉴런 중 어떤 것은 잘 흥분해서 친한 친구처럼 그 소문을 퍼뜨리는 데 도움을 주고 싶어 한다. 다른 뉴런은 억제적이어서 기본적으로 조용히 있으라고 말한다. (A) 그리고 뉴런은 여러 다른 이웃이나 멀리 떨어진 친구와 그러한 대화를 나눌 때마다, 말을 퍼뜨리거나 침묵하라는 메시지를 기억하여, 그 소문이 다시 돌아올 때 뉴런은 더 확실하게 반응한다. 이것은 반복적인 상호 발화를 통해 뉴런 간의 연결이 강화되었기 때문이다.

Solution Guide

뉴런의 활성화를 결정하는 것은 정보 활동의 합이라는 내용의 주어진 글 다음에, 이를 this activity로 가리키는 문장으로 시작하여 자세히 설명하는 (B)가 오고, 이러한 활동이 연쇄 반응을 일으키는 것은 이웃에 소문을 퍼뜨리는 것과 비슷하다는 내용의 (C)가 이어지는 것이 자연스럽다. (A)의 첫 문장은 (C)에서 이웃에 소문을 퍼뜨리는 경우와 그렇지 않은 경우를 다시 한번 언급하고 있으므로 (A)가 그 뒤를 잇는 것이 글의 순서로 가장 적절하다.

Structure in Focus

- **It is** [the combined activity of information {coming in}] **that** determines [whether a neuron is active or not].
  첫 번째 [ ]는 It is와 that 사이에 놓여 그 의미가 강조되고 있고, 그 안의 { }는 information을 수식하는 분사구이다. 두 번째 [ ]는 determines의 목적어 역할을 하는 명사절이다.
- In effect, each neuron is a bit like a microprocessor [because it computes the combined activity of all the other neurons {it is connected to}].
  [ ]는 이유를 나타내는 부사절이며, 그 안의 { }는 all the other neurons를 수식하는 관계절이다.

21

정답 ②

소재 질료인(質料因)과 동력인(動力因)

해석 전통적인 경제학은 '생산 요소'라는 말을 사용한다. 생산 요소는 어떤 생산물을 만드는 데 필요한 생산 공정에 투입되는 요소이다. 예를 들어 피자를 만들려면 요리사, 오븐이 있는 주방, 원재료가 필요하다. 그러나 그것을 가만히 생각해 보면 요리사와 주방은 몇 가지 근본적인 면에서 원재료와 다르다는 것을 분명히 알 수 있을 것이다. 요리사와 주방은 피자를 만든 후에 비록 단지 조금 더 닳긴 하지만 이전과 거의 동일하다. 그러나 원재료는 남김없이 모두 사용되어 먼저 피자 자체로 변하고 그런 다음 그 후 빠르게 쓰레기로 변한다. 요리사와 주방은 피자에 물리적으로 담기지 않지만 원재료는 그렇다. 수천 년 전 아리스토텔레스는 이 중요한 차이를 논의해 원인(요인)을 변형되는 것인 '질료인(質料因)'과 그 과정에서 자신은 변형되지 않고 변형을 일으키는 것인 '동력인(動力因)'으로 나누었다. 원재료는 질료인(質料因)이고, 요리사와 주방은 동력인(動力因)이다.

Culture Note

material cause vs. efficient cause(질료인 대 동력인) 아리스토텔레스가 세계의 현상과 변화를 설명한 4원인에 속하는 것들로, 질료인은 목적하는 형상을 이루는 바탕 재료를 말하고, 동력인은 사물을 생성하고 변화시키는 역할을 하는 것을 말한다. 예를 들어 조각의 재료로서 대리석이나 청동은 질료인이고, 건축에서의 건축가는 동력인에 해당한다.

Solution Guide

전통적인 경제학에서 사용되는 말인 생산 요소 간의 차이를 피자를 만드는 데 필요한 요소를 예로 들어 설명한 글이다. ② 뒤의 문장은 원재료가 남김없이 모두 사용되어 피자가 되었다가 쓰레기가 된다는 내용인데, however가 그 안에 사용되었다. ② 앞의 문장은 요리사와 주방은 원재료와 몇 가지 근본적인 면에서 다르다는 내용이어서 ② 뒤의 문장과의 논리적 연결이 어색하다. 주어진 문장은 요리사와 주방이 피자를 만든 후에 이전과 거의 동일하다는 내용으로 ② 뒤의 문장과 대조를 이루므로, 주어진 문장이 들어가기에 가장 적절한 곳은 ②이다.

Structure in Focus

- If you think about it carefully, however, you will clearly see [that the cook and kitchen are different in some fundamental ways from the raw ingredients].
  [ ]는 see의 목적어 역할을 하는 명사절이다.
- Thousands of years ago, Aristotle discussed this important distinction and divided causation (factors) into *material cause*, [that {which is transformed}], and *efficient cause*, [that {which causes the transformation without itself being transformed in the process}].
  두 개의 [ ]는 각각 *material cause*, *efficient cause*와 동격 관계이다. 두 개의 { }는 각각 that을 수식하는 관계절이다.

22

정답 ④

소재 자녀 양육에 드는 경제적 비용의 분담

해석 사회는 사망하는 구성원을 대체할 자녀를 길러야 하며, 그러지 않으면 그 사회는 두어 세대가 지나 소멸할 것이다. 그러므로 자녀 생산을 긍정적인 외부 효과로 생각할 수 있을 것이다. 자녀가 없는 사람들은 자녀가 있는 사람들의 자녀 양육 노동으로부터 혜택을 받는데, 그들은 나이가 들면서 살게 되는 다양한 연령대의 사회를 향유하고, 젊은 사람들의 노동력이 퇴직한 그들을 부양할 수 있다. 그렇다면 모두가 자녀를 기르는 데 드는 경제적 비용을 분담해야 하는가? 미국에서는 자녀를 교육하는 비용은 공교육 시스템을 통해 공동으로 떠맡지만, 자녀를 기르는 데 드는 대부분의 다른 비용은 부모의 사적인 비용으로 간주된다. 그러나 전 세계 약 절반의 국가에서는 자녀를 둔 가정에 직접 보조금을 지급함으로써 사회 전체가 자녀 양육에 드는 모든 비용의 책임 일부를 떠맡는다. 이러한 보조금은 그 나라 근로자의 중위 소득에 따라 정해지는 경우가 많은데, 예를 들어 정부는 두 자녀를 둔 어떤 가정에든 국가 중위 소득의 10퍼센트를 지급할 수도 있다.

Culture Note

median income(중위 소득) 중위 소득은 모든 가구를 소득 순으로 순위를 매겼을 때, 가운데를 차지하는 가구의 소득을 의미하는데, 대체적으로 중산층 가구 비중을 고려할 때는 경제 협력 개발 기구의 기준을 따르는 사례가 많다.

Solution Guide

자녀 양육에 드는 경제적 비용을 어떻게 분담해야 하는가에 대한 내용의 글이다. ④ 앞뒤에 있는, 각각 자녀를 기르는 데 드는 경제적 비용을 모두 분담해야 하는가를 묻는 내용과, 전 세계 약 절반의 국가에서는 직접 보조금을 지급하여 자녀 양육에 드는 모든 비용의 책임 일부를 떠맡는다는 내용을 however로 연결하는 것은 어색하다. 미국에서는 자녀를 교육시키는 비용은 공교육 시스템을 통해 공동으로 떠맡지만, 자녀를 기르는 데 드는 대부분의 다른 비용은 부모의 사적인 비용으로 처리된다는 내용의 주어진 문장이 ④에 들어가면 however가 사용되어 대조를 나타내는 ④ 뒤의 문장과 잘 호응이 되어 자연스럽게 내용이 연결되므로, 주어진 문장이 들어가기에 가장 적절한 곳은 ④이다.

Structure in Focus

- Those [who do not have children] benefit from the child-rearing labors of those [who **do**]; they enjoy a society of varied ages [in which to live as they grow older], and a labor force of younger people is available to support them in their retirement.
  첫 번째 [ ]는 Those를 수식하는 관계절이고, 두 번째 [ ]는 those를 수식하는 관계절이다. 두 번째 [ ] 안의 do는 have children을 대신한다. 세 번째 [ ]는 a society of varied ages를 수식하는 관계절이다.
- In about half of the world's states, however, the full society assumes [some of the responsibility for all costs of child rearing] by giving direct grants to families with children.
  [ ]는 assumes의 목적어 역할을 하는 명사구이다.

23

정답 ③

소재 영장류의 추상적 관계형 추론 능력

해석 영장류는 자연적인 환경에서, 특히 그들의 먹이 또는 사회 위계에서의 지위가 위태로운 경우에 정교한 형태의 추론을 할 수 있다. 그러나 그들의 관계형 추론이 얼마나 다방면적일 수 있을지는 불분명하다. 1940년대에 영장류학자 Harry Harlow는 흥미로운 발견을 했다. 일련의 실험에서 원숭이는 두 개의 시각적 물체 중 하나를 선택하는 법을 배웠는데, 그중의 하나에는 보상이 주어지고 다른 하나에는 보상이 주어지지 않았다. Harlow는 완전히 새로운 물체 두 개로 그 과제가 다시 시작될 때마다 원숭이들이 조금씩 더 빨리 배운다는 것을 놀라워하며 언급했다. 사실, 그들의 (과제) 수행은 수백 개의 새로운 물체 세트를 거치면서 계속 더 빨라졌고, 결국 원숭이들은 두 번째 시도부터는 계속 거의 완벽하게 반응할 수 있었다. Harlow는 반복적인 (물체의) 쌍을 거치는 동안 원숭이가 '배우는 법을 알게 되었다'고 주장했다. 원숭이는 각 쌍에서의 두 자극 사이의 관계에 대한 추상적인 무언가, 즉 한 자극에 보상이 주어지면 나머지 자극에는 보상이 주어지지 않는다는 것을 배운 것처럼 보인다. 이 지식을 새로운 쌍에 일반화함으로써, 그들은 한층 더 빠르게 배울 수 있었다. 비슷한 방식으로 실험을 거친 인간 아이들도 같은 능력을 보여 주었다.
→ Harry Harlow의 실험은 영장류가 인간과 마찬가지로 다른 맥락에서 추상적 관계형 추론을 적용할 수 있으며, 이는 자극에 더 많이 노출될수록 더 빠르게 일어난다는 사실을 보여 준다.

Solution Guide

보상을 받는 물체와 보상을 받지 못하는 물체를 구별하며, 새로운 물체 세트를 반복해서 보여 줬을 때 이를 더 빨리 구별해 내는 Harry Harlow의 원숭이 실험을 소개하는 내용의 글이다. 영장류가 한 쌍에서 배운 관계형 추론 지식을 새로운 쌍으로 일반화할 수 있고, 이런 일반화하는 능력은 물체의 쌍이 반복될수록 더 빨리 발휘되었다는 내용이므로, 빈칸 (A), (B)에 들어갈 말로 가장 적절한 것은 ③ '적용할 – 더 많이'이다.
① 수용할 – 간헐적으로
② 습득할 – 짧게
④ 설명할 – 규칙적으로
⑤ 거부할 – 반복적으로

Structure in Focus

- In a series of experiments, monkeys learnt to choose between two visual objects, [one of which was rewarded and one was **not**].
  [ ]는 two visual objects를 부가적으로 설명하는 관계절이다. not 뒤에는 rewarded가 생략되었다.
- Human children [tested in a comparable fashion] showed the same ability.
  [ ]는 Human children을 수식하는 분사구이다.

24~25

정답 24 ① 25 ⑤

소재 기억에 영향을 끼치는 스키마

해석 1930년대에 영국의 심리학자 Frederic Bartlett 경은, 우리는 우리가 경험하는 사건으로부터 세상에 대한 지식을 점차 축적하고, 그런 다음 이러한 경험은 그가 '스키마'라고 부른 체계적인 정신 구조 속에 결집된다는 의견을 제시했다. 그 결과, 이들 스키마(달리하면 'schemas')는 우리가 새로운 경험을 이해하고 그것을 기억하는 데 쓸 틀을 형성하는 데 도움이 되도록 사용된다. 이러한 방식의 한 가지 잠재적 단점은 우리의 현재 스키마에 맞지 않는 정보와 사건을 우리가 이해하고 기억하기가 상대적으로 어렵다는 것이다. Bartlett의 대표적인 실증 중 하나는 한 영국 대학생에게 특이한 북미 민간 설화를 제시하고 이를 외워서 기억하게 한 것이었다. 이 학생이 기억해서 쓴 글은 원본과 달리 더 짧고 많은 세부 사항을 생략했다. 그다음에 이 첫 번째 학생이 기억해서 쓴 글은 외워서 기억하도록 두 번째 학생에게 주어졌는데, 그 결과 그의 재현에서 더 많은 특이한 세부 사항이 빠졌지만, 다른 세부 사항이 추가되어, 겉보기에는 그 이야기를 영국인의 귀에 더 일관되고 더 이해하기 쉽게 만든 것 같았다. 이 절차는 연이은 10명의 학생이 이전의 재현물을 배우고 자신만의 설명을 만들어 낼 때까지 반복되었다. 연속 재현이 끝날 무렵에는 재현물이 훨씬 더 짧아지고 원작의 초자연적인 세부 사항이 없어졌으며 전체 이야기가 1930년대 영국 대학생들의 경험에 더 가까워졌다. 따라서 이 실증은 기억의 구성적 본질, 그리고 신념과 태도가 기억과 이해에 미치는 영향을 보여 준다. 소문은 Bartlett의 연구 결과와 반대인(→ 유사한) 일반적인 사례의 역할을 하는데, 이야기는 여러 번의 말을 거치면서 점진적으로 바뀐다. 잠시 은유로 되돌아가자면, 인간의 기억은 녹음기와 같지 '않다'!

Solution Guide

24 우리는 경험하는 사건으로부터 세상에 대한 지식을 축적하고, 이러한 경험은 스키마라고 부르는 체계적인 정신 구조 속에 결집되어 새로운 경험을 이해하고 그것을 기억하는 데 쓸 틀을 형성하는 데 도움이 되도록 사용되는데, 이것이 현재 스키마에 맞지 않는 정보와 사건을 이해하고 기억하는 것을 상대적으로 어렵게 해서 기억의 변화를 가져온다는 것을 Bartlett가 한 예시를 들어 보여 주고 있다. 따라서 글의 제목으로 가장 적절한 것은 ① '이전 지식이 기억에 어떻게 영향을 미치는가'이다.
② 소문이 인간관계에 어떻게 영향을 미치는가
③ 스토리텔링을 위한 새로운 경험의 필요
④ 기억력을 향상시키기 위해 해야 할 일
⑤ 이야기 구성에서 경험이 중요한 이유

25 현재 스키마에 맞지 않는 정보와 사건을 이해하고 기억하는 것이 상대적으로 어려워 자신들의 경험에 더 가깝게 이야기가 바뀐 것은 소문이 여러 번의 말을 거치면서 점진적으로 바뀌는 것과 유사할 것이므로, (e)의 counter는 similar와 같은 낱말로 바꾸어야 한다.

Structure in Focus

- In the 1930s, the English psychologist Sir Frederic Bartlett proposed [that we gradually build up our knowledge of the world from events {we experience}], and [that these experiences are then clustered in organized mental structures {he called "schemata}]."
  두 개의 [ ]는 and로 연결되어 proposed의 목적어 역할을 하는 명사절이고, 각 [ ] 안의 { }는 각각 events와 organized mental structures를 수식하는 관계절이다.
- One potential downside of this arrangement is [that **it** is relatively difficult {for us to understand and remember information and events 〈that do not fit our current schemata〉}].

[ ]는 is의 주격 보어 역할을 하는 명사절이다. [ ] 안에서 it은 형식상의 주어이고, { }는 내용상의 주어이다. { } 안의 〈 〉는 information and events를 수식하는 관계절이다.

- This first student's written recall was then given to a second student [to learn and recall] with the result [that more unusual details were dropped out of his reproduction, but other details were added, apparently to make the story more coherent and comprehensible to English ears].
  첫 번째 [ ]는 목적을 나타내는 to부정사구이고, 두 번째 [ ]는 the result와 동격 관계이다.

26~28

정답 26 ④ 27 ⑤ 28 ②

소재 불안한 비올라 연주자를 위한 조언

해석 (A) 젊은 비올라 연주가인 Mary는 Theresa Adams가 텍사스 주 San Antonio에서 열린 전국 음악 교육자 학회에서 발표를 하는 동안 바흐가 작곡한 느린 사라반드를 연주했다. 그 곡은 활을 드는 팔의 지속된 제어, 따뜻한 음색, 그리고 정확한 음높이를 필요로 한다. 매우 수줍어하고 있었기에, Mary는 교육자들이 이렇게 많이 모인 모임 앞에서 연주하며 눈에 띄게 남의 시선을 의식했다. 연주를 위해 리허설을 하는 동안, 그녀는 불안감을 조절하는 데 매우 어려움을 겪었다.

(D) Mary는 활이 떨리지 않게 하는 데 어려움을 겪었고, 그녀가 내는 음색은 가늘었고 긁는 듯한 소리가 났다. Theresa는 Mary가 자신이 연주하는 음악에 대해 따뜻한 느낌을 가지고 있지만 그것을 표현하기에 너무 어색함을 느껴 그것을 표현하지 못한다는 것을 알 수 있었다. Theresa는 자신이 Mary에게 어떤 지시를 했는지 청중이 알 수 없도록 은밀하게 Mary와 잠시 이야기했다. Theresa는 Mary에게 가장 좋아하는 바흐 곡 비올라 연주자가 누구인지 물었고, 그녀는 그 사람은 Martha Katz이며 자신은 그녀처럼 사라반드를 연주하고 싶다고 대답했다.

(B) 그런 다음 Theresa는 Mary에게 그녀의 연주를 녹화하는 비디오카메라가 무대 위쪽에 있다고 상상하라고 지시했다. Teresa는 Mary에게 그녀가 음이 맞지 않거나 음을 빼먹거나 음색이 엉망인지는 문제가 되지 않는다고 말했다. 오로지 중요한 것은 그녀가 바흐의 곡을 연주하면서 Martha Katz의 모습처럼 보여야 한다는 것이었다. Theresa는 Mary에게 카메라는 그녀가 보이는 방식을 기록할 뿐이며, 그녀가 내는 소리는 그녀가 본받고 싶어 하는 대상이 같은 곡을 연주한 CD에 의해 대체될 것이라고 말했다.

(C) Mary가 더는 자신이 어떻게 연주하는지에 관해 걱정할 필요가 없었으므로, 그녀는 연주 시간 동안 마음 놓고 자신을 Martha Katz의 역할 속으로 던져 넣었다. 그녀는 자신 있고, 편안하고, 위엄 있어 보였을 뿐만 아니라, 또한 활을 제어하고, 정확하게, 악구를 잘 구분해서 연주했다. 그녀는 바흐의 사라반드를 연주할 때 실질적으로 Martha Katz가 '되었다'. 청중은 그녀의 연주에 깜짝 놀랐으며, 그렇게나 뚜렷한 효과를 만들어 낸 어떤 지시를 Theresa가 그녀에게 했는지에 대해 알고 싶어 했다. 그리고 Mary는 자신이 Martha Katz라고 상상하기는 했지만, 자신이 여전히 비올라를 연주한 사람이라는 것을 깨달았다.

Solution Guide

26 주어진 글 (A)에서 Mary는 전국 음악 교육자 학회에서 연주하게 되었고, 불안감을 통제하는 데 어려움을 겪었음을 언급하고, 다음으로 (D)에서 Mary가 겪은 어려움을 구체적으로 언급한 다음, Theresa가 Mary의 불안감을 낮추기 위해 이야기를 하게 되었음을 제시한다. 그런 다음 (B)에서 Theresa는 Mary에게 비디오카메라를 상상하고, 카메라는 보이는 방식만 기록하고, 소리는 Mary가 본받고 싶어 하는 대상인 Martha Katz의 연주음으로 대체될 것이라 말했다는 내용으로 이어져야 한다. 다음으로 (C)에서 이제 걱정을 떨친 Mary가 훌륭한 연주를 했고, 실은 연주한 사람이 자신이라는 것을 깨달았다는 내용으로 연결되어야 글의 흐름이 자연스럽게 이어질 수 있다.

27 (a), (b), (c), (d)는 모두 Mary를 가리키고 (e)는 Martha Katz를 가리킨다.

28 Theresa는 Mary에게 카메라가 그녀의 모습만을 녹화하고 음은 CD로 대체한다고 상상하라고 말했으므로, 글에 관한 내용으로 적절하지 않은 것은 ②이다.

Structure in Focus

- [Being very shy], Mary was noticeably self-conscious [playing before this large gathering of educators].
  첫 번째 [ ]는 이유를 나타내는 분사구문이고, 두 번째 [ ]는 시간을 나타내는 분사구문이다.
- The audience was shocked by her playing and curious to know [what instructions Theresa had given her {that had produced such a marked effect}].
  [ ]는 know의 목적어 역할을 하는 명사절이고, 그 안의 { }는 what instructions를 수식하는 관계절이다.

TEST 2

본문 192~211쪽

01 ①	02 ②	03 ②	04 ⑤	05 ⑤	06 ⑤	07 ②
08 ②	09 ③	10 ④	11 ⑤	12 ④	13 ⑤	14 ③
15 ③	16 ①	17 ①	18 ④	19 ①	20 ③	21 ⑤
22 ②	23 ②	24 ①	25 ⑤	26 ②	27 ③	28 ⑤

01

정답 ①

소재 약사 직위 제안 거절

해석 Cole 씨께,

약사 직위를 제안해 주셔서 감사합니다. 저는 보건 의료에 대한 강한 열정과 환자의 삶에 긍정적인 영향을 미치고자 하는 열망이 있어서 이 직위는 저에게 매력적입니다. 그러나 제가 지난 인터뷰에서 간단히 말씀드렸듯이, 귀사가 현재 저의 가장 중요한 직업적 목표인 박사 학위를 위해 진행되고 있는 저의 공부를 위한 등록금 비용을 변제할 입장에 있지 않다는 것을 알게 되어 실망했습니다. 3월 14일에 저는 학비 변제가 포함된 복리 후생 제도가 있는 회사로부터 다른 직위를 제안받았습니다. 향후 2년 동안 이 비용이 상당할 것으로 예상하기 때문에 저는 이 직위를 수락하기로 했습니다. 이번 인터뷰에서 귀하께서 내어 주신 시간과 저에게 보여 주신 특별한 관심에 진심으로 감사드립니다. 다시 한 번 귀하의 배려에 감사드립니다.

Julie Robinson 드림

Solution Guide

약사 직위를 제안받았지만, 약학 박사 학위 취득을 위한 학비 지원을 하지 않는다는 것을 알고 제안을 거절하는 내용이므로, 글의 목적으로 가장 적절한 것은 ①이다.

Structure in Focus

- As I indicated in our last interview, however, I was disappointed to learn [that your company would not be in a position to reimburse tuition costs for my ongoing study toward a Doctor of Pharmacy degree, {currently a primary professional goal of mine}].
  [ ]는 learn의 목적어 역할을 하는 명사절이고, 그 안의 { }는 a Doctor of Pharmacy degree와 동격 관계이다.
- I sincerely appreciate the time [you have taken] and the special interest [you have shown in me] during the interview.
  두 개의 [ ]는 각각 the time과 the special interest를 수식하는 관계절이다.

02

정답 ②

소재 위험에 처한 Captain Hall

해석 어느 날, 유명한 북극 탐험가인 Captain Hall은 자신이 탐험하고 싶어 했던 어떤 섬을 방문하기 위해 작은 배를 타고 갔다. 그 배는 해안의 바위에 단단히 고정되어 있었다. 탐험을 마치고 돌아왔을 때, 그는 바닷물이 차올라 자신의 배를 뜨게 했고, 그 배는 전혀 손이 닿지 않게 되었다는 것을 알게 되었다. Captain Hall은 자신이 처한 극도의 위험을 두려워했다. 배는 그와 세상 사이를 연결하는 유일한 수단이었는데, 그의 손이 닿을 수 없는 지경에 이르게 되었다. 어떻게 해야 했을까? 이런 날씨에 배를 향해 헤엄치는 것은 불가능했다. 그는 가능해 보이는 유일한 것을 했다. 그는 자신의 부츠를 맸던 가죽끈을 풀어서 약 20피트 길이의 줄을 만들었다. 그는 그 줄의 끝에 무거운 돌을 묶고, 그 돌을 배 안으로 던져, 배를 해안으로 끌어당겼다. Captain Hall은 다시 한 번 그 배에 들어갔고, 자신이 피할 수 없는 굶주림에서 신발끈에 의해 구원되었다고 느꼈을 때 말로 표현할 수 없는 안도감이 들었다!

Solution Guide

Captain Hall이 섬 탐험을 마치고 배로 돌아왔을 때 조수가 차올라 자신의 배가 손이 닿지 않는 곳에 있는 것을 보고 두려움을 느꼈지만, 자신의 부츠 끈을 이용해 배를 다시 해안으로 끌어당겨서 배에 다시 타게 된 순간 안도했다는 내용의 글이므로, Captain Hall의 심경 변화로 가장 적절한 것은 ② '겁에 질린 → 안도하는'이다.

① 혼란스러워하는 → 부끄러워하는
③ 신이 난 → 확신에 찬
④ 무관심한 → 발랄한
⑤ 불안해하는 → 실망한

Structure in Focus

- One day, Captain Hall, [the famous Arctic explorer], went in a small boat [to visit a certain island {which he wanted to explore}].
  첫 번째 [ ]는 Captain Hall과 동격 관계이다. 두 번째 [ ]는 목적의 의미를 나타내는 to부정사구이고, 그 안의 { }는 a certain island를 수식하는 관계절이다.
- When he returned from his expedition, he discovered [the tide had risen and floated his boat, {which was quite out of reach}].
  [ ]는 discovered의 목적어 역할을 하는 명사절이고, 그 안의 { }는 his boat를 부가적으로 설명하는 관계절이다.

03

정답 ②

소재 새로운 과학, 기술의 발전과 더불어 발전하는 법

해석 지난 100년 동안 우리 세상에 일어난 변화에 대해 생각해 보라. 가장 먼저 떠오르는 것은 아마 지난 세기의 눈부신 과학적, 기술적 업적인 자동차, 항공기, 전화기, 라디오와 TV, 컴퓨터, 그리고 유전 공학일 것이다. 각각의 새로운 발전은 그에 따른 법률 변화의 필요성을 만들어 낸다. 예를 들어, 자동차를 둘러싸고 생겨난 방대한 양의 법률을 생각해 보라. 자동차의 제작 및 정비, 도로에서의 운전자 행동, 그리고 심지어 자동차가 어디에 주차될 수 있는지와 같은 문제를 규제하는 법규가 있다. 사실, 치안 판사 재판소가 재판하는 형사 사건의 거의 절반이 자동차 이용과 직접적으로 관련되어 있다. 도로의 교통량 증가와 그에 따른 교통사고의 끊임없는 증가는 또한 민법, 특히 불법 행위 및 보험에 관한 법 분야에서의 발전을 야기했다.

Solution Guide

지난 100년 동안 과학과 기술이 눈부시게 발전함에 따라 법도 그에 따라 발전했다는 것을 자동차를 사례로 들어 설명하는 내용의 글이다. 따라서 글의 요지로 가장 적절한 것은 ②이다.

Structure in Focus

- Think about the changes [that have taken place in our world over the past 100 years].
  [ ]는 the changes를 수식하는 관계절이다.
- Consider, for example, the vast body of law [which has grown up around the motor vehicle]: there are regulations [governing such matters as the construction and maintenance of motor vehicles, the conduct of drivers on the road and even where vehicles may be parked].
  첫 번째 [ ]는 the vast body of law를 수식하는 관계절이고, 두 번째 [ ]는 regulations를 수식하는 분사구이다.

04

정답 ⑤

소재 진리 추구와 도덕적 판단

해석 때로는 어떤 문제에 대한 진실을 추구하는 것이 그것을 추구하지 않는 것보다 도덕적으로 더 나쁠 것이다. 이것은 핵무기 연구의 경우에서처럼, 답 자체가 위험하거나 해로운 것으로 판명될 수도 있기 때문일 것이다. 그러나 그것은 또한 진실을 추구하는 방식이 위험하거나 해롭거나, 또는 그 결과와는 별개로 단순히 도덕적으로 잘못된 것이기 때문일 수도 있다. 나치나 Tuskegee 실험을 생각해 보라. 여기서 도덕적으로 나쁜 것은 추구되는 정보가 아니라, '그 정보가 추구되는 방식'이다. 그리고 우리는 그런 극적인 사례에 의존할 필요가 없다. 국립보건원과 국립과학재단은 인간 피실험자를 포함하는 모든 종류의 실험을 수반하는 현대 과학 연구를 엄격하게 감시한다. 특정 과학 정보를 얻을 수 있는 유일한 방법이 다른 사람에게 해를 끼치는 경우에, 우리는 일반적으로, 모든 것을 고려해 볼 때 당연히 그 정보를 추구할 가치가 없다고 생각한다. 따라서 특정 탐구 노선을 추구할지 결정할 때는 그 노선을 추구하는 것이, 도덕적인 것이든 (아니면) 다른 것이든 간에 우리의 다른 가치관과 충돌할 것인지 먼저 판단해야 한다.

Culture Note

Tuskegee experiment(Tuskegee 실험) 1932년부터 1972년까지 미국 Alabama 주 Tuskegee에서 수행된 악명 높고 비윤리적인 임상 연구로 많은 희생자를 낳았다. 이 연구는 연구 대상인 아프리카계 미국인 남성들을 치료하는 대신 그냥 방치하고 관찰함으로써 결국 128명이 사망하게 되었고, 이로 인해 인종 차별과 윤리적 모순의 상징으로 여겨지며 미국 의학계의 큰 오점으로 기록되었다.

Solution Guide

필자는, 도덕적으로 나쁜 것은 추구되는 정보가 야기하는 결과일 수도 있고, 그 정보가 추구되는 방식일 수도 있는데, 특정한 방식으로 진리를 추구할 때는 그 탐구가 추구하는 것이 다른 가치관과 충돌할 수 있는지 먼저 판단해야 한다고 주장하고 있다. 따라서 필자가 주장하는 바로 가장 적절한 것은 ⑤이다.

Structure in Focus

- Consider the Nazi or Tuskegee experiments: **it is** not [the information pursued] **that** is morally bad here, but [*the manner in which that information is pursued*].
  「it is ~ that ...」에 의해 두 개의 [ ]가 강조되고 있다. 그 두 개의 [ ]는 「not ~ but ...」에 의해 연결되어 있는데, 'but+두 번째 [ ]'가 끝으로 이동한 형태이다.
- In cases [where the only way {in which we can obtain certain scientific information} is harmful to other people], we generally feel — rightly — [that the information is not worth pursuing, all things considered].
  첫 번째 [ ]는 cases를 수식하는 관계절이고, 그 안의 { }는 the only way를 수식하는 관계절이다. 두 번째 [ ]는 feel의 목적어 역할을 하는 명사절이다.

05

정답 ⑤

소재 유년 시절 경험의 제한을 받는 희생자

PART Ⅲ 테스트편

해석 부모로서 우리는 자녀에게 허용해야 할 자유에 대해 토론하는 데 수없이 많은 시간을 쓴다. 자유가 너무 많으면 나쁜 행동을 초래할 수도 있는 반면, 충분치 않으면 그들의 성장을 억누를 수도 있다. 어느 정도가 허용되어야 할까? 나는 자유에 관한 토론을 할 때 항상 서커스 코끼리를 떠올린다. 코끼리는 새끼일 때 4피트 길이의 쇠사슬이 달린 작은 말뚝에 묶여짐으로써 제한을 알게 된다. 코끼리는 자신의 자유가 그 작은 4피트에 제한된다는 것을 알도록 훈련받는다. 힘이 더 세지고 몸집이 더 커지면서도 코끼리는 여전히 그 4피트 밖에는 더 이상의 자유가 없다고 생각한다. 그 말뚝을 움직여 자유롭게 돌아다닐 수 있는 힘은 엄청나지만, 그것은 자신이 할 수 있다고 여기는 것 때문에 말뚝이나 사슬을 부수려는 시도를 하지 않을 것이다. 여러분도 스스로가 만든 구속의 희생자인가? 허용되지 않는다고 생각하기 때문에 4피트의 범위를 벗어나지 못하고 있지 않는가? 과감해지라. 여러분의 범위 밖으로 나가 성장할 수 있는지 살펴보라. 돌파구 없이는 변화가 있을 수 없다.

Solution Guide

새끼일 때 4피트 길이의 쇠사슬이 달린 작은 말뚝에 묶여 제한을 알게 된 서커스 코끼리는 힘이 더 세지고 몸집이 더 커지면서도 여전히 자신이 그 4피트 밖으로는 나갈 수 없다고 생각한다는 내용의 글이다. 따라서 밑줄 친 부분이 의미하는 바로 가장 적절한 것은 ⑤ '이전의 경험이 자신의 자유를 제한하는 희생자'이다.

① 개인적인 노력을 통해 자유를 성취하는 승리자
② 모든 상황에서 절대적 자유를 지지하는 자
③ 자유에 대한 책임을 강조하는 사상가
④ 유년 시절의 너무 많은 자유에 반대하는 비판가

Structure in Focus

- Although the power [to move that stake and run free] is immense, it will not attempt to break the stake or the chains because of [what it perceives as being able to].
  첫 번째 [ ]는 the power를 수식하는 to부정사구이고, 두 번째 [ ]는 because of의 목적어 역할을 하는 명사절이다.

06

정답 ⑤

소재 인종 이데올로기

해석 인종 이데올로기를 완화하는 가장 효과적인 방법은 다양한 인종적 배경을 가진 사람들을 한데 모아 서로를 개인으로서 대할 수 있게 하고 이데올로기가 사람들의 중요한 측면과 그들 삶의 현실을 보기 어렵게 한다는 것을 발견할 수 있게 하는 상황에 두는 것이다. 그러나 이는 교사, 코치, 고용주가 흑인의 타고난 신체적 재능과 인지 능력 부족에 대한 근거 없는 믿음을 유지할 때 어렵다. 사회과학자 Ellis Cashmore는 한 주요 신문사에서 기사를 쓰는 한 흑인 기자로부터 전화를 받은 경험으로 이를 분명히 보여 준다. 그 기자는 왜 아무도 자신이 절대적 진리라고 믿는 것, 즉 흑인 운동선수는 '타고난 장점'을 가지고 있다는 것을 실제로 표현하지 않는지 물었다. 유능한 흑인 기자가 이 결함이 있는 이론을 믿었다는 사실 자체가 그것이 가진 힘과 인종 이데올로기에 기반한 기대에서 벗어나기 어렵다는 것을 보여 주는 증거이다. 그러한 근거 없는 믿음이 사회에서 신뢰성을 유지하면, 흑인은 신체적 능력보다는 정신적 능력을 요구하는 학업, 업무 및 기타 활동에 적합하지 않거나 불필요하다고 여겨진다.

Solution Guide

유능한 흑인 기자가 흑인에 대한 인종 이데올로기를 벗어나지 못하는 질문을 던진 사례를 단적인 예로 들어 인종 이데올로기에서 벗어나기가 얼마나 어려운 일인지를 설명하는 내용의 글이다. 따라서 글의 주제로 가장 적절한 것은 ⑤ '흑인에 관한 인종 이데올로기를 벗어나는 것의 어려움'이다.

① 미디어가 인종에 관한 고정관념에 미치는 영향
② 직장 내 인종 다양성의 필요
③ 인종 편견에 대한 도전에서 교육의 역할
④ 인종 간의 조화 촉진에서 스포츠의 중요성

Structure in Focus

- [The most effective way to defuse racial ideology] is [to bring people from different ethnic backgrounds together under conditions {that enable them to 〈deal with one another as individuals〉 and 〈discover that ideologies obscure important aspects of people and the realities of their lives〉}].
  첫 번째 [ ]는 문장의 주어이고, 두 번째 [ ]는 is의 주격 보어 역할을 하는 to부정사구이다. { }는 conditions를 수식하는 관계절이고, 두 개의 〈 〉는 and로 연결되어 to에 이어져 enable의 목적격 보어 역할을 한다.
- The very fact [that a talented black journalist believed this defective theory] is evidence [to {its power} and {the difficulties in escaping expectations based on racial ideology}].
  첫 번째 [ ]는 The very fact와 동격 관계이다. 두 번째 [ ]는 evidence를 수식하는 전치사구이고, 그 안의 두 개의 { }는 and로 연결되어 전치사 to의 목적어 역할을 한다.

07

정답 ②

소재 협상의 기술

해석 협상가는 선택 사항을 수락하는 것의 매력도를 높여 그것을 더 마음에 들도록 만들 수 있다. 이는 부정적인 면보다 긍정적인 면을 강조하는 문제이다. 직원에게 동기를 부여하기 위한 전통적인 당근과 채찍 전술의 말로 하자면, 그 접근법은 채찍을 더 크게 만들기보다는 당근을 더 매력적으로 만들어야 한다. 약속과 제안은 여러 방식으로 더 매력적으로 만들 수 있는데, 매력적인 특성을 극대화하고 부정적인 특성을 최소화하거나, 제안이 상대방의 요구를 어떻게 충족하는지 보여 주거나, 제안 수락에 따른 불이익을 줄이거나, 제삼자의 추천이나 사실에 근거한 증거를 제공하여 제안을 더 신뢰성 있게 만들거나, 또는 제안이 빨리 수락되지 않으면 만료되도록 제안에 기한을 설정하는 것이다. 많은 이들은 이런 것들이 할인 쿠폰, 1+1 행사, '오늘 한정' 판매, 추가 매력 요소와 유사한 일반적인 판매 요령이라고 주장할 것이다. 그것들은 그렇다! 협상가는 판매원이 제품을 판매하기 위해 사용하는 것과 동일한 기술을 사용할 수 있고 그렇게 해야 한다.

Culture Note

extra-added-attraction elements(추가 매력 요소) 제품이나 서비스에 추가적인 매력을 더하기 위해 사용되는 판매 전략으로, 여기에는 무료 선물이나 샘플, 보너스 기능이나 혜택, 한정된 시간 동안 제공되는 할인, 경품 행사, 유명인 인증, 또는 소셜 미디어 프로모션 등이 포함될 수 있다. 이는 흔히 할인이나 쿠폰과 같은 다른 판매 전략과 함께 사용되어, 제품이나 서비스에 대한 긴박함과 흥분을 조장하고, 이로 인해 매출과 수익 증가가 나타날 수 있다.

Solution Guide

협상가는 당근과 채찍 전술을 사용하여, 즉 위협과 회유의 전술을 사용하여 협상에 임해야 하는데, 채찍을 더 크게 만들기보다는 당근을 더 매력적으로 만들어야 한다는 내용의 글이다. 따라서 글의 제목으로 가장 적절한 것은 ② '협상에서는 위협을 강화하기보다는 제안을 달콤하게 하라'이다.

① 중립적인 입지 구축하기: 협상의 출발점
③ 협상에서 승리하기 위해 사실에 근거한 증거와 법적 권한을 모두 사용하라
④ 협상가가 직접 제삼자의 개입을 추구하는 경우
⑤ 정해진 양의 자원을 배분하는 과정으로서의 협상

Structure in Focus

- Promises and offers can be made more attractive in several ways: [maximizing the attractive qualities and minimizing the negative ones], [showing {how the offer meets the other party's needs}], [reducing the disadvantages of accepting the offer], [making offers more credible by providing third-party references or factual support], or [setting deadlines on offers so they expire if not accepted quickly].
  다섯 개의 [ ]는 several ways의 구체적 내용을 설명하는 동명사구이다. 두 번째 [ ] 안의 { }는 showing의 목적어 역할을 하는 명사절이다.
- Many would argue [that these are common sales tricks {similar to discount coupons, two-for-the-price-of-one offers, "today only" sales, and extra-added-attraction elements}].
  [ ]는 argue의 목적어 역할을 하는 명사절이고, 그 안의 { }는 common sales tricks를 수식하는 형용사구이다.

08

정답 ②

소재 클라리넷 연주자 Benny Goodman

해석 Benny Goodman은 역대 가장 위대한 클라리넷 연주자 중 한 명이다. 1909년 시카고에서 태어난 그는 10세에 레슨을 받기 시작했다. 타고난 재능을 바탕으로 그는 빠르게 발전하여 곧 전문적으로 연주하게 되었다. 그는 뉴올리언스 재즈에 큰 영향을 받았고, 그것은 평생 그의 음악에 중요한 역할을 했다. 16세에 그는 시카고의 Ben Pollack 오케스트라에 입단했는데, 그것은 당시 미국 최고의 밴드 중 하나였다. 그는 곧 음반 녹음을 하게 되었고, 얼마 지나지 않아 자신만의 밴드를 결성했다. Goodman은 1935년 이전에도 비교적 잘 알려져 있었지만, 정말로 그의 경력을 크게 도약하게 한 것은 바로 로스앤젤레스의 Palomar Ballroom에서 생긴 그의 스타일의 변화였다. 그리고 몇 년 후, 그는 뉴욕시의 카네기 홀에서 연주하게 되었다. 당시에 이것은 재즈 오케스트라에게 처음 있는 일이었다. 그 연주회는 엄청난 성공을 거두었다. 수년간 전문적 관객의 관심만 끌고 나서, 재즈가 마침내 성공하여 주류 관객에게 받아들여지고 있었다.

Solution Guide

뉴올리언스 재즈에 큰 영향을 받았다(He was strongly influenced by New Orleans jazz, ~)고 했으므로, 글의 내용과 일치하지 않는 것은 ②이다.

Structure in Focus

- [Born in 1909 in Chicago], he began taking lessons at the age of 10.
  [ ]는 주절의 주어 he의 부수적 상황을 나타내는 분사구문이다.
- Although Goodman was relatively well known before 1935, **it was** [the change in his style {that occurred in the Palomar Ballroom in Los Angeles}] **that** really caused his career to take off.

PART Ⅲ 테스트편

[ ]는 it was와 that절 사이에 놓여 그 의미가 강조되고 있다. 그 안의 { }는 the change in his style을 수식하는 관계절이다.

09

정답 ③

소재 연령 집단별 소득층 점유율

해석 위 도표는 1971년과 2021년 미국 성인의 각 소득층 점유율(%)을 연령 집단별로 보여 준다. 18세에서 29세의 미국 성인 사이에서, 상위 소득층의 점유율은 1971년에서 2021년까지 5퍼센트포인트 증가했고, 반면에 그들의 중간 소득층 점유율은 같은 기간에 12퍼센트포인트 감소했다. 1971년의 중간 소득층에서, 30세에서 44세 미국 성인의 점유율이 다른 어떤 연령 집단의 점유율보다 더 높았다. 1971년에는 3분의 2가 넘는 45세에서 64세 미국 성인이 중간 소득층이었고, 2021년에는 그 연령 집단의 절반이 넘는 사람들이 같은 소득층에 있었다. 하위 소득층에서 65세 이상 미국 성인의 점유율은 1971년 54퍼센트에서 2021년 37퍼센트로 떨어졌고, 반면에 같은 기간의 중간 소득층에서 그들의 점유율은 39퍼센트에서 47퍼센트로 상승했다. 하지만 65세 이상의 미국 성인은 2021년에 3명 중 1명이 넘게 하위 소득층인 유일한 연령 집단이었다.

Solution Guide

1971년에 45세에서 64세 성인은 60퍼센트, 2021년에 49퍼센트가 중간 소득층에 속해 각각 3분의 2와 절반에 미치지 못하므로, 도표의 내용과 일치하지 않는 것은 ③이다.

Structure in Focus

- However, American adults 65 and older were the only age group [in which more than one-in-three adults were in the lower-income tier in 2021].
  [ ]는 the only age group을 수식하는 관계절이다.

10

정답 ④

소재 어린이 퀼트 챌린지

해석 **2024 어린이 퀼트 챌린지**

재미있고 신나는 도전에 참여할 준비가 되셨나요?
그렇다면 어린이 퀼트 챌린지에 참여하여 여러분의 창의력과 디자인 실력을 뽐내 보세요.

대회 지침

1. 이 대회는 15세 이하의 모든 청소년이 참여할 수 있습니다.
2. 이 대회는 대회 참가 신청서를 제출하는 맨 처음 50명으로 제한됩니다.
3. 퀼트는 지름이 45인치보다 더 크면 안 됩니다. 퀼트 작업은 손이나 기계로 해도 됩니다.
4. 대회 참가자는 퀼트를 우편으로 제출해야 하며, 그것은 8월 9일까지 도착해야 합니다.
5. 퀼트는 9월 5일부터 7일까지 The Great Wisconsin Quilt Show에서 전시될 것입니다. 수상자는 9월 7일, 토요일에 그 쇼에서 발표될 것입니다.
6. 상위 3명의 우승자에게는 1등 300달러, 2등 200달러, 3등 100달러의 상금이 수여될 것입니다.

Solution Guide

수상자는 9월 7일, 토요일 Show에서 발표된다(Winners will be announced at the Show on Saturday, September 7.)고 했고 9월 7일은 퀼트 쇼 마지막 날이므로, 안내문의 내용과 일치하지 않는 것은 ④이다.

Structure in Focus

- The contest is limited to the first 50 people [who submit a contest entry form].
  [ ]는 the first 50 people을 수식하는 관계절이다.

11

정답 ⑤

소재 Brownstone House 자선 자원봉사 클리닉

해석 **Brownstone House 자선 자원봉사 클리닉**

Brownstone House 자선 자원봉사 클리닉은 건강한 생활 방식을 장려하는 데 중점을 두는 비영리 단체인 Brownstone House의 많은 계획 중 하나입니다. 이 클리닉은 곤궁에 처한 사람들에게 기본적인 의료 서비스와 지원을 제공하는 자원봉사자들이 직원으로 구성되어 있으며, 2016년 개원 이래 10,000명이 넘는 환자를 진료했습니다.

세부 정보

- 토요일 및 일요일, 오전 9시 ~ 오후 1시에 문을 엽니다.
- 장소: Brownstone House 2층 210호실 (West Bellfort Avenue 555번지)
- 비용: 첫 방문 때 8달러, 그리고 이후 방문마다 5달러
- 클리닉은 예약으로만 운영됩니다. 예약을 잡거나 취소하려면, 주중에 Brownstone House 700-123-4567로 전화 주십시오.

참고

- 의사의 개인 사무실이나 휴대 전화로 의사에게 직접 연락을 시도하지 말아 주십시오.

더 많은 정보를 원하시면, cyn@brownstonehouseinc.org로 우리에게 이메일을 보내주시기 바랍니다.

Solution Guide

의사의 개인 사무실이나 휴대 전화로 직접 연락을 시도하지 말아 달라고 했으므로, 안내문의 내용과 일치하는 것은 ⑤이다.

Structure in Focus

- The Brownstone House Charity Volunteer Clinic is one of the many initiatives of Brownstone House, [a nonprofit organization {that focuses on promoting healthy lifestyles}].
  [ ]는 Brownstone House와 동격 관계이고, 그 안의 { }는 a nonprofit organization을 수식하는 관계절이다.
- The clinic [is staffed by volunteers {who provide basic medical care and support to those in need}] and [has served more than 10,000 patients since opening in 2016].
  두 개의 [ ]는 and로 연결되어 문장의 술어 역할을 한다. 첫 번째 [ ] 안의 { }는 volunteers를 수식하는 관계절이다.

12

정답 ④

소재 인간이 다른 종과 관계를 맺는 방식

해석 크리족 사냥꾼의 세계관에서는 인간이 사냥을 통제하지 않는다. 물고기와 사냥감은 단순히 잡히도록 그곳에 있는 것이 아니다. 그보다는 사람들에게 자기 자신을 기꺼이 제공함으로써 (또는 반대로 사냥꾼에게 자기 자신을 허락하지 않음으로써) 사냥의 성공을 통제하는 것은 바로 동물이다. 크리족은 동물들이 사람들이 아는 것과 같은 것을 알고 그 지식을 사람들에게 전하고 공유할 수 있다고 생각한다. 인간과 동물은 호혜 관계에 있는데, 마치 인간이 다른 인간과의 관계에서 그런 것과 꼭 마찬가지이다. 실제로 인류학자들은 훨씬 더 보편적으로 근대와 포스트 모던의 문화를 포함하여 모든 문화에서 사람들이 서로 관계를 맺는 방식과 다른 종과 관계를 맺는 방식 사이에 지대한 관계가 있다고 주장한다.

Solution Guide

④ 주절에 쓰인 are in a relationship of reciprocity의 반복을 피하기 위해 사용되었으므로 do를 are로 고쳐야 한다.

① take의 대상인 The fish and game을 의미상의 주어로 하여 목적을 나타내는 수동형의 to부정사구가 쓰인 것은 어법상 적절하다.

② offering을 수식하는 부사에 해당하므로 어법상 적절하다.

③ knowing이 이끄는 동명사구와 and로 연결되어 전치사 with의 목적어로 기능하는 동명사구를 이끄는 being은 어법상 적절하다.

⑤ the ways를 수식하는 관계절을 이끄는 관계사로 that이 쓰인 것은 어법상 적절하다.

Structure in Focus

- The Cree credit animals with [knowing the same things {that people know}] and [being able to communicate and share {that knowledge with people}].
  두 개의 [ ]는 and로 연결되어 전치사 with의 목적어 역할을 하는 동명사구이다. 첫 번째 [ ] 안의 { }는 the same things를 수식하는 관계절이다. 두 번째 [ ] 안의 { }는 communicate와 share에 공통으로 이어진다.
- Indeed, anthropologists argue even more generally [that in all cultures, including those {that are modern and postmodern}, there are profound connections between the ways {that people engage with each other and with other species}].
  [ ]는 argue의 목적어 역할을 하는 명사절이고, 그 안의 첫 번째 { }는 those를 수식하는 관계절이며, 두 번째 { }는 the ways를 수식하는 관계절이다.

13

정답 ⑤

소재 원격 근무를 통한 새로운 고용의 창출

해석 우리의 인터넷 경제에서 가사 전담 부모에게 새로운 직장 선택권이 생겼다. 지난 수십 년 동안 많은 여성들이 자영업을 해왔다. 그러한 방식은 근무 시간과 근무일에 더 큰 유연성을 제공한다. 원격 근무의 증가는 그들을 위한 기회를 더욱 늘릴 수 있을 것이다. Withinwork와 같은 인터넷 플랫폼은 일자리를 구하는 근로자가 이력서를 올리고 근로자를 구하는 고용주가 그들이 할 일을 게시하므로, 쌍방 간의 플랫폼이다. 인공 지능(AI) 알고리즘은 여기서 어떤 사람이 보는 일련의 일자리를 수집하여 제시함으로써 핵심적인 매칭 역할을 한다. 나는 Withinwork에서 프로필을 설정하고 AI가 내게 제안한 (내가) 선택할 수 있는 일에 깊은 인상을 받았다. 모든 쌍방 간의 매칭 플랫폼과 마찬가지로, 지원자가 더 많은 채용 정보를 볼수록 그 사람이 그 플랫폼에서 가치를 발견할 가능성은 더 높아진다. 이런 의미에서, 원격 근무가 사회적으로 높은 지위의 활동으로 성장함에 따라, 이 과정은 자체적인 힘을 잃을(→ 얻을) 것이다.

Solution Guide

인터넷 경제에서 가사 전담 부모에게 새로운 직장 선택권이 생겨서 근무 시간과 근무일에 더 큰 유연성이 생기게 되었다는 내용의

PART Ⅲ 테스트편

글이다. Withinwork와 같은 쌍방향 플랫폼으로 인해 고용주와 근로자 간의 연결이 더 수월해지고, 이로 인해 원격 근무가 사회적으로 높은 지위를 차지하는 활동으로 성장함에 따라 그런 과정이 힘을 얻게 될 것임을 추론할 수 있다. 따라서 ⑤의 lose를 gain과 같은 낱말로 바꾸어야 한다.

Structure in Focus

- Internet platforms such as Withinwork are two-sided platforms as workers [seeking employment] post their resumes and employers [seeking workers] post their tasks.
  첫 번째 [ ]는 workers를 수식하는 분사구이고, 두 번째 [ ]는 employers를 수식하는 분사구이다.
- I [set up my profile on Withinwork] and [was impressed with the alternative tasks {that I was offered by the AI}].
  두 개의 [ ]는 and로 연결되어 문장의 술어 역할을 한다. 두 번째 [ ] 안의 { }는 the alternative tasks를 수식하는 관계절이다.

14

정답 ③

소재 사회적 약자 우대 정책

해석 사회적 약자 우대 정책의 적절한 수혜 대상에 대한 상당한 논쟁이 존재한다. 미국에서 사회적 약자 우대 정책을 지지하는 사람들은 많은 소수 집단에 적용될 수 있도록 적용 범위를 확대함으로써 그러한 프로그램을 지지하는 정치적 기반을 넓히기를 바랐다. 그러나 실제로는 어떤 이들의 마음에서 더 넓어진 적용 범위는 정부 차별의 가장 명백한 피해자, 즉 아프리카계 미국인과 아메리카 원주민을 돕기 위해 의도된 프로그램을 지지하는 도덕적 논거를 약화하였다. 어떤 이들은 맥락이 중요하다고 주장한다. 따라서 아시아계 미국인과 여성은 일반적으로 대학교의 전체 학생 중에서 불충분하게 대표되지 않기 때문에, (그렇다고 해서 이들을 제한 대상으로 지목해서는 안 되지만) 그들을 위한 사회적 약자 우대 입학은 이제 부적절할 것이다. 반면에 기업 임원이나 대학교 교수진 중, 흑인, 아시아계, 라틴계, 여성은 모두 과거에 배제의 상황에 직면했고 오늘날에 여전히 불충분하게 대표되고 있으므로, 이 영역에서는 네 집단 모두 사회적 약자 우대 정책의 수혜 대상이어야 한다.

Solution Guide

사회적 약자 우대 정책의 적용 범위에 관한 한 가지 주장에 대한 핵심 논거가 빈칸에 들어가야 한다. 현재의 (사회적) 맥락을 고려하여 사회적 약자 우대 정책의 적용 범위를 과거와는 달리해야 한다는 주장이 이어지는 것으로 보아, 빈칸에 들어갈 말로 가장 적절한 것은 ③이다.

① 예산
② 성별
④ 교육
⑤ 성격

Structure in Focus

- Considerable debate exists [as to the appropriate beneficiaries of affirmative action].
  [ ]는 Considerable debate를 수식하는 전치사구이다.
- In practice, however, the wider coverage has diluted, in the minds of some, [the moral argument {in favor of a program 〈intended to help the most obvious victims of governmental discrimination: African Americans and Native Americans〉}].
  [ ]는 diluted의 목적어 역할을 하는 명사구이고, 그 안의 { }는 the moral argument를 수식하는 전치사구이며, 그 안의 〈 〉는 a program을 수식하는 분사구이다.

15

정답 ③

소재 기술 혁신으로 인한 창조적 파괴

해석 기술 혁신에 기인한 실업에 대한 예측은 산업 혁명이 시작된 이래로 되풀이되어 왔다. 그러나 반복되는 현실은 창조적 파괴를 통한 경제 성장이라는 것이었다. 그렇다, 기계는 많은 일자리를 파괴했으며, 흔히 새로운 일자리가 너무 늦거나 구할 수 없는 실직 노동자에게 자주 치명적인 영향을 미쳤다. 그러나 시간이 지나면서 일자리 파괴는 새롭고 대개는 더 나은 일자리와 더 높은 소득으로 들어간 노동력과 자본을 풀어 놓았다. 그것은 기술이 노동, 특히 저숙련 노동을 '대체하기도' 하고 노동을 '보완하기도' 해서, 즉 그것을 더 생산적으로 만들기도 해서, 노동의 새로운 수요를 만들어 내기 때문이다. 건성으로 관찰하는 사람들은 흔히 '기계가 인간 노동을 대체하는 정도를 과장하는' 경향이 있었고, 이는 쉽게 관찰할 수 있었는데, 그들은 '남아 있을 인간 노동에 대한 수요를 반복적으로 과소평가했다.'

Solution Guide

기술 혁신이 실업을 초래하긴 했으나 시간이 지나면서 더 나은 일자리와 더 높은 소득으로 들어간 노동력과 자본을 풀어 놓았는데 이는 기술이 노동의 새로운 수요를 만들어 내기 때문이라는 것이 글의 중심 내용이므로, 빈칸에 들어갈 말로 가장 적절한 것은 ③이다.

① 아이디어 생산

② 확장된 마케팅
④ 통제된 자유
⑤ 다양화된 수요

Structure in Focus

- That is because technology **both** [*substitutes* for labor — in particular, less-skilled labor —] **and** [*complements* labor, or makes it more productive], [thus generating new demand for labor].
  첫 번째와 두 번째 [ ]는 「both ~ and ...」로 대등하게 연결되어 because가 유도하는 부사절의 술어 역할을 한다. 세 번째 [ ]는 앞 절의 상황에서 비롯된 결과를 나타내는 분사구문이다.
- Casual observers have often tended "to overstate the extent of machine substitution for human labor," [which was readily observable]; they "repeatedly underestimated the demand for the work of human beings [that would remain]."
  첫 번째 [ ]는 machine substitution for human labor를 부가적으로 설명하는 관계절이고, 두 번째 [ ]는 the demand for the work of human beings를 수식하는 관계절이다.

16

정답 ①

소재 컴퓨터 음악에서 손놀림과 음의 관계

해석 음악용 장비가 악기가 되는 가장 일반적인 상황은 라이브 공연에서다. 피아노 연주는 일반적으로 실시간 연주와 관련되는데, 컴퓨터 기반 악기는 점점 더 실시간으로 연주되고 있다. 예를 들어, 라이브 전자 음악가 공연에서 노트북 컴퓨터는 키보드 신시사이저, 그루브 박스, 턴테이블에도 우선해서 점점 더 많이 사용된다. 컴퓨터 연주에서 달라지는 한 가지는 손놀림과 음의 관계가 때로 덜 직접적이라는 것이다. 어쿠스틱 악기 연주에서는 음악가의 손놀림이 음으로 바뀐다. 피아노나 신시사이저 건반을 누르거나 기타의 지판에 손가락을 슬라이드 하는 것을 포함해서 많은 악기는 일대일의 손놀림 대 음 관계를 갖고 있는데, 각각은 손놀림을 곧바로 들을 수 있는 결과로 바꾼다. 한 번의 마우스 손놀림이나 파라미터 조작이 리듬 파트의 복잡성이나 음악적인 목소리의 전체 앙상블의 음색과 음량을 바꾸는 경우에, 많은 전자 및 컴퓨터 기반 악기는 일대다의 손놀림 대 음 관계를 갖는다.

Culture Note

slide(슬라이드 주법) 기타줄을 짚은 손가락을 지판에 밀착한 채로 위아래 방향으로 쭉 미끄러뜨리듯 슬라이드 하여 음 사이의 전환을 매끄럽게 이어 주는 주법

Solution Guide

어쿠스틱 악기 연주에서는 피아노 건반을 누르거나 기타의 지판에 손가락을 슬라이드 하는 음악가의 손놀림이 직접적인 소리를 내지만, 컴퓨터 음악 연주는 마우스의 움직임이나 파라미터 조작이 리듬 파트나 전체 앙상블의 음색과 음량을 바꾸는 경우, 동작과 소리의 관계에 있어서 일대다의 관계가 있다고 했으므로, 빈칸에 들어갈 말로 가장 적절한 것은 ①이다.
② 결과로 하나의 매체에 음성, 시각 또는 텍스트가 모두 있을 수 있다는
③ 음악가는 손놀림을 사용하여 자신을 더 명확하게 표현할 수 있다는
④ 클래식 음악에서 컴퓨터를 악기로 사용할 수 있다는
⑤ 컴퓨터 음악 제작은 수고를 줄이고 다양한 가능성을 제공한다는

Structure in Focus

- [The most common situation {in which musical equipment becomes an instrument}] is in live performance.
  [ ]는 문장의 주어 역할을 하는 명사구이고, 그 안의 { }는 The most common situation을 수식하는 관계절이다.
- One thing [that changes in computer performances] is [that the gestural relationship with sound is sometimes less direct].
  첫 번째 [ ]는 One thing을 수식하는 관계절이고, 두 번째 [ ]는 is의 주격 보어 역할을 하는 명사절이다.

17

정답 ①

소재 불확신과 주장의 강도

해석 두 명의 Northwestern University 마케팅 연구자인 David Gal과 Derek Rucker는 사람들이 확신하지 못하게 만들기 위해 프레이밍 기술을 사용하여 연구를 수행했다. 예를 들어, 그들은 한 집단에게는 그들이 완전히 확신에 차 있던 때를 기억하라고 말했고, 다른 집단에게는 그들이 의심으로 가득 찼던 때를 기억하라고 말했다. 그런 다음 그들은 참가자들에게 그들이 고기를 먹는 사람인지, 채식주의자인지, 엄격한 채식주의자인지, 아니면 그 밖의 사람인지, 이것이 그들에게 얼마나 중요한지, 그리고 그들이 자신의 의견을 얼마나 확신하는지를 물었다. 불확신의 시기를 기억하도록 요청받았던 사람들은 자신의 식생활 선택에 대해 확신이 더 적었다. 그러나 자신이 먹는 방식으로 먹도록 다른 누군가를 설득하기 위해 자신의 믿음을 쓰라고 요청받았을 때, 그들은 자신의 선택에 대해 확신했던 사람들보다 더 많고 더 강력한 주장을 쓰곤 했다. Gal과 Rucker는 그 연구를 (예를 들면

PART Ⅲ 테스트편

매킨토시 컴퓨터 선호 대 윈도즈 컴퓨터 선호와 같이) 여러 다른 주제들을 가지고 수행했으며 비슷한 결과를 발견했다. 확신이 더 적을 때, 사람들은 단호해지고 훨씬 더 강하게 주장하곤 했다.

Solution Guide

David Gal과 Derek Rucker의 실험에서, 불확실한 기분이 들도록 프레이밍 된 사람들은 더 단호하고 더욱 강하게 주장하곤 했다는 내용이 제시되므로, 빈칸에 들어갈 말로 가장 적절한 것은 ①이다.

② 자신의 의견에 대한 더 적은 증거를 찾곤
③ 그들의 의견을 더욱 기꺼이 바꾸곤
④ 연구자들의 의도를 더 강하게 의심하곤
⑤ 그들의 선택에 대한 근거가 되는 세부 사항을 덜 기억하곤

Structure in Focus

- For example, they told one group [to remember a time {when they were full of certainty}], and the other group [to remember a time {when they were full of doubt}].
  두 개의 [ ]는 told의 목적격 보어 역할을 하는 to부정사구이다. 두 개의 { }는 각각 a time을 수식하는 관계절이다.
- However, when asked to write their beliefs [to persuade someone else to eat the way {they **did**}], they would write more and stronger arguments than those [who were certain of their choice].
  첫 번째 [ ]는 목적을 나타내는 to부정사구이고, 그 안의 { }는 the way를 수식하는 관계절이며, did는 ate을 대신한다. 두 번째 [ ]는 those를 수식하는 관계절이다.

18

정답 ④

소재 일시적인 미디어 단식의 필요성

해석 우리의 음식, 음료, 습관 중 일부로부터 잠시 휴식을 취하는 것, 즉 '단식하는' 것이 때로는 바람직한 것과 마찬가지로, 미디어 단식도 여러분의 신체에 좋을 수도 있다. 일정 시간 언플러그드 상태로 보내 보면 미디어 사용 습관의 장단점을 명료하게 알 수 있다. 전자기기 없는 생활은 끊임없는 주의 산만, 온라인 광고, 인공 청색광에서 여러분이 잠시 벗어나게 해 준다. 여러분은 신체 활동, 대면 상호 작용, 그리고 심지어 고독과 같은 다른 것들을 위한 더 많은 시간을 가질 것이다. (가장 중요한 것은 여러분이 대면 의사소통, 컴퓨터 매개 의사소통, 또는 그 둘의 어떤 조합을 하기로 선택할 때 무엇을 얻고 무엇을 잃는가에 관해 주의 깊게 생각하는 것이다.) 여러분은 또한 커뮤니케이션 시대의 삶이 이전의 생활, 그리고 세상과 연결하고 소통하는 방식과 어떻게 다른지 비판적으로 고찰할 기회를 갖게 될 것이다.

Solution Guide

첫 문장에서 일시적으로 미디어의 사용을 중단하는 미디어 금식이 신체에 좋을 것이라고 전제한 다음, 그것의 유익한 점으로서 자신의 미디어 관행 점검, 미디어의 부정적 측면으로부터의 자유, 다른 것들을 위한 시간 확보, 커뮤니케이션 시대의 생활에 관한 고찰 기회를 제시하는 내용의 글이므로, 여러 의사소통 방식의 장단점을 숙고하는 것이 중요하다는 내용의 ④는 글의 전체 흐름과 관계가 없다.

Structure in Focus

- In the same way [that **it** is sometimes advisable {to take a momentary break, or "fast," from some of our food, beverages, and habits}], a media fast may be good for your system.
  [ ]는 the same way를 수식하는 관계절이다. 관계절 내에서 it은 형식상의 주어이고, { }는 내용상의 주어이다.
- You'll also have the opportunity [to reflect critically on {how life in the Communication Age differs from older modes of living and connecting and engaging with the world}].
  [ ]는 the opportunity의 구체적 내용을 설명하는 to부정사구이고, 그 안의 { }는 on의 목적어로 쓰인 명사절이다.

19

정답 ①

소재 대중의 존경을 중시하는 나르시시스트

해석 자존감과 대중의 존경을 구분할 수 있는 한, 후자가 더 중요한 것 같다. 나르시시스트의 최우선시되는 동기는 다른 사람들로부터 사회적 인정을 받는 것인 것 같다. (A) 즉, 그들은 다른 사람들이 자신을 존경하게 만드는 방법을 찾는 데 많은 시간과 에너지를 소모한다. 다른 사람의 존경보다는 호감을 받는 면에서는 그들은 다소 무관심하다. 즉, 나르시시스트는 호감을 얻는 데 관심이 있는 정도가 다른 어떤 사람보다 더 많지도 더 적지도 않다. (C) 하지만 존경을 받는 것은 그들에게 매우 중요하다. (아마도 이미 자기 자신의 좋은 자질을 은밀히 확신하고 있기 때문에) 일반적으로 그들은 자신에게 무언가를 증명하는 데 지나치게 관심이 있는 것 같지는 않지만, 다른 사람들에게 자신의 우월성을 보여 주는 데는 상당히 관심이 있다. (B) 예를 들어, 어려운 과제를 다루며 자신이 얼마나 유능한지 알아볼 기회가 주어지면, 나르시시스트는 아무도 보지 않을 때는 최소한의 노력을 기울이는데, 이는 자신의 탁월함을 자신에게 입증하는 데 별로 관심이 없다는 신

호이며, 반면에 다른 사람이 보고 있으면 그들은 돋보이기 위해 최대한의 노력을 기울인다.

Solution Guide

나르시시스트의 최우선시되는 동기는 대중의 존경, 즉 사회적 인정을 받는 것이라고 화제를 제시하는 주어진 글 다음에, 이 내용을 환언하면서 한편으로 그들이 다른 사람들의 호감을 얻는 데는 다소 무관심하다는 내용의 (A)가 이어져야 한다. (A)의 내용과는 대조적으로 나르시시스트는 자신의 우월성을 보여 주어 다른 사람들의 존경을 받는 것을 중요하게 생각한다는 내용의 (C)가 온 후, 그것의 구체적인 사례를 설명하는 (B)가 이어지는 것이 글의 순서로 가장 적절하다.

Structure in Focus

- That is, they **spend** much of their time and energy **seeking** [ways to get others to admire them].
  「spend ~ -ing」는 '~을 …하는 데 소모하다'의 의미를 나타낸다. [ ]는 seeking의 목적어 역할을 하는 명사구이다.
- For example, [if given a chance {to tackle a difficult task and find out how good they are}], narcissists put forth minimal effort if no one is looking, [which is a sign {that they do not really care about demonstrating their brilliance to themselves}], [whereas if others are watching, they put forth maximum effort in order to shine].
  첫 번째 [ ]는 조건을 나타내는 분사구문으로, 의미를 명확히 하기 위해 접속사를 명시했다. 그 안의 { }는 a chance의 구체적 내용을 설명하는 to부정사구이다. 두 번째 [ ]는 주절의 내용을 부가적으로 설명하는 관계절이고, 그 안의 { }는 a sign과 동격 관계이다. 세 번째 [ ]는 대조를 나타내는 부사절이다.

20

정답 ③

소재 등반과 윤리

해석 등반과 철학이 교차하는 한 가지 명백한 영역은 등반의 규범적인 차원, 즉 등반가의 윤리적이거나 비윤리적인 행동과 관련된 것이다. 등반에서의 윤리적 문제 중 일부에는 더 일반적인 도덕 원칙의 직접적인 연장이 수반된다. (B) 예를 들어, 여러분의 등반 업적에 관해 거짓말하는 것은, 성과에 대해 거짓말을 하는 것이 일반적으로 잘못이기 때문에 잘못이며, 절벽에서 불필요하게 다른 사람을 위험에 빠뜨리는 것은, 더 일반적으로는 다른 사람을 불필요하게 위험에 빠뜨리는 것이 항상 잘못이기 때문에 잘못이다. (C) 그러나 다른 윤리적인 문제들은 등반에 고유한 요인들을 수반하므로, 그런 까닭에 더 광범위한 도덕 규칙을 적용하여 해결될 수 없다. 줄을 타고 내려올 때 (바위에) 볼트를 설치하는 것은 잘못인가? 전통적인 (등반) 구간에서 먼저 설치된 장비를 쓰는 것은 속이는 것인가? (A) 이러한 종류의 질문에는 더 광범위한 도덕 규칙들이 어떤 직접적인 방식으로도 적용되지 않고, 등반가들은 등반의 상황 속에서 무엇이 옳은지 그른지를 스스로 알아내야 한다.

Solution Guide

주어진 글은 등반의 윤리적 문제 중 일부에는 더 일반적인 도덕 원칙의 직접적인 연장이 수반된다고 언급한다. 다음으로 (B)에서 그 사례 두 가지를 제시하고, (C)에서 이런 방식으로 해결될 수 없는 등반의 고유 요인과 관련된 다른 윤리적 문제들이 있음을 언급하고 그런 사례 두 가지를 제시하고 난 다음, (A)에서 these sorts of questions로 (C)의 문제를 받아, 이러한 문제들은 등반의 맥락 안에서 파악되어야 함을 언급해야 글의 흐름이 자연스럽게 연결될 수 있다.

Structure in Focus

- [One obvious area {where climbing and philosophy intersect}] **is** with regard to the normative dimension of climbing — the ethical or unethical behavior of climbers.
  [ ]는 문장의 주어 역할을 하는 명사구이고, 술어동사는 is이다. [ ] 안의 { }는 One obvious area를 수식하는 관계절이다.
- However, other ethical issues [involve factors {that are unique to climbing}] and thus [cannot be resolved by invoking broader moral rules].
  두 개의 [ ]는 and로 연결되어 문장의 술어를 이룬다. 첫 번째 [ ] 안의 { }는 factors를 수식하는 관계절이다.

21

정답 ⑤

소재 지각에 수반된 시각적 자극 처리 과정

해석 감각과 지각은 거의 항상 함께 일어난다. 그러나 연구자들은 그 두 가지가 어떻게 함께 작용하는지 알아내기 위해 각 과정을 개별적으로 연구해 왔다. 지각은 상향식 처리 과정을 통해 생길 수 있는데, 그런 과정은 환경으로부터의 물리적 자극에서 시작하여 그러한 자극을 신경 자극으로 바꾸는 변환을 거치면서 진행된다. 그 신호는 잇따라서 더 복잡한 뇌 영역으로 전달되고, 궁극적으로 시각적 자극의 인식으로 이어진다. 예를 들어, 여러분이 가장 친한 친구의 얼굴을 볼 때, 여러분의 눈은 빛 에너지를 신경 자극으로 변환하는데, 그 자극은 뇌로 들어와 시각 영역으로 간다. 이 정보는 시각적 자극을 감지하고 궁극적으로 그것의 지각을 위한 기초를 형성한다. 그러나, 지각에 똑같이 중요한 것은 하향식 처리 과정인데, 그 과정은 이전에 습득한 지식을 포함한다. 그 결과, 여러분이 가장 친한 친구의 얼굴을 볼 때, 얼굴이, 특히 여러분에게 친숙한 얼굴이 어떻게 생겼는지에 대한 정보를 저장하는 뇌 영역은 여러분이 특정한 시각적 자극을 지각하고 인식하는 데 도움을 줄 수 있다.

Solution Guide

지각은 감각을 통한 자극이 뇌 영역으로 전달되는 상향식 처리 과정을 통해 일어나지만, 뇌에 저장된 정보가 자극을 지각하고 인식하는 데 도움을 주는 하향식 처리 과정도 중요하다는 내용의 글이다. 주어진 문장에서 하향식 처리가 지각에 중요한 역할을 한다고 했는데, ⑤의 앞부분까지는 상향식 처리 과정을 설명하는 내용이고, ⑤의 바로 다음 문장은 하향식 처리가 자극을 지각하고 인식하는 데 도움이 된다는 내용이므로, 주어진 문장이 들어가기에 가장 적절한 곳은 ⑤이다.

Structure in Focus

- Equally important to perception, however, is [top-down processing, {which involves previously acquired knowledge}].

  [ ]는 문장의 주어 역할을 하는 명사구인데, 형용사구가 문두에 오면서 동사 is가 주어 앞에 놓이는 어순이 되었다. { }는 top-down processing을 부가적으로 설명하는 관계절이다.
- As a result, when you look at your best friend's face, brain regions [that store information about what faces look like, particularly {**those** ⟨that are familiar to you⟩}], can help you to perceive and recognize the specific visual stimulus.

  [ ]는 brain regions를 수식하는 관계절이다. [ ] 안의 { }는 앞의 faces에 대해 부가적으로 설명하는 명사구이고, 그 안의 ⟨ ⟩는 those를 수식하는 관계절이다.

22

정답 ②

소재 성 주류화

해석 유럽 연합은 1990년대 후반부터 정책 입안에서 성 불평등을 해결하기 위한 주요 전략으로 성 주류화를 받아들였다. 그것은 정책 과정의 모든 단계(설계, 실행, 모니터링, 평가)에 성 인지 관점을 통합하는 것으로 정의된다. 성 주류화는 모든 정책이 사회 및 인구 통계학적 집단에 다르게 영향을 미쳐, 결과적으로 불평등한 권력관계를 형성하고 유지할 가능성이 있다는 이해를 바탕으로 한다. 예를 들어, 성 주류화는 남성의 법적 권리로서의 육아 휴직이나 여성이 주로 종사하는 직종(예컨대, 간호직)에서의 남성을 위한 노동 정책과 같은, 남성의 경험을 명시적으로 고려할 수도 있다. 성 주류화는 건강 관리에도 적용되어 여성과 남성의 건강 관리 요구를 동등하게 증진할 수 있다. 많은 국가에서 관상 동맥 심장 질환은 남성적 식견을 통해 정의되어 예방에서 회복에 이르기까지 의료의 모든 영역에 영향을 미친다. 이는 여성의 심장 건강에 대한 요구를 간과하는 결과를 초래할 뿐만 아니라, 헤게모니 남성성 모델에 맞는 것으로 보이지 않는 남성에게 부정적으로 영향을 미칠 수도 있다.

Culture Note

hegemonic masculinity(헤게모니 남성성) 사회적으로 구성된 남성성으로, 가부장제에서 권위 있는 남성성을 대표한다.

Solution Guide

주어진 문장은 모든 정책이 사회 및 인구 통계학적 집단에 다르게 영향을 미쳐 불평등한 권력관계를 형성하고 유지할 가능성이 있다는 성 주류화의 기반이 되는 개념을 설명한다. 따라서 이 문장 바로 앞에는 성 주류화의 일반적 정의가 언급되어야 하고, 바로 뒤에는 구체적인 사례가 제시되어야 한다. 따라서 주어진 문장이 들어가기에 가장 적절한 곳은 ②이다.

Structure in Focus

- Gender mainstreaming is based on the understanding [that all policies have the potential to impact social and demographic groups differently, {thus creating and sustaining unequal power relations}].

  [ ]는 the understanding과 동격 관계이다. { }는 앞에서 기술된 내용의 결과로 일어나는 상황을 기술하는 분사구문이다.
- **Not only does this** lead to overlooking women's heart health needs, but it also may negatively impact men [who do not seem to fit the model of hegemonic masculinity].

  부정어구 Not only로 문장이 시작되어 조동사 does가 주어 this 앞에 놓이는 어순이 되었다. [ ]는 men을 수식하는 관계절이다.

23

정답 ②

소재 뉴런의 경쟁과 뇌의 재구조화

해석 전통적인 교과서 그림은 뇌의 뉴런이 병에 든 콩 모양 젤리처럼 행복하게 서로 나란히 들어차 있다고 암시하지만, 만화에 속지 말라. 뉴런은 생존을 위한 경쟁에서 헤어나지 못한다. 인접한 국가와 마찬가지로 뉴런도 자기 영역을 차지하고 끈질기게 방어한다. 그것은 신경계의 모든 수준에서 영역과 생존을 위해 싸우며 각 뉴런 그리고 뉴런 간의 각 연결부가 자원을 얻으려고 싸운다. 뇌의 수명 내내 경계 전쟁이 맹렬히 계속됨에 따라, 지도는 한 사람의 경험과 목표가 항상 뇌의 구조에 반영되는 방식으로 다시 그려진다. 회계사가 피아니스트가 되기 위해 자기 직업을 그만두면, 손가락에 전적으로 할애된 신경계 영역이 확장될 것이며, 그녀가 현미경 사용 전문가가 되면, 그녀가 찾는 작은 세부 사항을 위해 시각 피질은 더 높은 해상도를 발달시킬 것이며, 그녀가 조향사가 되면 냄새를 맡는 데 할당된 그녀의 뇌 영역이 확대될 것이다.

→ 뉴런은 존재를 위해 끊임없이 서로 싸우며, 그것은 사람의 경험과 목표에 기반하여 뇌 구조의 개인화로 이어진다.

Solution Guide

뉴런은 인접한 국가와 마찬가지로 자신의 영역을 차지하고 방어하려 하며, 영역과 생존을 위해 경쟁하므로, 한 사람의 경험과 목표의 변화에 따라 뇌의 재구조화가 계속 이루어진다는 내용이므로, 빈칸 (A), (B)에 들어갈 말로 가장 적절한 것은 ② '싸우며 – 개인화'이다.

① 싸우며 – 통합
③ 연결하며 – 단순화
④ 연결하며 – 재생
⑤ 협력하며 – 분화

Structure in Focus

- [As the border wars rage through the lifetime of a brain], maps are redrawn in such a way [that the experiences and goals of a person are always reflected in the brain's structure].
  첫 번째 [ ]는 시간을 나타내는 부사절이고, 두 번째 [ ]는 such a way를 수식하는 관계절이다.
- ~; if she becomes a microscopist, her visual cortex will develop higher resolution for the small details [she seeks]; ~.
  [ ]는 the small details를 수식하는 관계절이다.

24~25

정답 24 ① 25 ⑤

소재 도로 혼잡 통행료 징수제

해석 싱가포르에서는, 도로 혼잡 통행료 징수제로 인해 도로에서 시속 40마일의 속도를 낼 수 있으리라고 항상 기대할 수 있다. 부자는 이것을 감당할 여유가 있을 가능성이 더 높지만, 버스도 이 속도를 낼 수 있으며, 버스의 규모의 경제로 인해 이것은 이 속도를 내는 데 드는 1인당 이동 비용을 낮춘다. 통근에 드는 전체 비용에는 휘발유, 주차비, 도로 사용료에 대한 자기 부담 경비뿐만 아니라, 손실된 시간의 가치도 포함된다. 교통 정체로 인해 출퇴근에 15분이 아니라 30분이 걸리면, 통근자는 15분을 손해 본 것이다. 경제학자들은 그러한 시간 손실을 그 사람 시급의 절반으로 평가하는 경험 법칙을 채택했다. 예를 들어, 내가 시간당 80달러를 받는데 교통 체증에 갇혀 15분을 손해 본다면, 나는 손실된 시간으로 10달러(0.25×80×0.5)를 잃는 것이다.

교통 정체로 인한 그러한 시간 손실을 줄이기 위해, 스톡홀름, 런던, 싱가포르와 같은 도시에서는 도로 혼잡 통행료 징수제를 채택했다. 그러한 도시의 운전자들은 더 빠른 속도로 이동하고 시간을 절약하지만, 교통량이 절정에 달하는 시간대에 이동하려면 더 많은 돈을 자비로 지불해야 한다. 도로 혼잡 통행료 징수제를 채택한 도시가 그렇게 적은 이유에 대한 한 가지 설명은 행동 경제학에 초점을 맞추고 있는데, 즉 사람들은 도로가 무료인 것에 익숙해 있다는 것이다. 경제학자에게 이것은 당혹스러운 설명인데, 정체된 도로로 인해 우리는 우리의 귀중한 시간을 잃기 때문이다. 이 시간 비용은 무료 도로를 무료로 사용할 수 없다는 것을 의미한다. 도로 혼잡 통행료 징수제에 대한 동의(→ 반대)의 두 번째 설명은 많은 가난한 사람들이 운전을 하는데, 그들은 도로 이용료를 지불하기보다는 자신의 시간을 사용해 통근 비용을 지불하기를 선호한다는 것이다.

Culture Note

economies of scale(규모의 경제) 기업이 생산량을 늘릴수록 생산 단가가 감소하는 현상을 말한다. 규모의 경제는 기업이 생산량을 늘릴수록 고정 비용을 분산시킬 수 있고 생산 효율성을 높일 수 있기 때문에 발생하며, 이런 이유로 기업의 경쟁력 강화와 수익성 향상을 도모할 수 있다.

Solution Guide

24 교통 정체로 인한 통근자의 시간 손실을 줄이기 위해 세계 몇몇 도시에서 도로 혼잡 통행료 징수제를 채택했는데, 그것의 취지와, 돈을 내고 속도를 더 내는 것에 대한 논쟁점을 기술하고 있다. 따라서 글의 제목으로 가장 적절한 것은 ① '도로 혼잡 통행료 징수제: 시간이 돈보다 더 귀중한가?'이다.

② 도로에서의 시간 손실에 대한 다양한 보상책
③ 도로 혼잡 통행료 징수제를 시행하기에는 지나치게 많은 행정 업무
④ 도로 혼잡의 근본적인 원인에 대한 분석
⑤ 통근 시간 단축을 위한 노력: 승산 없는 싸움

25 도로 혼잡 통행료 징수제에 반대하는 두 번째 설명은 가난한 사람들은 도로 이용료를 지불하기보다는 긴 통근 시간을 기꺼이 감내하여 통근 비용을 지불하기를 선호한다는 내용이므로, (e)의 agreement를 opposition과 같은 낱말로 바꾸어야 한다.

Structure in Focus

- Drivers in such cities [move at higher speeds and save time] but [must pay more money out of pocket to

travel at peak use times].
두 개의 [ ]는 but으로 연결되어 문장의 술어 역할을 한다.

- A second explanation for the opposition to road pricing is [that many poor people drive and they prefer to pay for their commute {using their time rather than paying a road use fee}].
[ ]는 is의 보어 역할을 하는 명사절이다. 그 안의 { }는 pay for their commute에 부수하는 상황을 나타내는 분사구문이다.

26~28

정답 26 ② 27 ③ 28 ⑤

소재 코코넛 나무에서 배운 교훈

해석 (A) 어느 더운 오후에 어린 William과 그의 아빠는 먼지가 날리는 마을 길을 지나가고 있었다. 그때가 건기여서, 어린 William은 마을 길 전체가 쓸쓸하고 황량해 보인다고 생각했다. 한참을 걷고 나서, 그는 아빠에게 잠시 쉬기 위해 어디서 멈추자고 부탁했다. 주위를 둘러보았지만, 어린 William과 그의 아빠는 쉴 수 있는 편안한 곳을 찾지 못했다. 쉴 만한 어떤 곳도 찾지 못해, 그들은 어쩔 수 없이 뜨겁고 눈부신 태양 아래에서 계속 걸어야만 했다.
(C) 몇 분을 걸은 후에, 어린 William과 그의 아빠는 저 멀리 떨어진 데 있는, 불타는 태양을 막아 주는 그늘을 제공할 수 있는 커다란 코코넛 나무를 보았기 때문에, 그 나무에 도착하기 위해 더 빨리 걷기 시작했다. "아빠, 아빠랑 저랑 저 나무까지 경주할래요?"라고 어린 William이 아빠에게 물었다. 짧게 미소를 지어 보인 후, 그는 경주에 동의했고, 셋까지 셌을 때, 달리기 선수처럼 잽싸게 출발하는 어린 William의 모습을 지켜보았다.
(B) 어린 William 모르게 그의 아빠는 그를 이기게 했다. 그는 자기가 그 거대한 코코넛 나무에 먼저 도달했기 때문에 기뻐서 껑충껑충 뛰었다. 어린 William과 그의 아빠는 하루 종일 걷느라 매우 지쳐서 깊은 안도의 한숨을 내쉬었다. 그들은 자신들이 가지고 있던 모든 것을 땅에 내려놓았고, 그 거대한 코코넛 나무 아래에 누웠는데, 그 나무는 태양으로부터 그들을 보호해 주었다. 그리고 그들은 공중의 시원한 바람을 맞았다.
(D) 그때, 그들은 배가 고프기 시작했다. 어린 William은 그 거대한 코코넛 나무를 올려다보며 "이 거대한 코코넛 나무는 쓸모없어요. 우리가 먹을 수 있는 코코넛이 하나도 없잖아요."라고 말했다. "내 귀여운 어린 William, 우리 주변의 사람들과 사물에 감사하지 않는 것은 좋지 않단다. 이 나무는 네가 쓸모없다고 말하고 있지만, 뜨거운 태양으로부터 우리를 구해줬잖니."라고 그의 아빠가 대답했다. 어린 William은 자신이 누웠던 자리에서 조용히 일어나 나무를 향해 고개를 돌렸다. 그는 태양으로부터 자신들을 보호해 준 그 나무에게 감사를 표했다. 그 코코넛 나무가 어린 William과 그의 아빠에게 더 상쾌한 바람을 선사하기 시작했다.

Solution Guide

26 어느 더운 오후에 마을 길을 지나가던 어린 William과 그의 아빠는 쉴 곳을 찾지 못하고 계속 걸어야 했다는 내용의 주어진 글 (A) 다음에, 불타는 태양으로부터 그들이 시원하게 쉴 수 있는 코코넛 나무가 멀리 떨어진 곳에 있는 것을 발견하고 그곳에 빨리 도착하기 위해 어린 William이 아빠에게 경주를 제안하는 (C)가 이어져야 한다. 그다음에는 하루 종일 걷느라 지친 어린 William과 그의 아빠가 코코넛 나무에 도착하여 쉬는 내용의 (B)가 이어지고, 배가 고파진 어린 William이 그 코코넛 나무가 열매가 없어서 쓸모없다며 불평하자, 그의 아빠가 자신들을 뜨거운 햇볕에서 구해 준 코코넛 나무에 감사해야 한다고 말하고 이 말에 따르는 어린 William의 모습이 언급된 (D)가 그 뒤를 잇는 것이 글의 순서로 가장 적절하다.

27 밑줄 친 (a), (b), (d), (e)는 모두 어린 William을 가리키지만, (c)는 그의 아빠를 가리킨다.

28 글 (D)에서 어린 William이 코코넛 나무에 자신과 아빠가 먹을 수 있는 코코넛이 하나도 없어서 쓸모없다고 했으므로, 글에 관한 내용으로 적절하지 않은 것은 ⑤이다.

Structure in Focus

- They dropped all [that they had with them] on the ground and lay down under the huge coconut tree, [which protected them from the sun].
첫 번째 [ ]는 all을 수식하는 관계절이고, 두 번째 [ ]는 the huge coconut tree를 부가적으로 설명하는 관계절이다.
- After a few minutes' walk, little William and his dad saw a huge coconut tree far off in the distance [that could provide shade from the burning sun], so they started walking faster to reach the tree.
[ ]는 a huge coconut tree far off in the distance를 수식하는 관계절이다.
- ~, "**it** is not good [to be ungrateful to people and things around us].
it은 형식상의 주어이고, [ ]는 내용상의 주어이다.

TEST 3 본문 212~231쪽

01 ③	02 ④	03 ③	04 ⑤	05 ⑤	06 ⑤	07 ①
08 ②	09 ⑤	10 ⑤	11 ⑤	12 ④	13 ⑤	14 ②
15 ①	16 ②	17 ③	18 ④	19 ③	20 ③	21 ③
22 ④	23 ④	24 ⑤	25 ③	26 ⑤	27 ②	28 ④

01

정답 ③

소재 임시 피클볼 경기장 마련 계획

해석 회원분들께
지역 사회의 건강과 사회적 유대를 증진하기 위한 저희 공원의 노력을 항상 지지해 주셔서 감사합니다. 공지한 바와 같이, 봄철이 허락하는 대로 Lions Park에서의 공사가 시작될 예정입니다. 올여름에 시내에서 피클볼 경기를 할 수 있는 대체 장소로, Green Valley Road 201번지에 위치한 Rose Park의 아스팔트로 포장된 표면에 세 개의 피클볼 코트용 라인이 그려질 것입니다. Lions Park에서 썼던, 휴대용 네트와 여분의 공을 담은 파란색 장비 보관함도 거기로 이전될 것입니다. 그 보관함의 잠금을 해제하는 비밀번호는 주민 센터 안내대에 전화하여 받으실 수 있습니다. 대체 피클볼 코트와 관련하여 질문이 있으시면, mperkins@ShakopeeMN.gov로 Mark Perkins에게 연락 주시기를 바랍니다. 올여름에 Lions Park에 새로운 피클볼 전용 코트가 완공되기를 기대합니다.
Mark Perkins 드림

Solution Guide

Lions Park의 공사 관계로 Rose Park에 임시로 피클볼 경기장을 마련할 것임을 회원들에게 알리는 내용이므로, 글의 목적으로 가장 적절한 것은 ③이다.

Structure in Focus

- As an alternative place [to play pickleball in town this summer], the lines for three pickleball courts will be painted on the blacktop surface at Rose Park, [located at 201 Green Valley Road].
  첫 번째 [ ]는 an alternative place를 수식하는 to부정사구이다. 두 번째 [ ]는 Rose Park를 부가적으로 설명하는 분사구이다.
- The combination [to unlock the bin] can be obtained by calling the front desk at the community center.
  [ ]는 The combination을 수식하는 to부정사구이다.

02

정답 ④

소재 기차역에서 기다림 후에 만난 아빠

해석 Weston역에서 기차에서 내렸는데 아버지의 흔적이 없었을 때, 나는 일이 잘 풀리지 않으리라고 짐작했어야 했다. 나는 겨우 열다섯 살이었고, 아버지가 나타나지 않으면 결코 집에 돌아갈 수 없었다. 나는 승강장을 정처 없이 왔다 갔다 했다. 기다림은 영원처럼 느껴졌고, 나는 그에게 나쁜 일이 생긴 건 아닌지 걱정스럽게 생각하기 시작했다. 잠시 후, 역무원 중 한 명이 내게 다가와 내가 괜찮은지 물었다. 나는 괜찮다고 대답했지만, 속으로는 걱정이 커지고 있었다. 그때 나는 왼쪽을 휙 보고 아빠를 알아보았다. 바로 그 순간, 나의 모든 걱정이 사라졌다. "아빠!"라고 나는 소리쳤다. 나는 바닥에서 내 작은 가방을 낚아채 그에게 달려갔다. 그는 내 머리를 헝클어 놓고 나를 자신에게로 가까이 끌어당기면서, "기다리게 해서 미안해, 아들아."라고 말했다. "집에 가자." 그가 미소 지었고, 나는 훨씬 더 큰 미소로 그의 미소에 화답했다.

Solution Guide

기차역에 내렸으나 아버지가 없었고, 그를 계속 기다려도 그가 나타나지 않자 걱정스러운 마음이었으나, 아빠를 만난 후 걱정이 사라지고 기분 좋게 미소 지을 수 있었다는 내용의 글이므로, 'I'의 심경 변화로 가장 적절한 것은 ④ '걱정하는 → 안도하는'이다.
① 몹시 화가 난 → 만족스러워하는
② 자신감 있는 → 초조한
③ 무관심한 → 아주 신이 난
⑤ 부끄러운 → 자랑스러운

Structure in Focus

- I should have guessed [things were not going to go well] [when {I stepped off the train at Weston Station} and {there was no sign of my father}].
  첫 번째 [ ]는 guessed의 목적어 역할을 하는 명사절이다. 두 번째 [ ]는 시간을 나타내는 부사절이고, 그 안에서 두 개의 { }가 and로 연결되어 when에 이어진다.
- ~, and I began to anxiously wonder [if something bad had happened to him].
  [ ]는 wonder의 목적어 역할을 하는 명사절이다.

03

정답 ③

소재 지속 가능한 도시 조성을 위한 도시 농업

해석 도시 농업은 단순히 소득을 올리거나 소규모 식량 생산 활동을 하는 관행에서 벗어나 활력이 넘치는 도시 공동체를 만드는 데 가장 중요한 에너지 절약 자원으로서 지역의 식량 생산을 촉진하는 데 초점을 맞춘 더 지속 가능한 관행으로 변화하고 있다. 식량 안보와 식품 안전이 전 세계적으로 식량의 입수 가능성과 보건과 관련하여 부담을 일으키고 있는 인구 증가와 함께 도시가 해결해야 할 문제가 되면서 그것은 도시 계획에 훨씬 더 중요해질 필요가 있다. 현재 관행에서, '도시 농업'이라는 용어는 반드시 식량 생산 자체가 지속 가능한 방법론이나 절차에 기반한다는 것을 의미하지는 않지만, 생태에 기반을 둔 접근법과 결합되면 그렇다. 오늘날 도시에서 천연자원 감소에 대한 인식이 생기고 환경 저하가 진행되면서, 도시 농업은 더 지속 가능한 도시를 만들기 위한 해결책의 중요한 부분으로서 생태에 기반을 둔 체제를 도시에 다시 도입하는 데 새로운 의미를 띠고 있다. 이것은 식량을 도시 체제의 필수적인 부분으로 생각하는 패러다임의 전환을 진정 필요로 한다.

Solution Guide

현대 도시가 직면한 식량 안보와 식품 안전 문제의 해결책으로 제시되는 도시 농업은 지속 가능한 도시 조성을 가능하게 하므로 생태 기반형 도시 농업을 활용할 필요가 있다는 내용의 글이므로, 글의 요지로 가장 적절한 것은 ③이다.

Structure in Focus

- Urban agriculture is moving from just a practice for earning an income and small food-producing activities to a more sustainable practice [that focuses on promoting local food production as an energy-saving resource {that is central to creating vital urban communities}].
  [ ]는 a more sustainable practice를 수식하는 관계절이고, 그 안의 { }는 an energy-saving resource를 수식하는 관계절이다.
- In current practice, the term *urban agriculture* does not necessarily mean [that food production itself is based on a sustainable methodology or procedure] but [when combined with an ecological-based approach] it **does**.
  첫 번째 [ ]는 mean의 목적어 역할을 하는 명사절이고, 두 번째 [ ] 안에서는 when과 combined 사이에 it is가 생략된 것으로 이해할 수 있다. does는 means that ~ procedure를 대신한다.

04

정답 ⑤

소재 어린아이가 할 수 없는 결정에 대한 처리

해석 일부 부모에게는 어린아이를 마치 그들이 나이가 훨씬 더 많은 것처럼 대하는 경향이 있다. 그들은 마치 자신의 아이가 나이 이상으로 성숙하다는 인상을 주고 싶어 하는 것 같다. 그들은 어린아이가 너무 어려 결정할 수 없는 문제에 관해 결정을 내리도록 요구한다. 아이가 이런 상황에 처하면, 때때로 아이는 부모가 자신에게 하기를 바라는 것을 할 것이고, 때로는 그저 "싫어."라고 말할 것이다. 이것은 자신의 권위를 보여 주고 자신의 힘을 드러내려는 아이의 시도이다. 결코 어린아이는 자신이 너무 어려 내릴 수 없는 결정을 하도록 요구받아서는 안 된다. 부모가 결정을 내린 다음 아이에게 지시해야 한다. 예를 들어, 부모는 아이가 그만 놀고 밥을 먹어야 한다고 생각하면, 아이에게 "이제 밥 먹고 싶니?"라고 물어서는 안 된다. 부모가 아이에게 장난감을 치우고 밥 먹을 준비를 하라고 말해야 한다. 부모는 아이가 낮잠을 자야 한다고 생각하면, 아이에게 "낮잠 자고 싶니?"라고 물어서는 안 된다. 부모가 아이에게 낮잠을 잘 시간이라고 말해야 한다.

Solution Guide

일부 부모에게는 아이가 너무 어려 결정할 수 없는 문제에 관해 결정을 내리도록 요구하는 경향이 있는데, 그런 결정은 부모가 내린 다음 아이에게 지시해야 한다는 내용의 글이다. 따라서 필자가 주장하는 바로 가장 적절한 것은 ⑤이다.

Structure in Focus

- They ask a small child to make decisions about matters [he is too young to decide].
  [ ]는 matters를 수식하는 관계절이다.
- When a child is put in this situation, [sometimes he will do {what the parent wants him to do}], and [sometimes he will simply say, "No]."
  주절에 해당하는 두 개의 [ ]는 and에 의해 연결되어 있다. 첫 번째 [ ] 안의 { }는 do의 목적어 역할을 하는 명사절이다.

05

정답 ⑤

소재 신경 과학과 인문 과학의 만남

해석 나는 신경 과학과 인문 과학을 거대한 Alp(알프스산맥의 한 산)의 양쪽 반대편에서 힘차게 터널을 뚫고 들어가는 두 명의 매우 작은 광부와 비슷하다고 생각한다. Alp의 자기 쪽에 있는 신경 과학자는 반대쪽에 있는 인문학자가 내는 굴 파는 소리에 많이 귀를 기울이지 않지만, 일부 인문학자, 인문학에서 뇌가 하는 역할에 관심이 있는 이들은 반대쪽의 신경 과학자가 말하고 있는 것에 매우 열심히 귀를 기울인다. 우리는 희망을 안고 아주 많은 연구자들에게 의존한다. 우리는 우리를 괴롭히는 질문에 대한 해답을 그들로부터 얻기를 바란다. 우리가 비록 두 집단으로 나누어져 있긴 하지만, 신경 과학자들과 인문 과학에 속한 우리는 같은 희망을 공유하고 있다. 비록 산으로 인해 왜소해 보이지만, 우리의 굴 파기 작업이 거대한 Alp의 한가운데서 만나, 그곳에서 이 신비롭고 매혹적인 보물, 즉 '마음'을 알아내기를 우린 바란다. 우린 바란다.

Solution Guide

신경 과학과 인문 과학은 거대한 Alp(알프스산맥의 한 산)의 양쪽 반대편으로 나누어져 있기는 하지만, 각 학문이 그 산의 한가운데서 만나 두 학문이 연구하는 마음에 대한 이해가 한데 모이기를 바란다는 내용의 글이다. 따라서 밑줄 친 부분이 글에서 의미하는 바로 가장 적절한 것은 ⑤ '신경 과학과 인문 과학에서의 마음에 대한 이해가 한데 모일 것이다.'이다.

① 인문 과학과 신경 과학이 더 전문화될 것이다.
② 인문학자는 신경 과학자보다 더 빨리 발견할 것이다.
③ 신경 과학과 인문 과학의 연구 방향이 바뀔 것이다.
④ 인문 과학과 신경 과학은 이전보다 더 많은 문제에 직면할 것이다.

Structure in Focus

- I think of neuroscience and the human sciences as like two very small miners [energetically tunnelling in from opposite sides of an immense Alp].
  [ ]는 two very small miners를 수식하는 분사구이다.
- ~, some humanists, [those {concerned with the brain's role in the arts}], listen very closely to [what the neuroscientists on the other side are saying].
  첫 번째 [ ]는 some humanists와 동격 관계이고, 그 안의 { }는 those를 수식하는 분사구이다. 두 번째 [ ]는 전치사 to의 목적어 역할을 하는 명사절이다.

06

정답 ⑤

소재 타고난 음악적 재능에 대한 믿음

해석 현대 방송 미디어는 음악 연주 능력을 타고난 재능으로 설명하는 것을 영구화하는 데 기여했을 수도 있다. '제2의 모차르트'가 흔한 호칭인, 비범한 아동 연주자의 발견은, 높은 수준의 음악적 학습이 어떻게 환경적, 교육적, 그리고 경제적 요인의 흔치 않은 풍성한 결합에서 기인했는지 보도하는 것보다 훨씬 더 좋은 기삿거리가 된다. 그러나 단순한 미디어 선정주의를 넘어서, 재능에 대한 믿음은 다른 흥미로운 효과를 제공한다. 음악적 재능이 있는 사람에게 특별함이라는 명칭을 부여하는 것은 콘서트 경험을 환상적이고 심지어 초자연적인 사건으로 바꿀 수 있다. 게다가, 연주자 스스로가 '영재'라는 호칭으로부터 이점을 얻을 수 있다. 특별하다는, 혹은 심지어 신의 축복을 받았다는 느낌은 연주자의 자존감과 동기 부여에 기여할 수 있고, 결과적으로 많은 '재능 있는' 연주자는 자신의 재능을 길러야 한다는 의무를 느끼는데, 이는 그들이 자신감과 성공에 대한 기대감을 가지고 자신들의 음악 활동에 다가가게 해 준다.

Solution Guide

미디어에 의한, 타고난 음악적 재능에 대한 믿음은 콘서트 경험을 환상적인 사건으로 바꿀 수 있고, 음악가의 자존감과 동기부여에 기여하고, 재능 계발에 대한 의무를 느끼게 해서, 그가 자신감과 성공에 대한 기대를 가지고 음악 활동을 하게 해 준다는 내용의 글이다. 따라서 글의 주제로 가장 적절한 것은 ⑤ '미디어로 인해 강화된 타고난 음악적 재능에 대한 믿음의 긍정적 효과'이다.

① 재능이 있는 음악가에 치중해서 방송하는 것의 문제점
② 음악 콘서트 홍보를 위한 방송 미디어 활용의 잠재력
③ 연습이 완벽을 만든다고 믿는 것의 심리적 이점
④ 창의적 지능 향상에서 음악 교육의 중요성

Structure in Focus

- [The discovery of an exceptional child performer — "the next Mozart" is a common label] — **makes** for a much better story than reporting [how advanced musical learning has resulted from an unusually plentiful combination of environmental, educational, and economic factors].
  첫 번째 [ ]는 문장의 주어 역할을 하는 명사구이고, 술어동사는 makes이다. 두 번째 [ ]는 reporting의 목적어 역할을 하는 명사절이다.
- ~; consequently, many "talented" musicians feel an obligation [to nurture their gift], [which allows them {to approach their musical activities with confidence and the expectation of success}].
  첫 번째 [ ]는 an obligation의 구체적 내용을 설명하는 to부정사구이다. 두 번째 [ ]는 many "talented" musicians ~ their gift의 내용을 부가적으로 설명하는 관계절이고, 그 안의 { }는 allows의 목적격 보어 역할을 하는 to부정사구이다.

07

정답 ①

소재 휴대 전화가 재정의한 공간 개념

해석 많은 사람은 사람들이 대기 구역에서 휴대 전화를 자주 사용하는 것을 목격해 왔다. 그것은 무료한 시간을 보내는 방법이긴 하지만, 또한 보통 공간이라고 부르기에 미약하거나 공간으로 제대로 정의되지 않은 것 안에 공간을 만들어 내는 방법이기도 하

PART Ⅲ 테스트편

다. 휴대 전화 불통 지역의 가장자리 공간은 또한 전화를 걸거나 문자를 보내기에 가장 적합한 장소이기도 하다. 따라서 사람들이 무선 셀 기지국과의 교신이 끊겼다가 공항에 착륙하거나 터널을 빠져나오면, 그들은 전화를 걸거나 문자를 보낼 가능성이 더 많다. 휴대 전화는, 가령 콘서트에 갔는데 다른 사람들이 그 콘서트의 일부(나 전체)를 들을 수 있도록 그들에게 전화하는 사람처럼, 멀리 떨어져 있는 사람과 공간을 공유하는 데 사용될 수 있다. 극단적으로는, 사람들이 휴대 전화를 통한 다른 사람과의 상호 작용에 너무 몰두해서 자신이 점유하는 물리적 공간 속의 사람들과의 소통이 끊어질 수도 있다. Sherry Turkle은 이것을 '함께 있는 혼자'라고 부르고, 다른 이들은 이러한 행동의 특성을 나타내기 위해 '부재의 존재'라는 용어를 사용했다.

Solution Guide

사람들은 통화를 하거나 문자를 보내는 등 휴대 전화를 사용하면서 어떤 공간 안에 또 다른 공간을 만들거나 먼 곳에 있는 누군가와 한 공간을 공유할 수도 있는 반면, 휴대 전화 속 사람들과의 상호작용에 몰두하다가 정작 물리적 공간을 함께 점유하고 있는 사람들과의 소통은 끊길 수도 있다는 내용의 글이다. 따라서 글의 제목으로 가장 적절한 것은 ① '휴대 전화는 우리의 물리적 공간을 어떻게 재정의하는가?'이다.

② 디지털 기기는 에티켓 규칙을 어떻게 바꾸고 있는가?
③ 디지털 변화: 더 지속 가능한 미래를 향해
④ 연결 끊김: 그것의 원인과 해결 방법
⑤ 우리가 기술로부터 더 많은 것을 기대하면서도 서로에게 덜 기대하는 이유

Structure in Focus

- ~ but it is also a way [to create a space within {what is often a weak or poorly defined space}].
  [ ]는 a way를 수식하는 to부정사구이고, 그 안의 { }는 전치사 within의 목적어 역할을 하는 명사절이다.
- At the extreme, people may be **so** immersed in the interaction with others on a mobile phone, **that** they lose contact with those in the physical space [they occupy].
  '매우 ~해서 …하다'라는 의미의 「so ~ that ...」이 사용되었다.
  [ ]는 the physical space를 수식하는 관계절이다.

08

정답 ②

소재 W. E. B. DuBois

해석 W. E. B. DuBois(1868~1963)는 아프리카계 미국인 사회학자로 테네시주에 있는 Fisk 대학교를 졸업했고, Harvard 대학교에서 박사 학위를 취득한 최초의 아프리카계 미국인이 되었다. 그 후 그는 Atlanta 대학교에서 미국의 두 번째 사회학과를 설립했다. 그는 곧 많은 다른 일 중에서도 두 개의 학술지를 창간하고 다수의 책과 소논문을 집필하는 것을 포함한 매우 왕성한 학문적 경력을 시작했다. 그는 미국의 인종 문제에 대한 연구와 저술에 집중했다. 그러나 동시에 그는 자신의 방대한 지식을 사회를 개선하는 데 적용하기 위해 열심히 노력했다. 그는 인종 평등을 위해 싸우는 아프리카계 미국인 지식인 단체인 Niagara Movement를 설립했다. 또한 National Association for the Advancement of Colored People(전미 유색인종 지위 향상 협회)(NAACP)의 설립을 도왔고, 그것의 영향력 있는 잡지인 *Crisis*를 편집하기도 했다. 나중에는 인종 평등을 달성하기 위해 심지어 물리력의 사용을 옹호하기도 했다. 결국 인종 관계의 개선을 거의 보지 못하고, 그는 1961년에 아프리카 국가 가나로 이주했고, 그곳에서 2년 후 사망했다.

Solution Guide

DuBois는 Atlanta 대학교에서 미국의 두 번째 사회학과를 설립했다(Then, at Atlanta University, he founded the nation's second department of sociology.)고 했으므로, 글의 내용과 일치하지 않는 것은 ②이다.

Structure in Focus

- He soon began a highly productive academic career [that included, among many other things, {founding two scholarly journals} and {writing numerous books and articles}].
  [ ]는 a highly productive academic career를 수식하는 관계절이다. 두 개의 { }는 and로 연결되어 included의 목적어 역할을 하는 동명사구이다.
- Finally, seeing little improvement in race relations, he moved in 1961 to the African nation of Ghana, [where he died 2 years later].
  [ ]는 the African nation of Ghana를 부가적으로 설명하는 관계절이다.

09

정답 ⑤

소재 미국 영화계의 무대 뒤 주요 역할에 종사한 여성의 비율

해석 위 도표는 2015년부터 2021년까지 가장 높은 수익을 올린 250편의 미국 영화에서 무대 뒤 주요 역할에서 일한 여성의 비율과 2021년의 그 여성들의 비율을 역할별로 보여 준다. 2015년 대비 2016년과 2017년에는 가장 높은 수익을 올린 250편의 미국 영화에서 일한 여성의 비율이 더 낮았으나 2018년에는

더 높았다. 2021년 가장 높은 수익을 올린 250편의 미국 영화에서 일한 여성의 비율은 전체의 4분의 1을 차지했다. 같은 해에 이 영화들에서 여성 책임 프로듀서의 비율은 여성 프로듀서의 비율보다 더 낮았다. 2021년에 가장 높은 수익을 올린 250편의 미국 영화에서 여성 감독과 작가의 비율은 각각 17퍼센트였던 반면 전체 편집자 중 22퍼센트가 여성이었다. 같은 해에 무대 뒤 주요 역할 중에서, 영화 촬영 기사의 여성 비율은 가장 낮았는데 작가로 일한 여성 비율의 3분의 1 미만이었다.

Solution Guide

2021년 무대 뒤 주요 역할에서 영화 촬영 기사로 일한 여성의 비율(6퍼센트)은 작가로 일한 여성의 비율(17퍼센트)의 3분의 1을 넘는다. 따라서 ⑤는 도표의 내용과 일치하지 않는다.

Structure in Focus

- In the same year, the percentage of female executive producers in these films was lower than **that** of female producers.
  that은 the percentage를 대신한다.

10

정답 ⑤

소재 Limber 대학 여름 소프트볼 캠프

해석 **Limber 대학 여름 소프트볼 캠프**

Limber 대학은 6월 14일부터 16일까지 연례 소프트볼 캠프를 주최하게 되어 매우 기쁩니다.

두 가지 캠프 수업이 있습니다:

캠프 수업	A	B
나이	4~7세	8~18세
시간	오전 9시~ 오전 11시 30분	오전 10시~ 오후 2시
비용(1인당)	80달러	160달러

캠프 참가자는 글러브와 배트를 지참하고 야구화를 착용해야 합니다. 또한 자외선 차단제, 물병, 여분의 옷/양말을 지참하는 것이 좋습니다.

Camp B 참가자는 점심 도시락을 가져와야 합니다. (점심시간은 매일 오전 11시 30분입니다.)

간식과 음료는 구매하실 수 있습니다.

캠프에 등록하시려면, Jessica Kershaw 코치에게 jessica.kershaw@limbercollege.edu로 문의하십시오.

Solution Guide

간식과 음료는 구매하여 이용할 수 있다고 했으므로, 안내문의 내용과 일치하지 않는 것은 ⑤이다.

Structure in Focus

- [To sign up for the camp], please contact coach Jessica Kershaw at jessica.kershaw@limbercollege.edu.
  [ ]는 목적의 의미를 나타내는 to부정사구이다.

11

정답 ⑤

소재 Sunflower 공원 가족 야영

해석 **Sunflower 공원 가족 야영**

올여름 재미 가득한 가족 야영을 경험하고 싶다면, Sunflower 공원 가족 야영에 참여하세요! 자연 산책, 낚시 대회, 캠프파이어 놀이 등과 같은 활동이 있을 것입니다!

날짜: 8월 10일 토요일 ~ 8월 11일 일요일

비용: 4인 가족 35달러, 추가 야영객 1명당 5달러

등록 마감일: 8월 7일

장소: Sunflower 공원

일반 정보:

- 공원에 입장하는 차량은 공원 레크리에이션 출입증이 필요합니다.
- 가족당 소형 텐트 2개 또는 중형 텐트 1개까지 가져올 수 있습니다.
- 체크인은 토요일 정오에 시작됩니다. 체크아웃은 일요일 오전 11시입니다.
- 저희 직원이 트레일러로 여러분의 장비를 야영지로 운반하고 야영지에서 운반해 나옵니다. 짐 싣는 시간은 토요일 정오부터 오후 1시까지, 일요일 오전 9시부터 오전 11시까지입니다.

마감일 전에 등록하여 자리를 예약하세요. 그곳에서 뵙기를 바랍니다!

Solution Guide

직원이 트레일러로 야영객의 장비를 야영지로 운반하고 야영지에서 운반해 나올 것(Our staff will transport your equipment to and from the campsite in a trailer.)이라고 했으므로, 안내문의 내용과 일치하는 것은 ⑤이다.

Structure in Focus

- There will be activities [such as a nature walk, fishing competition, campfire games and more]!
  [ ]는 activities를 수식하는 전치사구이다.

12

정답 ④

소재 고급품이라는 믿음의 심리적 영향

해석 우리가 피상적인 증거에 근거해 매우 쉽게 감명을 받아 판단을 내리긴 하지만, 때로는 고급스러움이 우리의 행복을 향상시키는 자신감의 심리적 증진을 제공한다. 유명 디자이너가 만든 옷을 입으면 우리가 자신에 대해 더 나은 기분이 들 수 있고, 이는 그리고 자기 강화가 된다. 우리는 자신의 고급 의류를 입으면 특별하다고 느끼고 그에 따라 행동한다. 고급품은 우리 뇌의 쾌락 중추를 밝힌다. 여러분이 비싼 와인을 마시고 있다고 생각하면, 여러분이 정확히 똑같은 와인을 싸구려라고 생각할 때 그것을 마시는 것에 비해, 그것의 맛이 더 좋을 뿐만 아니라 쾌락 경험과 관련된 뇌의 가치 평가 기관이 더 활성화되는 것을 보인다. 여기서 중요한 것은 실제 고급품이 아니라 믿음이다. Harvard 대학교 경영 대학원의 교수인 Francesca Gino는 유명 디자이너 제품 선글라스의 모조품이라고 믿는 (하지만 실제로는 진품인) 것을 착용하는 사람들은 사기꾼인 것처럼 느끼고 시험에서 부정행위를 할 가능성이 더 높다는 것을 알아냈다. 여러분이 성공할 때까지 속일 수는 있겠지만, 마음 깊은 곳에서는, 우리가 그러는 경우에, 우리 중 많은 이들이 사기꾼인 것처럼 느낀다.

Solution Guide

④ wore의 목적어 역할을 하는 명사절을 이끌면서 그 절 안의 동사 believed의 목적어 역할도 해야 하므로 which를 선행사를 포함하는 관계사 what으로 고쳐야 한다.

① make의 목적격 보어 feel의 주체인 us와 같은 대상을 가리키므로 재귀대명사 ourselves는 적절하다.

② associated의 수식을 받는 the brain's valuation system은 동사 associate의 목적어로 이해되므로 과거분사 associated는 적절하다.

③ 주어 역할을 하는 명사절 What's important here 뒤에 이어지는 술어동사 is는 적절하다.

⑤ 앞에 나온 동사 fake를 대신하는 do는 적절하다.

Structure in Focus

- ~, but sometimes luxury provides a psychological boost to confidence [that improves our well-being].
  [ ]는 a psychological boost to confidence를 수식하는 관계절이다.
- Francesca Gino, [a professor at Harvard Business School], found [that people {who wore 〈what they believed to be fake designer brand sunglasses (but were in fact genuine)〉} felt like frauds and were more likely to cheat on tests].
  첫 번째 [ ]는 Francesca Gino와 동격 관계이다. 두 번째 [ ]는 found의 목적어 역할을 하는 명사절이다. [ ] 안의 { }는 people을 수식하는 관계절이고, { } 안의 〈 〉는 wore의 목적어 역할을 하는 명사절이다.

13

정답 ⑤

소재 어류 남획으로 인해 파생되는 문제

해석 어류 남획은 대체로 어장에서의 과도한 노력과 능력의 결과이다. 너무나도 흔히, 어장 관리자는 어획 노력을 통제하지 못했고, 그 결과 지속 불가능한 수준의 어획량을 초래했다. 이것은 관리가 참여자의 수나 고도의 개별적 노력을 제한하지 않는 개방형 어장에 특별한 문제였다. 이러한 상황에서는, 경제적 유인이 장기적인 지속 가능한 이용보다 단기적인 이기적 이용을 선호하는데, 어류 자원을 복원하기 위해 현재 어획량을 희생하는 것의 경제적 이익은 단기적 요구(지불해야 할 청구서)에 비해 인지하기 어렵고, 장기적 이익은 어장이 회복되면 신규 진입자와 나누어야 할 수도 있기 때문이다. 더 많은 사람이 어장에 진입하거나 자신의 어획 능력을 향상할수록 개별 어부의 미래 어획량은 감소한다. 흔히 이것은 심지어 자원이 감소할 때도 개인별 어획량을 유지하거나 심지어 증가하려는 경쟁을 조장한다. 이에 대응하여, 관리자는 어획기를 연장할(→ 단축할) 수도 있는데, 그러면 참여자들은 자신의 어획 성능을 높이고, 노력이 시간상 집중되어, 때로 '고기잡이 경쟁' 또는 '고기잡이 시합'을 초래하게 된다.

Solution Guide

어류 남획으로 인해 파생되는 문제에 대한 글이다. 참여자들이 자신의 어획 성능을 높이고, 노력이 시간상 집중되어, 고기잡이 경쟁을 하는 상황이 이어지고 있는 것으로 보아, 관리자는 어획기를 단축할 수 있다는 내용이 언급되어야 한다. 따라서 ⑤의 lengthen을 shorten과 같은 낱말로 바꾸어야 한다.

Structure in Focus

- Too often, fishery managers have been unable to control fishing effort, [resulting in unsustainable levels of catch].
  [ ]는 주절이 기술하는 상황에서 비롯된 결과를 나타내는 분사구문이다.
- This has been a particular problem for open-access fisheries [where management does not limit {the number of participants} or {high individual effort}].
  [ ]는 open-access fisheries를 수식하는 관계절이고, 두 개의 { }는 or로 연결되어 limit의 목적어 역할을 한다.

14

정답 ②

소재 숙제의 의미

해석 일반적으로 '숙제'는 수업 시간 외에 수행하도록 계획된 모든 지정 과제로 구성된다. '숙제'라는 단어가 설명하지 않는 것은 과제의 질이나 양이며, 그것이 어휘 전쟁으로 바뀌어 숙제에 대한 토론을 어렵게 만드는 현실이다. 예를 들어, 두 사람이 자기 자녀의 숙제에 대해 논의하는 경우에, 어떤 사람은 무의미한 연습 문제지에 대해 불평할 수도 있고, 상대방은 성찰하거나 창작하도록 학생을 유도하는 신중하게 공들여 만든 활동을 맘에 들어 한다. 그러나 구체적인 활동의 이름을 밝히는 대신에, 그들은 둘 다 그 과업을 단순히 '숙제'라고만 부른다. 그래서 한 부모는 도대체 왜 어느 누가 (무의미한) 숙제의 지지자가 될지 의아해하는데 다른 한 부모는 부모가 왜 자녀가 집에서 (유의미하고 창의적인) 일을 하는 것을 원하지 '않을지' 이해할 수 없다. 두 부모 중 누구도 숙제에 대해 같은 말을 사용하지 않기 때문에 상대방의 관점을 이해하지 못한다.

Solution Guide

숙제라는 단어가 수업 시간 외에 수행하도록 지정된 모든 과제로 구성되어 그 의미가 너무 넓어서 각자 다른 의미로 이해되기 때문에 숙제에 대한 토론이 어렵게 된다는 사실을 부모 사이의 논쟁 사례를 들어 제시하고 있으므로, 빈칸에 들어갈 말로 가장 적절한 것은 ②이다.

① 관계
③ 책임
④ 투자
⑤ 예의

Structure in Focus

- For example, [if two people discuss their children's homework], **one** could be railing against mindless worksheets while **the other** is in favor of carefully crafted activities [prompting students to reflect or create].
  첫 번째 [ ]는 조건을 나타내는 부사절이다. 둘 중 하나는 one, 나머지 하나는 the other로 지칭하는 표현이 사용되었다. 두 번째 [ ]는 carefully crafted activities를 수식하는 분사구이다.
- And so one parent wonders [why on earth anyone would be a proponent of (mindless) homework] while the other can't understand [why a parent *wouldn't* want their child to do (relevant and creative) work at home].
  두 개의 [ ]는 각각 wonders와 understand의 목적어 역할을 하는 명사절이다.

15

정답 ①

소재 아프리카계 미국인 교외화의 의도치 않은 결과

해석 미국의 사회학자 William Julius Wilson은 아프리카계 미국인의 교외화의 의도치 않은 결과는 도심 지역이 귀중한 역할 모델을 잃은 것이라고 주장했다. 고소득 소수 집단이 도시 중심부를 떠남에 따라, 남아 있는 젊은이들은 일해서 소득 상향 이동성을 달성한 성인 남성을 보거나 교류할 가능성이 더 적을 것이다. 개발 경제학 연구는, 도미니카 공화국의 데이터를 가지고, 젊은이들이 더 많은 교육을 받음으로써 가능한 임금 인상에 대한 정보를 얻으면, 이러한 정보가 젊은이들의 교육 성취도를 높인다는 것을 상세히 기록했다. 이에 대한 설명은 젊은이들이 자신과 비슷하게 생겼으면서 높은 수준의 교육 또한 달성한 사람들과 결코 교류하지 않으면 교육의 경제적 이점을 과소평가할 가능성이 더 높다는 것이다. 따라서 상향으로 이동하는 사람들의 교외화는 도심 지역의 동료 효과에 사회적 영향을 미친다.

Solution Guide

미국 내 소수 집단인 아프리카계 미국인이 교외로 이동하는 것은 남아 있는 젊은이들이 교육을 통해 좋은 일자리를 얻어 상승하는 소득 이동성을 달성한 성인을 보거나 교류할 가능성이 더 적어진다는 내용의 글이다. 따라서 빈칸에 들어갈 말로 가장 적절한 것은 ①이다.

② 다양한 갈등을 해결한
③ 교육에 너무 많은 돈을 지출한
④ 사회적 불의에 무관심해진
⑤ 높은 수준의 불평등으로 고생한

Structure in Focus

- American sociologist William Julius Wilson has argued [that an unintended consequence of African American suburbanization has been {that inner cities have lost valuable role models}].
  [ ]는 argued의 목적어 역할을 하는 명사절이고, 그 안의 { }는 been의 보어 역할을 하는 명사절이다.
- The explanation for this is [that young people are more likely to underestimate the economic benefits of education when they never interact with people {who look like them and have also attained a high level of education}].
  [ ]는 is의 보어 역할을 하는 명사절이고, 그 안의 { }는 people을 수식하는 관계절이다.

16

정답 ②

소재 라디오의 소형화

해석 1950년대 광고주들은 베이비붐 세대에게 다가가는 데 관심이 있었기 때문에, 많은 라디오 방송국은 특히 그들을 소리쳐 불렀던 디스크자키와 함께 로큰롤이라는 음악을 틀었다. 다른 방송국들은 다양한 스타일의 음악과 디스크자키로 다양한 연령층을 목표로 삼았다. 특정 음악 선호에 초점을 맞춘 이러한 새로운 종류의 방송국은 라디오가 이제 그 어느 때보다 휴대가 더 쉬워졌기 때문에 인기를 끌었다. 1948년에 Audion 진공관을 위한 훨씬 더 작은 대체물인 트랜지스터가 개발되면서 라디오 수신기의 소형화가 이루어졌다. 이제 라디오는 그야말로 사람들이 공원으로, 해변으로, 또는 어디로든지 하루 종일 가지고 다닐 수 있는 물건이 되었다. 갑자기 그 매체는 새로운 생명을 얻었고, 기업들은 서둘러 새로운 면허를 취득했다. 1946년에 약 1,000개였던 방송국 수는 1950년대 중반에 거의 3,500개로 급격히 증가했다. 이 중 가장 큰 비율은 특정 유형의 음악을 틀었다.

Solution Guide

특정 음악 선호에 초점을 맞춘 새로운 종류의 방송국이 인기를 끌게 된 이유가 빈칸에 들어가야 한다. 트랜지스터 개발 덕분에 라디오의 소형화를 이룰 수 있었고, 그로 인해 사람들이 하루 종일 어디든지 라디오를 가지고 다닐 수 있게 되었다는 것이 그 이유로 제시되고 있으므로, 빈칸에 들어갈 말로 가장 적절한 것은 ②이다.

① 청취자들의 사연을 특별히 포함했기
③ 세대 간 연결고리로 작동했기
④ 새로운 음악가들을 위한 무대가 되었기
⑤ 청취자들에게 그들이 좋아하는 음악을 공짜로 제공했기

Structure in Focus

- [Because advertisers in the 1950s were interested in reaching baby boomers], many radio stations played music called rock 'n' roll with disc jockeys [that specifically called out to them].
  첫 번째 [ ]는 이유를 나타내는 부사절이고, 두 번째 [ ]는 disc jockeys를 수식하는 관계절이다.
- The development in 1948 of the transistor, [a much smaller replacement for the Audion vacuum tube], led to the miniaturization of radio receivers.
  [ ]는 the transistor와 동격 관계이다.

17

정답 ③

소재 친구 사귀기

해석 Arthur Aron과 내가 진행한 연구에서 우리는 컴퓨터로 작동하는 가짜 데이트 서비스를 만들었는데, 대학생들이 연애 대신에 교우를 찾을 수 있도록 돕는 것이 그 목표였다. 모든 실험 대상자들은 자신의 관심사를 등재했고, 우리는 일주일 후에 되돌아가서 그들에게 다른 사람이 작성한 약력을 검토하고 그 사람이 좋고 그 사람을 만나고 싶은지 판단하도록 요청했다. 그들 중 절반은 우리의 매우 신뢰할 수 있는 짝 찾아 주기 프로그램이 이 새로운 사람이 그들에게 이상적인 짝이라고 판단했다는 말을 들었다. 나머지 절반은 아무 말도 듣지 못했다. 친구 관계가 가능한지 여부에 관한 정보를 전혀 제공받지 못했을 때, 사람들은 자신과 매우 비슷한 관심사를 가진 사람을 선호했다. 그러나 친구 관계가 될 가능성이 높다는 말을 들었을 때는 다른 관심사로 자신을 보완하는 사람을 선호했다. 즉, (친구) 관계가 가능하다고 확신할 때 사람들은 독특하고 흥미로우며 자신의 시야를 넓힐 수 있는 기회를 제공하는 사람과 시간을 보내고 싶어 했다.

Solution Guide

제시된 실험에서 친구 관계가 가능한지 여부에 관한 정보를 제공받지 못한 사람들은 자신과 비슷한 관심사를 가진 사람을 선호했지만, 친구 관계의 가능성이 높다는 말을 들은 사람들은 자신과 다른 관심사를 가진 사람을 선호했다고 언급하고 있으므로, 빈칸에 들어갈 말로 가장 적절한 것은 ③이다.

① 그들의 친한 친구가 질투할 것이라고 느낄
② 다양한 배경 출신의 친구들이 이미 있을
④ 약력에 근거하여 후보를 판단할 수 없을
⑤ 짝 찾아 주기 알고리즘에 관한 정보를 받지 못했을

Structure in Focus

- All the subjects listed their interests, and we returned a week later to ask them to [review a profile {written by another person}] and [judge {whether they liked and wanted to meet them}].
  두 개의 [ ]는 and로 연결되어 to에 이어져 ask의 목적격 보어 역할을 하는 to부정사구를 이룬다. 첫 번째 { }는 a profile을 수식하는 분사구이다. 두 번째 { }는 judge의 목적어 역할을 하는 명사절이다.
- That is, when people were confident [that a relationship was possible], they wanted to spend time with people [who were unique, interesting], and [who offered a chance for them to expand their horizons].
  첫 번째 [ ]는 confident의 의미를 보충한다. 두 번째와 세 번

째 [ ]는 and로 연결되어 people을 수식하는 관계절이다.

18

정답 ④

소재 현재 현실을 조직하는 은유적 개념

해석 많은 우리 활동(논쟁, 문제 해결, 시간 할당 등)은 본질적으로 은유적이다. 그런 활동을 특징짓는 은유적 개념은 우리의 현재 현실을 조직한다. 새로운 은유는 새로운 현실을 창조하는 힘을 가지고 있다. 이것은 우리가 우리의 경험을 은유 측면에서 이해하기 시작할 때 일어나기 시작할 수 있고, 그것은 우리가 그것(은유)의 측면에서 행동하기 시작할 때 더 깊은 현실이 된다. 새로운 은유는 우리가 우리 행동의 근거로 삼는 개념 체계에 들어오면, 그 개념 체계, 그리고 그 체계가 만들어 내는 인식과 행동을 바꿀 것이다. 많은 문화적 변화는 새로운 은유적 개념의 도입과 예전의 은유적 개념의 상실에서 발생된다. (죽은 은유는 매우 자주, 그리고 매우 오랜 기간 동안 사용되어 그것의 원래 비유적 의미가 희미해진 대중적인 은유이다.) 예를 들어, 전 세계 문화의 서구화는 부분적으로 시간이 돈이라는 은유를 그 문화에 도입하는 것의 문제이다.

Solution Guide

은유적 개념은 우리의 현재 현실을 조직하고, 새로운 은유는 새로운 현실을 창조한다는 내용의 글이다. ④는 매우 오랜 기간 동안 매우 자주 사용되어 비유적 의미가 희미해진 대중적인 은유가 죽은 은유라는 내용이다. 따라서 문화적 변화의 원인으로 새로운 은유적 개념의 도입으로 인한 오랜 은유적 개념의 상실을 언급한 ③과 세계 문화의 서구화의 원인으로 시간이 돈이라는 은유의 도입을 언급한 ⑤ 사이의 ④는 글의 흐름상 어색하다. 따라서 글의 전체 흐름과 관계가 없는 문장은 ④이다.

Structure in Focus

- If a new metaphor enters the conceptual system [that we base our actions on], it will alter that conceptual system and the perceptions and actions [that the system gives rise to].
  첫 번째 [ ]는 the conceptual system을 수식하는 관계절이고, 두 번째 [ ]는 the perceptions and actions를 수식하는 관계절이다.
- A dead metaphor is a popular metaphor [that has been used **so** frequently and for **such** an extended period **that** its original figurative meaning has faded].
  [ ]는 a popular metaphor를 수식하는 관계절이다. 그 안에 '매우 ~해서 …하다'라는 의미의 「so[such] ~ that ...」이 사용되었다.

19

정답 ③

소재 사냥을 통한 동물 피해 통제

해석 동물 피해 통제 옹호론자들은 흔히 '사냥감 동물'의 특징을 '유해 동물 종'이라고 묘사한다. 예를 들어, 사슴은 가축을 죽이지는 않지만, 교외에서 뜰을 파괴하고, 질병을 옮기고, 자동차 사고를 유발하고, 여타 형태의 피해를 가한다고 비난을 받는다. (B) 따라서 스포츠 사냥을 하는 사람들은 대중의 지지를 받으며 사슴을 죽이는 것이 허용되는데, 어쨌든 사슴과의 충돌 사고에 연루되기를 원하는 사람은 아무도 없다. 사슴과 관련해서는 안타깝게도, 사냥이 사슴의 개체 수를 반드시 통제하는 것은 아니다. 그것들(사슴의 개체 수)은 사냥철이 끝나면 자원에 대한 경쟁이 줄어들기 때문에 곧 원래대로 되돌아갈 수 있다. (C) 그리고 물론, 그것들의 자연 포식자의 상당수를 말살한 동물 피해 통제 조치도 또한 그것들의 많은 개체 수에 한몫한다. 도로변 울타리 사용뿐만 아니라 더 책임감 있는 운전, 속도 제한, 경고 표지판, 도로변 반사경과 같은, 사슴이 유발할 수 있는 피해를 방지할 수많은 방법이 있다. (A) 그러나 개발업자들이 교외 지역에 계속 건축하는 한 인간과 야생동물이 접촉하게 될 것이라는 사실은 사라지지 않는다. 안타깝게도, 동물 피해 통제 프로그램에는 이런 문제를 해결하는 단 한 가지 방법이 있는데, 그것은 사냥이다.

Solution Guide

사슴을 사례로 들어 동물 피해 통제 옹호론자들이 사냥감 동물을 유해 동물 종으로 묘사해서 비난한다는 주어진 글 뒤에는, 그 결과로 스포츠 사냥을 하는 사람들에게 사슴을 죽이는 것이 허용된다는 내용을 So로 이끄는 (B)가 이어져야 한다. 글 (B) 마지막에 사슴의 개체 수가 사냥철이 지나면 곧 원래대로 되돌아간다는 내용이 언급되었으므로, 그다음에는 사슴 개체 수의 증가의 또 다른 원인으로 사슴의 자연 포식자를 말살한 동물 피해 통제 조치를 추가하는 (C)가 이어져야 한다. 글 (C) 마지막에 사냥 외의 사슴의 피해 방지 방법을 제시하고 있는데, 이런 방법이 있음에도 불구하고 개발업자들의 교외 지역 건축으로 인해 인간과 야생동물의 접촉이 지속된다는 내용을 역접의 접속사 Yet으로 이끌며, 아쉽게도 동물 피해 통제 프로그램은 사냥만을 문제 해결 방법으로 삼는다는 내용의 (A)가 그 뒤를 잇는 것이 글의 순서로 가장 적절하다.

Structure in Focus

- Yet the fact remains [that as long as developers continue to build in suburban areas, humans and wildlife will come into contact].
  [ ]는 the fact와 동격 관계이다.
- And, of course, the animal damage control measures [that wiped out many of their natural predators] also

play a role in their large numbers.
[ ]는 the animal damage control measures를 수식하는 관계절이다.

20

정답 ③

소재 적합성 향상과 유전자 빈도

해석 하나의 유전자는 그것의 보유자가 비 보유자보다 어떤 적합성 향상 행동을 수행할 가능성을 더 크게 함으로써 빈도가 증가할 수 있다. (B) 예를 들어 많은 종의 암컷은 수컷의 구애 표현의 질을 토대로 짝을 선택한다. 수컷들의 구애 표현이 질에서 다르고 유전적 차이가 그 (구애) 표현 차이의 기초가 된다면, 그 우월한 표현을 위한 유전자는 빈도가 증가할 것이다. 물론 구애 행동이 적합성에 영향을 주는 유일한 행동은 아니다. (C) 부모가 자녀에게 주는 돌봄의 양에서 다르다면, 돌봄의 양이 자녀의 생존 능력에 영향을 준다면, 그리고 유전적 차이가 자녀 돌보기에서의 이러한 차이의 기초가 된다면, 그렇다면 더 많은 양의 돌봄을 위한 유전자는 빈도가 증가할 것이다. (A) 따라서 하나의 유전자가 어떤 적합성 향상 행동의 가능성을 더 크게 하는 한, 그 유전자는 한 개체군에서 빈도가 증가할 것이고, 그 결과 그 행동 또한 빈도가 증가할 수 있을 것이다. 이러한 이유로, 생물학자들은 빈번히 진화 생물학의 관점에서 볼 때 "행동 형질은 어떤 다른 부류의 특질과 다름없다."라고 말한다.

Solution Guide

유전자 빈도는 적합성 향상 행동에 영향을 미칠 때 증가한다는 내용의 주어진 글 다음에는, 그 사례로 구애 표현의 질에 관한 내용을 제시하는 (B)가 이어져야 한다. 그다음에는 (B)의 마지막 문장과 관련하여 구애 표현의 질뿐만 아니라 자녀 돌보기의 양도 적합성 향상에 영향을 미쳐 유전자 빈도가 증가한다는 내용의 (C)가 이어지고, 이 두 가지 사례를 통해 도출된 유전자 빈도와 적합성 향상 행동의 상관관계를 요약하는 내용의 (A)로 이어지는 것이 글의 순서로 가장 적절하다.

Structure in Focus

- So, [**as long as** a gene makes some fitness-enhancing behavior more likely], [that gene will increase in frequency in a population], and [as a result the behavior may increase in frequency as well].
  첫 번째 [ ]는 '~하는 한'이라는 의미를 나타내는 「as long as ~」에 의해 유도되는 부사절이다. 두 번째와 세 번째 [ ]가 and로 연결되어 주절을 이룬다.
- [If parents differ in the quantity of care {they give to their offspring}], [if the quantity of care affects the viability of offspring], and [if a genetic difference underlies this difference in parental care], then the gene for higher quantity care will increase in frequency.
  세 개의 [ ]는 and로 연결된 조건의 부사절이다. 첫 번째 [ ] 안의 { }는 care를 수식하는 관계절이다.

21

정답 ③

소재 이동성 증가와 문화 정체성 상실

해석 포스트모더니티의 한 특징은 자발적이든 강요되든 세계적인 인구의 이동성 증가이다. 사회 전체의 이주, 난민 문제, 이주 노동자의 유입으로 인해 글로벌 다문화 사회가 형성되면서 어떤 국가도 합리적으로 동질적인 문화적 정체성이나 일련의 문화적 규범을 정의하는 데 어려움을 겪고 있다. 아메리카의 '용광로' 이미지의 실패 사례는 현저한 예이다. 미국은 항상 이민자들의 국가였으나 그 나라는 용케도, 최소한 제2차 세계대전까지지는, 전체로서 그 자체에 대한 의식을 유지했는데, 유럽 출신의 영어 사용 국가라는 것이었다. 하지만 아시아계, 아프리카계, 그리고 라틴계의 새로운 이주는 이러한 이미지에 도전했고 그 국가의 중심적인 문화 정체성을 규정하는 것을 거의 불가능하게 만들었다. 게다가 아메리카의 경험은 또한 세계의 다른 지역들에서도 기준이 되었다. 사람들의 정체성은 조각나고, 복수화되고, 혼합되었고, 과거에 침묵하고 주변적 지위로 내쫓겼던 인구 집단이 갑자기 역사적, 문화적 무대의 중심으로 옮겨왔다.

Solution Guide

주어진 문장은 미국은 이민자의 국가임에도 최소한 제2차 세계대전까지 문화 정체성을 유지하고 있었다는 내용을 담고 있다. 따라서 이 문장 바로 앞에는 미국의 문화 정체성과 관련된 내용을 도입하는 문장이 있어야 하고, 바로 뒤에는 미국의 국가 정체성과 관련하여 제2차 세계대전 이후의 상황을 설명하는 내용의 문장이 이어져야 한다. 따라서 주어진 문장이 들어가기에 가장 적절한 곳은 ③이다.

Structure in Focus

- [The migration of whole societies, the problem of refugees, the incorporation of migrant workers], have created a global, multicultural society [that challenges the ability of any nation {to define a reasonably homogeneous cultural identity or a set of cultural norms}].
  첫 번째 [ ]는 문장의 주어 역할을 하는 명사구이고, 두 번째 [ ]는 a global, multicultural society를 수식하는 관계절이다. { }는 the ability of any nation의 구체적 내용을 설

명하는 to부정사구이다.

- But new migrations — Asian, African, and Latino — [have challenged this image] and [made **it** almost impossible {to define a central cultural identity for the nation}].
  두 개의 [ ]가 and로 연결되어 문장의 술어 역할을 한다. it은 형식상의 목적어이고, { }는 내용상의 목적어이다.

22

정답 ④

소재 연안 해역에서의 인간의 영향

해석 상업적 어업이 더 깊은 심해에서 이루어지지 않기 때문에 인간의 영향은 바다의 상층 500미터에서 가장 직접적이다. 사실, 지질 채취와 항구 및 풍력 발전 단지 건설은 일반적으로 수심 50미터 이하의 바다에서 이루어진다. 얕은 연안 바다에서, 인간의 영향은 매우 뚜렷한데, 심지어 지구의 외딴 지역에서도 그러하다. 남극해의 동물은 많고 수십 년 동안 상업적 이용으로부터 보호받아 왔지만, 20세기 초반의 사냥은 생태계를 더는 자연 그대로의 생태계로 간주할 수 없을 정도로 바꾸었다. 이것이 지구상에 자연 그대로와 비슷한 연안 바다가 남아 있지 않다고 말하는 것은 아니다. 북서부 하와이의 섬들이 한 가지 사례가 될 수 있는데, 그곳은 인간이 거주한 적이 없고 단지 매우 드물게 어로 원정만을 경험한 적이 있다. 그런 장소는 거의 없는데, 사실 아마도 1퍼센트 미만의 해수면이 어로나 다른 종류의 교란 활동으로부터 완전히 보호받고 있을 것이다.

Solution Guide

얕은 연안 바다에서 인간이 생태계에 많은 영향을 미쳐서 자연 그대로의 생태계를 교란하고 있다는 내용의 글이다. ④ 바로 앞 문장은 사냥으로 인해 생태계가 더는 자연 그대로의 생태계로 간주될 수 없는 정도로 바뀐 것에 관한 내용이고 ④ 바로 뒤 문장은 인간의 영향이 거의 없었던 북서부 하와이의 섬들이 해당 사례로 제시되고 있으므로, 자연 그대로와 비슷한 연안 바다가 지구상에 존재할 수 있다는 내용의 주어진 문장이 ④에 들어가야 글의 흐름이 자연스러워진다. 따라서 주어진 문장이 들어가기에 가장 적절한 곳은 ④이다.

Structure in Focus

- ~, yet hunting in the early part of the twentieth century changed the ecosystem to a degree [that **it** can no longer be considered a pristine ecosystem].
  [ ]는 a degree를 수식하는 관계절이다. 그 안의 it은 the ecosystem을 대신한다.
- A case may be made for the northwest Hawaii islands, [which have never been inhabited by humans and only very rarely have experienced fishing expeditions].
  [ ]는 the northwest Hawaii islands를 부가적으로 설명하는 관계절이다.

23

정답 ④

소재 새로운 신념과 그에 일치되는 기억

해석 Michael Ross, Cathy McFarland, Garth Fletcher가 수행한 간단한 실험에서, 대학생들은 자주 양치질하는 것의 중요성을 주장하는 설득력 있는 메시지를 받았다. 그 메시지를 받은 후에, 학생들은 양치질에 대한 태도를 바꾸었다. 말할 필요도 없이 이것은 놀라운 일이 아니다. 하지만 놀라웠던 것은 이것이다. 나중에 같은 날 다른 상황에서 학생들은 "지난 2주 동안 양치질을 몇 번이나 했습니까?"라는 질문을 받았다. 그 메시지를 받은 학생들은 대조군의 학생들보다 훨씬 더 자주 이를 닦았다고 기억했다. 학생들은 연구자를 속이려고 한 것이 아니었는데, 그들이 거짓말을 할 이유가 없었기 때문이다. 그들은 단지 기억을 돕기 위한 휴리스틱으로 자신의 새로운 태도를 사용하고 있던 것뿐이었다. 어떤 의미에서 학생들은 이제 막 그 분별 있는 행동이 무엇일지 알게 되었음에도 불구하고 자신이 항상 분별 있고 합리적인 방식으로 행동했다고 믿을 필요가 있었다.

→ (인용한) 글의 실험에 따르면, 양치질에 대한 학생들의 태도는 자주 양치질을 하는 것에 대한 설득력 있는 메시지에 의해 영향을 받았는데, 이는 그들이 새로운 믿음과 일치하도록 자신의 기억을 수정하게 했다.

Solution Guide

대학생들은 자주 양치질하는 것의 중요성을 주장하는 설득력 있는 메시지를 받은 후 양치질에 대한 태도를 바꾸었는데, 놀라운 것은 그 새로운 양치질에 대한 태도에 맞게 과거의 기억을 수정했다는 내용이므로, 빈칸 (A), (B)에 들어갈 말로 가장 적절한 것은 ④ '영향을 받았는데 – 일치하도록'이다.

① 예측되었는데 – 관련이 없도록
② 표현되었는데 – 일치하도록
③ 예측되었는데 – 섞이도록
⑤ 영향을 받았는데 – 관련이 없도록

Structure in Focus

- In a simple experiment [conducted by Michael Ross, Cathy McFarland, and Garth Fletcher], college students received a persuasive message [arguing the importance of frequent tooth brushing].

첫 번째 [ ]는 a simple experiment를 수식하는 분사구이고, 두 번째 [ ]는 a persuasive message를 수식하는 분사구이다.

- They were simply using their new attitudes as a heuristic [to help them remember].
  [ ]는 a heuristic을 수식하는 to부정사구이다.

24~25

정답 24 ⑤ 25 ③

소재 일반적인 믿음에 기대는 오류에 맞서는 과학

해석 여러분 자신의 삶에서 일반적인 믿음에 기대는 오류에 관해서 말하자면, 과학자들은 항상 더 나은 결론에 도달하기 위해 노력하고 있고, 그것은 여러분이 개인으로서 적어도 자동적으로 하는 일이 아니고, 더 나아가 그것은 여러분의 기관 또한 그다지 잘하는 일은 아니라는 점을 명심하라. 여러분은 과학에서 귀무가설이라고 부르는 것을 찾지 않는다. 즉, 어떤 것을 믿으면, 여러분은 그것이 자신의 가정에 어떻게 필적하는지 확인하기 위해 반대되는 증거를 좀처럼 찾지 않는다. 그것이 도시 괴담, 민담, 미신, 기타 등등의 원인이다. 의심하는 마음을 갖는 것은 여러분의 장점이 아니다. 기업이나 기타 기관에서는 그 기관의 잘못에 주의를 기울이는 업무를 담당하는 부서를 좀처럼 따로 두지 않는다. 과학에서와 달리, 대부분의 인간 사업에서는 단순한 불만 처리 부서가 아니라 조직이 올바른 길을 가고 있는지 묻는 부서처럼 운영에서 최악의 것을 찾는 데 전념하는 특별 부서를 포함한다(→ 두지 않는다). 모든 인간의 노력은 체계적으로 잠시 멈추어 현재 그것이 틀렸는지 물어봐야 한다. 두뇌를 능가하려면 두개골에서 끊임없이 작동하는 그 부서가 필요하다. 과학적 방법의 교훈을 빌려서 여러분의 개인 생활에 그것을 적용하는 것이 바람직하다. 여러분이 바느질하고 골프를 치고 고양이 동영상을 검색하는 동안, 과학은 (눈에 안 뜨이게) 뒤로 물러나서 여러분의 어리석음에 맞서 싸우고 있다. 인간이 하는 다른 어떤 일도 이만큼 열심히 싸우고 있지 않거나 적어도 싸워서 이기고 있지는 않다.

Culture Note

null hypothesis(귀무가설) 우리가 증명하고자 하는 가설의 반대되는 가설을 의미한다. 이에 반해, 대립가설은 우리가 증명 또는 입증하고자 하는 가설을 말한다. 가설 검증 과정에서, 'A 물질이 위암을 유발한다.'라는 가설을 입증할 때 'A 물질은 위암을 유발하지 않는다.'라는 귀무가설을 설정한다. 귀무가설이 틀렸다는 것을 통해서 'A 물질이 위암을 유발한다.'는 대립가설이 성립하는 것을 증명하게 된다. 가설이 참이 아님을 증명하는 것이 참임을 증명하는 것보다 상대적으로 수월하기 때문에 귀무가설을 도입한다.

Solution Guide

24 일반적인 믿음에 기대는 오류(common belief fallacy)에 빠지지 않기 위해서는 우리의 삶에 과학적 사고방식 및 과학적 방법, 즉 과학을 적용해야 한다는 내용의 글이므로, 글의 제목으로 가장 적절한 것은 ⑤ '잘못된 일반적인 믿음을 피하기 위해 여러분의 삶에 과학을 적용하라'이다.

① 일반적인 믿음은 과학을 보완한다
② 과학은 가치중립적인 분야가 아니다
③ 상식은 여러분의 일상을 부드럽게 유지한다
④ 직관과 과학적 증거 중에 어떤 것이 더 강력한가?

25 기업이나 기타 기관에서는 그것의 잘못에 주의를 기울이는 업무를 담당하는 부서를 따로 두는 경우가 거의 없다는 바로 앞 문장의 내용을 확장하는 내용이 되어야 하므로, (c)의 include를 leave out과 같은 낱말로 바꾸어야 한다.

Structure in Focus

- That is, when you believe in something, you rarely seek out evidence to the contrary [to see {how it matches up with your assumptions}].
  [ ]는 목적을 나타내는 to부정사구이고, { }는 see의 목적어 역할을 하는 명사절이다.
- Corporations and other institutions rarely set aside a division [tasked with paying attention to the faults of the agency].
  [ ]는 a division을 수식하는 분사구이다.
- Unlike in science, most human undertakings leave out [a special department {devoted to looking for the worst in the operation}] — [not just a complaint department, but a department that asks if the organization is on the right path].
  첫 번째 [ ]는 leave out의 목적어 역할을 하는 명사구이고, 그 안의 { }는 a special department를 수식하는 분사구이다. 두 번째 [ ]는 첫 번째 [ ]를 구체적으로 설명한다.

26~28

정답 26 ⑤ 27 ② 28 ④

소재 Madeleine의 수업을 받게 된 Jill

해석 (A) Jill은 매우 병약한 아이였지만, 항상 유명한 댄서 Madeleine Sharp처럼 되기를 원해 왔다. 어느 날 Jill과 그녀의 엄마는 Bromley의 Bell 호텔 무도회장에서 하는 소녀 대상의 Madeleine Sharp 씨의 수업에 갔다. Madeleine Sharp는 키가 크고 날씬했으며 힘이 넘쳤다. 여덟 명의 다른 어린 소녀들이 있었는데, 그들은 모두 그녀의 지시를 따르기 위해 Madeleine이 하는 한마디 한마디에 귀를 기울이고 점프를 했다. Madeleine은 Jill에게 다가와 "자, Jill이 뭘 할 수 있는지 보자."라고 말했다.

Jill은 모든 댄서들에게 대표적인 첫 번째 규칙인 바를 잡는 법부터 시작했다. Madeleine Sharp는 "얘야, 절대 그것을 꽉 잡아서는 안 돼."라고 말했다.

(D) 그녀는 Jill에게 계속 단호하게 말했다. "손을 그 위에 가볍게 얹으렴. 그건 너의 균형을 잡아 주기 위해 거기 있는 것이지, 생명줄로 있는 게 아니야. 양발을 바깥쪽으로 향하게 해. 이건 발만 그래야 하는 것이 아니라 네 다리 전체가 바깥쪽으로 향하도록 엉덩이에서 시작해야 해. 좋아." Madeleine Sharp는 그녀의 댄서로서의 가능성을 살펴보고 싶었다. 그래서 그녀는 피아노 연주자에게 서정적인 곡을 연주해 달라고 부탁하고 나서, "Jill, 얘야, 네가 뛰며 즐기는 모습과 음악이 네게 뭘 하라고 말하는지를 내가 보게 해 줘."라고 말했다. 그 당시 Jill은 그것을 몰랐지만, Madeleine Sharp는 매우 존경을 받았고, 그로 인해 그녀의 수업에 들어가는 것은 매우 경쟁이 치열했다.

(C) 그래서 Jill의 엄마는 자신의 딸이 춤을 추는 동안 몹시 긴장했는데, 특히 몇 명의 다른 어머니들이 그곳에서 계속 머물러 이 새로 온 아이가 어떻게 할지 지켜보았기 때문이었다. Jill은 음악에 도취되어 방 이곳저곳을 나는 듯이 뛰어다녔다. 일 분 정도 후 Madeleine은 박수를 쳤고, Jill은 그녀 앞에서 멈춰 서서, 희망을 가득 안고, 숨을 헐떡이며 그녀를 올려다보았다.

(B) Madeleine은 한쪽 팔로 Jill을 감싸 안고 Jill의 엄마에게 돌아와서, "Jill을 매우 가르치고 싶어요. 금요일에 다시 올 수 있으신가요?"라고 말했다. 그들은 몇 마디를 더 주고받았지만, Jill은 어떤 것도 듣지 못했다. Jill의 머리는 오후에 있었던 일들과 그녀 앞에 놓인 흥분되는 새로운 세상으로 너무도 번잡했다. 그녀는 엄마가 "어서 가자, 얘야. 집에 가서 네 아빠에게 말씀드리자!"라고 말하는 것을 거의 알아채지 못했다. 하지만 그녀의 목소리가 Jill의 정신을 들게 했을 때, Jill은 양팔로 엄마를 껴안았다.

Solution Guide

26 주어진 글 (A)는 Jill이 엄마와 함께 유명한 댄서 Madeleine Sharp를 찾아가 그녀에게 자신의 춤 동작을 보여 주기 시작하는 내용인데, Madeleine이 Jill에게 춤 동작에 대해 조언을 해 주는 내용과 그녀의 수업을 들어가는 것은 매우 경쟁이 치열하다는 내용의 (D)가 그 뒤에 이어져야 한다. 그다음에는 그 때문에 Jill이 춤을 추고 있는 동안 그녀의 엄마가 몹시 긴장했고, Jill이 춤을 마치고 Madeleine의 반응을 기대하는 내용의 (C)가 이어지고, 금요일에 다시 와 달라는 Madeleine의 제안에 Jill이 무척 기뻐하는 내용의 (B)가 그 뒤를 잇는 것이 글의 순서로 가장 적절하다.

27 밑줄 친 (a), (c), (d), (e)는 모두 Madeleine을 가리키지만, (b)는 Jill을 가리킨다.

28 글 (C)에서 Jill의 엄마는 자신의 딸이 춤을 추는 동안 몹시 긴장했다고 했으므로, 글에 관한 내용으로 적절하지 않은 것은 ④이다.

Structure in Focus

- Jill was quite a sickly child, but she had always wanted to be like Madeleine Sharp, [a famous dancer].
  [ ]는 Madeleine Sharp와 동격 관계이다.
- ~, "Jill, dear, let me [see you run and enjoy yourself] and [see {what the music tells you to do}]."
  두 개의 [ ]는 and로 연결되어 let의 목적격 보어 역할을 한다. 두 번째 [ ] 안의 { }는 see의 목적어 역할을 하는 명사절이다.

한눈에 보는 정답

Part Ⅰ 유형편

	G	01	02	03	04	05	06	07	08	09	10	11	12
01	①	④	④	②	③								
02	①	④	⑤	③	①								
03	①	⑤	③	⑤	⑤								
04	⑤	③	①	③	②								
05	④	⑤	④	②	②								
06	②	④	⑤	⑤	⑤								
07	⑤	⑤	④	②	⑤								
08	④	⑤	⑤	⑤	④								
09	②	⑤	⑤	④	④								
10	③	④	④	③	④								
11	②	④	⑤	②	②								
12	④	⑤	④	⑤	⑤								
13	②	②	①	④	①	③	②	③	③	⑤	②	②	③
14	③	④	③	③	③								
15	④	⑤	③	①	③	②	⑤						
16	③	⑤	⑤	④	⑤	④	④						
17	①	①	①	②	④								
18	01 ② 02 ⑤	④	⑤	③	④	②	③	①	②				
19	01 ⑤ 02 ③ 03 ③	②	③	④	④	③	④	③	③	⑤	④	⑤	④

Part Ⅱ 주제·소재편

	G	01	02	03
20	④	③	①	⑤
21	④	②	④	⑤
22	①	④	②	④
23	⑤	③	⑤	④
24	④	④	⑤	③
25	⑤	②	②	⑤
26	④	⑤	⑤	②
27	①	④	③	②
28	④	⑤	④	④
29	③	⑤	③	④
30	④	①	①	③
31	⑤	⑤	②	④

Part Ⅲ 테스트편

Test 1	01	02	03	04	05	06	07	08	09	10
	⑤	⑤	③	②	④	⑤	②	②	⑤	④
	11	12	13	14	15	16	17	18	19	20
	④	⑤	⑤	③	④	①	⑤	④	②	③
	21	22	23	24	25	26	27	28		
	②	④	③	①	⑤	④	⑤	②		

Test 2	01	02	03	04	05	06	07	08	09	10
	①	②	②	⑤	⑤	⑤	②	②	③	④
	11	12	13	14	15	16	17	18	19	20
	⑤	④	⑤	③	③	①	①	④	①	③
	21	22	23	24	25	26	27	28		
	⑤	②	②	①	⑤	②	③	⑤		

Test 3	01	02	03	04	05	06	07	08	09	10
	③	④	③	⑤	⑤	⑤	①	②	⑤	⑤
	11	12	13	14	15	16	17	18	19	20
	⑤	④	⑤	②	①	②	③	④	③	③
	21	22	23	24	25	26	27	28		
	③	④	④	⑤	③	⑤	②	④		